# HANDBOOK OF REAL ESTATE AND MACROECONOMICS

# Handbook of Real Estate and Macroeconomics

*Edited by*

Charles Ka Yui Leung

*Department of Economics and Finance, City University of Hong Kong, Kowloon Tong, Hong Kong*

Edward Elgar
PUBLISHING

Cheltenham, UK • Northampton, MA, USA

© Charles Ka Yui Leung 2022

Cover image: Pierre Blaché on Unsplash.

All rights reserved. No part of this publication may be reproduced, stored in a retrieval system or transmitted in any form or by any means, electronic, mechanical or photocopying, recording, or otherwise without the prior permission of the publisher.

Published by
Edward Elgar Publishing Limited
The Lypiatts
15 Lansdown Road
Cheltenham
Glos GL50 2JA
UK

Edward Elgar Publishing, Inc.
William Pratt House
9 Dewey Court
Northampton
Massachusetts 01060
USA

A catalogue record for this book
is available from the British Library

Library of Congress Control Number: 2022934521

This book is available electronically in the **Elgar**online
Economics subject collection
http://dx.doi.org/10.4337/9781789908497

ISBN 978 1 78990 848 0 (cased)
ISBN 978 1 78990 849 7 (eBook)

Printed and bound by CPI Group (UK) Ltd, Croydon, CR0 4YY

# Contents

| | | |
|---|---|---|
| *List of contributors* | | vii |
| *Introduction to the* Handbook of Real Estate and Macroeconomics<br>Charles Ka Yui Leung | | x |

PART I   REAL ESTATE-RELATED WEALTH AND MACROECONOMICS

| 1 | Real estate market and consumption: macro and micro evidence of Japan<br>*Kazuo Ogawa* | 2 |
|---|---|---|
| 2 | The Bank of Japan as a real estate tycoon: large-scale REIT purchases<br>*Takahiro Hattori and Jiro Yoshida* | 21 |
| 3 | Land and macroeconomics<br>*Prasad Sankar Bhattacharya* | 39 |

PART II   HOUSING PRICE DYNAMICS AND AFFORDABILITY

| 4 | Affordable housing conundrum in India<br>*Piyush Tiwari and Jyoti Shukla* | 83 |
|---|---|---|
| 5 | Residential location and education in the United States<br>*Eric A. Hanushek and Kuzey Yilmaz* | 106 |
| 6 | Testing for real estate bubbles<br>*Eric Girardin and Roselyne Joyeux* | 137 |
| 7 | Disaggregating house price dynamics<br>*Rose Neng Lai and Robert A. Van Order* | 165 |
| 8 | The effect of macroeconomic uncertainty on housing returns and volatility: evidence from US state-level data<br>*Reneé van Eyden, Rangan Gupta, Christophe André and Xin Sheng* | 206 |

PART III   FINANCIAL CRISIS AND STRUCTURAL CHANGE

| 9 | Financial crisis and the U.S. mortgage markets – a review<br>*Sumit Agarwal and Sandeep Varshneya* | 240 |
|---|---|---|
| 10 | Is housing still the business cycle? Perhaps not.<br>*Richard K. Green* | 269 |
| 11 | International macroeconomic aspect of housing<br>*Joe Cho Yiu Ng* | 284 |

| 12 | How did the asset markets change after the Global Financial Crisis? *Kuang-Liang Chang and Charles Ka Yui Leung* | 312 |

PART IV  NON-RESIDENTIAL REAL ESTATE

| 13 | From the regional economy to the macroeconomy *Santiago M. Pinto and Pierre-Daniel G. Sarte* | 338 |
| 14 | Industrial parks and urban growth: a political economy story in China *Matthew E. Kahn, Jianfeng Wu, Weizeng Sun and Siqi Zheng* | 359 |
| 15 | Pension funds and private equity real estate: history, performance, pathologies, risks *Timothy J. Riddiough* | 371 |
| 16 | A mayor's perspective on tackling air pollution *Shihe Fu and V. Brian Viard* | 413 |

*Index* 438

# Contributors

**Sumit Agarwal** is Low Tuck Kwong Distinguished Professor of Finance at the Business School and Professor of Economics and Real Estate at the National University of Singapore.

**Christophe André** is a senior economist at the Organisation for Economic Co-operation and Development (OECD) in Paris. He now heads the Korea-Sweden desk in the OECD Economics Department.

**Prasad Sankar Bhattacharya** is Senior Lecturer in Economics at the Department of Economics, Deakin University, Australia.

**Kuang-Liang Chang** is Professor in the Department of Political Economy at National Sun Yat-San University in Taiwan.

**Shihe Fu** is Professor of Economics at Xiamen University, China. He received his PhD in economics from Boston College in 2005.

**Eric Girardin** is Professor of Economics at Aix-Marseille University's School of Economics, Aix-Marseille University, France, and Visiting Professor at HSBC-Peking University Business School (United Kingdom campus).

**Richard K. Green** is Professor in the Price School of Public Policy, Marshall School of Business, and Department of Economics at the University of Southern California, where he is also Director of the Lusk Center for Real Estate.

**Rangan Gupta** is Professor at the Department of Economics, University of Pretoria, South Africa.

**Eric A. Hanushek** is the Paul and Jean Hanna Senior Fellow at the Hoover Institution of Stanford University. He has authored or edited 24 books along with over 250 articles.

**Takahiro Hattori** is Project Assistant Professor at the Graduate School of Public Policy, University of Tokyo. He is also a visiting scholar in the Ministry of Finance, Japan.

**Roselyne Joyeux** is Professor in Economics in the Faculty of Business and Economics at Macquarie University in Sydney, Australia. She has been appointed to the Australian Research Council College of Experts.

**Matthew E. Kahn** is the Bloomberg Distinguished Professor of Economics and Business at Johns Hopkins University and Director of the university's 21st Century Cities Initiative.

**Rose Neng Lai** is Professor in Finance and Dean of Honours College at the University of Macau. She was awarded the 2019 International Real Estate Society Achievement Award.

**Charles Ka Yui Leung** is Associate Professor at the City University of Hong Kong. He received the Fulbright Scholarship (Research) and his research can be found on several websites, such as https://ideas.repec.org/e/ple96.html.

**Joe Cho Yiu Ng** received his PhD from the City University of Hong Kong. He received the 2019 Fulbright RGC Hong Kong Research Scholar Award and visited Virginia Tech in the United States. His research can be found at https://orcid.org/0000-0002-8702-2813.

**Kazuo Ogawa** has been Professor of the College of Foreign Studies of Kansaigaidai University since 2017. He was awarded the Nikkei Prize for Excellent Books in Economic Science.

**Santiago M. Pinto** joined the Federal Reserve Bank of Richmond in 2012 and is now a senior economist and policy advisor in the Research Department.

**Timothy J. Riddiough** holds the James A. Graaskamp Chair and is Professor of Real Estate and Urban Land Economics at the University of Wisconsin – Madison. He is a past president of the American Real Estate and Urban Economics Association.

**Pierre-Daniel G. Sarte** is a senior advisor in the Research Department and has been with the Richmond Fed since 1996. He currently serves as Associate Editor of the Journal of Monetary Economics and has served as a co-editor of Economics Letters.

**Xin Sheng** is Senior Lecturer at Lord Ashcroft International Business School, Anglia Ruskin University, United Kingdom.

**Jyoti Shukla** is Lecturer in Property at the University of Melbourne, Australia.

**Weizeng Sun** is Associate Professor at the School of Economics, Central University of Finance and Economics, China.

**Piyush Tiwari** is Professor of Property at University of Melbourne, Australia. He has served as a member of the International Property Measurement Standards Committee of the International Property Measurement Standards Coalition.

**Reneé van Eyden** is Professor at the Department of Economics, University of Pretoria, South Africa. She has served as Secretary of the African Econometric Society and has been appointed to Skills Development Projects of the United Nations.

**Robert A. Van Order** holds the Oliver Carr Chair in Finance and Real Estate at George Washington University and is Professor of Finance and Economics. He received the George Bloom Distinguished Service Award: American Real Estate and Urban Economics Association in 2007.

**Sandeep Varshneya** is a finance PhD candidate at NUS Business School, National University of Singapore. He also received his CFA Charter in the year 2008 from the CFA Institute, United States.

**V. Brian Viard** is Associate Professor of Strategy and Economics at Cheung Kong Graduate School of Business in China. He received his PhD in business economics from the University of Chicago in 2000.

**Jianfeng Wu** is Associate Professor at the China Center for Economic Studies, Fudan University.

**Kuzey Yilmaz** is Associate Professor at the Department of Economics of Cleveland State University. His work has appeared in leading journals.

**Jiro Yoshida** is Associate Professor of Business at the Pennsylvania State University and Guest Associate Professor of Economics at the University of Tokyo, among other positions.

**Siqi Zheng** is the STL Champion Professor of Urban and Real Estate Sustainability at the Center for Real Estate and Department of Urban Studies and Planning at Massachusetts Institute of Technology (MIT). She established and is Faculty Director of the MIT Sustainable Urbanization Lab.

# Introduction to the *Handbook of Real Estate and Macroeconomics*
## Charles Ka Yui Leung

The following story occurred during my visit to the Hoover Institution (2018–19). A seminar speaker began by "apologizing" that his talk may not be "very macro." A senior faculty at Stanford University responded that there is *no boundary of macroeconomics*, implying there should not be much worry about "not macro enough."

This book is a collection of papers relating to real estate and macroeconomics. Given the "definition" of macroeconomics offered by that Stanford economist, I can put any topic in this book without an apology. Still, I feel obligated to provide some background for the emergence of the macro-real estate literature. Therefore, this introduction aims to facilitate the communication between the authors and readers of this book by mentioning some related contributions and not provide another survey on the macro-real estate literature. The chapters of this book provide outstanding reviews of different strands of the literature already. The objectives of the book are simple:

1. What should real estate economists know about macroeconomics?
2. What should macroeconomists know about real estate?
3. What general audience should know about the interactions between real estate and macroeconomics?

Although classical economists do not discuss housing, perhaps except David Ricardo relating trade policy to land prices (Leung, 2004), recent decades have witnessed a structural change. Literature on real estate (e.g., housing, commercial properties, land) and macroeconomics relate to each other (Baxter, 1996; Ben-Shafar et al., 2008; Edelstein and Kim, 2004; Greenwood and Hercowitz, 1991; Leung, 2004; Leung and Quigley, 2007; Mera and Renaud, 2000). The growth of that literature was further stimulated by the 2008 Global Financial Crisis (GFC) (Bardhan et al., 2012; Davis and Van Nieuwerburgh, 2014; Leung and Chen, 2017; Leung and Ng, 2019; Malpezzi, 2017; McMillen, 2011; Piazzesi and Schneider, 2016).

On the other hand, the change in the research frontier does not seem to be very visible in the teaching of economics. For instance, the standard introductory "macroeconomics" textbooks only loosely suggest that the fluctuation of house prices could lead to a wealth effect, affecting consumption and gross domestic product (GDP). It begs the question whether, if housing wealth fluctuations can lead to a significant "wealth effect," households should be cautious as they allocate their wealth to housing. Yet standard introductory textbooks typically skip the decision process of how families make portfolio decisions, choosing between housing and other alternatives.

Much research effort has been devoted to addressing this question. Part I of this book examines the real estate-related wealth effect. For instance, Ogawa (Chapter 1, this volume) employs both aggregate and panel household data and exploits different statistical tools to help us understand the wealth effect in the context of Japan. The justifications are clear. A theoretical discussion of the wealth effect may sound too abstract for the general audience. Hence, putting the wealth effect in a particular context may help readers understand the issue. Japan experienced the so-called "bubble burst" in the early 1990s, where both the stock price and real estate prices (land and housing) suffered significant downward adjustments. Arguably, Japan has not fully recovered from that "shock." Therefore, a case study of the wealth effect of Japanese real estate may be a good starting point.

Wealth is not an exclusive privilege of the private sector; governments can also acquire real estate-related wealth. For instance, Japan adopted unconventional monetary policies even before the United States and Euro areas (Dell'Ariccia et al., 2018; Fukuda, 2019; Westelius, 2021). Hattori and Yoshida (Chapter 2) examine the Bank of Japan's purchase of real estate investment trusts (REITs). Since REITs are relatively simple assets, some potential motives of holding stocks do not apply. Hattori and Yoshida study the intraday transactions and conclude that the evidence is consistent with the hypothesis that the Bank of Japan attempts to decrease the risk premiums.

Land is perhaps one of the most basic forms of wealth. Since the seminal work of Ricardo (1817), much has been written on the economics of land. More recently, researchers also notice the implications of land price fluctuations on the macroeconomy (e.g., Deng et al., 2021; Leung and Chen, 2006; Liu et al., 2013, 2016). Bhattacharya (Chapter 3) explains how the land market is related to macroeconomic variables. His chapter also provides evidence that some land reforms can promote urbanization.

Another essential issue bridging real estate and macroeconomics is housing affordability. Economists have studied housing affordability for decades, and now it has become a global concern (Gong and Leung, 2021; Green and Malpezzi, 2003; Leung and Tang, 2021; Leung et al., 2020; Malpezzi, 2020; Quigley and Raphael, 2004; Yao, 2020; Yılmaz and Yesilırmak, 2020). Part II of this book examines the issue from different angles. For instance, Tiwari and Shukla (Chapter 4) study housing affordability in India. India has the second-largest population globally and the level of economic development significantly differs across regions. Hence, it is easy to imagine that housing affordability can be an issue in India. However, India's data are not always accessible, and its institutions are not always well understood. Tiwari and Shukla present a clear picture of the situation and make a policy recommendation.

On the other hand, if housing units are being traded in the market, high housing prices must reflect the demand for specific population segments. One possibility is that the residential residence is tied to the "right of education" (O'Sullivan, 2018). In many countries, local pre-college public education is often provided to "residents" only. Recent research has confirmed that human capital investment has long-term consequences, especially in the early years (Attanasio et al., 2020; Cunha and Heckman, 2007, 2008). Therefore, from a macroeconomic perspective, quality education is vital for economic performance (Hanushek and Woessmann, 2015, 2016; Hanushek et al., 2017). Hanushek and Yilmaz (Chapter 5) review the literature on the interaction between residential decisions and schooling choice. While their chapter focuses on the United States, some lessons apply to other countries as well.

Other chapters of this book shed light on different aspects of the "affordability puzzle." For example, one explanation for unaffordable housing is that the housing prices deviate from the "economic fundamentals." Statistically, there are different approaches to verify this hypothesis. For instance, one can test whether there is a "bubble" in housing prices. The asset price bubble is often cited as one reason for Japan's "lost decades" (Ito, 2003; Okina et al., 2001;

Ueda, 2012). Girardin and Joyeux (Chapter 6) provide a comprehensive literature review and examine whether such a bubble exists in the Japanese data.

Perhaps, more fundamentally, what kind of "house price dynamics" is normal? And what is not? The macroeconomic approach often assumes a single housing market and focuses on the dynamics of national house prices (e.g., Davis and Heathcote, 2005; Favilukis et al., 2017; Leung, 2007, 2014). Macroeconomists distinguish a regular regime from a sunspot regime (Lubik and Schorfheide, 2003, 2004). The macroeconomic approach of housing would state whether the housing market is in a normal state or a bubble state (Chen, 2001; Phillips et al., 2011). It is also possible that there is more than one "normal state," with none of them being a bubble state, with the housing market switching between them (Chang et al., 2011, 2012, 2013). Real estate economists, on the other hand, pay attention to cross-sectional heterogeneity. Lai and Van Order (Chapter 7) review the literature which employs the conventional panel data approach to study whether a bubble exists. They consider both the time series (i.e., house price changes in different periods) and cross-sectional variations (i.e., house price differences across other regions within the same time frame).

Like the earlier theoretical models (Davis and Heathcote, 2005; Leung, 2007, 2014), the traditional panel data method often assumes a constant variance. In practice, the world keeps changing. The recent pandemic illustrates this point. At the beginning of the outbreak, the threat of COVID-19 was underestimated. Unfortunately, the number of causalities increased rapidly, and the world fell into panic. The implementation of vaccines brings hope to many, and the degree of uncertainty seems to have eased. Van Eyden et al. (Chapter 8) employ cutting-edge techniques and study the house price dynamics when the level of uncertainty changes over time. They find that macroeconomic uncertainty will spill over to housing market volatility in most states of America. Their results suggest another channel where the macroeconomy and the housing market are linked.

Yet another possibility is that the housing market experiences a permanent change, often labeled as a "structural break" in the economics literature. A natural candidate to consider would be the 2008 GFC. Since the GFC involved the housing market and mortgage-backed securities, it quickly became a shared research interest among macroeconomists and real estate researchers. Many authors have studied the GFC (Gorton and Metrick, 2012; Lo, 2012), and Part III of this book is devoted to it. Agarwal and Varshneya (Chapter 9) review the recent micro-evidence and shed light on the different explanations of the GFC.

The GFC may indeed mark a structural break in both the housing market and the macroeconomy. For instance, Green (1997) shows that residential investment is a "leading indicator" of GDP in the United States. This provided another bridge between the housing market and the macroeconomy. Green (Chapter 10) finds that the relationship vanished after the 2008 GFC. This result is consistent with Leung and Ng (2019), which examines the statistical relationships between housing market variables and macroeconomic variables in the United States. They find that the correlations have, in general, weakened since the GFC. Ng (Chapter 11) finds that such "structural change" has occurred in other OECD countries after the GFC. Also, Chang and Leung (Chapter 12) compare the statistical distribution of asset returns in the United States. They also find that the housing indices suggest that housing as an asset has become riskier since the GFC, while the stock market indices indicate that the stock market has become safer.

Part IV of this book collects several chapters on non-residential real estate, which should be the topic of a whole book, or even books. The invited authors skillfully present some concise chapters to give a glimpse of the different aspects. As earlier chapters have explored the "disaggregate house price dynamics," one would naturally ask why other regions have different house price dynamics. One potential explanation is that the underlying economic structure is different in the first place. It leads to the question of why people or firms would choose certain areas rather than others. Pinto and Sarte (Chapter 13) connect the regional economics and macroeconomics literature. They show the implications of locational choices made by households and firms on the macroeconomy.

If regional economics matters, it is natural to ask whether or what the government can do. Kahn et al. (Chapter 14) explain a particular class of "regional economic policy," namely, the industrial parks established in China. They evaluate the possible misallocation of capital due to those policies and draw some lessons from the policy experiments.

The global aging issue may have significant economic implications (Acemoglu and Restrepo, 2017; Bloom et al., 2010; Cooley and Henriksen, 2018). The economics literature has studied the pension system for decades (Auerbach and Kotlikoff, 1987; Cooley and Soares, 1999; Feldstein and Liebman, 2002; Kotlikoff, 1992). Economists are also aware that commercial real estate plays a role in economic growth and business cycle movements (Davis et al., 2020; Gort et al., 1999; Kan et al., 2004; Kwong and Leung, 2000). Riddiough (Chapter 15) shows how commercial real estate and its securitization could impact retirement financing.

The World Health Organization (2020) estimates that around 7 million people have died of air pollution. The economics literature has also provided evidence that pollution diminishes economic performance (Graff Zivin and Neidell, 2013). Fu and Viard (Chapter 16) consider the effect of air pollution from a mayor's perspective and naturally connect the pollution issue to traffic congestion and other urban problems.

I want to stress that the topics explored in this book are by no means exhaustive. Moreover, several new developments have not been covered (e.g., Duca et al., 2017; Kehoe et al., 2019; Kindermann et al., 2021; Krishnamurthy and Li, 2021). Nonetheless, this book would facilitate more communication between macroeconomics and real estate economics.

I want to take this opportunity to thank all my teachers, coauthors, previous and current colleagues, especially Eric Hanushek, who have helped me for years, long before this project started. I also learned a lot from the colleagues in the Asian Real Estate Society, especially Ko Wang and Yuichiro Kawaguchi. There are too many to thank for those who have helped in the process. I will miss many names no matter how hard I try. First, I thank all the contributors of this book for their willingness to share their insights and wisdom. I also thank those who have read different chapters of this book at various stages, such as Nan-Kuang Chen, Julan Du, Yifan Gong, Vikas Kakkar, Fred Kwan, Jennifer Lai, David Leung, Lingxiao Li, Edward Tang, Chi Man Yip, Yuxi Yao, and others who prefer to remain anonymous. Some contributors also read chapters other than their own. This project began when I was visiting the Hoover Institution, whose hospitality is gratefully acknowledged. I am also grateful to Alan Sturmer and colleagues at Edward Elgar for their patience and help throughout the whole process. And I would like to thank those who have prayed for me over the years. Perhaps this book is a part of the answer.

# REFERENCES

Acemoglu, D. and P. Restrepo (2017). "Secular stagnation? The effect of aging on economic growth in the age of automation," *American Economic Review*, 107(5), 174–179.

Attanasio, O., C. Meghir, and E. Nix (2020). "Human capital development and parental investment in India," *Review of Economic Studies*, 87, 2511–2541.

Auerbach, A. and L. J. Kotlikoff (1987). *Dynamic Fiscal Policy*, Cambridge: Cambridge University Press.

Bardhan, A., R. Edelstein, and C. Kroll (Eds) (2012). *Global Housing Markets: Crises, Policies, and Institutions*, New York: John Wiley.

Baxter, M. (1996). "Are consumer durables important for business cycles," *Review of Economics and Statistics*, 78(1), 147–155.

Ben-Shafar, D., C. Leung, and S. E. Ong (Eds) (2008). *Mortgage Market Worldwide*, Oxford: Blackwell.

Bloom, D. E., D. Canning, and G. Fink (2010). "Implications of population ageing for economic growth," *Oxford Review of Economic Policy*, 26(4), 583–612.

Chang, K. L., N. K. Chen, and C. K. Y. Leung (2011). "Monetary policy, term structure and real estate return: Comparing REIT, housing and stock," *Journal of Real Estate Finance and Economics*, 43, 221–257.

Chang, K. L., N. K. Chen, and C. K. Y. Leung (2012). "The dynamics of housing returns in Singapore: How important are the international transmission mechanisms?" *Regional Science and Urban Economics*, 42, 516–530.

Chang, K. L., N. K. Chen, and C. K. Y. Leung (2013). "In the shadow of the United States: The international transmission effect of asset returns," *Pacific Economic Review*, 18(1), 1–40.

Chen, N. K. (2001). "Asset price fluctuations in Taiwan: Evidence from stock and real estate prices 1973 to 1992," *Journal of Asian Economics*, 12(2), 215–232.

Cooley, T. F. and E. Henriksen (2018). "The demographic deficit," *Journal of Monetary Economics*, 93(C), 45–62.

Cooley, T. F. and J. Soares (1999). "A positive theory of social security based on reputation," *Journal of Political Economy*, 107(1), 135–160.

Cunha, F. and J. Heckman (2007). "The technology of skill formation," *American Economic Review*, 97(2), 31–47.

Cunha, F. and J. Heckman (2008). "Formulating, identifying and estimating the technology of cognitive and noncognitive skill formation," *Journal of Human Resources*, 43(4), 738–782.

Davis, M. and J. Heathcote (2005). "Housing and the Business Cycle," *International Economic Review*, 46(3), 751–784.

Davis, M. and S. Van Nieuwerburgh (2014). "Housing, finance and the macroeconomy," Working paper No. 20287, National Bureau of Economic Research, www.nber.org/papers/w20287

Davis, J. S., K. X. D. Huang, and A. Sapci (2020). "Imperfect substitutability in real estate markets and the effect of housing demand on the macroeconomy," Globalization Institute Working Papers 401, Federal Reserve Bank of Dallas.

Dell'Ariccia, G., P. Rabanal, and D. Sandri (2018). "Unconventional monetary policies in the Euro Area, Japan, and the United Kingdom," *Journal of Economic Perspectives*, 32(4), 147–172.

Deng, Y., Y. Tang, P. Wang, and J. Wu (2021). "Spatial misallocation in housing and land markets: Evidence from China." Mimeo.

Duca, J. V., P. H. Hendershott, and D. C. Ling (2017). "How taxes and required returns drove commercial real estate valuations over the past four decades," *National Tax Journal*, 70(3), 549–584.

Edelstein, R. and K. H. Kim (2004). "Special issue on housing and the macroeconomy: The nexus," *Journal of Housing Economics*, 13(4), 247–248.

Favilukis, J., S. C. Ludvigson, and S. Van Nieuwerburgh (2017). "The macroeconomic effects of housing wealth, housing finance, and limited risk sharing in general equilibrium," *Journal of Political Economy*, 125(1), 140–223.

Feldstein, M. and J. B. Liebman (2002). "Social security," in A. J. Auerbach and M. Feldstein (eds), *Handbook of Public Economics*, Volume 4, New York: Elsevier, pp. 2245–2324.

Fukuda, S. (2019). "The effects of Japan's unconventional monetary policy on Asian stock markets," *Public Policy Review (Ministry of Finance, Japan)*, 15(1), 1–19.

Gong, Y. and C. K. Y. Leung (2021). "When education policy and housing policy interact: Can they correct for the externalities?" *Journal of Housing Economics*.

Gort, M., J. Greenwood, and P. Rupert (1999). "Measuring the rate of technological progress in structures," *Review of Economic Dynamics*, 2(1), 207–230.

Gorton, G. and A. Metrick (2012). "Getting up to speed on the financial crisis: A one-weekend-reader's guide," *Journal of Economic Literature*, 50(1), 128–150.

Graff Zivin, J. and M. Neidell (2013). "Environment, health, and human capital," *Journal of Economic Literature*, 51(3), 689–730.

Green, R. (1997). "Follow the leader: How changes in residential and non-residential investment predict changes in GDP," *Real Estate Economics*, 25(2), 253–270.

Green, R. and S. Malpezzi (2003). *A Primer on U.S. Housing Markets and Housing Policy*, Washington, DC: Urban Institute.

Greenwood, J. and Z. Hercowitz (1991). "The allocation of capital and time over the business cycle," *Journal of Political Economy*, 99(6), 1188–1214.

Hanushek, E. and L. Woessmann (2015). *The Knowledge Capital of Nations: Education and the Economics of Growth*, Cambridge, MA: MIT Press.

Hanushek, E. and L. Woessmann (2016). "Knowledge capital, growth, and the East Asian miracle," *Science*, 351(6271), 344–345.

Hanushek, E., J. Ruhose, and L. Woessmann (2017). "Knowledge capital and aggregate income differences: Development accounting for US states," *American Economic Journal: Macroeconomics*, 9(4), 184–224.

Ito, T. (2003). "Retrospective on the bubble period and its relationship to developments in the 1990s," *World Economy*, 26(3), 283–300.

Kan, K., S. K. S. Kwong, and C. K. Y. Leung (2004). "The dynamics and volatility of commercial and residential property prices: Theory and evidence." *Journal of Regional Science*, 44(1), 95–123.

Kehoe, P. J., V. Midrigan, and E. Pastorino (2019). "Debt constraints and employment," *Journal of Political Economy*, 127(4), 1926–1991.

Kindermann, F., J. Le Blanc, M. Piazzesi, and M. Schneider (2021). "Learning about housing cost: Survey evidence from the German house price boom," NBER Working Paper No. 28895.

Kotlikoff, L. J. (1992). *Generational Accounting: Knowing Who Pays, and When, for What We Spend*, New York: Free Press.

Krishnamurthy, A. and W. Li (2021). "Dissecting mechanisms of financial crises: Intermediation and sentiment," NBER Working Paper No. 27088.

Kwong, S. K. S. and C. K. Y. Leung (2000). "Price volatility of commercial and residential property," *Journal of Real Estate Finance and Economics*, 20(1), 25–36.

Leung, C. K. Y. (2004). "Macroeconomics and housing: A review of the literature," *Journal of Housing Economics*, 13(4), 249–267.

Leung, C. K. Y. (2007). "Equilibrium correlations of asset price and return," *Journal of Real Estate Finance and Economics*, 34, 233–256.

Leung, C. K. Y. (2014). "Error correction dynamics of house price: An equilibrium benchmark," *Journal of Housing Economics*, 25, 75–95.

Leung, C. K. Y. and N. K. Chen (2006). "Intrinsic cycles of land price: A simple model," *Journal of Real Estate Research*, 28(3), 293–320.

Leung, C. K. Y. and N. K. Chen (2017). "A special issue on housing, credit markets, and the macroeconomy: An introduction," *Taiwan Economic Review*, 45(1), 1–3.

Leung, C. K. Y. and C. Y. J. Ng (2019). "Macroeconomic aspects of housing," in J. H. Hamilton, A. Dixit, S. Edwards, and K. Judd (Eds), *Oxford Research Encyclopedia of Economics and Finance*, Oxford: Oxford University Press.

Leung, C. K. Y. and J. Quigley (2007). "Special issue on macroeconomics, regulation, and housing: Introduction," *Journal of Housing Economics*, 16, 99–101.

Leung, C. K. Y. and E. C. H. Tang (2021). "The dynamics of the house price-to-income ratio: Theory and evidence," *Contemporary Economic Policy*.

Leung, C. K. Y., C. Y. J. Ng, and E. C. H. Tang (2020). "Why is the Hong Kong housing market unaffordable? Some stylized facts and estimations," *Quarterly Bulletin*, Central Bank of the Republic of China (Taiwan), 42(1), 5–58.

Liu, Z., P. Wang, and T. Zha (2013). "Land-price dynamics and macroeconomic fluctuations," *Econometrica*, 81(3), 1147–1184.

Liu, Z., J. Miao, and T. Zha (2016). "Land prices and unemployment," *Journal of Monetary Economics*, 80(C), 86–105.

Lo, A. W. (2012). "Reading about the financial crisis: A twenty-one-book review," *Journal of Economic Literature*, 50(1), 151–178.

Lubik, T. A. and F. Schorfheide (2003). "Computing sunspot equilibria in linear rational expectations models," *Journal of Economic Dynamics and Control*, 28(2), 273–285.

Lubik, T. A. and F. Schorfheide (2004). "Testing for indeterminacy: An application to U.S. monetary policy," *American Economic Review*, 94(1), 190–217.

Malpezzi, S. (2017). "Residential real estate in the U.S. financial crisis, the Great Recession, and their aftermath," *Taiwan Economic Review*, 45(1), 5–56.

Malpezzi, S. (2020). "Housing 'affordability' and responses during times of stress: A brief global review," Paper presented at the City University of Hong Kong Housing Affordability Workshop.

McMillen, D. (2011). "Special issue: The effect of the housing crisis on state and local government finances," *Regional Science and Urban Economics*, 41(4), 305.

Mera, K. and Renaud, B. (2000). *Asia's Financial Crisis and the Role of Real Estate*, New York: M. E. Sharpe.

O'Sullivan, A. (2018). *Urban Economics*, 9th ed, New York: McGraw Hill.

Okina, K., M. Shirakawa, and S. Shiratsuka (2001). "The asset price bubble and monetary policy: Japan's experience in the late 1980s and the lessons: Background paper," *Monetary and Economic Studies*, 19(S1), 395–450.

Phillips, P. C. B., Y. Wu, and J. Yu (2011). "Explosive behavior in the 1990s Nasdaq: When did exuberance escalate asset values?" *International Economic Review*, 52(1), 201–226.

Piazzesi, M. and M. Schneider (2016). Housing and macroeconomics, Working paper No. 22354, National Bureau of Economic Research, www.nber.org/papers/w22354

Quigley, J. M. and Raphael, S. (2004). "Is housing unaffordable? Why isn't it more affordable?" *Journal of Economic Perspectives*, 18, 191–214.

Ricardo, D. (1817). *On the Principles of Political Economy and Taxation*, reprinted by Batoche Books in 2001.

Ueda, K. (2012). "Deleveraging and monetary policy: Japan since the 1990s and the United States since 2007," *Journal of Economic Perspectives*, 26(3), 177–202.

Westelius, N. (2021). "Twenty years of unconventional monetary policies: Lessons and way forward for the Bank of Japan," IMF, www.imf.org/en/Publications/WP/Issues/2020/11/08/Twenty-Years-of-Unconventional-Monetary-Policies-Lessons-and-Way-Forward-for-the-Bank-of-49765

World Health Organization (2020). "Air pollution," www.who.int/health-topics/air-pollution#tab=tab_1

Yao, Y. (2020). "Accounting for the decline in homeownership among the young," paper presented at the City University of Hong Kong Housing Affordability Workshop.

Yılmaz, K. and M. Yesilırmak (2020). "Access to transportation, residential segregation, and economic opportunity," paper presented at the City University of Hong Kong Housing Affordability Workshop.

# PART I

# REAL ESTATE-RELATED WEALTH AND MACROECONOMICS

# 1. Real estate market and consumption: macro and micro evidence of Japan
*Kazuo Ogawa*

## 1  INTRODUCTION

The real estate market in Japan has been turbulent over three decades. Figure 1.1 shows the Urban Land Price Index of residential land of the six major cities and other cities. The residential land price of the six major cities soared from September 1986 to September 1990 of the bubble period at 22.5 percent per annum. After the land price peaked in September 1990, the bubble burst. The land price plummeted from September 1990 to September 1993 at 15.9 percent per annum. The land price kept on falling for 15 consecutive years. Although fall of the land price came to an end in March 2005, the subsequent growth rate of land price is only 0.3 percent per annum. The residential land price in those other cities exhibits a similar trend, but its fluctuations are far milder.

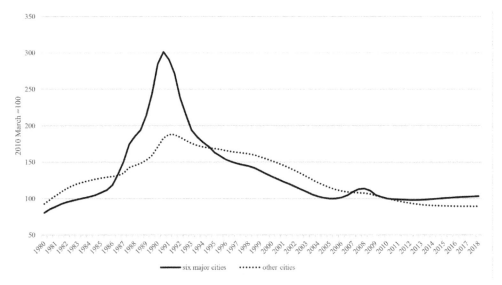

*Source*: Japan Real Estate Institute, Urban Land Price Index.

*Figure 1.1    Urban Land Price Index: residential land*

It has been argued that excessive fluctuations of land price affected the performance of the Japanese economy to a large extent. In fact, the annual real gross domestic product growth rate from 1986 to 1990 was 5.5 percent, but it fell sharply to only 1.0 percent from 1990 to 2018. The purpose of this study is to investigate the extent to which a shock in the real estate market affected consumption spending. Panel 1 of Figure 1.2 shows the market value of land assets held by Japanese households from 1994 to 2007 and panel 2 shows the revaluation accounts (capital gains or losses) of land assets. The Japanese households incurred large capital losses in the late 1990s to the early 2000s. The simple correlation coefficient between the rate of change in residential land price and revaluations is 0.8472. Therefore it is quite likely that an adverse shock in the real estate market had large negative effects on consumption.

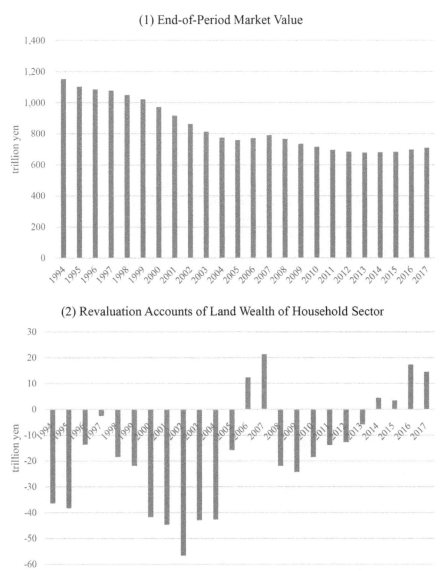

Source: Economic and Social Research Institute, Annual Report of National Accounts.

Figure 1.2    Land wealth of household sector

This study contributes to the literature twofold. First, it pins down the channels through which a shock in the real estate market is propagated to consumption spending. There are two competing channels through which a shock in the real estate market or change in land price affects consumption.[1] One channel is well known as the *wealth effect channel*. The life cycle permanent income hypothesis of consumption (LCY-PIH) states that total wealth, which consists of financial wealth, tangible wealth and human wealth, is an important determinant of consumption. A shock in land price affects consumption by changing tangible wealth. The other channel is called the *collateral channel*. The balance sheet conditions of debtors affect the cost of raising external funds under capital market imperfections. When there exists asymmetric information between debtors and creditors, it will drive a wedge between the cost of external finance and internal finance, called an *external finance premium*. An external finance premium reflects the creditor's cost of collecting the debtor's information and monitoring the debtor's behavior and the cost arising from an adverse selection problem or moral hazard problem. The premium for external funds influences the cost of external funds and thereby affects the economic activities of the debtor. Furthermore, the external finance premium is inversely associated with the borrower's collateralizable net worth. Therefore, an adverse shock in land price has negative effects on the consumer's net worth, which raises the external finance premium and reduces borrowing as well as consumption.[2,3] Using quarterly time series data, we estimate the vector regression (VAR) model to examine which channel is more important in propagating a shock in land price to consumption.

The other contribution is to quantify the effects of a shock in land price on consumption with precision. The use of time series data prevents us from measuring precisely the extent to which a shock in land price affects consumption due to multicollinearity. Therefore, we use panel data for households to quantify the effects of a shock in the land price market on consumption by estimating consumption function.

Let us preview our findings. First, we estimate a five-variate VAR model including consumption and residential land price, with quarterly data from 1980 to 2018. We find that a positive shock in land price gives rise to a persistent increase in consumption. However, once the channel from land price to consumer borrowing is shut off, the effects of a shock in the land price on consumption are dampened to a large extent. This evidence shows that the channel through which a shock in land price is transmitted to consumption is the collateral channel. Second, we reestimate the VAR model with the same specification by dividing the sample period into two: 1980 to 2002 and 2003 to 2018. The former subsample corresponds to the turbulent period including the bubble and the lost decades, while the latter corresponds to the period when a non-performing loans problem is somehow overcome after the financial revitalization program in 2002. For the former period, we still find that collateral channel was at work, but not for the latter period.

To estimate the effect of a shock in land price on consumption with precision, we use the panel data of the Japan Household Panel Survey (KHPS/JHPS) collected by the Panel Data Research Center at Keio University. The sample period covers nine years from 2009 to 2017. Our estimates of the marginal propensity to consume (MPC) out of housing wealth are from 0.0097 to 0.0146, slightly larger than the estimates of the previous studies. Moreover, we find that housing wealth has a significantly positive effect on the consumption of young households, but the effect of housing wealth on the consumption of old households is insignificant in some cases. Our evidence shows that the collateral channel is still at work for young households even after the non-performing loan problem is worked out. We failed to detect the collateral channel from aggregate time series data due to a heterogeneous response of household consumption to housing wealth.

This study is organized as follows. The next section provides a literature survey of past studies that have examined the effects of the performance of the real estate market on consumption in Japan. Section 3 estimates the effect of residential land price on consumption based on the VAR model, using aggregate time series data. Section 4 estimates the consumption function of the LCY-PIH, using panel data of households and measuring the effect of house wealth on consumption. Section 5 concludes the study.

## 2 LITERATURE SURVEY: RELATIONSHIP BETWEEN THE REAL ESTATE MARKET AND CONSUMPTION IN JAPAN

In the literature researchers have investigated the relationship between the performance of the real estate market and consumption by estimating the consumption function with housing wealth as one of the explanatory variables. Ogawa et al. (1996b) estimate the LCY-PIH consumption function with different types of wealth as explanatory variables. Their concern is what types of wealth are relevant in consumption decisions of households. They estimate the consumption function using pooled data of prefectural cross-sections for three different years (1980, 1985 and 1990). They construct their data set mainly from the *Annual Report of Prefectural Accounts* by the Cabinet Office. Their estimates of MPC out of tangible wealth are not significant and sometimes take a negative value.

Hori and Shimizutani (2004) also measure the MPC out of the real asset capital gains for individual house owners and condominium owners. They use micro-level data from the Japanese Panel Survey of Consumption conducted by the Institute of Household Economy (Kakei-Keizai-Kenkyu-Sho) from 1993 to 1999. Their estimates of the MPC out of real asset capital gains are about 0.1 and 0.05, respectively, but none are significant.

Ogawa and Wan (2007) estimate the consumption functions of total expenditure with several wealth variables. They use resampled micro data from the National Survey of Family Income and Expenditure. The survey is conducted every five years and their study is based on the waves from 1989, 1994 and 1999. The virtue of using the data in these three waves is coverage of two entirely different periods: the bubble and the lost decades. The wealth variables are liquid wealth, total wealth and net wealth. Total wealth is the sum of the savings balance, land equity and home equity at market prices. The MPC out of total wealth and net wealth is statistically significant but the estimates are quite small, 0.0002 to 0.0003.

Muellbauer and Murata (2011) and Aron et al. (2012) estimate the consumption function with real land price, using the aggregate social network analysis data from 1961 to 2008. They find that real land price had significantly negative effects on consumption and argue that in countries where consumer access to credit is restricted, these restrictions can enhance the negative effect of higher house prices on consumption because saving for a housing deposit needs to be higher.

Naoi (2014) estimates the consumption function derived from reference-dependent preferences, using the KHPS/JHPS for eight years from 2004 to 2011. His evidence supports the theoretical prediction that consumption response to household wealth is larger when optimal consumption levels are lower than reference points. His estimates of the effects of housing wealth on consumption are significant and range from 0.0065 to 0.0079 when consumption levels are below reference points, but are insignificant and much lower when consumption levels are above reference points.

Hori and Niizeki (2017) provide the most comprehensive study estimating the MPC of housing wealth from consumption function. They use cross-sectional data of the Japanese Family Income and Expenditure Survey (FIES) over the period of 1983 to 2012. The data cover about 500,000 households. They make a painstaking effort to construct individual housing wealth. For example, they estimate the value of residential land assets owned by individual households by multiplying the land area (square meters) of their homes reported in the FIES by the price of residential land at the closest survey location in the *Land Market Value Publication* (Chika-koji) provided by the Ministry of Land, Infrastructure, Transport and Tourism. They find that the MPC out of housing wealth is approximately 0.0059–0.0082 for total consumption. Following the methodology of Campbell and Cocco (2007), they further find that the consumption response of older households to housing wealth is larger than that of younger households, which they argue supports the pure wealth effects hypothesis. Hori and Niizeki (2017) provide the only study that compares the validity of the pure wealth effect and the collateral effect of housing wealth.

To sum up, the effects of housing wealth on consumption have been estimated to be lower in Japan than their counterparts in western countries. The MPCs out of housing wealth are 0.02 to 0.043 in the United States (Bostic et al., 2009; Caceres, 2019; Juster et al., 2006), 0.09 to 0.14 in the United Kingdom (Disney et al., 2010), 0.02 to 0.024 in Italy (Guiso et al., 2006; Paiella, 2007) and 0.02 in Spain (Bover, 2005).[4] The MPC out of housing wealth in Japan is at the most 0.01 and our estimates presented here are slightly larger than previously. As for the channel through which a shock in land price is propagated to consumption, our evidence differs from Hori and Niizeki (2017) in that the collateral channel is at work throughout our sample period.

## 3 TIME SERIES EVIDENCE: REAL ESTATE MARKET AND CONSUMPTION

To the best of the author's knowledge, there are no studies that investigate the relationship between the performance of the real estate market and consumption in Japan based on the VAR model. The virtue of the VAR model is that we can identify the channels through which a shock in the real estate market is propagated to a change in consumption. We estimate the VAR model that consists of five variables: total consumption, disposable income, liquid wealth, consumer borrowing and residential land price. Disposable income and liquid wealth are two important determinants of consumption. Residential land price affects consumption in two ways. First, a change in residential land price changes the housing wealth of households, which in turn affects consumption (wealth effect). Second, a rise in residential land price mitigates the borrowing constraints of households and increases consumption (collateral effect). Note that in the latter channel residential land price affects consumption spending via consumer borrowing. We test the validity of the collateral channel by comparing two VAR models. In one model we estimate the fully unconstrained five-variate VAR model and in the other model the channel from residential land price to consumer borrowing is shut off by imposing zero restrictions on the coefficient estimates of land price in the consumer borrowing equation. If the effect of land price on consumption is weakened when the channel from residential land price to consumer borrowing is shut off, then the collateral channel is at work.

Table 1.1    Results of the augmented Dickey–Fuller unit root test and Phillips–Perron test

| Level | Augmented Dickey–Fuller test | Phillips–Perron $Z_t$ test |
| --- | --- | --- |
| Residential land price | −3.277* | −1.832 |
| Consumer borrowing | −1.796 | −1.452 |
| Disposable income | −1.593 | −1.452 |
| Liquid wealth | −3.008 | −2.625 |
| Consumption | −0.970 | −0.885 |
| *Growth rate* | | |
| Residential land price | −4.243*** | −2.209 |
| Consumer borrowing | −3.530** | −3.051 |
| Disposable income | −3.779** | −8.590*** |
| Liquid wealth | −4.645*** | −4.200*** |
| Consumption | −4.982*** | −6.566*** |

*Note*: Lag order is taken as two. A trend term is included in the regression. *, **, ***: significant at the 10%, 5% and 1% levels, respectively.

However, if the effect of land price on consumption remains unaltered, then the wealth effect channel is at work.[5]

Let us describe the variables we use in estimation. Consumption is real final consumption expenditure of households. Disposable income is real net disposable income of households. Consumption and disposable income are taken from the Annual Report of National Accounts. Liquid wealth is the sum of cash currency, deposits, trust, securities investment trusts and securities. Consumer borrowings are borrowings from private financial institutions. Liquid wealth and consumer borrowings are taken from the Flow of Funds Accounts of the Bank of Japan. All the variables are deflated by final consumption expenditure and seasonally adjusted. Residential land price is the Urban Land Price Index of residential land in the six major cities, taken from the Japan Real Estate Institute. The original land price series is available only for March and September, so we interpolate the land price index for June and December. The sample period is from the first quarter of 1980 to the first quarter of 2018.

Table 1.1 shows the results of the augmented Dickey–Fuller unit root test and Phillips–Perron test of five variables in the VAR model. The null hypothesis that the variable contains a unit root is not rejected at the conventional significance level for any variables. Table 1.1 also shows the results of the unit root test of five variables in terms of growth rate. This time the null hypothesis is rejected decisively. Therefore, we estimate the VAR model in terms of growth rate of variables.[6] The optimal lag order is chosen using the three-model selection criteria for VAR models. The three criteria are the Akaike information criteria, the Bayesian information criteria and the Hannan–Quinn information criteria. We finally choose the lag length to be two.

First, we estimate an unconstrained five-variate VAR model for the whole sample. The stability condition of the VAR model is satisfied.[7] The order of five variables is residential land price, consumer borrowing, disposable income, liquid wealth and consumption.[8]

Table 1.2 shows the variance decomposition of consumption. The fraction of 10-year-ahead forecast-error variance of consumption that can be attributed to both disposable income and liquid wealth is about 19 percent each, while the fraction attributed to residential land price is 8.2 percent. Table 1.3 shows the variance decomposition of consumer borrowing. About 40

8  Handbook of real estate and macroeconomics

Table 1.2   Variance decomposition of consumption: first quarter 1980-first quarter 2018

| Year | Consumption (%) | Residential land price (%) | Consumer borrowing (%) | Disposable income (%) | Liquid wealth (%) |
|---|---|---|---|---|---|
| 1 | 91.8 | 2.9 | 2.9 | 1.6 | 0.8 |
| 2 | 85.1 | 2.6 | 2.5 | 3.6 | 6.2 |
| 3 | 73.7 | 2.8 | 2.2 | 11.5 | 9.7 |
| 4 | 65.9 | 3.2 | 2.8 | 14.1 | 14.0 |
| 5 | 58.9 | 3.7 | 3.9 | 16.5 | 16.9 |
| 6 | 54.3 | 4.3 | 5.3 | 17.4 | 18.7 |
| 7 | 50.9 | 5.2 | 6.5 | 18.0 | 19.3 |
| 8 | 48.6 | 6.1 | 7.5 | 18.3 | 19.4 |
| 9 | 46.9 | 7.2 | 8.3 | 18.5 | 19.2 |
| 10 | 45.5 | 8.2 | 8.9 | 18.6 | 18.8 |

Table 1.3   Variance decomposition of consumer borrowing: first quarter 1980-first quarter 2018

| Year | Consumption (%) | Residential land price (%) | Consumer borrowing (%) | Disposable income (%) | Liquid wealth (%) |
|---|---|---|---|---|---|
| 2 | 0.0 | 1.6 | 90.7 | 0.9 | 6.7 |
| 3 | 0.0 | 6.0 | 81.5 | 3.2 | 9.2 |
| 4 | 0.2 | 12.4 | 73.7 | 4.6 | 9.1 |
| 5 | 0.2 | 19.5 | 66.3 | 5.9 | 8.1 |
| 6 | 0.2 | 25.8 | 59.9 | 6.8 | 7.2 |
| 7 | 0.2 | 30.9 | 54.8 | 7.6 | 6.5 |
| 8 | 0.2 | 34.6 | 50.9 | 8.2 | 6.1 |
| 9 | 0.2 | 37.2 | 48.1 | 8.7 | 5.8 |
| 10 | 0.3 | 38.9 | 46.2 | 9.1 | 5.6 |

percent of 10-year-ahead forecast-error variance of consumer borrowing is explained by residential land price. These results imply that the collateral channel is important in propagating a shock in land price to consumption by way of consumer borrowing. Figure 1.3 depicts the impulse response of consumption to a one standard deviation shock to residential land price together with the associated 95 percent confidence intervals.[9,10] Consumption is increased by 0.11 percentage points two years after a positive unexpected shock to residential land price and the positive effect persists for 10 years after the shock. Figure 1.3 also depicts the impulse response of consumption to a one standard deviation shock to the other three variables: disposable income, consumer borrowing and liquid wealth.[11] A rise in consumption is statistically significant after a positive shock of each variable. Consumption increases by 0.42 percentage points two years after a positive shock to disposable income, 0.22 percentage points five years after a positive shock to consumer borrowing and 0.36 percentage points three years after a positive shock to liquid wealth.

Now we estimate the constrained five-variate VAR model by shutting off the channel from residential land price to consumer borrowing. This exercise can test the validity of the collateral channel. If the impulse response of consumption to a one standard deviation shock to residential land price is lower than the unconstrained case, then the collateral channel plays an important role through which a shock in residential land price is propagated to consumption

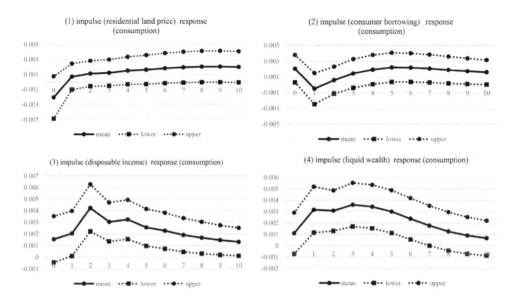

Figure 1.3   Impulse response functions: 1st quarter 1980–first quarter 2018

via consumer borrowing. However, if the impulse response of consumption to a shock to residential land price remains unaltered, housing wealth effect à la the LCY-PIH is at work. Figure 1.4 depicts the impulse response of consumption to a one standard deviation shock to residential land price when the channel from residential land price to consumer borrowing is shut off.[12] An increase in consumption is insignificant and much smaller than in the case with endogenous consumer borrowings. This evidence shows that the collateral channel plays a vital role in propagating a shock in residential land price to consumption.[13]

Our sample period covers nearly four decades and includes a variety of events that affected the real estate market, such as the asset bubble, the lost decades, the global financial crisis and Abenomics.[14] Therefore, it is an interesting exercise to examine whether there was a structural break where the transmission mechanism of a shock in residential land price to consumption changed. For that purpose we reestimate the five-variate VAR model for two subsamples. The first subsample covers the most turbulent periods including the bubble period and the lost decades, while the second subsample corresponds to the recovery phase of the real estate market. We break the whole sample period into two by the year 2002 when the financial revitalization program took place under the Koizumi Administration and the non-performing loan ratio of large financial institutions fell thereafter.

Table 1.4 shows the variance decomposition of consumption for the first subsample. The fraction of 10-year-ahead forecast-error variance of consumption that can be attributed to residential land price is 18.8 percent, much higher than the case of the whole sample period, and the fractions attributed to disposable income and liquid wealth are 6.0 percent and 14.5 percent, respectively, much lower than the case of the whole sample period. Table 1.5 shows the variance decomposition of consumer borrowing. More than half (51.6 percent) of 10-year-ahead forecast-error variance of consumer borrowing is explained by residential land price. These results confirm that the collateral channel is important in propagating a shock in land price to consumption in the former subsample.

## 10  Handbook of real estate and macroeconomics

(1) Unconstrained 5-variate VAR model

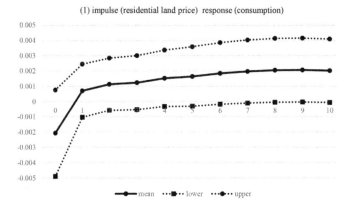

(2) Shut-off of the channel from land price to consumer borrowing

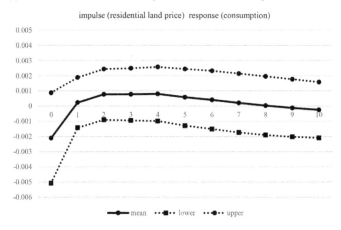

*Figure 1.4*   Impulse response functions: first quarter 1980–first quarter 2018

*Table 1.4*   Variance decomposition of consumption: first quarter 1980–fourth quarter 2002

| Year | Consumption (%) | Residential land price (%) | Consumer borrowing (%) | Disposable income (%) | Liquid wealth (%) |
|---|---|---|---|---|---|
| 1 | 82.0 | 2.0 | 15.8 | 0.1 | 0.1 |
| 2 | 82.2 | 2.7 | 14.6 | 0.1 | 0.4 |
| 3 | 77.3 | 3.8 | 14.6 | 3.3 | 1.0 |
| 4 | 72.2 | 5.6 | 15.0 | 3.6 | 3.6 |
| 5 | 65.8 | 8.0 | 14.9 | 4.8 | 6.4 |
| 6 | 60.3 | 10.5 | 15.1 | 5.1 | 9.0 |
| 7 | 55.5 | 13.0 | 15.0 | 5.5 | 11.0 |
| 8 | 51.6 | 15.2 | 14.9 | 5.7 | 12.5 |
| 9 | 48.4 | 17.2 | 14.9 | 5.9 | 13.6 |
| 10 | 45.8 | 18.8 | 14.8 | 6.0 | 14.5 |

Table 1.5  Variance decomposition of consumer borrowing: first quarter 1980-fourth quarter 2002

| Year | Consumption (%) | Residential land price (%) | Consumer borrowing (%) | Disposable income (%) | Liquid wealth (%) |
|---|---|---|---|---|---|
| 2 | 0.2 | 11.1 | 75.5 | 0.2 | 13.1 |
| 3 | 1.0 | 24.7 | 55.4 | 2.2 | 16.7 |
| 4 | 0.8 | 35.1 | 43.4 | 2.8 | 17.9 |
| 5 | 0.7 | 42.8 | 34.8 | 3.5 | 18.1 |
| 6 | 0.7 | 47.7 | 29.3 | 4.1 | 18.2 |
| 7 | 0.7 | 50.4 | 25.8 | 4.7 | 18.4 |
| 8 | 0.7 | 51.7 | 23.7 | 5.2 | 18.8 |
| 9 | 0.7 | 52.0 | 22.5 | 5.6 | 19.2 |
| 10 | 0.8 | 51.6 | 21.9 | 6.0 | 19.6 |

Table 1.6  Variance decomposition of consumption: first quarter 2003-first quarter 2018

| Year | Consumption (%) | Residential land price (%) | Consumer borrowing (%) | Disposable income (%) | Liquid wealth (%) |
|---|---|---|---|---|---|
| 1 | 93.5 | 0.5 | 0.4 | 5.0 | 0.5 |
| 2 | 74.9 | 0.7 | 3.6 | 13.6 | 7.3 |
| 3 | 61.0 | 0.8 | 4.3 | 22.5 | 11.4 |
| 4 | 57.9 | 2.6 | 4.2 | 23.2 | 12.1 |
| 5 | 58.3 | 3.7 | 4.0 | 22.3 | 11.6 |
| 6 | 58.2 | 3.9 | 4.0 | 22.2 | 11.7 |
| 7 | 57.3 | 3.9 | 3.9 | 22.7 | 12.1 |
| 8 | 56.1 | 4.7 | 3.9 | 23.0 | 12.4 |
| 9 | 55.0 | 6.2 | 3.8 | 22.8 | 12.3 |
| 10 | 54.0 | 7.9 | 3.7 | 22.4 | 12.1 |

Table 1.6 shows the variance decomposition of consumption for the latter subsample. The fraction of 10-year-ahead forecast-error variance of consumption that can be attributed to residential land price is only 7.9 percent, much lower than the case of the former subsample period, and the fraction attributed to disposable income is 22.4 percent, much higher than the former subsample period. Table 1.7 shows the variance decomposition of consumer borrowing for the latter subsample period. The 10-year-ahead forecast-error variance of consumer borrowing cannot be explained by residential land price. The contribution of residential land price to the 10-year-ahead forecast-error variance of consumer borrowing is only 1.8 percent. Thus we can conclude that residential land price affects consumption by way of the wealth effect in the latter subsample.

Our evidence shows that the collateral channel plays an important role in propagating a shock in residential land price to consumption in the former subsample. We can also confirm this evidence by comparing the impulse response of consumption to a shock to residential land price in an unconstrained VAR model with the impulse response pattern when the channel from residential land price to consumer borrowing is shut off.

Figure 1.5 depicts two impulse response patterns of consumption to a one standard deviation shock to residential land price for the former subsample. One is the unconstrained case and the other is the case where the channel from residential land price to consumer borrowing is shut

12    Handbook of real estate and macroeconomics

Table 1.7    Variance decomposition of consumer borrowing: first quarter 2003-first quarter 2018

| Year | Consumption (%) | Residential land price (%) | Consumer borrowing (%) | Disposable income (%) | Liquid wealth (%) |
|---|---|---|---|---|---|
| 2 | 0.0 | 0.4 | 94.8 | 1.8 | 3.0 |
| 3 | 0.5 | 0.3 | 92.7 | 2.1 | 4.3 |
| 4 | 0.5 | 0.3 | 92.6 | 2.5 | 4.1 |
| 5 | 0.5 | 0.3 | 91.7 | 2.5 | 5.0 |
| 6 | 0.6 | 0.4 | 89.6 | 2.5 | 6.9 |
| 7 | 0.8 | 0.5 | 88.0 | 2.4 | 8.3 |
| 8 | 0.9 | 0.7 | 87.3 | 2.4 | 8.7 |
| 9 | 1.1 | 1.1 | 86.8 | 2.4 | 8.6 |
| 10 | 1.1 | 1.8 | 85.9 | 2.5 | 8.7 |

(1) Unconstrained 5-variate VAR model

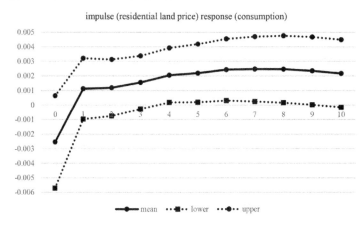

(2) Shut-off of the channel from land price to consumer borrowing

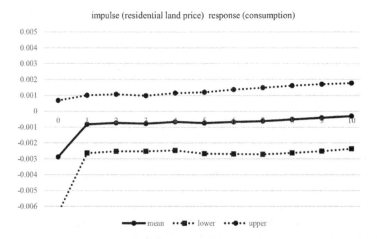

Figure 1.5    Impulse response functions: first quarter 1980–fourth quarter 2002

(1) Full 5-variate VAR model

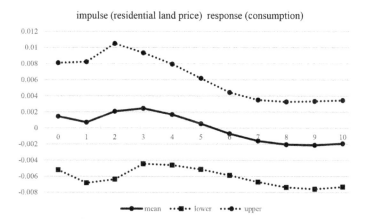

(2) Shut-off of the channel from land price to consumer borrowing

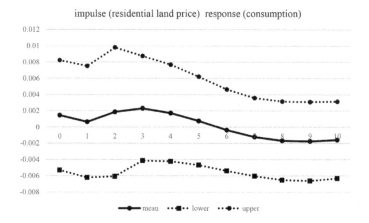

*Figure 1.6    Impulse response functions: first quarter 2003–first quarter 2018*

off.[15] In the unconstrained VAR model consumption is increased by 0.20 percentage points four years after a positive shock to residential land price and the positive effect persists for ten years after the shock. On the other hand, when the channel from residential land price to consumer borrowing is shut off, the increase in consumption is almost nil.

Figure 1.6 compares two impulse response patterns of consumption to a one standard deviation shock to residential land price for the latter subsample.[16] The impulse response patterns of the two cases are very similar. The response of consumption to a shock in residential land price is not so large. The largest response of consumption, which is 0.24–0.25 percentage points, comes three years after a positive shock to residential land price and is dampened quickly thereafter.

## 4  PANEL DATA EVIDENCE: THE REAL ESTATE MARKET AND CONSUMPTION

We estimate the effects of a change in the real estate market on consumption, using panel data on households. Use of panel data enables us to obtain precise estimates of the effects of a change in housing wealth on consumption since the panel data set is free from multicollinearity. We use the panel data of the KHPS/JHPS. The KHPS has been implemented every year since 2004 for 4,000 households and 7,000 individuals nationwide. An additional survey on a cohort of about 1,400 households and 2,500 individuals started from 2007 to compensate for sample dropout. The JHPS is a new survey targeting 4,000 male and female subjects nationwide in parallel with the KHPS.

The KHPS and JHPS are suitable for estimating the effect of a change in housing wealth on consumption since they record the self-reported market value of land plots and residential buildings. We use the KHPS/JHPS for the period of 2009 to 2017 since after-tax annual income is available only after 2009. The total number of households who own their houses and reported the market value of their houses and land plots as well as their outstanding housing loans was 8,396.

The consumption function we estimate is a LCY-PIH type with two wealth variables, liquid financial wealth and housing wealth including residential house and land. We also add socio-economic variables to the list of explanatory variables. The consumption function is specified as follows:

$$\left(\frac{C}{Y}\right)_{it} = \alpha_0 + \alpha_1 \left(\frac{1}{Y}\right)_{it} + \alpha_2 \left(\frac{LW}{Y}\right)_{it} + \alpha_3 \left(\frac{HW}{Y}\right)_{it} + \sum_{j=1}^{n} \beta_j (Z_j)_{it} + u_{it}. \qquad (1.1)$$

Explanations of the variables used in estimation are in order. The total consumption expenditure $(C)_{it}$ is the real total consumption expenditure of household $i$ in January of year $t$ multiplied by 12 to obtain an annual figure and divided by the final consumption expenditure deflator. The after-tax annual income $(Y)_{it}$ is the real after-tax annual income of the household in the previous year $t-1$. The liquid financial wealth $(LW)_{it}$ is the sum of deposits and securities divided by the final consumption expenditure deflator.

The housing wealth $(HW)_{it}$ is the sum of the self-reported market value of housing and land plots, which is divided by the final consumption expenditure deflator. The socio-economic variables $(Z)_{it}$ include the following household attributes: household size and binary working status comprising no paid work, self-employed, professional, work without any employee relationship and non-regular wage worker. Finally we add year dummies to represent common shocks that hit the sampled households.[17]

We discard the households whose consumption–income ratio, liquidity–wealth–income ratio and housing–stock–income ratio are smaller than the 1st percentile or greater than the 99th percentile. The total number of households used for estimation is 7,481. Table 1.8 shows the descriptive statistics of the major variables. The self-reported market value of land plots and housing is 15.0 million yen and 10.1 million yen, respectively, and the mortgage loan balance is 16.9 million yen. The proportion of households who have negative equity is 31.0 percent.

Table 1.8    Descriptive statistics of major variables in panel data set

| Item | Mean | Median | Standard deviation |
|---|---|---|---|
| Age | 48.2 | 47 | 11.15 |
| Household size | 3.8 | 4 | 1.29 |
| Market value of housing (10,000 yen) | 1009.9 | 900 | 808.47 |
| Market value of land plot (10,000 yen) | 1502.4 | 1000 | 1431.90 |
| Mortgage loan balance (10,000 yen) | 1689.5 | 1500 | 1280.85 |
| Market value of liquid assets (10,000 yen) | 555.5 | 300 | 1085.58 |
| After-tax annual income (10,000 yen) | 602.1 | 550 | 308.71 |
| Annual consumption expenditure (10,000 yen) | 387.9 | 330 | 296.60 |
| Proportion of respondents who have spouse (%) | 89.7 | | |
| Proportion of respondents who performed paid work (%) | 82.7 | | |
| Self-employed (%) | 7.5 | | |
| Professional (%) | 1.0 | | |
| Worker at family business (%) | 2.4 | | |
| Working at home, consigned worker or subcontractor (%) | 2.2 | | |
| Wage worker (%) | 70.5 | | |
| Full-time, regular employee (%) | 46.6 | | |
| Non-regular employee (%) | 23.3 | | |
| Proportion of respondents who have negative equity (%) | 31.0 | | |
| Proportion of respondents who have no liquid wealth (%) | 19.7 | | |

*Source*: Panel Data Research Center at Keio University, Japan Household Panel Survey.

We estimate Equation 1.1 under two different statistical models to see the robustness of the estimation results, especially the coefficient estimates of housing wealth. The statistical specifications we employ are panel regression and panel IV regression. The first panel of Table 1.9 shows the estimation results for the whole sample.[18] In the third and fourth columns, we estimate the MPCs out of liquid financial wealth separately for the households likely to be liquidity-constrained and unconstrained households.[19] The coefficient estimate of liquid financial wealth is significantly positive for possibly liquidity-constrained households, irrespective of model specifications. The MPC out of financial wealth is from 0.0281 to 0.0510. The coefficient estimate of housing wealth is also estimated with high precision. The MPC out of housing wealth hovers around 0.01.

Our estimates of the MPC out of housing wealth are slightly larger than those in the previous studies, but lower than their international counterparts. In contrast the MPC of liquid wealth is comparable with those of other advanced economies. For example, the MPCs out of financial wealth are 0.003 to 0.19 in the United States (Caceres, 2019; Dynan and Maki, 2001; Juster et al., 2006) and 0.04 to 0.092 in Italy (Guiso et al., 2006; Paiella, 2007). Why is the MPC out of housing wealth smaller in Japan, while the MPC out of financial wealth in Japan is comparable with the international counterparts? Financial markets in advanced countries are equally well developed, so households can easily liquidate their liquid wealth in financial markets to increase consumption. However, the resale market for home equity is less developed in Japan than in the United States and European countries, and thus the means to capitalize gains on home equity for consumption is somewhat limited, which might explain smaller MPCs out of housing wealth in Japan.[20]

In the previous section we could not detect the collateral channel after 2002 using aggregate time series data. Failure to detect the collateral channel might be due to heterogeneity in the

## 16   Handbook of real estate and macroeconomics

Table 1.9   Estimation results of consumption function by panel data

| | Whole sample | | | | | Younger household | | | | | Older household | | | |
|---|---|---|---|---|---|---|---|---|---|---|---|---|---|---|
| | Panel regression | Panel regression (IV) | Panel regression | Panel regression (IV) | Panel regression | Panel regression (IV) | Panel regression | Panel regression (IV) | Panel regression | Panel regression (IV) | Panel regression | Panel regression (IV) | Panel regression | Panel regression (IV) |
| 1/income | 233.9554*** (51.61) | 216.2932*** (53.26) | 233.8587*** (51.65) | 216.3534*** (53.27) | 238.0735*** (48.58) | 222.5142*** (50.08) | 236.7256*** (48.23) | 221.7525*** (50.23) | 225.3602*** (23.55) | 207.4953*** (26.38) | 226.7929*** (23.66) | 207.2576*** (26.38) |
| Liquid wealth/income | 0.0319*** (4.89) | 0.01784*** (2.12) | | 0.0119 (1.14) | | 0.0202 (1.37) | | 0.0040 (0.23) | 0.0418*** (4.46) | 0.0150 (1.41) | | 0.0068 (0.47) |
| Liquid wealth/income (unconstrained households) | | | 0.0096 (1.11) | | 0.0131 (1.16) | | −0.0174 (−1.28) | | | | | |
| Liquid wealth/income (constrained households) | | | 0.0510*** (6.26) | 0.0281** (2.20) | | | 0.0452*** (3.16) | 0.0531** (2.19) | | | 0.0548*** (4.89) | 0.0312* (1.94) |
| Housing wealth/income | 0.0117*** (4.06) | 0.0100*** (2.59) | 0.0119*** (4.13) | 0.0097** (2.50) | 0.0143*** (3.83) | 0.0111* (1.93) | 0.0146*** (3.92) | 0.0100* (1.89) | 0.0070 (1.44) | 0.0089 (1.50) | 0.0070 (1.45) | 0.0083 (1.40) |
| Household size | 0.0302*** (3.38) | 0.0370*** (7.29) | 0.0309*** (3.46) | 0.0376*** (7.35) | 0.0151 (1.19) | 0.0177*** (2.61) | 0.0161 (1.28) | 0.0201*** (3.08) | 0.0377*** (2.57) | 0.0511*** (6.48) | 0.0387*** (2.64) | 0.0523*** (6.60) |
| *Working status* | | | | | | | | | | | | |
| No paid work | −0.0153 (−0.56) | −0.0328* (−1.86) | −0.0482* (−1.69) | −0.0477* (−1.94) | −0.0255 (−0.80) | −0.0073 (−0.36) | −0.0615* (−1.84) | −0.0423 (−1.41) | 0.0186 (0.36) | −0.0632** (−2.15) | −0.0175 (−0.32) | −0.0953** (−2.28) |
| Self-employed | 0.0188 (0.39) | 0.0325 (1.25) | 0.0210 (0.44) | 0.0341 (1.31) | −0.0157 (−0.26) | 0.0926** (2.52) | −0.0152 (−0.25) | 0.0980*** (2.75) | 0.0782 (0.92) | −0.0304 (−0.80) | 0.0786 (0.92) | −0.0269 (−0.71) |
| Professional | −0.1264 (−1.09) | −0.0890 (−1.32) | −0.1216 (−1.05) | −0.0891 (−1.32) | 0.1009 (0.76) | 0.0007 (0.01) | 0.1081 (0.82) | −0.0008 (−0.01) | −0.7091*** (−3.14) | −0.1960* (−1.85) | −0.7010*** (−3.11) | −0.1981* (−1.87) |
| Work without any employee relationship | −0.0035 (−0.08) | −0.0148 (−0.39) | −0.0036 (−0.80) | −0.0262 (−0.65) | 0.0282 (0.52) | 0.0527 (1.17) | −0.0139 (−0.25) | 0.0279 (0.57) | −0.0491 (−0.63) | −0.1260* (−1.92) | −0.0788 (−1.00) | −0.1502** (−2.15) |
| Non-regular worker | −0.0099 (−0.41) | −0.0342** (−2.23) | −0.0382 (−1.50) | −0.0458** (−2.21) | −0.0126 (−0.44) | −0.0151 (−0.87) | −0.0433 (−1.44) | −0.0445* (−1.79) | −0.0095 (−0.21) | −0.0667** (−2.46) | −0.0402 (−0.83) | −0.0923** (−2.54) |
| Constant | 0.1140*** (2.84) | 0.1033*** (3.43) | 0.1263*** (3.14) | 0.1053*** (3.46) | 0.1656*** (2.99) | 0.1203*** (3.22) | 0.1808*** (3.26) | 0.1251*** (3.36) | 0.1088 (1.64) | 0.1484*** (2.94) | 0.1180* (1.77) | 0.1529*** (3.01) |
| R-squared | 0.3362 | 0.3857 | 0.3934 | 0.3860 | 0.4062 | 0.4823 | 0.4079 | 0.4813 | 0.2501 | 0.2966 | 0.2520 | 0.2982 |
| Sargan statistics[a] | | 8.684 (0.12) | | 8.631 (0.12) | | 7.910 (0.16) | | 7.918 (0.16) | | 11.77 (0.04) | | 11.54 (0.04) |
| Stochastic model | fixed effect | random effect | fixed effect | random effect | fixed effect | random effect | fixed effect | random effect | fixed effect | random effect | fixed effect | random effect |

*Note:* The number in parenthesis is the t-value. The coefficient estimates of year dummies are suppressed. [a] The number in parenthesis of Sargan statistics is the p-value. The instruments we use for liquid-wealth-income ratio and housing-wealth-income ratio are one-year-lagged liquid wealth and housing wealth and five dummy variables for the firm size of the workplace of the household head. *, **, ***: significant at the 10%, 5% and 1% levels, respectively.

response of household consumption to land price. To pursue this issue further, we estimate the consumption function separately for younger households and older households. When the pure housing wealth channel is at work, older households with shorter remaining lifetimes over which to annuitize housing wealth should have a larger MPC out of housing wealth than younger households. The second and third panels of Table 1.9 show the estimation results of consumption function for younger households and older households, respectively. A younger household is defined as a household whose head is below 50 years old. The housing wealth exerts a significantly positive effect on the consumption of younger households, irrespective of model specification. In contrast, the response of consumption of older households to housing wealth is insignificant in all specifications.[21] This evidence indicates that younger households are likely to face borrowing constraints and housing wealth plays a collateral role in mitigating borrowing constraints. Weak response of consumption to housing wealth for older households might suggest that housing wealth is viewed as a bequest by older households.[22]

## 5   CONCLUDING REMARKS

This study is an empirical attempt to investigate the relationship between the performance of the real estate market and consumption in Japan. The contribution of this study to the literature is twofold. First, we investigate the channel through which a change in residential land price affects consumption. Using the quarterly time series over nearly four decades from 1980 to 2008, we estimate the VAR model including a change in land price and consumption to find the transmission mechanism of changes in land price to consumption. We find that the collateral channel plays an important role in propagating a shock in land price to consumption by way of consumer borrowing in the bubble period and the lost decades.

The other contribution is to estimate the effect of housing wealth on consumption with high precision, using the panel data of households. Using the panel data of the KHPS/JHPS from 2009 to 2017, we estimate the consumption function with two wealth variables: liquid wealth and housing wealth. Our estimates of MPC out of housing wealth is 0.0097 to 0.0146, consistent with the estimates obtained in past studies.

Moreover, we find that the housing wealth had a significantly positive effect on the consumption of younger households, but the effect of housing wealth on the consumption of older households was insignificant in some specifications. Our evidence shows that the collateral channel is still at work for younger households even after the non-performing-loan problem is worked out.

Overall, evaluation of the effects of the performance of the real estate market on the Japanese economy needs additional investigation into the channel through which a shock in land price is propagated to firms' activities. Past studies show that the collateral channel played a vital role in propagating a shock in land price to corporate investment. Reexamination of the collateral channel in the corporate sector after the lost decades would be an interesting avenue of future research.

## NOTES

1. There is a third explanation for positive correlation between house prices and consumption, which is called common factor hypothesis. King (1990) and Pagano (1990) argue that an upward revision to expected future incomes simultaneously increased the demand for housing services and consumption in the United Kingdom. This common factor hypothesis is not tested in this study. See Attanasio et al. (2009) for more details of this hypothesis.
2. The collateral channel lays emphasis on the relationship between land price and the *borrower*'s collateralizable net worth. However, a change in land price can also affect the expected cost of default for *lenders*. The expected cost of default may depend on whether the loan is secured and if so on the value of collateral. Ogawa and Kitasaka (2000) showed that the optimal loan supply of a value-maximizing banking firm depends on land price as well as the profit margin of the interest rate. In other words the land price also plays an important role in the bank's loan supply decision. Thus the collateral channel hypothesis in this chapter incorporates the behavior of both borrowers and lenders.
3. Some studies argue that the collateral channel plays an important role in explaining the long stagnancy of investment by Japanese firms in the 1990s. The borrowing of Japanese firms increased enormously in the late 1980s secured by land. Land used to be perfect for collateral in Japan under the expectation that the land price would never fall. In other words land was a useful device to reduce the external finance premium. In fact, based upon the aggregated time series data, Ogawa et al. (1996a) find that the external finance premium is reduced by appreciation of land value in the late 1980s for non-manufacturing industries that are composed of a number of small firms. Contrary to expectations, land price fell sharply in the1990s, which eroded firms' collateralizable net worth with the loan outstanding almost intact, which raised the external finance premium considerably and thereby decreased investment. Ogawa and Suzuki (1998) find a non-linearity in this effect with the panel data of Japanese listed companies in the machinery sector from 1970 to 1993. Gan (2007) finds evidence that the firms with larger land holdings before the burst of the land price bubble in Japan faced a more severe credit constraint in the subsequent period based on the data set of Japanese listed companies. By employing a unique data set on firms' land transactions and overall investment in Japan during the period of 1997–2006, Hazama and Uesugi (2015) find that the fixed tangible asset investment is positively associated with the growth rate of land prices, which is evidence for a collateral channel. Using the data set on Japanese small and medium enterprises in the 1980s and 1990s, Ogura (2015) shows that the collateral constraint is binding when the price of a collateralizable asset is declining, whereas it is not when the price is rising.
4. See Paiella (2009) for an extensive survey of the evidence on the relationship between house prices and consumer spending.
5. Chen and Leung (2007) argue that the relationship between economic fundamentals and land price might be non-linear. If this is the case, then applying a linear VAR would lead to a biased estimation, and regime-switching VAR that takes account of non-linearity between economic fundamentals and land price would be preferable. To examine the applicability of regime-switching VAR, we estimated the two-state Markov switching dynamic model, respectively, for each dependent variable of the five-variate VAR model. Then we calculated the correlation coefficients of one-period-ahead probability of being in a given state among five variables to see whether the regime-switching VAR model was applicable. If the correlation coefficients between the probabilities of being in a given state of five variables were significant, then we could go ahead and apply the regime-switching VAR model. It turned out that the correlation coefficient was significant only between consumer borrowing and consumption, which implies that the switching point varied across variables. Therefore we did not pursue the regime-switching VAR model.
6. We could not detect any cointegration relations among five variables. Therefore, we did not estimate the vector error correction model.
7. Note that a VAR model is stable if all moduli of the eigenvalue of the estimated models are strictly less than unity. See Hamilton (1994, pp. 260-261).
8. The five-variate VAR model can also be estimated by reordering the variables as follows: disposable income, consumer borrowing, residential land price, liquid wealth and consumption. The estimated results remain essentially unaltered.

9. Confidence intervals are estimated from 5,000 bootstrap replications of the estimated VAR model.
10. A one standard deviation shock to residential land price is 1.26 percentage points.
11. A one standard deviation shock to disposable income, consumer borrowing and liquid wealth is 1.45 percentage points, 1.33 percentage points and 2.49 percentage points, respectively.
12. A one standard deviation shock to residential land price is 1.27 percentage points.
13. The collateral channel is also supported by data from other countries. For example, see the evidence for the United States provided by Cooper (2013) and for Australia and Canada provided by Atalay et al. (2014) and Windsor et al. (2015).
14. Abenomics is the comprehensive economic policy package adopted by former prime minister Shinzo Abe to sustainably revive the Japanese economy from the lost decades.
15. A one standard deviation shock to residential land price is 1.55 percentage points.
16. A one standard deviation shock to residential land price is 0.44 percentage points.
17. We do not include the age variable as an explanatory variable since linear combinations of year dummies are closely correlated with the age variable.
18. The coefficient estimates of year dummies are not shown in the table to save space.
19. The households likely to be liquidity constrained are those with the working status of no work, work without any employee relationship and non-regular wage worker.
20. The Ministry of Land, Infrastructure, Transport and Tourism reports that the proportion of used homes out of total home transactions in Japan was 14.5 percent in 2018, which is much lower than the United States (81 percent) and the United Kingdom (85.9 percent).
21. Caceres (2019) also finds that younger individuals tend to have a significantly larger MPC than older cohorts. The MPC out of housing wealth for those aged 25 to 44 years is 0.08, while it is less than 0.04 for those aged 65 years or older. There is an interestingly contrasting result obtained by Chen and Wang (2011). They examine the effect of housing and stock wealth on consumption, using Taiwan's household survey data for 1996–2006. They find that the effect of housing wealth is insignificant for middle-aged and old households, while negatively significant for young households and renters. The overall effect of housing wealth is insignificant. A possible explanation is that the used market for home equity in Taiwan is relatively small and the means to capitalize gains on home equity for consumption are limited.
22. Using the same data set from JHPS for 2006 to 2015, Iwata and Yukutake (2017) also find that changes in housing wealth do not significantly increase elderly consumption. They argue that the elderly homeowners cannot release part of their housing wealth as cash. Rather, elderly homeowners leave their housing assets to their children and in exchange receive cash to fund consumption.

# REFERENCES

Aron, J., Duca, J.V., Muellbauer, J. and Murata, K. (2012). "Credit, Housing Collateral, and Consumption: Evidence from Japan, the U.K. and the U.S.," *Review of Income and Wealth*, Vol. 58, No. 3, pp. 397–423.

Atalay, K., Whelan, S. and Yakes, J. (2014). "House Prices, Wealth and Consumption: New Evidence from Australia and Canada," *Review of Income and Wealth*, Vol. 62, No.1, pp. 69–91.

Attanasio, O.P., Blow, L., Hamilton, R. and Leicester, A. (2009). "Booms and Busts: Consumption, House Prices and Expectations," *Economica*, Vol. 76, pp. 20–50.

Bostic, R., Gabriel, S., and Painter, G. (2009). "Housing Wealth, Financial Wealth and Consumption: New Evidence from Micro Data," *Regional Science and Urban Economics*, Vol. 39, No.1, pp. 79–89.

Bover, O. (2005). "Wealth Effects on Consumption: Microeconometric Estimates from the Spanish Survey of Household Finances," Documentos de Trabajo No. 0522, Banco de España.

Caceres, C. (2019). "Analyzing the Effects of Financial and Housing Wealth on Consumption Using Micro Data," IMF Working Paper WP/19/115.

Campbell, J.Y. and Cocco, J.F. (2007). "How Do House Prices Affect Consumption? Evidence from Micro Data," *Journal of Monetary Economics*, Vol. 54, pp. 591–621.

Chen, N.K. and Leung, C.K.Y. (2007). "Asset Price Spillover, Collateral and Crises: with an Application to Property Market Policy," *Journal of Real Estate Finance and Economics*, Vol. 37, pp. 351–385.

Chen, N.K. and Wang, H.J. (2011). "The Effect of Changes in Asset Prices on Private Consumption," *Quarterly Bulletin*, Central Bank of CBC (Taiwan), Vol. 33, No. 1, pp.7–40 (in Chinese).

Cooper, D. (2013). "House Price Fluctuations: The Role of Housing Wealth as Borrowing Collateral," *Review of Economics and Statistics*, Vol. 95, No. 4, pp. 1183–1197.

Disney, R., Gathergood, J. and Henley, A. (2010). "House Price Shocks, Negative Equity and Household Consumption in the United Kingdom," *Journal of the European Economic Association*, Vol. 8, No. 6, pp. 1179–1200.

Dynan, K. and Maki, D. (2001). "Does Stock Market Wealth Matter for Consumption?" FEDS Working Paper No. 2001-21, Board of Governors of the Federal Reserve System.

Gan, J. (2007). "A Collateral, Debt Capacity, and Corporate Investment: Evidence from a Natural Experiment," *Journal of Financial Economics*, Vol. 85, pp. 709–734.

Guiso, L., Paiella, M. and Visco, I. (2006). "Do Capital Gains Affect Consumption? Estimates of Wealth Effects from Italian Household Behavior," in Klein, L. (ed.), *Long Run Growth and Short Run Stabilization: Essays in Memory of Albert Ando (1929–2002)*. Cheltenham, U.K. and Northampton, MA, U.S.A.: Edward Elgar Publishing.

Hamilton, J.D. (1994). *Time Series Analysis*. Princeton, NJ: Princeton University Press.

Hazama, M and Uesugi, I. (2015). "Heterogenous Impact of Real Estate Prices on Firm Investment," RIETI Discussion Paper 15-E-091.

Hori, M. and Niizeki, T. (2017). "Housing Wealth Effects in Japan: Evidence Based on Household Micro Data," ESRI Discussion Paper Series No. 339.

Hori, M. and Shimizutani, S. (2004). "Asset Holding and Consumption: Evidence from Japanese Panel Data in the 1990s," *Seoul Journal of Economics*, Vol. 17, No. 21, pp. 153–179.

Iwata, S. and Yukutake, N. (2017). "Housing Assets and Consumption among the Japanese Elderly," Faculty of Economics, Toyama University, Working Paper No. 308.

Juster, T., Lupton, J., Smith, J. and Stafford, F. (2006). "The Decline in Household Saving and the Wealth Effect," *Review of Economics and Statistics*, Vol. 88, No. 1, pp. 20–27.

King, M. (1990). "Discussion," *Economic Policy*, Vol. 11, pp. 383–387.

Muellbauer, J. and Murata, K. (2011). "Consumption, Land Prices and the Monetary Transmission Mechanism in Japan," in Hamada, K., Kashyap, A.K. and Weinstein, D. (eds), in *Japan's Bubble, Deflation and Long-term Stagnation*, Cambridge, MA: MIT Press, pp. 175–216.

Naoi, M. (2014). "Housing Wealth, Reference-Dependent Preferences and Household Consumption," *Keio Journal of Economics*, Vol. 106, No. 4, pp. 473–487 (in Japanese).

Ogawa, K. and Kitasaka, S. (2000). "Bank Lending in Japan: Its Determinants and Macroeconomic Implications," in Hoshi, T. and Patrick, H. (eds), *Crisis and Change in the Japanese Financial System*, Berlin: Kluwer Academic Publishers, pp. 159–199.

Ogawa, K. and Suzuki, K. (1998). "A Land Value and Corporate Investment: Evidence from Japanese Panel Data," *Journal of the Japanese and International Economies*, Vol. 12, No. 3, pp. 232–249.

Ogawa, K. and Wan, J. (2007). "Household Debt and Consumption: A Quantitative Analysis Based on Household Micro Data for Japan," *Journal of Housing Economics*, Vol. 16, pp. 127–142.

Ogawa, K., Kitasaka, S., Yamaoka, H. and Iwata, Y. (1996a). "A Borrowing Constraint and the Role of Land Asset in Japanese Corporate Investment Decision," *Journal of the Japanese and International Economies*, Vol. 10, No. 2, pp. 122–149.

Ogawa, K., Kitasaka, S., Yamaoka, H. and Iwata, Y. (1996b). "An Empirical Re-Evaluation of Wealth Effect in Japanese Household Behavior," *Japan and the World Economy*, Vol. 8, No. 4, pp. 423–442.

Ogura, Y. (2015). "Investment Distortion by Collateral Requirements: Evidence from Japanese SMEs," RIETI Discussion Paper 15-E-050.

Pagano, M. (1990). "Discussion," *Economic Policy*, Vol. 11, pp. 387–390.

Paiella, M. (2007). "Does Wealth Affect Consumption? Evidence for Italy," *Journal of Macroeconomics*, Vol. 29, No. 1, pp. 189–205.

Paiella, M. (2009). "The Stock Market, Housing and Consumer Spending: A Survey of the Evidence on Wealth Effects," *Journal of Economic Surveys*, Vol. 23, No. 5, pp. 947–973.

Windsor, C., Jaaskela, J.P. and Finlay, R. (2015). "Housing Wealth Effects: Evidence from an Australian Panel," *Economica*, Vol. 82, pp. 552–577.

# 2. The Bank of Japan as a real estate tycoon: large-scale REIT purchases

*Takahiro Hattori and Jiro Yoshida*

## 1 INTRODUCTION

The Bank of Japan (BOJ) enhanced its unconventional monetary policy in October 2010 by purchasing equity exchange-traded funds (ETFs) and public real estate investment trusts (REITs) in addition to the open market operations of Japanese Government Bonds (JGBs). These equity purchase programs are unprecedented in the history of central banking.[1] In April 2013, the BOJ started a new policy regime called quantitative and qualitative monetary easing (QQE), in which the BOJ further increased the asset purchase amount and started new fixed-price JGB purchase operations (Hattori and Yoshida, 2020). After ten years of continued REIT purchases, the BOJ has become one of the largest owners of public REITs. The BOJ issued the Report of Possession of Large Volume to 21 REITs by February 6, 2020, because it owned more than 5 percent of the outstanding shares. However, the BOJ's specific purchase behavior is not publicly known.

The objective of our study is to unveil the BOJ's behavior of purchasing REIT shares. We use both the BOJ's daily purchase report and intraday REIT return data. Using the linear probability model (LPM) and the Cox hazard model with time-varying covariates, we find that the BOJ tends to start purchasing REIT shares when it observes a significantly negative REIT return over the previous night and during the morning market on the Tokyo Stock Exchange (TSE). In particular, the BOJ strongly responds to a REIT return below the 30th percentile of historical overnight and morning returns. The BOJ continues purchasing REIT shares daily until either overnight or morning returns become positive. Thus, we conclude that the BOJ applies a counter-cyclical intervention rule based on the overnight and morning returns. However, general stock market returns do not impact the BOJ's REIT purchase decisions. Furthermore, we find that the lunchtime and afternoon returns are more likely to be positive on the day of the BOJ's intervention. This result suggests that the BOJ's purchase orders positively affect REIT returns after the morning market.

The BOJ's program to purchase REITs and ETFs is unique among central banks' large-scale asset purchase (LSAP) programs. Most LSAPs—first deployed by the BOJ in 2001—are targeted to long-maturity bonds such as government bonds and mortgage-backed securities (MBSs). These LSAPs are used to lower long-term interest rates and stimulate firms' and consumers' spending when the short-term policy rate is near the zero lower bound. However, both REIT shares and ETFs are risky equity securities traded on a stock exchange. The primary objective of REIT/ETF purchases is to decrease various risk premiums by attracting more funds into the financial markets and stabilizing the economy (Shirakawa, 2010). Thus, this program can be understood as an extension of LSAPs that aim to decrease risk premiums.[2]

Although the BOJ does not discuss the specific mechanism to decrease risk premiums, extant studies suggest that the BOJ's ETF purchases can reduce equity risk premiums by increasing stock prices (Barbon and Gianinazzi, 2019; Charoenwong et al., 2021; Harada and Okimoto, 2021). A higher stock price implies a lower risk premium if the risk-free rate is unchanged around the zero lower bound. For the BOJ's operations to affect stock prices, there must be limits to arbitrage between the stock market and other financial markets. Otherwise, the BOJ's additional demand for stocks will be spread across all financial markets through arbitrage. Thus, this stock price impact is analogous to LSAP's effect through the scarcity channel (D'Amico et al., 2012; Hamilton, 2018; Krishnamurthy and Vissing-Jorgensen, 2011, 2013). The scarcity channel hypothesis states that a central bank's LSAP can affect long-term bond prices if bond markets are segmented by investors' preferred maturity habitats (Greenwood and Vayanos 2014; Modigliani and Sutch, 1966; Vayanos and Vila, 2009; Wallace, 1981).

The BOJ can potentially reduce REIT risk premiums further through additional channels. For example, if the marginal REIT investor is less diversified than the marginal ETF investor, the BOJ's REIT purchases can reduce the marginal investor's exposure to REIT risks and thus the equilibrium price of REIT risks. This channel is analogous to the capital-constraints channel for the Fed's purchase of mortgage-backed securities (MBSs). When MBS investors are capital-constrained, MBS yields include premiums corresponding to underdiversification. When a central bank purchases MBSs, these capital-constraint premiums will decrease (Krishnamurthy and Vissing-Jorgensen, 2013). Also, REIT share purchases can decrease REITs' credit risk by reducing leverage (the default risk channel).

Our finding that the BOJ purchases REIT shares after observing a significant negative return suggests that the BOJ aims to mitigate large decreases in REIT share prices. Moreover, REIT shares are more likely to increase after the morning market on the day of the BOJ's purchase operation. This purchasing behavior and the intraday price dynamics are consistent with the BOJ's key objective to decrease various risk premiums because a higher REIT share price is associated with a lower expected REIT equity premium. However, the program may create a side-effect on the price discovery function of the financial market. If REIT market prices do not incorporate negative information fully, investors' assessment of the economic condition may be biased.

The remainder of this chapter is organized as follows. Section 2 describes the BOJ's unconventional monetary policy, and Section 3 explains the Japanese REIT market. Then, Section 4 describes the data, Section 5 details our empirical strategy and Sections 6 and 7 present our empirical results. Section 8 concludes.

## 2 BANK OF JAPAN'S UNCONVENTIONAL MONETARY POLICY

The BOJ pioneered in adopting an unconventional monetary policy. It was the first central bank to use forward guidance in 1999 when it adopted the zero interest rate policy. After the global financial crisis, the BOJ set up in October 2010 the fund to purchase REITs and ETFs. The BOJ states three objectives of purchasing risky assets. First, the BOJ aims to stimulate both firms' and households' spending by decreasing funding costs through the reduction of long-term interest rates and various risk premiums. Second, the BOJ expects investors and financial institutions to increase their portfolio allocations to risky assets such as stocks, REITs and loans to ease the private sector's funding. Third, the BOJ aims to eliminate deflationary expectations and decrease real interest rates.

In April 2013, the BOJ started QQE to achieve a 2 percent inflation rate measured by the consumer price index. The "quantitative" component corresponds to the change in the BOJ's target from the uncollateralized overnight call rate (i.e., price) to the monetary base (i.e., quantity). The BOJ targeted to increase the monetary base by approximately 60–70 trillion Japanese yen (JPY) each year.[3] Two years after starting QQE, the BOJ almost doubled the monetary base by holding more JGBs on its balance sheet. Subsequently, the BOJ further accelerated the monetary base growth from October 2014.

The "qualitative" component corresponds to open-market operations for almost all securities except for municipal, government-guaranteed and government agency bonds. For example, the BOJ purchases longer-term government bonds, commercial papers, corporate bonds, ETFs and REITs. The BOJ also applied negative ten basis points to private banks' current accounts at the BOJ (January 2016) and launched a new fixed-price JGB purchase program in September 2016 (Hattori and Yoshida, 2020).

The BOJ started purchasing REITs through trust in October 2010 up to a limit of 50 billion JPY, which was increased later by 10 billion JPY in April 2012. Under QQE starting in 2013, the BOJ changed the limit to an annual purchase amount of 30 billion JPY. From October 2014, the BOJ tripled the annual purchase amount to 90 billion JPY under QQE2. The BOJ's REIT holdings and ownership ratio increased significantly during QQE2 (Figure 2.1). In 2019, the BOJ's ownership ratio became approximately 3.5 percent of the 16 trillion JPY market capitalization of REITs. The maximum ownership proportion for each REIT is 10 percent, which was increased in December 2015 from 5 percent. The BOJ holds all assets it purchased under QQE, including ETFs, REITs and JGBs. This buy and hold policy is not unique to the BOJ; for example, the Fed did not sell bonds or MBSs under QE until it started to decrease its balance sheet in October 2017. The BOJ is still increasing its asset base because it has not

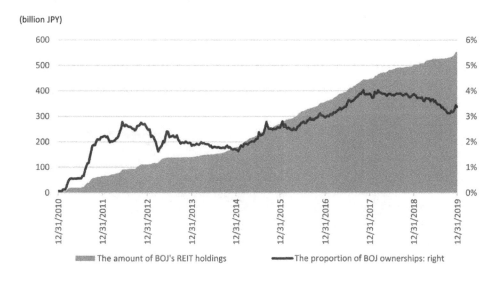

*Source*: Bloomberg.

*Figure 2.1* The BOJ's REIT holdings

yet achieved its inflation rate target. Thus, the BOJ does not consider tapering or "quantitative tightening."

The BOJ sets several conditions for an REIT to be purchased. It must trade for more than 200 days with an annual trading value of 20 billion JPY or more. The BOJ also applies the collateral standards set forth in the Guidelines on Eligible Collateral (Policy Board Decision on October 13, 2000):[4] (1) publicly offered bonds issued by a firm must be rated AA or higher by an eligible rating agency, and (2) principal investment objects of a firm should be real estate (including leaseholds, superficies and asset-backed securities).

The BOJ does not make an advance notice about the specific date of a REIT purchase operation, although it announces the annual budget and the daily ex-post purchase record. The BOJ submits a REIT purchase order through the designated trust banks without public notice. This operation method contrasts with the BOJ's regular JGB auctions, for which the BOJ makes an announcement each month of the purchase amount and frequency for the following month (Hattori, 2020).

## 3    THE JAPANESE REIT MARKET

Japanese REITs were established in 2000 by the amendment to the Act on Investment Trusts and Investment Corporations. The first two REITs—Nippon Building Fund and Japan Real Estate—were listed on the TSE in September 2001. Figure 2.2 depicts the growth of the Japanese public REIT market in terms of the number of listed REITs and their market capitalization. The initial growth period until 2007 was followed by a contraction period between 2010 and 2012 due to the global financial crisis starting in 2007 and the Great East Japan Earthquake in 2011. However, there has been another period of steady market growth since 2012. As of January 31, 2020, 64 REITs were listed with the total market capitalization of

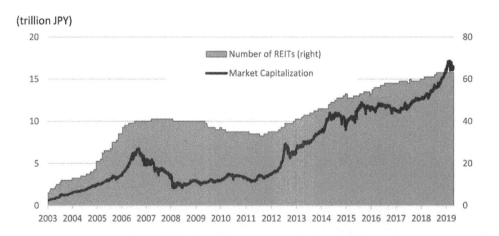

*Source*: Bloomberg.

*Figure 2.2*    *Number and market capitalization of REITs*

17 trillion JPY, which accounts for approximately 3 percent of the market capitalization of TOPIX. The Japanese REIT market is now the second-largest REIT market in the world after the United States REIT market. Of the 19.2 trillion JPY assets under management, office properties are 41.6 percent, retail properties are 17.6 percent, industrial properties are 16.0 percent, residential properties are 14.4 percent and hotel properties are 8.4 percent.

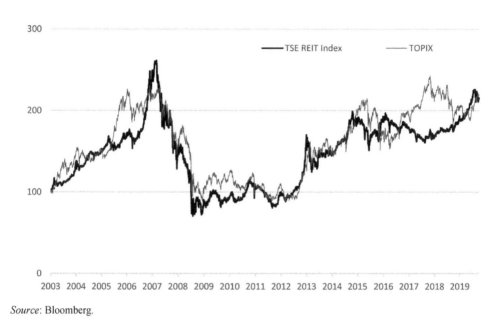

*Source*: Bloomberg.

*Figure 2.3*     *TOPIX and REIT price returns*

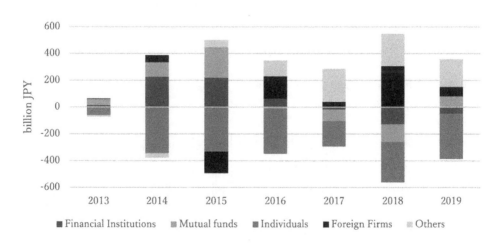

*Source*: Bloomberg.

*Figure 2.4*     *Net purchase amount by investor type*

26  *Handbook of real estate and macroeconomics*

Figure 2.3 depicts the TOPIX and the TSE-REIT Index (ex-dividends) between 2003 and 2020. After a sharp decrease between 2007 and 2008, the REIT Index generally exhibits an upward trend until 2019. The two indexes generally moved in tandem, but they started to diverge around 2014.

Figure 2.4 depicts the net purchase amount by investor type between 2013 and 2019. Throughout this period, individuals have been net sellers, whereas foreign investors have been net buyers since 2016. Other institutions have been increasing the net purchase amount since 2015. In 2019, sellers were individuals (338 billion JPY) and financial institutions (47 billion JPY), whereas buyers were mutual funds (81 billion JPY), foreign firms (69 billion JPY) and others (208 billion JPY). The BOJ's annual net purchase amount of 90 billion JPY is sizable in the market.

## 4   DATA

We obtain the dates and amounts of the BOJ's REIT purchase operations from the BOJ's website. Figure 2.5 depicts the size of daily operations (panel A) and the number of operations for each month (panel B). Before QQE2 (until September 2014), the size of each operation

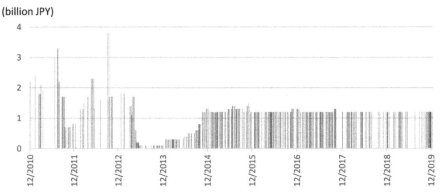

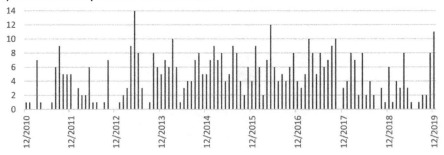

*Source*: Bank of Japan

*Figure 2.5*   The BOJ's REIT purchase operations

varied significantly, and the operations were irregular. Under QQE2, the size of each operation became almost constant at 1.2 billion JPY, and more than one operation took place almost every month. The average number of operations is 2.5 before QQE2 and 5.3 under QQE2.

We use the TSE-REIT Index to compute REIT returns from April 2013 to December 2019. We divide each trading day into four subperiods: the overnight period (from 15:00 on the previous trading day to 09:00), the morning market (from 09:00 to 11:30), lunchtime (from 11:30 to 12:30) and the afternoon market (from 12:30 to 15:00).

Table 2.1 shows the descriptive statistics of the TSE-REIT Index ex-dividend returns. The mean daily return is 2.1 bps, with a standard deviation of 95.7 bps. Periodic returns tend to be slightly lower and less volatile while the market is closed (overnight and lunchtime) than while the market is open.

Table 2.1   Tokyo Stock Exchange REIT Index returns

| Periods | Observations | Mean | Standard deviation | Minimum | Maximum |
|---|---|---|---|---|---|
| Daily | 1,654 | 0.00021 | 0.00957 | -0.07340 | 0.05713 |
| Overnight (15:00–09:00) | 1,654 | -0.00027 | 0.00423 | -0.02002 | 0.02028 |
| Morning market (09:00–11:30) | 1,654 | 0.00016 | 0.00567 | -0.03282 | 0.05087 |
| Lunchtime (11:30–12:30) | 1,654 | -0.00018 | 0.00116 | -0.01029 | 0.00642 |
| Afternoon market (12:30–15:00) | 1,654 | 0.00049 | 0.00585 | -0.04671 | 0.05772 |

Note: This table shows the descriptive statistics of the TSE-REIT Index returns from April 2013 to December 2019.
Source: Bloomberg.

Table 2.2 shows the deciles of TSE-REIT Index returns for each subperiod. For our empirical analysis, we construct a dummy variable for each decile group: for example, returns less than the 10th percentile, returns greater than or equal to the 10th percentile and less than the 20th percentile, etc.

Table 2.2   Percentiles of Tokyo Stock Exchange REIT Index returns

| Percentiles | Daily | Overnight (15:00–09:00) | Morning market (09:00–11:30) | Lunchtime (11:30–12:30) | Afternoon market (12:30–15:00) |
|---|---|---|---|---|---|
| 10th | -0.00909 | -0.00457 | -0.00555 | -0.00139 | -0.00514 |
| 20th | -0.00547 | -0.00249 | -0.00315 | -0.00092 | -0.00318 |
| 30th | -0.00329 | -0.00158 | -0.00180 | -0.00061 | -0.00185 |
| 40th | -0.00162 | -0.00080 | -0.00081 | -0.00037 | -0.00071 |
| 50th | 0.00017 | -0.00012 | 0.00014 | -0.00016 | 0.00036 |
| 60th | 0.00172 | 0.00057 | 0.00104 | 0.00006 | 0.00144 |
| 70th | 0.00341 | 0.00129 | 0.00218 | 0.00028 | 0.00261 |
| 80th | 0.00596 | 0.00225 | 0.00346 | 0.00058 | 0.00395 |
| 90th | 0.00946 | 0.00386 | 0.00556 | 0.00103 | 0.00631 |

Note: This table shows TSE-REIT Index return deciles for each of the four subperiods. The sample period is from April 2013 to December 2019.
Source: Bloomberg.

## 5  EMPIRICAL STRATEGY

### 5.1  Linear Probability Model

We first estimate the following LPM to analyze the BOJ's REIT purchase decisions by using the daily data.

$$\mathbb{I}_t = \alpha_1 + \sum_{i=\{N,A,L,P\}} \beta_1^i r_t^i + \varepsilon_{1,t}, \qquad (2.1)$$

where $\mathbb{I}_t$ denotes the dummy variable that takes a value of one if the BOJ purchases REIT shares at date t and takes zero otherwise. The explanatory variable $r_t^i$ denotes TSE-REIT Index returns during subperiod $i$, as defined in Section 4. The subperiods consist of the overnight period $(N)$, the morning market $(A)$, lunchtime $(L)$ and the afternoon market $(P)$. $\varepsilon_{1,t}$ denotes the error term. A negative coefficient $\beta_1^i$ indicates that the BOJ is more likely to purchase REIT shares on date $t$ if a REIT return is smaller (more negative) during subperiod $i$.

The second variation includes lagged REIT returns:

$$\mathbb{I}_t = \alpha_2 + \sum_{i=\{N,A,L,P\}} \beta_2^i r_t^i + \gamma_2^i r_{t-1}^i + \varepsilon_{2,t}. \qquad (2.2)$$

By testing the statistical significance of $\beta_2^i$ and $\gamma_2^i$, we can identify whether the BOJ responds to returns on the same day or the previous day.

The third variation includes TOPIX returns to test whether the BOJ responds to REIT returns or stock returns:

$$\mathbb{I}_t = \alpha_3 + \sum_{i=\{N,A,L,P\}} \beta_3^i r_t^i + \delta_3^i s_t^i + \varepsilon_{3,t}, \qquad (2.3)$$

where $s_t^i$ denotes TOPIX returns for subperiod $i$. A statistically significant coefficient $\beta_3^i$ indicates that the BOJ responds to REIT returns after controlling for the response to TOPIX returns. The fourth variation includes lagged terms for both REIT and TOPIX returns:

$$\mathbb{I}_t = \alpha_4 + \sum_{i=\{N,A,L,P\}} \beta_4^i r_t^i + \gamma_4^i r_{t-1}^i + \delta_4^i s_t^i + \theta_4^i s_{t-1}^i + \varepsilon_{4,t}. \qquad (2.4)$$

In the previous specifications, the estimated coefficient $\beta_4^i$ is a local linear approximation of the potentially non-linear effect of REIT returns. To estimate a non-linear effect, we use the return decile dummy variables that we define in Section 4. By using the sixth-decile group (between the 50th and 60th percentiles) as the reference group, we estimate the following equation for each subperiod $i = \{N, A, L, P\}$:

$$\mathbb{I}_t = \alpha_5^i + \sum_{d=\{1,\ldots,5,7,\ldots,10\}} \beta_5^{i,d} r_t^{i,d} + \varepsilon_{5,t}^i, \qquad (2.5)$$

where $r_t^{i,d}$ denotes the dummy variable that takes a value of one if a subperiod-$i$ return on date $t$ is in decile-group $d$ and takes zero otherwise. Thus, the coefficient $\beta_5^{i,d}$ represents the incremental probability of the BOJ's purchase when a return is in the $d$ th-decile group as opposed to the sixth-decile group.

## 5.2  Cox Hazard Model with Time-Dependent Covariates

An issue with an LPM is that it ignores the conditional nature of the BOJ's decision making. In other words, it does not distinguish consecutive daily purchases from a single purchase. To analyze the BOJ's decision conditional on a sequence of its past decisions, we estimate the Cox hazard model (Cox, 1972). When $T$ denotes the random failure time after a period of survival, the survival function of time $t$ is defined as:

$$S(t) \equiv \Pr(T \geq t) = \int_t^\infty f(u) du,$$

where $f(u) \equiv \lim_{\Delta u \to 0} \frac{1}{\Delta u} \Pr(u \leq T < u + \Delta u)$ is the density function. Then, the hazard function that represents an instantaneous rate of failure conditional on survival up to $t$ is defined as:

$$\lambda(t) \equiv \lim_{\Delta t \to 0} \frac{1}{\Delta t} \Pr(t \leq T < t + \Delta t | T \geq t) = \frac{f(t)}{S(t)}.$$

When covariates impact the failure time, most studies assume a Cox proportional hazard model with time-invariant covariate vector $X$:

$$\lambda(t|X) = \lambda_0(t) e^{X\beta},$$

where $\lambda_0(t)$ denotes the baseline hazard function. We allow for a time-dependent covariate vector $X(t)$ (for example, Fisher and Lin, 1999; Zhang et al., 2018; Dirick et al., 2019):

$$\lambda(t|X(t)) = \lambda_0(t) e^{X(t)\beta_6}. \qquad (2.6)$$

For covariates, we use contemporaneous and lagged TSE-REIT subperiod returns as in Equation 2.2: $X(t)\beta_6 = \sum_{i=\{N,A,L,P\}} \beta_6^i r_t^i + \gamma_6^i r_{t-1}^i$.

We analyze both starting and stopping decisions by defining two different failure events. To analyze the BOJ's starting decision, we treat a consecutive period of BOJ inaction as survival and the first day of REIT purchases as a failure. In this specification, a negative coefficient $\beta_6^i$ indicates that a lower (more negative) return is associated with a larger hazard rate of starting purchases conditional on no purchases up to the previous day. In the second specification to analyze the stopping decision, we reverse survival and failure; we treat a consecutive period of BOJ purchases as survival and the first day of inaction as a failure. In this specification, a positive coefficient $\beta_6^i$ indicates that a higher (more positive) return is associated with a larger hazard rate of stopping purchases conditional on a series of purchases up to the previous day.

## 6  REIT PURCHASE BEHAVIOR

In analyzing the BOJ's REIT purchase behavior, we primarily focus on the coefficient on overnight returns because it clearly represents a causal relationship. We also use the coefficient on morning returns because we believe the BOJ submits REIT purchase orders during

Table 2.3   Linear probability model for the entire sample period

|  | (1) | (2) | (3) | (4) |
|---|---|---|---|---|
| TSE-REIT Index |  |  |  |  |
| Overnight | −39.118 *** | −38.180 *** | −40.066 *** | −38.734 *** |
|  | (−11.549) | (−11.937) | (−9.957) | (−10.487) |
| Morning | −30.372 *** | −30.258 *** | −30.251 *** | −30.419 *** |
|  | (−8.560) | (−8.539) | (−8.986) | (−9.241) |
| Lunchtime | 33.814 *** | 34.318 *** | 37.120 *** | 37.825 *** |
|  | (3.424) | (3.510) | (3.889) | (4.071) |
| Afternoon | 0.948 | 1.225 | 1.115 | 1.227 |
|  | (0.657) | (0.855) | (0.689) | (0.769) |
| Lagged overnight |  | −5.696 *** |  | −3.921 |
|  |  | (−2.569) |  | (−1.447) |
| Lagged morning |  | −2.464 |  | −1.700 |
|  |  | (−1.369) |  | (−0.924) |
| Lagged lunchtime |  | −12.949 |  | −15.712 |
|  |  | (−1.445) |  | (−1.664) * |
| Lagged afternoon |  | 3.622 |  | 3.452 |
|  |  | (1.319) |  | (1.327) |
| TOPIX |  |  |  |  |
| Overnight |  |  | 1.006 | 0.530 |
|  |  |  | (0.592) | (0.311) |
| Morning |  |  | −0.015 | −0.016 |
|  |  |  | (−0.009) | (−0.010) |
| Lunchtime |  |  | −5.325 | −5.993 |
|  |  |  | (−0.977) | (−1.085) |
| Afternoon |  |  | −0.156 | 0.247 |
|  |  |  | (−0.089) | (0.147) |
| Lagged overnight |  |  |  | −1.229 |
|  |  |  |  | (−0.833) |
| Lagged morning |  |  |  | −2.997 * |
|  |  |  |  | (−1.951) |
| Lagged lunchtime |  |  |  | 5.151 |
|  |  |  |  | (1.054) |
| Lagged afternoon |  |  |  | 0.434 |
|  |  |  |  | (0.201) |
| N | 1654 | 1654 | 1654 | 1654 |
| Adjusted R-squared | 0.336 | 0.341 | 0.335 | 0.341 |

*Note*: This table shows the estimation results of Equations 2.1 through 2.4. The dependent variable is the dummy variable for the BOJ's REIT purchases. The covariates are TSE-REIT Index and TOPIX returns during the overnight period (from 15:00 on the previous trading day to 09:00), the morning market (from 09:00 to 11:30), lunchtime (from 11:30 to 12:30) and the afternoon market (from 12:30 to 15:00). Lagged returns are for the previous trading day. The sample period is from April 2013 to December 2019. The t-statistics are in parentheses based on Newey and West (1987) standard errors. ***, ** and * denote statistical significance at the 1%, 5% and 10% levels, respectively.

lunchtime. Although the data do not allow us to determine precisely when the BOJ submits orders, it is likely before the afternoon market opens because the BOJ conducts other JGB open-market operations at either 09:20 or 12:50. As we discuss below, our estimation result suggests that the BOJ submits orders during lunchtime.

Table 2.3 shows the estimation results of the LPM (Equations 2.1, 2.2, 2.3 and 2.4).[5] Column 1 shows that the probability of BOJ purchases is strongly negatively associated with overnight and morning returns (−39.118 and −30.372, respectively). These negative associations do not change when we include lagged REIT returns (Column 2), TOPIX returns (Column 3) and lagged REIT and TOPIX returns (Column 4). Lagged returns largely have insignificant coefficients. As returns are measured in percentage points, a one percentage point lower return during the overnight period or the morning market is associated with 39 and 30 percentage point larger probabilities of pur-

*Table 2.4 Linear probability model by subperiod*

|  | Before QQE October 2021–March 2013 | QQE before yield curve control April 2013–September 2016 | QQE under yield curve control October 2016–December 2019 |
|---|---|---|---|
| **TSE REIT Index** |  |  |  |
| Overnight | −26.676 *** | −33.194 *** | −55.492 *** |
|  | (−5.820) | (−9.038) | (−7.983) |
| Morning | −6.664 * | −24.426 *** | −55.162 *** |
|  | (−1.783) | (−9.256) | (−12.014) |
| Lunchtime | −3.742 | 34.285 *** | 34.306 *** |
|  | (−0.560) | (3.079) | (2.414) |
| Afternoon | 9.331 | 0.618 | 3.496 |
|  | (1.629) | (0.351) | (0.935) |
| Lagged overnight | 2.089 | −4.405 | −3.489 |
|  | (0.530) | (−1.497) | (−0.740) |
| Lagged morning | 2.043 | −0.434 | −5.242 |
|  | (1.079) | (−0.214) | (−1.466) |
| Lagged lunchtime | 1.860 | −19.957 * | 1.278 |
|  | (0.374) | (−1.916) | (0.072) |
| Lagged afternoon | 4.770 | 3.714 | −2.625 |
|  | (1.061) | (1.389) | (−0.793) |
| **TOPIX** |  |  |  |
| Overnight | −4.498 * | −2.086 | 3.368 |
|  | (−1.929) | (−0.986) | (1.468) |
| Morning | −4.597 | 0.380 | −0.617 |
|  | (−1.610) | (0.211) | (−0.221) |
| Lunchtime | −5.200 | −7.560 | 2.084 |
|  | (−0.740) | (−0.999) | (0.285) |
| Afternoon | 3.631 | 0.685 | −3.768 |
|  | (0.989) | (0.377) | (−0.862) |
| Lagged overnight | −2.459 | −2.141 | 0.534 |
|  | (−1.255) | (−1.162) | (0.269) |
| Lagged morning | −1.192 | −2.503 | −2.319 |
|  | (−0.442) | (−1.334) | (−0.813) |
| Lagged lunchtime | 2.932 | 2.832 | 6.094 |
|  | (0.344) | (0.485) | (0.768) |
| Lagged afternoon | −1.841 | 0.577 | −1.656 |
|  | (−0.529) | (0.257) | (−0.410) |
| N | 560 | 859 | 793 |
| Adjusted R-squared | 0.266 | 0.354 | 0.395 |

*Note*: This table shows the estimation results of Equation 2.4 for three subperiods. The dependent variable is the dummy variable for the BOJ's REIT purchases. The covariates are TSE-REIT Index and TOPIX returns during the overnight period (from 15:00 on the previous trading day to 09:00), the morning market (from 09:00 to 11:30), lunchtime (from 11:30 to 12:30) and the afternoon market (from 12:30 to 15:00). Lagged returns are for the previous trading day. The sample period is from April 2013 to December 2019. The t-statistics are in parentheses based on Newey and West (1987) standard errors. ***, ** and * denote statistical significance at the 1%, 5% and 10% levels, respectively.

chases, respectively. This negative coefficient for overnight returns indicates a causal relationship because an overnight return is determined at the beginning of the morning market. A comparable magnitude of the coefficient on morning returns suggests that the BOJ also observes returns during the morning market before making a purchase decision.

Table 2.4 shows the estimation results of Equation 2.4 for three subperiods. Before QQE (from October 2010 to March 2013), the negative coefficients on overnight and morning returns were smaller in magnitude than those for the entire sample period. The size of these coefficients became significantly larger under QQE (from April 2013 and September 2016), and even larger under the yield curve control regime (from October 2016 and December 2019). TOPIX and lagged returns are not associated with the BOJ's purchase decision in any subperiod. The BOJ seems to have established and strengthened its purchase rule over time.

Table 2.5 and Figure 2.6 show the estimation result of Equation 2.5 regarding the non-linear effect of returns on the BOJ's behavior. For overnight returns, the estimated coefficients are positive and statistically significant for the first, second and third decile groups. When an overnight return is significantly negative and in the first decile group, the BOJ is 52.6 percentage points more likely to purchase REITs than in the reference case of the sixth decile group. In the second and third decile groups, the coefficients monotonically decrease to 0.287 and 0.166, respectively. In contrast, the coefficients for the seventh through tenth decile groups are negative and statistically significant. Thus, when an overnight return is significantly positive, the BOJ is less likely to purchase REITs. A similar result is obtained for morning returns. The coefficients are positive and monotonically decreasing for the first (0.560) through the fourth (0.081) decile groups, whereas they are negative and decreasing for the seventh ($-0.063$) through the tenth ($-0.143$) decile groups.

*Table 2.5*   Linear probability model based on return decile dummies

| Return decile groups | Overnight | Morning | Lunchtime | Afternoon |
|---|---|---|---|---|
| < 10th | 0.526 *** | 0.560 *** | 0.152 *** | 0.031 |
|  | (10.92) | (10.08) | (2.17) | (0.57) |
| 10th–20th | 0.287 *** | 0.503 *** | 0.015 | −0.044 |
|  | (5.98) | (10.21) | (0.35) | (−0.91) |
| 20th–30th | 0.166 *** | 0.256 *** | 0.013 | 0.003 |
|  | (3.60) | (5.14) | (0.33) | (0.06) |
| 30th–40th | 0.026 | 0.081 ** | 0.035 | −0.051 |
|  | (0.63) | (2.14) | (0.90) | (−1.08) |
| 40th–50th | 0.032 | −0.002 | 0.075 | −0.091 * |
|  | (0.65) | (−0.06) | (1.77) | (−1.91) |
| 50th–60th | Reference | Reference | Reference | Reference |
|  | (omitted) | (omitted) | (omitted) | (omitted) |
| 60th–70th | −0.123 *** | −0.063 ** | 0.069 | 0.006 |
|  | (−3.13) | (−2.16) | (1.62) | (0.12) |
| 70th–80th | −0.133 *** | −0.109 *** | 0.163 *** | 0.004 |
|  | (−3.46) | (−3.73) | (4.00) | (0.08) |
| 80th–90th | −0.126 *** | −0.119 *** | 0.235 *** | 0.049 |
|  | (−3.30) | (−3.79) | (4.92) | (0.96) |
| > 90th | −0.161 *** | −0.143 *** | 0.303 *** | 0.098 * |
|  | (−3.82) | (−4.44) | (3.99) | (1.90) |
| N | 1654 | 1654 | 1654 | 1654 |
| Adjusted R-squared | 0.210 | 0.272 | 0.032 | 0.008 |

*Note*: This table shows the estimation result of Equation 2.5. The dependent variable is the dummy for REIT purchases, and the independent variables are dummy variables for return decile groups. Return decile groups are calculated for each of the overnight period (from 15:00 on the previous trading day to 09:00), the morning market (from 09:00 to 11:30), lunchtime (from 11:30 to 12:30) and the afternoon market (from 12:30 to 15:00). The sample period is from April 2013 to December 2019. The t-statistics are in parentheses based on Newey and West (1987) standard errors. ***, ** and * denote statistical significance at the 1%, 5% and 10% levels, respectively.

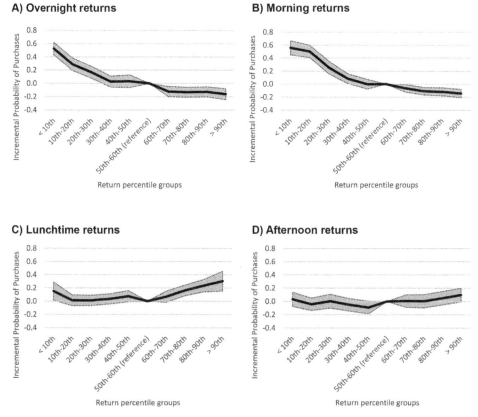

*Note*: This figure depicts the estimated coefficients from Table 2.3. The vertical axis shows the incremental probability of the BOJ's purchase relative to the baseline probability for the sixth decile group. Return decile groups are calculated for each of the overnight period (from 15:00 on the previous trading day to 09:00), the morning market (from 09:00 to 11:30), lunchtime (from 11:30 to 12:30) and the afternoon market (from 12:30 to 15:00). The sample period is from April 2013 to December 2019.

*Figure 2.6    Incremental probability of purchases by return decile groups*

Table 2.6 shows the estimated coefficient vector $\beta_6$ in Equation 2.6 for the Cox hazard model of starting decisions (that is, when a failure is defined as the start of the BOJ's REIT purchases). The reported coefficients are the natural logarithm of the hazard ratio for a one basis point higher return. Consistent with the results from the LPMs, overnight returns and morning returns have negative coefficients that are statistically significant at the 1 percent level. Thus, after a period of inaction, the BOJ is more likely to start purchasing REIT shares when overnight and morning returns are negative. For a one basis point lower return during the overnight period and the morning market, the hazard function is 1.8 and 1.1 percent larger, respectively (the log hazard ratio is 0.018 and 0.011, respectively). No lagged return is statistically significant.

Table 2.7 shows the estimated coefficient vector $\beta_6$ in Equation 2.6 for the Cox hazard model of stopping decisions (that is, when a failure is defined as the end of consecutive REIT

*Table 2.6    Cox hazard model of starting decisions*

|  | (1) | (2) |
|---|---|---|
| Overnight | −0.018 *** | −0.018 *** |
|  | (−12.93) | (−12.13) |
| Morning | −0.011 *** | −0.011 *** |
|  | (−11.51) | (−11.03) |
| Lunchtime | 0.014 *** | 0.014 *** |
|  | (2.48) | (2.39) |
| Afternoon | −0.001 | −0.001 |
|  | (−0.83) | (−0.79) |
| Lagged overnight |  | −0.002 |
|  |  | (−1.34) |
| Lagged morning |  | 0.000 |
|  |  | (−0.37) |
| Lagged lunchtime |  | 0.001 |
|  |  | (0.36) |
| Lagged afternoon |  | −0.001 |
|  |  | (−1.01) |
| N | 1,222 | 1,222 |

*Note*: This table shows the estimation result of Equation 2.6 for the Cox hazard model of starting decisions. A failure is defined as the start of the BOJ's REIT purchases after a period of inaction. REIT returns are measured in basis points. The sample period is from April 2013 to December 2019. The z-statistics are in parentheses. ***, ** and * denote statistical significance at the 1%, 5% and 10% levels, respectively.

*Table 2.7    Cox hazard model of stopping decisions*

|  | (1) | (2) |
|---|---|---|
| Overnight | 0.004 *** | 0.005 *** |
|  | (3.47) | (3.81) |
| Morning | 0.004 *** | 0.004 *** |
|  | (4.81) | (5.00) |
| Lunchtime | −0.001 | −0.002 |
|  | (−0.12) | (−0.28) |
| Afternoon | 0.000 | 0.000 |
|  | (−0.07) | (−0.38) |
| Lagged overnight |  | 0.003 ** |
|  |  | (1.97) |
| Lagged morning |  | 0.002 |
|  |  | (1.25) |
| Lagged lunchtime |  | 0.006 |
|  |  | (1.27) |
| Lagged afternoon |  | −0.001 |
|  |  | (−1.50) |
| N | 431 | 431 |

*Note*: This table shows the estimation result of Equation 2.6 for the Cox hazard model of stopping decisions. A failure is defined by the end of the BOJ's REIT purchases after consecutive daily purchases. REIT returns are measured in basis points. The sample period is from April 2013 to December 2019. The z-statistics are in parentheses. ***, ** and * denote statistical significance at the 1%, 5% and 10% levels, respectively.

purchases). The coefficients on overnight and morning returns are positive and statistically significant at the 1 percent level. Thus, after consecutive daily purchases, the BOJ is more likely to stop operations when overnight and morning returns are positive. For a one basis point higher return, the hazard function is 0.4 percent larger (that is, the log hazard ratio is 0.004). The coefficient is statistically insignificant for lagged returns.

## 7   THE EFFECT ON REIT SHARE PRICES

We use the same empirical models from Equations 2.1 to 2.6 to infer the effect of the BOJ's purchases on REIT share prices. As we discussed in the previous section, the BOJ is likely to submit orders during lunchtime. Thus, the coefficients on lunchtime and afternoon returns are likely driven by the causal effect of the BOJ purchases on REIT share prices.

Table 2.3 for Equations 2.1, 2.2, 2.3 and 2.4 shows that the coefficient on lunchtime returns is positive and statistically significant. A one percentage point larger lunchtime return is associated with a 33.8 percentage point larger probability of a BOJ operation. This positive association suggests that the afternoon market tends to start at higher REIT share prices after the BOJ submits a purchase order during lunchtime. This positive association between BOJ operations and lunchtime returns is observed only under QQE (Table 2.4). With this linear specification, the coefficient on afternoon returns is positive but statistically insignificant regardless of periods.

Based on return decile groups (Table 2.5 and Figure 2.6), the coefficients are significantly positive for large returns during lunchtime and the afternoon market. For example, in the tenth decile group of lunchtime returns, the coefficient is 0.303 and statistically significant at the 1 percent level. Similarly, the coefficient on the tenth decile group of afternoon returns is 0.098 and statistically significant at the 10 percent level. Thus, the BOJ's REIT purchases are likely to cause unusually large positive returns, especially during lunchtime.

Furthermore, Table 2.6 shows that the start of daily REIT purchases after a period of inaction causes significantly positive lunchtime returns. The first of the consecutive purchases probably has a large price effect because investors update their conditional expectations of subsequent purchases. Table 2.7 shows that the end of consecutive REIT purchases does not have a significantly negative effect on REIT share prices during lunchtime or the afternoon. This is probably because the BOJ stops purchasing REIT shares only after they observe significantly positive returns overnight and in the morning market. This result implies that the BOJ's operation is effective not only on the day of operation but rather persistently.

## 8 CONCLUSION

Our study is the first to analyze the BOJ's REIT share purchase program. It is an unprecedented program among other LSAP programs around the world. Our main finding is that the BOJ purchases REIT shares in a highly discretionary manner rather than on a regular schedule. Using an LPM and the Cox proportional hazard model with time-varying covariates, we find that the BOJ tends to start purchasing REIT shares when it observes a significantly negative return over the previous night and during the morning market on the TSE. The BOJ stops purchasing REIT shares when either overnight or morning returns become significantly positive. Furthermore, the BOJ's REIT share purchases are associated with significantly positive REIT returns during lunchtime and the afternoon market, suggesting a significant effect on REIT share prices. Moreover, the price effect is persistent because stopping consecutive purchases does not affect REIT share prices negatively. This study contributes to the literature by revealing how the BOJ affects real estate equity prices as part of its unconventional monetary policy.

## NOTES

1. The Swiss National Bank also holds United States corporate shares, but its aim is to control foreign exchange rates rather than interest rates and risk premiums.
2. A major difference is that the BOJ has been making advance announcements of the exact date of JGB auctions since March 2017, whereas the BOJ purchases REITs and ETFs without announcements.
3. This description is based on the release in April 2013. For more information, see www.boj.or.jp/en/announcements/release_2013/k130404a.pdf and www.boj.or.jp/en/announcements/press/koen_2013/data/ko130412a1.pdf.
4. See www.boj.or.jp/en/mopo/measures/term_cond/yoryo18.htm/.
5. We also estimate Equation 2.2 by using REIT spreads over TOPIX returns. The result is shown in the Appendix.

## REFERENCES

Barbon, A. and Gianinazzi, V. 2019. Quantitative Easing and Equity Prices: Evidence from the ETF Program of the Bank of Japan. *Review of Asset Pricing Studies* 9 (2): 210–255.

Charoenwong, B., Morck, R. and Wiwattanakantang, Y. 2021. Bank of Japan Equity Purchases: The (Non-)Effects of Extreme Quantitative Easing. *Review of Finance* 25(3): 713–743.

Cox, D.R. 1972. Regression Models and Life Tables (with Discussion). *Journal of the Royal Statistical Society: Series B* 34: 187–220.

D'Amico, S., English, W., López-Salido, D. and Nelson, E. 2012. The Federal Reserve's Large-Scale Asset Purchase Programmes: Rationale and Effects. *The Economic Journal* 122: 415–446.

Dirick, L., Bellotti, T., Claeskens, G. and Baesens, B. 2019. Macro-Economic Factors in Credit Risk Calculations: Including Time-Varying Covariates in Mixture Cure Models. *Journal of Business and Economic Statistics* 37 (1): 40–53.

Fisher L.D. and Lin, D.Y. 1999. Time-Dependent Covariates in the Cox Proportional-Hazards Regression Model. *Annual Review of Public Health* 20: 145–57.

Greenwood, R., Vayanos, D. 2014. Bond Supply and Excess Bond Returns. *Review of Financial Studies* 27(3): 663–713.

Hamilton, J.D. 2018. The Efficacy of Large-Scale Asset Purchases When the Short-Term Interest Rate Is at Its Effective Lower Bound. *Brookings Papers on Economic Activity* 49 (2 (Fall)): 543–554.

Harada, K. and Okimoto, T. 2021. The BOJ's ETF Purchases and Its Effects on Nikkei 225 Stocks. *International Review of Financial Analysis* 77: 101826.

Hattori, T. 2020. The Impact of Quantitative and Qualitative Easing with Yield Curve Control on the Term Structure of Interest Rates: Evidence from Micro-Level. *Economics Letters*.

Hattori, T. and Yoshida, J. 2020. Yield Curve Control. *SSRN*: 3396251.

Krishnamurthy, K. and Vissing-Jorgensen, A. 2011.The Effects of Quantitative Easing on Interest Rates. Brookings Papers on Economic Activity, Fall.

Krishnamurthy, K. and Vissing-Jorgensen, A. 2013. The Ins and Outs of LSAPs. Kansas City Federal Reserve Symposium on Global Dimensions of Unconventional Monetary Policy.

Modigliani, F. and Sutch, R. 1966. Innovations in Interest Rate Policy. *American Economic Review* 56 (2): 178–197.

Newey, W. and West, K. 1987. A Simple, Positive Semi-Definite, Heteroskedasticity and Autocorrelation Consistent Covariance Matrix. *Econometrica* 55 (3): 703–708.

Shirakawa, M. 2010. Japan's Economy and Monetary Policy. Speech at the Kisaragi-kai Meeting in Tokyo, November 4, Bank of Japan.

Vayanos, D. and Vila, J.L. 2009. A Preferred-Habitat Model of the Term Structure of Interest Rates. NBER Working Paper 15487, 1–2.

Wallace, N. 1981. A Modigliani-Miller Theorem for Open-Market Operations. *American Economic Review* 71(3): 267–274.

Zhang, Z., Reinikainen, J., Adeleke, K.A., Pieterse, M.E. and Groothuis-Oudshoorn, C.G.M. 2018. Time-Varying Covariates and Coefficients in Cox Regression Models. *Annals of Translational Medicine* 6 (7): 121–130.

## APPENDIX

We estimate Equation 2.2 by using REIT spreads over TOPIX returns instead of controlling for TOPIX returns directly as in Equations 2.3 and 2.4. The result is consistent with that for Equation 2.4 shown in Table 2.3.

*Table 2A.1    Linear Probability Model based on REIT spreads over TOPIX returns*

|  | Coefficient | Coefficient |
|---|---|---|
| Overnight (spread) | −2.319 | −1.983 |
|  | (−1.081) | (−0.938) |
| Morning (spread) | −12.290 *** | −12.257 *** |
|  | (−6.654) | (−6.339) |
| Lunch (spread) | 13.363 * | 14.195 ** |
|  | (1.95) | (2.046) |
| Afternoon (spread) | 3.96 ** | 4.089 ** |
|  | (2.19) | (2.255) |
| L.overnight (spread) |  | 1.784 |
|  |  | (1.033) |
| L.morning (spread) |  | −1.282 |
|  |  | (−0.817) |
| L.lunch (spread) |  | −0.799 |
|  |  | (−0.133) |
| L.afternoon (spread) |  | 3.924 *** |
|  |  | (2.373) |
| N | 1654 | 1654 |
| Adjusted R-squared | 0.046 | 0.048 |

*Note*: This table shows the estimation results of Equations 2.1 and 2.2 by replacing REIT returns with REIT spread over TOPIX returns. The dependent variable is the dummy variable for the BOJ's REIT purchases. Returns are measured during the overnight period (from 15:00 on the previous trading day to 09:00), the morning market (from 09:00 to 11:30), lunchtime (from 11:30 to 12:30) and the afternoon market (from 12:30 to 15:00). Lagged returns are for the previous trading day. The sample period is from April 2013 to December 2019. The t-statistics are in parentheses based on Newey and West (1987) standard errors. ***, ** and * denote statistical significance at the 1%, 5% and 10% levels, respectively.

# 3. Land and macroeconomics
*Prasad Sankar Bhattacharya*

## 1 INTRODUCTION

How is land going to impact macroeconomic decisions? This question, though quite broad, remains very important for economists and policy makers alike given the fact that land is one of the fundamental factors of production. In both classical and neoclassical growth models (Lewis, 1954; Nichols, 1970), land plays an important role as a crucial input in the production process.[1] Generally, land is used as a static input in production from a macroeconomic perspective (stock variable) since land sizes are given within a country's geographical boundary. However, the distribution of land varies both within and across countries, and often these distributions are shaped by policy interventions like land reform (Lipton, 2009), land zoning (Rossi-Hansberg, 2004) and land redevelopment (mostly in urban settings) to name a few. Land usage also varies a lot within and across countries, where some lands are earmarked as agricultural land, fallow land, pasture land, forest land and urban land.

In stages of growth, land plays an important role as the initial growth of countries is primarily driven by agricultural sector growth, which is directly linked with land (Johnston and Mellor, 1961; Lewis, 1954). Nichols (1970) shows that savings can be bolstered with land holdings and associated price increase in land. This remains true for both urban and rural land, with urban land becoming more price sensitive as cities expand and rural land reaping the benefit of conversion of farmland to residential land as cities expand. Within a broader perspective, Hayami and Ruttan (1985) argue that agricultural growth is fundamental to economic development with the hypothesis that agricultural productivity growth is the key driver for agricultural output and subsequent economic growth. Given the fact that almost 75 percent of people in the world, especially in developing countries, are reliant on agricultural income (Binswanger-Mkhize et al., 2009; World Bank, 2008), it is of first-order importance to understand how land plays a critical role in boosting income and growth over time in a number of countries across the world. In developing countries, often land is the only tangible asset which people have that would give them a subsistence income both in the current period (Schultz, 1964) and in the future period. Thus, giving access and rights over land through land reforms became one of the fundamental policy decisions in developing countries (Lipton, 2009; King, 1977) after the Second World War.

A vast literature focuses on tenure security of land and its consequence on agricultural productivity and income (Arnot et al., 2011). The idea is that with improved tenure security, tenants will have the incentive to enhance agricultural productivity by applying more labor-intensive organic manure to land (Besley, 1995; Jacobi and Mansuri, 2008). Land titles (an indicator of tenure security) can also be used as collateral to obtain credit for improving agricultural investment (Feder, 1988). Similarly, enhanced tenure security in terms of land titles would stimulate land market transactions and lead to efficient allocation of land to willing farmers (Place, 2009; Deininger and Feder, 2001).

The emphasis on agricultural production stems from the fact that it reduces poverty (Christiaensen et al., 2011) and more so at a very low level of development (Bourguignon and Morrison, 1998; Datt and Ravallion, 1996). It could also provide the capital necessary to finance growth in other sectors, like the industrial sector of the economy, through land tax revenues (Ghatak and Ingersent, 1984; Schiff and Valdez, 1992).

## 1.1　Land and Urban Macroeconomic Concepts

In addition to the channels mentioned above, land plays a crucial role in urban settings as well.[2] In urban areas, land is needed for a number of reasons including organizing production (particularly industrial and manufacturing goods production like setting up factories, etc.), residential purposes, transportation, recreational use (urban parklands, etc.) and facilitating transactions in the services sector by setting up offices and workplaces. Evans (2004) concentrates on the economic theory of the land market and highlights the importance of urban land supply for development. Leung (2004) and Leung and Ng (2019) provide overviews of the macroeconomic issues involving the housing market. One pertinent concept in urban economics in the broad sense is the nexus between house prices and short-run business cycles in developed countries (Baxter, 1996; Davis and Heathcote, 2005; Del Negro and Otrok, 2007; Goodhart and Hofmann, 2008; Greenwood and Hercowitz, 1991; Leamer, 2007).

A number of recent studies focus on land price dynamics and house prices. Nichols (1970) proves that savings can be bolstered with land holdings and associated price increases in land in the urban setting where urban land prices increase with the expansion of cities. In an influential paper, Liu et al. (2013) show that land price fluctuations are interlinked with macroeconomic volatility where land is used as collateral in firms' credit constraints. Similarly, Davis and Heathcote (2007) find that house price fluctuations are primarily linked with land price dynamics across different locations in the United States (USA). Piazzesi and Schneider (2016) survey the literature on housing and macroeconomics and find that land price increase was one of the primary factors for house price increase. There are heterogeneities in price increases, with lower land prices increasing at a much faster rate than the already high land prices (Kuminoff and Pope, 2013), especially in the 2000s boom in the USA. Focusing on a number of advanced economies, Knoll et al. (2017) report that house prices rose significantly after the Second World War period in a number of industrial countries due to a substantial increase in land prices. Thus, land plays an important role in determining house price dynamics, a very pertinent concept in macroeconomics.

## 1.2　The Focus of the Chapter

In this chapter, we concentrate on providing new evidence in relation to the above topics, focusing on transformation from a rural setting to urban development. In particular, we investigate if particular types of land reform implementation involving rural land across the world could usher in enhanced urbanization over time. The specific reforms are the measures implemented with the motives of fully transferring end user rights to land to the beneficiaries. Bhattacharya et al. (2019) document such major reforms across the world and we choose four of these focusing on transferring end user rights: (1) distribution of land; (2) consolidation of rural land; (3) privatization of mainly state-owned farmland; and (4) restitution of land.[3] The underlying idea is that these reforms will lead to possible land market development in the future where willing buyers and sellers participate and land-related transactions happen without any state or government direction.

In addition, where end user rights are not fully transferred, such as reforms focusing on improving tenure security arrangements as well as legally recognizing customary, indigenous, community, religious and traditional practices on land in terms of its use, this could also be used as a potential signal towards facilitating land market-related transactions. These motives for land reforms from Bhattacharya et al. (2019) will also be used to analyze their possible positive impact in developing land market-oriented transactions, which in turn could facilitate economic development or urbanization.

Land market development over time may lead to enhanced urbanization as reform beneficiaries have the option to quit farming altogether if they decide to do so, with the marginal cost of farming becoming more than the marginal benefit attained. This sort of progression is also in line with the changes in the production structure of the economy, where more emphasis will be given to industrial production and service sector activities over and above the agricultural sector as the economies progress. Thus, a priori, we would expect that end user right transfer motives would be positively related to urbanization, a proxy for urban development and economic growth (Nunn and Qian, 2011). On the other hand, as a falsification exercise, we would expect that the reforms where end user rights are not transferred may not lead to such positive outcomes.

In the empirical strategy, we use a quasi-experimental setup and employ a flexible event-study design and differences-in-differences (DiD) technique to identify the causal effect of land reform implementation motives involving end user rights transfers on urbanization. The empirical specifications control for pertinent factors influencing urbanization as a failure to do so would lead to omitted variable bias. A number of falsification/placebo results are also presented to bolster the baseline findings. The results show very positive support for our conjectured hypothesis that end user rights motives land reform implementations, where user rights are transferred fully or partially, would lead to enhanced urbanization. In addition, the empirical analysis uses novel data on the nominal farmland price index reported in Knoll et al. (2017) for developed countries and find that end user rights-focused land reforms played a positive role in enhancing farmland prices. This indicates plausible land market demand-side mechanisms of such land reform implementations.

The rest of the chapter is organized as follows. In Section 2, we discuss how land, economic growth and development issues are related by looking at the rural setting. Section 3 presents studies analyzing links between land and urban indicators like house prices. In Section 4, we provide the rationale behind the new empirical evidence presented. Section 5 describes the underlying data and descriptive statistics. Section 6 elaborates the empirical strategy. All empirical results and discussions are presented in Section 7. Section 8 concludes the chapter after highlighting pertinent policy choices and avenues for future research.

## 2 LAND AND MACROECONOMICS: RURAL PERSPECTIVE

### 2.1 Land, Agricultural Productivity and Growth

Land plays a crucial role in agriculture-driven growth in the early stages of economic development (Weil and Wilde, 2009). Bezemer and Heady (2008) provide an overview of how agriculture drives economic growth. There is, however, considerable debate regarding the importance of agriculture in enhancing growth (Tsakok and Gardner, 2007; Valdés and Foster, 2010). One set of studies (Tiffin and Irz, 2006; Timmer, 2008; Gollin et al., 2002) finds that the agriculture sector is fundamental to development and economic growth by enhancing value added in agriculture and improving the gross domestic product (GDP) in a number of countries across the world.

There are a number of channels through which agricultural productivity can be improved. The first channel would be more investment in land by providing more inputs in the production process including organic manure. Besley (1995) and Jacobi and Mansuri (2008) proxy one particular investment in land with the "use of farmyard manure" as the empirical measure of investment in the cases of Ghana and Pakistan, respectively. These enhanced investments, in turn, are linked with improved property rights over land with the intuition that increased property rights over land provide incentives for farmers to invest more in lands they formally own and for which they have end user rights. Goldstein and Udry (2008) investigate this particular channel in Ghana and find that people with more local-level political connections have more access to secure property rights over land and, subsequently, they invest more in their land to improve productivity and associated income. There are a number of studies showing that incomplete property rights over land leads to underinvestment in agricultural land (Besley, 1995; Jacobi and Mansuri, 2008; Jacobi et al., 2002). Note that Johnston and Mellor (1961) also mention improved land security as a precondition for the development of the agricultural sector.

Second, agricultural productivity can be improved by a spurt in agricultural investment through increased borrowing with land as a collateral if there is perfect tenure security over land (Feder, 1988). In such instances, land plays the role of a tangible asset based on which more credit can be obtained to improve agricultural investment (Besley and Ghatak, 2010; Croppenstedt et al., 2003; Dethier and Effenberger, 2011).

Third, productivity can be improved by facilitating land market transactions, where willing buyers and sellers participate in the land market without any government intervention (Deininger et al., 2017). These market mechanisms would work effectively in situations where property rights over land are well defined and end user rights are given via land titling. In addition, such transactions would bode well for land rental markets (Holden et al., 2008; Jin and Jayne, 2013).

On the contrary, papers by Ban et al. (1980) and Fane and Warr (2003) do not find the supremacy of the agricultural sector in fostering economic growth in South Korea and Indonesia, respectively. Gardner (2005) also supports this with a cross-country study of 85 countries.

## 2.2   Land Tenure Security and Its Impact on Growth and Development

Given the importance of land tenure security on agricultural productivity, it would be good to analyze how tenure security affects productivity. Arnot et al. (2011) provide an interesting overview of studies on tenure security. They posit that both the content and assurance aspects of tenures should be looked into carefully, but also clarify that the content angle is empirically more tractable with measures like legal title to land (Feder and Onchan, 1987; Smith, 2004). The type of tenure is also used as a proxy for tenure in a number of studies (Carter and Olinto, 2003; Gavian and Fafchamps, 1996; Otsuka et al., 2001; Place and Otsuka, 2002).

In the short run, having user rights will lead to more productive use of land simply because the landowner has the absolute ownership and can adopt more productive technologies to increase output/production without the fear of losing/usurping the final product. From the landowners' perspective, this brings in guaranteed income earning. Indeed, there is a voluminous literature documenting how agricultural output and productivity increase after successful implementation of land reforms (Bardhan and Mookherjee, 2007).

In the long run, end user rights will enable land market-related transactions with end users being the beneficiaries, free to sell or buy land in the market without unnecessary state or government interventions (ARD, 2008). These will probably usher in more investments in land by using land as collateral to obtain credits (Arnot et al., 2011). The property rights in land follow a vast literature which discusses the importance of property rights in general for bolstering economic growth (Barro 1991; Bohn and Deacon, 2000; Levine and Renelt 1992; Persson and Tabellini, 1994).

## 2.3    Recent Findings on Agriculture and Aggregate Productivity

In a series of influential papers, Restuccia et al. (2008) and Adamopoulos and Restuccia (2014, 2020) analyze potential factors affecting productivity in agriculture. They find that distortion in the allocation of factor inputs in agriculture has a profound impact on productivity. One of the candidate explanations for such disruption is the higher cost of inputs like fertilizers, which could be due to domestic production restrictions as well as higher import restrictions of such inputs (Restuccia et al., 2008). The other explanation boils down to restrictions on labor mobility (Restuccia et al., 2008), which may not be of that much importance in developing countries like India where there is substantial labor mobility across states during agricultural seasons. Moreover, some additional channels of distortion are scalability in regards to farm size (Adamopoulos and Restuccia, 2014) and inefficiency in land market transactions (Adamopoulos and Restuccia, 2020). This chapter's focus could be linked with the above papers by saying that land as an important factor input can be better allocated if there are end user rights. In fact, Adamopoulos and Restuccia (2020) show that embarking on land reforms in the absence of proper land market institutions could actually lead to a substantial decline in agricultural productivity, as happened in the Philippines.

## 3    LAND AND MACROECONOMICS: URBAN CONNECTIONS

In this section, we briefly review concepts involving land and macroeconomics from an urban perspective. Within urban economics, house prices and their dynamics play the most vital role, and especially after the subprime lending crisis and associated global financial crisis in 2008–2009, understanding house price dynamics and relevant factors has become one of the focal points in the macroeconomic research agenda (Adam and Woodford, 2012; Jorda et al., 2015). Thus, it is no wonder there are a number of detailed surveys that cover housing and macroeconomics in general (Leung, 2004), housing and macroeconomic issues focusing on land dynamics (Piazzesi and Schneider, 2016) as well as drivers of house prices and factors affecting interconnected economic activities like credit markets, house price expectations and financial stability (Duca et al., 2020).

Nichols (1970) provides one of the first studies showing that savings can be bolstered with land holdings and associated price increases in urban land where land prices increase with the expansion of cities. In an influential paper, Liu et al. (2013) show that land price fluctuations are interlinked with macroeconomic volatility where land is used as collateral in firms' credit constraints. Similarly, Davis and Heathcote (2007) show that house price fluctuations are primarily linked with land price dynamics across different locations in the USA.

Piazzesi and Schneider (2016) survey the literature on housing and macroeconomics and find that land price increase was one of the primary factors for house price increases. There are heterogeneities in price increases, with lower land prices increasing at a much faster rate than the already high land prices (Kuminoff and Pope, 2013), especially in the 2000s boom in the USA. Knoll et al. (2017) report that real (Consumer Price Index adjusted) house prices rose significantly after the Second World War in a number of industrial countries due to a substantial increase in residential land prices.[4] Knoll et al.'s finding echoes with results from Gyourko et al. (2013) and Glaeser and Ward (2009).

In a number of recent papers, Glaeser (2021) and Djankov et al. (2021) shed light on the property rights surrounding urban land markets and their effect on prices. Djankov et al. (2021) use data from 190 countries in the twenty-first century and find that property rights institutions have a significant impact on the allocation of urban land, and that these institutions show a drastic improvement over the last 16 years. Our chapter speaks to this evidence in the sense that we investigate whether major, path-breaking land reform implementations focusing on end users' rights being fully or partially transferred could be used to shape up land market institutions later. We present heterogeneity in regards to such institutions' impact on urbanization in 181 countries covering the twentieth century.

Glaeser (2021) analyzes a number of factors affecting the urban agglomeration happening in developing countries. He states that "development of many western cities relied on a nexus of property rights for landowners, including the right to build, buy, alienate, mortgage and rent, that are far more limited in many developing world cities" as one of the important lessons from the past. Thus, property rights and their various facets have far-reaching consequences for both developed and developing countries' urban landscapes. In this context, the research questions investigated in this chapter would be of interest to a number of stakeholders.

## 4    LAND REFORMS WITH END USER RIGHTS FULLY TRANSFERRED, INTERMEDIATE STEPS TOWARDS CREATING LAND MARKETS AND THEIR POTENTIAL IMPACT ON URBANIZATION: EMPIRICAL HYPOTHESES

Given the overview of how land plays an important role in both rural and urban settings, it would be interesting to investigate whether decisions like major land reform implementations usher in increased urbanization, an important indicator of growth and development in the extant literature. Land reforms are very effective in improving agricultural productivity and rural income in a number of countries (de Janvry et al., 2015) and there are numerous country-level studies showing the positive impact of land reform in reducing poverty, in India (Besley and Burgess, 2000), Ghana (Besley, 1995) and China (Deininger and Jin, 2007) to name a few.

Place (2009) provides an excellent overview of land tenures in the context of Africa and finds that the enhancing tenure decisions may have beneficial impacts on agricultural productivity, depending on the underlying macroeconomic conditions within which the tenures operate. One of the crucial channels of improving agricultural productivity is through increased investment in agricultural land when there are secure land tenure rights (Goldstein and Udry, 2008). This follows a vast literature (De Soto, 2000; North and Thomas, 1973) focusing on the importance of well-defined and secure property rights over land for economic development.

## 4.1     Hypothesis 1

In line with the above, we analyze the impact of a particular set of land reforms where end users' rights in land were transferred to the beneficiaries. The investigation is based on the conjecture that properly transferred end user rights usher in land market transactions, which, in turn, hasten economic growth and development.

We use urbanization as the empirical measure for development. This is a widely used proxy for economic development and growth in a number of recent studies. Nunn and Qian (2011) point out that urbanization and per capita income are closely interlinked based on studies by Acemoglu et al. (2002, 2005) and DeLong and Shleifer (1993). Thus, urbanization can be used as an outcome or dependent variable.

Given that the focus is on land reforms transferring end user rights in rural land and ushering in probable land market transactions across rural and urban settings, we would like to have an outcome variable that resonates closely with the transition process. Urbanization, measured as the proportion of urban population to the total population, is a good outcome variable as it shows the propensity to transfer to a more urban setup if the urban population is growing more in comparison to the total population. Taking a look at the data, we find overwhelming support that urbanization was growing over the years across all countries in the data sample. Thus, one testable hypothesis will be the positive incentive for urbanization if end user rights are transferred, *ceteris paribus*.

## 4.2     Hypothesis 2

What happens if end users' rights in land are not transferred but the land tenure security is improved so that farmers have more guarantees about future income based on land-tiling activities? Similarly, instead of transferring land user rights, if the authorities start recognizing traditional and informal land tenure arrangements as legal arrangements and thus facilitate intermediate land transactions, what would be the possible impact on long-term growth and development? Note that the above two types of land reform arrangements do not involve the physical transfer of land, and thus, these land reform motives could be easily implemented without causing a lot of friction amongst stakeholders like landlords and land-dependent tenants. These two particular types of reforms have therefore been implemented widely across the world, and especially in a number of developing countries in Asia, Africa and Latin America. Improving tenure security is also pursued extensively in a number of countries in the Organisation for Economic Co-operation and Development like the United Kingdom, Germany and France.

Thus, based on the above argument, where complete end user arrangements are not given fully but some positive intermediate steps are taken to signal the start of market-oriented land transactions, we would expect that these initiatives would also positively usher in more urbanization, *ceteris paribus*. There may be a time lag in terms of such impact as these are in-between steps towards creating a fully functioning market. If this is true, then we can reckon that positive impact will be fully realized as we move away from the time when such reforms were initially implemented.

## 4.3 Hypothesis 3

In addition, we use the nominal agricultural farmland price index from Knoll et al. (2017) as another outcome variable. Knoll et al. (2017) report farmland prices for 11 advanced countries only, thus restricting our analysis to a handful of developed economies. Though constrained in terms of sample size, the outcome variable suits our intuition in regards to land market development due to end user rights being transferred to beneficiaries. With end user rights, the beneficiaries have the opportunity to participate in the land market by buying and selling land based on the market demand and supply dynamics. If the supply side of land is determined by the arable land area, then end users' rights will encourage the demand side of the market as more willing beneficiaries participate in that market. They may demand more land as they can invest more or try to scale up their production or they can sell land if the marginal cost of production remains too high to match the marginal benefit. Thus, if we could control for supply-side factors by looking at the arable land area in particular and the number of rural people in general, then a priori, end user rights transferring land reform would enhance the price of farmland. This is an additional hypothesis which could be tested in the empirical analysis.

## 5  DATA AND DESCRIPTIVE STATISTICS

### 5.1 Dependent Variable

The main outcome variable is urbanization, which is measured as the proportion of urban population to total population. We use urbanization in a logarithmic scale as the dependent variable with the relevant data collated from the World Development Indicators (WDIs) of the World Bank. We use urbanization as the main dependent variable to check Hypotheses 1 and 2. Later, in another empirical specification (described below), the nominal price index of farmland prices from Knoll et al. (2017) is employed as an additional dependent variable to test the third hypothesis.

Later, we use manufacturing valued added as a percentage of GDP from the WDIs as an alternative measure for urbanization to check the robustness of our main results pertaining to Hypotheses 1 and 2.

### 5.2 Explanatory Variables: Major Land Reform Implementations

The land reform implementation variables are from the major land reform dataset compiled at the world level by Bhattacharya et al. (2019).[5] The reforms are categorized as major if these measures (land reform acts) changed the agrarian structure of the economy substantially by setting new directions and changing rules for land ownership, land tenure and land user rights.

Bhattacharya et al. (2019) categorized 12 different motives for land reform, out of which four are of particular interest for us in the empirical analysis as they transfer the end user rights to land to the beneficiaries. These four particular reforms are employed to test the proposed Hypothesis 1.

1. *Distribution*: This is listed as a major reform where the land title is transferred to the new owner. In particular, the transfer of the ownership or end user rights of state lands to beneficiaries is classified as the distribution motive of land reform. Distribution generally takes place by giving empty public land to the landless (or land-poor) as part of traditional land reforms. However, in some countries, previously uninhabited lands may be given to colonizers or squatters (Paraguay, 1904 and Brazil, 1964 and 1998) as part of land settlement programs. We consider both of the above cases as distribution. In regards to formerly communist countries, transfer of the former collective lands to ordinary people (former workers) are also listed as distribution since end user rights were given to the beneficiaries (Albania, 1991 and Armenia, 1991).
2. *Consolidation*: The consolidation objective also transfers end user rights to beneficiaries and generally spans the European region. However, a number of developing countries like India (1953, 1960 and 1970), Rwanda (2005) and Turkey (1984) also employed this land reform motive. Early consolidation efforts in Europe can be traced back to the fourteenth century (Bavaria, 1353) and some consolidation efforts that were initiated in the nineteenth century spilled over to the twentieth century (e.g., Austria, 1899). In the traditional sense, consolidation refers to the reparceling of fragmented lands into unitary land blocks. In such instances, farmers retain their ownership and tenure rights with consolidation aimed at improving their land use. Consolidation may occur through agreement or enforcement and it can have a national or regional scope (Portugal's 1962 reform was concentrated on the country's northwest); however, we did not distinguish these in our coding. The modern consolidation paradigm encompasses rural integrated development steps, where land use is enhanced through irrigation, new roads, soil conservation and other infrastructure development. We list both traditional and modern consolidation concepts as a single consolidation motive.
3. *Privatization*: Privatization is another case of transfer of user rights which refers to the sale of state-owned farmland to the beneficiaries. Typically a dissolution method of the collectivist mode of agriculture, privatization is used in some of the erstwhile socialist countries (Bulgaria, 1991, Czechoslovakia, 1991 and Poland, 1991) in combination with other forms of dissolution. In some cases, the law may enable the parliament to sell lands of religious importance (Israel, 2009). In other instances, the state can sell previously expropriated lands as happened in Taiwan in 1951 and again in 1953 involving former Japanese-owned lands.
4. *Restitution*: Restitution is the last motive of the transfer of end user rights in our empirical analysis. Under restitution, the state/authority returned the previously collectivized land or a similar size of land back to its former owners or their descendants following the collapse of communism (Bulgaria, Czechia, Estonia, Latvia, Lithuania and Romania). However, several countries did not elect to restitute collectivized lands, or restituted them only partially. In some instances, the collectivized lands had no claimants even though they were offered to be restituted (e.g., Estonia, 1991). In contrast, quite a few formerly communist countries collectivized land only minimally during communism (Poland). In other cases,

previously nationalized/expropriated (not necessarily collectivized) lands were returned by the state/authority with the transfer of end user rights to beneficiaries (Algeria, 1990 and South Africa, 1994).
5. *Combination of above four motives*: In the empirical analysis, we also include another motive, which is the combination of the above four end user motives, and use this as another combined category of the end user rights transfer motive. The idea is that the combination of all four end user rights transfer motives would give us a uniform, all-encompassing picture of end user rights being transferred to the beneficiaries.

In addition, the following two major land reforms are used to test the proposed Hypothesis 2. These reforms do not transfer physical lands to beneficiaries and, most importantly, full end user rights to lands are also not transferred. We conjecture that these kinds of reforms with partial end user rights being transferred could be treated as signals for creating land market-facilitating institutions. We could think about such reforms as stepping stones in ushering in full-scale land market transactions.

1. *Tenure security improvement*: The tenure security improvement is in relation to tillers of the land (tenants and/or sharecroppers) with the key feature that the land title rests with the landowner, and not with the tenant and/or sharecropper. However, the tenants can still make their own private and long-term decisions on agricultural activity with the security they receive. The landowner may also be the state, where the state gives greater tenure security to farmers (Ethiopia, 1997), provides extended leases (Georgia, 1998, Croatia, 1991 and Israel 1960) or gives the opportunity for land sharing (Moldova, 1991 and Russia, 1990). As an example of greater tenure security in which the land is owned by private persons, Europe exhibits several tenure security improvement acts that give tenants more rights with longer-term leases and enabling faster land dispute claims (France, 1946, Netherlands, 1937 and 1958).[6]
2. *Recognition of customary/indigenous/community/religious/traditional (CICRT) land rights*: This particular land reform motive does not involve the transfer of end user rights to the beneficiaries; rather, the recognition of CICRT rights aims at formalizing the previously informal land rights and moving the CICRT lands into the formal sector. Recognition of CICRT land rights has the potential to improve farmers' decision making in agricultural activity. In a number of countries, especially in the developing world, informal rights to land may exist collectively or privately. The key difference between these is that the former refers to collective rights under customary, indigenous, community, religious as well as traditional rules, while the latter refers to informal private individual/household rights. The law may recognize either CICRT ownership rights (Niger, 1961) or only private rights (Mozambique, 1997). We coded both of the recognitions as CICRT rights.

In addition, two falsification exercises are also presented with major land reform implementation motives where end user rights are not transferred to the beneficiaries at all, neither fully (as proposed in Hypothesis 1) nor partially (as per Hypothesis 2). These are briefly outlined below.

1. *Pro-poor land reform*: This particular set of land reforms is primarily targeted at poor beneficiaries without transferring end user rights, but it includes both physical transfer of land as well as non-physical transfer of land. Specifically, an act or directive is deemed to

be pro-poor if it is specifically targeted at the poor or if one of the major beneficiaries is the poor. In particular, an act or directive is listed as pro-poor if the source documentation mentions one of the following keywords regarding the targets and beneficiaries of the reform: landless; poor; landless agricultural labor; bonded labor; marginal farmers; reduce poverty; peasants; subsistence peasants; subsistence farmers. In addition, we consider squatters as poor (Costa Rica, 1961 and Jamaica, 1968).[7]

2. *Combination of three motives, landholding ceiling imposition, expropriation and redistribution*: In the last falsification check, we combine three motives from the Bhattacharya et al. (2019) paper, which are often used together in implementation. The first motive imposes an upper ceiling on the quantity of land to be held by landlords, primarily in the context of developing countries in Africa (e.g., Namibia, 1995 and Somalia, 1975), Latin America (e.g., Bolivia, 1953, Brazil, 1964, Cuba, 1959 and Dominican Republic, 1962) and South Asia (e.g., China, 1947, Japan, 1946, South Korea, 1950 and Taiwan, 1953). The land-holding ceiling imposition is implemented to smooth out highly unequal land ownership between landlords and intended beneficiaries without transferring land user rights. The second motive for expropriation involves the confiscation of private land from landlords (excluding confiscation of land for collective or communism-type decision making) above the imposed ceilings with or without compensation. The third motive, redistribution, generally takes places after land ceiling imposition and expropriation with the confiscated/expropriated lands taken over and above the upper ceiling being transferred to the poor by the ruler/state. Interestingly, redistribution also comes with the transfer of end user rights to land. However, since the above three motives are used together with the first two motives (landholding ceiling imposition and expropriation) where end user rights are not transferred, we use the combination of the above three together as a combined motive, treating it as one where end user rights are not transferred fully.

### 5.3     Control Variables

We use a number of control variables from the extant literature (Nunn and Qian, 2011). The first specification (outlined in Section 6) controls for pertinent variables for urbanization, namely, the number of people in an urban area and urban population growth, which are directly linked with the outcome variable as increasing urban population means increasing urbanization. Similarly, urban population growth rate determines the proportion of urban population in the total population. These two variables are collated from the WDIs. In addition, we also control for the gross agricultural production index from the Food and Agricultural Organization statistical database with the intuition that more agricultural production would indicate more agricultural income-earning opportunities and thus would limit the propensity to urbanize.

In the second specification (more information is provided in Section 6) involving a nominal farmland price index from a set of developed countries as an outcome variable, we control for two key variables: (1) the arable land area, as it signals the effective land available for cultivation and could be interpreted as the supply-side indicator of the land market; and (2) the level of rural population (in logarithmic scale) with the idea that the level of rural population has a positive bearing on farmland prices as a bigger rural population means increased pressure on farmland. The arable land area is taken from the Food and Agricultural Organization website and the rural population numbers are from the WDIs.

## 5.4 Descriptive Statistics

Table 3.1 provides the descriptive statistics for all variables used in the empirical analysis.

*Table 3.1    Descriptive statistics*

| Variables | Mean | Standard deviation | Minimum | Maximum | Observations |
|---|---|---|---|---|---|
| *Dependent variables* | | | | | |
| Urbanization | 49.749 | 24.854 | 2.077 | 100.000 | 9,864 |
| Nominal farmland price index | 62.124 | 75.119 | 0.0001 | 547.5 | 846 |
| *Independent variables (land reform implementation motives)* | | | | | |
| Distribution | 0.083 | 0.274 | 0 | 1 | 19,502 |
| Consolidation | 0.046 | 0.211 | 0 | 1 | 19,502 |
| Privatization | 0.021 | 0.144 | 0 | 1 | 19,502 |
| Restitution | 0.010 | 0.100 | 0 | 1 | 19,502 |
| Combined end user motive | 0.137 | 0.344 | 0 | 1 | 19,502 |
| Tenure security implementation | 0.129 | 0.335 | 0 | 1 | 19,502 |
| CICRT recognition | 0.045 | 0.208 | 0 | 1 | 19,502 |
| Pro-poor | 0.188 | 0.391 | 0 | 1 | 19,502 |
| Combined motive of land ceiling, expropriation and redistribution | 0.196 | 0.397 | 0 | 1 | 19,502 |
| *Control variables* | | | | | |
| Urban population | 127,000,00 | 402,000,00 | 8029 | 761,000,000 | 9,861 |
| Urban population growth rate | 3.086 | 3.181 | −187.142 | 48.935 | 9,860 |
| Gross agricultural production index | 81.946 | 51.754 | 5.67 | 1104.66 | 8,871 |
| Arable land area (hectares) | 7,517.14 | 22,293.88 | 0.2 | 189244 | 8,792 |
| Rural population | 165,000,00 | 754,000,00 | 2159 | 881,000,000 | 9,612 |

*Note*: Urbanization is measured as the proportion of urban people out of the total population. The land reform motives take the value of 1 from the year in which they are implemented; otherwise, the motives are counted as 0.

A quick glance at the descriptive statistics reveals the sample size difference in terms of the dependent and control variables with respect to the independent variables. This is due to the fact that most of the dependent and control variables are from 1960 onward, whereas the independent variables span 1900–2010. However, this will not have any bearing on the empirical analysis as we will be looking at the effect of implementation once it is done and often this covers the post-1960 period.

Taking a look at the independent variables, we see considerable heterogeneity in regards to their diagnostics. The land reform implementation with end users' rights transferred shows the mean hovering between 0.01 (restitution) and 0.08 (distribution), pointing towards more distribution-specific implementation in comparison to the restitutions. Interestingly, the combination of all four end user motives depict a healthy mean of

0.137, which is even higher than the tenure security improvement motive mean of 0.129. Note that the tenure security improvement motive is related to the partial transfer of end user rights in land. Similarly, the CICRT recognition motive is also linked with the partial transfer of end user rights in land, which shows the mean value of 0.045.

In this connection, note that the combined motive of land ceiling imposition, expropriation and redistribution reveals the highest mean of 0.196 among all the land reform motives used in the analysis. This means that this particular combined motive is used quite frequently in the data sample. Thus, a falsification exercise involving this particular land reform variable could reveal the largest negative effect in the ensuing empirical analysis. The same point could be validated for the pro-poor land reform motive, another reform variable employed in the falsification exercise.

## 6  EMPIRICAL STRATEGY

We will be using the land reforms as exogenous shocks in a quasi-experimental setup with the idea that these sorts of reforms are path-breaking, significant changes and they do not occur frequently. We exploit the variation in major land reform implementations over time across countries noting the fact that different countries at different points in time implemented major land reforms.[8] In addition, there are heterogeneities in regards to motives of land reforms implemented, viz. some land reforms give end user rights to reform beneficiaries such as reforms focusing on land distribution, land consolidation, privatization of state-owned lands and land restitution. In contrast, in land reforms where improving tenure security is the main aim and land reforms which formally recognize informal land transaction decisions through community, indigenous and religious norms, end user rights are not fully given to the beneficiaries. Thus, and as hypothesized earlier (see Section 4), one would expect to see marked differences between outcome variables if end user rights are fully or partially transferred versus reforms where end user rights are not considered at all. The intuition is to identify the causal effect of these differential motives of land reforms by looking at the significant breaks in the outcome variables after implementation.

One could use a traditional DiD estimator to identify the causal effect of major land reform implementation on the outcome variables. However, the traditional, single-coefficient DiD estimator is effective when the treatment (in this case, land reform implementation) occurs only once, between the pre-period and post-period, thus generating fixed treated and control units or countries (Goodman-Bacon, 2018). If the treatment varies over time, i.e., with some countries implementing land reform at time t and some other countries implementing land reform at time t + n, where n could be 1 or 50 or 70 or 90 (for instance, the first major land reform implementation in the USA occurred in 1902, but in Canada, a neighbor of the USA, the first major land reform implementation occurred in 1973), or in the quite distant past, then this can be viewed as multiple treatments or experiments (Goodman-Bacon, 2018). In such instances, already treated countries can be seen as controls for later treated countries since their treatment status does not change. However, with changes in treatment effects or land reform implementations over time, these get subtracted from the DiD estimate, leading to biased results in the single-coefficient DiD estimates (Goodman-Bacon, 2018).

## 6.1 Baseline Model

To alleviate such concerns involving single-coefficient DiD estimators, we employ a flexible event-study model as in Jacobson et al. (1993), Stevenson and Wolfers (2006) and Bhalotra et al. (2019):

$$Y_{it} = \alpha + \sum_{j=2}^{10} \beta_j^{lead} LR_i \times 1\{lead_t = j\} + \sum_{m=0}^{15} \beta_m^{lag} LR_i \times 1\{lag_t = m\} + \delta.Z_{it} + \varphi_i + \sigma_t + \varepsilon_{it}, \quad (3.1)$$

where the main outcome variable, $Y_{it}$, is urbanization (measured as the proportion of urban population out of total population) in country *i* at time *t*. The main independent variable is denoted by *LR*, which represents land reform implementation in country *i*. *LR* takes the value of 1 if a country ever implemented a particular kind of land reform, and using the event-study design, we interact this land reform with a set of leads and lags based on the year the land reform was implemented. We use 10 periods for leads and 15 periods for lags, keeping in mind that these major land reform implementations did not occur very frequently, and thus deciphering the impact of a particular land reform implementation within a period of 10 years before and 15 years after is a reasonable time frame to analyze its impact on the outcome variable.[9] In the baseline model, we also use appropriate controls (denoted by $Z_{it}$) to address possible omitted variable bias.

These controls include urban population, growth rate of urban population and, importantly, an index of agricultural production, which measures the value of gross agricultural production in countries over time. Note that agricultural production would be influenced by factors like inputs used, soil quality, level of mechanization, access to credit, etc. As agricultural production increases, so does the income-earning opportunity from tilling the land, and this may discourage people from moving to urban areas in search of livelihoods. Thus, agricultural production would act as a deterrent towards urbanization. In addition, we also control for unobservable factors using country fixed effects ($\varphi_i$) and year fixed effects ($\sigma_t$). All standard errors are clustered at the country level following the suggestion of Bertrand et al. (2004).

The coefficients of interest will be the estimates of $\beta^{lag}$ as they capture the effects after land reform implementations. The lead variables can be used to check and test for any pre-trends which are very important in the underlying identification assumption of no parallel pre-trends (Bhalotra et al., 2019).[10] Freyaldenhoven et al. (2019) point out that the absence of such pre-trends can be taken as a test of exogeneity of the policy variable, which is the land reform implementation in our context (described in detail in the next paragraph). Note that this test should be judged as partial as it can only identify parallel pre-trends but cannot actually test for counterfactuals (Bhalotra et al., 2019; Kahn-Lang and Lang, 2018).

Our main independent variables involve land reform implementations where full end user rights were transferred to the beneficiaries. Since full end user rights could accentuate land market-related transactions, among other alternatives, we expect that these implementations would spur the urbanization incentives. Thus, we anticipate that the lagged estimates will be positive and significant after the implementation years for these particular land reform motives. We use five particular land reform implementation motives involving transfer of end user rights from the Bhattacharya et al. (2019) paper, viz. (a) distribution of state-owned lands to beneficiaries, (b) consolidation of private land, (c) privatization of state-owned farmland, (d) restitution of land and (e) a combination of the four motives to decipher the overall impact of such land reforms.[11] Taking option (e) where we pool together a number of different categories of motives is prudent given the fact that this will give us a broad, overall picture of the land reform policies implemented to transfer end users' rights.

Based on the conjectured Hypothesis 2, we also present results with two motives where full end user rights were not transferred to the beneficiaries, rather the land tenure arrangements were made more transparent and secure so that the end users enjoyed the certainty of income earned over land in a more secure way and for a more prolonged period of time. We could treat these kinds of reforms as showing the stepping stones towards more land market-friendly transactions by partially recognizing user rights to land rather than fully recognizing end user rights to land in deference to Hypothesis 1. These are: (1) land reform implementation with tenure security improvement as the only motive and (2) land reform implementation where the motive is to legally recognize informal land-related transactions using community norms, indigenous procedures as well as religious beliefs.

Since we envisage that end user rights on land would lead to more urbanization, we provide two falsification or placebo results with alternative land reform implementation motives where end user rights are not transferred to the beneficiaries, be it fully or partially. These are: (1) land reforms that are targeted explicitly at the rural poor and (2) land reforms that are implemented with the motives of imposing land ceilings, expropriation and redistribution. This second set of reforms in (2) is treated as a combined motive as often the redistributive land reforms follow the staged process of imposing land ceilings first, followed by expropriation with or without compensation for the landholders from whom the lands are expropriated over the stipulated land ceilings and, lastly, redistribution of expropriated land to the intended beneficiaries. In these two falsification instances, we expect either muted or negative effects on the outcome variable – urbanization.

## 6.2 The Two-Way Differences-in-Differences Model

After reporting the above flexible event-study estimates, we also provide estimates from the two-way DiD model, keeping in mind that the DiD estimates reported may not be unbiased due to the change in implementation variable over time across countries, as mentioned in Section 6.1. Thus, in all likelihood, the DiD estimates will under-report the true impact of the land reform implementation variables. Nevertheless, the DiD estimates will provide important effects in regards to the magnitudes of the land reform implementations undertaken. In these specifications, the independent variable (land reform implementation) takes the value 1 from the year or time period the land reform is implemented until the end of the data sample; otherwise, it takes the value 0. Similar to Equation 3.1, this model is also estimated with appropriate controls, country-specific fixed effects and time effects and the standard errors are clustered at the country level.

## 6.3 Additional Specification

We use the following specification to decipher the impact of land reform implementation involving end user rights on land prices (as conjectured in Hypothesis 3 in Section 4) for 11 developed countries from the Knoll et al. (2017) paper. We employ the nominal farmland price index as the land price variable from the above paper as the outcome variable.

$$LP_{it} = \theta + \sum_{g=2}^{10} \lambda_g^{lead} LR_i \times 1\{lead_t = g\} + \sum_{h=0}^{15} \lambda_h^{lag} LR_i \times 1\{lag_t = h\} + \psi.M_{it} + \pi_i + \mu_t + \gamma_{it}, \quad (3.2)$$

where LP stands for the nominal index of farmland prices from the Knoll et al. (2017) paper. Similar to Equation 3.1, the coefficients of interests will be the $\lambda^{lag}$ estimates as these capture the effect of post-land reform implementation on land prices. With end user rights over land, there is a possibility of improved land market transactions and this would be captured by the positive impact on land prices for farmland. The intuition is that end user rights will either signal or facilitate easy transactions involving land as willing buyers and sellers would be able to buy or sell land when needed. In such instances, we could interpret end user rights as facilitating or creating demand in the land market, and as a result, the prices will shore up over time in countries where such reforms are implemented.

In regards to the supply side of the land market, we control for the arable land area, as it signals the effective land available for cultivation. This will have a primary impact on the rural land or farmland prices. We expect the estimates associated with the arable land area to be negative, especially when the rural farmland prices are used as the dependent variable. In addition, the level of rural population (in logarithmic scale) is used as another control variable, with the idea being that the level of rural population would have a bearing on the farmland prices. The a priori expectation is that the number of rural people will influence rural farmland prices positively. Moreover, similar to Equation 3.1, the unobserved heterogeneities are addressed with country and year fixed effects and the standard errors are clustered at the country level.

Given the nature of land reform implementation in developed countries with end user rights (primarily consolidation and very few privatizations), we will provide results with two different motives of implementation, (1) consolidation and (2) combined end user motive. No falsification results could be presented due to the nature of land reform motives implemented in these developed countries.

# 7 RESULTS AND DISCUSSION

## 7.1 Main Results: The Impact of Various End User Rights Motives for Land Reform Implementation on Urbanization

### 7.1.1 Results for Hypothesis 1

The following figures present results from Equation 3.1 where we concentrate on the impact of land reform implementations where full end users' rights were transferred on the outcome variable of interest – urbanization. These represent testing for Hypothesis 1. The figures are reproduced for comparison purposes in Appendix A.

Figure 3.1 shows some support to the postulated hypothesis that land reform implementation with the distribution motive where end user rights are transferred is associated with higher urbanization, especially after five years. Thus, the distribution motive plays a role in ushering in urbanization, and this could be attributed to possible land market-related transactions taking place after transferring end user rights in such implementations. There appears to be no pre-trends looking at the period before the land reform implementation, so the identification strategy mentioned in Section 6.1 seems to be working.

Figure 3.2 provides much stronger support to the postulated hypothesis, with the consolidation land reform implementation showing positive support to the urbanization outcome if we take a look at the relevant lagged variables. Thus, consolidation land reforms with transfer of end user rights matter for urbanization, and the effect shows up after just two years of the reforms being implemented. However, there appears to be some significant pre-trends, thus violating the no-pre-trends assumption for identification. In such instances, we can say that the

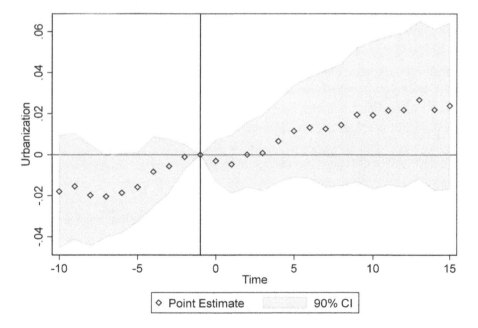

*Figure 3.1*　*The impact of distributive motive land reform implementation on urbanization*

56  *Handbook of real estate and macroeconomics*

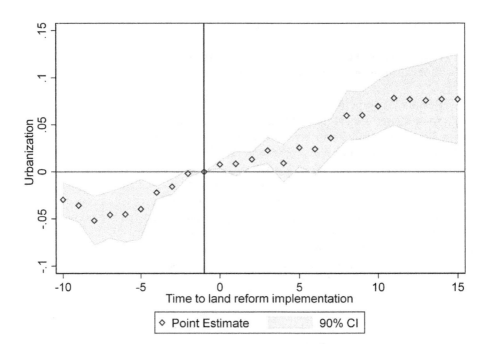

*Figure 3.2*   *The impact of consolidation motive land reform implementation on urbanization*

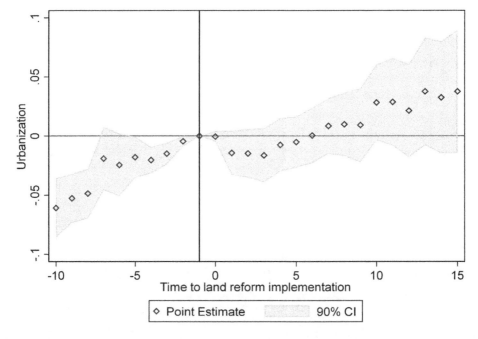

*Figure 3.3*   *The impact of privatization motive land reform implementation on urbanization*

consolidation-motive land reform implemented is strongly correlated with the outcome variable – urbanization. Consolidation-type reforms are pursued in both developed and developing countries with full transfer of end users' rights. It appears that consolidation did usher in land market development which impacted urbanization as per Hypothesis 1, but the effect could not be treated as causal.

The privatization-motive land reform implementation, as depicted in Figure 3.3, however, shows no statistically significant impact on urbanization. Thus, even if end user rights are transferred with the privatization motive, this does not necessarily lead to more people flocking towards urban centers over time. The result points to heterogeneities in the impact of the particular motives on the outcome variable.

Figure 3.4 shows strongest support for the proposed hypothesis, especially after looking at the post-reform period from six years onwards. Thus, the restitution motive land reforms which were implemented with full transfer of end users' rights remain instrumental in creating land market-type transactions. These transactions, in turn, impact the level of urbanization in a positive and significant way. The figure also shows no statistically significant pre-trends; thus, identification is achieved for this particular land reform implementation variable. Note that restitution-type reforms are prevalent in former Soviet Union countries after the disintegration of the union. Thus, these particular type of reforms, which happened mainly in the 1990s, could be devised in such a way that full end user rights in land were transferred easily, which later hastened urbanization.

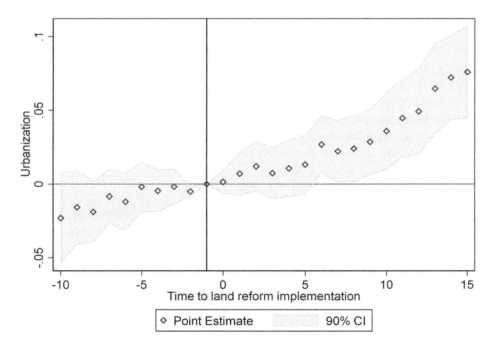

*Figure 3.4*   The impact of restitution motive land reform implementation on urbanization

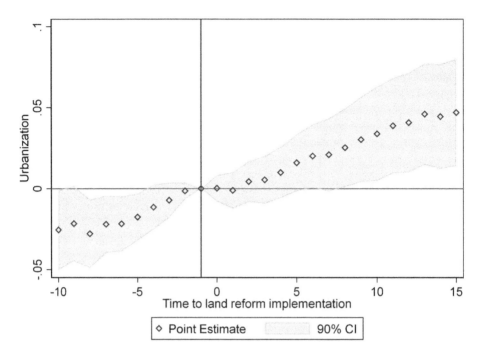

*Figure 3.5    The impact of combined end user rights motives land reform implementation on urbanization*

Figure 3.5 reveals the land reform implementations where combined end user rights were transferred (i.e., a combination of reform motives of distribution, privatization, consolidation and restitution). There is very strong support for urbanization Hypothesis 1, especially five years after reform implementation; thus, giving end user rights to rural land could usher in land market-type transactions and that would lead to more urbanization. This could happen as, with end user rights, the beneficiaries have the option to invest more in their own land or participate in land market transactions where land can be bought and sold freely if they wish to quit agricultural production. In this instance, the second hypothesis seems to be a more plausible alternative for the beneficiaries to pursue. The pre-trends also show no apparent support (which is confirmed by the statistical significance of the lagged variables) for parallel trends; thus, identification is achieved. This finding is in line with Deininger et al. (2017) who highlighted full transfer of property rights in land as an important driver of the land market.

Taking all of the above findings together, we find the strongest support for Hypothesis 1 when end user rights are transferred as a bundle in the combined motive and where end user rights are given through the restitution channel. These findings are in line with a number of country-specific results mentioned in the brief overview of the literature above. It is interesting to note that the country-specific findings are supported with the broad macroeconomic dataset that we are using in this chapter.

In regards to Hypothesis 2 with partial transfer of end user rights, there is very good support from the CICRT recognition motive as a stepping stone towards facilitating land market transactions. Given that this motive of reform is prevalent in a number of developing countries, especially in Africa, Latin America and South East Asia, we find it heartening to see causal support of our hypothesis covering a large swathe of developing countries.

Focusing on Hypothesis 3 with 11 developed countries, we find that combined end user rights and consolidation-type reforms did indeed signal mature land market development by hiking up the land price, a phenomenon documented in the extant literature.

### 7.1.2 Results for Hypothesis 2

The following two figures present results from tenure security improvement-type reforms and CICRT recognition land reforms. We know that these categories of reform do not fully transfer the end user rights, rather these are treated as stepping stones for creating land market transaction arrangements by partially recognizing end users' rights. Thus, we would expect a positive impact, if any, from such types of reform, not immediately, but with some passage of time after such reforms have taken place. In addition, the magnitude of the impact may not be as large in comparison to reforms where end user rights are fully transferred.

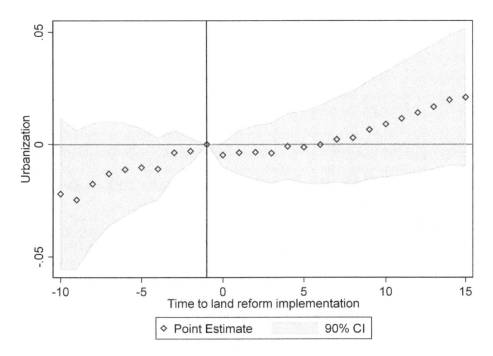

*Figure 3.6*   *The impact of improving tenure security motive land reform implementation on urbanization*

Taking a look at Figure 3.6 and keeping in mind the above brief points regarding the characteristics of such reforms, we find muted support for urbanization as a result of tenure security improvement-type reforms, especially after eight years of cumulative implementation. The coefficients remain statistically insignificant, albeit positive. Thus, land reforms with tenure security improvements do not affect urbanization, probably due to the ambiguous nature of end user rights.

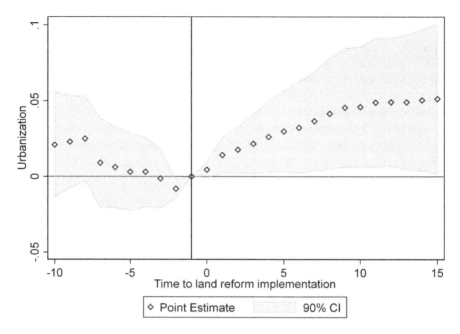

*Figure 3.7  The impact of CICRT recognition motive land reform implementation on urbanization*

However, Figure 3.7 shows remarkable support for Hypothesis 2 in the sense that giving CICRT recognition improves the propensity to urbanize after this particular land reform is implemented. Thus, partial transfer of end users' rights through CICRT recognition could be used as a stepping stone towards facilitating land market transactions. Given that CICRT recognition is often used in developing countries in Latin America, Africa and South East Asia, this particular finding has important policy implications. The pre-trends do not show any statistically significant impact, making CICRT recognition land reform a causal factor for urbanization and long-term economic development.

### 7.2  Falsification Results: The Impact of Non-End User Rights Motives Land Reform Implementation on Urbanization

The following figures show the falsification or placebo-type results involving two different types of land reform implementation where end user rights are not transferred either fully or partially. If our conjecture is true, then the falsification exercise will yield neither statistically significant results nor positive results for the outcome variable (urbanization) involving the end user rights reported earlier.

The falsification findings from Equation 3.1 are presented. Figure 3.8 shows implementation for pro-poor land reforms and Figure 3.9 presents land reform implementation with the combined motive of land ceiling imposition, expropriation and redistribution.

A quick look at Figure 3.8 reveals that the pro-poor motive land reform implementations have no positive and statistically significant impact on urbanization. This shows a clear support of baseline results in Hypotheses 1 and 2 in terms of falsification. There is no pre-trend

Land and macroeconomics 61

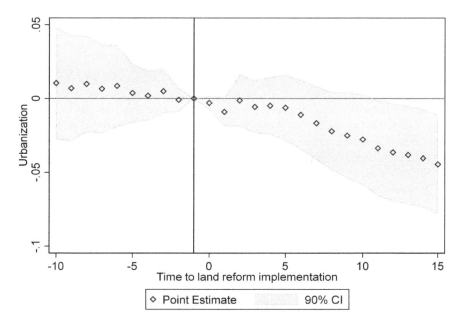

*Figure 3.8*     *Falsification result: the impact of pro-poor motive land reform implementation on urbanization*

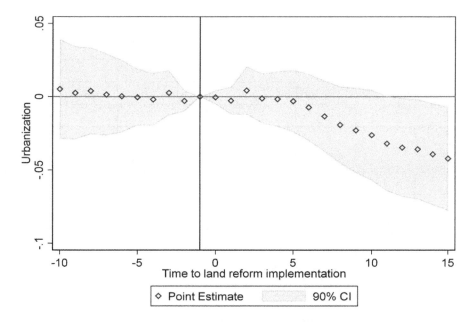

*Figure 3.9*     *Falsification result: the impact of combined land ceiling imposition, expropriation and redistribution motive land reform implementations on urbanization*

detected and the post-reform coefficients are all showing negative impact on urbanization. Thus, pro-poor-type reforms where there are no full or partial transfer of end user rights would not create any land market setup incentives and would not reveal any positive bearing on long-run growth and development.

The findings from Figure 3.9 also support our main conjecture as the post-implementation of the combined motive of land ceiling imposition, expropriation and redistribution reveals a negative and statistically insignificant impact on urbanization. Thus, for this instance as well where end user rights are not fully or partially transferred, the land reform implementation has no positive bearing on the outcome variable – urbanization. The falsification results presented, therefore, lend credence to Hypotheses 1 and 2.

## 7.3   Results from the Two-Way Differences-in-Differences Estimation

We present the following results from the DiD estimation after controlling for country- and year-specific fixed effects as well as relevant controls used in Equation 3.1.

Table 3.2   *Differences-in-differences estimation results for land reform implementations with end users' rights transferred fully and partially*

| Independent variables (land reform implementation motives with end users' rights) ↓ | Dependent variable |||||||
|---|---|---|---|---|---|---|---|
| | Urbanization | Urbanization | Urbanization | Urbanization | Urbanization | Urbanization | Urbanization |
| *End user rights fully transferred (Hypothesis 1)* | | | | | | | |
| Distribution | 0.042*** (2.03) | | | | | | |
| Consolidation | | 0.093*** (5.40) | | | | | |
| Privatization | | | 0.100*** (2.63) | | | | |
| Restitution | | | | 0.066 (1.29) | | | |
| Combination of above four motives together | | | | | 0.056*** (2.71) | | |
| *End user rights partially transferred (Hypothesis 2)* | | | | | | | |
| Tenure security improvement | | | | | | 0.052** (1.95) | |
| CICRT recognition | | | | | | | 0.039 (1.25) |
| R-squared | 0.8744 | 0.8743 | 0.8748 | 0.8738 | 0.8750 | 0.8754 | 0.8745 |
| Sample size | 8728 | 8728 | 8728 | 8728 | 8728 | 8728 | 8728 |
| Number of countries | 181 | 181 | 181 | 181 | 181 | 181 | 181 |
| Mean of the dependent variable | 49.749 | 49.749 | 49.749 | 49.749 | 49.749 | 49.749 | 49.749 |
| Controls | ✓ | ✓ | ✓ | ✓ | ✓ | ✓ | ✓ |
| Fixed effects | ✓ | ✓ | ✓ | ✓ | ✓ | ✓ | ✓ |
| Time effects | ✓ | ✓ | ✓ | ✓ | ✓ | ✓ | ✓ |

*Note*: The relevant t-statistics are reported in parentheses. ***, ** and * denote 99%, 95% and 90% significance levels, respectively. The R-squared reported are *within R-squared*. All regressions include country-specific fixed effects and time effects as well as controls. The controls are: (1) the level of urban population (in natural logarithmic scale), (2) the urban population growth rate and (3) the gross agricultural production index (in natural logarithmic scale).

The DiD estimates from Table 3.2 show support for the main conjectured hypothesis in Hypothesis 1. The land reform implementations where end user rights are fully transferred show positive and statistically significant effects on urbanization in a majority of cases. One exception is that of the restitution-motive land reform, which shows a statistically insignificant yet positive result. The statistical insignificance could be attributed to the small number of restitution-motive land reforms as compared to other types of land reform. Note that the results resonate with the recent findings in Glaeser (2021) where he mentions that property rights in land hasten the development of urban cities, especially in developed countries.

In regards to the magnitudes, the effects translate to around 1.7 percent in terms of constant elasticity for distributive land reform implementation, i.e., one successful distributive land reform implementation will increase urbanization by 1.7 percentage points. Similarly, for the consolidation and privatization motives, these constant elasticities are 1.03 and 0.05 percent, respectively. Taking the combined motive, the elasticity hovers around 3 percent. Even if the numbers seem small, note that the land reform implementations in consideration do not happen frequently; thus, from that perspective, the constant elasticities show quite considerable and statistically significant effects over time across countries.

Taking a look at the DiD estimates pertaining to Hypothesis 2 with end users' rights partially transferred, there is also positive support for the conjectured idea that partially transferred property rights in land could also usher in urbanization. The tenure security improvement motive yields a positive and statistically significant impact on urbanization. This lends credence to the idea that even partial transfer of end user rights could signal a positive improvement towards the creation of land market transaction arrangements. These arrangements would in turn help long-run growth and development. The CICRT recognition motive, though positive in sign, is not statistically significant. Thus, even if recognition of customary, indigenous, community, religious and traditional land rights could be used as a marker for land market recognition activities, these could not yield statistically significant estimates for urbanization.

Note that the above positive estimates could be interpreted as potential land market development markers as mentioned by Deininger et al. (2017) and discussed at length by Deininger and Feder (2001) as well as by Binswanger-Mkhize et al. (2009).[12] This would not be the case had the lands been physically transferred without explicitly giving end users rights as our falsification exercise shows with two particular motives of land reform, i.e., pro-poor and a combination of land ceiling, expropriation and redistribution. For these later two cases of reform, the land users would be primarily interested in tilling the land for consumption purposes, whereas giving end users rights to land as hypothesized in Hypotheses 1 and 2 could open the window of opportunity for such lands to be used as investment purposes over and above consumption decisions.

The control variables used (but not reported in Table 3.2) show expected signs and statistical significance as conjectured before. The level of urban population remains positive and statistically significant in all specifications. Similarly, the value of the agricultural production index remains negative and statistically significant in all specifications, showing that the improvement in agricultural production and associated income-earning opportunities slow down the level of urbanization. The growth rate of the urban population remains positive albeit not statistically significant, indicating more of a level impact (through number of urban people) than a change or growth effect.

### 7.3.1 Checking Hypotheses 1 and 2 with an alternative outcome variable

We use manufacturing value added as a percentage of GDP from the WDIs as an alternative outcome variable to test Hypotheses 1 and 2.[13] The idea is to analyze whether land reforms with end user rights fully and partially transferred usher in urbanization, then whether these land reforms also affect manufacturing which would be important given that user rights are needed to start effective production activities. The event analysis graphs for this analysis are reported in Appendix B.

Taking a look at the graphs in Appendix B, we do not find any immediate causal support from land reforms with end users' rights transferred fully or partially driving the manufacturing valued-added activities. This could be attributed to at least three potential explanations. The first is paucity of such data from the WDIs, with the sample size dropped to half if manufacturing value added as a percentage to GDP is used as the outcome variable instead of the urbanization measure. The second could be that the link between urbanization and manufacturing value added is quite small, with the correlation hovering around 0.28 for the dataset we have used. This means that manufacturing value added as an alternative indicator for urbanization could not be used comprehensively as a viable alternative to the urbanization measure. Finally, manufacturing valued added could be primarily driven by technological improvement over time as proposed in the economic growth literature, rather than the enhancement in property rights involving land. Thus, it may not be surprising that we could not find any causal support for Hypotheses 1 and 2 using event study-based analysis with manufacturing value added as an alternative outcome variable.

## 7.4 Results from the Land Price Variable as Dependent Variables (Hypothesis 3)

In the following section, we present results from estimating Equation 3.2 for 11 developed countries in the sample for two particular land reform implementations, (1) consolidation and (2) combined-motive end user right-transferring reforms. The data sample for nominal farmland prices is taken from the Knoll et al. (2017) paper and we estimate Equation 3.2 with the nominal farmland index as the dependent variable.

### 7.4.1 Results from the nominal farmland price index as the dependent variable

Figures 3.10 and 3.11 show the impact of consolidation and combined end user rights motives land reform implementation on the nominal farmland price index for 14 advanced countries.

Figure 3.10 reveals some interesting findings. First, there appear to be no statistically significant pre-trends, which helps in regards to causal interpretation. Second, there is a statistically significant and positive impact on nominal farmland prices, which means there is strong support for the conjectured hypothesis that some particular end user transfer-oriented land reforms like consolidation facilitate the demand side of the land market and this in turn positively influences agricultural land prices. Third, the effect dies down from 11 years onwards, signaling that only end user rights transfer may not last long in hiking up demand, and other market-enabling transactions, decisions or institutions should be put in place to keep up the demand. Overall, consolidation-motive land reform implementation has a positive and statistically significant causal impact on farmland prices over the short to medium term.

Figure 3.11 shows the impact of combined end user rights land reform implementation on the farmland price index. Similar to the Figure 3.10 result, we find a positive and statistically significant effect from combined end user rights land reform implementation on the nominal

*Land and macroeconomics* 65

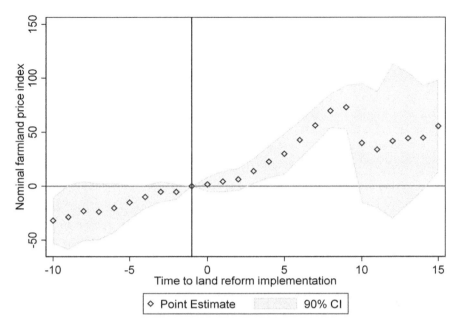

*Figure 3.10    The impact of consolidation motive land reform implementation on the nominal farmland price index in developed countries*

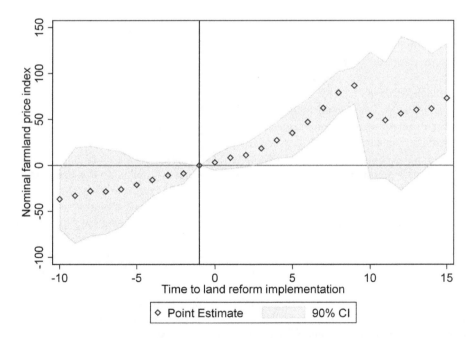

*Figure 3.11    The impact of combined end user motives land reform implementation on the nominal farmland price index in developed countries*

farmland price index and the effect remains consistent even after 10 periods. Thus, these combinations of end user rights point towards possible land market demand creations, which in turn influence nominal farmland prices positively. This finding is in line with recent evidence from Djankov et al. (2021).

Taking all the empirical evidence presented above, we find good support for our three proposed hypotheses outlined in Section 4. Thus, land reform implementations focusing on transferring end users' rights either fully or partially could be used to usher in land market-related transactions. This, in turn, would facilitate more urbanization in a number of countries. In addition, it would have a positive bearing on farmland prices in developed countries.

## 8 CONCLUDING REMARKS

This chapter provides a broad overview of important issues in macroeconomics involving land. Land and macroeconomics is a wide-ranging concept to cover within a chapter. Thus, we limit our attention to three interconnected themes. The first theme focuses on pertinent concepts involving rural land and its consequences on macroeconomic indicators like growth and development. Then, in the second theme, we delve into the issues of urban land and its dynamics in mainly urban contexts like house prices and urban development, keeping in mind that housing and real estate issues also encompass economic growth and development. The last theme presents new empirical evidence where we investigate how a particular type of land reform implementation involving the transfer of end users' rights to beneficiaries either fully or partially could usher in one interesting driver of development, namely, urbanization.

The empirical strategy uses a quasi-experimental setup involving a flexible event-study design and the DiD technique to identify the causal effect of land reform implementation motives involving end user rights transfer on urbanization using the recently developed major land reform database by Bhattacharya et al. (2019). In addition, the empirical analysis also uses novel data on agricultural farmland prices reported by Knoll et al. (2017) and found that the end user rights-focused land reforms played a positive role in enhancing farmland prices, indicating plausible land market demand-side mechanisms of such land reform implementations.

In regards to policy implications, the chapter's discussion and empirical analysis show that there could be some interesting policy decisions that policy makers or governments may consider. The first would be the reforms encouraging land market development in rural areas by helping set up institutions supporting land-related transactions including transfer of property rights to land in rural areas. Note that Djankov et al. (2021) point to such effectiveness of institutions in the global context. Second, policy makers could devise proper mechanisms to boost the smooth conversion of rural land to urban land, thus increasing the supply of urban land for development purposes and ameliorating possible business cycle fluctuations involving urban land. Finally, appropriate fiscal policies could be undertaken to boost planned urban development in developing countries which would be environmentally sustainable for future generations.

Future research could focus on the channels behind land reform implementation with end user rights transferred fully or partially and how these impact land market development through changes in land or assets as well as income inequality.

## ACKNOWLEDGMENTS

I would like to thank the anonymous reviewer for insightful comments on the earlier version of the chapter. I would also like to thank the editor for giving me the opportunity to contribute to the book. Charles provided very good suggestions and comments in the early stages of this chapter's draft. I am also very thankful to him for kind reminders which helped me to complete the chapter within a reasonable amount of time. All standard disclaimers apply.

## NOTES

1. If journal publication is considered an important indicator of academic knowledge pertaining to the field, then it is interesting to note that the *Land Economics* journal started publication in 1925.
2. Just for reference, the top field journal in urban economics, the *Journal of Urban Economics*, started publication in 1974. The *Journal of Housing Economics*, another journal focusing on housing economics in particular, started publishing in 1991.
3. Additional details about these motives are provided in Section 5.
4. The countries are: Australia, Belgium, Canada, Denmark, Finland, France, Germany, Japan, Netherlands, Norway, Sweden, Switzerland, United Kingdom and the United States.
5. The following discussion on the land reform dataset relies heavily on the data appendix accompanying Bhattacharya et al. (2019).
6. Additional information regarding this particular motive is in Bhattacharya et al.'s (2019) appendix.
7. Please refer to Bhattacharya et al.'s (2019) appendix for more information regarding this specific category of land reform.
8. There are instances where countries implemented more than one particular land reform over the 1900–2010 time period. However, we are using only the very first land reform implementation in the empirical analysis.
9. We employ different lag and lead combinations as alternative checks and the findings remain qualitatively similar. These results are available upon request.
10. The first lead is omitted as the baseline category.
11. Note that Bhattacharya et al. (2019) also state that redistributive land reforms were implemented with the transfer of end user rights. However, given the fact that redistributive land reforms were often implemented with two other land reform motives, viz. imposing land holding ceilings and expropriating the surplus land beyond such ceilings and subsequently redistributing it, we are not treating redistributive land reform as a separate category with exclusive end user rights transferred in the analysis.
12. I would like to thank the referee for raising this important point in the report.
13. We thank an anonymous reviewer for suggesting this alternative robustness check.

## REFERENCES

Acemoglu, D., Johnson, S. and Robinson, J.A. 2002. Reversal of Fortune: Geography and Institutions in the Making of the Modern World Income Distribution. *Quarterly Journal of Economics*, 117(4), 1231–1294.

Acemoglu, D., Johnson, S. and Robinson, J.A. 2005. The Rise of Europe: Atlantic Trade, Institutional Change and Economic Growth. *American Economic Review*, 95(3), 546–579.

Adam, K. and Woodford, M. 2012. Robustly Optimal Monetary Policy in a Micro Founded New Keynesian Model. *Journal of Monetary Economics*, 59(5), 468–487.

Adamopoulos, T. and Restuccia. D. 2014. The Size Distribution of Farms and International Productivity Differences. *American Economic Review*, 104(6), 1667–1697.

Adamopoulos, T. and Restuccia, D. 2020. Land Reform and Productivity: A Quantitative Analysis with Micro Data. *American Economic Journal: Macroeconomics*, 12(3), 1–39.

ARD, 2008. Land Tenure and Property Rights Reports. Prepared for USAID.
Arnot, C.D., Luckert, M. and Boxall, P. 2011. What Is Tenure Security? Conceptual Implications for Empirical Analysis. *Land Economics*, 87(2), 297–311.
Ban, S.H., Moon, P.Y. and Perkins, D.H. 1980. *Studies in the Modernization of Republic of Korea: 1945–1975 Rural Development*. London and Cambridge, MA: Council on East Asian Studies and Harvard University Press.
Bardhan, P. and Mookherjee, D. 2007. Land Reform and Farm Productivity in West Bengal. http://ibread.org/bread/sites/default/files/0704conf/bread0704_bardhan_mookherjee.pdf
Barro, R. 1991. Economic Growth in a Cross-Section of Countries. *Quarterly Journal of Economics*, 106(2), 407–443.
Baxter, M. 1996. Are consumer durables important for business cycles? *Review of Economics and Statistics*, 78, 147–155.
Bertrand, M., Duflo, E. and Mullainathan, S. 2004. How Much Should We Trust Differences-in-Differences Estimates? *Quarterly Journal of Economics*, 119(1), 249–275.
Besley, T. 1995. Property Rights and Investment Incentives: Theory and Evidence from Ghana. *Journal of Political Economy*, 103(5), 903–937.
Besley, T. and Burgess, R. 2000. Land Reform, Poverty Reduction, and Growth: Evidence from India. *Quarterly Journal of Economics*, 115(2), 389–430.
Besley, T. and Ghatak, M. 2010. Property Rights and Economic Development. *Handbook of Development Economics*. Amsterdam: Elsevier.
Bhalotra, S., Clarke, D., Gomes, J.F. and Venkataramani, A. 2019. Maternal Mortality and Women's Political Participation. *CEPR Discussion Paper No. 14339*, Centre for Economic and Policy Research.
Bhattacharya, P.S., Mitra, D. and Ulubasoglu, M.A. 2019. The Political Economy of Land Reform Enactments: New Cross-National Evidence (1900–2010), *Journal of Development Economics*, 139, 50–68.
Bezemer, D. and Headet, D. 2008. Agriculture, Development, and Urban Bias. *World Development*, 36(8), 1342–1364.
Binswanger-Mkhize, H.P., Bourguignon, C. and Brink, R. van den. 2009. *Agricultural Land Redistribution: Toward Greater Consensus*. Washington, DC: World Bank.
Bohn, H. and Deacon, R.T. 2000. Ownership Risk, Investment, and Resource Use. *American Economic Review*, 90(3), 526–549.
Bourguignon, F. and Morrison, C. 1998. Inequality and Development: The Role of Dualism. *Journal of Development Economics*, 57(2), 233–257.
Carter, M.R. and Olinto, P. 2003. Getting Institutions "Right" for Whom? Credit Constraints and the Impact of Property Rights on the Quantity and Composition of Investment. *American Journal of Agricultural Economics*, 85(1), 173–186.
Christiaensen, L., Demery, L. and Kuhl, J. 2011. The (Evolving) Role of Agriculture in Poverty Reduction: An Empirical Perspective. *Journal of Development Economics*, 96(2), 239–254.
Croppenstedt, A., Demeke, M. and Meschi, M.M. 2003. Technology Adoption in the Presence of Constraints: The Case of Fertilizer Demand in Ethiopia. *Review of Development Economics*, 7(1), 58–70.
Datt, G. and Ravallion, M. 1996. How Important to India's Poor Is the Sectoral Composition of Economic Growth? *World Bank Economic Review*, 10(1), 1–25.
Davis, M.A. and Heathcote, J. 2005. Housing and the Business Cycle. *International Economic Review*, 46(3), 751–784.
Davis, M.A. and Heathcote, J. 2007. The Price and Quantity of Residential Land in the United States. *Journal of Monetary Economics*, 54(8), 2595–2620.
de Janvry, A., Emerick, K., Gonzalez-Navarro, M. and Sadoulet, E. 2015. Delinking Land Rights from Land Use: Certification and Migration in Mexico. *American Economic Review*, 105(10), 3125–3149.
De Soto, H. 2000. *The Mystery of Capital: Why Capitalism Triumphs in the West and Fails Everywhere Else*. New York: Basic Books.
Deininger, K. and Feder, G. 2001. Land Institutions and Land Markets. In *Handbook of Agricultural Economics*, Vol. 1A, edited by Bruce L. Gardner and Gordon C. Rausser, 287–331. Amsterdam: Elsevier.
Deininger, K. and Jin, S. 2007. Securing Property Rights in Transition: Lessons from Implementation of China's Rural Land Contracting Law. *World Bank Policy Research Working Paper No. 4447*, Washington DC: World Bank.
Deininger, K., Sara Savastano, S. and Xia, F. 2017. Smallholders' land access in Sub-Saharan Africa: A New Landscape? *Food Policy*, 67, 78–92.
Del Negro, M. and Otrok, C. 2007. 99 Luftballons: Monetary Policy and the House Price Boom across U.S. States. *Journal of Monetary Economics*, 54(7), 1962–1985.

DeLong, J.B. and Shleifer, A. 1993. Princes and Merchants: City Growth before the Industrial Revolution. *Journal of Law and Economics*, 36(2), 671–702.
Dethier, J.-J. and Effenberger, A. 2011. Agriculture and Development: A Brief Review of the Literature. *World Bank Policy Research Working Paper 5553*, Washington, DC: World Bank.
Djankov, S., Glaeser, E.L., Perotti, V. and Shleifer, A. 2021. Property Rights and Urban Form. *National Bureau of Economic Research Working Paper No. 28793*, NBER.
Duca, J.V., Muellbauer, J. and Murphy, A. 2020. What Drives House Price Cycles? International Experience and Policy Issues. *Journal of Economic Literature*, 59(3), 773–864.
Evans, A.W. 2004. *Economics, Real Estate and the Supply of Land*. Oxford: Blackwell.
Fane, G. and P. Warr. 2003. How Economic Growth Reduces Poverty: A General Equilibrium Analysis for Indonesia. In *Perspectives on Growth and Poverty*, edited by R. van der Hoeven and A. Shorrocks, 217–234. WIDER: United Nations University.
Feder, G. 1988. *Land Policies and Farm Productivity in Thailand*. Baltimore, MD: Johns Hopkins University Press.
Feder, G. and Onchan, T. 1987. Land Ownership Security and Farm Investment in Thailand. *American Journal of Agricultural Economics*, 69(2), 311–320.
Freyaldenhoven, S., Hansen, C. and Shapiro, J.M. 2019. Pre-Event Trends in the Panel Event-Study Design. *American Economic Review*, 109(9), 3307–3338.
Gardner, B.L. 2005. Causes of Rural Economic Development. *Agricultural Economics*, 32(S1), 21–41.
Gavian, S. and Fafchamps, M. 1996. Land Tenure and Allocative Efficiency in Niger. *American Journal of Agricultural Economics*, 78(2), 460–471.
Ghatak, S. and Ingersent, K. 1984. *Agriculture and Economic Development*. Brighton: Wheatsheaf Harvester Press.
Glaeser, E.L. 2021. What Can Developing Cities Today Learn from the Urban Past? *National Bureau of Economic Research Working Paper No. 28814*, NBER.
Glaeser, E.L. and Ward, B.A. 2009. The Causes and Consequences of Land Use Regulation: Evidence from Greater Boston. *Journal of Urban Economics*, 65(3), 265–78.
Goldstein, M. and Udry, C. 2008. The Profits of Power: Land Rights and Agricultural Investment in Ghana. *Journal of Political Economy*, 116(6), 981–1022.
Gollin, D., Parente, S. and Rogerson, R. 2002. The Role of Agriculture in Development. *American Economic Review*, 92(2), 160–164.
Goodhart, C. and Hofmann, B. 2008. House Prices, Money, Credit, and the Macroeconomy. *Oxford Review of Economic Policy*, 24(1), 180–205.
Goodman-Bacon, A. 2018. Difference-in-Differences with Variation in Treatment Timing. *National Bureau of Economic Research Working Paper No. 25018*, NBER.
Greenwood, J. and Hercowitz, Z. 1991. The Allocation of Capital and Time over the Business Cycle. *Journal of Political Economy*, 99, 1188–1214.
Gyourko, J., Mayer, C. and Sinai, T. 2013. Superstar Cities. *American Economic Journal: Economic Policy*, 5(4), 167–199.
Hayami, Y. and Ruttan, V.W. 1985. *Agricultural Development: An International Perspective*, Second Edition. Baltimore, MD: Johns Hopkins University Press.
Holden, S., Otsuka, K. and Place, F. 2008. *The Emergence of Land Markets in Africa: Impacts on Poverty, Equity, and Efficiency*. Washington, DC: Resources for the Future and EfD.
Jacobi, H.G. and Mansuri, G. 2008. Land Tenancy and Non-Contractible Investment in Rural Pakistan. *Review of Economic Studies*, 75(3), 763–788.
Jacobi, H.G., Li, G. and Rozelle, S. 2002. Hazards of Expropriation: Tenure Insecurity and Investment in Rural China. *American Economic Review*, 92(5), 1420–1447.
Jacobson, L.S., LaLonde, R.J. and Sullivan, D.G.1993. Earnings Losses of Displaced Workers. *American Economic Review*, 83(4), 685–709.
Jin, S. and Jayne, T.S. 2013. Land Rental Markets in Kenya: Implications for Efficiency, Equity, Household Income, and Poverty. *Land Economics*, 89(2), 246–271.
Johnston, B.F. and Mellor, J.W. 1961. The Role of Agriculture in Economic Development. *American Economic Review*, 51(4), 566–593.
Jorda, O., Schularick, M. and Taylor, A.M. 2015. Leveraged Bubbles. *Journal of Monetary Economics*, 76(S), S1–S20.
Kahn-Lang, A. and Lang, K. 2018. The Promise and Pitfalls of Differences-in-Differences: Reflections on "16 and Pregnant" and Other Applications. *National Bureau of Economic Research Working Paper 24857*, NBER.
King, R. 1977. *Land Reform: A World Survey*. London: G. Bell & Sons.
Knoll, K., Schularick, M. and Steger, T. 2017. No Price Like Home: Global House Prices, 1870–2012. *American Economic Review*, 107(2), 331–353.

Kuminoff, N.V. and Pope, J.C. 2013. The Value of Residential Land and Structures during the Great Housing Boom and Bust. *Land Economics*, 89(1), 1–29.

Lipton, M. 2009. *Land Reform in Developing Countries Property Rights and Property Wrongs*. Abingdon: Routledge.

Leamer, E.E. 2007. Housing *Is* the Business Cycle. *Proceedings of the Economic Policy Symposium, Jackson Hole, Wyoming*, 149–233. Federal Reserve Bank of Kansas City.

Levine, R. and Renelt, D. 1992. A Sensitivity Analysis of Cross-Country Growth Regressions. *American Economic Review*, 82(4), 942–963.

Leung, C.K.Y. 2004. Macroeconomics and Housing: A Review of the Literature. *Journal of Housing Economics*, 13(4), 249–267.

Leung, C.K.Y. and Ng, C.Y.J. 2019. Macroeconomic Aspects of Housing. *Oxford Research Encyclopaedia of Economics and Finance*. Oxford: Oxford University Press.

Lewis, A.W. 1954. Economic Development with Unlimited Supplies of Labour. *Manchester School*, 22, 139–191.

Liu, Z., Wang, P. and Zha, T. 2013. Land-Price Dynamics and Macroeconomic Fluctuations. *Econometrica*, 81(3), 1147–1184.

Nichols, D.A. 1970. Land and Economic Growth. *American Economic Review*, 60(3), 332–340.

North, D. and Thomas, R. 1973. *The Rise of the Western World: A New Economic History*. Cambridge: Cambridge University Press.

Nunn, N. and Qian, N. 2011. The Potato's Contribution to Population and Urbanization: Evidence from a Historical Experiment. *Quarterly Journal of Economics*, 126, 593–650.

Otsuka, K., Suyanto, S., Sonobe, T. and Tomich, T.P. 2001. Evolution of Land Tenure Institutions and Development of Agroforestry: Evidence from Customary Land Areas of Sumatra. *Agricultural Economics*, 25(1), 85–101.

Persson, T. and Tabellini, G. 1994. Is Inequality Harmful for Growth? *American Economic Review*, 84(3), 600–621.

Piazzesi, M. and Schneider, M. 2016. Housing and Macroeconomics. *National Bureau of Economic Research Working Paper No. 22354*, NBER.

Place, F. 2009. Land Tenure and Agricultural Productivity in Africa: A Comparative Analysis of the Economics Literature and Recent Policy Strategies and Reforms. *World Development*, 37(8), 1326–1336.

Place, F. and Otsuka, K. 2002. Land Tenure Systems and Their Impacts on Agricultural Investments and Productivity in Uganda. *Journal of Development Studies*, 38(6), 105–128.

Restuccia, D., Yang, D.T. and Zhu, X. 2008. Agriculture and Aggregate Productivity: A Quantitative Cross-Country Analysis. *Journal of Monetary Economics*, 55(2), 234–250.

Rossi-Hansberg, Esteban. 2004. Optimal Urban Land Use and Zoning. *Review of Economic Dynamics*, 7, 69–106.

Schiff, M. and Valdez, A. 1992. The Plundering of Agriculture in Developing Countries. Washington, DC: World Bank.

Schultz, T.W. 1964. *Transforming Traditional Agriculture*. New Haven, CT. Yale University Press.

Smith, R.E. 2004. Land Tenure, Fixed Investment and Farm Productivity: Evidence from Zambia's Southern Province. *World Development*, 32(10), 1641–1661.

Stevenson, B. and Wolfers, J. 2006. Bargaining in the Shadow of the Law: Divorce Laws and Family Distress. *Quarterly Journal of Economics*, 121(1), 267–288.

Tiffin, R. and Irz, X. 2006. "s Agriculture the Engine of Growth? *Agricultural Economics*, 35, 79–89.

Timmer, C.P. 2008. Agriculture and Pro-Poor Growth: An Asian Perspective. *Asian Journal of Development Economics*, 5(1), 1–27.

Tsakok, I. and Gardner, B. 2007. Agriculture in Economic Development: Primary Engine of Growth or Chicken and Egg? *American Journal of Agricultural Economics*, 89(5), 1145–1151.

Valdés, A. and Foster, W. 2010. Reflections on the Role of Agriculture in Pro-Poor Growth. *World Development*, 38(10), 1362–1374.

Weil, D.N. and Wilde, J. 2009. How Relevant Is Malthus for Economic Development Today? *American Economic Review: Papers and Proceedings*, 99(2), 255–260.

World Bank. 2008. *World Development Report 2008: Agriculture for Development*. Washington, DC: World Bank.

# APPENDIX A

All event-study analysis figures reported in Section 7 are reproduced here with a 95 percent confidence interval (CI) for comparison purposes.

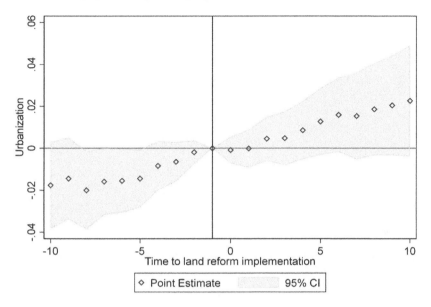

*Figure 3A.1   The impact of distributive motive land reform implementation on urbanization*

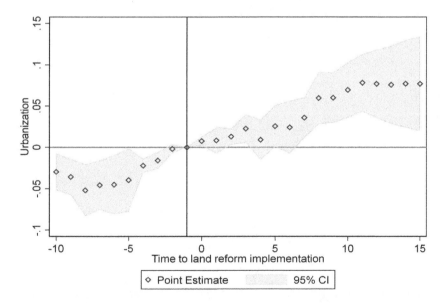

*Figure 3A.2   The impact of consolidation motive land reform implementation on urbanization*

72  *Handbook of real estate and macroeconomics*

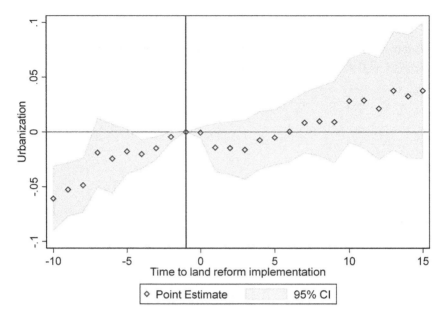

*Figure 3A.3*   *The impact of privatization motive land reform implementation on urbanization*

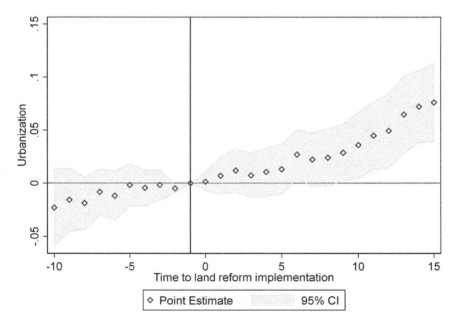

*Figure 3A.4*   *The impact of restitution motive land reform implementation on urbanization*

Land and macroeconomics 73

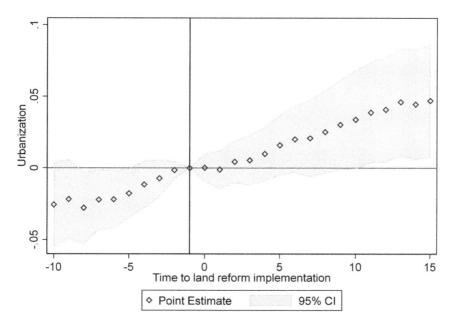

*Figure 3A.5  The impact of combined end user rights motives land reform implementation on urbanization*

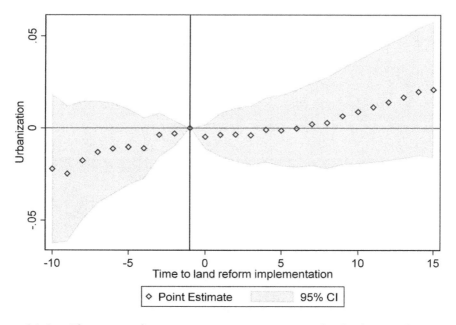

*Figure 3A.6  The impact of improving tenure security motive land reform implementation on urbanization*

74  *Handbook of real estate and macroeconomics*

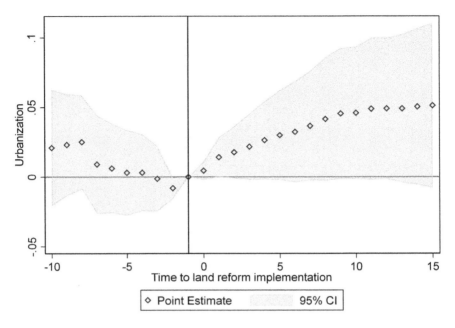

*Figure 3A.7*  The impact of CICRT recognition motive land reform implementation on urbanization

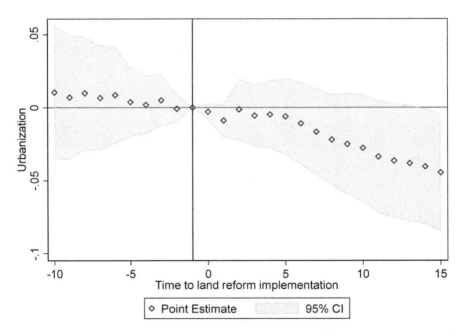

*Figure 3A.8*  The impact of pro-poor motive land reform implementation on urbanization

Land and macroeconomics 75

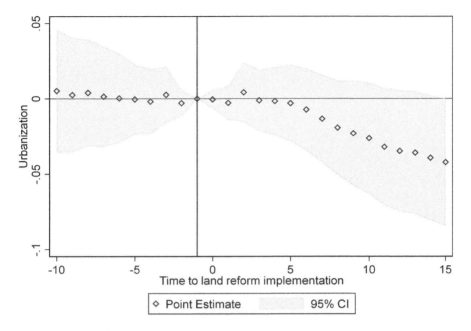

*Figure 3A.9*   The impact of combined land ceiling imposition, expropriation and redistribution motive land reform implementation on urbanization

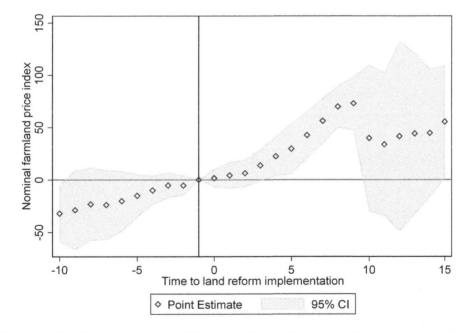

*Figure 3A.10*   The impact of consolidation motive land reform implementation on nominal farmland price index in developed countries

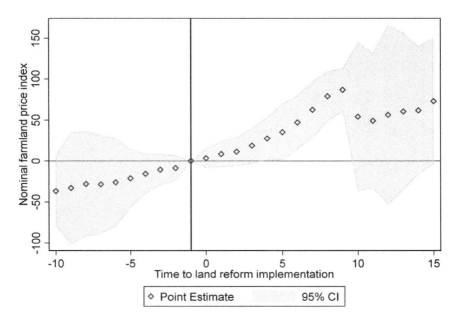

*Figure 3A.11    The impact of combined end user motives land reform implementation on nominal farmland price index in developed countries*

# APPENDIX B

The event-analysis figures here are generated with manufacturing value added as a percentage of GDP as an alternative indicator for urbanization. All figures are reported with 90 percent confidence intervals.

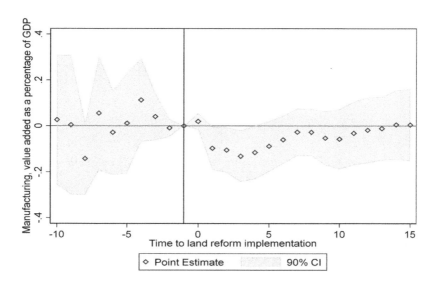

*Figure 3B.1*   The impact of distributive motive land reform implementation on manufacturing, value added as a percentage of GDP

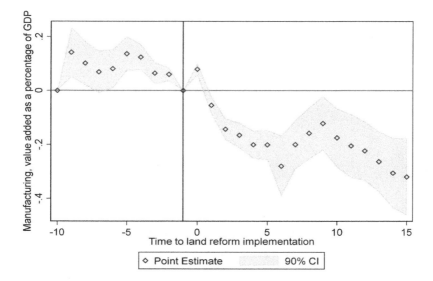

*Figure 3B.2*   The impact of consolidation motive land reform implementation on manufacturing, value added as a percentage of GDP

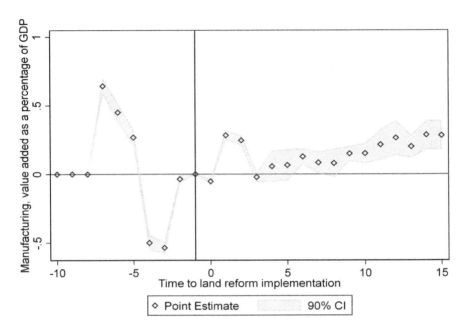

*Figure 3B.3*   *The impact of privatization motive land reform implementation on manufacturing, value added as a percentage of GDP*

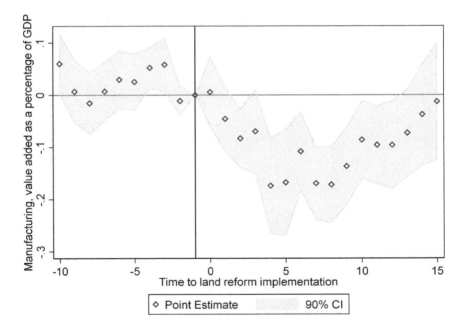

*Figure 3B.4*   *The impact of restitution motive land reform implementation on manufacturing, value added as a percentage of GDP*

*Land and macroeconomics* 79

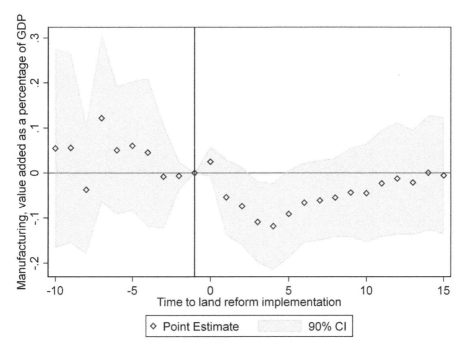

*Figure 3B.5  The impact of combined end user motives land reform implementation on manufacturing, value added as a percentage of GDP*

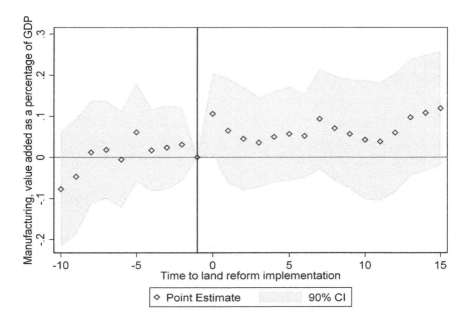

*Figure 3B.6  The impact of tenure security improvement motive land reform implementation on manufacturing, value added as a percentage of GDP*

80  *Handbook of real estate and macroeconomics*

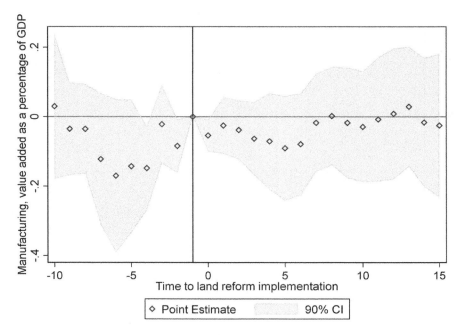

*Figure 3B.7*  *The impact of CICRT recognition motive land reform implementation on manufacturing, value added as a percentage of GDP*

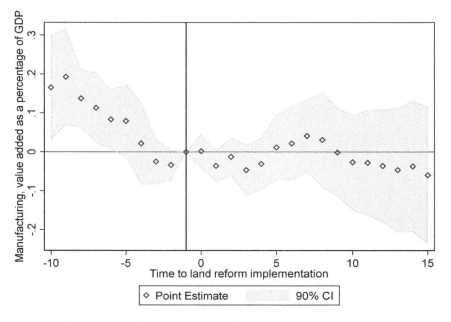

*Figure 3B.8*  *The impact of pro-poor motive land reform implementation on manufacturing, value added as a percentage of GDP*

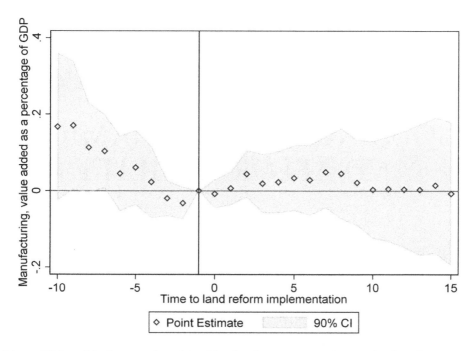

*Figure 3B.9*   The impact of combined land ceiling, expropriation and redistribution motive land reform implementation on manufacturing, value added as a percentage of GDP

# PART II

# HOUSING PRICE DYNAMICS AND AFFORDABILITY

# 4. Affordable housing conundrum in India
*Piyush Tiwari and Jyoti Shukla*

## 1 INTRODUCTION

Understanding the welfare implications of housing policy has been an important area of urban policy research (Leung et al., 2019). Research suggests that the economic growth agenda is intertwined with education policy, affordable housing policy and local public finance, where property tax is the largest component (Leung et al., 2019). However, what constitutes a good housing policy is still an area of active research. In a review of housing policies in a comparative context, Fahey and Norris (2011) argue that housing has two aspects to it: a capital asset (dwelling unit) and the service that the dwelling unit provides (accommodation that housing provides). In conventional social housing policy research, the social element of housing provision is thought of as rental housing, as social housing or rental subsidy for private tenants (Fahey and Norris, 2011). However, housing ownership can also be thought of as an area of intervention by the state to help low-income households achieve homeownership, justified on the grounds that ownership brings forward saving and investment in housing to active stages of the lifecycle to the benefit of later stages when mortgages are paid off and housing costs are low (Fahey et al., 2004). Most housing policies are designed to incentivise homeownership. There is a volume of studies that examines the impact of housing policies on homeownership, house prices, mortgage debt and financial stability (Davis and van Nieuwerburgh, 2015). Results from these studies indicate that some of these policies, such as mortgage interest subvention or mortgage interest tax deductibility, have had counter-objective outcomes. Moreover, the impact of policies such as mortgage interest subvention or subsidies for the development of affordable housing on macroeconomy is not well understood (Pinto and Sarte, 2020). There are studies which argue that these policies distort the market in favour of homeownership which crowds out household investment from other productive uses and has negative consequences for the economy (Gervais, 2002). On the other hand, Chambers et al. (2009) argue that, assuming budget neutrality, removing mortgage interest deduction increases homeownership as the average tax rate declines. There is a general consensus in the literature that the effect of subsidies (tax or interest rate provided through intermediaries) on homeownership is regressive as tenure is mediated by existing socio-demographic inequalities (Kurz and Blossfeld, 2004), has a distortionary effect on housing markets and results in lower welfare for low-income households (Floetotto et al., 2012; Jeske et al., 2013).

Most of these studies have examined the effect of housing policies in developed countries, which have deeper housing markets. There is a paucity of literature on examining housing markets and policies in developing countries like India which present different institutional characteristics. Some stylized facts for India are: a large rural population, a high homeownership rate (particularly in rural areas), very low penetration of mortgages, a very small tax base and substantial regional differences in economic structure and output. This makes it difficult to contextualize results from the literature to the Indian housing market. This chapter presents a brief review of the housing situation in India at the sub-national (states and union territories

(UTs)) level. Due to significant economic and cultural differences across states and UTs, this review will provide nuanced insights into the housing problem for housing policies and programmes to consider in their design and implementation. The chapter clarifies the nature of the housing problem in India and presents institutional housing characteristics (that affect the demand and supply side of housing) at the regional level that have an impact on the inadequacies that households experience. Recent housing policy and its efficacy is also discussed but an economic analysis of policies based on quantitative traditions is not conducted. This could be an agenda for future research.

Starting with the oft cited notion of a housing shortage, based on the 2011 census (ORGCC, 2020), the Technical Group on Urban Housing Shortage was constituted by the Government of India to advise them in the preparation of the Twelfth Five Year Plan (2012–2017) and this estimated a shortage of 18.78 million housing units for 2012 (MoHUPA, 2012). This macro number captured the imagination of policy makers and developers, more so because it was nearly 17 per cent of existing urban housing stock. The 2011 census also reported that about 9 per cent of houses were vacant, and an additional 18 per cent were not in use exclusively for residential purposes, together comprising 27 per cent of housing stock (ORGCC, 2020). In this context, shortage at the macro level is a bizarre notion as it hides the nature and factors that can affect gaps in housing. The Technical Group on Urban Housing Shortage defined housing shortage as the sum of households residing in houses in a dilapidated condition, households living in congested conditions and homeless households. These components of inadequacy in housing are not comparable and cannot be added to present a comprehensive housing shortage number as has been done by the Technical Group. For example, a household living in a congested house is not in the same situation with regard to their housing inadequacy as a homeless household. Summing up the different natures of housing inadequacies implicitly promotes construction of new housing as a solution. Tiwari et al. (2021) argue that households adjust inadequacies through (1) moving to and buying a new house, (2) rebuilding an existing home, (3) adding an extension to an existing home and (4) repairing an existing home. They estimate the probability of household housing inadequacy adjustment choice using microeconomic data for India. The results illustrate that rebuilding, extending and repairing are more common than moving and buying a new house. This makes it important that different components of inadequacies are understood separately. The word 'inadequacy' rather than 'shortage' has been used deliberately here because inadequacy illustrates deviation of the desired from the actual and this may or may not translate into new housing needs, which is the usual interpretation of a housing shortage. Where new households[1] are formed or where households need to be housed, a new unit is required, but where there is a mismatch between the desired and the actual, it generates a need to extend or upgrade an existing unit but not for a new house to be built, unless an extension or upgrading of an existing house is not possible. Failure to recognize this aspect has resulted in policies that implicitly promote new construction despite only partially meeting the gap between the desired[2] and the actual, and this often leads to unoccupied houses.

The housing debate in India has conspicuously omitted discussion on the regional dimension of the housing shortage, let alone housing inadequacy. Although housing is a state subject and any policy needs implementation through different states and their agencies, regional specificities have been missing from policy discourses, particularly those which are formulated by the national government such as the flagship policy of the current central government, *Pradhan Mantri Awas Yojana* (PMAY, translated as Prime Minister Housing Scheme), which aims to achieve housing for all by 2022 through assistance provided to economically weaker sections (EWSs) of society. An assessment of state-wise distribution of assisted housing (presented later) illustrates, however, that the beneficiaries of this central government policy have been households in those states which are economically better off. This highlights the importance of understanding housing inadequacy at the regional or state level.

The objectives of this chapter are two-fold: (1) to provide an overview of the state of housing and (2) to examine the nature and causes of housing inadequacy in India at the state level. A review of the central government housing scheme, PMAY, is also presented with the intention of identifying shortcomings for policies and providing a roadmap for future policies.

The rest of the chapter is organized as follows: Section 2 presents a brief literature review. Section 3 presents the macro context for housing in India. Section 4 discusses the regional disparity in economic growth. Section 5 examines regional variation in the housing gap and its nature. This section also discusses the question of affordability. Sections 6 and 7 discuss various demands (availability and access to formal finance) and supply-side factors (efficiency of planning approvals) at the state level that are necessary mitigants of the housing gap. Section 8 assesses the effectiveness of PMAY and Section 9 presents a discussion and concludes.

## 2 LITERATURE

The literature presented in this section relates to Indian housing markets and to the specific issue of housing shortages, housing inadequacy and mechanisms that households adopt to mitigate their housing inadequacies.

Population growth, rising affluence and a declining cost of home purchase for those who can access formal finance has led to a substantial increase in the share of property holdings (in value terms) of households at the macroeconomic level (Purfield, 2007). However, most asset purchases, including housing, are financed by households' own savings rather than through bank finance or capital markets (Purfield, 2007). The nexus of supply-induced housing demand has resulted in a growth in investment in housing that is largely concentrated towards luxury investment housing purchased by higher income groups while leaving a large proportion of EWS, low-income group (LIG) and middle-income group (MIG) households crowded out of the market (Singh, 2013). Despite significant activity in the housing market as noted by Purfield (2007), the lopsidedness of private housing development has not ameliorated housing inadequacies – which are interpreted as housing shortage in policy circles in India.

While the housing shortage has been an issue for policy making, the academic literature on understanding and modelling the housing shortage has been limited. The Technical Group of the Government for the Twelfth Five Year Plan (2012–17) has estimated a housing shortage based on estimates of homelessness, congestion and obsolescence, as discussed later. There are studies that have critiqued estimates of the housing shortage by the Technical Group. Singh (2013) criticizes the estimates as they use the same norm related to congestion and obsolescence for the whole country without recognition of regional/state differences. Singh (2013) emphasizes the importance of state/region-level estimations of the housing shortage as there are cultural, climatic and geographical differences across states which impact preferences towards the formation of households, size of houses, type of houses and building materials used and these affect housing demand. According to the United Nations Committee on Economic, Social and Cultural Rights, the essential components of adequate housing are: legal security of tenure; availability of services, material, facilities and infrastructure; affordability; habitability; accessibility; location; and cultural adequacy. In Recommendation No. 115 of 1961 of the International Labour Organization on workers' housing, Singh et al. (2017) derived criteria for adequate housing in rural areas. Based on a survey of 15 villages and projecting it to the national level, Singh et al. (2017) estimated that 140 million households in rural areas did not live in adequate houses in 2011, a much higher number compared to government housing shortage estimates of 40 million houses in rural India. Tiwari and Rao (2016) have also estimated the housing shortage to be much higher than government estimates.

Over the last two decades, microeconomic studies have been conducted that analyse the determinants of housing demand in India (see Ahmad, 2019; Roy, 2018, 2021; Tiwari and Parikh, 1998; Tiwari et al., 1999). These conclude that housing demand is income- and price-inelastic. Changes in income and house prices do not result in significant changes in housing consumption, particularly for homeowners, due to the huge transaction costs involved in such adjustments (Roy, 2021). Tiwari et al. (2021) argue that the choice for adjustment in the housing consumption disequilibrium depends on a household's financial position, the characteristics of the household and the house. The nature of construction required for adjustment and the location also have an impact on choice.

Highlighting housing market imperfections in India, Singh (2013) points towards incomplete information in terms of a lack of a data base on mortgages, transparency in transactions and proper laws, robust indices for benchmarking, which makes it difficult to undertake rigorous market analysis. The absence of a regulator or regulators to supervise non-financial aspects of the housing market has resulted in housing being developed in an ad hoc and unplanned manner across the country (Singh, 2013).

Harish (2016) highlights the lack of discussion on rental housing, particularly in government policy discourse on affordable housing. They find a strong positive correlation between the urban workforce participation rate and the percentage of rental housing and argue that facilitating rental housing (both public and private) would be an essential enabler for household and city economic development. The public housing system in cities where it has been tried has failed due to fiscal and institutional challenges. Various innovative mechanisms (such as land lease to households living in slums on public land; land tax parity between ownership and rental housing; parity on electricity and water changes between ownership; and rental tenures such as hostels) are necessary to facilitate rental housing development and provisions (Harish, 2016).

On the supply of affordable housing, Ram and Needham (2016) have investigated the challenges that developers face in supplying affordable housing and their survey results identify land availability, lengthy planning processes and a lack of formal finance for EWS and LIG households as the top three reasons. They argue that instruments such as higher floor area ratio norms for projects with affordable housing, transferable development rights which provide extra floor area ratio that are not tied to location and can be applied elsewhere and tax exemptions for developers for affordable housing construction can reduce the cost of affordable housing.

Sengupta (2010) emphasizes that incremental self-building is a common and traditional method of housing production in India, especially in rural parts of the country, but finds little mention of this in housing policies. High land price, lack of tenure security in slums, discouragement from the government to undertake self-builds in informal settlements and a lack of formal finance have hindered self-build housing production resulting in housing poverty – a state caused by the inadequacy of housing and unaffordability (Sengupta, 2010). In the context of low-income households living in slums, despite an unfavourable institutional framework for self-builds, Nakamura (2014) finds that households living in non-notified slums are more likely to adjust their housing consumption through self-builds in an incremental manner, much more than their counterparts living in notified slums. The difference between notified and non-notified slums is that the former is recognized by the government and has better tenure security. Households in slums (notified and non-notified) largely spend their own savings on construction as access to formal finance is poor. Tiwari et al. (2021) found that households living in notified slums tend to reconstruct their dwelling units as their financial position improves while those living in non-notified slums tend to adjust their housing consumption through repair and maintenance. In the long run, the nature of housing that results from the incremental self-build construction process is durable housing.

The short literature review presented in this section highlights the importance of understanding the nature of the housing problem, processes that households adopt to adjust deviation between current and optimal housing requirements, the role of government affordable housing programmes and the role of state-level financial and non-financial institutions in facilitating access to optimal housing for a household at the state level (district, block or village level, though preferable, would be difficult due to a lack of disaggregated data).

## 3  THE MACRO CONTEXT FOR HOUSING IN INDIA

The last three decades have seen an acceleration in economic growth in India (World Bank, 2020). The per capita income grew 3.5 times during this period (World Bank, 2020). The growth in income in cities has been much faster than in villages (Sengupta, 2019). The phenomenal growth has also been accompanied by an increase in inequalities across income, consumption expenditure and wealth, which is far more pronounced in cities than in villages (Himanshu, 2019). The income share of the top 10 per cent is 56 per cent (World Inequality Lab, 2018), while the bottom 50 per cent has an income share of less than 15 per cent (Himanshu, 2019). The rise in income has not resulted in an increase in household savings. In fact, household savings as a percentage of gross domestic product (GDP) have steadily declined from 24 per cent in 2011–2012 to 17 per cent in 2017–2018 (Ministry of Finance, 2020). The share of savings in the form of physical assets in total household savings has also declined (Prakash et al., 2020). Sengupta (2019) attributes the decline in savings to a rise in expenditure on services such as education, travel and healthcare, which are not translating into demand for consumer durables and assets. Youth unemployment is also high, which is eroding household savings (Sengupta, 2019).

Historically, the homeownership rate in India has been high. The homeownership rate in 2018 was 85 per cent. The rural homeownership rate was 96 per cent while the urban rate was 63 per cent (NSS, 2019). These rates are similar to countries which are largely agrarian. Compared to 2012, the homeownership rate in cities increased in 2018 (NSS, 2019). With urbanization and prosperity, aspirations for homeownership in cities will increase further. The average addition of new housing stock at the national level during 2001–2011 was 8.1 million per year (ORGCC, 2020). The addition to urban housing stock was 3.9 million per year during 2001–2011, almost half of the newly added stock (ORGCC, 2020). While this is in line with the urbanization trend (29 per cent of population lives in cities), the rate of new housing in cities during 2001–11 was much faster than the urbanization trend. Though the next census is yet to commence, based on the 69th and 76th rounds of National Sample Surveys, it appears that the new addition to stock since 2011 has slowed down substantially. The decline is much greater in urban India. As per the 76th round of the National Sample Survey, only 4.3 million houses were added in 2017, of which 1.3 million were in urban and 3 million were in rural areas (NSS, 2019).

Tiwari and Rao (2016) estimated the housing shortage for rural and urban India. Following earlier practices of reporting shortages, they estimated that the housing shortage in 2011 in rural India was 28.87 million and in urban India the housing shortage was 21.87 million units. More than these numbers, what is interesting in their estimates is the breakup of the housing shortage. This is presented in Table 4.1.

*Table 4.1    Housing need in India in 2011*

| Factors taken for assessing housing shortages | Rural housing shortage (million) | Urban housing shortage (million) |
|---|---|---|
| Number of non-durable houses | 10 | 3 |
| Shortage due to congestion[a] | 10.86 | 15.09 |
| Shortage due to obsolescence[b] | 7.18 | 2.84 |
| Homeless population | 0.83 | 0.94 |
| Total | 28.87 | 21.87 |

*Notes*:
[a] This is calculated by multiplying the number of households with an appropriate 'congestion factor', which is defined as the percentage of houses in which at least one couple does not have a separate room to live in. This includes households in which couples are sharing a room with at least one other member aged 10 years or more. The congestion factor in rural India is 6.5% and in urban India 19.1% (Tiwari and Parikh, 2012).
[b] This is calculated by multiplying the number of households with an appropriate 'obsolescence factor', which is defined as the percentage of households living in dwelling units aged 40–80 years that are in bad condition plus the percentage of households living in structures aged more than 80 years, irrespective of the condition of the structure. The obsolescence factor in rural India is 4.3% and in urban India 3.6% (Tiwari and Parikh, 2012).
*Source*: Tiwari and Rao (2016).

The extent to which PMAY has complemented or substituted the new housing stock formation will be seen during the 2021 census but the programme claims to have assisted in the construction, finance and improvement of 10 million houses for low-income households in urban India during the 2015–2019 period. However, only 3.2 million houses that have been assisted are completed.

*Table 4.2    Average sale price of houses/apartments in India*

| House/Apartment value | Second quarter of 2018 | Second quarter of 2019 |
|---|---|---|
| Less than 5 million | 45% | 52% |
| 5–10 million | 55% | 30% |
| Above 10 million |  | 18% |

*Source*: Knight Frank (2019).

It appears that while there is some shift in the type of income groups for which houses are being added through the market (Table 4.2), the overall new addition to housing stock post-2011 has been slower than in the previous decade.

*Affordable housing conundrum in India* 89

*Table 4.3    Housing affordability for various income groups in urban India*

| Income group | Defined affordability | | | | Affordability status in 2020 | |
| --- | --- | --- | --- | --- | --- | --- |
| | Monthly income of household (in Indian Rupees (INR) 2020) | House size (m$^2$) | Affordability 1: House price (rent/EMI) as percentage of monthly income | Affordability 2: Ratio of house price to annual income of household | House price (rent) as percentage of monthly income | Ratio of house price to annual income of household (in 2020) |
| Below poverty line | 6,720 | 30 | 5 | 2 | 174 | 50 |
| Economically weaker section | <25,000 | 30 | 20 | 3 | 93 | 27 |
| Low-income group | 25,000–50,000 | 60 | 30 | 4 | 31 | 9 |
| Middle-income group | 50,000–100,000 | 120 | 30–40 | 5 | 16 | 4 |
| Higher middle-income group | 100,000–150,000 | 150 | 30–40 | 5 | 9 | 3 |
| High-income group | 200,000 | >150 | 30–40 | 5 | 6 | 2 |

*Note*: Column 2: incomes associated with income groups are based on PMAY norms. Column 3: housing norms considered for assistance under PMAY. Columns 4 and 5: affordability criteria proposed by various committees, see Tiwari and Rao (2016). Column 6: rent is assumed to be 3.5% of house cost. Column 7: house price considered here is Rs 4 million, which is the current value of a dwelling unit considered by Tiwari and Rao (2016) adjusted using the National Housing Bank residential index.

Table 4.2 illustrates that the target segment for a large proportion of new housing in the private development market is the higher income group. While overall housing affordability has improved, as shown by the declining house price to income ratio (see Palayi and Priyaranjan, 2018), new houses are still unaffordable for a large segment of society. Table 4.3 presents the housing affordability status for various income groups in urban India. The second column in Table 4.3 is the income range for households in particular groups as defined by PMAY for their programmes. Columns 3 and 4 are affordability criteria for different income groups suggested by the Parekh and Wadhwa Committees (Tiwari and Rao, 2016). For households who are below the poverty line, the ratio of housing rent to monthly income is 174 per cent and house price to annual income is 50 per cent. The affordability status of EWSs is also highly stressed (Table 4.3). While rental housing is affordable for LIGs (with a rent to monthly income ratio of 31 per cent), the ownership of housing is unaffordable (with a house price to annual income ratio of 9). Home ownership is affordable to households in the higher middle-income and high-income groups. Since the distribution of number of households by income groups in Table 4.3 is not available, an estimate has been made to provide the scale of the problem. Keelery (2020) of Statistica presents estimates of the number of households by income categories defined as strugglers (with an income less than Rs 2300 per month), the next billion (income Rs 2300–7700 per month), aspirers (income Rs 7700–15400), affluent (income Rs 15400–30800) and elite (with income above Rs 30800 per month) for 2016. Based on their household distribution data, an estimated 25 million households (one quarter of urban households) would be in the strugglers category in urban India in 2016. This category corresponds to those who are in EWSs and below the poverty line in Table 4.3. There are another

38 million urban households who are estimated to be in the 'next billion' group defined by Keelery (2020), which corresponds to the low-income group in Table 4.3. New housing is unaffordable for these households as well. Low-income households can afford rental housing in urban areas.

Palayi and Priyaranjan (2018) compute affordability status by different income groups in 49 cities.[3] Their results indicate that EWS households can afford a new house in only five cities, LIG households can afford one in only five cities, MIG households can afford one in nine cities and HMIG in 18 cities.

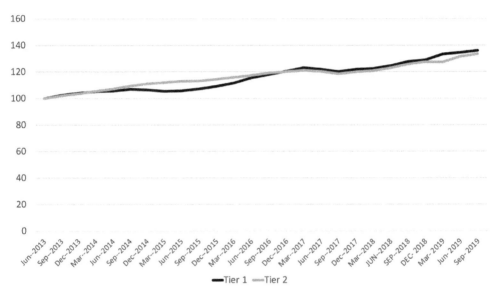

*Source*: Based on NHB data.

*Figure 4.1*    House price index in Tier 1 and Tier 2 cities

Figure 4.1 presents the National Housing Bank (NHB) house price index trend from 2013 to 2019. The NHB tracks house prices in 50 cities. We have aggregated these cities in two categories: Tier 1 (metropolitan cities) and Tier 2 (capital cities of states that are not metropolitan cities and cities on the fringes of metropolitan cities). House prices during this period have seen slow growth across all cities in India. An average growth of 20 per cent over six years is below the inflation rate. While the growth in house prices has been slower, base house values are quite high making housing unaffordable, as discussed earlier.

The housing need presented in Table 4.1 ignores how Indian households attempt to bridge the deviation between their current and desired housing. Housing shortage (Table 4.1) has four components: non-durable houses, obsolescence, congestion and homelessness. Other than homelessness, the components of the housing shortage do not necessarily require new houses. The problems of non-durability and obsolescence of houses are addressed by households through incremental reconstruction using durable materials. Congestion is partially addressed by extending existing houses. A cumulative housing shortage is thus a misguiding concept. As per the National Sample Survey 69th round survey data (for the year 2011–2012) on housing conditions collected by the Ministry of Statistics and Programme Implementation India, the proportions of rural houses with durable, semi-durable and undurable structures are 65.8 per cent, 24.6 per cent and 9.6 per cent, respectively. In contrast, the proportions in the urban areas are 93.6 per cent, 5 per cent and 1.4 per cent, respectively (NSS, 2014). The first important observation is that households undertake construction activity to adjust their housing disequilibrium. As per the National Sample Survey 65th Round survey of housing conditions, approximately 10 per cent of the households undertook a construction activity in the preceding 365 days in 2008–2009 (12 per cent in rural areas and 4 per cent in urban areas) to adjust their housing, with only about 1 per cent of the constructions remaining under progress at the end of the period (NSS, 2010). Of all the completed constructions, nearly 72 per cent relate to alterations, improvements or major repairs. The proportion of construction of new buildings and addition to floor space is about 14 per cent each. Self-built houses constituted 0.37 million in urban and 2.52 million in rural India (NSS, 2010). In this context, it would be important for policies aimed at improving housing conditions to focus on these modes of adjustment in housing to be effective. However, as discussed later, policies and markets have generally favoured building new stock over extensions or upgrades.

Various affordable housing programmes have been instituted in India to address the housing needs since 2007 but with limited success. For a review, see Tiwari and Rao (2016) and NHB (2018). Among others, the main problem of these programmes was fragmentation in implementation and lack of a clear objective. In 2015, the new central programme PMAY was launched which aimed to provide 50 million affordable houses (20 million in urban and 30 million in rural India) by 2022. The PMAY Urban programme provides central assistance to urban local bodies (ULBs) and other implementation agencies of states and UTs and has four components:

1. In situ rehabilitation of existing slum dwellers using land as a resource through private participation.
2. Credit-linked subsidy scheme implemented through prime lending institutions and monitored by central nodal agencies, namely the NHB and the Housing and Urban Development Corporation.
3. Affordable housing in partnership.
4. Subsidies for beneficiary-led individual house construction/enhancement.

The programme resulted in the sanctioning of 10.3 million affordable houses in urban areas by December 2019. A large part of the assistance has been sought for beneficiary-led individual house construction/enhancement, which supports the view that many households adjust deviation in housing consumption through extensions and upgrades.

The PMAY Rural programme aims to assist in the provision of durable houses for the homeless and those living in non-durable houses through cash assistance. The scheme also facilitates beneficiaries in availing of institutional finance. By March 2019, 10 million houses had been approved for assistance, of which 8.5 million have been completed. These are largely related to upgrades of current houses.

The second aspect of understanding housing disequilibrium, which is ignored when we discuss housing inadequacies at the national level, is the regional dimension. India has 29 states and seven UTs. These states have different levels of urbanization, economic growth and prosperity and different economic structures. Housing conditions are different across the states and UTs, and some are better than others. Hence to understand housing in India, we need to investigate states and UTs; this is the focus of this chapter.

## 4  REGIONAL DISPARITY IN ECONOMIC GROWTH

There is disparity in economic growth across states and UTs, as shown in Figure 4.2, which plots the growth in net state domestic product. The thick black line is the growth rate for India as a whole and the other lines are for states and UTs. The figure shows the differences in growth across states. These differences were far more pronounced during the earlier periods on the chart but have become narrower during the later periods. During 2012–2013 and 2013–2014 few states were driving growth in the country, but in later periods many more states have contributed to national growth. Excluding the extreme growth rates for some states in earlier periods of the chart, the growth band in 2012–2013 was 6 to 19 per cent but in 2017–2018 the band narrowed to 10 to 19 per cent.

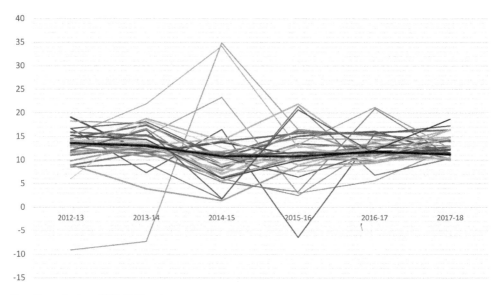

*Note*: Current prices, 2011–2012 series.

*Figure 4.2    Growth in net domestic product*

## 5  REGIONAL DIMENSION OF AFFORDABILITY AND HOUSING INADEQUACIES

Using per household net state domestic product for states and UTs in India[4] as a proxy for average household income and a house price to income ratio of 5.0 for middle-income households, the maximum affordability level for this group has been estimated (Figure 4.3). The average value of a house affordable to middle-income households should be around 2.8 million rupees in 2017–2018.

Table 4.4 presents the average price of a middle-income household house of 120 square meters (as stipulated in PMAY eligibility guidelines for middle-income households for the credit-linked subsidy scheme) in eight cities in India. If viewed in conjunction with Figure 4.3,

*Affordable housing conundrum in India* 93

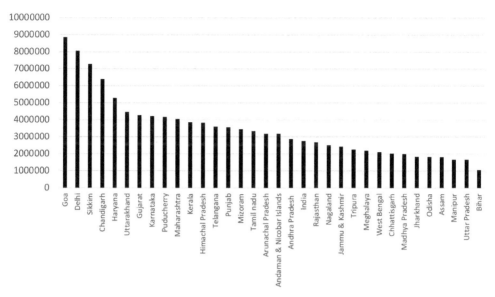

*Note*: The desired value of a house is calculated using an affordability ratio (house price/annual income) of 5. The value is derived by multiplying per household net state domestic product by the affordability ratio of 5.

*Figure 4.3* Housing affordability for middle-income households, 2017–2018

*Table 4.4* Average house price in major cities

| City, state | Average price of 120m² house (million rupees), 2018 |
|---|---|
| Amdavad, Gujarat | 3.67 |
| Bengaluru, Karnataka | 6.05 |
| Chennai, Tamil Nadu | 5.67 |
| Hyderabad, Telangana | 5.28 |
| Kolkata, West Bengal | 4.21 |
| Mumbai, Maharashtra | 9.29 |
| National Capital Region of Delhi | 5.48 |
| Pune, Maharashtra | 5.65 |

*Note*: Using weighted average house price per square meter for the second quarter of 2018 from Knight Frank (2018).

except in the National Capital Region of Delhi and Amdavad (Gujarat), the average house is not affordable to middle-income households.

Table 4.5 presents estimates of average house prices for a 120 square meter house in Tier 1 and Tier 2 cities in India by income group. This indicates that houses, even in Tier 2 cities, are unaffordable to middle-income households in states that are on the right side of India in Figure 4.3.

Focusing on housing inadequacies, the first step would be to review housing size norms that have been adopted for the implementation of PMAY in India. PMAY has used an income-based approach to determine the size of an affordable house. The size of an affordable dwelling unit for EWS and LIG households is 30 square metres. For MIG households, the size

Table 4.5  Price of houses for different income groups

|  | House price – Tier 1 cities (million rupees) | House price – Tier 2 cities (million rupees) |
| --- | --- | --- |
| Economically weaker sections | 4.95 | 2.14 |
| Low income | 5.25 | 2.44 |
| Middle income | 6.00 | 3.19 |
| Higher-middle income | 6.90 | 4.09 |
| High income | 8.25 | 5.44 |

*Source*: Based on a survey of developers.

Table 4.6  Indicators of overcrowding in housing

| Area per person (m²) | Number of people |
| --- | --- |
| More than 10 | 2 |
| 9–10 | 1.5 |
| 7–9 | 1 |
| 5–7 | 0.5 |
| Less than 5 | 0 |

*Source*: Adapted from Ramalhete et al. (2018).

of the dwelling unit is 60 square meters. For higher middle- and high-income households, the size of the dwelling is 120 and 150 square meters, respectively. An income-based approach ignores the main cause of inadequacy, which is the size of a household and part of the requirement that is linked to lifecycle situations.

As an absolute minimum requirement for housing size, it is important to look at the minimum housing size necessary to overcome crowding. World Health Organization Housing and Health Guidelines (WHO, 2018) suggest that:

> household crowding is a condition where the number of occupants exceeds the capacity of the dwelling space available, whether measured as rooms, bedrooms or floor area, resulting in adverse physical and mental health outcomes. The level of crowding relates to the size and design of the dwelling, including the size of the rooms, and to the type, size and needs of the household, including any long-term visitors.

Measures adopted across countries for crowding differ substantially and depend on the economic status of a country. UN-Habitat considers overcrowding to be when there are more than three persons per habitable room. A similar measure is used by the Argentinian National Institute of Statistics and Censuses. These measures exclude common amenity areas. Developed economies have more generous norms. As per the American Crowding Index, crowding occurs when there is more than one person per room. The United Kingdom, Canada and Eurostat use measures which are nuanced according to the number of married/cohabiting couples, the age of children and the number of people in a household (WHO, 2018). The World Health Organization also presents indicators of overcrowding based on the area of bedroom per person (Table 4.6). Children under 12 months were not considered and those between 1–10 years of age were considered as 0.5 (Ramalhete et al., 2018). ICF International states that overcrowding occurs if the area (including circulation, porches and other similar spaces) per person is less than 15.23 square meters per person (Ramalhete et al., 2018).

There are no specific norms for per person housing area required or number of bedrooms required from a crowding point of view. We adopt ICF international norms as they are comprehensive, including size of bedrooms and the circulation area. The minimum housing size for an average household in various states is presented in Figure 4.4. This is computed by multiplying the ICF International norm of 15.23 square meters per person with average household size in urban areas, rural areas and overall for states and UTs in India. Due to differences in household sizes in rural and urban areas, there are some differences in the minimum size of housing requirements as per crowding norms. The minimum house size to meet crowding norms ranges between 60 square meters in Tamil Nadu to 90 square meters in Uttar Pradesh.

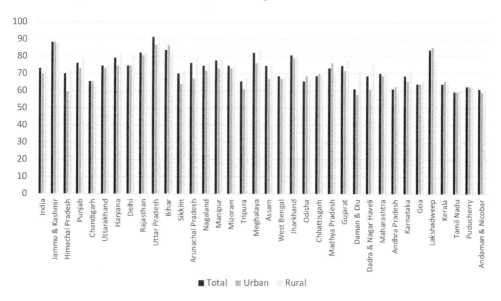

*Figure 4.4*    Minimum housing size for average household, 2011

The inverse relation between income and household size has been investigated by Tripathi (2018). An important interpretation of Figure 4.4 is that the states (such as Uttar Pradesh, Bihar or Jharkhand) that have lower incomes have requirements for larger size houses as the household sizes in these states are bigger. The deviation from the optimum in poorer states will be much larger while the affordability is low.

## 6    REGIONAL VARIATION IN ACCESS TO FINANCE

Access to finance is necessary to supplement households' own equity to purchase or construct a house. The overall penetration of mortgage finance in India is low (Figure 4.5). The outstanding housing loans of commercial banks and housing finance institutions (HFIs) as a percentage of GDP is about 10 per cent (NHB, 2018). About 55 per cent of credit is provided by banks and the rest by specialized HFIs (NHB, 2018). The penetration of commercial banking varies across states. Poorer states like Bihar, Uttar Pradesh, Jharkhand, Madhya Pradesh, West

96    Handbook of real estate and macroeconomics

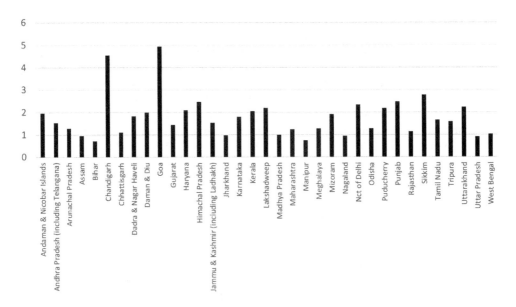

*Figure 4.5    Commercial bank branches per 10,000 persons*

Bengal and states in the northeast such as Assam, Manipur and Nagaland have one or less than one bank branch per 10,000 persons. Many of these states have higher rural populations.

The other institutions in housing finance are 91 specialized HFIs. Before banks were permitted to lend for housing, HFIs were the dominant lenders. The spread of HFIs in states is also limited to states which are considered economically better off (Figure 4.6).

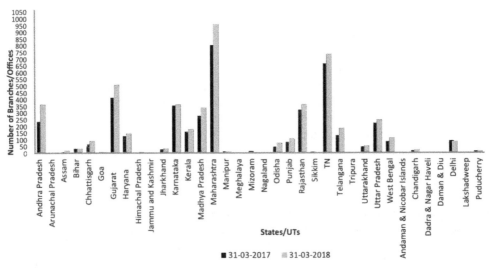

*Source*: NHB (2018).

*Figure 4.6    Branches/offices of registered housing finance institutions*

NHB (2018) reports that 96 per cent of disbursed funding by HFIs in 2017–18 was for the purchase of a new or resale house or the construction of a new house. Only 4 per cent of the total disbursement was for upgrades of existing homes. In terms of distribution of size of loans, the biggest growth was in the upper loan segment (NHB, 2018).

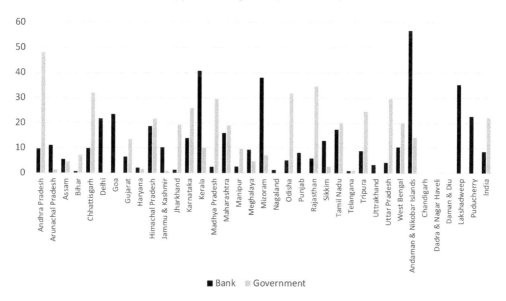

*Figure 4.7* Proportion of households undertaking construction who accessed government or bank finance, 2018

Access to finance has affected the way in which households adjust their deviations in housing requirements. As shown in Figure 4.7, as per the 76th round of the National Sample Survey conducted in 2018, only a small proportion of households who undertook construction accessed bank finance. In general, the role of bank finance in financing household construction activity is low. The states which have low penetration of banks (Figure 4.5) are also the ones where the use of bank finance for construction is much lower than other states. In some states such as Uttar Pradesh, low bank finance is partially offset by government finance. Newly formed states like Andhra Pradesh have a higher proportion of households accessing bank and government sources of finance.

The consequence of a lack of formal finance for construction activity is that the proportion of households who undertake these activities to adjust their deviation of current housing from optimal is low (Figure 4.8). What is interesting, however, is that a higher proportion of households in poorer states and states in the northeast use incremental construction activities to adjust their housing requirements (inadequacies and quality) than in economically better-off states. This may also be because of better housing conditions in better-off states.

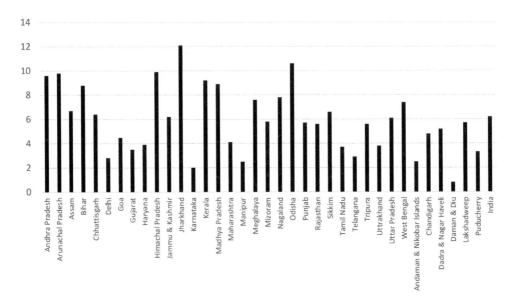

*Figure 4.8    Proportion of households who undertake construction activity during 2018*

## 7    REGIONAL VARIATION IN LOCAL GOVERNANCE, PLANNING APPROVAL

The capacity of ULBs to deliver on affordable housing programmes depends on their financial strength. The total revenue per capita for municipalities in various states is presented in Figure 4.9 (Ahluwalia et al., 2019). The figure also presents revenues from own sources. The difference between total and own revenue is transfers from the state to ULBs. For municipal sustainability it is important that own sources of revenue are strong. The per capita revenue in general is low, which limits the capacity of ULBs to undertake any housing programme on their own or jointly with the central government. PMAY requires that housing programmes are implemented through ULBs and state implementing agencies. The distribution of sanctioned PMAY houses does indicate that states where municipalities are financially strong have been able to implement these programmes but then this builds in a self-selection bias towards economically well-off states.

The learning process has also been a stumbling block for implementing housing projects. As shown in Table 4.7, due to the time taken in getting various approvals across select cities, it can take more than a year to get a project off the ground. Various layers of planning approvals also lead to rent-seeking opportunities, which all add up to the cost of affordable housing.

*Affordable housing conundrum in India* 99

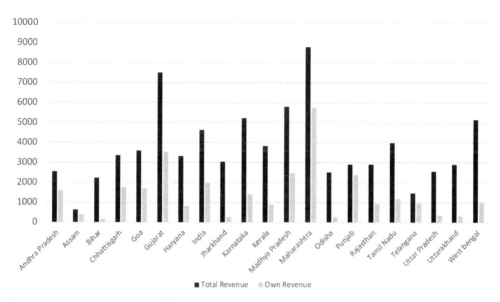

Source: Based on Ahluwalia et al. (2019).

*Figure 4.9    Municipal revenue per capita, 2017–2018, in rupees*

*Table 4.7    Major approvals required for housing construction projects and time taken*

|  | Maharashtra (Mumbai) | Gujarat (Amdavad) | Odisha (Bubhneshwar) | Tamil Nadu (Chennai) | Haryana |
|---|---|---|---|---|---|
| Non-agriculture permission/land conversion | 3 months (+) | 2 months | 3–6 months | 9 months | 6 months |
| Ownership certificate | 15 days | 60 days | 6–12 months | 12 months | 3 days |
| Building layout approval | 1 month | 6 months | 6–12 months | 45 days | 6 months |
| Commencement certificate | 15–30 days | 2–3 months | 6 months | 1–4 months | 6–9 months |
| Archaeological Survey of India | 6 months | Over 1 year | 3–24 months |  | 2 months |
| Airport Authority of India | 3–4 months | 6 months | 6–12 months | 1–2 months | 3 months |
| Environment | 3+ months | 1 year | 30 days to 1 year | 4–8 months | 2 years |
| Building completion and occupancy certificate | 3 months | 3–4 months | 6–12 months | 3–6 months | 1 year |

Source: Federation of Indian Chambers of Commerce approval process for real estate projects.

## 8    REGIONAL VARIATIONS IN IMPLEMENTATION OF PMAY

As of December 2019, 10.3 million houses in urban India have been sanctioned under four PMAY schemes (in situ slum redevelopment, credit-linked subsidy scheme, affordable housing in partnership and beneficiary-led construction) since 2015 (MoHUA, 2019). While there is a quantum jump in the yearly number of sanctions granted, the completion rate is low. On average 25 million houses were sanctioned each year between 2016–19 but the completion rate was only 7 million housing units per year (MoHUA, 2019). The largest progress has been under the beneficiary-led construction scheme which saw 6 million houses being sanctioned for construction. The scheme provides assistance of 0.15 million rupees to households in EWS categories to either construct new houses or to enhance existing houses on their own. Given the amount of assistance, it is fair to expect that a large proportion of construction under this scheme would have been for extensions. What is important to highlight here is that the number of households that have benefitted from the credit-linked subsidy scheme is merely 0.8 million, a reflection of the poor penetration of the financial system in India. The progress of in situ slum redevelopment is also not significant as only 0.46 million houses have been sanctioned under this category (MoHUA, 2019).

Further analysis indicates that states with higher populations have a higher share of PMAY-sanctioned houses, as expected. However, what is counterintuitive is that the states with higher per capita income (measured as per capita state domestic product) have a higher share of sanctioned houses per state domestic product. The correlation coefficient between per capita income and PMAY houses per state net domestic product is −0.44. The distribution of PMAY houses normalized by state net domestic product and PMAY houses normalized by population is further illustrated in Figures 4.10 and 4.11, which present state-sanctioned PMAY houses.

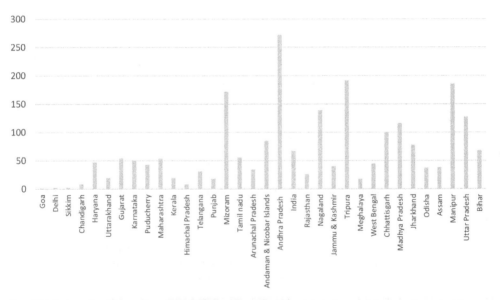

*Note*: This is the ratio of the number of PMAY houses sanctioned in a state to the net state domestic product in billion rupees for 2017–2018 (current prices, 2011–2012 series).

*Figure 4.10*   Number of sanctioned PMAY houses normalized by state net domestic product

The financing of PMAY projects indicates that ULBs in only a few states, such as Karnataka, Gujarat, Maharashtra, Odisha and Tamil Nadu, have been able to contribute to the project cost.

*Affordable housing conundrum in India* 101

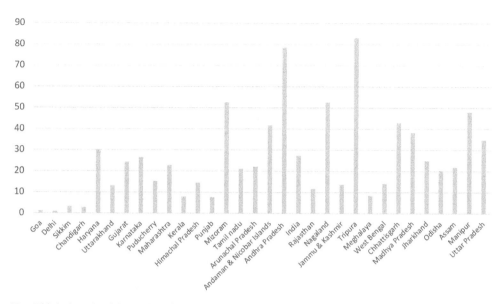

*Note*: This is the ratio of the number of PMAY houses sanctioned in a state to state urban population in thousands based on the 2011 census. Andhra Pradesh includes Telangana here as Telangana was not a separate state in the 2011 census.

*Figure 4.11    Number of PMAY houses normalized by state urban population*

The contribution share is, however, very small. ULBs do not have the financial capacity to bear the cost of a project, which has resulted in heavy reliance on state funding.

## 9    DISCUSSION AND CONCLUSION

This chapter examines the nature of the housing problem in India. In a departure from past approaches that focus on housing needs, we argue that a better approach to understand housing issues in India is to investigate the housing gap, which is the deviation of actual housing from the desired. Moreover, since there are state-level differences in economic and institutional conditions, it is argued that an analysis at the sub-national level is more appropriate. As housing is a state subject in the Constitution, a state-level analysis would highlight state-specific differences and efficacy in the implementation of housing programmes.

Housing inadequacies arise from congestion, obsolescence and poor quality of housing and the responses to adjust these range from improvements/upgrades, extensions and rebuilds to moving to an existing or new house that meets the household requirements. Given the complex nature of housing inadequacies and mechanisms for adjustments, it is meaningless to combine these in a single measure called 'need' or 'shortage'. Recognition of the complexity also allows programmes to adopt a multi-faceted approach.

A state-wise affordability analysis indicates that new housing is unaffordable to a large proportion of the population across states. The issue is extenuated further in economically poor states, which are populous and also lack financial penetration. The data indicate that a number of households undertake self-builds to incrementally improve their housing condition, largely financed through their own savings. Research suggests that houses can be affordable even if average house prices are high, provided distribution of supplied houses is over a wide price range (Malpezzi, 2019). This has been missing in the new supply of houses in India as there has been a shortage of low-income housing. Given that households have a tendency to adjust their housing consumption incrementally as they accumulate savings, policies that encourage the development of smaller houses with the possibility for extension later on would improve the affordability of new houses for low- and middle-income households.

The central government programme, PMAY, which aims to achieve housing for all by 2022 by focusing on EWS and LIG households, has made significant progress towards its target but there are gaps that need to be looked into for better implementation. The analysis of the data indicates that the distribution of assisted households is skewed more towards better-off states. One of the reasons is that the programme requires that besides beneficiaries, states and ULBs also contribute financially to access central government assistance. This builds in a bias towards those states that are economically well off. Other components of the programme like a credit-linked subsidy scheme also suffer because of poor financial sector penetration in EWSs.

What comes out clearly from the analysis is that policies need to align with actual practice. Demand-side policies such as a credit-linked subsidy scheme will work when the supply of new housing is elastic. The literature argues that subsidized finance complemented with elastic housing supply would help lower-income households (Malpezzi, 2019), but inefficiencies in the formal financial system that limit access to credit for low-income households may not result in the intended outcomes. Unless financial access for low-income households is improved, the benefit of a credit subsidy cannot be realized by poor households. Supporting self-builds is a better approach than a focus on new housing. The relative success of beneficiary-linked construction also points to the viability of this approach.

Housing market and institutional reforms are necessary for addressing housing problems in India. Steps to enhance the penetration of formal finance are necessary. While it is out of scope of the present chapter to outline those steps, a comprehensive analysis of the financial sector is needed. Models like hub and spoke or the business correspondent model of the Reserve Bank of India could be further investigated to enhance financial penetration.

New development or upgrades require a facilitating planning regime. The current development approval process needs be reformed as it is too cumbersome, time consuming and expensive. This chapter did not explore tenure and tenure-related approaches but it is imperative that the development of the rental housing market needs to be prioritized in programmes.

The literature suggests that house prices and high rents are one aspect of unaffordability, while the other dimension is stagnant income growth for lower-income households. Economic growth in states has been robust but income inequality has also risen. Housing policy would need to be intertwined with policies that improve incomes to improve affordability (Malpezzi, 2019).

## NOTES

1. A 'household' is a group of persons who normally live together and take their meals from a common kitchen unless the exigencies of work prevent any of them from doing so. Persons in a household may be related or unrelated or a mix of both.

2. A desired house is one that a household wishes for, which is very specific to a household depending on their preferences. This is a utopian state, which gets constrained by budget, household composition, affordability, access to resources including finance, supply of housing and facilitating government policies and programmes. These constraints determine the housing that gets consumed by a household. There is a state which is intermediate between the actual and desired, referred to here as optimal housing, which is based on certain norms related to health and other things and determines what the housing consumption to meet these norms should be. In this chapter, we refer to optimal housing as desired housing. Norm-based optimal housing allows us to look at the housing question at the sub-national level from the perspective of the 'gap' between optimal and actual housing consumption.
3. An affordable house is defined as one where household monthly expenditure on housing (comprising loan repayments) to monthly income does not exceed 30 per cent. In their calculation of an affordable house, Palayi and Priyaranjan (2018) consider different sizes of house for different income groups. Defined by PMAY for their credit-linked subsidy scheme, an eligible house for subsidy is 30 square meters for EWS, 60 square meters for LIG, 120 square meters for MIG and 150 square meters for HMIG households. Palayi and Priyaranjan (2018) compute affordability on the basis of these sizes of house for different income groups. It may be argued that differentiating housing size by income group without considering household size is a crude way of defining housing requirements and in some ways underestimates affordability for lower-income households.
4. Per household net state domestic product is calculated by multiplying per capita state domestic product by average household size. A better measure of average household income in a state would be average household disposable income (i.e. household income including social benefits net of taxes and social contribution) rather than per household net state domestic product. There could be differences between household disposable income and household net state domestic product because not all income generated by production in a state is distributed to households. Some is retained by firms or governments or may be appropriated by non-residents. Since the data on household disposable income are not available for states, per household state domestic product is used as a proxy.

# REFERENCES

Ahluwalia, I.J., Mohanty, P.K., Mathur, O., Roy, D., Khare, A. and Mangla, S. (2019), 'State of Municipal Finances in India', Indian Council for Research on International Economic Relations, New Delhi.

Ahmad, S. (2019), 'Housing Poverty and Inequality in Urban India', in Heshmati Almas, Maasoumi Esfandiar and Wan Guanghua (Eds), *Economic Studies in Inequality, Social Exclusion and Well-Being*, New York: Springer, 107–122.

Chambers, M., Garriga, C. and Schlagenhauf, D.E. (2009), 'Accounting for Changes in the Homeownership Rate', *International Economic Review*, 50(3), 677–726.

Davis, M.A. and van Nieuwerburgh, S. (2015), 'Housing Finance and the Macroeconomy', NBER Working Paper 20287, National Bureau of Economic Research, Cambridge, MA.

Fahey, T. and Norris, M. (2011), 'Housing in the Welfare State: Rethinking the Conceptual Foundations of Comparative Housing Policy Analysis', *International Journal of Housing Policy*, 11(4), 439–452.

Fahey, T., Nolan, B. and Maitre, B. (2004), 'Housing Expenditures and Income Poverty in EU Countries', *Journal of Social Policy*, 33(3), 437–454.

Floetotto, M., Kirker, M. and Stroebel, J. (2012), 'Government Intervention in the Housing Market: Who Wins, Who Loses?', Working Paper, Stanford University, Stanford, CA.

Gervais, M. (2002), 'Housing Taxation and Capital Accumulation', *Journal of Monetary Economics*, 49(7), 1461–1489.

Harish, S. (2016), 'Public Social Rental Housing in India: Opportunities and Challenges', *Economic and Political Weekly*, 60(5), 49–56.

Himanshu (2019), 'Inequality in India: A Review of Levels and Trends', WIDER Working Paper 2019/42, United Nations University World Institute for Development Economics Research, Helsinki.

Jeske, K., Krueger, D. and Mitman, K. (2013), 'Housing, Mortgage Bailout Guarantees and the Macro Economy', *Journal of Monetary Economics*, 60(8).
Keelery, S. (2020), 'Households by Annual Income Brackets India 2010–2025', Statistica, www.statista.com/statistics/482584/india-households-by-annual-income/, accessed 3 July.
Knight Frank (2018), 'India Real Estate: Residential and Office', July–December, Knight Frank India.
Knight Frank (2019), 'India Real Estate: Residential and Office', July–December, Knight Frank India.
Kurz, K. and Blossfeld, H.-P. (Eds) (2004), *Home Ownership and Social Inequality in Comparative Perspective*, Stanford, CA: Stanford University Press.
Leung, C.K.Y., Ng, C. and Yiu, J. (2019), 'Macroeconomic Aspects of Housing', in *The Oxford Research Encyclopedia of Economics and Finance*, Oxford: Oxford University Press.
Malpezzi, S. (2019), 'Myths and Realities of Affordable Housing: Some International Lessons', Presentation to University College London Conference, The Case of Affordable Housing: A Global Perspective on Financing and Institutional Ownership, 12 September 2019, www.ucl.ac.uk/bartlett/construction/sites/bartlett/files/myths_and_realities_of_affordable_housing_2019.pdf, accessed 15 February 2021.
Ministry of Finance (2020), *Economic Survey of India 2019–2020*, New Delhi: Ministry of Finance, Government of India.
MoHUA (2019), *Urban Transformation through Housing for All*, New Delhi: Ministry of Housing and Urban Affairs, Government of India.
MoHUPA (2012), *Report on the Technical Group on Urban Housing Shortage (2012–2017)*, New Delhi: Ministry of Housing and Urban Poverty Alleviation, Government of India, September.
Nakamura, S. (2014), 'Impact of Slum Formalization on Self-Help Housing Construction: A Case of Slum Notification in India', *Urban Studies*, 1–25.
NHB (2018), 'Report on Trends and Progress of Housing in India', National Housing Bank, Mumbai.
NSS (2010), 'Housing Condition and Amenities in India 2008–09', Report No. 535 (65/1.2/1), National Sample Survey Office, Ministry of Statistics and Programme Implementation, Government of India, New Delhi.
NSS (2014), 'Drinking Water, Sanitation, Hygiene and Housing Condition in India', Report No. 556 (69/1.2/1), National Sample Survey Office, Ministry of Statistics and Programme Implementation, Government of India, New Delhi.
NSS (2019), 'Drinking Water, Sanitation, Hygiene and Housing Condition in India', Report No. 584 (76/1.2/1), National Sample Survey Office, Ministry of Statistics and Programme Implementation, Government of India, New Delhi.
ORGCC (2020), 'Census of India 2011', Office of the Registrar General and Census Commissioner, India, Ministry of Home Affairs, Government of India, New Delhi, https://censusindia.gov.in/2011-common/censusdata2011.html, accessed 3 July 2020.
Palayi, A. and Priyaranjan, N. (2018), 'Affordable housing in India', *Reserve Bank of India Bulletin*, January, 13–25.
Pinto, S. and Sarte, P.G. (2020), 'From the Regional Economy to the Macroeconomy', Global Research Unit Working Paper 2020-014, City University of Hong Kong.
Prakash, A., Ekka, A.P., Praiyadarshi, K., Bhowmick, C. and Thakur, I. (2020), 'Quarterly Estimates of Households' Financial Assets and Liabilities', *RBI Bulletin*, June.
Purfield, C. (2007), 'India: Asset Prices and the Macroeconomy', IMF Working Paper, WP/07/221, Asia and Pacific Department, International Monetary Fund, Washington, DC.
Ram, P. and Needham, B. (2016), 'The Provision of Affordable Housing in India: Are Commercial Developers Interested?', *Habitat International*, 55, 100–108.
Ramalhete, I., Farias, H. and Pinto, R.D.S. (2018), 'Overcrowding and Adequate Housing: The Potential of Adaptability', *International Journal of Architectural and Environmental Engineering*, 12(12), 1203–1213.
Roy, D. (2018), 'Housing Demand in Indian Metros: A Hedonic Approach', *Journal of Housing International Markets and Analysis*, 13(1).
Roy, D. (2020), 'Shortage and Demand for Housing of Low-Income Urban Households', Indian Council for Research on International Economic Relations, New Delhi.
Sengupta, J. (2019), 'People Are Saving Less', Commentary, Observer Research Foundation, www.orfonline.org/research/people-are-saving-less-53101/, accessed 20 April 2020.

Sengupta, U. (2010), 'The Hindered Self-Help: Housing Policies, Politics and Poverty in Kolkata, India', *Habitat International*, 34, 323–331.
Singh, C. (2013), 'Housing Market in India: A Comparison with the US and Spain', Working Paper 406, Indian Institute of Management, Bangalore.
Singh, S., Swaminathan, M. and Ramachandran, V.K. (2017), 'Housing Shortages in Rural India', *Review of Agrarian Studies*, 54–72.
Tiwari, P. and Parikh, J. (1998), 'Affordability, Effective Demand and Housing Policy in Urban India', *Urban Studies*, 35, 2111–2129.
Tiwari, P. and Parikh, J. (2012), 'Global Housing Challenge: A Case Study of CO2 Emissions in India', *SPANDREL Journal*, 96–104.
Tiwari, P. and Rao, J. (2016), 'Housing Markets and Housing Policies in India', ADBI Working Paper 565, Asian Development Bank Institute, Tokyo.
Tiwari, P., Parikh, K. and Parikh, J. (1999), 'Effective Housing Demand in Mumbai (Bombay) Metropolitan Region', *Urban Studies*, 36, 1783–1809.
Tiwari, P., Shukla, J. and Ramaswamy, S. (2021), 'Financial Constraints to Adequate Housing: An Empirical Analysis of Housing Consumption Disequilibrium and Households' Decisions towards Meeting Housing Requirements in India', *International Journal of Housing Policy*.
Tripathi, S. (2018), 'Does Higher Economic Development Reduce Household Size? Evidence from India', MPRA Paper 86684, University Library of Munich, Germany.
World Bank (2019), 'GDP Growth (%)', https://data.worldbank.org/indicator/NY.GDP.MKTP.KD.ZG, accessed 3 July 2020.
World Bank (2020). Online data: India, https://data.worldbank.org/country/india, accessed 23 March 2022.
World Inequality Lab (2018), 'World Inequality Report 2018', World Inequality Database.
WHO (2018), 'WHO Housing and Health Guidelines', World Health Organization, Geneva.

# 5. Residential location and education in the United States

*Eric A. Hanushek and Kuzey Yilmaz*

## 1 INTRODUCTION

The educational story in the United States (U.S.) is thoroughly intertwined with residential location.[1] Poverty, race, and schooling are very highly correlated with location, and the institutional structure of public education decision making in the U.S. leads to a close linkage of location, housing, and education. As a result, residential decisions have added implications for households. Moreover, the reliance on the local tax for a large portion of school funding implies that the governmental grant system has an important effect on both locational decisions and on educational outcomes. This chapter provides a theoretical and empirical discussion of the interaction of location and schooling.

Education in the U.S. is provided by local school districts that operate with considerable autonomy. Funding is provided by a combination of local, state, and federal revenues with the level of spending and the performance of schools varying significantly across school districts. Matched against this institutional backdrop are processes of locational decisions by households that have an outcome of residential location (and implicitly school district) being closely related to the race and income of families. While accepting this outcome of individual locational decisions, governments – through financing of districts and other approaches such as providing broadened school choice to families – pursue interventions that at least in part represent an effort to ameliorate the adverse effects of location on minority and low-income families. Whether or not these interventions are successful depends partially on whether they correctly anticipate the behavior of individuals, since individuals respond to the incentives set up by governmental policies.

In order to understand the nature of the U.S. locational environment, we begin with an overview of the relevant theoretical arguments on both location and local public good provision. The two primary relevant models involve urban location theory and Tiebout choice of governmental services. While each has its strengths, neither provides a clear picture of the underlying individual choice or of the outcomes of policy interventions. Following a discussion of the evidence for these models and of the shortcomings of them, we then discuss several areas of the interaction of policy and locational decisions. In the schooling area, the form of government finance of local schools, the interventions to prevent the segregation of schools, and the movement to consolidate local school districts represent perhaps the largest and most significant governmental interventions that involve the intersection of schools and location. Additionally, a different set of governmental interventions – those involving increased school choice – can be thought of as a method of reducing the linkage of location and schooling.

The objective throughout is to identify the state of the art in both theoretical and empirical analyses of schools and location. As part of this explanation, a key element is noting areas where currently relevant modeling and evidence are insufficient.

## 2  RESIDENTIAL LOCATION CHOICE AND OUTCOMES

The residential location behavior of households was analyzed in a microeconomic framework in the early models of the literature. Later, the theory was extended to a general equilibrium framework. A key aspect of the recent literature for residential location models is the general equilibrium nature of residential and school choices. Any government intervention alters the economic incentives for households, so when households respond by changing their residential and school choices, general equilibrium effects occur that might be large in size and may lead to unintended consequences.

Interestingly, two separate streams of literature have emerged over time and have survived as mostly independent lines of research: urban location models and community choice (Tiebout) models. This artificial separation originated from the policy issues that each literature studied. In urban location models, a household's residential location is determined by the trade-off between accessibility (i.e. location) and space. These models examine the equilibrium and optimal patterns of residential land use. In community choice models, the residential location (i.e. community) of a household is determined by public goods along with the price (i.e. taxes) that a community offers. In these models, the public good is usually education, and these models are used to study issues in the financing of schools. Realizing that those two literatures are artificially separated, some scholars provide a joint treatment of them. This basic model permits investigating how accessibility and public goods interact in a metropolitan area and provides a more realistic framework to analyze school district finance policies. In the following subsections, we will provide a literature survey of the three literatures and the analysis of education finance policies, as well as a literature survey for the outcomes of residential choice in the last subsection.

### 2.1  Urban Location Models

As urban problems began to rise in the 1950s, researchers and policy makers intensified their efforts to develop a comprehensive theory of modern urban systems. Among many urban problems, it was observed that within the U.S. metropolitan areas, poverty was concentrated in central cities as the population suburbanized: the poor lived in central cities while the rich lived in suburban areas.[2] As a result, urban location models came into existence to explain urban land use patterns. The pioneers of modern urban location theory were Alonso (1964), Mills (1967, 1972), Muth (1969), and Kain (1975), with their models of land markets that generalized the 1826 work of Johann Von Thünen on the theory of agricultural land use. In the basic urban location model, all employment opportunities are offered by the firms located in the Central Business District (CBD) and workers commute to their workplaces in the CBD from the surrounding residential areas. The model allows households to differ by income. More importantly, it relies on Von Thünen's concept of bid-rent curves and predicts that households are stratified by distance and income from the CBD and that the spatial ordering of households is determined by the relative steepness of the bid-rent curves. Basically, there are two opposing forces that determine the relative steepness of bid-rent curves and, hence, the location of households: commuting costs and the demand for housing. The further away a household's residential location from the CBD is, the higher the commuting cost is. More importantly, the locations far away from the CBD are less attractive for the rich because the rich value commuting time more highly than the poor. As a result of higher commuting costs, the housing rent must fall with distance from the CBD. The model also argues that the rich are attracted to residential locations further away from the CBD because they want to buy more land and land is cheaper at those locations. Overall, the latter force dominates the former force (i.e. the income elasticity of housing demand exceeds the income elasticity of marginal commuting cost) and the rich live further away from the CBD (suburbs) while the poor reside in locations around the CBD (central city). This model is the cornerstone of modern land use theory in urban location models but has been extended in a variety of dimensions (e.g. see LeRoy and Sonstelie, 1983; Brueckner, 1987; Straszheim, 1987; Fujita, 1989; Glaeser and Kahn, 2004).

Wheaton (1977) provided early empirical evidence that the standard urban location model cannot explain the concentration of poverty in central cities: his paper shows that the two opposing forces mentioned above are approximately equal in size, implying an indeterminate pattern of location by income. In more recent work, Glaeser et al. (2008) found that the housing-based force is far weaker than the time-cost force, which is just the opposite of the crucial assumption in standard urban location models. In other words, the urban location model would imply the concentration of the rich around the CBD, in contradiction to the U.S. land use pattern.

One solution to this puzzle has been offered by LeRoy and Sonstelie (1983): the role of public transportation as an alternative transport mode choice. They extend the Alonso-Muth model to incorporate two competing modes of commuting: automobile and bus. They show that when the fast automobile was introduced it was adopted by the rich, and the poor relied on slow, cheap buses. This choice lessens the commuting cost for the rich, resulting in the movement of the rich to the suburbs. The empirical support for their argument later comes from Glaeser et al. (2008) as discussed above. Their explanation revolves around better access to public transportation. Central cities have high population densities required for a convenient, frequent public transit service, so those cities naturally attract the poor population, which must rely on this transit mode. Their inclusion of the public transportation mode as an alternative to the automobile is innovative because their extended urban location model also addresses the problem of central city decline and resurgence.

Although standard urban location models assume that employment is centralized and offered at the CBD, urban employment has been suburbanizing for a long time.[3] One important extension is the incorporation of multiple workplaces into urban location models, which is a fundamental empirical feature of today's urban landscape. There are two main literatures dealing with (1) models with endogenously determined employment location (e.g. Mills, 1972; Fujita and Ogawa, 1982; Henderson and Slade, 1993; Anas and Kim, 1996), and (2) models that assume an exogenously determined spatial location pattern for employment and explore its effects on other aspects of resource allocation in urban areas (e.g. White, 1976, 1999; Sullivan, 1986; Sivitanidou and Wheaton, 1992; Hotchkiss and White, 1993; Ross and Yinger, 1995). The incorporation of decentralized employment into urban modeling is explored in depth in White (1999).

An important change in the U.S. residential pattern over the last century is the generally increasing suburbanization of the population (Boustan and Shertzer, 2013). Urban location theory has also produced an interesting series of papers on this issue and provided a number of different explanations for the suburbanization of population in the U.S. This change, it has been argued, was driven in large part by falling commuting costs (LeRoy and Sonstelie, 1983; Baum-Snow, 2007; Garcia-López, 2010) and rising incomes (Margo, 1992). Another strand of literature concerns the possible role of the age of the housing stock and the filtering mechanism (Glaeser and Gyourko, 2005; Rosenthal, 2008; Brueckner and Rosenthal, 2009). Additionally, Boustan (2010) and Boustan and Margo (2013) argue that suburbanization may also have been motivated by distaste for racial (or income) diversity.

First detected in the late 1960s, regentrification described the return of some affluent households to cities, causing an increase in housing prices and property tax revenue. Although regentrification occurred on a far smaller scale in comparison to the pre-1970s suburbanization trend that shaped today's urban residential patterns, regentrification has kept pace and had its own effect on the spatial distribution of households across metropolitan areas. As the "back-to-city" trend continues in many U.S. cities, regentrification has received greater attention from both scholars and policy makers. One possible explanation for regentrifaction is offered by LeRoy and Sonstelie (1983) as mentioned above: access to public transportation as an alternative means of commuting to the workplace, with some rich suburbanites moving downtown and making use of public transportation. Other explanations given in the literature are (1) those of Brueckner et al. (1999) and Couture and Handbury (2019), who argued that the presence of non-tradable service amenities (e.g. restaurants and nightlife) and topographical and historical amenities (such as an attractive river or beautiful buildings) in the city center may attract the rich more strongly than the poor; (2) those of Brueckner and Rosenthal (2009), who argued that the age of housing stock affects patterns of location by income, and regentrification is ultimately driven by the passage of time and associated aging and obsolescence of housing stock; (3) racial differences in amenity valuations of downtown neighborhoods and improvements in suburban labor market opportunities for unskilled workers (Baum-Snow and Hartley, 2020); (4) policies of urban renewal and environmental regulations (Gamper-Rabindran and Timmins, 2011; González-Pampillón et al., 2019); and (5) the rising value of high-skilled workers' time (Su, 2019).

After the 2008 crisis, declining cities such as Detroit have led to an interesting series of work from urban economists. Rosenthal and Ross (2015) review recent studies that consider and explain the tendency for neighborhood and city-level economic status to rise and fall. Their main message is that many locations exhibit extreme persistence in economic status. Moreover, Brooks and Lutz (2016) confirm this finding, and their evidence suggests that both public forces (zoning) and private forces (agglomeration) generate self-reinforcing effects that lead to this persistence. Owens et al. (2020) present a model with residential externalities to study the urban structure of Detroit and conclude that neighborhood development requires the coordination of developers and residents, without which it may remain vacant even with sound fundamentals.

## 2.2   Community Choice Models

To explain the flight of the rich from central cities, others pointed a finger at urban social problems such as low-quality public schools, racial preferences, crime, and fiscal amenities[4] (see Mieszkowski and Mills, 1993; Mills and Lubuele, 1997; Cullen and Levitt, 1999; Katz et al., 2001; Boustan, 2010; Baum-Snow and Lutz, 2011). The role of local public goods, especially education, in residential choice has received a great deal of attention from researchers (see, for example, Oates, 1969; Fischel, 2006b; Nechyba, 2006). A separate line of residential location models has emerged from the central insight of Tiebout (1956) and builds upon the analytical framework developed in Ellickson (1971). These models were mainly used to study issues in school finance policy, and for the sake of tractability, they ignored the location aspect of residential location choice in urban location models. In these models, households vote with their feet to shop for the community that best satisfies their preferences for local public good where the provision of local public good becomes efficient. These models predict the sorting of households by income into communities.[5]

In the school finance literature, Inman (1978) was among the first to carry out a quantitative comparison of education finance systems in the context of an explicit model. In a series of papers, Fernández and Rogerson (1995, 1996, 1998, 2003) later contrast education finance systems by using a political economy approach: the tax rate and amount of public good provided in a community are determined by the vote of residents in a community. By using such a political economy approach, Epple et al. (1983, 1984, 1993), Epple and Romer (1991), and Epple and Sieg (1999) also analyze the properties of multi-community models, where taxation of housing is used to finance a local public good – education. In addition to these, Glomm and Ravikumar (1992) and Silva and Sonstelie (1995) compare various state and local finance systems, whereas Nechyba (1996) and de Bartolome (1997) examine foundation systems in the finance of schools.

Even though the incorporation of political economy into these models is innovative, it comes at a cost: the existence of equilibrium becomes problematic. Epple et al. (1983, 1984, 1993) develop conditions that involve restrictions on preferences and the technology of public good supply under which equilibrium exists and provide some computational examples to illustrate the way those conditions guarantee the existence of an equilibrium. Reviews of residential sorting models are provided by Boadway and Tremblay (2012) and Brulhart et al. (2015).

Epple and Platt (1998) estimate a model with idiosyncratic preferences for locations and find that these explain most of the location decisions of households. Considering explicitly job accessibility as in Epple and Platt (1998), Bayer and McMillan (2012) find that the dispersion of jobs and the heterogeneity of the housing stock act as strong brakes on the tendency for households to segregate by race, education, and income.

In many countries, private schools are offered as an alternative to public education.[6] Rangazas (1995), Nechyba (2000), and Ferreyra (2007) introduce private schools into community choice models and study the effect of vouchers. Moreover, Nechyba (2003) extends his general equilibrium model in Nechyba (1999) to investigate the impact of school finance policies on mobility and quality and enrollment in private and public schools.

### 2.3 Hybrid Residential Choice Models

One important prediction of community choice models is that households sort themselves into communities by their income and tastes and that identical households would live in the same community.[7] This is an important shortcoming of these models, given that communities are empirically heterogeneous.[8] One reason for this counterfactual result in these models is that they are essentially designed to deal with spaceless economies, ignoring spatial problems such as land use, journey to work, geographical allocation of households, etc.[9] This omission raises questions about whether the models can support analyses of issues in educational finance policy. In the U.S., education is financed significantly through property taxes on housing. Thus, community choice models need to model households' decision making on housing. However, housing is different from other goods: it has an important attribute, namely accessibility, that is explicitly modeled and studied in urban location models.[10] De Bartolome and Ross (2003) and Hanushek and Yilmaz (2007b) offer early papers attempting to combine those two artificially separated modeling perspectives to provide a more realistic modeling of residential location decision.[11]

Hanushek and Yilmaz (2007b, 2013) develop a model that incorporates both locational motivations – accessibility (urban location models) and public goods (community choice models) – simultaneously and find an equilibrium with outcomes more consistent with empirical observation. Their models yield an equilibrium that differs sharply from those found in either urban location models or community choice models. Communities in fact have a mixture of people with different incomes and people with different preferences for schools. They develop both monocentric city and polycentric city models with two school districts. Households, differing in their incomes as well as the valuation they place on education, choose a school district (a quality of education and property tax package), a location in that school district, the consumption of a composite commodity, housing size,[12] and leisure. Households commute to their workplaces, and commuting has both time and pecuniary costs.[13] Land is assumed to be owned by absentee landlords whose sole objective is to maximize their revenue from the land. As for education, school districts use local property taxes to finance schools. The property tax rate in each school district is assumed to be determined by majority voting. An education production function that includes both peer effects and expenditure per pupil as inputs is introduced into the model. In their model, housing prices are a function of location and community characteristics among other things, and endogenously determined. Their model is complex and rich. As a result, they need to rely on computational techniques to find the equilibrium. They later use this model to study the impact of school finance policy on the quality of education that communities provide along with tax price, welfare of households, and spatial distribution of households across metropolitan areas. Their model is interesting in the sense that households are mobile and respond to altered incentives.

By extending a hybrid model with the introduction of private schools, Hanushek et al. (2011) study how a private school option affects school quality, housing prices, and the spatial distribution of households in metropolitan areas. The paper finds that private schools and district autonomy may benefit public schoolers and poorer communities, and monetary inputs may fail to increase the quality of public schools. The paper recommends that policy makers extend choices for households rather than restrict them.

## 2.4   Analytical Approaches

The urban location models that are used to explain the concentration of poverty in central cities and spatial distribution of population across metropolitan areas have a fairly simple structure and are tractable from a modeling perspective. Similarly, the community choice models that are mainly used for studying school finance policies have a simple structure as well. The models that provide a unified treatment of those two separated streams of literature have a much more realistic set up and better prediction than both urban location models and community choice models: they consider households' joint choice of a place to reside along with other dimensions such as the size of the dwelling, accessibility, local public goods (e.g. education), and a set of taxes to finance local public goods. Moreover, those models consider peer effects that result from social interaction with other households in their community. Every good thing comes at a cost and, in this case, the cost is that the model becomes highly complicated and researchers need to use computational methods to solve their highly complex models. As the simulation-based model becomes more complicated, researchers need to impose more specific parametrization to be able to solve the model.

In the case of assessing school finance policies, it is difficult to ignore the interplay between household location decisions and the quality of schooling they obtain. Residential location choices are influenced by public school considerations, and schooling outcomes are determined by the composition of households in the school district, the boundaries of which are geographically defined. Community choice models are thought to be a good representation of metropolitan areas in the U.S., most of which have many school districts or local governments differentiated by public goods and taxes. Households vote with their feet, picking the community that best provides the public good of their preference. The major implication of households' mobility and fragmented government structures is that they increase the efficiency in the production of public good (education). In reality, communities are typically more limited, households have preferences for multiple goods that are related to location (e.g. proximity to workplace), and schooling itself may not be efficiently provided. Simulation models[14] seem to be one step in the right direction because they permit multiple jurisdictions with a range of attributes. Epple and Nechyba (2004) summarize much of the progress that has been made in both empirical and theoretical fiscal federalism literature and provide an overview of stylized facts regarding fiscal decentralization around the world.

Education occupies a central position in the policies of governments, and it is heavily subsidized around the world. Glomm et al. (2011) review the literature on the models of public funding for education. This literature is interesting in the sense that there is a political economy side where households with conflicting interests vote and determine the level of public spending on education. Another important aspect of the models they discuss is the availability of private education as an alternative, which generates non-single-peaked preferences over school funding levels for voters. These models are later used to study school finance policies. Even though their objective is to provide a review of theoretical models, they also include simulation-based models and empirical literature that is relevant to the theoretical models they discuss in their review.

An alternative promising area of research, structural estimation, estimates theoretical models in which household optimizing behavior is included directly into the estimation of household preferences for school quality. Based on a vertical sorting model, Epple and Sieg (1999) use observed differences in the distribution of income within and across neighborhoods to identify the marginal willingness to pay for a public good. Others (e.g. Bayer et al., 2007b) have used horizontal sorting models to value school qualities across neighborhoods. In a general equilibrium model, Ferreyra (2007) studies private school vouchers and residential choices. The decision-making process is static in these models, and some researchers have attempted to make it dynamic. Bayer et al. (2016) propose a model that employs a panel of micro-data to estimate willingness to pay for neighborhood amenities. Relying on the synthetic cohort assumption, Caetano (2019) estimates a dynamic model of school quality valuation. Both models, however, use partial equilibrium models in the estimation. In a recent paper, Mastromonaco (2014) builds a dynamic general equilibrium model of residential location choice and uses it to find the equilibrium consequences of changes in public school quality. Additionally, Zheng and Graham (2020) use an overlapping generations model to examine the intergenerational implications of various housing policies. These analyses offer an interesting and innovative perspective, but also require a series of necessary simplifications.

## 2.5 Evidence on the Outcomes of School Choice

So far, our discussion has emphasized the residential decision making of households. However, many policy discussions revolve around the outcomes of residential choice. There are two major research lines, each of which has received a great deal of attention from both policy makers and researchers: (1) the capitalization of school quality and taxes into housing prices and (2) the impact of extended choice on school quality. We will review each one in turn.

### 2.5.1 The capitalization of school quality into housing prices

In the U.S., the K-12 system is highly decentralized and local property taxes are the main source of funding for public schools.[15] School quality is an important factor in the residential location choice of households. As predicted by both urban location models and community choice models, the advantages of a residential location are capitalized into housing prices. For instance, school quality and taxes are capitalized into house prices in line with the predictions of community choice models. Therefore, house prices provide a window for the demand for school quality. Beginning with Oates (1969), scholars have tried to find the value households place on school quality and property taxes by using a wide range of methods and data sets.

In the early years, researchers relied on per pupil spending as a measure of school quality (e.g. Oates, 1969; Pollakowski, 1973; McMillan and Carlson, 1977; Brueckner, 1979).[16] Moreover, they mainly use aggregate data, and their dependent variable is average housing prices. Later studies include various school quality measures in their regressions. In the literature, there is no consensus as to whether output-based school qualities perform better than input-based quality measures (e.g. Clark and Herrin, 2000; Seo and Simons, 2009). Other branches of this literature try to distinguish the effect of school quality from the effects of other neighborhood amenities influencing house prices by adding neighborhood variables to regression models (e.g. Pollakowski, 1973; Bayer et al., 2007b), and by controlling for location and using instrumental variables methods (e.g. Downes and Zabel, 2002). With respect to location controls, one particular line of research includes school boundary fixed effects by considering houses located on attendance district boundaries (e.g. Black, 1999; Weimer and Wolkoff, 2001; Kane et al., 2003; Gibbons and Machin, 2008; Zahirovic-Herbert and Turnbull, 2008; Dhar and Ross, 2012; Imberman and Lovenheim, 2016). Even though the size of the capitalization of better schools is subject to debate, this literature finds that better schools raise housing prices.

The empirical literature on the capitalization of school quality into house prices is reviewed in various places (Machin, 2011; Black and Machin, 2011; Nguyen-Hoang and Yinger, 2011). Although there are so many measures of school quality available, there nonetheless remains some uncertainty about exactly how consumers get their information about schools (see Downes and Zabel, 2002). Figlio and Lucas (2004) find that state school grade reports affect households' residential locations and house prices. Even with information about state school grade reports or test scores at a school, the household may have trouble sorting out the "value added" of schools, since test scores are affected by families and peers in addition to schools. Using the Norwegian data to examine whether access to school choice affects housing prices, Machin and Salvanes (2016) utilize the policy change of removing catchment areas and find that housing valuation sensitivity is reduced, which proves parents value better-performing schools.

The disagreements and open questions in this literature highlight the empirical relevance of the theoretical models' building on location and school quality. The variation in results appears partly related to methodology, but full reconciliation has yet to occur.

### 2.5.2 The impact of Tiebout choice on school efficiency

In community choice models, households vote with their feet and pick the best community that satisfies their preferences for education. A household's ability to participate in school choice introduces pressure on public schools (Tiebout competition), and Tiebout competition leads to the efficient provision of education. From studies across different metropolitan areas, it appears that competition among school districts is an important contributor to the quality of public schools. Borland and Howsen (1992) find that competition has positive effects on student achievement in the state of Kentucky. Hoxby (2000) extends this literature by considering the possibility that school district performance could influence the number of school districts in metropolitan areas. To address the potential endogeneity problem due to endogenous district formation, she builds instruments from the natural boundaries (streams and rivers) of metropolitan areas. Her paper finds that Tiebout choice produces more productive schools. This issue is not without its controversy, however, as different interpretations have been presented by Rothstein (2005), and the analytical methods of Hoxby have been debated (Rothstein, 2007; Hoxby, 2007).

Community choice models have strong assumptions and, in reality, some of those assumptions do not necessarily hold. For instance, the decision to move for a household is a complex decision and based on many factors such as accessibility to workplace, pollution levels, safety, and natural surroundings. Additionally, moving to change their school district is very costly for a household. As a result, school districts exert monopoly power (Merrifield, 2001). School choice programs such as charter schools (Cordes, 2018; Baude et al., 2020) or school vouchers (Friedman, 1962) diminish the monopoly power held by public schools and, therefore, lead to better and cost-efficient schools (Friedman and Friedman, 1980; Chubb and Moe, 1990). Recently, Urquiola (2016) reviews the literature on school competition.

## 3 INTERACTION OF POLICY AND LOCATIONAL DECISIONS

The previous sections have described key elements of the interaction of location and schooling, both from a theoretical and an empirical viewpoint. In contrast, while that discussion emphasizes the behavior of households in choosing a location, a range of policy decisions have explicitly been based on location but for the most part assuming that households will not react to the policies. These policies aim to alter the attractiveness of a local school district but generally ignore any general equilibrium effects from household behavior. Here we review some of the more important policies affecting the location–schooling equilibrium.

### 3.1 State Funding of Schools and School Finance Court Cases

The funding of schools has been jointly determined by federal, state, and local decision making. We begin with an overall description of the funding of schools. There are some generalizations across states, even though there are in fact large variations across states in the pattern of the funding of schools.

While most governmental appropriation decisions are made by the relevant executive and legislative branches of government, school funding is one area where the courts have also been heavily involved. This court involvement has frequently called for a redistribution of the funding of schools across districts within a state and as such has altered the fiscal (and possibly educational) attractiveness of districts.

The federal funding of schools has been relatively small and has focused on extra funds for disadvantaged children or for special education. Federal support of schools has increased in recent years, partially linked to greater funding under school accountability. Nonetheless, ignoring the recessionary uptick, federal funds remain less than 10 percent of total revenues (see Figure 5.1). As they vary with the characteristics of students, they have much of the character of funding that follows the child, regardless of locational choice.

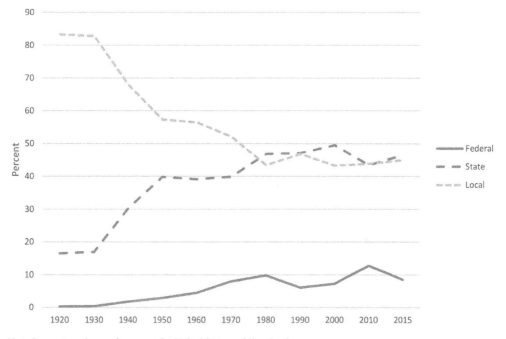

*Note*: Percentage shares of revenues for United States public schools.
*Source*: U.S. Department of Education (2018).

*Figure 5.1*     *Sources of United States school revenue*

The U.S. education system is unique around the world in the degree of local control that has been granted to local governments. This local control is seen in a variety of dimensions, but perhaps the most important is the ability of local school districts to raise funds for schools. As seen in Figure 5.1, in recent decades the funding from state sources and from local sources has been roughly equal. In most states, local districts are given the ability to use the property tax, and thus the local property tax is a major source of funding for education.[17] Not surprisingly, property tax bases vary from one district to another, and this variation has contributed to an educational system characterized by enormous total spending variation across states and districts in spending levels.

The overall pattern of school financing has been heavily influenced by the results of state school finance court cases. These court decisions sometimes require changes in funding and other times do not, but they have led to a general increase in the state share of spending.

*Table 5.1    Sources of state school revenue in 2015, in percent*

|  | Federal | State | Local |
| --- | --- | --- | --- |
| Average | 8.5 | 46.5 | 45.0 |
| Minimum | 4.2 | 24.9 | 3.9 |
| Maximum | 14.9 | 90.1 | 66.8 |

*Note*: This table reflects the range of revenue sources across states in 2015.
*Source*: U.S. Department of Education (2019).

The pattern of school revenues does, however, differ noticeably across states. As Table 5.1 shows, while in the extreme (in Illinois) two-thirds of revenues come from localities, only 4 percent do at the minimum (in Vermont). Federal revenues also vary noticeably, depending on the overall level of spending in each state and on the proportion of students from poor families.

The character of state funding is, however, pivotal in determining the distribution of educational spending across districts. All states distribute state revenue for education to local school districts, both as basic support and, almost universally, as categorical grants for specific funding needs. An important element of state aid is helping to narrow the gaps in education spending across school districts. Flat grants are the oldest and simplest form of aid, providing a uniform amount of aid per student or teacher. As opposed to their objective to provide some minimum level of education expenditure, historically the grants were ineffective at reducing the variance in funding due to their small amounts. The most common scheme, foundation grants, is aimed at guaranteeing a minimum level of spending: they do so by providing larger state funding to districts with less fiscal capacity as identified by lower tax bases. The exact formula and level of funding differ significantly across states, but the formulae typically require local districts to contribute the foundation spending level in varying amounts depending on their capacity as measured by the property tax base. Districts can then generally further supplement the basic funding with their own property tax receipts. District power equalization programs match grant programs with the aim that the program will make it possible for any district, whatever its tax base, to spend the same amount of money from the same tax effort identified by the property tax rate. The final grant scheme – categorical aid – is given for specific expenditure categories such as special education, transportation, buildings, textbooks, and equipment.

Clearly the state funding program has direct implications for the geography of funding – and changes in state policies (that occur rather frequently) have immediate ramifications for the tax and spending policies of individual districts. Implicitly this means that state policies directly impact the fiscal and educational attractiveness of districts leading, among other things, to changes in housing values through differential capitalization. While these general equilibrium effects are almost certainly substantial in the case of major funding decisions, there has been limited analysis of them.

However, as suggested, the courts have also been significant actors in the determination of the level and distribution of school funding across districts.[18] A variety of parties have instituted court proceedings claiming that the legislated funding formula violates constitutional requirements for funding schools. While the division is sometimes fuzzy, these court cases fall into two major groupings: equity cases and adequacy cases. In the simplest terms, equity cases are focused on the distribution of funding across districts, while adequacy cases are focused on the level of funding. Some existing cases have, however, had elements of both.

### 3.1.1 Equity cases

In the early 1970s, parents began to file lawsuits against state governments to require states to equalize spending per pupil among districts, reasoning that the quality of education a child receives should not be a function of the wealth of the community in which he or she resides (the principle of wealth neutrality).[19] *Serrano* v. *Priest* (1974) was the first successful court case related to state school finance equity.[20] John Serrano sued the State of California about the low quality of the local high school's education program. Serrano cited the very large difference between two school districts in Los Angeles, Beverly Hills and Baldwin Park. Beverly Hills used its large property tax base to spend more per student while charging a lower property tax rate than Baldwin Park. In ruling in favor of Serrano, state court judges in California overturned the state's existing system of school finance. The court ruled that the existing property tax system violated the equal protection clause of the state's constitution.

*San Antonio School District* v. *Rodriguez* (1973), filed on behalf of some children living in districts with low per pupil property valuations in Texas, was a similar case to *Serrano*.[21] It differed, however, in that the case was brought in a federal court and relied on the equal protection clause of the U.S. constitution alone. The U.S. Supreme Court ruled that education is not a fundamental right guaranteed to U.S. citizens by the federal constitution. There are two major implications from the Rodriguez decision. First, the federal courts would do nothing to promote equalization of spending across states. Second, any fiscal reform of the school finance system must come from state governments and state courts.

The state court cases frequently led to dramatic changes in the distribution of funding across local districts. While changing the funding going to individual districts, these court rulings also changed the fiscal attractiveness of individual districts by changing the benefits and tax costs of individual districts. As a result, these court cases also had direct implications of the capitalization of schooling into the housing prices of districts. Nonetheless, this impact on housing prices has not been adequately researched.

### 3.1.2 Adequacy cases

A different kind of court case followed the "equity" cases epitomized by *Serrano*. The Kentucky Supreme Court took the dramatic and unprecedented step in 1989 of declaring the entire state system of elementary and secondary school education unconstitutional under the state constitution for failing to provide all children with an adequate education.[22] Adequacy, as defined in Kentucky and a large number of subsequent court cases, involves both identifying desired educational outcomes required by a state constitution and setting a path to meet the standard. The typical court remedy for a finding that the state financing was inadequate was to require states to increase their funding of schools, sometimes very dramatically. These court cases proved to be very successful, with a string of victories for plaintiffs between 1989 and 2005 in many state courts including New York, New Jersey, and Wyoming.

Interestingly, after 2005, the pattern of state court rulings completely reversed, leading to a significant number of plaintiff losses.[23] Thus, there appears to be a recent reluctance among the courts to intervene in school funding.

For our purposes, it is clear that these cases had a very different impact on location and schooling. Unlike the equity cases that were designed to change the geographic pattern of the funding of schools, these cases were more aimed at the level of funding rather than the distribution. Nonetheless, in rewriting finance laws, the distribution of funding is invariably affected along with the level of funding.

*Table 5.2    School finance court cases and Supreme Court decisions through 2018*

| Type of case | Supreme Court decision | |
|---|---|---|
| | For plaintiffs | For defendants |
| Equity | 21 | 24 |
| Adequacy | 20 | 18 |
| Both | 18 | 15 |

*Note*: Decisions for the plaintiffs call for state changes in school finance funding statutes; decisions for the defendants leave school finance funding statutes unchanged. An additional 12 cases were heard by the relevant state supreme court but remanded to a lower court for further consideration.
*Source*: Hanushek and Lindseth (2009), updated by author.

Table 5.2 summarizes the court cases decided through 2018.[24] All cases are separate actions in state courts. With 117 total cases, it is clear that some states have had multiple court cases. Before 1989, all cases involved equity – the distribution of funds across districts. After 1989, some involved just adequacy – the overall level of spending – and some were a mixture of equity and adequacy. As seen, decisions have been almost evenly split between those for the plaintiffs that found the school finance system to violate the state constitution and those for the defendants that found no constitutional violation.

There is a large body of research that investigates the impact of school finance reforms on the distribution of school resources. In his work, Fischel (1989, 2006a) finds that California's *Serrano* decision equalizing school spending contributed to the property tax limitation of Proposition 13 and subsequently to relative declines in California spending on education (compared to other states). Later, Murray et al. (1998) find that successful litigation reduced inequality in the amount spent per student by raising spending in the poorest districts while leaving spending in the richest districts unchanged. It thereby increased aggregate spending on education. States accomplished this by providing less state funds to property-rich districts and more funds to property-poor districts, while allowing property-rich districts to increase their local contributions. Moreover, reform led states to fund additional spending through higher state taxes. More generally, Hoxby (2001) demonstrates that school finance equalization schemes can level spending up or down, depending on the price and income effects they impose. Strikingly, it appears that some students from poor households in states such as California or New Mexico would actually have better-funded schools if their states did not attempt such complete equalization.

The relationship of court actions and student outcomes is generally different. Early investigations of the effects of expenditure equalization from the courts generally do not find implications for the equalization of outcomes.[25] Clark (2003) finds that, while Kentucky's Education Reform Act did have a significant equalizing effect on school spending, it did not have an equalizing effect on student achievement between rich and poor school districts.

Card and Payne (2002), on the other hand, find evidence that the equalization of educational expenditures across school districts narrows the distribution of education spending and correspondingly narrows the distribution of SAT scores among children of diverse socioeconomic backgrounds. More recently, Jackson et al. (2016) use decisions in court cases as a source of exogenous variation in school spending and then examine how funding affects longer-term outcomes. In a similar type approach, Lafortune et al. (2017) investigate how both court decisions and legislative changes in funding alter the relative funding of poor districts and in turn how that affects achievement. Nonetheless, the impact of school finance court cases on student performance remains unclear.

An alternative approach to studying the impact of these fiscal changes is the general equilibrium simulation modeling in Hanushek and Yilmaz (2007a, 2007b). They consider how households respond to various funding policies including both funding equalization across districts and district power equalization and find that welfare and achievement are generally reduced by these policies. After governmental involvement, the rich are pushed to subsidize more households and the marginal price for a better education rises. Moreover, due to the redistribution of school resources, the quality of education in the community with a better education goes down and the gap with the other community becomes smaller. The rich end up getting a relatively lower quality of education, even though they have a demand for a community with a better education. As a result, they are worse off. The poor side of the story is interesting and actually justifies why a general equilibrium model provides a better framework to study issues in educational finance. Due to the higher marginal price for a better education, some richer households move to the poorer community, causing an increase in rents. The poor are worse off due to higher rents and the fact that their preferred level of quality of education is lower than what they have after the policy. Individual incentives respond to the policies set up by the government, and the distortion created by incentives cannot be ignored.

### 3.2   School Desegregation

Perhaps the largest social policy of the U.S. in the second half of the twentieth century was the racial desegregation of schools. This policy had direct ramifications for both urban location and schools. In *Brown* v. *Board of Education of Topeka* (1954), the U.S. Supreme Court declared that legally enforced (*de jure*) racial segregation was unconstitutional.[26] Before then, a number of states maintained legal segregation of schools by race. However, over the late 1950s and early 1960s, the progress in desegregating schools was not substantial. Empowered by the Civil Rights Act of 1964, the Department of Health, Education, and Welfare had the power to withhold federal funding from school districts that discriminated on the basis of race. The following year, with the passage of the Elementary and Secondary Education Act of 1965, the department issued its first desegregation guidelines for receipt of federal funds, requiring school districts to submit a court order or a voluntary desegregation plan as evidence of non-discrimination.[27] The federal courts also became more active in desegregation in 1968, when the U.S. Supreme Court decision in *Green* v. *County School Board of New Kent County* finally called for dismantling the dual school system. This Supreme Court ruling set desegregation guidelines for voluntary desegregation and for court-ordered plans.[28] The decisions required the desegregation of schools in areas where local governments pursued a policy of explicit segregation. Court cases also moved from areas that had segregation laws (*de jure* segregation) to ones where the existing patterns of housing and schools led to segregation (*de facto* segregation). In 1973's *Keyes* v. *School District No. 1* (Denver), the U.S. Supreme Court extended the obligation to desegregate to school districts with de facto rather than de jure segregation. The policies of courts toward desegregation clearly affect the interaction of housing and schools (e.g. see Boustan, 2010; Baum-Snow and Lutz, 2008).

The policies toward desegregation have actually changed dramatically over time. While the courts were expansive in their rulings through the 1970s, they began to retreat on requiring added desegregation after that.[29] At the height of court involvement, hundreds of districts in the U.S. were under court orders or had a voluntary agreement on various actions to reduce racial segregation, and these often required extra funding of districts under desegregation orders.

Two trends, however, directly impacted the force of these orders. First, in a series of U.S. Supreme Court rulings (notably *Milliken* and *Jenkins*), it became established that desegregation orders applied within districts but not across them.[30] Second, some of the court decisions accelerated the suburbanization of the white population – a situation often dubbed "white flight."[31] Thus some of the suburbanization trends identified previously were actually reinforced by court actions.

Finally, the federal courts moved away from desegregation orders. Perhaps the end of the era of court involvement was the U.S. Supreme Court decisions in 2007 that banned voluntary race-based policies.[32] At the same time remaining aspects of prior agreements and court orders have also been disappearing. In his work, Lutz (2005) finds that dismissal of a court-ordered desegregation plan results in a gradual, moderate increase in racial segregation and an increase in black dropout rates and black private school attendance.

Court orders clearly had a big impact on the character of schools after *Brown* in 1954. Schools became substantially less segregated (Welch and Light, 1987; Clotfelter, 2004; Reber, 2005; Baum-Snow and Lutz, 2008). Almost all of the school segregation in the most recent period has come from residential segregation across districts (as discussed above); see Rivkin and Welch (2006). Due to demographic changes (largely increases in the Hispanic population), racial exposure (say, blacks to whites) has decreased even though measures of concentration have not (Rivkin, 2016).

The larger question is the educational impact of school segregation. A mounting body of evidence suggests that school segregation has negative impacts on black achievement (Angrist and Lang, 2004; Guryan, 2004; Hanushek and Raymond, 2005; Hanushek and Rivkin, 2009; Hanushek et al., 2009).

### 3.3   School District Consolidation

The twentieth century saw a dramatic consolidation of school districts. In 1937 there were 119,000 separate public school districts. Today there are less than 14,000.[33] There has been some work considering the reasons for consolidation (e.g. Kenny and Schmidt, 1994; Brasington, 1999; Gordon and Knight, 2009) and the impact of consolidation on costs (Duncombe and Yinger, 2005). On the benefit side of consolidation, large districts have economies of scale because they can provide libraries, sport facilities, administration, and so forth on a district-wide basis. On the cost side, large districts combine different individuals with different preferences (heterogeneity) who must compromise to share a school district and agree on common educational policies. Specifically, Tiebout sorting is based on the notion that individuals prefer to interact with people who are similar to themselves in tastes for public goods. Now, they must interact with people different from themselves. A trade-off between economies of scale and heterogeneity helps to explain the consolidation pattern of local jurisdictions in the U.S.

For our purposes, however, it is important to point out the implications of this and other trends for the operation of schools and for the interaction with families. Over the same period, funding of education also changed dramatically, as described previously. In 1930 less than 0.5 percent of revenues for elementary and secondary schools came from the federal government, and less than one-fifth came from states, leaving over 80 percent to be raised locally. Some in fact view this finding in earlier periods as benefit taxation, where residents pay varying taxes in accordance with the perceived performance of schools (Fischel, 2006a). As noted previously, local share has fallen to roughly 45 percent – the same as state share.

Taking those trends together, it is reasonable to assume that parents were much closer to what was going on in the schools 75 years ago than they are today. Likewise, school administrators in the small districts of the past, supported largely by local funds, almost certainly paid closer attention to the needs and desires of the families they served. School district consolidation has effectively moved decision making and management of education away from the local population. Moreover, larger districts with larger populations mean that there are more diverse preferences among parents for what they want in their schools. Thus, the administration of any district necessarily requires compromises among the various interests.

The influence of parents and local administrators has also changed because of the overall centralization of decision making that has been occurring over the past century. As states have become more prominent in the funding of schools, they have also moved toward more centralized decision making about the operation of schools. That is understandable because, if states are going to fund schools, they have a responsibility not to waste their (or the federal government's) funds. The overall result of the trends in government revenue and administration of education is that school decisions have migrated away from parents and local voters and toward state bureaucracies.

Tiebout suggested that parents could satisfy their desire for local governmental services by shopping for the jurisdiction that provided the services that best met their individual desires.[34] Thus, by living in the same area, parents with similar desires could group together to ensure more homogeneous demands. Moreover, since one aspect of schools involves how effectively they use their resources, competition for consumers could put competitive pressures on school districts to improve their performance and efficiency. The idea of shopping across alternative jurisdictions does, however, require that there be a large number of districts so that there is a sufficient range of choice. It also becomes very complicated when parents have multiple interests. For example, some parents may, in addition to schools, have desires with respect to welfare payments, hospital coverage, police, and safety or with respect to accessibility to jobs. Selection of place of residence on the basis of school districts may compete with or fail to satisfy the other interests of the family. Particularly, much of the consolidation of districts occurs across relatively rural districts, where the range of choice is limited by population density.

A significant percentage of housing decisions involve finding a location that meets demands for commuting to work, as in the standard location model. With decentralized workplaces, different jurisdictions become more or less attractive, and that makes parents' choices much more complicated than simply choosing a school (Hanushek and Yilmaz, 2007b).[35]

122   *Handbook of real estate and macroeconomics*

Finally, for a variety of reasons, the public schools in adjacent jurisdictions may not look too different from one another. Central state restrictions; the limited viewpoints of school personnel in terms of curricula, pedagogy, and effective administration; and other things could lead schools to be quite similar in approach, curricula, and goals. The contraction of choices of different school districts when subsumed by the other choice aspects of residential location thus puts natural limits on how widespread any version of school choice such as Tiebout's might be.

### 3.4   School Choice Options

A final element of location and schools is the availability of school choice options. One of the direct implications of allowing broader selection among schools by families is that the closeness of the relationship of location and school quality is reduced. Choice options follow the ideas originally set out by Friedman (1962) when he argued for using vouchers to fund schools. Individuals would have the ability to shop among schools using a government voucher.

One thing that has been happening over time is substantial changes in the percentage of students actively choosing what kind of school they attend. As recently as 2000, 85 percent of students went to the traditional public school to which they were assigned (Figure 5.2).[36] By 2016, one-quarter of students made choices concerning the sector of instruction. Private schooling has been constant at roughly 10 percent, with the vast majority being religiously based. However, charter schools – public schools that are not controlled by local districts –

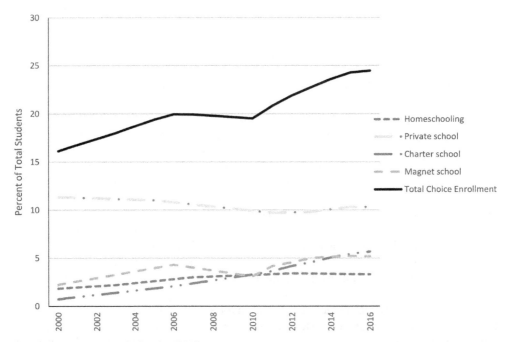

*Source*: U.S. Department of Education (2018).

*Figure 5.2*   Students attending school of choice

have grown significantly (Baude et al., 2020). Perhaps most surprising has been a rising share of students who are homeschooled.

Recent U.S. experiences with school choice include the introduction of a limited voucher program in Milwaukee, the introduction of a more broadly accessible program in Cleveland, the U.S. Supreme Court's affirmation of such policies, the use of vouchers in Washington, DC, and the introduction of a variety of private voucher programs. These experiences have been discussed and analyzed in a variety of different places and are under fairly constant revision.[37] While these voucher programs have generally found positive achievement effects and have been very popular with parents, they have not greatly expanded over time.

### 3.4.1    Homeschooling

There has been a considerable surge in homeschooling, i.e. students not attending regular public or private school. A significant number of parents have simply withdrawn their children from the regular public schools and taken personal responsibility for their education. Estimates put the number of homeschoolers at 1.7 million children or over 3 percent of all school children in 2016, although there is some uncertainty about the numbers involved.[38] Unfortunately, however, little is known about this in terms of movements of children in and out of homeschool environments or of their performance trends. The full impacts on homeschooling as a result of school closures during the pandemic are also unknown.

### 3.4.2    Intradistrict open enrollment

A particularly popular version of public school choice involves an open enrollment plan, under which, for example, students could apply to go to a different school in their district rather than the one to which they are originally assigned. In a more expansive version, no initial assignment is made at all, and students apply to an ordered set of district schools. A common version of this has been the use of magnet schools that offer a specialized focus such as college preparation or the arts. Forms of open enrollment plans were the response of a number of districts in southern states to the desegregation orders flowing from *Brown* v. *Board of Education*. In general, simple open enrollment plans were not found to satisfy the court requirements for desegregation of districts, but magnet schools (with racial balance restrictions) became a reasonably common policy approach.[39] In 2016, 5 percent of all students attended magnet schools.[40]

These programs do not, however, offer much school competition. First, the flow of students is heavily controlled. For example, the first caveat is always "if there is space at the school," but the desirable public schools virtually never have space. Second, large urban school systems where there is a natural range of options frequently face other restrictions, such as racial balance concerns, that severely constrain the outcomes that are permitted. Third, and most important, these plans seldom have much effect on incentives in the schools. The competitive model of vouchers envisions that schools that are unable to attract students will improve or shut down. That threat provides an incentive to people in the schools to perform well or to potentially lose their jobs. In a district with open enrollment, personnel in undersubscribed schools generally still have employment rights and simply move to another school with more students, diminishing the effect of competitive incentives.

### 3.4.3 Interdistrict open enrollment

Another variant of open enrollment plans permits students in a city to attend any public school in the state. Conceptually, this could offer some competitive incentives. If a district lost sufficient students through out-migration, it could be left with less funding and could be forced to reduce its workforce. Again, however, the reality does not bring to bear many of the potentially positive effects of competition. In the first instance, voluntary interdistrict enrollment typically requires the approval of the boards of the schools a student is exiting and entering, meaning that the parents can face significant hurdles in making choices. The "if there is space at the school" clause generally stops all but some token movement. In addition, because of complicated formulas for school funding that mix federal, state, and local dollars, the funding following the choice student is typically less than the full funding for a student in the receiving district, meaning that any district accepting students is asking its residents to subsidize the education of students whose families reside and thus pay school taxes outside the district. The funding of transfers is also complicated by the common practice of basing current-year funding on prior-year enrollment or attendance figures, or both.

### 3.4.4 Charter schools

The rise of charter schools has introduced an element of choice in schooling that promises to better mimic a genuine voucher program. As they are creatures of the separate states and operate in different ways according to state rules, there is no common model of a charter school. The essential features are that they are public schools but ones that are allowed to operate to varying degrees outside of the normal public school administrative structures. To the extent that they survive through their ability to attract sufficient numbers of students, they are schools of choice. They differ widely, however, in the rules for their establishment, in the regulations that apply to them, in the financing that goes with the students, and in a host of other potentially important dimensions.[41] Some states, for example, impose a variety of requirements about teacher certification, curriculum, acceptance of special education students, and the like—advertised as "leveling the playing field"—in order to ensure that charter schools do not offer any true innovation and competition. Other states, however, remove a substantial amount of regulation and truly solicit innovation and competition.[42]

Despite the regulatory diversity surrounding them, charter schools can nonetheless offer true competition to the traditional government schools, because they can draw students away from poorly performing schools. Employment rights typically do not transfer between charters and existing school districts so there is potentially pressure on school personnel to attract students. Moreover, we see that charters are truly susceptible to the necessary downside of competition in that a substantial number of attempted charters do not succeed in the marketplace.[43]

Since the nation's first charter school legislation was enacted into law in Minnesota in 1991, some 45 states and the U.S. Congress, on behalf of the District of Columbia, have enacted legislation that provides for charter schools. In the nation as a whole, charter schools increased from a handful in 1991 to more than 7,000 schools serving 3 million students, or approximately 5.6 percent of the public school population, in 2016.[44]

In some places, charters have become quite significant. For example, in the 2017–2018 school year, 45 percent of students in the District of Columbia, 17 percent of students in Arizona, 13 percent of students in Colorado, and 10 percent of students in California attended charter schools.[45]

What do we know about the performance of charter schools? In a study of assessing the quality of charter schools, Hanushek et al. (2007) find that the average quality in the charter sector is not significantly different from that in regular public schools but there is considerable heterogeneity in terms of performance. This overall performance has, however, improved as the market for charter schools has become more established (Baude et al., 2020). The heterogeneity of achievement impact across states is readily seen with a national study, the largest to date of charter schools (CREDO, 2013). That study finds that overall charter schools have improved compared to their earlier study (CREDO, 2009).[46] The improvement is not uniform, however, and the results across states and local districts differ significantly. Importantly, charter schools are most prevalent in urban centers,[47] and they also appear most effective in urban settings (CREDO, 2015).

There is a recent body of literature (e.g. see Mehta, 2017; Ferreyra and Kosenok, 2018; Walters, 2018; Singleton, 2019) that explicitly models the supply and demand of charter schools and uses the estimated models to identify the treatment effect of charter schools and/ or evaluate the impact of various policies on the performance of charter schools. The structural model in Mehta (2017) renders a comprehensive and internally consistent picture of treatment effects when there may be general equilibrium effects of school competition. Additionally, Singleton (2019) evaluates the effects of funding policies that provide funding for more needy, low-income students and presents evidence that this policy skews the distribution of students served by charters towards low-cost populations by influencing where charter schools decide to open and whether they survive.

## 4   CONCLUSIONS

The study of location and schooling has been a vibrant area of research. The institutional structure of U.S. schools – where local districts have considerable fiscal and policy autonomy – highlights the importance of the joint consideration of location and education.

On the theoretical side, the area has been marked by the historic development of distinct treatments of household decisions. Urban locational models focus on household choices that are driven by accessibility and housing prices. Tiebout models of public good choice, on the other hand, have households focusing exclusively on the public services offered by different jurisdictions. The separation of these models is in part the result of a desire to have models that yield analytical solutions. However, recent advances in more complex models solved by simulation techniques have expanded this work to incorporate more realistic household behavior.

Two of the strong lines of empirical analyses growing out of this locational modeling are the investigation of how the attractiveness of different locations is capitalized into housing prices and how competition among districts affects the efficiency of school provision. There are natural and productive extensions that exist for both lines of research.

With the overview of models that link location and schooling, it is possible to consider some of the major policy changes that have occurred over the past half century. First, state governments – often driven by the courts – have made some dramatic changes in the financing of local schools. These changes alter the fiscal attractiveness of different areas, which the previous locational models suggest will lead to individual behavioral changes. Unfortunately, the existing literature on the impacts of these policy changes has seldom considered these behavioral changes and the resulting impact of them. Second, perhaps the largest policy change in

U.S. schools has been the desegregation of the schools. These actions, largely driven by the federal courts, have distinct locational impacts. The existing empirical work focuses on family movements, largely "white flight" from central cities. The impact on the subsequent patterns of education has been much less studied. Indeed, the theoretical models discussed here focus almost exclusively on income and do not adequately treat race and location. Third, the U.S. has seen the dramatic consolidation of local school districts over the twentieth century. While work has helped to understand the forces behind this consolidation, there is virtually no existing work on the educational impacts.

Finally, within the context of how schools and locations are determined, a number of policy actions have been aimed directly at lessening the impact of residential location. These actions generally fall under the heading of school choice, where expanded options of choosing specific schools help to break the link between residential location and schooling opportunities. In this area, our knowledge is rapidly expanding in large part because the policies have been moving quickly.

In sum, recent work has greatly expanded our understanding of how household locational choices impact the educational opportunities that are available. At the same time, this work has also highlighted a variety of areas where research is missing but vital to policy decisions that are currently being made.

## NOTES

1. This chapter updates and extends Hanushek and Yilmaz (2011).
2. The suburbanization of population in metropolitan areas drew considerable attention from early researchers (Mills, 1972, 1992; Mills and Price, 1984; Margo, 1992; Mieszkowski and Mills, 1993; Mills and Lubuele, 1997).
3. See Glaeser and Kahn (2001, 2004) for a discussion of patterns of American cities.
4. Nechyba and Walsh (2004) argue that homogeneous suburban communities allow high-income households to escape redistributive central-city taxation while improving the quality of public goods.
5. Black (1999), Bayer et al. (2007a), and Calabrese et al. (2006) find that the driving force for sorting in the U.S. metropolitan areas rests in the differences in public good provision and demographic characteristics.
6. There are studies about how private education affects spending on public education (e.g. Epple and Romano, 1996; Glomm and Ravikumar, 1998; Alesina et al., 2001). This literature is based on political economy models and also needs to overcome the problem of multi-peaked preferences over school funding levels.
7. Fernández and Rogerson (1996) find an equilibrium in which the middle-income households live in both communities while the rich and the poor reside exclusively in the community with high- and low-quality local public education, respectively.
8. In his paper, Davidoff (2005) reports that the sorting by income, generated by the differences in tax and spending policies, into communities is far from complete. These differences account for only approximately 2 percent of the variation in household income.
9. Another possible explanation for the observed within-community heterogeneity is the presence of heterogeneous unobserved factors such as locational preference and home attachment.
10. Epple et al. (2010) provide sufficiency conditions under which models that assume a single housing price in each community continue to apply in the presence of location-specific amenities that vary both within and across communities.
11. A review of alternative modeling approaches is provided by Epple and Nechyba (2004), Nechyba (2006), and Hanushek and Yilmaz (2011). This literature ignores any of the short-run dynamics or the interactions with the macroeconomy (e.g. Leung, 2004; Leung and Ng, 2019).

12. Suburban communities also use land use controls to exclude the poor from rich communities. See Hanushek and Yilmaz (2015) for a study of land use controls in a general equilibrium setup.
13. For a model with public transportation as an alternative mode of commuting, see Yilmaz (2019, 2020): households can commute to their workplaces by either an automobile or a bus, and the choice of the mode of transportation is endogeneous in the model.
14. A thorough review of theoretical and simulation-based model literature is provided by Nechyba (2006).
15. The share of school district revenues that state and local governments provide for K-12 has changed significantly over the last century. Today, states play a large and increasing role in school funding. See Yilmaz (2019) for a study of this policy shift.
16. Unfortunately, the literature on expenditure as a measure of quality is inconclusive and fails to find a relationship between school inputs and outputs (Hanushek, 2003).
17. See Yilmaz (2020) for the financing history of the U.S. K-12 education system.
18. Early analysis by Murray et al. (1998) showed that court cases raised the level of state spending. Subsequent analyses have used these spending increases to consider the impact of spending on outcomes; see, for example, Jackson et al. (2016).
19. The initial legal arguments were presented in Coons et al. (1970). A history and interpretation of the many legal cases can be found in Hanushek and Lindseth (2009).
20. *Serrano* v. *Priest*, 557 P.2d 929 (Calif. 1976).
21. *San Antonio Independent School District* v. *Rodriguez*, 411 U.S. 1 (1973).
22. *Rose* v. *Council for Better Education*, 790 S.W.2d 186 (Ky. 1989). The details and issues of these decisions are discussed in Hanushek and Lindseth (2009).
23. As these court cases are ongoing, it is difficult to predict the future path. See Hanushek and Lindseth (2009).
24. This tabulation updates and extends the information in Hanushek and Lindseth (2009) to 2018.
25. Downes (1992, 2004), Hanushek and Somers (2001), Cullen and Loeb (2004), Duncombe and Johnston (2004), and Flanagan and Murray (2004). See also Greene and Trivitt (2008).
26. *Brown* v. *Board of Education*, 347 U.S. 483 (1954).
27. See Cascio et al. (2009) on the impact.
28. For a history and analysis of court interventions to desegregate schools, see Armor (1995).
29. See the history of court involvement in desegregation through the mid-1990s in Armor (1995).
30. The *Miliken* decision in Michigan restricted interdistrict remedies to situations where the surrounding districts were parties to the segregative acts (*Milliken* v. *Bradley*, 418 U.S. 717, 744–746 (1974)). This was extended in *Jenkins* (*Missouri* v. *Jenkins*, 515 U.S. 70 (1995)) where interdistrict funding in the case of Kansas City, Missouri, was eliminated because the other districts and the state were not party to the segregation itself. See Hanushek and Lindseth (2009).
31. See Coleman et al. (1975), Clotfelter (1976, 2001), Fairlie and Resch (2002), Boustan (2010), Cascio and Lewis (2012), and Rivkin (2016).
32. See Linn and Welner (2007) for a discussion of various aspects of this.
33. U.S. Department of Education (2019).
34. Internationally, there is evidence that school performance is greater when local schools are given more autonomy in decision making (Hanushek et al., 2013).
35. The overall welfare implications in Hanushek and Yilmaz (2007a, 2007c) depend on the specification and parametrization of the model. Based on a model modified from the one in Hanushek and Yilmaz (2007a), Gong and Leung (2020) find that whether school consolidation has a positive effect on welfare depends on how extreme the sorting pattern is in the baseline.
36. Note that these shares of students with choice do not include a number of districts that allow or require students to choose among the traditional public schools. As all students stay within the traditional public schools, there is no pressure on the school district to try to keep the students. This feature differs from the other forms of choice with the exception of magnet schools. Magnet schools offer specialty curricula (academic, the arts, or another vocational focus), and they offer an alternative to the traditional schools.
37. Evaluations of Milwaukee vouchers and others can be found in Rouse (1998) and Peterson et al. (2002). The DC voucher program in particular has been the subject of considerable political turmoil since it comes under the jurisdiction of the U.S. Congress. The most recent evaluation of DC

vouchers finds improvements in student reading achievement but not math achievement through the introduction of vouchers; see Wolf et al. (2009, 2013). For more general evidence on choice, see Egalite and Wolf (2016).
38. U.S. Department of Education (2019).
39. Armor (1995).
40. U.S. Department of Education (2019).
41. See Finn et al. (2000) on the early history. A description along with current data can be found at https://charterschoolcenter.ed.gov/what-charter-school#history, accessed July 3, 2020.
42. Center for Education Reform (2003).
43. Center for Education Reform (2002).
44. U.S. Department of Education (2019).
45. U.S. Department of Education (2019).
46. Some locations do, however, develop much better-performing charter schools. More specific analyses of New York City charter schools find consistently better performance of students in charter schools (CREDO, 2010; Hoxby et al., 2009). Importantly, because these studies use different methodologies while finding very similar results, the reliability of the findings is enhanced.
47. U.S. Department of Education (2019).

# REFERENCES

Alesina, Alberto, Edward Glaeser, and Bruce Sacerdote. 2001. "Why Doesn't the United States Have a European-Style Welfare State?" *Brookings Papers on Economic Activity*, no. 2: 187–254.

Alonso, William. 1964. *Location and Land Use*. Cambridge, MA: Harvard University Press.

Anas, Alex, and Ikki Kim. 1996. "General Equilibrium Models of Polycentric Urban Land Use with Endogenous Congestion and Job Agglomeration." *Journal of Urban Economics* 40, no. 2 (September): 232–256.

Angrist, Joshua D., and Kevin Lang. 2004. "Does School Integration Generate Peer Effects? Evidence from Boston's Metco Program." *American Economic Review* 94, no. 5 (December): 1613–1634.

Armor, David J. 1995. *Forced Justice: School Desegregation and the Law*. New York: Oxford University Press.

Baude, Patrick L., Marcus Casey, Eric A. Hanushek, Gregory R. Phelan, and Steven G. Rivkin. 2020. "The Evolution of Charter School Quality." *Economica* 87, no. 345 (January): 158–189.

Baum-Snow, Nathaniel. 2007. "Did Highways Cause Suburbanization?" *Quarterly Journal of Economics* 122, no. 2 (May): 775–805.

Baum-Snow, Nathaniel, and Daniel Hartley. 2020. "Accounting for Central Neighborhood Change, 1980–2010." *Journal of Urban Economics* 117 (May): 103228.

Baum-Snow, Nathaniel, and Byron Lutz. 2008. "School Desegregation, School Choice and Changes in Residential Location Patterns by Race." Finance and Economics Discussion Series 2008-57. Washington, DC: Federal Reserve Board (August).

Baum-Snow, Nathaniel, and Byron F. Lutz. 2011. "School Desegregation, School Choice, and Changes in Residential Location Patterns by Race." *American Economic Review* 101, no. 7 (December): 3019–3046.

Bayer, Patrick, and Robert McMillan. 2012. "Tiebout Sorting and Neighborhood Stratification." *Journal of Public Economics* 96, no. 11 (December): 1129–1143.

Bayer, Patrick, Fernando Ferreira, and Robert McMillan. 2007a. "A Unified Framework for Measuring Preferences for Schools and Neighborhoods." *Journal of Political Economy* 115, no. 4 (August): 588–638.

Bayer, Patrick, Fernando Ferreira, and Robert McMillan. 2007b. "A Unified Framework for Measuring Preferences for Schools and Neighborhoods." *Journal of Political Economy* 115, no. 4 (August): 588–638.

Bayer, Patrick, Robert McMillan, Alvin Murphy, and Christopher Timmins. 2016. "A Dynamic Model of Demand for Houses and Neighborhoods." *Econometrica* 84, no. 3 (May): 893–942.

Black, Sandra E. 1999. "Do Better Schools Matter? Parental Valuation of Elementary Education." *Quarterly Journal of Economics* 114, no. 2 (May): 577–599.

Black, Sandra E., and Stephen Machin. 2011. "Housing Valuations of School Performance." In *Handbook of the Economics of Education*, edited by Stephen Machin Eric A. Hanushek and Ludger Woessmann. New York: Elsevier: 485–519.

Boadway, Robin, and Jean-François Tremblay. 2012. "Reassessment of the Tiebout Model." *Journal of Public Economics* 96, no. 11 (December): 1063–1078.

Borland, Melvin V., and Roy M. Howsen. 1992. "Student Academic Achievement and the Degree of Market Concentration in Education." *Economics of Education Review* 11, no. 1 (March): 31–39.

Boustan, Leah P. 2010. "Was Postwar Suburbanization 'White Flight'? Evidence from the Black Migration." *Quarterly Journal of Economics* 125, no. 1 (February): 417–443.

Boustan, Leah P., and Robert A. Margo. 2013. "A Silver Lining to White Flight? White Suburbanization and African-American Homeownership, 1940–1980." *Journal of Urban Economics* 78 (November): 71–80.

Boustan, Leah p., and Allison Shertzer. 2013. "Population Trends as a Counterweight to Central City Decline, 1950–2000." *Demography* 50, no. 1 (February): 125–147.

Brasington, David M. 1999. "Joint Provision of Public Goods: The Consolidation of School Districts." *Journal of Public Economics* 73, no. 3 (September): 373–393.

Brooks, Leah, and Byron Lutz. 2016. "From Today's City to Tomorrow's City: An Empirical Investigation of Urban Land Assembly." *American Economic Journal: Economic Policy* 8, no. 3 (August): 69–105.

Brueckner, Jan K. 1979. "Property Values, Local Public Expenditure and Economic Efficiency." *Journal of Public Economics* 11, no. 2 (March): 223–245.

Brueckner, Jan K. 1987. "The Structure of Urban Equilibria: A Unified Treatment of the Muth-Mills Model." In *Handbook of Regional and Urban Economics*, edited by Edwin S. Mills. Amsterdam: North-Holland: 821–845.

Brueckner, Jan K., and Stuart S. Rosenthal. 2009. "Gentrification and Neighborhood Housing Cycles: Will America's Future Downtowns Be Rich?" *Review of Economics and Statistics* 91, no. 4 (November): 725–743.

Brueckner, Jan K., Jacques-François Thisse, and Yves Zenou. 1999. "Why Is Central Paris Rich and Downtown Detroit Poor? An Amenity-Based Theory." *European Economic Review* 43, no. 1 (January): 91–107.

Brulhart, Marius, Sam Bucovetsky, and Kurt Schmidheiny. 2015. "Taxes in Cities: Interdependence, Asymmetry, and Agglomeration." In *Handbook of Regional and Urban Economics*, edited by Gilles Duranton, Vernon Henderson, and William Strange. Amsterdam: North Holland: 1123–1196.

Caetano, Gregorio. 2019. "Neighborhood Sorting and the Value of Public School Quality." *Journal of Urban Economics* 114 (November): 103193.

Calabrese, Stephen, Dennis Epple, Thomas Romer, and Holger Sieg. 2006. "Local Public Good Provision: Voting, Peer Effects, and Mobility." *Journal of Public Economics* 90, no. 6–7: 959–981.

Card, David, and A. Abigail Payne. 2002. "School Finance Reform, the Distribution of School Spending, and the Distribution of SAT Scores." *Journal of Public Economics* 83, no. 1 (January): 49–82.

Cascio, Elizabeth U., and Ethan G. Lewis. 2012. "Cracks in the Melting Pot: Immigration, School Choice, and Segregation." *American Economic Journal: Economic Policy* 4, no. 3: 91–117.

Cascio, Elizabeth, Nora Gordon, Ethan Lewis, and Sarah Reber. 2009. "Paying for Progress: Conditional Grants and the Desegregation of Southern Schools." NBER WP14869. Cambridge, MA: National Bureau of Economic Research (April).

Center for Education Reform. 2002. *Charter School Closures: The Opportunity for Accountability*. Washington, DC: Center for Education Reform.

Center for Education Reform. 2003. *Charter School Laws across the States: Ranking Score Card and Legislative Profiles*. Washington, DC: Center for Education Reform (January).

Chubb, John E., and Terry M. Moe. 1990. *Politics, Markets and America's Schools*. Washington, DC: Brookings Institution.

Clark, David E., and William E. Herrin. 2000. "The Impact of Public School Attributes on Home Sale Prices in California." *Growth and Change* 31, no. 3 (Summer): 385–407.

Clark, Melissa. 2003. "Education Reform, Redistribution, and Student Achievement: Evidence from the Kentucky Education Reform Act." Mimeo, Mathematica Policy Research (October).

Clotfelter, Charles T. 1976. "School Desegregation, 'Tipping,' and Private School Enrollment." *Journal of Human Resources* 22, no. 1 (Winter): 29–50.

Clotfelter, Charles T. 2001. "Are Whites Still Fleeing? Racial Patterns and Enrollment Shifts in Urban Public Schools." *Journal of Policy Analysis and Management* 20, no. 2 (Spring): 199–221.

Clotfelter, Charles T. 2004. *After Brown: The Rise and Retreat of School Desegregation.* Princeton, NJ: Princeton University Press.

Coleman, James S., Sara D. Kelley, and John A. Moore. 1975. "Trends in School Integration, 1968–73." Paper 722-03-01. Washington, DC: Urban Institute.

Coons, John E., William H. Clune, and Stephen D. Sugarman. 1970. *Private Wealth and Public Education.* Cambridge, MA: Belknap Press of Harvard University Press.

Cordes, Sarah A. 2018. "In Pursuit of the Common Good: The Spillover Effects of Charter Schools on Public School Students in New York City." *Education Finance and Policy* 13, no. 4: 484–512.

Couture, Victor, and Jessie Handbury. 2019. "Urban Revival in America, 2000 to 2010." NBER Working Paper Series No. 24084. Cambridge, MA: National Bureau of Economic Research (November).

CREDO. 2009. *Multiple Choice: Charter School Performance in 16 States.* Stanford, CA: Center for Research on Education Outcomes, Stanford University.

CREDO. 2010. *Charter School Performance in New York City.* Stanford, CA: Center for Research on Education Outcomes, Stanford University.

CREDO. 2013. *National Charter School Study 2013.* Stanford, CA: Center for Research on Education Outcomes, Stanford University.

CREDO. 2015. *Urban Charter School Study: Report on 41 Regions.* Stanford, CA: Center for Research on Educational Outcomes.

Cullen, Julie B., and Steven D. Levitt. 1999. "Crime, Urban Flight, and the Consequences for Cities." *Review of Economics and Statistics* 81, no. 2 (May): 159–169.

Cullen, Julie B., and Susanna Loeb. 2004. "School Finance Reform in Michigan: Evaluating Proposal A." In *Helping Children Left Behind: State Aid and the Pursuit of Educational Equity*, edited by John Yinger. Cambridge, MA: MIT Press: 215–249.

Davidoff, Thomas. 2005. "Income Sorting: Measurement and Decomposition." *Journal of Urban Economics* 58, no. 2 (September): 289–303.

de Bartolome, Charles A.M. 1997. "What Determines State Aid to School Districts? A Positive Model of Foundation Aid as Redistribution." *Journal of Policy Analysis and Management* 16, no. 1 (Winter): 32–47.

de Bartolome, Charles A.M., and Stephen L. Ross. 2003. "Equilibria with Local Governments and Commuting: Income Sorting vs Income Mixing." *Journal of Urban Economics* 54: 1–20.

Dhar, Paramita, and Stephen L. Ross. 2012. "School District Quality and Property Values: Examining Differences along School District Boundaries." *Journal of Urban Economics* 71, no. 1 (January): 18–25.

Downes, Thomas A. 1992. "Evaluating the Impact of School Finance Reform on the Provision of Public Education: The California Case." *National Tax Journal* 45, no. 4 (December): 405–419.

Downes, Thomas A. 2004. "School Finance Reform and School Quality: Lessons from Vermont." In *Helping Children Left Behind: State Aid and the Pursuit of Educational Equity*, edited by John Yinger. Cambridge, MA: MIT Press: 284–313.

Downes, Thomas A., and Jeffrey E. Zabel. 2002. "The Impact of School Characteristics on House Prices: Chicago 1987–1991." *Journal of Urban Economics* 52, no. 1 (July): 1–25.

Duncombe, William, and Jocelyn M. Johnston. 2004. "The Impacts of School Finance Reform in Kansas: Equity Is in the Eye of the Beholder." In *Helping Children Left Behind: State Aid and the Pursuit of Educational Equity*, edited by John Yinger. Cambridge, MA: MIT Press: 148–193.

Duncombe, William, and John Yinger. 2005. "Does School District Consolidation Cut Costs?" Center for Policy Research, Maxwell School Syracuse University (November).

Egalite, Anna J., and Patrick J. Wolf. 2016. "A Review of the Empirical Research on Private School Choice." *Peabody Journal of Education* 91, no. 4 (2016/08/07): 441–454.

Ellickson, Bryan. 1971. "Jurisdictional Fragmentation and Residential Choice." *American Economic Review* 61, no. 2 (May): 334–339.

Epple, Dennis, and Thomas Nechyba. 2004. "Fiscal Decentralization." In *Handbook of Regional and Urban Economics*, edited by J. Vernon Henderson and Jacques-François Thisse. Amsterdam: Elsevier: 2423–2480.

Epple, Dennis, and Glenn J. Platt. 1998. "Equilibrium and Local Redistribution in an Urban Economy When Households Differ in both Preferences and Incomes." *Journal of Urban Economics* 43, no. 1 (January): 23–51.

Epple, Dennis, and Richard E. Romano. 1996. "Ends against the Middle: Determinating Public Service Provision When There Are Private Alternatives." *Journal of Public Economics* 62, no. 3 (November): 297–325.

Epple, Dennis, and Thomas Romer. 1991. "Mobility and Redistribution." *Journal of Political Economy* 99: 828–858.

Epple, Dennis, and Holger Sieg. 1999. "Estimating Equilibrium Models of Local Jurisdictions." *Journal of Political Economy* 107, no. 4 (August): 645–681.

Epple, Dennis, Radu Filimon, and Thomas Romer. 1983. "Housing, Voting, and Moving: Equilibrium in a Model of Local Public Goods with Multiple Jurisdictions." In *Research in Urban Economics*, edited by J.V. Henderson. Greenwich, CT: Jai Press: 59–90.

Epple, Dennis, Radu Filimon, and Thomas Romer. 1984. "Equilibrium among Local Jurisdictions: Toward an Integrated Treatment of Voting and Residential Choice." *Journal of Public Economics* 24, no. 3 (August): 281–308.

Epple, Dennis, Radu Filimon, and Thomas Romer. 1993. "Existence of Voting and Housing Equilibrium in a System of Communities with Property Taxes." *Regional Science and Urban Economics* 23: 585–610.

Epple, Dennis, Brett Gordon, and Holger Sieg. 2010. "Drs. Muth and Mills Meet Dr. Tiebout: Integrating Location-Specific Amenities into Multi-Community Equilibrium Models." *Journal of Regional Science* 50, no. 1 (February): 381–400.

Fairlie, Robert W., and Alexandra M Resch. 2002. "Is There 'White Flight' into Private Schools? Evidence from the National Educational Longitudinal Survey." *Review of Economics and Statistics* 84, no. 1 (February): 21–33.

Fernández, Raquel, and Richard Rogerson. 1995. "On the Political Economy of Education Subsidies." *Review of Economic Studies* 62, no. 2: 249–262.

Fernández, Raquel, and Richard Rogerson. 1996. "Income Distribution, Communities, and the Quality of Public Education." *Quarterly Journal of Economics* 111, no. 1 (February): 135–164.

Fernández, Raquel, and Richard Rogerson. 1998. "Public Education and Income Distribution: A Dynamic Quantitative Evaluation of Education-Finance Reform." *American Economic Review* 88, no. 4 (September): 813–833.

Fernández, Raquel, and Richard Rogerson. 2003. "Equity and Resources: An Analysis of Education Finance Systems." *Journal of Political Economy* 111, no. 4 (August): 858–897.

Ferreyra, Maria Marta. 2007. "Estimating the Effects of Private School Vouchers in Multidistrict Economies." *American Economic Review* 97, no. 3: 789–817.

Ferreyra, Maria Marta, and Grigory Kosenok. 2018. "Charter School Entry and School Choice: The Case of Washington, D.C." *Journal of Public Economics* 159(March): 160–182.

Figlio, David N., and Maurice E. Lucas. 2004. "What's in a Grade? School Report Cards and the Housing Market." *American Economic Review* 94, no. 3 (June): 591–604.

Finn, Chester E., Jr., Bruno V. Manno, and Gregg Vanourek. 2000. *Charter Schools in Action: Renewing Public Education*. Princeton, NJ: Princeton University Press.

Fischel, William A. 1989. "Did Serrano cause Proposition 13?" *National Tax Journal* 42 (December): 465–474.

Fischel, William A. 2006a. "The Courts and Public School Finance: Judge-Made Centralization and Economic Research." In *Handbook of the Economics of Education*, edited by Eric A. Hanushek and Finis Welch. Amsterdam: North Holland: 1277–1325.

Fischel, William A., ed. 2006b. *The Tiebout Model at Fifty: Essays in Public Economics in Honor of Wallace Oates*. Cambridge, MA: Lincoln Institute of Land Policy.

Flanagan, Ann E., and Sheila E. Murray. 2004. "A Decade of Reform: The Impact of School Reform in Kentucky." In *Helping Children Left Behind: State Aid and the Pursuit of Educational Equity*, edited by John Yinger. Cambridge, MA: MIT Press: 195–214.

Friedman, Milton. 1962. *Capitalism and Freedom*. Chicago, IL: University of Chicago Press.
Friedman, Milton, and Rose Friedman. 1980. *Free to Choose: A Personal Statement*. San Diego, CA: Harcourt.
Fujita, Masahisa. 1989. *Urban Economic Theory: Land Use and City Size*. New York: Cambridge University Press.
Fujita, Masahisa, and Hideaki Ogawa. 1982. "Multiple Equilibria and Structural Transition of Non-Monocentric Urban Configurations." *Regional Science and Urban Economics* 12, no. 2 (May): 161–196.
Gamper-Rabindran, Shanti, and Christopher Timmins. 2011. "Hazardous Waste Cleanup, Neighborhood Gentrification, and Environmental Justice: Evidence from Restricted Access Census Block Data." *American Economic Review* 101, no. 3 (May): 620–624.
Garcia-López, Miquel-Àngel. 2010. "Population Suburbanization in Barcelona, 1991–2005: Is Its Spatial Structure Changing?" *Journal of Housing Economics* 19, no. 2 (June): 119–132.
Gibbons, Stephen, and Stephen Machin. 2008. "Valuing School Quality, Better Transport, and Lower Crime: Evidence from House Prices." *Oxford Review of Economic Policy* 24, no. 1 (March): 99–119.
Glaeser, Edward l., and Joseph Gyourko. 2005. "Urban Decline and Durable Housing." *Journal of Political Economy* 113, no. 2 (April): 345–375.
Glaeser, Edward L., and Matthew E. Kahn. 2001. "Decentralized Employment and the Transformation of the American City." In *Brookings-Wharton Papers on Urban Affairs, 2001*, edited by William G. Gale and Janet Rothenberg Pack. Washington, DC: Brookings: 1–47.
Glaeser, Edward L., and Matthew E. Kahn. 2004. "Sprawl and Urban Growth." In *Handbook of Regional and Urban Economics*, edited by J. Vernon Henderson and Jacques-François Thisse. Amsterdam: Elsevier: 2481–2527.
Glaeser, Edward L., Matthew E. Kahn, and Jordan Rappaport. 2008. "Why Do the Poor Live in Cities? The Role of Public Transportation." *Journal of Urban Economics* 63, no. 1 (January): 1–24.
Glomm, Gerhard, and B. Ravikumar. 1992. "Public vs. Private Investment in Human Capital: Endogenous Growth and Income Inequality." *Journal of Political Economy* 100, no. 4 (August): 818–834.
Glomm, Gerhard, and B. Ravikumar. 1998. "Opting out of Publicly Provided Services: A Majority Voting Result." *Social Choice and Welfare* 15: 187–199.
Glomm, Gerhard, B. Ravikumar, and Ioana C. Schiopu. 2011. "The Political Economy of Education Funding." In *Handbook of the Economics of Education*, Vol. 4, edited by Eric A. Hanushek, Stephen Machin, and Ludger Woessmann. Amsterdam: North Holland: 615–680.
Gong, Yifan, and Charles Ka Yui Leung. 2020. "When Education Policy and Housing Policy Interact: Can They Correct for the Externalities?" *Journal of Housing Economics* 50 (December): 101732.
González-Pampillón, Nicolás, Jordi Jofre-Monseny, and Elisabet Viladecans-Marsal. 2019. "Can Urban Renewal Policies Reverse Neighborhood Ethnic Dynamics?" *Journal of Economic Geography* 20, no. 2: 419–457.
Gordon, Nora, and Brian Knight. 2009. "A Spatial Merger Estimator with an Application to School District Consolidation." *Journal of Public Economics* 93, no. 5–6: 752–765.
Greene, Jay P., and Julie R. Trivitt. 2008. "Can Judges Improve Academic Achievement?" *Peabody Journal of Education* 83, no. 2 (April): 224–237.
Guryan, Jonathan. 2004. "Desegregation and Black Dropout Rates." *American Economic Review* 94, no. 4 (September): 919–943.
Hanushek, Eric A. 2003. "The Failure of Input-Based Schooling Policies." *Economic Journal* 113, no. 485 (February): F64–F98.
Hanushek, Eric A., and Alfred A. Lindseth. 2009. *Schoolhouses, Courthouses, and Statehouses: Solving the Funding-Achievement Puzzle in America's Public Schools*. Princeton, NJ: Princeton University Press.
Hanushek, Eric A., and Margaret E. Raymond. 2005. "Does School Accountability Lead to Improved Student Performance?" *Journal of Policy Analysis and Management* 24, no. 2 (Spring): 297–327.
Hanushek, Eric A., and Steven G. Rivkin. 2009. "Harming the Best: How Schools Affect the Black-White Achievement Gap." *Journal of Policy Analysis and Management* 28, no. 3 (Summer): 366–393.
Hanushek, Eric A., and Julie A. Somers. 2001. "Schooling, Inequality, and the Impact of Government." In *The Causes and Consequences of Increasing Inequality*, edited by Finis Welch. Chicago, IL: University of Chicago Press: 169–199.

Hanushek, Eric A., and Kuzey Yilmaz. 2007a. "The Complementarity of Tiebout and Alonso." *Journal of Housing Economics* 16(2), no. 2 (June): 243–261.

Hanushek, Eric A., and Kuzey Yilmaz. 2007b. "Schools and Location: Tiebout, Alonso, and Government Policy." National Bureau of Economic Research Working Paper 12960. Cambridge, MA: NBER (March).

Hanushek, Eric A., and Kuzey Yilmaz. 2007c. "Schools and Location: Tiebout, Alonso, and Government Policy." *Journal of Economic Theory* 15, no. 6: 829–855.

Hanushek, Eric A., and Kuzey Yilmaz. 2011. "Urban Education, Location, and Opportunity in the United States." In *Oxford Handbook of Urban Economics and Planning*, edited by Nancy Brooks, Kieran Donaghy, and Gerrit-Jan Knaap. Oxford: Oxford University Press: 583–615.

Hanushek, Eric A., and Kuzey Yilmaz. 2013. "Schools and Location: Tiebout, Alonso, and Governmental Finance Policy." *Journal of Public Economic Theory* 15, no. 6 (December): 829–855.

Hanushek, Eric A., and Kuzey Yilmaz. 2015. "Land Use Controls, Fiscal Zoning, and the Local Provision of Education." *Public Finance Review* 43, no. 5 (September): 559–585.

Hanushek, Eric A., John F. Kain, Steve G. Rivkin, and Gregory F. Branch. 2007. "Charter School Quality and Parental Decision Making with School Choice." *Journal of Public Economics* 91, no. 5–6 (June): 823–848.

Hanushek, Eric A., John F. Kain, and Steve G. Rivkin. 2009. "New Evidence about *Brown v. Board of Education*: The Complex Effects of School Racial Composition on Achievement." *Journal of Labor Economics* 27, no. 3 (July): 349–383.

Hanushek, Eric A., Susanne Link, and Ludger Woessmann. 2013. "Does School Autonomy Make Sense Everywhere? Panel Estimates from PISA." *Journal of Development Economics* 104: 212–232.

Hanushek, Eric A., Sinan Sarpça, and Kuzey Yilmaz. 2011. "Private Schools and Residential Choices: Accessibility, Mobility, and Welfare." *B.E. Journal of Economic Analysis and Policy: Contributions* 11, no. 1: article 44.

Henderson, Vernon, and Eric Slade. 1993. "Development Games in Non-Monocentric Cities." *Journal of Urban Economics* 34, no. 2 (September): 207–229.

Hotchkiss, David, and Michelle J. White. 1993. "A Simulation Model of Decentralized Metropolitan Area." *Journal of Urban Economics* 34: 159–185.

Hoxby, Caroline M. 2000. "Does Competition among Public Schools Benefit Students and Taxpayers?" *American Economic Review* 90, no. 5 (December): 1209–1238.

Hoxby, Caroline M. 2001. "All School Finance Equalizations Are Not Created Equal." *Quarterly Journal of Economics* 116, no. 4 (November): 1189–1231.

Hoxby, Caroline M. 2007. "Does Competition among Public Schools Benefit Students and Taxpayers? Reply." *American Economic Review* 97, no. 5 (December): 2038–2055.

Hoxby, Caroline M., Sonali Murarka, and Jenny Kang. 2009. *How New York City's Charter Schools Affect Achivement*. Cambridge, MA: New York City Charter Schools Evaluation Project (September).

Imberman, Scott A., and Michael F. Lovenheim. 2016. "Does the Market Value Value-Added? Evidence from Housing Prices after a Public Release of School and Teacher Value-Added." *Journal of Urban Economics* 91 (2016/01/01/): 104–121.

Inman, Robert P. 1978. "Optimal Fiscal Reform of Metropolitan Schools." *American Economic Review* 68, no. 1 (March): 107–122.

Jackson, C. Kirabo, Rucker C. Johnson, and Claudia Persico. 2016. "The Effects of School Spending on Educational and Economic Outcomes: Evidence from School Finance Reforms." *Quarterly Journal of Economics* 131, no. 1 (February): 157–218.

Kain, John F. 1975. *Essays on Urban Spatial Structure*. Cambridge, MA: Ballinger Publishing.

Kane, Thomas J., Douglas O. Staiger, and Gavin Samms. 2003. "School Accountability Ratings and Housing Values [with Comments]." *Brookings-Wharton Papers on Urban Affairs*: 83–137.

Katz, Lawrence F., Jeffrey R. Kling, and Jeffrey B. Liebman. 2001. "Moving to Opportunity in Boston: Early Results of a Randomized Mobility Experiment." *Quarterly Journal of Economics* 116, no. 2 (May): 607–654.

Kenny, Lawrence W., and Amy B. Schmidt. 1994. "The Decline in the Number of School Districts in the U.S.: 1950–1980." *Public Choice* 79, no. 1–2 (April): 1–18.

Lafortune, Julien, Jesse Rothstein, and Diane Whitmore Schanzenbach. 2017. "School Finance Reform and the Distribution of Student Achievement: Online Appendix." *American Economic Journal: Applied Economics* 10, no. 2: 1–26.

LeRoy, Stephen F., and Jon Sonstelie. 1983. "Paradise Lost and Regained: Transportation Innovation, Income, and Residential Location." *Journal of Urban Economics* 13, no. 1 (January): 67–89.

Leung, Charles Ka Yui. 2004. "Macroeconomics and Housing: A Review of the Literature." *Journal of Housing Economics* 13, no. 4 (December): 249–267.

Leung, Charles Ka Yui, and Cho Yiu Joe Ng. 2019. "Macroeconomic Aspects of Housing." *Oxford Research Encyclopedias: Economics and Finance*.

Linn, Robert L., and Kevin G. Welner, eds. 2007. *Race-Conscious Policies for Assigning Students to Schools: Social Science Research and the Supreme Court Cases*. Washington, DC: National Academy of Education.

Lutz, Byron. 2005. " Post Brown vs. the Board of Education: The Effects of the End of Court-Ordered Desegregation." Finance and Economics Discussion Series 2005-64. Washington, DC: Federal Reserve Board.

Machin, Stephen. 2011. "Houses and Schools: Valuation of School Quality through the Housing Market." *Labour Economics* 18, no. 6 (December): 723–729.

Machin, Stephen, and Kjell G. Salvanes. 2016. "Valuing School Quality via a School Choice Reform." *Scandinavian Journal of Economics* 118, no. 1 (January): 3–24.

Margo, Robert A. 1992. "Explaining the Postwar Suburbanization of Population in the United States: The Role of Income." *Journal of Urban Economics* 31, no. 3 (May): 301–310.

Mastromonaco, Ralph. 2014. "A Dynamic General Equilibrium Analysis of School Quality Improvments." Mimeo.

McMillan, Melville, and Richard Carlson. 1977. "The Effects of Property Taxes and Local Public Services upon Residential Property Values in Small Wisconsin Cities." *American Journal of Agricultural Economics* 59, no. 1 (February): 81–87.

Mehta, Nirav. 2017. "Comptetition in Public School Districts: Charter School Entry, Student Sorting, and School Input Determination." *International Economic Review* 58, no. 4: 1089–1116.

Merrifield, John D. 2001. *The School Choice Wars*. Lqanham, MD: Rowman-Littlefield.

Mieszkowski, Peter, and Edwin S. Mills. 1993. "The Causes of Metropolitan Suburbanization." *Journal of Economic Perspectives* 7, no. 3: 135–147.

Mills, Edwin S. 1967. "An Aggregate Model of Resource Allocation in a Metropolitan Area." *American Economic Review* 57: 197–210.

Mills, Edwin S. 1972. *Studies in the Structure of the Urban Economy*. Washington, DC: Resources for the Future.

Mills, Edwin S. 1992. "The Measurement and Determinants of Suburbanization." *Journal of Urban Economics* 32, no. 3 (November): 377–387.

Mills, Edwin S., and Luan Sendé Lubuele. 1997. "Inner Cities." *Journal of Economic Literature* 35, no. 2 (June): 727–756.

Mills, Edwin S., and Richard Price. 1984. "Metropolitan Suburbanization and Central City Problems." *Journal of Urban Economics* 15, no. 1 (January): 1–17.

Murray, Sheila E., William N. Evans, and Robert M. Schwab. 1998. "Education-Finance Reform and the Distribution of Education Resources." *American Economic Review* 88, no. 4 (September): 789–812.

Muth, Richard F. 1969. *Cities and Housing: The Spatial Pattern of Urban Residential Land Use*. Chicago, IL: University of Chicago Press.

Nechyba, Thomas J. 1996. "A Computable General Equilibrium Model of Intergovernmental Aid." *Journal of Public Economics* 62: 363–397.

Nechyba, Thomas J. 1999. "School Finance Induced Migration Patterns: The Impact of Private School Vouchers." *Journal of Public Economic Theory* 1, no. 1: 5–50.

Nechyba, Thomas J. 2000. "Mobility, Targeting, and Private-School Vouchers." *American Economic Review* 90, no. 1 (March): 130–146.

Nechyba, Thomas J. 2003. "Centralization, Fiscal Federalism and Private School Attendance." *International Economic Review* 44, no. 1: 179–204.

Nechyba, Thomas J. 2006. "Income and Peer Sorting in Public and Private Schools." In *Handbook of the Economics of Education*, edited by Eric A. Hanushek and Finis Welch. Amsterdam: North Holland: 1327–1368.

Nechyba, Thomas J., and Randall P. Walsh. 2004. "Urban Sprawl." *Journal of Economic Perspectives* 18, no. 4 (Fall): 177–200.

Nguyen-Hoang, Phuong, and John Yinger. 2011. "The Capitalization of School Quality into House Values: A Review." *Journal of Housing Economics* 20, no. 1 (March): 30–48.

Oates, Wallace E. 1969. "The Effects of Property Taxes and Local Public Spending on Property Values: An Empirical Study of Tax Capitalization and the Tiebout Hypothesis." *Journal of Political Economy* 77, no. 6 (November/December): 957–971.

Owens, Raymond, III, Esteban Rossi-Hansberg, and Pierre-Daniel Sarte. 2020. "Rethinking Detroit." *American Economic Journal: Economic Policy* 12, no. 2 (May): 258–305.

Peterson, Paul E., William G. Howell, Patrick J. Wolf, and David E. Campbell. 2002. "School Vouchers: Results from Randomized Experiments." In *The Economics of School Choice*, edited by Caroline M. Hoxby. Chicago, IL: University of Chicago Press.

Pollakowski, Henry O. 1973. "The Effects of Property Taxes and Local Public Spending on Property Values: A Comment and Further Results." *Journal of Political Economy* 81, no. 4 (July–August): 994–1003.

Rangazas, Peter. 1995. "Vouchers in a Community Choice Model with Zoning." *Quarterly Review of Economics and Finance* 35, no. 1 (Spring): 15–39.

Reber, Sarah J. 2005. "Court-Ordered Desegregation: Successes and Failures Integrating American Schools since *Brown versus Board of Education*." *Journal of Human Resources* 40, no. 3 (Summer): 559–590.

Rivkin, Steve G. 2016. "Desegregation since the Coleman Report: Racial Composition of Schools and Student Learning." *Education Next* 16, no. 2 (Spring): 29–37.

Rivkin, Steven G., and Finis Welch. 2006. "Has School Desegregation Improved Academic and Economic Outcomes for Blacks?" In *Handbook of the Economics of Education*, edited by Eric A. Hanushek and Finis Welch. Amsterdam: North Holland: 1019–1049.

Rosenthal, Stuart S. 2008. "Old Homes, Externalities, and Poor Neighborhoods: A Model of Urban Decline and Renewal." *Journal of Urban Economics* 63, no. 3 (May): 816–840.

Rosenthal, Stuart S., and Stephen Ross. 2015. "Cycles and Persistence in the Economic Status of Neighborhoods and Cities." In *Handbook of Regional and Urban Economics*, edited by Gilles Duranton, Vernon Henderson, and William Strange. Amsterdam: North Holland: 1047–1120.

Ross, Stephen L., and John Yinger. 1995. "Comparative Static Analysis of Open Urban Models with a Full Labor Market and Suburban Employment." *Regional Science and Urban Economics* 25, no. 5 (October): 575–605.

Rothstein, Jesse. 2005. "Does Competition among Public Schools Benefit Students and Taxpayers? A Comment on Hoxby (2000)." NBER Working Paper 11215. Cambridge, MA: National Bureau of Economic Research.

Rothstein, Jesse. 2007. "Does Competition among Public Schools Benefit Students and Taxpayers? Comment." *American Economic Review* 97, no. 5 (December): 2026–2037.

Rouse, Cecilia Elena. 1998. "Private School Vouchers and Student Achievement: An Evaluation of the Milwaukee Parental Choice Program." *Quarterly Journal of Economics* 113, no. 2 (May): 553–602.

Seo, Youngme, and Robert A. Simons. 2009. "The Effect of School Quality on Residential Sales Price." *Journal of Real Estate Research* 31, no. 3 (June): 307–328.

Silva, Fabio, and Jon Sonstelie. 1995. "Did Serrano Cause a Decline in School Spending?" *National Tax Journal* 48, no. 2 (June): 199–215.

Singleton, John D. 2019. "Incentives and the Supply of Effective Charter Schools." *American Economic Review* 109, no. 7 (July): 2568–2612.

Sivitanidou, Rena, and William C. Wheaton. 1992. "Wage and Rent Capitalization in the Commercial Real Estate Market." *Journal of Urban Economics* 31, no. 2 (March): 206–229.

Straszheim, Mahlon. 1987. "The Theory of Urban Residential Location." In *Handbook of Regional and Urban Economics*, edited by Edwin S. Mills. Amsterdam: North-Holland: 717–757.

Su, Yichen. 2019. "The Rising Value of Time and the Origin of Urban Gentrification." Research Department Working Paper 1913. Dallas: Federal Reserve Bank of Dallas (October 31).

Sullivan, Arthur M. 1986. "A General Equilibrium Model with Agglomerative Economies and Decentralized Employment." *Journal of Urban Economics* 20, no. 1 (July): 55–75.
Tiebout, Charles M. 1956. "A Pure Theory of Local Expenditures." *Journal of Political Economy* 64, no. 5 (October): 416–424.
U.S. Department of Education. 2018. *Digest of Education Statistics, 2017*. Washington, DC: National Center for Education Statistics.
U.S. Department of Education. 2019. *Digest of Education Statistics 2018*. Washington, DC: National Center for Education Statistics.
Urquiola, Miguel. 2016. "Competition among Schools: Traditional Public and Private Schools." In *Handbook of the Economics of Education*, Vol. 5, edited by Eric A. Hanushek, Stephen Machin, and Ludger Woessmann. Amsterdam: North Holland: 209–237.
Walters, Christopher R. 2018. "The Demand for Effective Charter Schools." *Journal of Political Economy* 126, no. 6 (December): 2179–2223.
Weimer, David L., and Michael J. Wolkoff. 2001. "School Performance and Housing Values: Using Non-Contiguous District and Incorporation Boundaries to Identify School Effects." *National Tax Journal* 54, no. 2 (June): 231–253.
Welch, Finis, and Audrey Light. 1987. *New Evidence on School Desegregation*. Washington, DC: U.S. Commission on Civil Rights.
Wheaton, William C. 1977. "Income and Income Residence: An Analysis of Consumer Demand for Location." *American Economic Review* 67, no. 4 (September): 620–631.
White, Michelle J. 1976. "Firm Suburbanization and Urban Subcenters." *Journal of Urban Economics* 3: 323–343.
White, Michelle J. 1999. "Urban Areas with Decentralized Employment: Theory and Empirical Work." In *Handbook of Regional and Urban Economics*, edited by Paul Cheshire and Edwin S. Mills. Amsterdam: North Holland: 1375–1412.
Wolf, Patrick J., Babette Gutmann, Michael Puma, Brian Kisida, Lou Rizzo, and Nada Eissa. 2009. *Evaluation of the DC Opportunity Scholarship Program: Impacts after Three Years*. Washington, DC: Institute for Education Sciences (March).
Wolf, Patrick J., Brian Kisida, Babette Gutmann, Michael Puma, Nada Eissa, and Lou Rizzo. 2013. "School Vouchers and Student Outcomes: Experimental Evidence from Washington, DC." *Journal of Policy Analysis and Management* 32, no. 2 (April): 246–270.
Yilmaz, Kuzey. 2019. "The Role of Government in Regentrification." *Papers in Regional Science* 98, no. 1: 575–594.
Yilmaz, Kuzey. 2020. "States and School Finance." *Regional Science Policy and Practice* 12, no. 3 (June): 539–549.
Zahirovic-Herbert, Velma, and Geoffrey K. Turnbull. 2008. "School Quality, House Prices and Liquidity." *Journal of Real Estate Finance and Economics* 37, no. 2 (August): 113–130.
Zheng, Angela, and James Graham. 2020. "Public Education Inequality and Intergenerational Mobility." Available at http://dx.doi.org/10.2139/ssrn.3092714 (September 20).

# 6. Testing for real estate bubbles
*Eric Girardin and Roselyne Joyeux*

## 1 INTRODUCTION

Real estate prices matter. Housing is the major component of household wealth (Englund et al., 2002) and large changes in household consumption are often driven by sharp movements in house prices (Pavlidis et al., 2009). 'Macroeconomic' asset price bubbles are those which are large enough to impact macroeconomic variables (Filardo, 2004). In the aftermath of the Global Financial Crisis (Duca et al., 2010; Levitin and Wachter, 2012; Wachter, 2015), a consensus has been built (Duca et al., 2017) that the bursting of real estate bubbles contributes in a major way to persistent downturns (Herring and Wachter, 1999; Bordo and Haubrich 2012; Crowe et al., 2013), not simply amplifying them (like during the Great Depression; Green and Wachter, 2007), but even representing the initial impulse (as for the Great Recession associated with the Global Financial Crisis (Duca et al., 2010; Levitin and Wachter, 2012; Wachter, 2015) or for the East Asian crisis (Herring and Wachter, 1999)). Bubbles which generate systemic risk are especially harmful, in as much as they can substantially contribute to the collapse of the whole financial system (Brunnermeier and Oehmke, 2013; Brunnermeier et al., 2020). The aftermath of the burst of a bubble can be long lasting, as illustrated by Japan's lost decades associated with its 'asset market hangover' (Higgins and Osler, 1997). Housing bubbles in China (Deng et al., 2017; Glaeser et al., 2017) in the new millennium have also raised a lot of concern due in particular to the (often) large share of the real estate sector in aggregate growth. Accordingly, it is important to have access to methods enabling us to try and detect bubbles in real estate prices.

This chapter has three objectives. First, we will aim at determining theoretically how a potential bubble component can be extracted from real estate prices. Second, we will search for the appropriate strategy and methodology in order to econometrically detect the periods when such a component is present. Finally, we will aim at illustrating the applicability of such a strategy for a major country's housing market – Japan's.

House prices contain a rational bubble if investors are willing to pay more for the real estate unit than they know is justified by the value of the discounted stream of rents because they expect to be able to sell the unit at an even higher price in the future. Given the abundance of research dealing with bubbles in financial assets, it is tempting to simply transpose its methods to the real estate market. However, real estate presents specific features as an asset; specificities which need to be carefully accounted for when trying to identify a possible bubble component in real estate prices. Real estate assets differ from stocks since their supply is endogenous, short-selling is very difficult and transaction costs are high. Houses, flats, offices, logistics and commercial premises are very heterogenous in terms of their characteristics, location and unobserved costs. Rents differ sharply from dividends in many dimensions. The market for real estate is both a market for real estate assets and a market for the physical use of real estate.

Stylized facts about the real estate markets have been established and rationalized by Glaeser and Nathanson (2015). The theory of asset market bubbles was surveyed by Scherbina and Schlusche (2014) and matching reviews for real estate market bubbles were provided by Glaeser and Nathanson (2015) and Scherbina and Schlusche (2012). Detecting bubbles in asset markets has been an ongoing challenge, which empirical methods have for long been unable to meet. We will focus here on econometric tests of real estate bubbles. The early econometric methods, as surveyed by Gurkanyak (2008), exclusively aimed at testing for the presence of rational bubbles in the context of the present value model (see West, 1988b, and Camerer, 1999, on the earlier literature). Such methods initially led to four streams of research, from the variance bounds tests of Shiller (1981) and LeRoy and Porter (1981) and West's tests of bubbles (1987, 1988a) to integration/cointegration-based tests (Diba and Grossman, 1988a, 1988b) and Evans's (1991) criticism of this approach and tests of collapsing bubbles. These, and further tests up to the early 2010s, were surveyed by Homm and Breitung (2012). Gurkanyak (2008) also discusses intrinsic bubbles, their econometric detection and related models of regime-switching fundamentals.[1]

The history of sharp rises in real estate prices, either buildings or land, is rich and picturesque (Shiller, 2007; Glaeser, 2013). However, there is a long way between such observations and their characterization as real estate bubbles. Many economists conceptualize bubbles as situations in which the real estate asset price surpasses the asset's fundamental value, and the asset becomes overvalued. Prices serve as signals of market conditions, derived by demand and supply. The increase in price signals a shortage of supply; eventually, supply increases, the price drops and there is a new equilibrium in price and quantity. However, in times of bubbles, prices may not serve as good signals and, thus, may not reflect market conditions or changes in the underlying value of the asset. In other words, the bubble sends out a signal that the asset is more valuable than it actually is. The difficulty faced by this approach is that the fundamental value of a real estate asset is not easy to measure. Generally, we think of the fundamental value of a real estate asset as the expectation of a stream of payments in the form of rents to the owner over time, discounted to present value. Accordingly, to evaluate the presence of a bubble, we should compare the price of a real estate asset to such a measure of the fundamental value. The comparison is typically between real estate price indexes and indexes on the amount charged to rent a similar real estate unit. If rents are also rising sharply, ensuring reasonable movements in the price-to-rent ratio, at first sight there would not seem any reason to conclude that a bubble is present. However, periods of explosive behaviour in price-to-rent ratios are not necessarily bubbles since this ratio should be matched against the relative cost of buying versus renting. The price of a house is not the only determinant of the cost of owning it; rising house prices do not necessarily indicate that homeownership has become more expensive relative to renting, but may reflect the fact that something has changed in the fundamental value of the house. The correct measure to use, as a comparison for rents, is the imputed annual rental cost of owning a home, a variant of the 'user cost', which is particularly difficult to measure.

Accordingly filtering out the price-to-rent ratio from movements in user cost should enable us to assess whether a real estate asset is overvalued. However, such a diagnostic of overvaluation would only correspond to the detection of a bubble if the deviation of the price-to-rent ratio from user cost proved to be explosive. This implies that, to empirically detect the presence of a bubble, we need first to decompose the price-to-rent ratio into a fundamental and a non-fundamental component. However, this non-fundamental component is unobservable. Existing literature thus suggests first estimating the fundamental component. Then one should assess the explosive character of this non-fundamental component; a component computed as the difference between the log price-to-rent ratio and the fundamental component.

We will present methodologies applied to test for the presence of rational bubbles in real estate markets. The most common bubble detection technique, proposed by Phillips, Shi and Yu (PSY) (2015a, 2015b) will enable us to detect the origination and termination dates of bubbles by testing for the presence of mildly explosive roots. Tests for real estate bubbles generally start with proxies of the bubble component, such as the price-to-rent ratio. A deeper analysis involves the most recent techniques proceeding in two steps: first filtering out the effect of fundamentals from the price-to-rent ratio; and then testing for the possibly mildly explosive character of the residual, non-fundamental, component.

Different methods can be used to decompose the price-to-rent ratio into its fundamental and non-fundamental components. They all require unbiased forecasts of future streams of rent growth and other relevant fundamentals. Vector-autoregressive (VAR) models can be used to forecast fundamental variables such as rent growth and interest rate, as in Campbell et al. (2009). Their approach requires the estimation of a VAR model, including the specification of the fundamentals in a structural form, the availability of house prices and rents in dollar value rather than as indexes and the calibration of some unknown parameters. Phillips and Shi's (2021) new approach only requires the estimation of a single-equation reduced-form model, which can be implemented with house price and rent indexes. We use their method and estimate the model with the instrumental variable method (IVX), as proposed by Magdalinos and Phillips (2009), where the explanatory variables are highly persistent and endogenous, and which has been shown to be valid by Kostakis et al. (2015). We also rely on a further extension of this instrumental-variable estimation suggested by Yang et al. (2020) to the case where the error terms are autocorrelated and heteroskedastic, and the regressors are persistent.

Our illustration of the use of the two-step method in the case of the housing market in Japan over the last four decades will show to what extent it is important to conduct a prior filtering of the price-to-rent ratio from the influence of fundamentals before testing for the presence of explosive bubbles. Indeed, we need to determine whether this enables researchers both to avoid misleading signals about spurious bubbles and to detect bubbles which may be hidden from observers who would exclusively focus on the raw price-to-rent ratio.

This chapter makes three contributions. First, we provide a review of the recent literature on bubble testing in real estate markets. Second, starting from a theoretical overview of real estate assets and how they differ from financial assets, we assess the latest econometric methodology to detect real estate bubbles. Third, in the case of Japan's house prices, we focus on a two-step econometric strategy to first filter out the fundamental component using the IVX-AR method based on a single-equation model. We then test for the possible explosive character of the (non-fundamental) residual.

The remainder of this chapter is structured as follows. In Section 2 we will consider what to search for when enquiring about the presence of bubbles in real estate markets. After reviewing the multiple ways in which real estate assets differ from financial assets, we will examine theoretically how fundamentals, associated with the user costs of housing, can be filtered out from the price-to-rent ratio in order to identify a residual component which can be a candidate to qualify as a bubble. Section 3 will present the two-step matching econometric strategy which first operates such a filtering out based on a single-equation model and then tests for the possible explosive character of the (non-fundamental) residual. We will illustrate the empirical implementation of such a two-step procedure in the case of Japan in Section 4, contrasting it with bubble detection on the raw price-to-rent ratio. Finally, Section 5 will conclude.

## 2 WHAT TO SEARCH FOR?

Detecting bubbles in financial assets is no easy task. However, the complexity of the search for bubbles in the real estate markets is compounded by the fact that such markets differ from financial, in particular stock, markets in multiple ways, as we will explain first. At a theoretical level, as reviewed next, diverse mechanisms have been proposed to rationalize booms and busts in real estate markets as well as macroeconomic variables. In an operational way, attempts to detect the presence of bubbles in real estate markets have relied on the prior need to ascertain fundamentals in order to detect departure of prices from their level implied by the rational valuation formula, and to determine to what extent such departures are explosive.

### 2.1 Real Estate versus Financial Assets

Five dimensions of the specificity of the real estate market need to be emphasized: the endogeneity of supply with respect to demand movements; the lack of short-selling and the high level of transaction costs, which hamper contrarian strategies in front of sharply rising real estate prices; the dual nature of real estate markets; the heterogeneity of housing units; and the differences between rents and dividends.

#### 2.1.1 Endogenous supply
Endogenous supply[2] of new real estate assets, which can sharply dampen price booms, makes the latter assets very different from most financial assets (Shiller, 2007), the supply of which is usually treated as exogenous, except in special circumstances (internet start-ups; see Hall, 2003).

Two theories explain elastic price booms. The lag in delivery of new supply due to construction time implies that delivery can take place at the end of a price boom, accelerating the bust (Glaeser, 2013), which is often ignored by speculators; but this depends heavily on the share of such new supply in the existing housing stock, a share which can be small in markets like the US. In the alternative theory (Nathanson and Zwick, 2017), elastic price booms typically take place in areas with a currently elastic, but soon to be inelastic, supply (Glaeser and Nathanson, 2015).

#### 2.1.2 Lack of short-selling and high transaction costs
Limits of arbitrage inherent to real estate assets, involving in particular the extreme difficulty of short-selling associated with asset heterogeneity, may be a source of deviation from the fundamental value (as in Schleifer and Vishny, 1997, general analysis). In the stock market, for example, with short-selling, people who think the market is overpriced and headed for a fall can borrow shares and sell them at the current high futures price (Miller, 1977). If share prices do indeed fall later, they can buy back the shares at a lower price and repay the loan, with a profit. Short-selling can be one of the forces preventing bubble formation or at least mitigating their rise, but it is not feasible to place such negative bets in the housing market. Indeed, borrowing a house and selling it while committing to buying it back subsequently in

order to pay back the loan, is not common practice. As expressed by Shiller in a blunt way: 'Without short-sellers, there is nothing to stop a group of ignorant investors – who get some ill-conceived idea that a certain investment is just terrific – from bidding up prices to extravagant levels. In the housing market, that poses an enormous problem' (Shiller, 2015).

The difficulty of short-selling in the housing market is especially enhanced by the absence of interchangeability (Nathanson and Zwick, 2017). Given the very large heterogeneity among houses, shorting is unlikely, since it would imply borrowing a house from someone else, and selling it with a promise to buy it back later. Besides, simple arbitrage, such as postponing purchase, may be difficult to implement in practice since this generates extra risk in the household's portfolio (Glaeser and Gyourko, 2009).

It may seem that an investor convinced of the overvaluation of house prices could short residential real estate investment trusts (REITs) which both invest in residential properties and are exchange traded. However, far from being consistently correlated with housing prices, REIT prices tend to behave like stock prices, and REITs are substantially different from houses. An alternative means for professional investors to profit from correctly forecasting home price declines, widely used during the Global Financial Crisis, relies on the use of mortgage derivatives such as collateralized debt obligations. However, there is a big difference between mortgages and homes, and such investors have in no way managed to prevent the emerging housing bubble to grow out of proportion.

In addition, transaction costs in real estate markets are many times higher than in stock markets (Case and Shiller, 2004), hampering arbitrage by investors who could pursue a contrarian strategy during periods with 'excessive' real estate price rises.

### 2.1.3 Dual nature of real estate markets

Another way in which the real estate market differs from other asset markets is due to its duality. It is both a market for real estate assets and a market for the physical use of real estate. Real estate, comprising the value of all outstanding buildings and land (built or vacant), represents the largest single component of a nation's wealth, as well as, in dynamic terms, the largest component of national investment (DiPasquale and Wheaton, 1996). The rationale for distinguishing real estate as an asset and as space becomes apparent when owners do not occupy the buildings which they own. The rent for space in the market for property use is driven by the needs of tenants, as well as by the type and quality of available buildings. At the same time, buildings bought and sold between investors in the capital market determine the asset price of space (DiPasquale and Wheaton, 1996).

### 2.1.4 Housing unit heterogeneity

The homogeneity of financial assets (and most other securities) is at variance with the high heterogeneity of real estate assets across locations as well as structures. The fragmentation of real estate markets is a major reason for the slow fall in real estate prices after the end of a boom (Glaeser and Nathanson, 2015). A sharp fall in financial asset prices can take place within a day, while a similar proportional fall in real estate prices would take months or years. Such slow falls are rationalized by the loss aversion of individual investors in real estate assets (Genovese and Mayer, 2001) who are very reluctant to lower their asking price even when they observe a collapse in the market. Real estate assets, such as housing units, differ from each other in three dimensions: among homes, neighbourhoods and unobserved costs (Glaeser and Nathanson, 2015). In the United States, in the late 2000s, only less than one-fifth of rentals units were single-family detached units, while the proportion was close to two-thirds for owner-occupied units (Glaeser and Gyourko, 2009). In addition, owner-occupied units are more likely to be situated outside central cities.

### 2.1.5 Rents versus dividends

It is tempting to focus on rents as a convenient proxy for fundamentals in the housing market, in analogy with the role of dividends as presumably anchoring stock prices. However, rents differ from dividends in at least four important respects (Taipalus, 2012). First, real estate prices generally rise before rises in rents, while rises in stock prices signal a rise in expected earnings, themselves corresponding to higher expected dividends. Second, rents are negotiated between owner and tenant while a firm's board decides on the amount of dividends. Third, in the stock market there is nothing similar to rent controls which prevent rent from responding to house price movements. Finally, while the dividend received by the shareholder matches the amount paid out by a firm, there is a large spread between the rent paid by a tenant and the return on her investment obtained by the owner (Mayer, 2006).

Overall, the real estate market has major characteristics which make it different from the stock market and make even more complex the attempt to match price developments in real estate markets with the predictions of the efficient market approach.

## 2.2 Theory of Housing Price Boom-Busts and Bubble Typology

### 2.2.1 Why do cycles in housing prices matter?

Real estate bubbles, when they burst, can generate macroeconomic downturns via three main channels (Duca et al., 2017). First, over and above usual wealth effects of changes in gross housing wealth, changes in the ability to borrow against housing wealth can inflate loan-to-value ratios above their value at the time of house purchase. Mortgage-debt-overhang effects depress consumption either via a reduction in discretionary income or by inducing extra savings in order to minimize the risk of incurring future late payment penalties. Finally, damage to the financial system, in an extension to the real estate sector of the financial accelerator of Bernanke et al. (1996), arises from the fact that loans, extended during booms, become non-performing. The resulting destruction of their capital makes banks unable to meet capital requirements, leading them to tighten credit standards and reduce lending in general.

The theoretical modelling of booms and busts[3] in the housing market is often based on expectation-driven cycles. Such a framework, based on the model of the housing market developed by Iacoviello and Neri (2010), was put forward by Lambertini et al. (2013). News shocks[4] trigger a joint boom in housing prices and bank credit to households, via the rise in the borrowing capacity of debtors due to their increasing housing wealth, acting as a financial accelerator. At the macroeconomic level, a bust is generated by economic outcomes which fail to match expectations about future economic conditions. In other words, while positive news shocks bring borrowing above its equilibrium level, their sudden reversal leads to a downward revision in real and financial decisions (see also Kermani, 2013; Kanik and Xiao, 2014).

Another line of theoretical research rationalizes booms and busts when agents, holding heterogeneous expectations about the state of long-run fundamentals, decide to revise their views because of social dynamics (Burnside et al., 2016). Agents with tighter priors are the principal candidates to convert other agents to their beliefs. When optimistic agents are correct, then booms are not followed by busts.[5] Factors other than 'news shocks' can drive real estate cycles. In a simple dynamic stochastic general equilibrium model proposed by Leung (2014) the reduced-form dynamics is consistent with the error-correction model estimated by Malpezzi (1999) and Capozza et al. (2004). Furthermore, Chen and Leung (2007) propose a framework in which the combination of large shocks and collateral constraints drives large-scale bankruptcy, generating regime-switching dynamics in house prices (similar to the evidence presented by Chang et al., 2011). In a model where agents imperfectly know the market, put forward by Kuang (2014), in as much as agents both learn and trade, cycles appear in both house prices and credit. Focusing on the formation of expectations in the presence of regime switching in the real estate market, Chen et al. (2015) show that the anticipation of a possible change in regime may impact the behaviour of agents, and thus alter the dynamics of aggregate output and housing prices.

Real estate cycles are often closely associated with banking cycles (Herring and Wachter, 1999). The banking system indeed plays a major role in the determination of real estate prices and their rise above fundamentals. A rise in the price of real estate generates a gain in the value of bank capital for banks owning real estate. In turn, this leads to a rise in the value of loans collateralized by real estate and may be conducive to a lower perception of the risk of real estate lending. Finally, the ensuing increase in the supply of credit to the real estate industry feeds real estate price inflation further.

### 2.2.2 Bubble types

From a theoretical perspective, the major distinction opposes rational to non-rational bubbles (Brzezicka, 2021). Within the rational bubble approach a first divergence comes from opposite assumptions with respect to information which can be either symmetric or asymmetric (Brunnermeier, 2001). Symmetry of information is assumed under the standard model. With asymmetry in access to information, 'not all investors know that the other investors know there is a bubble' (Wöckl, 2019). The presence of short-sale restrictions can lead to bubbles within such a setting (Allen et al., 1993). Rational bubbles are either intrinsic or explosive. With an intrinsic bubble (Froot and Obstfeld, 1991) the increase in price is driven by an over-reaction to fundamentals, in a non-linear but deterministic way. With explosive bubbles the increase in the house price is generated by stochastic price dynamics, and is orthogonal to fundamentals. Finally, agency-based models represent a fourth type of rational bubble. The latter models exploit the incentive problems faced by institutions, money managers and information intermediaries, with three types: herding, limited liability and misaligned incentives of information intermediaries (Scherbina and Schlusche, 2014; Wöckl, 2019).

Non-rational bubbles are usually explained by behavioural factors or within demand models. Behavioural factors encompass differences of opinion/heterogenous beliefs, feedback trading, biased self-attribution by investors and conservatism bias against negative news (within the context of real estate markets, see Scherbina and Schlusche, 2012; more broadly refer to Wöckl, 2019).

What Filardo (2004) labels 'macroeconomic' asset price bubbles are those which are large enough to impact macroeconomic variables. Such a perspective disregards three types of more minor phenomena. First, deviations from fundamentals simply corresponding to conventional error terms in asset pricing equations. Second, asset price anomalies that arise from issues of market microstructure in particular sub-classes of assets. Third, small short-lived bubbles that might be generated by bandwagon effects, fads, herding, positive feedback trading or information cascades. When such phenomena are restricted to a small sector, their impact on the economy as a whole is likely to be small. In a related but different perspective, bubbles which generate systemic risk are singled out by Brunnermeier et al. (2020). Such bubbles are especially harmful, in as much as they can be a major factor in the collapse of the whole financial system. This perspective leaves aside bubbles which do generate substantial financial losses but have only limited macroeconomic implications (Brunnermeier and Oehmke, 2013; Brunnermeier et al., 2020).

### 2.2.3 Bubbles and the present-value model

When real estate prices rise sharply, some observers, viewing real estate as an efficient market, consider that such rising prices are based on 'new information' and do not interpret them as worrying. However, doubts have widely been raised with respect to the applicability of the efficient markets theory, due to the abundance of evidence on departures from such information efficiency, associated with so-called anomalies.

Features of house prices such as a rapid rise, 'a speculative focus on future price increases rather than the asset's cash flow, and an eventual drop in prices' (Smith and Smith, 2006), are only loose signs of overvaluation. Indeed, a rise in housing prices can be associated with a rise in fundamentals, or with a prior undervaluation (past prices consistently below fundamental value). A sharp drop in prices can take place even when not preceded by a bubble.

Fama's (1965) definition of bubbles, as prices of assets which 'run well above or below the intrinsic value', offers a necessary, though not sufficient, condition for the presence of bubbles. A related view is proposed by Stiglitz (1990) who considered that 'if the reason that the price is high today is only because investors believe that the selling price is high tomorrow – when "fundamental" factors do not seem to justify such a price – then a bubble exists'.

### 2.2.4 House price versus the cost of ownership

The specificity of real estate assets is that the fundamental value can be assessed empirically by computing either the flow of rents or the user cost (Glaeser and Nathanson, 2015). The part of the return of owning a house analogous to the dividend on a stock comes from the rent the owner saves by living in the house rent-free,[6] while the capital gain is generated by the house price appreciation. The price-to-rent ratio, analogous to the price–earnings ratio for equities, aims at mirroring the relative cost of owning as opposed to renting. The rationale is that, with high house prices relative to rents, prospective homeowners will rather decide to rent. The demand for houses will fall towards being better aligned with rents. It is tempting to argue that persistently high price-to-rent ratios reflect not the fundamental rental value but unrealistic expectations of price gains in the future, signalling the presence of a 'bubble' (Himmelberg et al., 2005).

However, one should not consider as equivalent a house price and the cost of owning it. Besides, house prices respond more sharply to changes in fundamentals at times with either low real long-term interest rates or high expected price growth. Accordingly, it is not because house price growth accelerates that a bubble is present. It is thus not possible to assess housing costs by limiting the assessment of pricing in the housing market to price-to-rent or price-to-income[7] ratios since they might lead us to wrongly conclude that an exuberance is present in the housing market when the price of housing is actually reasonable. An evaluation of the cost of home ownership should be based on the user cost of housing, as proxied by the imputed annual rental cost of house ownership (Meese and Wallace, 1994; Case and Shiller, 2004; Himmelberg et al., 2005). The condominium market has lower transaction costs and higher liquidity than the market for houses, and as such may be more vulnerable to overvaluation and overbuilding driven by speculation from investors. A countervailing factor is that very few professional investors invest in single-family homes, implying that bubbles are less likely for flats' prices (Shiller, 2006).

We will consider as a necessary condition for a bubble that the market price of real estate assets is far above the present value of the anticipated earning capacity, or cash flow, from that asset. In the case of the real estate market, the present-value model has to be used with care since, as emphasized by Smith and Smith (2006), home buyers in general would not calculate the present value.

## 2.2.5 Fundamentals and bubbles

In the linear asset pricing model (Head et al., 2014) the price of housing is treated as if it were a standardized security. In the temporal user cost model[8] all buyers, typically homeowners, are assumed to pay a single price of housing.

The definition of the one-period gross return ($Q_{t+1}$) from investment in housing is:

$$Q_{t+1} = (P_{t+1} + R_{t+1}) / P_t \tag{6.1}$$

where $P$ denotes the real housing price and $R$ real housing rent. Based on the approximation proposed by Campbell and Shiller (1988a, 1988b), and a Taylor series expansion of order one, the logarithm of the price of housing can be expressed as (Kim and Kim, 2016; Shi, 2017):

$$p_t = \varphi + \lambda p_{t+1} + (1-\lambda) r_{t+1} - q_{t+1} \tag{6.2}$$

where $q_{t+1}, p_{t+1}$ and $r_{t+1}$ represent the logarithm of respectively $Q_{t+1}, P_{t+1}$ and $R_{t+1}$; and we note
$\varphi = [-\log(\lambda) + (1-\lambda)(\pi - \phi)]$, and $\lambda = [e^\pi / (e^\pi + e^\phi)]$, with $\pi$ and $\phi$ the sample means of $p$ and $r$, respectively. Under the perfect-foresight assumption, the house price can be rewritten as:

$$p_t = [\varphi / (1-\lambda)] + (1-\lambda) \sum_{j=0}^{\infty} \lambda^j r_{t+1+j} - \sum_{j=0}^{\infty} \lambda^j q_{t+1+j} + B_t \tag{6.3}$$

with

$$B_t = \lim_{j \to \infty} \lambda^j p_{t+1} = (1/\lambda) B_{t-1} \tag{6.4}$$

we get from Equation 6.3:

$$p_t - r_t = F_t + B_t \tag{6.5}$$

In the absence of bubbles, conditional upon information available at $t$, the expected value of the fundamental component, $F_t$, of the price-to-rent ratio should be equal to the present discounted value of the expected flow of future housing services and the expected future returns on housing investments (Campbell et al., 2009), as follows:

$$E_t(F_{t+1}) = [\varphi/(1-\lambda)] + E_t\left[\sum_{j=0}^{\infty}\lambda^j(r_{t+1+j} - q_{t+1+j})\right] \quad (6.6)$$

The future returns on housing investment can themselves be divided between the risk-free interest rate in the future and the future premia over such a risk-free real interest rate paid to housing investment. The dynamic Gordon growth model (Campbell and Shiller, 1988a, 1988b; applied to the real estate market by Plazzi et al., 2010) assumes that the housing price is simply equal to the discounted flow of rents, allowing time variation in both the required return on housing and rents. This time variation generates the changes in the housing price over time.

When the return to housing is decomposed into a real risk-free interest rate, noted $i$, and the premium over such a rate ($\rho = q - i$), the fundamental part of the logarithm of the price-to-rent ratio includes components[9] representing both costs and offsetting benefits of home ownership (Hendershot and Slemrod, 1982; Poterba, 1984), jointly composing the user cost of ownership. Such a user cost has three elements, the first with a positive sign and the last two with negative ones: first, the expected present value of the future growth of rents; second, the opportunity cost of owning a house, proxied by the expected present value of the real interest rate on a risk-free bond; finally, the compensation to homeowners for the higher risk associated with owning versus renting, in the form of the expected present value of a risk premium. If the housing market is in equilibrium, absent bubbles, the price-to-rent ratio should be equal to the user cost of ownership, as in Equation 6.7. In a widely used simplification of the latter, suggested for instance by Himmelberg et al. (2005), the housing premium is not time varying.

$$p_t - r_t = \theta + E_t\left[\sum_{j=0}^{\infty}\alpha^j \Delta r_{t+1+j} - \sum_{j=0}^{\infty}\alpha^j i_{t+1+j} - \sum_{j=0}^{\infty}\alpha^j \rho_{t+1+j}\right] \quad (6.7)$$

Since the bubble component satisfies the sub-martingale property (Diba and Grossman, 1988a):

$$E_t(B_{t+1}) = \frac{1}{\lambda}B_t, \frac{1}{\lambda} > 1. \quad (6.8)$$

Absent bubbles, the component $B_t$ would converge to zero when $j$ in Equation 6.4 becomes infinite, and only $F_t$ would drive the log of the price-to-rent ratio.[10] In contrast, an active bubble corresponds to the violation of the transversality condition (a condition under which $\lim_{j\to\infty}\lambda^j p_{t+j} = 0$), and the sub-martingale property (Equation 6.8) would be satisfied by the bubble $B_t$. The bubble would represent a non-stationary gap between the observed price-to-rent ratio and its stationary fundamental value corresponding to the present-value model (Kishor and Morley, 2015).

The bubble process, satisfying Equation 6.8, is likely to be non-linear. Periodically collapsing bubbles are generally considered to alternate between an expanding/explosive regime, noted as regime 2, and a non-exploding/collapsing regime, regime 1 (Van Norden and Schaller, 1993; Balke and Wohar, 2009). The bubble regimes are governed by a Markov-switching model, with the probabilities of maintenance of the explosive and non-explosive regimes, noted $\kappa$ and $\varphi$ respectively, expressed as:

$$P[S_{t+1}=2 \mid S_t = 2] = \kappa$$
$$P[S_{t+1}=1 \mid S_t = 1] = \varphi$$

where $S$ is the regime.

Within the non-explosive regime ($S_{t+1} = 1$), allowing for slow collapse, the bubble evolves according to:

$$B_{t+1} = \theta B_t + \beta + \mu_{t+1}^b$$

A bubble evolves within its explosive regime ($S_{t+1} = 2, S_t = 2$) as:

$$B_{t+1} = \frac{1}{\kappa}\left[\frac{1}{\lambda} - (1-\kappa)\theta\right]B_t - \frac{(1-\kappa)\beta}{\kappa} + \mu_{t+1}^B$$

For a bubble which moves out of the non-exploding and into the exploding regime, corresponding to ($S_{t+1} = 2, S_t = 1$), we have:

$$B_{t+1} = \frac{1}{(1-\varphi)}\left[\frac{1}{\lambda} - \varphi\theta\right]B_t - \frac{\varphi\beta}{1-\varphi} + \mu_{t+1}^B$$

This theoretical analysis implies that limiting an assessment of overvaluation in a housing market to the observation of price-to-rent ratios is potentially misleading. It is only by filtering price-to-rent ratios from movements in user costs that a proper assessment of such an overvaluation can be made.

## 3    HOW TO SEARCH FOR BUBBLES?

In Section 2 we saw that the log price-to-rent ratio could be decomposed in two components, the fundamental component $F_t$ and the bubble component $B_t$ which satisfies the sub-martingale property and is periodically collapsing. To test for the presence of a bubble we need to test whether $B_t$ is explosive. The difficulty is that $B_t$ is not observable. The approaches which have been taken in the applied literature either use a proxy for $B_t$ or try to estimate the fundamental component. The estimation of the fundamental component is not straightforward since it requires unbiased forecasts of future streams of the fundamental variables such as rent growth and real interest rates. The non-fundamental component, calculated as the difference between the log price-to-rent ratio and the fundamental component, includes not only the bubble component but also the forecast errors and the estimation errors.

In this section we present methodologies applied to test for the presence of rational bubbles in housing markets. We start with testing bubbles on proxies of the bubble component. We then explore the most recent techniques developed to filter out the effect of fundamentals from the price-to-rent ratio and test for the possible explosive character of the residuals. In the subsequent section we apply and compare those methodologies when testing for the presence of bubbles in the Japanese housing real estate market.

## 3.1  Testing for Bubbles in the Price-to-Rent Ratio

Since the bubble component is not observable we can choose to apply explosive unit root tests during the expansionary phase to proxies such as house prices themselves or the price-to-rent ratio. The most common bubble detection technique is the PSY (Phillips et al., 2015a, 2015b) test. It can be used to find the origination and termination dates of bubble rises by testing for the presence of mildly explosive roots in house prices normalized by fundamentals (Phillips et al., 2015a). The PSY method to detect bubbles is based on a double recursive test procedure with a flexible window. It uses data only up to the point of interest and may be used as an ex ante real time dating procedure. It provides an early warning diagnostic for monitoring asset markets which is essential for policy makers and regulators. When applied to a price-to-rent ratio the real time detection is only constrained by the frequency of the data. When applied to the price-to-rent ratio filtered out of the effect of fundamentals we are restricted by the availability of data on the fundamentals, which are often quarterly.

The PSY test can be applied directly on the log price-to-rent ratio. The PSY test is a right-tailed version of the Augmented Dickey–Fuller (ADF) test. It enables us to detect the origination and termination of bubble expansion periods. There are many other explosive root tests, including the recursive method of Phillips, Wu and Yu (Phillips et al., 2011) and the CUSUM strategy of Homm and Breitung (2012), but the PSY has been shown to outperform these tests when multiple bubbles occur in the data, as documented by Harvey et al. (2020). The PSY test is constructed by estimating the ADF statistic recursively on subsamples, thereby ensuring the test is robust to structural breaks or regime switching.

We denote by $r_1$ and $r_2$ the fractional beginning and ending points of a subsample; the resulting ADF statistics are denoted $ADF_{r_2}^{r_1}$. The ADF statistic is calculated on a sequence of backward increasing samples. The minimum window size $r_0$ is set to $(0.01+1.8/\sqrt{T})$ where $T$ is the total sample size. The ADF statistic series for observation $[rT]$ is denoted by $\left\{ ADF_{r_2}^{r_1} \right\}_{r_2=r}^{r_1 \in [0, r-r_0]}$. $SADF_r$ is defined as the sup value of the ADF sequence and is the appropriate statistic to test whether a process is mildly explosive:

$$SADF_r = \max\left\{ ADF_{r_2}^{r_1} : r_2 = r \text{ and } r_1 \in [0, r-r_0] \right\}.$$

The bubble origination (and termination) dates can be consistently estimated by using the first sequential observation for which the SADF statistic is above (below) its corresponding critical value (Phillips and Shi, 2020). This is the case even in the presence of multiple bubbles if the time span between two bubbles is longer than $r_0$.

Harvey et al. (2016) develop a wild bootstrapping procedure to calculate the critical values to reduce the probability of size distortion if conditional or unconditional heteroskedasticity is present. This is particularly relevant when applying the PSY test to the non-fundamental component of the price-to-rent ratio as established below.

Although it is straightforward to apply the PSY test to the price-to-rent ratio one should keep in mind that this test is designed to detect whether the bubble component satisfies the sub-martingale property. Specifically, the PSY test assumes an asymptotically negligible drift. This assumption is appropriate for the bubble component but not for the fundamental component. The fundamental component is made up of the following series, many of them I(1) (or near integrated) and with a non-zero drift: population, real gross disposable income, consumer price inflation (*CPI*), real total credit to the private non-financial sector, population and housing starts among others. During a speculative bubble both prices and price-to-rent ratios are explosive since the bubble component will dominate; however, the performance of the PSY test will be affected by the presence of the highly persistent series in the fundamental component.

### 3.2 Testing for Bubbles on the Filtered Price: The PSY-IVX Procedure

Different methods can be used to decompose the price-to-rent ratio into its fundamental and non-fundamental components. They all require unbiased forecasts of future streams of rent growth and other relevant fundamentals. Campbell et al. (2009) and Shi (2017) use a VAR model to forecast those variables and then obtain the non-fundamental component by subtracting the forecasted fundamentals from the log price-to-rent ratio. The drawback from such an approach is that it requires the estimation of a VAR model including the specification of the fundamentals in a structural form. This requires the availability of house prices and rents in dollar value; indexes are not appropriate. Calibration of some unknown parameters is also needed.

Phillips and Shi (2021) introduce a new approach without these shortcomings. It will be referred to as PSY-IVX. The PSY-IVX procedure only requires the estimation of a single-equation reduced-form model. To estimate the fundamental component, we regress the growth rate of the price-to-rent ratio on the macroeconomic and housing sector-specific fundamentals (rents, real interest rate, bank credit, real personal disposable income, population, employment and supply factors). Since the explanatory variables are persistent and endogenous, we need to construct instrumental variables for the fundamental variables which are less persistent. This is the basic idea behind the instrumental variable (IVX) method. The IVX-AR method extends this instrumental-variable estimation to the case where the error terms are autocorrelated and heteroskedastic. From this regression the fundamental component can be estimated and used to extract the bubble component of the price-to-rent ratio. House price and rent indexes may be used to estimate this equation.

Magdalinos and Phillips (2009) propose the IVX method to estimate models where the explanatory variables are highly persistent and endogenous. They construct instrumental variables with a lower degree of persistence than the original regressors, which eliminate the endogeneity issue. Kostakis et al. (2015) show that it is possible to conduct inference in this context since the IVX Wald tests have a standard chi-squared distribution and are robust to regressors with varying degrees of persistence even in the presence of heteroskedasticity. These tests stay valid when the regressors are mildly explosive.

Yang et al. (2020) extend this instrumental variable estimation to the case where the error terms are autocorrelated and heteroskedastic; this is the IVX-AR estimation method. They show that the Wald tests using the IVX-AR estimation method have good size properties even in small samples and notwithstanding the extent of serial correlation in the error terms and the persistence of the regressors.

We describe below step by step the PSY-IVX estimation procedure of Phillips and Shi (2021).

We denote by $y_t$ the growth rate of the log price-to-rent ratio, $y_t = \Delta p_t - \Delta r_t$. To decompose the growth of the price-to-rent ratio into a fundamental component and a non-fundamental component we estimate the model:

$$y_t = \alpha + \beta x_t + \varepsilon_t \tag{6.9}$$

$$x_t = d_x + \rho_x x_{t-1} + u_{xt} \quad \text{where } \rho_x = I_k + \frac{C_x}{T^\alpha} \tag{6.10}$$

where $x_t$ is a vector of $k$ fundamental variables including both housing demand and supply variables, $\alpha \in (0,1), C_x = \text{diag}(c_{x1},...,c_{xk})$, and $c_{xi} \leq 0$.

The elements of $x_t$ can be I(1), near integrated or mildly stationary. The error term in Equation 6.9 can be autocorrelated and conditionally heteroskedastic; we assume that $\varepsilon_t$ follows an AR($q$)-GARCH($m,n$) model.

The regressors can be highly persistent and endogenous due to the joint determination of $y_t$ and $x_t$. Therefore, we estimate the model using the IVX-AR method. The estimated fundamental component, $\hat{F}_t$, is equal to the cumulative sum of the fitted values $\hat{y}_t = \hat{\alpha} + \hat{\beta} x_t$ and the non-fundamental component is $e_t = p_t - r_t - \hat{F}_t$. The PSY test can then be applied to the non-fundamental component.[11]

Whereas the VAR approach constrains the number of included fundamental variables, this new approach allows for a possibly large set of such variables. It is easy to implement since it only requires the estimation of a single equation.

We illustrate below how to apply the PSY-IVX method to the Japanese housing market.

## 4 AN ILLUSTRATION: HOUSING NON-FUNDAMENTAL BUBBLE DETECTION FOR JAPAN

In our empirical application of the bubble detection procedure, we consider quarterly residential house prices for Japan from the first quarter of 1981 to the last quarter of 2019. It is more relevant to examine housing rather than land prices in Japan for two reasons (detailed by Ito and Hirono 1993). On the one hand, in Japan land prices are collected as fair assessment values in government surveys and are not a report of market transaction prices. On the other hand, an economic analysis of the housing market is concerned with the prices of assets, which enter the portfolios of either individual investors or small-size real estate companies, corresponding to housing units and not to unbuilt plots of land.

Our data sources are presented in the Appendix. The log price-to-rent ratio (*lprr*) in Japan, plotted in Figure 6.1, rose mildly in the early 1980s, then sharply, in two stages, from late 1986 to mid-1991, and mildly in a gradual way from mid-2013 onwards.

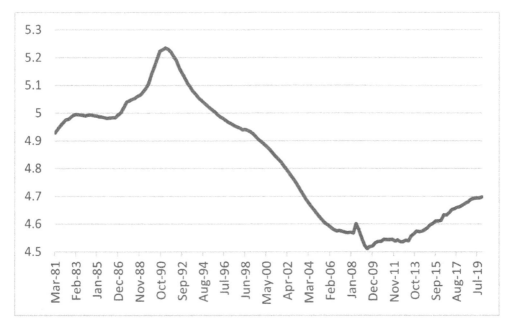

*Figure 6.1    Log of price-to-rent ratio*

### 4.1    Bubble Test on the Log Price-to-Rent Ratio

We plot in Figure 6.2 the bubble periods identified with the PSY test on the *lprr*, along with the log of the price-to-rent ratio. Highlighted areas correspond to periods of explosive behaviour as detected using 95 per cent critical values obtained from wild bootstrapping procedures.

There are two bubble periods: the third quarter of 1989 to the third quarter of 1990 and the third quarter of 2001 to the third quarter of 2005. The five-quarter-long bubble from summer 1989 corresponds to the late phase of the overheated housing market in Japan, well documented by many observers, who do not consider that it was present before 1988. This implies that some previous tests using PSY on the *lprr*, whose datings are reported in Table 6.1, such as by Hu and Oxley (2018) and Kholodilin and Michelsen (2018), are likely to imply a too early start of the bubble. With respect to the end of the bubble, those datings including periods later than mid-1991, such as Hu and Oxley (2018), Kholodilin and Michelsen (2018) and Pavlidis et al. (2015), should be considered with care, since the *lprr* started declining in the third quarter of 1991. The dating by Engsted et al. (2015) is very close to our detection of the 1989–1990 bubble, showing a similar duration, with a one-quarter lagged start, though it does thus include the third quarter of 1991 with a falling *lprr*. It is very surprising to see that Gomez-Gonzalez et al. (2018) are not able to detect any bubble in the *lprr* in the late 1980s.

It would be tempting to match the four year-long bubble we detect with the PSY test on the price-to-rent ratio from the third quarter of 2001 (confirming the dating by Pavlidis et al., 2015) with the time span of the pioneering use of quantitative easing by the Bank of Japan (Girardin and Moussa, 2011). Indeed, in March 2001, in order to provide ample liquidity to the banking system, the Bank of Japan's main operating policy target was changed to the commercial banks' balances with the Bank; a target which experienced a seven-fold rise up to

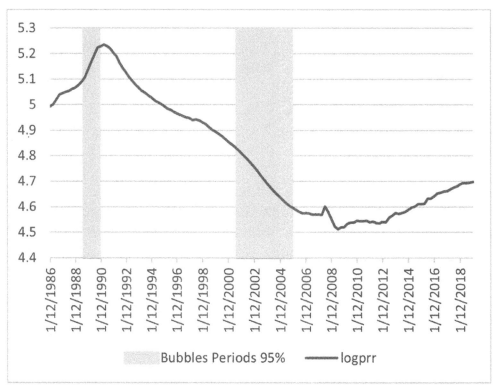

*Note*: The bubble periods are identified based on the SADF statistic sequence and the 95 per cent wild bootstrapping critical value sequence.

*Figure 6.2    The identified bubble periods (shaded) and the log of price-to-rent ratio*

*Table 6.1    Comparison of PSY detection of bubbles in Japan's housing price in previous work, using the price-to-rent ratio, 1980s to 2010s*

| PSY on *lprr* 1981Q1–2019Q4 | Engsted et al. (2015) *lprr* 1970Q1–2013Q4 | Gomez-Gonzalez et al. (2018) *lprr* 1970Q1–2015Q2 | Hu and Oxley (2018) lprr 1970Q1–1999Q4 | Kholodilin and Michelsen (2018) *lprr* 1970Q1–2018Q4 | Pavlidis et al. (2015) *lprr* 1975Q1–2013Q2 |
|---|---|---|---|---|---|
| 1989Q3–1990Q3 2001Q3–2005Q3 Falling *lprr* | 1989Q4–1990Q4 | | 1987Q2–1992Q2 | 1986Q1–1991Q4 | 1989Q4–1992Q1 2001Q3–2005Q4 |
| | | 2006Q2–2009Q1 2010Q3–2015Q2 | | 2015Q1–2017Q4 | |

*Note*: All studies quoted in this table use price-to-rent ratio (*lprr*) data from the Organisation for Economic Co-operation and Development except Pavlidis et al. (2015) who use Dallas-Fed data. The first column reports our own estimate.

December 2004. However, since over those four years the price-to-rent ratio kept declining, this period cannot qualify as a bubble. In the eyes of observers the first half of the 2000s was not characterized by the presence of a bubble in national housing prices in Japan. The leading real estate agent for international clients, Housing Japan (2021), indeed remarks that in the first years of the new millennium securitized real estate transactions focused on major cities, especially central Tokyo, 'but the overall market continued to languish'. Accordingly, the second bubble period detected by the PSY test on the price-to-rent ratio corresponds to a 'negative' bubble during a contractionary period, with an uninterrupted fall in *lprr* amounting to one-fifth. PSY recommend identifying ex post whether detected bubbles are in expansionary or contractionary phases.[12] Therefore, this period appears to be a crash in the price-to-rent ratio rather than a bubble.

Similarly, the lengthy bubble periods detected by some previous tests outside the late 1980s or early 2000s, such as 1981–1984 (as in Hu and Oxley, 2018) and 2011–2015 (Gomez-Gonzalez et al., 2018), should be considered with care since they often include episodes with falling price-to-rent ratios, such as in 1983 and 2011–2012.

### 4.2 Extracting the Fundamental Component

Most studies on the relationships between fundamentals and real estate prices in Japan have focused on the land market.[13] The high explanatory power of the high growth in bank loans, and to a lesser extent low interest rates, for land price inflation was especially emphasized by Ito and Iwaisako (1995) over the 1969–1993 sample, confirming descriptive evidence (Kanemoto, 1997; Sato, 2013). In analogy with work on liquidity-constrained investment by firms, bank lending plays a key role in financing the development projects which require land acquisition. Nakamura and Saita (2007) find that changes in the demographic factor and bank lending have an influence on the fluctuations of a weighted average of (real) land prices with annual data over 1965 to 2005.

Two major studies have examined the links between housing prices and macroeconomic fundamentals[14] in Japan in an international perspective. Hott and Monnin (2008), over quarterly data for 1960 to 2005, consider the gap between house prices and three fundamentals (aggregate income, construction and the mortgage rate), comparing Japan with four other countries. Caldera and Johansson (2013), also at a quarterly frequency over 1981 to 2005, find that real house prices (sourced from the Organisation for Economic Co-operation and Development (OECD)) respond significantly in the long run to households' disposable income (positively) and the stock of dwellings (negatively) but neither to a proxy for the mortgage rate nor to population (share of 25–44 years old). In the short run real house price inflation is only influenced (among these same four variables) by disposable income growth and changes in interest rates.

In order to decompose the price-to-rent ratio into its fundamental and non-fundamental components we take the main economic drivers for Japan to be the real mortgage rate, $i_t$, the logarithm of real rent, $lrrent_t$, the log of *CPI*, $lCPI_t$, the log real total credit to the private non-financial sector, $lrcredit_t$, the log of population, $lpop_t$, the log of real personal disposable income, $lRPDI_t$, the employment rate, $emp_t$ and the log of housing starts, $lworkstart_t$. Graphs for these variables are presented in Figure 6.3. Data descriptions and sources can be found in the Appendix. The rise in real bank credit, the fall in the real interest rate as well as the levelling off of housing starts at a high level are especially noticeable in the late 1980s.

Table 6.2 presents the IVX-AR-estimated $\beta$ parameters of Equation 6.9 for Japan. We consider two specifications for the explanatory variables in Equation 6.9. The first specification, PSY-IVX-4, includes only four variables, real rent, real bank credit, population and real

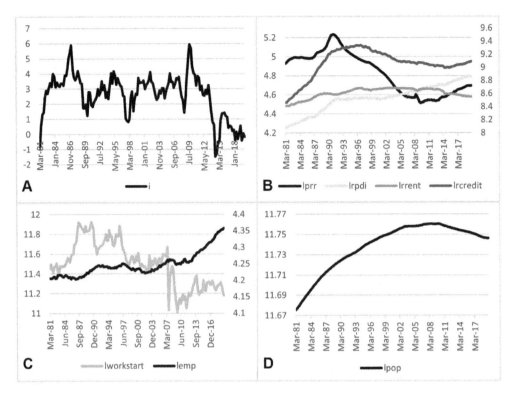

*Figure 6.3    Fundamentals*

*Table 6.2    IVX-AR estimates of the β parameters of the decomposition given in Equation 6.9*

| Method | lrcredit | lrent | lRPDI | lpop | lemp | i |
|---|---|---|---|---|---|---|
| PSY-IVX-4 | −0.0399** | 0.3183*** | 0.1201*** | −1.1716*** | | |
| PSY-IVX-6 | −0.0396** | 0.3029* | 0.1457* | −1.2270** | −0.0690 | −0.0415 |

*Note*: For both the IVX-4 and -6 models the optimal lag order *q* of the AR specification for the error term is selected as 2 quarters by the BIC. *, ** and *** indicate significance at the 10%, 5%, and 1% level, respectively.

personal disposable income. The $\beta$ coefficients are all significant at the 5 per cent significance level with the expected signs, except for the population coefficient which is negative (individual Wald tests robust to heteroscedasticity and autocorrelation are used to test for significance). This is not unexpected since the *lpop* graph has roughly a parabola shape, increasing until 2008 and decreasing thereafter, whereas *lprr* decreases from March 1991 until December 2009, and then increases. Hashimoto et al. (2020) argue that population declines in Japan have been larger in rural than in urban areas; thereby house prices have declined in rural areas but increased, especially after 2014, in urban areas. They also note the presence of an asymmetry, since house prices fall faster when population decreases than they rise with an increasing population (vindicating Glaeser and Gyourko's (2005) theoretical model). An increase in real disposable income by 1 per cent raises *prr* by 0.12 per cent; an increase in real rents by 1 per cent raises *prr* by 0.32 per cent; and an increase in real bank credit by 1 per cent decreases *prr* by 0.04 per cent. The second specification, PSY-IVX-6, incorporates six fundamental variables, augmenting the IVX-4 model with the real mortgage rate and the employment rate. The results including in addition the housing start variable are not presented since its coefficient is very insignificant (p-value is 0.72). Looking at Figure 6.3 we can see why this is the case. From March 2007 housing starts decrease abruptly until September 2009. They recover somewhat from 2012 but never to their pre-2007 level, even though real house prices did recover to reach that earlier level. For the six-variable specification the coefficients of the employment rate and the real mortgage rate are insignificant even at the 10 per cent level. The coefficients of the other variables are still significant at the 5 per cent level and of a similar magnitude as in the four-variable model.

Figure 6.4 displays the estimated non-fundamental component which eliminates the impact of the four included variables and the PSY bubble test results. Among the three bubble periods detected on the PSY-IVX-AR-4 residuals, the last quarter of 1988 to the second quarter of 1991, the last quarter of 2006 to the second quarter of 2007 and the first and second quarters of 2017, only the first one overlaps the first bubble period detected for *lprr*, the third quarter of 1989 to the third quarter of 1990, but not the second one, the third quarter of 2001 to the third quarter of 2005, reported in Table 6.1.

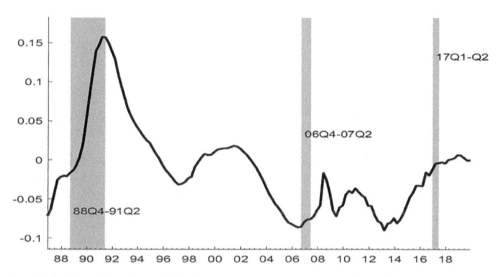

*Note*: The bubble periods are identified based on the SADF statistic sequence and the 95 per cent wild bootstrapping critical value sequence.

*Figure 6.4*    The estimated non-fundamental components (black line) and identified bubble periods from the PSY-IVX-4 method (shaded)

We examine the robustness of our detection of bubbles in the non-fundamental component by enlarging the set of fundamental variables to include two extra variables, the real mortgage rate and the employment rate, as in the PSY-IVX-6 specification.

The non-fundamental component rises in five episodes (Figure 6.5): in an uninterrupted way from mid-1988 up to mid-1991, from early 1997 to late 1998, from late 2006 to summer 2008, in 2009, and from 2013 to 2019. However, we detect an explosion in that component only during three episodes: the third quarter of 1988 to the second quarter of 1991, the third quarter of 2006 to the first quarter of 2007 and the first quarter of 2017.[15]

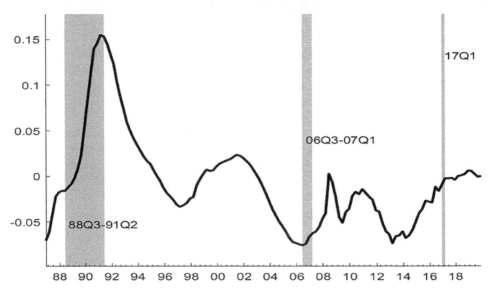

*Note*: The bubble periods are identified based on the SADF statistic sequence and the 95 per cent wild bootstrapping critical value sequence.

Figure 6.5    The estimated non-fundamental components (black line) and identified bubble periods from the PSY-IVX-6 method (shaded)

There is no major difference (comparing the shaded areas in Figures 6.4 and 6.5) made by the inclusion of the real mortgage rate and the employment rate among fundamentals. The three bubbles detected with the four-variable model are confirmed with the six-variable model, with a one-quarter shorter duration in 2017, a one-quarter earlier start and end for the second bubble and an unchanged ending date but a start one-quarter earlier for the late 1980s bubble.

Our detection of an explosive three-to-four-quarter-long period in the non-fundamental component, starting in the last (or third) quarter of 2006 (with six fundamental variables), does match the experience of practitioners and regulators as well as the findings of researchers on real estate markets in Japan in the mid-2000s. Housing Japan (2021) thus notes that, for practitioners, 'by 2006 it seemed once again that a bubble was beginning, so the Ministry of Finance moved again to restrict investment real-estate loans'. Subsequently, with the subprime crisis initiated in 2007, foreign investors disappeared from the Japanese real estate market and real estate prices once again slumped. This view is mirrored by regulators, as reflected in the Report of the Committee on Real Estate Investment Strategy (CREIS, 2010), which pointed to the wide 'recognition that there was a "real estate fund bubble" or "mini bubble" in the real estate investment market in downtown Tokyo just before the Lehman shock'. The same report deplores the lack of deep-enough empirical studies, stating that 'sufficient examination on whether that was true or not cannot be said to have been conducted in the past'. Academic studies, some of which were based on extremely careful constructions of price and rent data, such as Shimizu et al. (2015), using REIT stock market valuations instead of appraisal values, and rents on new contracts rather than on all contracts, also conclude that the 2006–2007 period stood out, in as much as the quick rise of their measure of Tobin's q (ratio of the market value over the replacement cost) for REIT values takes place in the second semester of 2006, up to mid-2007. In contrast, their appraisal-based price index only turns around in summer 2008.

The explosive episode for the non-fundamental component that we detect in the first semester of 2017 (both with four and six fundamental variables) was immediately preceded by the initiation of a new large round of economic stimulus, in the second half of 2016. The Bank of Japan introduced negative interest rates at the start of 2016 and adopted an even more accommodative monetary policy in September 2016 ('Quantitative and Qualitative Monetary Easing with Yield Curve Control'). Japan's central bank started controlling short- and long-term interest rates through market operations and expanding the monetary base to try and reach its desired level of inflation. The fiscal side of the stimulus included more government spending and a new postponement of a rise in the consumption tax rate. New housing loans from domestically licensed banks surged 27 per cent in 2016 compared to the previous year.

## 5    CONCLUSION

Bubbles arise on many different assets. We argue that their detection on real estate prices faces major challenges. The first challenge is to single out the features which make real estate prices different from the prices of other assets. The second challenge is to theoretically ascertain which should be the fundamental variables considered to be driving the dynamics in real estate prices. The third challenge is to design econometric methods which can both properly filter out fundamental movements from observed real estate prices and determine when the non-fundamental component starts, and stops, being mildly explosive.

We presented the recent techniques which meet the second and third series of challenges on the basis of a two-step approach. Their illustration with an application to Japanese data has shown how the focus on too-simple proxies of the non-fundamental component, such as the observed price-to-rent ratio, entails the risk of detecting spurious bubbles. Such spurious bubbles correspond to episodes when apparently excessive rises in the price-to-rent ratio are actually justified by the dynamics of underlying fundamentals. In contrast, explosive behaviour can be detected in the properly filtered-out non-fundamental component during periods when no explosive behaviour would be detected in the observed price-to-rent ratio.

The lessons from the present state of research on the empirical detection of bubbles in real estate prices are especially relevant for regulators and policy makers. After more than a decade with exceptionally large macroeconomic liquidity creation by central banks engaged in qualitative and quantitative easing, concerns have arisen for possible 'excessive' rises in asset prices in general, and real estate prices in particular. The sharp rises in housing prices in some countries (illustrated by the recent case of New Zealand, especially valuable coming from the country which pioneered inflation targeting) have led policy makers to wonder once again whether such excessive movements should be explicitly taken into account by monetary policy makers. The availability of techniques able to rigorously detect in real time the start and end of excessive moments in real estate prices is likely to be as useful in the future as it would have been during the multiple similar episodes in the past.

## NOTES

1. All these methods represent tests of rational bubbles. Behavioural models that allow for irrational pricing and associated 'irrational bubbles' were reviewed by Vissing-Jorgensen (2003).
2. Shiller (2015) reviews two centuries of real estate booms and busts, and Glaeser (2013) shows how real estate investors have repeatedly made the mistake of neglecting the supply response to rising prices.
3. For asset markets in general, see Martin and Ventura (2018).
4. According to Gomes and Mendicino (2015) news shocks explain a sizable fraction of the variation in house prices and other macroeconomic variables.
5. Ascari et al. (2013) put forward a partial disequilibrium dynamic model of the housing market in which the rational-expectations hypothesis is also relaxed in favour of a chartist-fundamentalist mechanism allowing for the endogenous development of bubbles.
6. Apart from rental savings from house ownership, one should also take into account factors which affect the cash flow, such as 'transaction costs, the down payment, insurance, maintenance costs, property taxes, mortgage payments, tax savings, and the proceeds if the home is sold at some point' (Smith and Smith, 2006).
7. As stressed by Smith and Smith (2006), affordability may be better measured by the ratio of mortgage payments to income than by the ratio of house prices to median income.
8. In an alternative cross-sectional or spatial setting, the no-arbitrage condition is such that the living cost in location X should be equal to the living cost in location Y augmented with the supplementary benefits associated with living in location X as opposed to location Y (Alonso, 1964).
9. Two other elements associated with tax policy may need to be included, involving first the cost of property taxes and second the mortgage and property taxes. However, as these are unlikely to vary over short periods, they can be neglected in a time series analysis of a national market.
10. The fundamental solution, where the value of the bubble is null at all times, corresponds to the present value-pricing approaches to housing prices, which can alternatively be called 'the standard model', or 'the market fundamentals model'. Four assumptions other than the absence of bubbles are embedded in this formulation of the present-value model (Gurkanyak, 2008): (1) there are no informational asymmetries; (2) the representative consumer is risk neutral; (3) the discount rate is constant; (4) the process generating rents is not expected to change.
11. The choice of fundamentals to estimate Equation 6.9 may affect the reliability of the PSY test. However, it is not possible to quantify through meaningful simulations the degree to which the PSY bubble detection test may be affected. What can be done is to compare the PSY test results using different sets of fundamental variables (see application in Section 4).
12. Phillips and Shi (2018) propose a reverse-recursion test for crash origination and termination. They recommend applying the PSY test to the data arranged in reverse order. Origination and termination dates can be estimated consistently using the PSY test. They show that this approach can detect multiple crashes.
13. Three other works should be mentioned. Nogushi (1994), using Japanese prefectures' data over 1977–1987, estimated the effect on real urban land prices of local real gross domestic product (positive), the share of secondary industry or tertiary industry in local gross domestic product, government bond yield (negative) and population growth rate (positive). Basile and Joyce (2001), over February 1971 to March 1991, using variance decomposition in a VAR, considered the effect on land prices of industrial production, the call rate and either broad money supply, commercial bank loans or loans to the real estate and construction sectors. Only output played a significant role. Krainer et al. (2010) contrasted the dynamics of commercial and residential land values in the early 1990s, which they rationalized with an original theoretical framework.
14. Ito and Hirono's (1993) analysis of the housing market is especially valuable but conducted from a microeconomic perspective and focused on the Tokyo market.
15. In Figures 6.4 and 6.5 we observe a sharp peak in the second quarter of 2008 which collapsed in the third quarter of 2008.

# REFERENCES

Allen, F., Morris, S., and Postlewaite, A. 1993, 'Finite bubbles with short-sales constraints', *Journal of Economic Theory*, vol. 61, no. 2, pp. 206–229.

Alonso, W. 1964, *Location and land use: Toward a general theory of land rent*. Cambridge, MA: Harvard University Press.

Ascari, G., Pescora, N., and Spelta, A. 2013, 'Boom and bust in housing market with heterogeneous agents', Manuscript, University of Pavia.

Balke, N.S., and Wohar, M.E. 2009, 'Market fundamentals versus rational bubbles in stock price: A Bayesian perspective', *Journal of Applied Econometrics*, vol. 24, pp. 35–75.

Basile, A., and Joyce, J.P. 2001, 'Asset bubbles, monetary policy and bank lending in Japan: An empirical investigation', *Applied Economics*, vol. 33, pp. 1737–1744.

Bernanke, B.S., Gertler, M., and Gilchrist, S. 1996, 'The financial accelerator and the flight to quality', *Review of Economics and Statistics*, vol. 78, no. 1, pp. 1–15.

Bordo, M.D., and Haubrich, J.G. 2012, 'Deep recessions, fast recoveries, and financial crises: Evidence from the American record', NBER working paper, 18194.

Brunnermeier, M.K. 2001, *Asset Pricing under Asymmetric Information: Bubbles, Crashes, Technical Analysis, and Herding*. Oxford: Oxford University Press.

Brunnermeier, M.K., and Oehmke, M. 2013, 'Bubbles, financial crises and systemic risk', in Constantinides, G.M., Harris, M., and Schultz, R.M. (eds), *Handbook of the economics of finance*, Part B, Chapter 18, pp. 1221–1288. New York: Elsevier.

Brunnermeier, M.K., Rother, S., and Schnabel, I. 2020, 'Asset price bubbles and systemic risk', *Review of Financial Studies*, vol. 33, pp. 4272–4317.

Brzezicka, J. 2021, 'Towards a typology of housing price bubbles: A literature review', *Housing, Theory and Society*, pp. 320–342.

Burnside, C., Eichenbaum, M., and Rebelo, S. 2016, 'Understanding booms and busts in housing markets', *Journal of Political Economy*, vol. 124, no. 4, pp. 1088–1147.

Caldera, A., and Johansson, A. 2013, 'The price responsiveness of housing supply in OECD countries', *Journal of Housing Economics*, vol. 22, pp. 231–249.

Camerer, C. 1999, 'Bubbles and fads in asset prices', *Journal of Economic Surveys*, vol. 3, no. 1, pp. 3–41.

Campbell, J., and Shiller, R. 1988a, 'The dividend-price ratio and expectations of future dividends and discount factors', *Review of Financial Studies*, vol. 1, no. 3, pp. 195–228.

Campbell, J., and Shiller, R. 1988b, 'Stock prices, earnings and expected dividends', *Journal of Finance*, vol. 43, no. 3, pp. 661–676.

Campbell, S.D., Davis, M.A., Gallin, J., and Martin, R.F. 2009, 'What moves housing markets? A variance decomposition analysis', *Journal of Urban Economics*, vol. 66, pp. 90–102.

Capozza, D.R., Hendershott, P.H., and Mac, C. 2004, 'An anatomy of price dynamics in illiquid markets: Analysis and evidence from local housing markets', *Real Estate Economics*, vol. 32, pp. 1–32.

Case, K.E., and Shiller, R.J. 2004, 'Is there a bubble in the housing market?' *Brookings Papers on Economic Activity*, vol. 2, pp. 299–342.

Chang, K.-L., Chen, N.K., and Leung, C.K.Y. 2011, 'Monetary policy, term structure and asset return: Comparing REIT, housing and stock', *Journal of Real Estate Finance and Economics*, vol. 43, pp. 221–257.

Chen, N.K., and Leung, C.K.Y. 2007, 'Asset price spillover, collateral and crises: With an application to property market policy', *Journal of Real Estate Finance and Economics*, vol. 37, pp. 351–85.

Chen, N.K., Cheng, H.L., and Chu, H.L. 2015, 'Asset price and monetary policy: The effect of expectations formation', *Oxford Economic Papers*, vol. 67, pp. 380–405.

CREIS 2010, Report of the committee on real estate investment strategy, Ministry of Land, Infrastructure, Transport and Tourism, Tokyo. www.mlit.go.jp/common/000140331.pdf

Crowe, C., Dell'Ariccia, G., Igan, D., and Rabanal, P. 2013, 'How to deal with real estate booms: Lessons from country experiences', *Journal of Financial Stability*, vol. 9, no. 3, pp. 300–319.

Deng, Y., Girardin, E., Joyeux, R., and Shi, S. 2017, 'Did bubbles migrate from the stock to the housing market in China between 2005 and 2010?' *Pacific Economic Review*, vol. 22, pp. 276–292.

Diba, B.T., and Grossman, H.I. 1988a, 'Explosive rational bubbles in stock prices?' *American Economic Review*, vol. 78, no. 3, pp. 520–530.

Diba, B.T., and Grossman, H.I. 1988b, 'The theory of rational bubbles in stock prices', *Economic Journal*, vol. 98, no. 392, pp. 746–754.

DiPasquale, D., and Wheaton, W.C. 1996, *Urban economics and real estate markets*. Englewood Cliffs, NJ: Prentice Hall.

Duca, J.V., Muellbauer, J., and Murphy, A. 2010, 'Housing markets and the financial crisis of 2007–2009: Lessons for the future', *Journal of Financial Stability*, vol. 6, no. 4, pp. 203–217.

Duca, J.V., Popoyan, L., and Wachter, S.M. 2017, 'Real estate and the great crisis: Lessons for macro-prudential policy', University of Pennsylvania, Wharton School.

Englund, P., Hwang, M., and Quigley, J.M. 2002, 'Hedging housing risk', *Journal of Real Estate Finance and Economics*, vol. 24, no. 1 pp. 67–200.

Engsted, T., Hvlid, S.J., and Pedersen, T.Q. 2015, 'Explosive bubbles in house prices? Evidence from OECD', *Journal of International Financial Markets, Institutions and Money*, vol. 40, pp. 14–25.

Evans, G.W. 1991, 'Pitfalls in testing for explosive bubbles in asset prices', *American Economic Review*, vol. 81, pp. 922–930.

Fama, E.F. 1965, 'The behavior of stock market prices', *Journal of Business*, vol 38, no. 1, pp. 34–105.

Filardo, A. 2004, 'Monetary policy and asset price bubbles: Calibrating the monetary policy trade-offs,' Bank for International Settlements Working Papers no. 155.

Froot, K.A., and Obstfeld, M. 1991, 'Intrinsic bubbles: The case of stock prices', *American Economic Review*, vol. 81, no. 5, pp. 1189–1214.

Genovese, D., and Mayer, C. 2001, 'Loss aversion and seller behavior: Evidence from the housing market', *Quarterly Journal of Economics*, vol. 116, no. 4, pp. 1233–1260.

Girardin, E., and Moussa, Z. 2011, 'Quantitative easing works: Lessons from the unique experience in Japan 2001–2006', *Journal of International Financial Markets, Institutions and Money*, vol. 21, no. 4, pp. 461–495.

Glaeser, E.L. 2013, 'A nation of gamblers: Real estate speculation and American history', *American Economic Review*, vol. 103, no. 3, pp. 1–42.

Glaeser, E.L., and Nathanson, C.G. 2015, 'Housing bubbles', in Duranton, G., Henderson, J.V., and Strange, W.C. (eds), *Handbook of regional and urban economics*, pp. 701–751. Amsterdam: Elsevier.

Glaeser, G.L., and Gyourko, J. 2005, 'Urban decline and durable housing', *Journal of Political Economy*, vol. 113, no. 2, pp. 345–375.

Glaeser, G.L., and Gyourko, J. 2009, *Rethinking federal housing policy*. Washington, DC: American Enterprise Institute.

Glaeser, G.L., Huang, W., Ma, Y., and Schleifer, A. 2017, 'A real-estate boom with Chinese characteristics', *Journal of Economic Perspectives*, vol. 31, no. 1, pp. 93–116.

Gomes, S., and Mendicino, C. 2015, 'Housing market dynamics? Any news', European Central Bank Working Paper no. 1775.

Gomez-Gonzalez, J.E., Gamboa-Abelaez, J., Hirs-Garzon, J., and Pinchao-Rosero, A. 2018, 'When bubble meets bubble: Contagion in OECD countries', *Journal of Real Estate Finance and Economics*, vol. 56, pp. 546–566.

Green, R.K., and Wachter, S.M. 2007, 'The housing finance revolution', Proceedings, Economic Policy Symposium, Jackson Hole, pp. 21–67.

Gurkanyak, R.S. 2008, 'Econometric tests of asset price bubbles: Taking stock', *Journal of Economic Surveys*, vol. 22, no. 1, pp. 166–186.

Hall, R.E. 2003, *Deal engines: The science of auctions, stock markets, and e-markets*. New York: W. Norton and Co.

Harvey, D.I., Leybourne, S.J., Sollis, R., and Taylor, A.R. 2016, 'Tests for explosive financial bubbles in the presence of non-stationary volatility', *Journal of Empirical Finance*, vol. 38, pp. 548–574.

Harvey, D.I., Leybourne, S.J., and Whitehouse, E.J. 2020, 'Date-stamping multiple bubble regimes', *Journal of Empirical Finance*, vol. 58, pp. 226–246.

Hashimoto, Y., Hong, G.H., and Zhang, X. 2020, 'Demographics and the housing market: Japan's disappearing cities', IMF working paper, no. 20-200.

Head, A., Lloyd-Ellis, H., and Sun, H. 2014, 'Search, liquidity, and the dynamics of house prices and construction', *American Economic Review*, vol. 104, no. 4, pp. 1172–1210.

Hendershot, P.H., and Slemrod, J. 1982, 'Taxes and the user cost of capital for owner-occupier housing', *Real Estate Economics*, vol. 10, no. 4, pp. 375–393.

Herring, R.J., and Wachter, S.M. 1999, 'Real estate booms and banking busts: An international perspective', Group of Thirty Occasional Paper, No. 58.

Higgins, M., and Osler, C. 1997, 'Asset market hangovers and economic growth', *Oxford Review of Economic Policy*, vol. 13, no. 3, pp. 110–134.

Himmelberg, C., Mayer C., and Sinai, C. 2005, 'Assessing house prices: Bubbles, fundamentals, and misperceptions', *Journal of Economic Perspectives*, vol. 19, no. 4, pp. 67–92.

Homm, U., and Breitung, J. 2012, 'Testing for speculative bubbles in stock markets: A comparison of alternative methods', *Journal of Financial Econometrics*, vol. 10, no. 1, pp. 196–231.

Hott, G., and Monnin, P. 2008, 'Fundamental real estate prices: An empirical estimation with international data', *Journal of Real Estate Finance and Economics*, vol. 36, no. 4, pp. 427–450.

Housing Japan 2021, *A history of Tokyo houses and real estate prices*. Tokyo: Housing Japan. https://housingjapan.com/buy/history/

Hu, Y., and Oxley, L. 2018, 'Bubble contagion: Evidence from Japan's asset price bubble of the 19880–90s', *Journal of the Japanese and International Economies*, vol. 50, pp. 89–95.

Iacoviello, M., and Neri, S. 2010, 'Housing market spillovers: Evidence from an estimated DSGE model', *American Economic Journal: Macroeconomics*, vol. 2, pp. 125–64.

Ito, T., and Hirono, K.N. 1993, 'Efficiency of the Tokyo housing market', *Bank of Japan Monetary and Economic Studies*, vol. 11, no. 1, pp. 1–32.

Ito, T., and Iwaisako, T. 1995, 'Explaining asset bubbles in Japan', NBER Working Paper no. 5358.

Kanemoto, Y. 1997, 'The housing question in Japan', *Regional Science and Urban Economics*, vol. 27, pp. 613–641.

Kanik, B., and Xiao, W. 2014, 'Housing boom-bust cycles, and monetary policy', Central Bank of Turkey Working Paper, 14/15.

Kermani, A. 2013, 'Cheap credit, collateral and the boom-bust cycle', in *Essays in macroeconomics and finance*, PhD thesis, MIT, June.

Kholodilin, K., and Michelsen, C. 2018, 'Signs of housing bubble in many OECD countries – lower risk in Germany', DIW Weekly Report, 30–31, pp. 275–285.

Kim, J.R., and Kim, G. 2016, 'Fundamentals and rational bubbles in the Korean housing market: A modified present-value approach', *Economic Modelling*, vol. 59, pp. 174–181.

Kishor, N.K., and Morley, J. 2015, 'What drives the price-rent ratio for the housing market? A modified present-value analysis', *Journal of Economic Dynamics and Control*, vol. 58, pp. 235–249.

Kostakis, A., Magdalinos, T., and Stamatogiannis, M.P. 2015, 'Robust econometric inference for stock return predictability', *Review of Financial Studies*, vol. 28, no. 5, pp. 1506–1553.

Krainer, J., Spiegel, M.M., and Yamori, N. 2010, 'Asset price persistence and real estate market illiquidity: Evidence from Japanese land values', *Real Estate Economics*, vol. 38, no. 2, pp. 171–196.

Kuang, P. 2014, 'A model of housing and credit cycles with imperfect market knowledge', *European Economic Review*, vol. 70, pp. 419–437.

Lambertini, L., Mendicino, C., and Punzi, M.T. 2013, 'Leaning against boom-bust cycles in credit and housing prices', *Journal of Economic Dynamics and Control*, vol. 37, pp. 1500–1522.

LeRoy, S.F., and Porter, R.D. 1981, 'The present value relation: Tests based on implied variance bounds', *Econometrica*, vol. 64, pp. 555–574.

Leung, C. 2014, 'Error-correction dynamics of house prices: An equilibrium benchmark', *Journal of Housing Economics*, vol. 25, pp. 75–95.

Levitin, A.J., and Wachter, S.M. 2012, 'Explaining the housing bubble', *Georgetown Law Journal*, vol. 100, no. 4, pp. 1177–1258.

Magdalinos, T., and Phillips, P.C.B. 2009, 'Limit theory for cointegrated systems with moderately integrated and moderately explosive regressors', *Econometric Theory*, vol. 25, pp. 482–526.

Malpezzi, S. 1999, 'A simple error-correction model of house prices', *Journal of Housing Economics*, vol. 8, pp. 27–62.

Martin, A., and Ventura, J. 2018, 'The macroeconomics of rational bubbles: A user's guide', *Frontier in Economics*, vol. 10, pp. 505–539.

Mayer, C. 2006, 'Where's the housing bubble? Comments', *Brookings Papers on Economic Activity*, vol. 1, pp. 51–59.

Meese, R., and Wallace, N. 1994, 'Testing the present value relation for housing prices: Should I leave my house in San Francisco', *Journal of Urban Economics*, vol. 35, pp. 155–172.
Miller, E.M. 1977, 'Risk, uncertainty, and divergence of opinion', *Journal of Finance*, vol. 32, no. 4, pp. 1151–1168.
Nakamura, K., and Saita, Y. 2007, 'Land prices and fundamentals', Bank of Japan Working Paper, 07-E-8.
Nathanson, C., and Zwick, E. 2017, 'Arrested development: Theory and evidence of supply-side speculation in the housing market', NBER Working Paper no. 23030.
Nogushi, Y. 1994, 'Land prices and house prices in Japan', in Nogushi, Y., and Poterba, J. (eds), *Housing markets in the United States and Japan*, pp. 11–28. Chicago, IL: University of Chicago Press.
Pavlidis, E., Paya, I., Peel, D., and Spiru, A.M. 2009, 'Bubbles in house prices and their impact on consumption: Evidence from the US', Lancaster University Management School, working paper no. 2009/025.
Pavlidis, E., Yusupova, A., Paya, I., Peel, D.A., Martinez-Garcia, E., Mack, A., and Grossman, V. 2015, 'Episodes of exhuberance in housing markets: In search of a smoking gun', *Journal of Real Estate Finance and Economics*, vol. 53, pp. 419–449.
Phillips, P.C.B., and Shi, S. 2018, 'Financial bubble implosion and reverse regression', *Econometric Theory*, vol. 34, no. 4, pp. 705–753.
Phillips, P.C.B., and Shi, S. 2020, 'Real time monitoring of asset markets: Bubbles and crises', in Hrishikesh, D.V. and Rao, C.R. (eds), *Handbook of statistics*, vol. 42, pp. 61–80. New York: Elsevier.
Phillips, P.C.B., and Shi, S. 2021, 'Diagnosing housing fever with an econometric thermometer', *Journal of Economic Surveys*, forthcoming.
Phillips, P.C.B., Wu, Y., and Yu, J. 2011, 'Explosive behavior in the 1990s Nasdaq: When did exuberance escalate asset values?' *International Economic Review*, vol. 52, no. 1, pp. 201–226.
Phillips, P.C.B., Shi, S., and Yu, J. 2015a, 'Testing for multiple bubbles: Historical episodes of exuberance and collapse in the S&P 500', *International Economic Review*, vol. 56, pp. 1043–1078.
Phillips, P.C.B., Shi, S., and Yu, J. 2015b, 'Testing for multiple bubbles: Limit theory of real-time detectors', *International Economic Review*, vol. 56, no. 4, pp. 1079–1134.
Plazzi, A., Torous, W., and Valkanov, R. 2010, 'Expected returns and expected growth in rents of commercial real estate', *Review of Financial Studies*, vol. 23, no. 9, pp. 3469–3519.
Poterba, J.M. 1984, 'Tax subsidies to owner-occupied housing: An asset-marlet approach', *Quarterly Journal of Economics*, vol. 99, no. 4, pp. 729–752.
Sato, H. 2013, 'The US real estate bubble: A comparison to Japan', *Japan and the World Economy*, vol. 15, no. 3, pp. 365–371.
Scherbina, A., and Schlusche, B. 2012, 'Asset bubbles: An application to residential real estate', *European Financial Management*, vol. 18, no. 3, pp. 464–491.
Scherbina, A., and Schlusche, B. 2014, 'Asset price bubbles: A survey', *Quantitative Finance*, vol. 14, no. 4, pp. 589–604.
Schleifer, A., and Vishny, R.A. 1997, 'The limits of arbitrage', *Journal of Finance*, vol. 52, no. 1, pp. 35–55.
Shi, S. 2017, 'Speculative bubbles or market fundamentals? An investigation of US regional housing markets', *Economic Modelling*, vol. 66, pp. 101–111.
Shiller, R.J. 1981, 'Do stock prices move too much to be justified by subsequent changes in dividends?' *American Economic Review*, vol. 71, pp. 421–436.
Shiller, R.J. 2006, 'Where's the housing bubble? Comments', *Brookings Papers on Economic Activity*, vol. 1, pp. 59–67.
Shiller, R.J. 2007, 'Historic turning points in real estate', Cowles Foundation Discussion Paper no. 1610.
Shiller, R.J. 2015, 'The housing market still isn't rational', *New York Times*, 24 July.
Shimizu, C., Diewert, W.E., Nishimura, K.G., and Watanabe, T. 2015, 'Estimating quality-adjusted commercial property price indices using Japanese REIT data', *Journal of Property Research*, vol. 32, no. 3, pp. 217–239.
Smith, M.H., and Smith, G. 2006, 'Where's the housing bubble?' *Brookings Papers on Economic Activity*, vol. 1, pp. 1–50.
Stiglitz, J.E. 1990, 'Symposium on bubbles', *Journal of Economic Perspectives*, vol. 4, no. 2, pp. 13–18.

Taipalus, K. 2012, 'Detecting asset price bubbles with time-series methods', Bank of Finland, Scientific Monographs, E:47-2012.

Van Norden, S., and Schaller, H. 1993, 'The predictability of stock market regime: Evidence from the Toronto stock exchange', *Review of Economics and Statistics*, vol. 75, no. 3, pp. 505–510.

Vissing-Jorgensen, A. 2003, 'Perspectives on behavioural finance: Does "irrationality" disappear with wealth? Evidence from expectations and actions', *NBER Macroeconomics Annual*, 139–194.

Wachter, S.M. 2015, 'The housing and credit bubbles in the United States and Europe: A comparison', *Journal of Money, Credit and Banking*, vol. 47, no. S1, pp. 37–42.

West, K.D. 1987, 'A specification test for speculative bubbles', *Quarterly Journal of Economics*, vol. 102, pp. 553–580.

West, K.D. 1988a, 'Dividends, innovations and stock price volatility', *Econometrica*, vol. 56, 37–61.

West, K.D. 1988b, 'Bubbles, fads and stock price volatility tests: A partial evaluation', *Journal of Finance*, vol. 43, no. 3, pp. 639–656.

Wöckl, I. 2019, 'Bubble detection in financial markets: A survey of theoretical models and empirical bubble detection tests', Manuscript, University of Graz. www.researchgate.net/publication/336085827_Bubble_Detection_in_Financial_Markets_-_A_Survey_of_Theoretical_Bubble_Models_and_Empirical_Bubble_Detection_Tests

Yang, B., Long, W., Peng, L., and Cai, Z. 2020, 'Testing the predictability of US housing price index returns based on an IVX-AR model', *Journal of the American Statistical Association*, vol. 115, no. 532, pp. 1–22.

# APPENDIX: DATA SOURCES

| | |
|---|---|
| *prr* | Housing price-to-rent ratio, base year 2015, and nominal rent index are sourced from the OECD, prices: Analytical House Price Indicators. |
| *i* | Real mortgage rate. Mortgage rate is the housing loan: corporation interest rate: private dwelling, sourced from the Japan Housing Finance Agency. We convert the monthly nominal mortgage rate to quarterly observations by averaging. The real mortgage rate is calculated as the nominal mortgage rate less inflation. |
| *Rent* | OECD, base year 2015, rent price index, seasonally adjusted. |
| *real_rent = rent/CPI_SA* | |
| *CPI* | Base year 2015, OECD, prices: comparative price level. *CPI_SA* is CPI seasonally adjusted using X-12. |
| *Bank_credit* | Total credit to private non-financial sector, adjusted for breaks, for Japan, billions of Japanese yen, quarterly, not seasonally adjusted. St-Louis Fed. |
| *RBank_credit = Bank_credit/CPI* | Real bank credit. |
| *Pop* | Population (1000s), Japanese Statistical Bureau, with an annual frequency interpolated to quarterly. |
| *RPDI* | Real personal disposable income, index base year 2005, OECD. |
| *Emp* | Employment rate: aged 15–64: all persons for Japan, per cent, seasonally adjusted. St-Louis Fed. |
| *Workstart* | Total dwellings and residential buildings, by stage of construction, started for Japan, number of permits, quarterly, seasonally adjusted. St-Louis Fed. |

# 7. Disaggregating house price dynamics
*Rose Neng Lai and Robert A. Van Order*

## 1  INTRODUCTION

Housing units are both consumption and investment assets, which means their values are not only about how much they cost to construct and maintain, but about how much expected return they generate in the future. Despite being only one element in investment markets, because housing units are owned by a majority of households in many countries and, hence, are a major source of household wealth, as well as creating household loans, housing markets can have big effects on the whole financial system. For example, while it is well known that investment in housing can be a good hedge against loss of wealth due to inflation, the burst of the United States (US) housing market bubble was also the trigger of the 2008–2009 Global Financial Crisis. Hence, it is important for both investors and regulatory bodies to have a good understanding of the causes of the rise and fall of housing prices.

As in other commodity markets, house price is governed by supply and demand. In some markets, however, double-digit vacancy rates and high house prices, such as in cities in China, coexist.[1] In this kind of booming market, there is often commentary that a bubble in the housing market has formed. "Bubbles are typically defined as periods in which asset prices run well above or below the intrinsic value" (Fama, 1965). Likewise, a bubble is defined as the part of the price that deviates from the housing market fundamentals (Case and Shiller, 1989, 2003). The usual result is that banks tend to overlend, despite the low quality of mortgagors (Loayza and Rancière, 2006), thus creating potential financial fragility. The bubble is then said to burst once the price plummets or there is a large correction back to the fundamentals. This is often followed by a prolonged distressed housing market and a distressed banking sector when the loans and mortgages become bad debts.

Hence, this chapter shows the importance of disaggregating house price dynamics in understanding which part of the housing price reflects the market fundamentals and which part is the bubble, so that regulatory bodies will be able to better prepare for any potential fragility in both the housing and the financial markets as a result of the bubble bursting. In particular, the fundamentals are built up over time, while the market conditions with bubbles are relatively short term. We show this by first introducing a theoretical model of the fundamentals of the housing markets following the Gordon Dividend Discount model. We then explain two types of econometric models that could be used to perform empirical studies of the markets. We illustrate these analyses with the housing markets in the US and China. These two countries are chosen for a few reasons. First, they are at present the two largest economies. Second, the US housing market is claimed to have been the trigger of the Global Financial Crisis. On the other hand, the Chinese markets have undergone a prolonged boom, and been widely described as having big bubbles; yet the bubbles have not really burst. We show how while both markets experienced booms, prices have risen with different characteristics and generated different outcomes so far. Disaggregation can be about factors affecting different markets within a country differently. Hence, the second attempt here is to analyze how different cities react to bubbles in the housing market.

This study by no means tries to exhaust all the types of explanation and models about housing bubbles. Instead, we review Lai and Van Order (2010, 2017, 2019) to illustrate how not admitting the existence of bubbles would reduce the usefulness of regulatory policies in balancing the boom and bust of the housing markets with the overall economy, and how not considering disaggregating the markets into different groups might reduce the usefulness of some policies. After all, one size does not fit all.

## 2  ON HOUSING BUBBLES

### 2.1  What They Are and Why

Assets are priced based on demand and supply. Higher demands drive prices up; increased supplies drive prices down. These up and down adjustments will be made until everyone, both buyers and sellers, agrees on the same price, the equilibrium price. This is easier said than determined. The question is *why* that amount of demand and supply. In the case of stocks, the price per share is what the shareholder is willing to pay today for what he/she can earn for the rest of the company's performance, i.e. the return on equity. Hence, the stock price reflects earnings in the future based on the best information about the earnings capability and growth of the company in the future, i.e. its "fundamentals." The stock market is where shares of many of the listed companies are traded. Occasionally, however, people might misjudge, for instance, because they are overly optimistic about the values of these companies, and therefore more willing to pay higher stock prices than the companies are actually worth. If everyone speculates that the price increase will be sustained, so that prices in the stock market keep surging to levels that are significantly above the companies' fundamentals, the bubble market is created. Hence, overconfidence (or bounded rationality) and speculation are two key causes of bubbles, although research has also shown that bubbles can exist without overconfidence, speculation, and uncertainty (see, for example, Smith et al., 1988; Lei et al., 2001; Levine et al., 2007).

Unlike more efficient stock markets where price adjustments are made very promptly, housing markets are much less efficient, and are therefore more prone to bubbles that last much longer. Housing markets also tend to be very cyclical, starting with demand build-ups pushing up the price, followed by developers rushing to build upon a shortage of supply, and then ending with oversupply and a price drop until demand starts to pick up again. Such a cycle will take years to complete. As described by Case and Shiller (2003):

> If expectations of rapid and steady future price increases are important motivating factors for buyers, then home prices are inherently unstable. Prices cannot go up rapidly forever, and when people perceive that prices have stopped going up, this support for their acceptance of high home prices could break down. Prices could then fall as a result of diminished demand: the bubble bursts.

With this, Shiller (2019) has already been warning the public of the next housing bubble burst since 2019 because, as he claimed, all assets have been overpriced, and a strong US economy does not imply it is healthy. His view is mostly concerned with narrative economics, which is basically the view that people's behavior and decision making can be seriously affected by stories and phenomena, rather than the traditional explanations using data and mathematical models and theories.[2] Figure 7.1 shows the average price indices of 44 metropolitan statistical areas (MSAs) for the period from January 2000 to December 2019. The housing prices start to increase from the trough in the first quarter of 2012 to a new high. This trend supports the argument of the existence of another bubble due to burst.

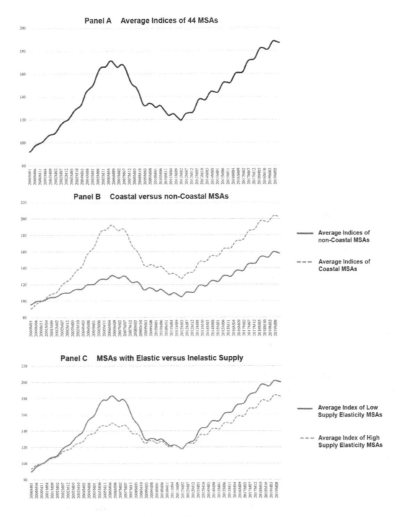

Source: Calculations from monthly house price indices from Freddie Mac for metropolitan statistical areas.

Figure 7.1  Price indices of the United States housing markets

Housing market bubbles can broadly be caused by an increase in the amount and ease of the supply of credit, usually associated with low interest rates and loose credit underwriting. Banks write mortgage contracts with more lenient standards to those who in the past might not be granted a mortgage. It also makes housing units more affordable with lower interest rates.

While this is good for homebuyers, it is also welcomed by speculators, driving up the market further. However, once liquidity dries up and/or interest rates go up, banks will be more careful in scrutinizing borrowers. Existing borrowers might also find it difficult to pay back their loans, and hence have to default. Investor confidence is gradually lost. Demand drops, prices plummet, and the bubble is burst.

Another cause of bubbles can be the behavior of investors. In addition to overly optimistic buyers who are willing to pay for overpriced assets, herding is another usually self-fulfilling phenomenon. Very often, people start to ignore their own information or rational judgment and follow others when they see these "winners" buying early and gaining a handsome profit upon selling. And when more "followers" gain as the prices continue to go up, more "followers" enter the market, pushing the prices further up. This is usually associated with keen persuasion from real estate brokers. Herding can also be on the supply side. DeCoster and Strange (2012) note that developers construct more housing units because they assume their competitors build based on valuable information about the market, which leads to overbuilding.

Examples of bubbles markets date back to the Dutch tulip mania in the seventeenth century when people started speculating on the prices of different tulips (Garber, 2000). A lot of farmers earned a whole lot of money by growing and selling tulips. Short-selling and contracts like futures were used. Some contracts could even change ownership ten times within one day. This speculation carried on until interest in buying the tulip bulbs suddenly died away, and prices plummeted. The bubble burst. The more recent bubbles include the Dot.Com bubble in the late 1990s when technology stocks, particularly those that had launched websites, were viewed and/or commented on as having very high earnings potential. A lot of these stocks had not even earned any income, and their price-earnings ratios were undefined. Once investors found that many of these companies could not deliver their ideas into real earning power, they lost confidence, the market had huge corrections in prices, and then the market crashed. The most recent is the 2006–2007 US housing bubble, in which the burst triggered the Global Financial Crisis in the second half of 2008 through 2009, leading not only to the Great Recession in the US, but also to economic shocks all over the world.

The problem with a bubble market is that it is often very difficult to realize whether the market boom is really due to a bubble or to strong performance. Economists therefore often claim that no one knows it is a bubble until it bursts. What is typical of a bubble is its very rapid formation (due to escalating prices) and then a very fast contraction when prices plummet due to extensive sell-offs when investors no longer believe the prices are realistic representations of the fundamentals.

Housing market bubbles tend to exist less frequently as stock market bubbles. However, because of high transaction costs and a lack of short-selling activities, housing market bubbles usually last longer. Glaeser and Nathanson (2015) did a thorough review of the various causes and theories of housing bubbles. In particular, they mention that housing market bubbles can be due to domination by "amateurs" who tend to be more "loss" averse and therefore not willing to sell at the low price that the market is willing to pay. As these "amateurs" herd to join the market during the boom, there are more loans than if the market is only filled with homeowners. As a result, when the bubble bursts many people lose their investments and cannot pay back the banks, and the banking sector is also in trouble. Housing bubbles are more prevalent in areas with inelastic supply, as the bubbles are supported by firstly strong demand and then a price surge, attracting more market participants, and then either an increase in supply or other liquidity-tightening conditions; demand shrinks, and finally the bubble bursts.

Glaeser and Nathanson (2015) also comment that policy makers should be cautious in containing bubbles and implementing macroeconomic policies to stabilize the markets as there could be serious consequences. Policies that support homeownership like those after 2002 in the US could lead to many homeowners losing their wealth because of the drop in value of their house while they are still indebted. In the 2006–2007 housing bubble, many homeowners lost their homes to foreclosure because they had no choice but to default their mortgages as housing price is usually correlated with personal income.

There have been many studies of stock market bubbles and housing bubbles. One of the earlier studies is Blanchard and Watson (1982) who suggest the stochastic bubbles model. This is later extended by Van Norden and Schaller (1993, 1996) and Van Norden (1996) to incorporate the time-varying relationship between returns and overpriced components. Another approach is Summers (1986), who proposes the fads model. Econometric models used to test bubbles for financial markets include testing for stationarity and cointegration in order to test for the presence of speculative bubbles in, for example, Diba and Grossman (1988) and Hamilton and Whiteman (1985) (although Evans (1991) also shows that by artificially introducing bubbles in the Monte Carlo simulations, these tests tend to reject the presence of bubbles too often). Baddeley (2005) shows that markets that are more prone to herding where financing and uncertainty are important determinants will tend to have bigger swings in booms and busts, and property markets are a typical example. Kindleberger and Aliber (2005) provide a good narration of the history of bubbles.

Studies of housing bubbles became readily available much later. Some examples are Chan et al. (2001), Capozza et al. (2004), Black et al. (2006), Hwang et al. (2006), Taipalus (2006), Coleman et al. (2008), Wheaton and Nechayev (2008), Case et al. (2011), Nneji et al. (2013), and Ling et al. (2015). Furthermore, according to Poterba (1984), market booms can be caused by inflation (see also Brunnermeier and Julliard, 2008). In this chapter, we introduce two types of econometric models that can be used to test the housing bubbles as covered in recent papers by Lai and Van Order (2010, 2017, 2019) for both the US markets and the Chinese markets.

## 2.2 The Case of the United States

The most recent housing bubble originated in 2001 when the US economy was in a recession after the Dot.Com bubble, and the Federal Reserve lowered the Fed funds rate 11 times from 6.5 percent all the way to 1.75 percent. More homes were bought, and home prices started to accelerate. Real estate brokers were able to attract many homebuyers to purchase their homes, with mortgage originators providing various sorts of mortgages that were less likely to be paid back, the so-called subprime and low document mortgages. Houses were bought because of the low mortgage rates and looser standards, in the hope that house prices would continue to rise. One type of loan, called "NINJA" loans, to people who have "no income, no job or assets" illustrates how easily loans were written. Mortgage originators, like banks, did not need to worry as much about default risks because they only originated the mortgages and were only indirectly responsible for default costs. The loans were then bundled together and sold as securities such as mortgage-backed securities, some of which were further bundled into collateralized debt obligations. As these securities were backed by mortgages and collateral such as housing units, which are usually considered to be the safest type of loan, and because most were structured, with subordinated pieces taking first losses, many securities were AAA rated by rating agencies. Whether their risks were actually that low is another story. As Glaeser and Nathanson (2015) mention, bubbles are much more likely to be created when the lenders "under-price default risk." In 2004, because the Securities Exchange Commission relaxed the net capital rule for investment banks like Goldman Sachs, Merrill Lynch, Bear Stearns, Morgan Staley, and Lehman Brothers, they were able to increase their leverage further. Funding supply from both securitization and these increasingly levered financial institutions became unlimited. Housing prices continued to rise.

The "American Dream" started to collapse when the Federal Reserve started to increase interest rates from 1 to 6.25 percent in the period 2004–2006 in order to cool down the overheated economy. As a result, the cost of short-term borrowing increased substantially. House prices started to drop, and property foreclosure began to increase in 2005. In 2007, many subprime mortgages defaulted, leading to the bankruptcy of investors and lenders, marking the burst of the housing bubble, which later led to the Global Financial Crisis. Figure 7.1 traces how house price indices surged from just above 90 points in January 2000 to over 170 points in mid-2006, dropping to 120 in March 2012. The cause of this bubble was of course the ease of funding and loose credit underwriting. Nevertheless, another driving force was herding. Seeing the house price upsurge, investors joined the market. The mortgage-backed securities and collateralized debt obligations were bought by many financial institutions with the aim of earning high returns, particularly because they were rated as high-quality debt securities. There was also serious herding among financial institutions.

Panels B and C of Figure 7.1 also show that markets did not boom at the same pace. In Panel B, the 44 MSAs are classified into a coastal group and non-coastal group. The former is made up of those with higher price growth and are mostly considered as bubble MSAs, while the latter group constitutes MSAs with lower growth and are mostly non-bubble MSAs. It is obvious that the coastal cities experienced much higher growth in the last housing bubble. The more recent data from the second half of 2012 also show higher price growth in coastal MSAs, although that of the non-coastal MSAs picks up in parallel. Panel C depicts the MSA group with more versus less elastic supply. As mentioned before, cities with inelastic supply tend to be more prone to the formation of bubbles. This is seen from the figure, albeit more obviously in the last bubble. Hence, it is important to disaggregate the country-wide data into different MSAs when studying bubble markets because their bubbles are formed differently, both in terms of speed and magnitude. Policy makers need to know their differences in order to set up policies to suit different needs from the markets.

## 2.3 The Case of China – Is There Really a Bubble?

After 40 years of the "open door" policy, China has gone from a poor country to the second largest economy in the world according to the World Bank. During its growth, it has become the world's factory with its cheap labor force. Gradually, it has also established relatively complete financial markets. Housing markets have been reformed from housing being provided by employers (typically state owned) to private ownership since 1998. With the constant expansion of the housing market in the early 2000s, many small developers have profited from building more housing units, and some have become big developers. As of 2019, the four largest Chinese real estate companies by revenue are Evergrande Group, Country Garden, Greenland Holdings, and Vanke.[3] Housing prices continue their increase as seen in Figure 7.2. In Panel A, the average price index of 80 cities (the list of cities is in Panel B of Tables 7.1A and 7.1B) shows a steady increase apart from a few hiccups at the end of 2008 and the

*Disaggregating house price dynamics* 171

beginning of 2009, after the Global Financial Crisis took place, and then in mid-2014 when there was oversupply and high vacancy rates.

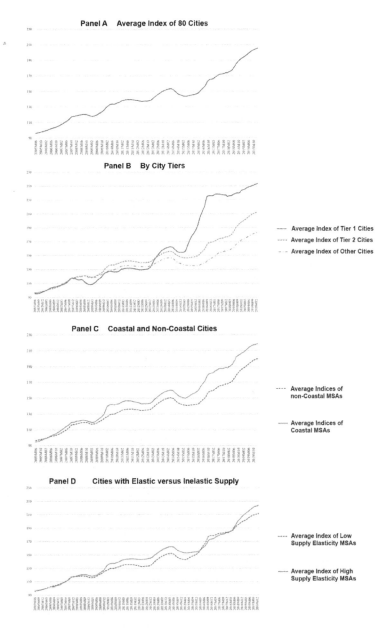

*Figure 7.2    Price indices of the Chinese housing markets*

## Table 7.1A  List of US metropolitan statistical areas in the study

| Bubble MSAs | | Non-bubble MSAs | |
|---|---|---|---|
| Anchorage | Salem | Akron | Fort Worth |
| Boston | San Diego | Ann Arbor | Gary |
| Fort Lauderdale | San Francisco | Atlanta | Greeley |
| Los Angeles | San Jose | Atlantic City | Houston |
| Miami | Seattle | Baltimore | Kansas City |
| New York | Tacoma | Boulder | Lake County |
| Phoenix | Tampa | Bremerton | Milwaukee |
| Portland | Honolulu | Chicago | Minneapolis |
| Riverside | Washington | Cincinnati | Philadelphia |
| | | Cleveland | Pittsburgh |
| | | Dallas | Racine |
| | | Denver | St. Louis |
| | | Detroit | Wilmington |
| | | Flint | |

*Classifications of MSAs into coastal versus inland and supply elasticities*

| MSA | Coastal | Supply elasticity | MSA | Coastal | Supply elasticity |
|---|---|---|---|---|---|
| Akron, OH | 0 | 2.59 | Mount Vernon-Anacortes, WA | 1 | |
| Ann Arbor, MI | 0 | 2.29 | Napa, CA | 1 | 1.14 |
| Atlanta-Sandy Springs-Roswell, GA | 0 | 2.55 | New Haven-Milford, CT | 1 | 0.98 |
| Atlantic City-Hammonton, NJ | 1 | | New York-Newark-Jersey City, NY-NJ-PA | 1 | 1.12 |
| Baltimore-Columbia-Towson, MD | 1 | 1.23 | Olympia-Tumwater, WA | 1 | |
| Boston-Cambridge-Newton, MA-NH | 1 | 0.86 | Oxnard-Thousand Oaks-Ventura, CA | 1 | |
| Bremerton-Silverdale, WA | 1 | | Philadelphia-Camden-Wilmington, PA-NJ-DE-MD | 0 | 1.82 |
| Bridgeport-Stamford-Norwalk, CT | 1 | | Providence-Warwick, RI-MA | 1 | 1.61 |
| Chicago-Naperville-Elgin, IL-IN-WI | 0 | 0.81 | Reading, PA | 0 | |
| Cleveland-Elyria, OH | 0 | 1.02 | Riverside-San Bernardino-Ontario, CA | 1 | 0.94 |
| Dallas-Fort Worth-Arlington, TX | 0 | 2.49 | San Francisco-Oakland-Hayward, CA | 1 | 0.68 |
| Detroit-Warren-Dearborn, MI | 0 | 1.24 | San Jose-Sunnyvale-Santa Clara, CA | 1 | 0.76 |
| Flint, MI | 0 | | Santa Cruz-Watsonville, CA | 1 | |
| Gainesville, FL | 1 | | Santa Rosa, CA | 1 | |
| Houston-The Woodlands-Sugar Land, TX | 0 | 2.3 | Seattle-Tacoma-Bellevue, WA | 1 | 1.045 |
| Kankakee, IL | 0 | | Sherman-Denison, TX | 0 | |
| Kingston, NY | 1 | | Trenton, NJ | 1 | |
| Los Angeles-Long Beach-Anaheim, CA | 1 | 0.63 | Vallejo-Fairfield, CA | 1 | 1.14 |
| Manchester-Nashua, NH | 1 | | Vineland-Bridgeton, NJ | 1 | |
| Miami-Fort Lauderdale-West Palm Beach, FL | 1 | 0.69 | Washington-Arlington-Alexandria, DC-VA-MD-WV | 1 | 1.61 |
| Michigan City-La Porte, IN | 0 | | Winchester, VA-WV | 1 | |
| Monroe, LA | 0 | | Worcester, MA-CT | 1 | 0.86 |

*Source*: Lai and Van Order (2017); supply elasticity from Saiz (2010).
*Note*: 0 = non-coastal; 1 = coastal.

Disaggregating house price dynamics    173

Table 7.1B    List of Chinese cities in the study

| City | Province | Tiers | Coastal | Supply elasticity | City | Province | Tiers | Coastal | Supply elasticity |
|---|---|---|---|---|---|---|---|---|---|
| Beijing | Beijing | Tier 1 |  | 0.53 | Guangzhou | Guangdong | Tier 1 | * | 12.62 |
| Shanghai | Shanghai | Tier 1 | * | 1.52 | Shenzhen | Guangdong | Tier 1 | * | 0.49 |
| Hefei | Anhui | Tier 2 |  | 13.03 | Wuxi | Jiangsu | Tier 2 |  |  |
| Chongqing | Chongqing | Tier 2 |  | 4.51 | Nanchang | Jiangxi | Tier 2 |  | 6.78 |
| Xiamen | Fujian | Tier 2 | * | 3.47 | Changchun | Jilin | Tier 2 |  | 5.4 |
| Fuzhou | Fujian | Tier 2 | * | 3.85 | Dalian | Liaoning | Tier 2 | * | 4.41 |
| Lanzhou | Gansu | Tier 2 |  | 4.9 | Shenyang | Liaoning | Tier 2 |  | 5.75 |
| Beihai | Guangxi | Tier 2 | * |  | Yinchuan | Ningxia | Tier 2 |  | 21.98 |
| Nanning | Guangxi | Tier 2 |  | 11.45 | Xining | Qinghai | Tier 2 |  | 37.05 |
| Guiyang | Guizhou | Tier 2 |  | 9.71 | Xian | Shaanxi | Tier 2 |  | 8.04 |
| Haikou | Hainan | Tier 2 | * | 8.83 | Qingdao | Shandong | Tier 2 | * | 2.89 |
| Sanya | Hainan | Tier 2 | * |  | Jinan | Shandong | Tier 2 |  | 2.68 |
| Shijiazhuang | Hebei | Tier 2 |  | 7.89 | Taiyuan | Shanxi | Tier 2 |  | 9.16 |
| Harbin | Heilongjiang | Tier 2 |  | 6.3 | Chengdu | Sichuan | Tier 2 |  | 4.36 |
| Zhengzhou | Henan | Tier 2 |  | 16.5 | Tianjin | Tianjin | Tier 2 | * | 5.1 |
| Wuhan | Hubei | Tier 2 |  | 4.66 | Urumqi | Xinjiang | Tier 2 |  | 16.71 |
| Changsha | Hunan | Tier 2 |  | 17.14 | Kunming | Yunnan | Tier 2 |  | -7.7 |
| Hohhot | Inner Mongolia | Tier 2 |  | 9.63 | Ningbo | Zhejiang | Tier 2 | * | 2.27 |
| Suzhou | Jiangsu | Tier 2 |  |  | Wenzhou | Zhejiang | Tier 2 | * |  |
| Nanjing | Jiangsu | Tier 2 |  | 3.42 | Hangzhou | Zhejiang | Tier 2 |  | 2.65 |

174  *Handbook of real estate and macroeconomics*

| City | Province | Tiers | Coastal | Supply elasticity | City | Province | Tiers | Coastal | Supply elasticity |
|---|---|---|---|---|---|---|---|---|---|
| Bengbu | Anhui | | | | Xuzhou | Jiangsu | | | |
| Anqing | Anhui | | | | Changzhou | Jiangsu | | | |
| Tongling | Anhui | | | | Yancheng | Jiangsu | | * | |
| Wuhu | Anhui | | | | Yangzhou | Jiangsu | | | |
| Quanzhou | Fujian | | * | | Ganzhou | Jiangxi | | | |
| Shantou | Guangdong | | * | | Jiujiang | Jiangxi | | | |
| Dongguan | Guangdong | | * | | Jilin | Jilin | | | |
| Foshan | Guangdong | | | | Weifang | Shandong | | | |
| Huizhou | Guangdong | | | | Yantai | Shandong | | * | |
| Shaoguan | Guangdong | | | | Weihai | Shandong | | * | |
| Zhanjiang | Guangdong | | * | | Zibo | Shandong | | | |
| Zhuhai | Guangdong | | * | | Linyi | Shandong | | | |
| Qinhuangdao | Hebei | | * | | Rizhao | Shandong | | | |
| Tangshan | Hebei | | | | Nanchong | Sichuan | | | |
| Baoding | Hebei | | | | Mianyang | Sichuan | | | |
| Pingdingshan | Henan | | | | Jinhua | Zhejiang | | | |
| Luoyang | Henan | | | | Huzhou | Zhejiang | | | |
| Changde | Hunan | | | | Jiaxing | Zhejiang | | | |
| Yueyang | Hunan | | | | Shaoxing | Zhejiang | | | |
| Nantong | Jiangsu | | * | | Taizhou | Zhejiang | | | |

*Note*: Supply elasticity is from Wang et al. (2012).

The housing boom in China shares causes similar to those in the US – government-motivated abundant money supply and low interest rates. What is unique in China is the extra force coming from local municipal governments. Due to the Global Financial Crisis, the government released an RMB 4 trillion (USD 586 billion) stimulus package to boost the economy by expanding credits and funding to local municipal governments to encourage spending on infrastructure. Added to this, local governments have to fulfill the tax policy of the central government. Since real estate developments offer higher returns, these local governments rely on selling land and enticing investments in building new apartment estates in order to boost their year-end performance.

Disaggregating the data as shown in Panel A of Figure 7.2 into different categories, it is easy to see that different cities grew at quite different paces. First, from Panel B, where cities are classified into the really booming four largest cities (Tier 1) and other cities (Tier 2, etc.), Tier 1 cities grew much faster than Tier 2 cities. Hence, applying any policies uniformly to all cities to mitigate housing bubbles might be successful in curbing the markets of Tier 1 cities on one hand, but dampen the markets in all other cities on the other. Note that the curve for Tier 1 cities below the other two groups during the period of the last quarter of 2007 to the last quarter of 2012 does not imply that the housing prices of these four Tier 1 megacities are lower than the other groups. Figure 7.2 only shows indices that started from 100 index points in the first month of the data in June 2005 when the housing prices of these cities were already higher than all other cities.

On the demand side, the Chinese are also famous for having high savings rates, but there are very few channels of investment. The stock markets tend to be volatile and not very efficient. Hence, a safer investment in which to store wealth is the property market. In addition, due to fast-growing housing prices, parents who have enough money have been incentivized to buy housing units for their children's use upon getting married in the future. This can partly explain the relatively high double-digit vacancy rate in China. The Chinese also have the perception that the Chinese government will regulate the markets such that there will not be a big price dive because the real estate industry constitutes so big a proportion of the economy that any downturn will trigger poor economic performance.

This may lead one to wonder why the housing boom has persisted for so long. Given easy credit, homebuyers have accumulated a lot of loans, increasing the default risk, and therefore the risk of the housing markets. This is nevertheless not quite applicable in China due to its culture. It is true that the prices have been so high that it is beyond the affordability of many Chinese. For instance, the price-to-income ratio in Tier 1 cities is 23 (Lin, 2019). However, for those who purchase the housing units, the typical downpayment has to be at least 20 percent during easy periods or 30 percent at other times. To cool down the markets, there are also policies requiring 40–50 percent downpayments for second homes, and full payment for additional units. Speculators often pay in cash. This means that the household leverage situation in the US is not occurring in China. In fact, the proportion of buyers who have mortgages in China is low. Glaeser et al. (2017) comment that as long as China continues to grow at a high speed, high housing prices can be justified because income grows faster than housing price.

Even though housing prices have surged by so much and have been widely agreed as constituting a bubble, whether the bubble will burst soon in the future is unclear. For example, Ahuja et al. (2010) claim that the market boom is due to factors of rapid urbanization and the culture of owning housing. Glaeser et al. (2017) also conclude that the Chinese housing bubble might not burst if the government takes the right measures. In fact, since the frenzy in 2008, the

176  *Handbook of real estate and macroeconomics*

central government has put forth different policies to curb the markets at different times. For instance, the purchase restrictions set in 2010 ("Guo-Shi-Tiao," that is "State 10 Measures," to distinguish them from the "Guo Ba Tiao," or "State 8 Measures," in 2005 and "Guo Liu Tiao," or "State 6 Measures" in 2006) prohibit households in Tier 1 cities to own more than one housing unit. Yet, in subsequent years, whenever there was a cool-down in the markets, the government would implement different measures to boost the markets, such as injecting more available funds to the banking sector, easing purchase restrictions, and so on. Hence, government intervention has allowed the apparent bubbles to stay afloat without reducing their size by much. Disaggregation in policies is crucial because of the heterogeneity of the cities as mentioned earlier. The Chinese government has done exactly that. Implementation of policies to curb the markets always starts from the easily overheated Tier 1 cities before similar policies, sometimes at different magnitudes, spread out to other cities. In other words, the puzzle is whether the markets are experiencing a bubble period; a bubble that does not burst might not actually be a bubble.

In the next sections, we show that our tests indeed do not show that the bubble will necessarily burst. Furthermore, like the studies for the US markets, we also classify the Chinese cities into different categories because these cities do not have the same pace of booming, and could therefore be open to different expanding or curbing policies. Zhi et al. (2019) confirm that it is important to perform bubble diagnostic tests because of the heterogeneity of the bubble characteristics across cities.

## 3  THEORETICAL AND EMPIRICAL MODELS

### 3.1  Model of the Fundamentals

"Fundamentals" in the context of real estate would be the perpetual flow of rents from the property. Given an information set, $\Omega_t$, the property price in equilibrium at time t should be equal to the rent obtained in the same period plus the present value of the price in the next period, that is

$$P_t = E(R_t | \Omega_t) + E(P_{t+1} / D_t | \Omega_t) \tag{7.1}$$

where $R_t$ is the imputed rent at time $t$. Imputed rent is the equivalent rent that the homeowner would pay if he/she were renting rather than owning, which in turn is the user cost, which equals the sum of the occupier's insurance, maintenance costs, depreciation, property tax, marginal income tax, and interest costs on the loans for the housing unit, as in Poterba (1984). $D_t$ is the risk-adjusted discount factor. For the imputed rent to be applicable to the model, it has to be measurable in the form of some market rent. Hence, the necessary condition is that the homeowner has to be indifferent between owning and renting. This way, complicated models with unstable demand and supply of housing across time and regions can be avoided, because the rent variable in our model can capture the underlying supply and demand factors, for instance due to inelastic supply, such as that mentioned in Glaeser et al. (2005), without having to depend on a particular model.

Since the price in the future is again the rent plus the present value of the price in the further future, iteratively, we have:

$$P_t = \sum_{i=0}^{\infty} E(R_{t+i} / D_{t+i}^i | \Omega_t) + \lim E(P_{t+1+i} / D_{t+1+i}^i | \Omega_t) \qquad (7.2)$$

The "fundamental" value is the price in Equation (7.2) where the second term represents the transversality condition, which hopefully approaches zero. That is

$$P_t = \sum_{i=0}^{\infty} E\left(R_{t+i} / D_{t+i}^i | \Omega_t\right). \qquad (7.3)$$

This means any test of the absence of bubbles is a test of the transversality condition, that is, whether the second term in (7.2) approaches zero. Note that Equation (7.3) incorporates a lot of correlations among the variables, for example that a rise in interest rates will cause a fall in property prices given the same rent. At the same time, however, the higher interest rate will lead to lower production, and therefore higher rent in the future. We can nevertheless simplify the model as follows.

Following the strand of literature that considers steady rent flow like dividends, according to the Gordon growth model, the price per unit of housing service at any time $t$, $P_t$ is the present value of all perpetual rental flow. That is

$$P_t = \frac{R_{t+1}}{\delta}. \qquad (7.4)$$

The term $\delta$ is the user cost, or "cap rate," of housing for each period. The user cost can vary over time, $t$, and can be expressed as

$$\delta_t = (1 - \tau_t) n_t - E(g) + d \qquad (7.5)$$

where $\tau_t$ is the marginal income tax rate at time $t$, $n_t$ is the nominal risk-free rate at the same period, $E(g)$ is the expected long-run rental growth rate (assumed constant), and $d$ is the sum of depreciation and risk premium (also assumed constant for simplicity). Deducting expected inflation rate (proxied by the expected consumer price index) from the nominal risk-free rate, Equation (7.5) becomes

$$\delta_t = \left[n_t - E(CPI_t)\right] - \left[E(g) - E(CPI_t)\right] - n_t \tau_t + d$$
$$= i_t - \left[E(g) - E(CPI_t)\right] - n_t \tau_t + d \qquad (7.6)$$

which can be interpreted as the real risk-free rate, $i_t$, net of expected real rent growth $E(g) - E(CPI_t)$, and tax-deducted mortgage payment and opportunity cost of equity, $n_t \tau_t$, plus depreciation and risk premium, $d$.

Inserting Equation (7.6) into Equation (7.4) and taking the logarithm and differencing on both sides, we have

$$p_t = r_{t+1} - \Delta \ln \left( i_t - \left[ E(g) - E(CPI_t) \right] - n_t \tau_t \right) \tag{7.7}$$

where $p_t$ is the growth rate of housing price and $r_{t+1}$ is the growth rate of rent.

## 3.2 Pricing Dynamics

According to Fama and French (1988) and Cutler et al. (1991), the logarithm of an asset market price is made up of the fundamental price, which is non-stationary, and predictable returns from past returns, which are stationary. Both these terms are autoregressive and are subject to different white noises. Hence, with a proxy for the fundamental price, the fads model for asset pricing is

$$p_{t+1} - p_t = \beta_0 + \beta_1 \left( p_t - p^x_t \right) + e_t$$

where $p_t$ is log of asset market price at time $t$, $p^x_t$ is the available proxy of the fundamental price, and $e_t \sim iid(0, \sigma_\omega^2)$. When this noise term is heteroscedastic, the fads model becomes similar to a regime-switching model in that it can appear to have two types of processes, either collapse or survive, and to be subject to two regime types. A more common notion of regime shift emphasizes discrete parameter shifts over different periods. We analyze models like this in Section 4.2.

Lai and Van Order (2010) provide an extension to this model with the error term being autoregressive. A regime shift is said to occur when the volatility of the error term increases and there is an increase in the "momentum" governed by the sum of the autoregression coefficients of the lagged error terms. Hence, the fundamental Equation (7.7) can be further approximated by

$$p - r = \alpha - \beta_i \Delta i + \beta_\pi \Delta \pi + \beta_n \Delta n_t + e_t \tag{7.8}$$

where $\alpha$ is a constant that allows rents and prices to have different trends, the $\beta$s are the coefficients from linearizing the terms, $\Delta \pi = \Delta \left[ E(g) - E(CPI_t) \right]$ is the long-run expected real rent growth, and $e_t$ is the disturbance term. The time factor is now incorporated in $\Delta n_t$. The $\beta$s in Equation (7.8) do not necessarily equal 1 because of tax and other factors such as cash-flow effects and lack of indexed mortgages that would be in $\Delta n_t$. A lagged approximation to Equation (7.8) is then

$$p_t = \alpha - \sum_{j=1}^{T} (\gamma^i_{t-j} \Delta i_{t-j} + \gamma^\pi_{t-j} \Delta \pi_{t-j}) + e_t \tag{7.9}$$

where $\rho_t$ is the house price growth rate minus rent growth rate. Equation (7.9) implies the constraint that a 1 percent growth in rent will lead to a 1 percent growth in house price in the long term. The residuals, $e_t$, are assumed to be an autoregressive process:

$$e_t = \sum_{j=1}^{T} \omega_{t-j} e_{t-j} + \upsilon_t \qquad (7.10)$$

where $\upsilon_t$ is *iid*. Note that the sum of $\omega_{t-j}$ will be greater than 1 if the bubble is explosive.

With this panel regression model (Equation (7.9)), Lai and Van Order (2017, 2019) test for the existence and magnitude of, and shifts in, momentum as measured by $\sum_t^T \omega_{t-j}$ in Equation (7.10). A positive sum implies momentum, while a negative sum implies mean reversion. Van Order and Dougherty (1991) test a rent-price model similar to the one developed in this chapter. Some research such as Capozza et al. (2004) studies bubbles as results of "overshooting" of estimated difference equations like Equation (7.7). Our work is similar to that of Chan et al. (2001), Black et al. (2006), Hwang et al. (2006), and Taipalus (2006), but is simpler than that of Chang et al. (2005), which estimates rents rather than using the market rent series data as in our model. Both types of work conclude that the fundamentals model is appropriate in explaining long-run price growth. Wheaton and Nechayev (2008) and Coleman et al. (2008) address regime shift in the bubble period.

### 3.3  The Pooled Mean Group Model

Equation (7.7) can also be expressed as

$$\frac{R_t}{P_t} = i_t - \pi_t + \alpha \qquad (7.11)$$

which is the long-run Gordon model where expected rents and prices move together. Hence, for estimation, Equation (7.11) can be expressed as

$$\frac{R_t}{P_t} = \gamma_i i_t - \gamma_\pi \pi_t + \alpha = c_t. \qquad (7.12)$$

Similar to Glaeser and Nathanson (2015), $R/P$ depends on past values of $R$, $P$, and $i$. Applying the Pooled Mean Group (PMG) and Mean Group (MG) estimation models of Pesaran et al. (1997, 1999), which are variations of the autoregressive distributed lag (ARDL) model (see Pesaran and Shin, 1999), we can decompose the influence of $R$, $P$, and $i$ on $R/P$ into long-run and short-run effects. PMG estimation identifies long-run relationships common to all cities and short-run dynamics of individual cities, while MG estimation allows both long-run and short-run relationships to be unique to individual cities.

Our model in Equation (7.12) can be represented as an ARDL in the form of

$$\Delta \rho_{c,t} = \lambda_c \rho_{c,t-1} + \sum_{j=0}^{q}\sum_{k=1}^{n} \delta^k_{c,j} \Delta x^k_{c,t-j} + \delta_c + \varepsilon_{c,t} \qquad (7.13)$$

where $\rho_{c,t} = \dfrac{R_{c,t}}{P_{c,t}}$ is the property rent-to-price ratio in city $c$, at time $t$

$\delta_c$ captures city-specific fixed effects
$x^k_{c,t-j}$ is the $k$th of $n$ regressors for city $c$
$\delta^k_{c,j}$ is the coefficient of the $k$th regressor for city $c$
$\lambda_{c,j}$ are scalars
$\varepsilon_{c,t}$ are the city-specific errors
$c$ represents panels or cities, $i = 1,2,\ldots,N$
$t$ represents time in quarters, $t = 1,2,\ldots,T$
$j$ is an indicator of lags;
   $j = 0,1,2,\ldots,l$ for lagged dependent variable
   $j = 0,1,2,\ldots,q$ lags for regressors

In error correction form, Equation (7.13) becomes

$$\Delta \rho_{c,t} = \phi_c \left\{ \rho_{c,t-1} - \sum_{k=1}^{n} \beta_c^k x_{c,t}^k \right\} - \sum_{j=0}^{q}\sum_{k=1}^{n} \delta^k_{c,j} \Delta x^k_{c,t-j} + \delta_c + \varepsilon_{c,t} \qquad (7.14)$$

where

$$\phi_c = -(1-\lambda_c), \quad \beta_c^k = \dfrac{\delta^k_{c,0}}{(1-\lambda_c)}.$$

This is the MG estimation. In the PMG estimation, $\beta_c^k = \beta^k$ for all cities such that Equation (7.14) becomes

$$\Delta \rho_{c,t} = \phi_c \left\{ \rho_{c,t-1} - \sum_{k=1}^{n} \beta^k x_{c,t}^k \right\} - \sum_{j=0}^{q}\sum_{k=1}^{n} \delta^k_{c,j} \Delta x^k_{c,t-j} + \delta_c + \varepsilon_{c,t}. \qquad (7.14')$$

The terms in the parentheses represent the long-run specification in the Gordon model, that is, $\rho_c = \sum_{k=1}^{n} \beta^k x_c^k - \delta_c / \phi_c$ represents the long-run equilibrium. The other terms are the allowance for different short-run adjustments for different cities. The intercept, $\delta_c$, is such that $\alpha_c = \delta_c / \phi_c$ is the long-run fixed effect of city $c$. The coefficient $\phi_c$ is the error correction term showing the speed of reversion to the long run, and should be negative. The double summation term can include lagged values of changes in the dependent variable and is the measure of momentum, which will disappear over time if the model is not explosive. This model is in accordance with what Glaeser and Nathanson (2015) describe as a bubble, which contains short-run momentum and long-run mean reversion.

Note that PMG and MG estimations are variations of ARDL models. Hence, it is necessary to check for panel unit root and cointegration before these estimations can be used. We follow different panel unit root tests for the rent-to-price ratio such as tests from Breitung (1999), Harris-Tzavalis (1999), Hadri (2000), Choi (2001), Im et al. (2003), and Breitung and Das (2005) for unbalanced time series data.

## 4 THE UNITED STATES HOUSING PRICE DYNAMICS

Lai and Van Order (2010, 2017, 2019) apply the idea of the Gordon model in Equation (7.7) to the US markets. In this section, we first discuss Lai and Van Order (2010) regarding the US housing bubble that burst in 2006–2007, which led to the Global Financial Crisis. Lai and Van Order (2017) extend this idea to break down the bubble as the short-run deviation from the long-run relationship with the PMG/MG estimation (which is also studied with a slightly different model specification in Lai and Van Order (2019) in order to compare the bubble situation in the Chinese markets, to be discussed in the next section).

### 4.1 Data Used

Both Lai and Van Order (2010) and (2017) use the Federal Housing Finance Administration quarterly house price indices, which are repeat sales house price indices for over 100 individual MSAs since 1980. The rent series is the "owner's equivalent rent of primary residence" from the Bureau of Labor Statistics. The local Consumer Price Indices are also from the Bureau of Labor Statistics. A total of 44 MSAs can be matched from these series. We first classify the MSAs into bubble and non-bubble MSAs according to their average annual growth rates in our sample period of 1980 to 2005 for Lai and Van Order (2010). There are 17 MSAs that grew faster than 2 percent and are thus classified as bubble MSAs. The other 27 MSAs are thus non-bubble MSAs. Noting that the bubble started its formation in 2000, we can also separate the sample into the pre- and post-1999 periods. The same bubble versus non-bubble MSA classification is subsequently used in Lai and Van Order (2017).

The 10-year Treasury rate is used as the nominal risk-free rate. The 10-year Treasury Inflation-Protected Securities (TIPS) which are indexed to inflation, but are available only after 1997, are also used as a proxy for real interest rates, with which we interpolate the series back to the last quarter of 1979. This rate did not work well for the Lai and Van Order (2010) model, but it is acceptable for some variations of the test models in Lai and Van Order (2017). For the latter research, we also added the Merrill Lynch one-year high yield rates minus the one-year Treasury rate to generate a yield spread to represent market-wide risk.

### 4.2 Regime Shift: Panel Regression

Lai and Van Order (2010) test for changes in regimes that are characterized by changes in the sum of coefficients and variances of the error terms in Equation (7.10) across periods. Table 7.2 reproduces the results with different lags of the explanatory variables – nominal

*Table 7.2A   Basic regression results for the fundamental equation (various lags)*

| Variables | 12 lags | 16 lags | 20 lags | 24 lags |
|---|---|---|---|---|
| *Coefficients of nominal interest* | | | | |
| Lag 1 | 0.3084 | 0.6500*** | 0.8360*** | 0.9408*** |
| 2 | 0.1308 | 0.1152 | 0.1056 | 0.1696 |
| 3 | 0.1220 | −0.0240 | −0.1080 | 0.2328 |
| 4 | 0.4172* | −0.0160 | 0.5108** | 0.7460*** |
| 5 | 0.3088 | 0.3340 | 0.5940** | 0.9840*** |
| 6 | 0.0080 | −0.2880 | −0.2800 | 0.0300 |
| 7 | 0.2140 | −0.1800 | −0.8640*** | −0.7160*** |
| 8 | −0.4960** | −1.2040*** | −1.2560*** | −1.1400*** |
| 9 | −0.0440 | −0.8600*** | −0.8360*** | −0.6720*** |
| 10 | −0.1840 | −0.5680*** | −0.6360*** | −0.6640*** |
| 11 | 0.1128 | −0.0680 | −0.1800 | −0.2360 |
| 12 | −0.1480 | −0.3280 | −0.5520** | −0.1800 |
| 13 | | −0.8880*** | −0.9800*** | −0.8040*** |
| 14 | | −1.6320*** | −1.5840*** | −1.1240*** |
| 15 | | −0.3880** | 0.0808 | 0.4784** |
| 16 | | −0.8040*** | −0.6960*** | −0.0840 |
| 17 | | | −0.8120*** | −0.1560 |
| 18 | | | −0.5840*** | −0.1200 |
| 19 | | | 0.0408 | 0.3864* |
| 20 | | | 0.4996** | 0.5624*** |
| 21 | | | | 1.0080*** |
| 22 | | | | 0.6584*** |
| 23 | | | | 0.4632** |
| 24 | | | | 0.7228*** |
| *Coefficients of rent growth* | | | | |
| Lag 1 | 0.1618*** | 0.1778*** | 0.1924*** | 0.1965*** |
| 2 | 0.1869*** | 0.2254*** | 0.2314*** | 0.2440*** |
| 3 | 0.2290*** | 0.2588*** | 0.2508*** | 0.2659*** |
| 4 | 0.2449*** | 0.1969*** | 0.1881*** | 0.2101*** |
| 5 | 0.2773*** | 0.1888*** | 0.1832*** | 0.2024*** |
| 6 | 0.3448*** | 0.2311*** | 0.2225*** | 0.2340*** |
| 7 | 0.3439*** | 0.2623*** | 0.2393*** | 0.2459*** |
| 8 | −0.0071 | 0.0860 | 0.0446 | 0.0438 |
| 9 | −0.0681 | 0.0678 | 0.0215 | 0.0102 |
| 10 | −0.1065** | 0.0731 | 0.0240 | 0.0015 |
| 11 | −0.0543 | 0.1531*** | 0.1021* | 0.0697 |
| 12 | 0.0351 | 0.3122*** | 0.2595*** | 0.2174*** |
| 13 | | 0.3224*** | 0.2697*** | 0.2150*** |
| 14 | | 0.3574*** | 0.3005*** | 0.2327*** |
| 15 | | 0.3367*** | 0.2826*** | 0.2009*** |
| 16 | | 0.1046*** | 0.0597* | −0.0362 |
| 17 | | | −0.0452*** | −0.1477*** |
| 18 | | | −0.0545*** | −0.1502*** |
| 19 | | | −0.0301*** | −0.1174*** |
| 20 | | | −0.0086 | −0.0871*** |
| 21 | | | | −0.0644*** |
| 22 | | | | −0.0419*** |
| 23 | | | | −0.0122 |
| 24 | | | | −0.0044 |
| Adjusted $R$-square | 0.079149 | 0.101218 | 0.1375 | 0.1562 |

*Note*: Regressors are lagged changes in 10-year Treasury and local rent growth (MSA fixed effects omitted); ***, **, * represent significance at 1, 5, and 10 percent, respectively.
*Source*: Lai and Van Order (2010).

*Disaggregating house price dynamics* 183

*Table 7.2B    Sums of coefficients of error equation*

| Fundamental model with 12 and 16 lags | | | | | | |
|---|---|---|---|---|---|---|
| | Fundamental Lag = 12 | | | Fundamental Lag = 16 | | |
| Category | Lag = 8 | Lag = 12 | Lag = 16 | Lag = 8 | Lag = 12 | Lag = 16 |
| Non-bubble MSA pre-1999 | 0.2862 (646.17) | 0.3793 (825.19) | 0.3567 (674.79) | 0.5651 (508.12) | 0.7056 (591.55) | 0.7239 (509.46) |
| Non-bubble MSA post-1999 | 0.7440 (259.64) | 0.7742 (168.22) | 0.8805 (56.48) | 0.8277 (132.28) | 0.8715 (118.08) | 0.9912 (80.24) |
| Differences | 0.4578 | 0.3949 | 0.5238 | 0.2626 | 0.1659 | 0.2673 |
| Bubble MSA pre-1999 | 0.5699 (169.09) | 0.5507 (191.43) | 0.4806 (221.50) | 0.5708 (128.89) | 0.5397 (220.74) | 0.4781 (144.18) |
| Bubble MSA post-1999 | 0.8502 (79.60) | 0.7293 (54.93) | 0.6270 (37.77) | 0.9028 (97.39) | 0.7951 (54.44) | 0.6677 (38.47) |
| Difference | 0.2803 | 0.1786 | 0.1464 | 0.332 | 0.2554 | 0.1896 |
| Fundamental model with 20 and 24 lags | | | | | | |
| | Fundamental lag = 20 | | | Fundamental lag = 24 | | |
| Category | Lag = 8 | Lag = 12 | Lag = 16 | Lag = 8 | Lag = 12 | Lag = 16 |
| Non-bubble MSA pre-1999 | 0.6071 (529.26) | 0.7110 (547.24) | 0.7315 (476.22) | 0.6360 (530.64) | 0.7364 (559.39) | 0.7537 (471.01) |
| Non-bubble MSA post-1999 | 0.8072 (123.82) | 0.8708 (102.41) | 0.9566 (51.91) | 0.7759 (128.47) | 0.8702 (97.57) | 0.8883 (54.02) |
| Differences | 0.2001 | 0.1598 | 0.2251 | 0.1399 | 0.1338 | 0.1346 |
| Bubble MSA pre-1999 | 0.5757 (129.93) | 0.5450 (227.52) | 0.5022 (146.30) | 0.6006 (128.62) | 0.5722 (231.14) | 0.5347 (149.40) |
| Bubble MSA post-1999 | 0.8983 (81.89) | 0.8139 (53.76) | 0.6498 (28.76) | 0.8810 (79.78) | 0.8133 (55.65) | 0.6703 (29.12) |
| Difference | 0.3226 | 0.2689 | 0.1476 | 0.2804 | 0.2411 | 0.1356 |

*Note:* Numbers in parentheses are $F$-statistics for testing $H_0$: Sum of the coefficients equals 1. All results reject the null hypothesis.

interest rates and rent growth. Table 7.2A depicts the panel regression results with the growth rate of house price minus growth rate of rent regressed on changes in 10-year Treasury rates and changes in city rental growth, both up to 12, 16, 20, and 24 lagged quarters, while Table 7.2B shows the averages of the sums of the coefficients of the error terms from Equation (7.10) for bubble MSAs and non-bubble MSAs, and for the periods pre- and post-1999, with different error term lags (8, 12, and 16). Table 7.2C shows whether the volatility of the errors in Equation (7.9) are different with different lagged variables, different periods, and bubble versus non-bubble MSAs. Finally, Table 7.2D exhibits the explanatory power of the panel regression models.

Variables in Table 7.2A show expected signs for most lags, generally negative for interest rate and positive for past rent growth, although models with more lags apparently perform better and the generated coefficients make more economic sense. Although not reported here, the non-bubble MSAs have almost zero constant terms while the bubble MSAs are about 1.5 percent. The coefficients suggest overshooting. For example, it is true that the coefficients of rental growth are positive in general across all four models with different lags, indicating that price appreciation is associated with rent increase. However, lags beyond about four years actually turn negative. Also, while interest rate shocks exhibit positive effects on price growth for one year and then turn negative, there is a sharp turn to positive five years later in the 24-lag model. This suggests a long-run effect of interest rates, albeit small. This is perhaps due to long-run supply adjustments.

Table 7.2B shows that all sums of coefficients of lagged error terms are positive, indicating autocorrelation. More interestingly, but as expected, these sums increased after 1999 by around 0.2 to 0.3 for non-bubble MSAs, but up to 0.8 for bubble MSAs. This means that momentum

## Table 7.2C  Test of differences in variance

### Comparing 12-lag versus 16-lag fundamental equations

| | Non-bubble MSAs | | | Bubble MSAs | | |
|---|---|---|---|---|---|---|
| | 12-lag fundamental | 16-lag fundamental | GQ test | 12-lag fundamental | 16-lag fundamental | GQ test |
| **8-lag residuals** | | | | | | |
| Pre-1999 | $1.61 \times 10^{-4}$ | $1.50 \times 10^{-4}$ | 1.07520 | $3.61 \times 10^{-4}$ | $2.98 \times 10^{-4}$ | 1.20986 |
| Post-1999 | $1.65 \times 10^{-4}$ | $1.09 \times 10^{-4}$ | 1.51334* | $1.91 \times 10^{-4}$ | $1.70 \times 10^{-4}$ | 1.12224 |
| Pre-/post-1999 test | 1.02281 | 1.37610 | | 1.89082* | 1.75388* | |
| **12-lag residuals** | | | | | | |
| Pre-1999 | $1.46 \times 10^{-4}$ | $1.44 \times 10^{-4}$ | 1.01623 | $3.02 \times 10^{-4}$ | $2.49 \times 10^{-4}$ | 1.21276 |
| Post-1999 | $1.27 \times 10^{-4}$ | $1.05 \times 10^{-4}$ | 1.21158 | $1.70 \times 10^{-4}$ | $1.57 \times 10^{-4}$ | 1.07893 |
| Pre-/post-1999 test | 1.15196 | 1.37340* | | 1.78437* | 1.58746* | |
| **16-lag residuals** | | | | | | |
| Pre-1999 | $1.41 \times 10^{-4}$ | $1.23 \times 10^{-4}$ | 1.15406 | $2.52 \times 10^{-4}$ | $2.18 \times 10^{-4}$ | 1.15502 |
| Post-1999 | $1.22 \times 10^{-4}$ | $1.02 \times 10^{-4}$ | 1.19612 | $1.92 \times 10^{-4}$ | $1.76 \times 10^{-4}$ | 1.09422 |
| Pre-/post-1999 test | 1.15831 | 1.20053 | | 1.31256* | 1.24346 | |

### Comparing 20-lag versus 24-lag fundamental equations

| | Non-bubble MSAs | | | Bubble MSAs | | |
|---|---|---|---|---|---|---|
| | 20-lag fundamental | 24-lag fundamental | GQ test | 20-lag fundamental | 24-lag fundamental | GQ test |
| **8-lag residuals** | | | | | | |
| Pre-1999 | $1.45 \times 10^{-4}$ | $1.44 \times 10^{-4}$ | 1.00520 | $2.95 \times 10^{-4}$ | $2.90 \times 10^{-4}$ | 1.01513 |
| Post-1999 | $1.15 \times 10^{-4}$ | $1.12 \times 10^{-4}$ | 1.02077 | $1.73 \times 10^{-4}$ | $1.69 \times 10^{-4}$ | 1.02275 |
| Pre-/post-1999 test | 1.26526 | 1.28485 | | 1.70605* | 1.71886* | |
| **12-lag residuals** | | | | | | |
| Pre-1999 | $1.40 \times 10^{-4}$ | $1.39 \times 10^{-4}$ | 1.00345 | $2.44 \times 10^{-4}$ | $2.40 \times 10^{-4}$ | 1.01880 |
| Post-1999 | $1.12 \times 10^{-4}$ | $1.10 \times 10^{-4}$ | 1.01870 | $1.62 \times 10^{-4}$ | $1.56 \times 10^{-4}$ | 1.03465 |
| Pre-/post-1999 test | 1.24361 | 1.26250 | | 1.50958* | 1.53305* | |
| **16-lag residuals** | | | | | | |
| Pre-1999 | $1.22 \times 10^{-4}$ | $1.19 \times 10^{-4}$ | 1.02404 | $2.16 \times 10^{-4}$ | $2.09 \times 10^{-4}$ | 1.03103 |
| Post-1999 | $1.09 \times 10^{-4}$ | $1.06 \times 10^{-4}$ | 1.02478 | $1.81 \times 10^{-4}$ | $1.77 \times 10^{-4}$ | 1.02488 |
| Pre-/post-1999 test | 1.11998 | 1.12078 | | 1.18985 | 1.18275 | |

*Note*: "GQ test" (Goldfeld–Quandt test) tests statistical difference between two fundamental equations. "Pre-/post-1999 test" is the test for statistical difference between the pre- and post-bubble periods. * The GQ test rejects the null hypothesis that variances are statistically the same at the 5 percent significance level (compared to an F-value of 1.3).

existed, and was stronger after 1999; although the bubble was not explosive because the sums are all less than 1 (hypothesis of existence of unit root has been tested negative, and omitted here). This shows a regime shift post-1999, with a non-explosive bubble. Since it might be likely that we do not see explosive bubbles because the cutoff point of 1999 is not appropriate, we also tried cutoff points of 2002 and 2003 when more housing units were sold. The results are similar. Looking at Table 7.2C, comparing the variances of the error terms from the panel regression (Equation (7.9)) with the Goldfeld–Quandt test, it is seen that changes in volatility are mostly found in bubble MSAs before and after 1999, and from bigger variances to smaller ones. That is, there was a regime shift in the bubble MSAs from higher market volatilities before 1999 to more stable regimes after 1999. Results from other cutoff periods echo these results.

Finally, because a lot of economic changes occurred after 2002, such as a sudden increase in subprime loans and decrease in interest rates as previously discussed, interest rates might have induced a big shock to the fundamentals, generating momentum, but only for that period when the low interest rates created a new class of mortgages, subprime mortgages, rather than applicable to the whole sample period in our tests. In other words, interest rates as an explanatory variable might actually be irrelevant in explaining the regime shift. Hence, we are curious if our panel regression model based on the Gordon model actually works after all. We compared the actual prices with the prices estimated from our model to see how much of the actual prices are explained by the model (with 20 lags, as shown in Table 7.2D, and 24 lags, with results available upon request) for different subperiods in the sample, all starting from 1990. The percentages of prices explained by the different explanatory variables are shown in Table 7.2D. For example, for the period 2000–2002 for bubble MSAs, the actual average cumulative log of price change is 0.26657 and the actual average cumulative rent is 0.12631. This means 0.12631/0.26657 = 47.38 percent of the price change is explained by rent change. The average difference between the growth rates of price and rent is 0.14027. Of this, 71.55 percent is explained by the panel regression model. Hence, a total of 85.03 percent is explained by both the rent growth and the "fundamentals." In other words, our panel regression models are able to explain the price growth quite satisfactorily, except for the 2003–2005 period, possibly when the market bubbles started to get really inflated.

Table 7.2D   Explanatory power of the fundamental model (without error equation)

| Period | Cumulative price changes | Cumulative rent changes | % of price change explained by rent change* | Cumulative growth rate difference | % of growth rate difference explained | Total % price change explained[†] |
|---|---|---|---|---|---|---|
| Non-bubble MSAs | | | | | | |
| 1990–1995 | 0.23361 | 0.18770 | 80.35 | 0.04590 | 281.90 | 135.74 |
| 1995–2000 | 0.22781 | 0.16358 | 71.80 | 0.06423 | 171.22 | 120.08 |
| 2000–2005 | 0.37557 | 0.15113 | 40.24 | 0.22444 | 55.65 | 74.79 |
| 2000–2002[‡] | 0.18644 | 0.10609 | 56.90 | 0.08036 | 81.45 | 92.00 |
| 2003–2005[‡] | 0.18913 | 0.04505 | 23.82 | 0.14408 | 41.26 | 54.44 |
| Bubble MSAs | | | | | | |
| 1990–1995 | 0.13553 | 0.18349 | 135.38 | −0.04796 | −386.07 | 271.99 |
| 1995–2000 | 0.22763 | 0.14794 | 64.99 | 0.07757 | 212.11 | 139.24 |
| 2000–2005 | 0.69539 | 0.21367 | 30.73 | 0.48171 | 40.48 | 58.18 |
| 2000–2002[‡] | 0.26657 | 0.12631 | 47.38 | 0.14027 | 71.55 | 85.03 |
| 2003–2005[‡] | 0.42882 | 0.08737 | 20.37 | 0.34145 | 27.72 | 40.76 |

Note: * "% of price change explained by rent change" is the percentage of average cumulative rent change constituting the average cumulative price change. [†] "Total % price change explained" refers to the proportion of price change explained by rent + fundamental model without error equation. [‡] Note that the cumulative changes on price, rent, and growth rate differences for the periods 2000–2002 and 2003–2005 do not add up to those for 2000–2005 because all the periods begin from one quarter prior to the period for the purpose of differencing. As such, adding the values of 2000–2002 and 2003–2005 double-counts quarter 4 of 2002.

In sum, the panel regression tests in Lai and Van Order (2010) conclude that there have always been bubbles in the form of disturbance generating momentum, but which were not explosive, and there was a regime shift in the post-1999 period in the form of increased momentum but not an increase in conditional volatility. This regime shifting is more significant in non-bubble MSAs, which also implies that bubble MSAs were always on the rise, albeit even higher after 1999. The drop in explanatory power after 2002 shows that the fundamentals did not explain much of the housing prices, perhaps because the "bubbles," which were chiefly started in 2003 and burst in 2006–2007, were more like random changes than momentum because of the several significant changes such as drop in interest rates and rise in subprime mortgages.

### 4.3  Long-/Short-Term Mechanisms: PMG/MG Estimation

In this section, testing the existence of bubbles in the US markets in Lai and Van Order (2017) is discussed. Unlike Lai and Van Order (2010) in which the dependent variable in the tests are the price-growth/rent-growth ratio, the regressands here are the opposite. Hence, coefficients of the explanatory variables suggested in the fundamental would generate opposite signs. Before running Equation (7.14) for MG estimation or Equation (7.14') for PMG estimation, we have to ensure that our rent-price ratio series is non-stationary using the various unit root tests, as mentioned in Section 3.3. Since MG and PMG estimations are ARDL models, we also have to verify the long-run relationship using the Westerlund (2007) panel cointegration test between rent-to-price ratio and the interest rate proxies. Our data pass all these tests. Hence, it is safe to run MG and PMG estimations (Equations (7.14) and (7.14')).

The long-run variables (the terms within the parentheses of Equations (7.14) and (7.14')) include combinations of nominal 10-year Treasury rates, 10-year Treasury rates minus rent growth, Merrill Lynch one-year high-yield spread, and/or TIPS. Short-run variables are from the lagged dependent variable (rent-to-price ratio) for the purpose of capturing the momentum, and the lagged long-run variables for the short-run effects. In some regressions, high yield rates minus rent growth and the 10-year Treasury rates minus rent growth are also included so as to control for the short-term effect from risky rates. As the price and rent data series are quarterly, we chose one, two, and four lags in the short-run components in Equations (7.14) and (7.14'). We found that the models with four lags, that is, up to one year, were most stable when applied to different variations of the model and subperiods.

As in the regime shift model, we also look into whether the residuals are autoregressive, and if so, whether they are explosive. We also study their volatilities as before. For the autoregression tests of the residuals, we tried with two, four, and eight lags. Note that we use far fewer lags in here than in the regime shift tests because the effects in the longer run will be incorporated in the long-run part of the MG and PMG estimation equations. With a longer period of data (also starting from 1980), we extend the residual autoregression tests to subperiods 1990–1999, 2000–2006, and 2007–2013, to represent the pre-bubble, bubble, and post-bubble periods. Also, due to the longer time period, the TIPS rate has much better explanatory power in these tests than in the regime shift tests.

Our discussion here will focus on the test model with combinations of 10-year TIPS, 10-year Treasury minus rent growth, 10-year Treasury as the long-term variable, and lagged values of changes in the ratio of rent-to-price index, yield spread, 10-year Treasury, and 10-year Treasury minus rent growth as short-term variables. Due to space limitations results from models with other variations are available upon request. Table 7.3 shows the results. Table

## Table 7.3A  PMG and MG estimation results

| | Model A1 PMG | Model A1 MG | Model A2 PMG | Model A2 MG | Model A3 PMG | Model A3 MG | Model A4 PMG | Model A4 MG |
|---|---|---|---|---|---|---|---|---|
| **Long-run variables** | | | | | | | | |
| 10-yr TIPs | 0.1428*** | 0.1549*** | 0.1571*** | 0.1602*** | 0.0728*** | 0.0812*** | 0.0749*** | 0.0814*** |
| 10Y- RentG | | | | | | | 0.5877 | 1.0854 |
| 10-year Treasury | 0.0061 | 0.0077 | 0.001 | 0.0061 | 0.0424*** | 0.0338*** | −0.5439 | −1.047 |
| **Short-run variables** | | | | | | | | |
| Error correction | −0.0268*** | −0.0348*** | −0.0268*** | −0.0350*** | −0.0268*** | −0.0362*** | −0.0271*** | −0.0423*** |
| $\Delta R_t P_{t-1}$ | 0.0433 | 0.0387 | 0.0496 | 0.0451 | 0.2005*** | 0.1924*** | 0.2001*** | 0.1809*** |
| $\Delta R_t P_{t-2}$ | 0.1073*** | 0.1052*** | 0.0999*** | 0.0986*** | 0.0745*** | 0.0795*** | 0.0740*** | 0.0764*** |
| $\Delta R_t P_{t-3}$ | 0.1677*** | 0.1694*** | 0.1651*** | 0.1671*** | 0.2002*** | 0.2043*** | 0.2000*** | 0.2025*** |
| $\Delta R_t P_{t-4}$ | 0.1301*** | 0.1317*** | 0.1270*** | 0.1292*** | 0.1538*** | 0.1605*** | 0.1525*** | 0.1548*** |
| $\Delta \text{Yield spread}_{t-1}$ | 0.0021*** | 0.0019*** | 0.0017*** | 0.0015*** | 0.0019*** | 0.0017*** | 0.0019*** | 0.0019*** |
| $\Delta \text{Yield spread}_{t-2}$ | 0.0016 | 0.0015 | 0.0018 | 0.0017 | 0.0011* | 0.0010* | 0.0011* | 0.0013* |
| $\Delta \text{Yield spread}_{t-3}$ | 0.0020** | 0.0019 | 0.0020* | 0.0019 | 0.0019*** | 0.0018** | 0.0019*** | 0.0020*** |
| $\Delta \text{Yield spread}_{t-4}$ | 0.0021*** | 0.0019*** | 0.0020*** | 0.0019*** | 0.0011* | 0.0011* | 0.0011* | 0.0012* |
| $\Delta 10Y_t$ | 0 | −0.0003 | −0.0001 | −0.0003 | 0.0001 | −0.0001 | 0.0001 | −0.0001 |
| $\Delta 10Y_{t-1}$ | −0.0018 | −0.0025 | | | 0.3565*** | 0.3619*** | 0.3689*** | 0.4514*** |
| $\Delta 10Y_{t-2}$ | 0.0082** | 0.0076** | | | 0.2145*** | 0.2267*** | 0.2242*** | 0.3012*** |
| $\Delta 10Y_{t-3}$ | −0.0004 | −0.0009 | | | 0.2646*** | 0.2748*** | 0.2718*** | 0.3268*** |
| $\Delta 10Y_{t-4}$ | −0.0026* | −0.0033** | | | 0.1144*** | 0.1235*** | 0.1192*** | 0.1589*** |
| $\Delta 10Y_{t-5}$ | −0.0003 | −0.0009 | | | 0.0379 | 0.0422 | 0.0403 | 0.0582 |
| $\Delta 10Y_t - \text{RentG}_t$ | | | −0.0033 | −0.0040* | −0.3572*** | −0.3631*** | −0.3697*** | −0.4536*** |
| $\Delta 10Y_{t-1} - \text{RentG}_{t-1}$ | | | 0.0089** | 0.0083** | −0.2072*** | −0.2199*** | −0.2170*** | −0.2950*** |
| $\Delta 10Y_{t-2} - \text{RentG}_{t-2}$ | | | −0.001 | −0.0015 | −0.2660*** | −0.2765*** | −0.2732*** | −0.3289*** |
| $\Delta 10Y_{t-3} - \text{RentG}_{t-3}$ | | | −0.0023 | −0.0030** | −0.1180*** | −0.1276*** | −0.1229*** | −0.1634*** |
| $\Delta 10Y_{t-4} - \text{RentG}_{t-4}$ | | | −0.0004 | −0.001 | −0.038 | −0.0429 | −0.0404 | −0.0595 |
| Constant | 0.0273*** | 0.0347*** | 0.0271*** | 0.0348*** | 0.0268*** | 0.0366*** | 0.0272*** | 0.0433*** |
| Log likelihood | 12707 | 12757 | 12702 | 12753 | 13859 | 13922 | 13859 | 13981 |
| Hausman test | 4.52 | | −2023.61 | | 1.08 | | 0.47 | |
| p-value | 0.1041 | | Invalid | | 0.5818 | | 0.9249 | |

Note: *, **, and *** denote significance at the 10, 5, and 1 percent levels, respectively. The variable 10 Y − RentG represents 10 year Treasury rates minus rent growth, yield spread is Merrill Lynch one-year high yield bond rates minus one-year Treasury rates. An insignificant value of the Hausman test indicates PMG is preferred to MG estimation. "Invalid" p-value is because of failure of the Hausman test.

Source: Lai and Van Order (2017).

7.3A lists the coefficients generated from the PMG and MG models with different long-run variables, while Table 7.3B summarizes the average of the sum of short-run coefficients for individual MSAs generated from the PMG estimation of Model A1. Table 7.3C provides the autoregression results of the residuals generated from Model A1, with various lags and in different subperiods, while Table 7.3D shows the sum of coefficients and their variances of the residual autoregression results. Table 7.3E provides the corresponding Goldfeld–Quandt tests for the changes in variance of the residuals. Finally, Table 7.3F lists the explanatory powers of the long-run and short-run components in Model A1.

Table 7.3B  Summary statistics of sum of short-run coefficients for individual MSAs from PMG estimation of Model A1 (individual MSAs in Table 7.1A)

|  | Error correction | | Sum of ($\Delta R/P$) | | Sum of ($\Delta$Yield spread) | | Constant | |
| --- | --- | --- | --- | --- | --- | --- | --- | --- |
|  | Non-bubble MSA | Bubble MSA | Non-bubble MSA | Bubble MSA | Non-bubble MSA | Bubble MSA | Non-bubble MSA | Bubble MSA |
| Average | −0.0229 | −0.0327 | 0.3495 | 0.5967 | 0.0055 | 0.0057 | 0.0048 | 0.0051 |
| Maximum | −0.0105 | −0.0119 | 0.8728 | 1.0877 | 0.0156 | 0.0122 | 0.0293 | 0.1443 |
| Minimum | −0.0379 | −0.1059 | −0.3830 | −1.2240 | −0.0008 | −0.0053 | −0.0158 | −0.0133 |

Source: Lai and Van Order (2017).

Table 7.3A shows that the results across the four models from both MG and PMG estimations are similar. PMG outperforms MG in most cases according to the low Hausman tests coupled with $p$-values higher than 10 percent. This means that the MSAs share the same influence from the long-run variables. Hence, our discussion in the following will be mostly based on the PMG results. The 10-year TIPS is the best performer among the long-run variables. The error correction coefficients are very consistent across models. A negative error correction coefficient of around −0.027 for quarterly frequency implies about 10.8 percent correction back to the long run each year. The momentum as expressed by the lagged rent-to-price ratios of up to four quarters is strong. On the other hand, the yield spread is mostly not significant. Inserting the 10-year Treasury and the 10-year Treasury minus rent growth individually does not show much effect; but when both are inserted, the results generate strange and difficult-to-interpret patterns. The constant term is the average of the fixed effects for all MSAs in the sample. Table 7.3B shows the averages, maxima, and minima of the sums of the short-run coefficients from Model A1 for the bubble and non-bubble MSAs. The more negative error correction coefficients from the bubble MSAs means that these MSAs correct back to the long run faster than the non-bubble counterparts, which makes the bubble MSAs look more like "growth stocks."

Table 7.3C shows the AR(2), AR(4), and AR(8) autoregression equations of the residuals from the PMG estimation of Model A1 for subperiods 1990–1998, 1999–2006, and 2007–2013, for all MSAs, bubble MSAs, and non-bubble MSAs. Table 7.3D sums the coefficients of all lags, and the corresponding variances of the residuals. In general, the sums of the coefficients are less than 1, meaning that the "bubbles" of these MSAs across all periods are not explosive, even though these sums are biggest in the 1999–2006 bubble period, and subsequently decrease after the Crisis. However, looking carefully into the different MSAs, the autoregressive effect of the residuals of the bubble MSAs after the bubble burst was much weaker. On the other hand, those of the non-bubble MSAs either did not change after the Crisis, or even increased. At the same time, the variances of the bubble MSA residuals are larger than those of their non-bubble counterparts, which is consistent with the finding

Table 7.3C  Residual autoregressive models from Model A1

|  | Two lags | | | Four lags | | | Eight lags | | |
|---|---|---|---|---|---|---|---|---|---|
|  | 1990–1998 | 1999–2006 | 2007–2013 | 1990–1998 | 1999–2006 | 2007–2013 | 1990–1998 | 1999–2006 | 2007–2013 |
| *All MSAs* | | | | | | | | | |
| $\varepsilon_{i,t-1}$ | 0.0315 | 0.1930*** | 0.0645** | -0.0301 | 0.0815*** | 0.0640** | -0.0346 | 0.0944*** | 0.0624** |
| $\varepsilon_{i,t-2}$ | 0.2819*** | 0.2590*** | -0.0058 | 0.2556*** | 0.2002*** | -0.0109 | 0.2509*** | 0.1979*** | -0.0332 |
| $\varepsilon_{i,t-3}$ | | | | 0.1639*** | 0.3992*** | 0.0913*** | 0.1458*** | 0.3658*** | 0.1011*** |
| $\varepsilon_{i,t-4}$ | | | | 0.0594** | -0.0206 | 0.0324 | 0.0342 | -0.0131 | 0.0209 |
| $\varepsilon_{i,t-5}$ | | | | | | | 0.0001 | -0.0547* | 0.1927*** |
| $\varepsilon_{i,t-6}$ | | | | | | | 0.0881*** | 0.0866*** | 0.0096 |
| $\varepsilon_{i,t-7}$ | | | | | | | 0.0632*** | -0.0726** | 0.0113 |
| $\varepsilon_{i,t-8}$ | | | | | | | -0.0437* | 0.0834*** | -0.0581** |
| Adjusted $R^2$ | 0.0819 | 0.134 | 0.00254 | 0.112 | 0.268 | 0.0104 | 0.123 | 0.28 | 0.0465 |
| *Bubble MSAs* | | | | | | | | | |
| $\varepsilon_{i,t-1}$ | 0.0503 | 0.1989*** | -0.0622 | -0.0434 | 0.0554 | -0.0555 | -0.0299 | 0.0676 | -0.0479 |
| $\varepsilon_{i,t-2}$ | 0.3711*** | 0.3025*** | 0.0165 | 0.3253*** | 0.2396*** | 0.0212 | 0.3523*** | 0.2645*** | 0.0178 |
| $\varepsilon_{i,t-3}$ | | | | 0.1914*** | 0.4802*** | 0.0722 | 0.1796*** | 0.4711*** | 0.0841* |
| $\varepsilon_{i,t-4}$ | | | | 0.0728* | -0.0499 | -0.0892** | 0.0407 | -0.0337 | -0.0737* |
| $\varepsilon_{i,t-5}$ | | | | | | | -0.0844** | -0.1008** | 0.1487*** |
| $\varepsilon_{i,t-6}$ | | | | | | | 0.0991** | 0.0424 | 0.0005 |
| $\varepsilon_{i,t-7}$ | | | | | | | 0.0981** | -0.0653 | -0.0621 |
| $\varepsilon_{i,t-8}$ | | | | | | | -0.1014*** | 0.0758 | -0.0909** |
| Adjusted $R^2$ | 0.142 | 0.168 | 0.000385 | 0.18 | 0.352 | 0.0103 | 0.203 | 0.357 | 0.0346 |
| *Non-bubble MSAs* | | | | | | | | | |
| $\varepsilon_{i,t-1}$ | -0.0598* | 0.1529*** | 0.3313*** | -0.0600* | 0.1220*** | 0.3156*** | -0.0709** | 0.1329*** | 0.2495*** |
| $\varepsilon_{i,t-2}$ | 0.0569* | 0.1123*** | -0.1462*** | 0.0649** | 0.0832** | -0.1691*** | 0.0497 | 0.0625* | -0.2344*** |
| $\varepsilon_{i,t-3}$ | | | | 0.0544* | 0.1602*** | 0.1193*** | 0.0374 | 0.1414*** | 0.1158*** |
| $\varepsilon_{i,t-4}$ | | | | -0.0412 | 0.0524 | 0.2118*** | -0.0308 | 0.0455 | 0.1525*** |
| $\varepsilon_{i,t-5}$ | | | | | | | 0.1154*** | -0.0339 | 0.2005*** |
| $\varepsilon_{i,t-6}$ | | | | | | | 0.0532* | 0.1148*** | 0.0549 |
| $\varepsilon_{i,t-7}$ | | | | | | | 0.0497* | -0.0541 | 0.1756*** |
| $\varepsilon_{i,t-8}$ | | | | | | | 0.0716*** | 0.1110*** | -0.0423 |
| Adjusted $R^2$ | 0.00563 | 0.0412 | 0.0962 | 0.0089 | 0.069 | 0.163 | 0.0317 | 0.0922 | 0.218 |

*Note:* *, **, and *** denote significance at the 10, 5, and 1 percent levels, respectively.
*Source:* Lai and Van Order (2017).

190  *Handbook of real estate and macroeconomics*

*Table 7.3D  Sum of coefficients and variances of residual autoregression estimation in Table 7.2B*

|  | Two lags | | | Four lags | | | Eight lags | | |
|---|---|---|---|---|---|---|---|---|---|
|  | 1990–1998 | 1999–2006 | 2007–2013 | 1990–1998 | 1999–2006 | 2007–2013 | 1990–1998 | 1999–2006 | 2007–2013 |
| *All MSAs* | | | | | | | | | |
| Sum of all coeff. | 0.3134 | 0.452 | 0.0587 | 0.4488 | 0.6603 | 0.1768 | 0.504 | 0.6877 | 0.3067 |
| Sum of sig. coeff. | 0.2819 | 0.452 | 0.0645 | 0.4789 | 0.6809 | 0.1553 | 0.5043 | 0.7008 | 0.2981 |
| Variance of res. | 0.00083 | 0.00060 | 0.00078 | 0.00080 | 0.00051 | 0.00078 | 0.00079 | 0.00051 | 0.00075 |
| *Bubble MSAs* | | | | | | | | | |
| Sum of all coeff. | 0.4214 | 0.5014 | −0.0457 | 0.5461 | 0.7253 | −0.0513 | 0.5541 | 0.7216 | −0.0235 |
| Sum of sig. coeff. | 0.3711 | 0.5014 | 0.0000 | 0.5895 | 0.7198 | −0.0892 | 0.5433 | 0.6348 | 0.0682 |
| Variance of res. | 0.00150 | 0.00115 | 0.00123 | 0.00144 | 0.00090 | 0.00122 | 0.00140 | 0.00091 | 0.00119 |
| *Non-bubble MSAs* | | | | | | | | | |
| Sum of all coeff. | −0.0029 | 0.2652 | 0.1851 | 0.0181 | 0.4178 | 0.4776 | 0.2753 | 0.5201 | 0.6721 |
| Sum of sig. coeff. | −0.0029 | 0.2652 | 0.1851 | 0.0593 | 0.3654 | 0.4776 | 0.2190 | 0.5626 | 0.6595 |
| Variance of res. | 0.00040 | 0.00025 | 0.00044 | 0.00040 | 0.00024 | 0.00041 | 0.00039 | 0.00023 | 0.00038 |

*Source:* Lai and Van Order (2017).

*Table 7.3E  Goldfeld–Quandt tests of variance of residuals from autoregression estimation in Table 7.3B*

|  | All MSAs | | | Bubble MSAs | | | Non-bubble MSAs | | |
|---|---|---|---|---|---|---|---|---|---|
|  | Two and four lags | Two and four lags | Two and eight lags | Two and four lags | Two and four lags | Two and eight lags | Two and four lags | Four and eight lags | Four and eight lags |
| 1990–1998 | 1.0315 | 1.0413 | 1.0095 | 1.0388 | 1.0609 | 1.0213 | 1.0012 | 1.0203 | 1.0191 |
| 1999–2006 | 1.1694*** | 1.1599*** | 1.0082*** | 1.2552*** | 1.2036** | 1.0429*** | 1.0229 | 1.0348 | 1.0116 |
| 2007–2013 | 1.0064 | 1.0412 | 1.0346 | 1.006 | 1.0231 | 1.017 | 1.0768 | 1.1472** | 1.0653 |
| Periods 1 and 2 | 1.3108*** | 1.4860*** | 1.4601*** | 1.3402*** | 1.6194*** | 1.5204*** | 1.5120*** | 1.5448*** | 1.5334*** |
| Periods 2 and 3 | 1.1150** | 1.1428*** | 1.1151** | 1.1354* | 1.0996 | 1.0949 | 1.3572*** | 1.2618*** | 1.2071*** |
| Periods 1 and 3 | 1.4615*** | 1.6983*** | 1.6282*** | 1.1804** | 1.4728*** | 1.3886*** | 2.0520*** | 1.9492*** | 1.8510*** |

*Note:* *, **, and *** denote significance at the 10, 5, and 1 levels, respectively.
*Source:* Lai and Van Order (2017).

*Disaggregating house price dynamics* 191

in the regime shift models. Furthermore, the variances during the bubble period 1999–2006 are smaller than in the pre-bubble and post-bubble periods. A possible explanation is that the markets are in general agreement with the rising prices, whereas opinions about the housing prices in other periods were more diverse. Again similar to the regime shift tests, Table 7.3E shows the Goldfeld–Quandt test results, which indicate that variances during the bubble period are different from other periods, and hence imply regime shifts, at least in volatility.

*Table 7.3F   Explanatory power of various components in Model A1*

|  | Mean | Maximum | Minimum | Max–min |
|---|---|---|---|---|
| *Non-bubble MSAs* | | | | |
| Long-run partial $R^2$ | 0.1324 | 0.4437 | 0.0299 | 0.4138 |
| Short-run partial $R^2$ | 0.5145 | 0.8857 | 0.3006 | 0.5851 |
| PMG model | 0.3034 | 0.7819 | 0.1301 | 0.6519 |
| Residual autregression | 0.5035 | 0.7636 | 0.2059 | 0.5577 |
| Total = PMG + residual AR(4) | 0.7345 | 0.9849 | 0.4137 | 0.5712 |
| *Bubble MSAs* | | | | |
| Long-run partial $R^2$ | 0.2313 | 0.5533 | 0.0667 | 0.4866 |
| Short-run partial $R^2$ | 0.6472 | 0.9150 | 0.2506 | 0.6644 |
| PMG model | 0.4198 | 0.7925 | 0.0902 | 0.7023 |
| Residual autregression | 0.3635 | 0.7956 | 0.0293 | 0.7663 |
| Total = PMG + residual AR(4) | 0.6790 | 0.9612 | 0.0464 | 0.9149 |

*Source*: Lai and Van Order (2017).

Finally, to show the explanatory power of the models, we calculate the estimated sums of squares of the models and compare them to the actual rent-to-price ratios. This is like the $R$-squares, or the coefficient of determination. To separate the explanatory power of the long-run and short-run components, we use the concept of coefficients of partial determination (Partial $r^2$). It should be noted that, according to Borcard (2002), adding the coefficients of partial determination from the short run and the long run does not generate the coefficient of determination. The results from Model A1 are shown in Table 7.3F. In particular, the PMG model explains the bubble MSAs better. Furthermore, the short-run components can explain the rent-to-price ratio more than the long-run components. Hence, with reference to Table 7.3A, the short-run explanatory power actually comes from the momentum (lagged rent-to-price ratio).

As mentioned earlier, cities with lower-supply elasticities are more prone to creating bubble markets because they tend to have larger short-run price momentum. Following Saiz (2010) that supply elasticities are inversely related to housing prices (see also Wheaton, 2015), we extract the same set of 34 cities as in Saiz (2010) and perform OLS regressions on the correlations between our momentum measures and those elasticities. Results in Figure 7.3 verify that supply elasticities are significantly negatively related to the momentum measures in our tests. More interestingly, the bubble MSAs were generally the ones with lower elasticities.

In sum, Lai and Van Order (2017) verify the findings in Lai and Van Order (2010) with PMG/MG estimations that can spread the effects into a long-run fundamental relationship and short-run momentum effects with a longer sample period from 1980 to 2013. First, the simple version of the Gordon model explains long-run behavior well. Second, the short run explains

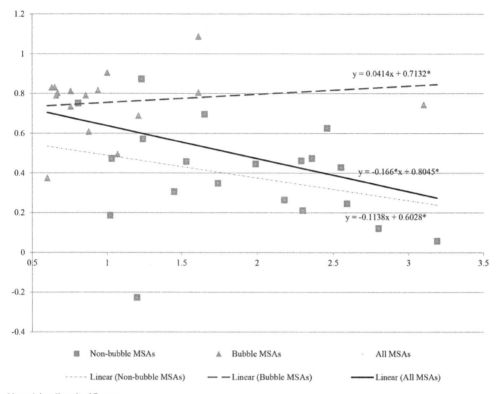

*Note:* * implies significance.
*Source:* Lai and Van Order (2017).

*Figure 7.3   Plots of the OLS regression and actual observations of sum of changes in rent-to-price ratio on supply elasticity*

the rent-to-price ratio better, and the effect comes mostly from the momentum, which is different across different cities, depending on their supply elasticities. It is the disaggregation of the house prices into long-run and short-run components that allows us to understand the part of the price explained by the fundamentals and the other part as a bubble.

## 5   CHINESE HOUSING PRICE DYNAMICS

### 5.1   Sample Data

In Lai and Van Order (2019), the PMG and MG estimations are applied to the US markets, but with more recent data (January 1980 and August 2016), and the Chinese markets. The aim is to find similarities between the two markets and therefore to see if there are any lessons the Chinese markets could learn from the bubble bursts in the US market in 2007. Note that because the Chinese data are in monthly series, the data for the US housing markets are different from before. In particular, monthly house price indices from Freddie Mac for MSAs and rent series from the monthly Owners' Equivalent Rent of Primary Residence from the Bureau of Labor Statistics are used. Furthermore, the interest rates are changed to five-year Treasury bonds and five-year TIPS, and there are differences between Merrill Lynch US Corporate AA Effective Yield and the one-year Treasury rate as credit spread. As the results for the US markets are mostly similar to the results explained in the previous section, we omit those test results and instead focus on the Chinese markets.

The monthly housing price and the rental data of the Chinese housing markets are obtained from the CityRE Data Technology Co.,[4] comprising data from housing for sale and lease for the first time for over 290 cities and areas in China starting from 2003. Prices and rents are per square meter for relatively homogeneous units.[5] We take the five-year Chinese government bonds from the National Interbank Funding Center as nominal long-term rates and five-year AAA corporate bond yields from the China Central Depository and Clearing Co. as a proxy for credit risk. Our data span from January 2009 to August 2016, which is not very long, due to limited availability. Nevertheless, this period is when the housing markets experienced constant rises in prices, which means not much would be lost for testing the existence of bubbles.

Our sample includes all four Tier 1 cities, all 36 Tier 2 cities, and 40 other cities as listed in Tables 7.1A and 7.1B. Chinese cities are classified as follows. The four Tier 1 cities, with the largest population and economic importance, are Beijing, Shanghai, Guangzhou, and Shenzhen. Tier 2 cities include capital cities of the 24 provinces, two autonomous municipalities (Tianjing and Chongqing), and 10 other cities. The 80 Chinese cities are also classified into coastal versus inland cities according to Yang and Chen (2014). There are puzzles about the representativeness of the rental market in China given its small size, since the homeownership rate is as high as 90 percent. Nevertheless, over the past five years, housing has become really unaffordable. With the support of the Chinese government, the rental market has greatly expanded, thus allowing rental rates to be more representative. In addition, because the qualities between rental units and units sold might not be comparable, the rent and price series may generate erroneous regression results. This is also not an issue in our case because our price and rent series are for relatively homogeneous units sold or leased *for the first time*. In fact, Wu et al. (2012) argue that owner-occupied housing and rental units in China are more homogenous than cities in other countries. Note that, unlike the tests for the US, we assume the rental growth rate is constant rather than calculating the real growth rates because the rates exhibit strong mean reversion and more or less constant rent growth.

## 5.2   Long-/Short-Term Mechanisms: PMG/MG Estimation

Table 7.4 shows the results of the PMG and MG estimation of the 80 Chinese cities. Not all of the variables that are inserted in the PMG/MG estimation models generate valid results. Fortunately, all the tests are valid and generate correct signs for the coefficients. The PMG dominates the estimations, with statistically significant long-run variables. In other words, all 80 cities share the same long-run influences from the long-run fundamental factors, and are different only in short-run dynamics. The error correction coefficients range from −0.075 to −0.096. This means a fast correction, especially relative to those for the US markets, because this almost 10 percent correction rate per month translates into a half-life of about seven months. Interest rates indeed exert influence in the short run as expected. What is interesting, though, are the negative signs of the momentum variables, significant of up to one-quarter. This implies that Chinese house prices actually have negative momentum. Together with the high

Table 7.4    PMG and MG estimation for determinants of rent-to-price ratio for 80 Chinese markets

|  | Model A1 |  | Model A2 |  | Model A3 |  | Model A4 |  |
|---|---|---|---|---|---|---|---|---|
|  | PMG | MG | PMG | MG | PMG | MG | PMG | MG |
| *Long-run variables* |  |  |  |  |  |  |  |  |
| Nom rates$_{-1}$ | 0.4802*** | 0.5791** | 0.5312*** | 0.7814** | 0.5958*** | 0.4104*** | 0.6545*** | 0.5607*** |
| *Short-run variables* |  |  |  |  |  |  |  |  |
| Error correction | −0.0750*** | −0.0962*** | −0.0779*** | −0.0957*** | −0.0877*** | −0.1039*** | −0.0962*** | −0.1169*** |
| $\Delta R/P_{-1}$ | −0.1974*** | −0.1900*** | −0.1853*** | −0.1833*** | −0.1739*** | −0.1769*** | −0.1851*** | −0.1858*** |
| $\Delta R/P_{-2}$ | −0.0701*** | −0.0672*** | −0.0736*** | −0.0743*** | −0.0644*** | −0.0690*** | −0.0591*** | −0.0634*** |
| $\Delta R/P_{-3}$ | −0.0303* | −0.0292* | −0.0550*** | −0.0551*** | −0.0632*** | −0.0673*** | −0.0436*** | −0.0475*** |
| $\Delta R/P_{-4}$ |  |  | −0.0189 | −0.0181 | −0.0217 | −0.0262 | −0.0342* | −0.0402** |
| $\Delta R/P_{-5}$ |  |  | 0.0241 | 0.0241 | 0.0117 | 0.0076 | 0.0008 | −0.0039 |
| $\Delta R/P_{-6}$ |  |  | 0.0115 | 0.0107 | 0.0062 | 0.0033 | −0.0058 | −0.0092 |
| $\Delta R/P_{-7}$ |  |  |  |  | 0.0182 | 0.0174 | 0.0095 | 0.008 |
| $\Delta R/P_{-8}$ |  |  |  |  | 0.0089 | 0.0082 | −0.0017 | −0.004 |
| $\Delta R/P_{-9}$ |  |  |  |  | 0.0186 | 0.0166 | 0.004 | 0.0034 |
| $\Delta R/P_{-10}$ |  |  |  |  |  |  | 0.0209 | 0.0224 |
| $\Delta R/P_{-11}$ |  |  |  |  |  |  | 0.0238* | 0.0256* |
| $\Delta R/P_{-12}$ |  |  |  |  |  |  | 0.0521*** | 0.0532*** |
| $\Delta$Nom rates$_{-1}$ | −0.0490*** | −0.0458*** | −0.0541*** | −0.0538*** | −0.0683*** | −0.0714*** | −0.0640*** | −0.0698*** |
| $\Delta$Nom rates$_{-2}$ | −0.0786*** | −0.0751*** | −0.0815*** | −0.0824*** | −0.0925*** | −0.0973*** | −0.0932*** | −0.0998*** |
| $\Delta$Nom rates$_{-3}$ | −0.0678*** | −0.0657*** | −0.0661*** | −0.0672*** | −0.0701*** | −0.0756*** | −0.0762*** | −0.0833*** |
| $\Delta$Nom rates$_{-4}$ |  |  | −0.0491*** | −0.0500*** | −0.0530*** | −0.0587*** | −0.0568*** | −0.0652*** |
| $\Delta$Nom rates$_{-5}$ |  |  | 0.0034 | 0.0023 | −0.006 | −0.0116 | −0.0212** | −0.0301** |
| $\Delta$Nom rates$_{-6}$ |  |  | −0.0265* | −0.0271* | −0.0369*** | −0.0417*** | −0.0529*** | −0.0607*** |
| $\Delta$Nom rates$_{-7}$ |  |  |  |  | −0.0310** | −0.0352*** | −0.0285** | −0.0359*** |
| $\Delta$Nom rates$_{-8}$ |  |  |  |  | −0.0571*** | −0.0601*** | −0.0659*** | −0.0721*** |
| $\Delta$Nom rates$_{-9}$ |  |  |  |  | −0.0048 | −0.0095 | −0.0219** | −0.0288*** |
| $\Delta$Nom rates$_{-10}$ |  |  |  |  |  |  | −0.0183** | −0.0240*** |
| $\Delta$Nom rates$_{-11}$ |  |  |  |  |  |  | −0.0257*** | −0.0304*** |
| $\Delta$Nom rates$_{-12}$ |  |  |  |  |  |  | 0.0034 | −0.0012 |
| Constant | 0.1268*** | 0.2210*** | 0.1174*** | 0.1747*** | 0.1142*** | 0.1444*** | 0.1125*** | 0.1460*** |
| Obs | 7,032 | 7,032 | 6,790 | 6,790 | 6,550 | 6,550 | 6,310 | 6,310 |
| No. of groups | 80 | 80 | 80 | 80 | 80 | 80 | 80 | 80 |
| Log likelihood | 6252 | 6308 | 6982 | 7045 | 7583 | 7647 | 8110 | 8184 |
| Hausman test | 0.16 |  | 0.49 |  | 1.5 |  | 0.84 |  |
| *p*-value | 0.6905 |  | 0.4834 |  | 0.2202 |  | 0.3585 |  |

*Source:* Lai and Van Order (2019).

error correction, this means that the Chinese housing markets are strongly mean-reverting. We also added yield spreads in the short-run component. Results were similar. In fact, even though PMG estimations outperform the MG estimations, results from the latter are very similar to those from PMG. Hence, we can be confident that the tests are in general stable and consistent.

It should be noted, though, that the long-run component of the tests on the Chinese markets should be considered with caution because of the short sample period. Recall that the US markets have slow reversion from short-run deviation back to the long-run phenomenon, and strong short-run momentum. The markets in China, on the other hand, correct from the short-run deviation very quickly, including the momentum. Robustness tests using China National Bureau of Statistics house price indices confirm the results.

## 5.3   Disaggregation

Disaggregation is the main theme of this chapter. In the two previous sections, we show how house price series comprise both the long-run fundamental and the short-run components that can be described as bubbles if there is strong momentum. This is the case in the US markets, but not apparent in the Chinese markets. Hence, it is important to disaggregate the house price series into long- and short-run components.

In the previous section on tests for the US housing markets, we also disaggregate the sample periods into pre-bubble and bubble periods, and classify cities into bubble cities (or MSAs) versus non-bubble cities. In the section above for the housing markets in China, we have not done either disaggregation yet. This section fulfills the function by testing different city categories, characterized by city tiers, coastal versus inland, and by supply elasticity. More interestingly, the Chinese housing market "bubbles" have not burst, and we saw that they behave differently from those in the US, at least in terms of the results from the PMG estimations. What we are curious about is whether this is true across cities, and how they are different. If some cities have bubbles but not others, the Chinese government should be really cautious. All these are covered in this section.

In order to facilitate comparison between US MSAs and Chinese cities, we performed the PMG/MG estimations like those in Section 4 but with slightly different regression models in order to facilitate comparison. A longer US time series is also available to allow us to compare the pre-bubble period, bubble period, and the post-bubble period. We also perform estimations for the coastal versus inland classification as well as the supply elasticity classifications. Summarized results are shown in Table 7.5. Detailed results are available upon request.

In the case of the US, coastal MSAs are also the ones with low supply elasticities (see Table 7.1A for the list). Many of them are also bubble MSAs. From Table 7.5A, coastal MSAs have faster corrections back to the long-run equilibrium than those inland MSAs, but not by much. In fact, the very small coefficients mean they revert very slowly. Other forces also have only negligible differences. However, when estimations are run on subperiods, there are indeed differences before the crisis that disappeared afterwards. In terms of differences in supply elasticities, a natural conjecture is that cities with low supply elasticities tend to have higher house price growth. Hence, we use the same set of cities as in Saiz (2010), resulting in 8 high-elasticity MSAs and 16 low-elasticity MSAs. From the sums of coefficients in Table 7.5B, as expected, MSAs with inelastic supply revert to long-term equilibrium faster, and have bigger momentum, albeit not by much. However, once the subsample periods are tested, the

*Table 7.5A    Coastal and inland MSAs*

|  |  | PMG ||||  MG ||||
|---|---|---|---|---|---|---|---|---|---|
|  |  | Error correction coefficient | Sum of ΔR/P | Sum of ΔTIPS_5Y | Constant | Error correction coefficient | Sum of ΔR/P | Sum of ΔTIPS_5Y | Constant |
| *Whole sample period Jan 1999–Aug 2016* |||||||||  |
| 3 lags | Inland | -0.0009 | 0.7205 | -0.0042 | 0.0005 | -0.0019 | 0.8055 | -0.0040 | 0.0016 |
|  | Coastal | -0.0019 | 0.9052 | -0.0057 | 0.0009 | -0.0027 | 0.8366 | -0.0052 | 0.0025 |
|  | Total | -0.0015 | 0.8422 | -0.0052 | 0.0007 | -0.0024 | 0.8260 | -0.0048 | 0.0022 |
| 6 lags | Inland | -0.0012 | 0.7537 | -0.0072 | 0.0008 | -0.0020 | 0.8278 | -0.0082 | 0.0009 |
|  | Coastal | -0.0019 | 0.9175 | -0.0055 | 0.0007 | -0.0026 | 0.8539 | -0.0043 | 0.0024 |
|  | Total | -0.0017 | 0.8616 | -0.0061 | 0.0007 | -0.0024 | 0.8450 | -0.0057 | 0.0019 |
| 9 lags | Inland | -0.0020 | 0.7945 | -0.0123 | 0.0015 | -0.0026 | 0.8548 | -0.0127 | 0.0012 |
|  | Coastal | -0.0026 | 0.9408 | -0.0073 | 0.0016 | -0.0032 | 0.8839 | -0.0068 | 0.0031 |
|  | Total | -0.0024 | 0.8909 | -0.0090 | 0.0016 | -0.0030 | 0.8740 | -0.0088 | 0.0025 |
| 12 lags | Inland | -0.0026 | 0.8175 | -0.0028 | 0.0035 | -0.0031 | 0.8701 | -0.0016 | 0.0033 |
|  | Coastal | -0.0030 | 0.9495 | 0.0031 | 0.0038 | -0.0036 | 0.8972 | 0.0021 | 0.0047 |
|  | Total | -0.0028 | 0.9045 | 0.0011 | 0.0037 | -0.0034 | 0.8880 | 0.0008 | 0.0042 |
| *Subsample periods* (for 2009–2016 coefficients are of MG instead of PMG) |||||||||  |
|  |  | Jan 1999–Dec 2006 |||| Jan 2009–Aug 2016 ||||
| 3 lags | Inland | −0.0010 | 0.5235 | −0.0039 | −0.0011 | −0.0095 | 0.6361 | −0.0019 | 0.0189 |
|  | Coastal | −0.0019 | 0.8311 | −0.0049 | −0.0013 | −0.0135 | 0.7389 | −0.0014 | 0.0207 |
|  | Total | −0.0016 | 0.7263 | −0.0046 | −0.0012 | −0.0121 | 0.7038 | −0.0016 | 0.0201 |
| 6 lags | Inland | −0.0009 | 0.5078 | −0.0056 | −0.0008 | −0.0120 | 0.7034 | −0.0097 | 0.0236 |
|  | Coastal | −0.0022 | 0.8679 | −0.0059 | −0.0009 | −0.0142 | 0.7623 | −0.0055 | 0.0249 |
|  | Total | −0.0018 | 0.7451 | −0.0058 | −0.0009 | −0.0134 | 0.7422 | −0.0069 | 0.0245 |
| 9 lags | Inland | −0.0009 | 0.5124 | −0.0089 | −0.0010 | −0.0201 | 0.7488 | −0.0229 | 0.0377 |
|  | Coastal | −0.0028 | 0.8726 | −0.0257 | −0.0016 | −0.0181 | 0.7864 | −0.0064 | 0.0304 |
|  | Total | −0.0021 | 0.7498 | −0.0199 | −0.0014 | −0.0188 | 0.7736 | −0.0120 | 0.0329 |
| 12 lags | Inland | −0.0008 | 0.4085 | −0.0102 | −0.0011 | −0.0256 | 0.7609 | −0.0196 | 0.0481 |
|  | Coastal | −0.0025 | 0.8497 | −0.0257 | −0.0019 | −0.0175 | 0.7812 | 0.0062 | 0.0308 |
|  | Total | −0.0019 | 0.6993 | −0.0204 | −0.0017 | −0.0203 | 0.7743 | −0.0026 | 0.0367 |

*Note*: Sum of short-run coefficients for individual US MSAs from PMG and MG estimation: Similar to Models A1 to A4 from Table 7.4.
*Source*: Lai and Van Order (2019).

results echo those in the coastal versus inland classification in that differences across MSAs occur only in the pre-bubble period.

In the case of Chinese cities, all four PMG models, as in Table 7.4, are run for Tier cities, coastal/inland cities, and cities with different supply elasticities, and results are shown in Table 7.6. Table 7.6 Panel A shows that the average error correction coefficients of the four Tier 1 cities are the least negative, indicating that these markets take longer to revert back to long-run equilibrium. The next slowest group is Tier 2 cities. Recall in the previous section that there is negative momentum in Chinese cities. It is interesting that this does not hold if we pick out the four Tier 1 cities; their momentums are all positive, although not large. Tier 2 cities have occasionally positive momentum, while the rest have really negative momentum. This verifies that, if bubbles existed, they would be in the Tier 1 and some of the Tier 2 cities. Furthermore, interest rates affect Tier 1 cities the least. Finally, the regression constants are positive, but

*Table 7.5B    24 MSAs by supply elasticity*

|  |  | PMG |  |  |  | MG |  |  |  |
|---|---|---|---|---|---|---|---|---|---|
|  |  | Error correction coefficient | Sum of ΔR/P | Sum of ΔTIPS_5Y | Constant | Error correction coefficient | Sum of ΔR/P | Sum of ΔTIPS_5Y | Constant |
| *Whole sample period Jan 1999–Aug 2016* |
| 3 lags | Low | −0.0020 | 0.8893 | −0.0074 | 0.0011 | −0.0025 | 0.7712 | −0.0058 | 0.0027 |
|  | High | −0.0012 | 0.7715 | −0.0041 | 0.0002 | −0.0021 | 0.8337 | −0.0032 | 0.0029 |
|  | Total | −0.0017 | 0.8500 | −0.0063 | 0.0008 | −0.0023 | 0.7920 | −0.0049 | 0.0027 |
| 6 lags | Low | −0.0020 | 0.9055 | −0.0066 | 0.0010 | −0.0026 | 0.7972 | −0.0063 | 0.0026 |
|  | High | −0.0014 | 0.7965 | −0.0061 | 0.0004 | −0.0024 | 0.8774 | −0.0080 | 0.0022 |
|  | Total | −0.0018 | 0.8692 | −0.0065 | 0.0008 | −0.0025 | 0.8240 | −0.0069 | 0.0024 |
| 9 lags | Low | −0.0025 | 0.9291 | −0.0070 | 0.0019 | −0.0032 | 0.8267 | −0.0109 | 0.0030 |
|  | High | −0.0023 | 0.8474 | −0.0109 | 0.0012 | −0.0030 | 0.9117 | −0.0150 | 0.0022 |
|  | Total | −0.0025 | 0.9019 | −0.0083 | 0.0017 | −0.0031 | 0.8550 | −0.0123 | 0.0028 |
| 12 lags | Low | −0.0027 | 0.9349 | 0.0046 | 0.0038 | −0.0036 | 0.8469 | −0.0024 | 0.0046 |
|  | High | −0.0031 | 0.8708 | −0.0018 | 0.0035 | −0.0035 | 0.9293 | −0.0037 | 0.0044 |
|  | Total | −0.0028 | 0.9135 | 0.0025 | 0.0037 | −0.0036 | 0.8744 | −0.0028 | 0.0045 |
| *Subsample periods* (for 2009–2016 coefficients are of MG instead of PMG) |
|  |  | Jan 1999–Dec 2006 |  |  |  | Jan 2009–Aug 2016 |  |  |  |
| 3 lags | Low | −0.0020 | 0.7766 | −0.0066 | −0.0012 | *−0.0115* | *0.6753* | *0.0007* | *0.0190* |
|  | High | −0.0012 | 0.5762 | −0.0034 | −0.0015 | *−0.0099* | *0.6182* | *−0.0003* | *0.0218* |
|  | Total | −0.0017 | 0.7098 | −0.0056 | −0.0013 | *−0.0109* | *0.6563* | *0.0004* | *0.0200* |
| 6 lags | Low | −0.0022 | 0.8083 | −0.0080 | −0.0009 | −0.0129 | 0.8230 | −0.0043 | 0.0241 |
|  | High | −0.0010 | 0.5428 | −0.0051 | −0.0012 | −0.0111 | 0.7208 | −0.0076 | 0.0206 |
|  | Total | −0.0018 | 0.7198 | −0.0070 | −0.0010 | −0.0123 | 0.7889 | −0.0054 | 0.0229 |
| 9 lags | Low | −0.0026 | 0.8061 | −0.0272 | −0.0018 | −0.0162 | 0.8553 | −0.0002 | 0.0301 |
|  | High | −0.0011 | 0.5506 | −0.0126 | −0.0011 | −0.0206 | 0.8023 | −0.0186 | 0.0356 |
|  | Total | −0.0021 | 0.7210 | −0.0223 | −0.0016 | −0.0177 | 0.8376 | −0.0063 | 0.0319 |
| 12 lags | Low | −0.0023 | 0.7887 | −0.0261 | −0.0019 | −0.0175 | 0.8473 | 0.0111 | 0.0335 |
|  | High | −0.0010 | 0.4367 | −0.0127 | −0.0011 | −0.0271 | 0.8409 | −0.0193 | 0.0486 |
|  | Total | −0.0019 | 0.6713 | −0.0216 | −0.0016 | −0.0207 | 0.8451 | 0.0010 | 0.0385 |

*Note*: Sum of short-run coefficients for individual US MSAs from PMG and MG estimation: Similar to Models A1 to A4 from Table 7.4.
*Source*: Lai and Van Order (2019).

smallest for Tier 1 cities, while "Others" tiers are the largest, suggesting less perceived risk and/or more expected growth in Tier 1 cities.

Table 7.6 Panel B summarizes the results of tests for the coastal and inland cities. Again, coastal cities correct to long-run equilibrium slower, and the constants are smaller, but not by much. Other coefficients are also comparable. Momentum is all negative. Finally, in terms of supply elasticities, we follow the estimates from Wang et al. (2012). Results are presented in Table 7.6 Panel C. Cities with low elasticity revert to long-run equilibrium slower than their counterparts. They are also the ones with positive momentum, and the constants are also smaller, as in the case of Tier 1 cities. This is however not true for the case of US markets.

Another interesting observation is on the autoregression of the residuals of both the US MSAs and the Chinese cities, as summarized in Table 7.7. As the data used here are monthly data, we use 6, 12, and 18 lags, unlike those used in the previous section. The sum of the coefficients of the lagged residuals of the US MSAs shown in Table 7.7A are in general

Table 7.6  Sum of short-run coefficients for individual Chinese cities from PMG estimation by city type

| PMG | | | Error correction coefficient | Sum of ΔR/P | Sum of Δ5Y | Constant |
|---|---|---|---|---|---|---|
| Panel A | By tiers | | | | | |
| 3 lags | | Tier 1 | −0.0247 | 0.1431 | −0.1017 | 0.0100 |
| | | Tier 2 | −0.0643 | −0.1083 | −0.1817 | 0.1143 |
| | | Others | −0.0896 | −0.5123 | −0.2172 | 0.1497 |
| | | Total | −0.0750 | −0.2977 | −0.1954 | 0.1268 |
| 6 lags | | Tier 1 | −0.0398 | 0.0591 | −0.1609 | 0.0138 |
| | | Tier 2 | −0.0648 | 0.0119 | −0.2002 | 0.1041 |
| | | Others | −0.0934 | −0.6110 | −0.3513 | 0.1397 |
| | | Total | −0.0779 | −0.2972 | −0.2738 | 0.1174 |
| 9 lags | | Tier 1 | −0.0403 | 0.0789 | −0.1822 | 0.0088 |
| | | Tier 2 | −0.0752 | −0.0031 | −0.3382 | 0.1039 |
| | | Others | −0.1037 | −0.5245 | −0.5172 | 0.1340 |
| | | Total | −0.0877 | −0.2597 | −0.4199 | 0.1142 |
| 12 lags | | Tier 1 | −0.0294 | 0.0810 | −0.0812 | −0.0002 |
| | | Tier 2 | −0.0878 | 0.1646 | −0.4607 | 0.1086 |
| | | Others | −0.1105 | −0.5928 | −0.6200 | 0.1274 |
| | | Total | −0.0962 | −0.2183 | −0.5214 | 0.1125 |
| Panel B | By coastal versus inland | | | | | |
| 3 lags | | Inland | −0.0783 | −0.3226 | −0.2033 | 0.1370 |
| | | Coastal | −0.0668 | −0.2361 | −0.1760 | 0.1015 |
| | | Total | −0.0750 | −0.2977 | −0.1954 | 0.1268 |
| 6 lags | | Inland | −0.0836 | −0.3201 | −0.3094 | 0.1291 |
| | | Coastal | −0.0637 | −0.2405 | −0.1855 | 0.0886 |
| | | Total | −0.0779 | −0.2972 | −0.2738 | 0.1174 |
| 9 lags | | Inland | −0.0917 | −0.2715 | −0.4483 | 0.1227 |
| | | Coastal | −0.0776 | −0.2302 | −0.3494 | 0.0931 |
| | | Total | −0.0877 | −0.2597 | −0.4199 | 0.1142 |
| 12 lags | | Inland | −0.1027 | −0.1908 | −0.5665 | 0.1239 |
| | | Coastal | −0.0801 | −0.2864 | −0.4095 | 0.0844 |
| | | Total | −0.0962 | −0.2183 | −0.5214 | 0.1125 |
| Panel C | By supply elasticity (Wang et al., 2012) | | | | | |
| 3 lags | | Low | −0.0437 | 0.0024 | −0.1611 | 0.0626 |
| | | High | −0.0702 | −0.2355 | −0.2230 | 0.1492 |
| | | Total | −0.0543 | −0.0928 | −0.1859 | 0.0972 |
| 6 lags | | Low | −0.0503 | 0.1481 | −0.2062 | 0.0640 |
| | | High | −0.0648 | −0.2193 | −0.2502 | 0.1284 |
| | | Total | −0.0561 | 0.0011 | −0.2238 | 0.0898 |
| 9 lags | | Low | −0.0587 | 0.1555 | −0.2859 | 0.0635 |
| | | High | −0.0771 | −0.2349 | −0.4032 | 0.1378 |
| | | Total | −0.0660 | −0.0006 | −0.3328 | 0.0932 |
| 12 lags | | Low | −0.0568 | 0.1457 | −0.2846 | 0.0583 |
| | | High | −0.0993 | 0.1695 | −0.5808 | 0.1551 |
| | | Total | −0.0738 | 0.1552 | −0.4031 | 0.0970 |

Source: Lai and Van Order (2019).

small. Many of them are also negative, indicating oscillations in the residual values. On the other hand, from Table 7.7B on Chinese cities, the sums are in general positive and large in magnitude, although still less than 1, that is, not explosive. This is more pronounced for coastal cities. Tier 1 and Tier 2 cities on the other hand do not have much autocorrelation. This leads to the puzzle of what makes up the "bubbles" that people believe exist. To see this, we check the explanatory powers of the models similar to the previous sections for the US markets.

*Disaggregating house price dynamics* 199

*Table 7.7A   Sums of significant coefficients of residual autoregression estimations: US MSAs*

| | PMG – three lags | | | PMG – six lags | | | PMG – nine lags | | | PMG – 12 lags | | |
|---|---|---|---|---|---|---|---|---|---|---|---|---|
| | AR(6) | AR(12) | AR(18) | AR(6) | AR(12) | AR(18) | AR(6) | AR(12) | AR(18) | AR(6) | AR(12) | AR(18) |
| Whole sample | −0.0998 | 0.0481 | 0.1399 | −0.1253 | −0.0636 | 0.0167 | 0.0520 | −0.0413 | −0.0789 | 0.0060 | −0.0512 | −0.0779 |
| Pre-Crisis period | −0.1484 | 0.1026 | 0.2663 | −0.1849 | 0.0020 | 0.1407 | −0.0082 | 0.0171 | 0.0553 | −0.0115 | 0.0054 | −0.0520 |
| Post-Crisis period | −0.0906 | −0.0810 | −0.0911 | −0.1478 | −0.1426 | −0.0993 | 0.0670 | −0.0453 | −0.1131 | −0.0425 | −0.1532 | −0.2776 |
| Coastal | −0.0488 | −0.0130 | 0.0081 | −0.0969 | −0.0273 | −0.0140 | 0.0833 | −0.0090 | −0.1082 | 0.0082 | −0.0580 | −0.0990 |
| Inland | −0.1084 | 0.0955 | 0.2812 | −0.1253 | −0.0706 | 0.1090 | | −0.1035 | −0.0114 | | −0.0809 | 0.0593 |
| High supply elasticity | −0.0970 | 0.0115 | 0.1285 | −0.1035 | −0.0656 | 0.0339 | | −0.1202 | −0.1158 | | −0.0599 | −0.0171 |
| Low supply elasticity | 0.0456 | 0.0818 | 0.0169 | −0.0836 | 0.0095 | 0.0664 | 0.0563 | 0.0888 | −0.0539 | 0.0436 | 0.0484 | −0.0416 |

*Source:* Lai and Van Order (2019).

*Table 7.7B   Sums of significant coefficients of residual autoregression estimations: Chinese cities*

| | PMG – three lags | | | PMG – six lags | | | PMG – nine lags | | | PMG – 12 lags | | |
|---|---|---|---|---|---|---|---|---|---|---|---|---|
| | AR(6) | AR(12) | AR(18) | AR(6) | AR(12) | AR(18) | AR(6) | AR(12) | AR(18) | AR(6) | AR(12) | AR(18) |
| All cities | 0.4819 | 0.7508 | 0.7107 | 0.2824 | 0.4793 | 0.5192 | 0.3097 | 0.5331 | 0.6120 | 0.6683 | 0.7953 | 0.7752 |
| Coastal | 0.7729 | *0.8572* | *0.8190* | 0.4377 | 0.6658 | 0.7096 | 0.4802 | *0.8014* | 0.7101 | *0.8726* | *0.9019* | 0.6753 |
| Inland | | −0.0324 | 0.1433 | | 0.0814 | 0.0852 | −0.0034 | −0.0028 | 0.0109 | | −0.0047 | 0.1016 |
| High supply elasticity | −0.0877 | 0.0773 | 0.1318 | | 0.1067 | 0.1010 | 0.0662 | 0.1500 | 0.0423 | | −0.1261 | −0.0071 |
| Low supply elasticity | 0.0680 | 0.1315 | 0.1745 | | 0.0035 | −0.0884 | | −0.0592 | −0.1900 | | −0.0609 | −0.1455 |
| Tier 1 | 0.0933 | 0.1977 | 0.2030 | 0.0984 | 0.3826 | 0.1742 | | | | | | |
| Tier 2 | | 0.2122 | 0.1583 | −0.0502 | 0.1913 | 0.1197 | | 0.1460 | 0.0204 | | −0.1340 | −0.1394 |
| Others | 0.5867 | 0.8126 | 0.8430 | 0.3449 | 0.4644 | 0.5488 | 0.3670 | 0.6535 | 0.7052 | 0.7678 | 0.7872 | *0.8278* |

*Source:* Lai and Van Order (2019).

*Table 7.8A    Measures of explanatory power of various models: partial R2s: US MSAs*

|  | Overall | Low-supply elasticity | High-supply elasticity | Coastal | Inland |
|---|---|---|---|---|---|
| *Subpanel A1: PMG with three lags in short run* | | | | | |
| Long Run Partial $R^2$ | 0.1713 | 0.2368 | 0.1636 | 0.2175 | 0.0820 |
| Short Run Partial $R^2$ | 0.8087 | 0.8819 | 0.7906 | 0.8786 | 0.6737 |
| PMG Model | 0.6695 | 0.6575 | 0.7483 | 0.7669 | 0.4813 |
| Residual Autoregression | 0.0367 | 0.0421 | 0.0342 | 0.0298 | 0.0500 |
| *Total = PMG + Residual* | *0.7062* | *0.6996* | *0.7825* | *0.7967* | *0.5313* |
| *Subpanel A2: PMG with six lags in short run* | | | | | |
| Long Run Partial $R^2$ | 0.2131 | 0.2652 | 0.2102 | 0.2632 | 0.1162 |
| Short Run Partial $R^2$ | 0.8255 | 0.8946 | 0.8071 | 0.8896 | 0.7014 |
| PMG Model | 0.6833 | 0.6718 | 0.7579 | 0.7725 | 0.5109 |
| Residual Autoregression | 0.0293 | 0.0343 | 0.0287 | 0.0246 | 0.0385 |
| *Total = PMG + Residual* | *0.7126* | *0.7060* | *0.7866* | *0.7971* | *0.5494* |

Source: Lai and Van Order (2019).

*Table 7.8B    Measures of explanatory power of various models: partial R2s: Chinese cities*

|  | Overall | Low-supply elasticity | High-supply elasticity | Coastal | Inland | Tier 1 | Tier 2 | Others |
|---|---|---|---|---|---|---|---|---|
| *Subpanel B1: PMG with three lags in short run* | | | | | | | | |
| Long-run partial $R^2$ | −0.0249 | 0.1206 | −0.0014 | 0.0149 | −0.0410 | 0.2515 | 0.0526 | −0.1223 |
| Short-run partial $R^2$ | 0.4048 | 0.3810 | 0.3656 | 0.4260 | 0.3963 | 0.4139 | 0.3584 | 0.4458 |
| PMG model | 0.4586 | 0.1682 | 0.1541 | 1.1443 | 0.1819 | 0.1658 | 0.1585 | 0.7579 |
| Residual autoregression | 0.1518 | 0.0595 | 0.0374 | 0.4390 | 0.0359 | 0.1023 | 0.0439 | 0.2537 |
| *Total = PMG + Residual* | *0.6104* | *0.2277* | *0.1915* | *1.5833* | *0.2178* | *0.2682* | *0.2025* | *1.0117* |
| *Subpanel B2: PMG with six lags in short run* | | | | | | | | |
| Long-run partial $R^2$ | 0.0635 | 0.0347 | 0.1350 | 0.1229 | 0.0042 | 0.3535 | 0.1147 | −0.0115 |
| Short-run partial $R^2$ | 0.4946 | 0.4823 | 0.5251 | 0.4748 | 0.5143 | 0.5791 | 0.4783 | 0.5008 |
| PMG model | 0.3057 | 0.2157 | 0.5286 | 0.3851 | 0.2262 | 0.2342 | 0.1940 | 0.4134 |
| Residual autoregression | 0.0388 | 0.0188 | 0.0883 | 0.0647 | 0.0129 | 0.0859 | 0.0225 | 0.0487 |
| *Total = PMG + Residual* | *0.3445* | *0.2345* | *0.6169* | *0.4498* | *0.2391* | *0.3201* | *0.2165* | *0.4621* |

Table 7.8A lists the average explanatory power for the US MSAs, while Table 7.8B is for the Chinese cities. For the US MSAs, the PMG estimation and the residual autoregression model in total explain 70–80 percent of the rent-to-price ratio. Within the PMG estimation, the long-run model explains 20 percent, while the short-run component explains much of the rest. On the other hand, the long-run component does not perform a significant enough job in explaining the rent-to-price ratios of the Chinese cities. This is perhaps due to the relatively short time series that hinders effective explanatory power of the long-run fundamentals. Nevertheless, while the short-run components are able to explain 40 percent, they are still not as much as what the US MSAs had. The residual autoregression part explains better than those for the US counterparts.

In sum, PMG estimation is more consistent for the US MSAs across different models and MSA categories than that for Chinese cities. This is true even if we shorten the time series to the same length as that of the Chinese sample period. These results seem to point to the fact that the US MSAs respond to the fundamentals and market forces in more or less the same ways. On the other hand, Chinese markets show very different characteristics. Even though house prices are on a continuous rise, only the four Tier 1 cities, of which three are also coastal cities, behave like bubble cities. Chinese housing markets are very often closely monitored by the government. The frequently imposed regulatory policies are always different in strength across different cities, such as stronger in coastal cities and weaker or non-existent in inland cities (these effects would have been embedded in the residuals in the estimation). Given close government intervention, it seems that the Chinese housing bubbles, even if they exist, will not burst and lead to big shocks to the economy and the financial sector.

## 6  CONCLUSIONS AND LESSONS LEARNT

The main purpose of this chapter is to show the importance of disaggregation in the study of housing markets. By reviewing Lai and Van Order (2010, 2017), we have shown in the sections above how housing prices can be disaggregated into the fundamentals explained by the Gordon model and the short run where bubbles are created when house prices deviate from this long-run fundamental. The long-run and short-run movements are shown both in regime shift models and PMG/MG estimation models. We show that the housing markets behave differently in different periods, particularly the time when there are bubbles. This is consistent with the well-researched proposition that housing markets are not efficient markets, and therefore can be forecasted.

All three research papers conclude that the US housing markets before the Global Financial Crisis experienced periods of momentum, creating non-explosive bubbles, which then burst in 2006–2007. There was a regime shift after 1999 when momentum increased, particularly for non-bubble MSAs. From Lai and Van Order (2019), the Chinese markets are mostly explained by random shocks and mean reversion, unlike the US markets which can best be explained by price momentum. This is very likely because of the frequent additions and removals of various government policies at times to curb, and at other times boost, the market. An easy conclusion is that US housing markets tend to have price chasing price, while those Chinese counterparts tend to have price chasing rent. It should be noted, however, that the data series for the Chinese markets are not long enough to draw confident conclusions as to whether the markets are less prone to bubbles than in the US, or are due to successful government policies that keep the markets buoyant.

The most significant contribution of these three studies is to point out that it is important to identify the potential bubbles based on lessons learnt from the past and take measures to ensure that the burst of the bubbles will not be too destructive, like the one leading in the US to the Global Financial Crisis. Disaggregation is crucial. As shown in our tests, bubble cities behave differently from non-bubble cities. Further analyses show that the bubble cities tend to be the ones that also have relatively inelastic supply, as discussed in numerous research papers mentioned earlier. Policy makers should pay attention to market movements in cities with inelastic supply to avoid bubble markets being contained too late. Further disaggregation can come from cities along the coasts, which are usually more attractive to settlers and therefore homebuyers, and hence are in higher demand, and are more populated. In other words, it is also important to distinguish policies for coastal versus inland cities. A uniform policy might result in overshooting in some less booming, or declining, markets.

## ACKNOWLEDGMENTS

We thank Rui-Hui Xu and Zongyuan Li for always providing very efficient and effective research assistance.

## NOTES

1. See "A Fifth of China's Homes Are Empty. That's 50 Million Apartments," Bloomberg, November 9, 2018, available from www.bloomberg.com/news/articles/2018-11-08/a-fifth-of-china-s-homes-are-empty-that-s-50-million-apartments.
2. See the interview entitled "This Is a Period of Abundance, But a Strong Economy Is not the Same as Healthy, Says Economist," by Calcalist, available from www.calcalistech.com/ctech/articles/0,7340,L-3776707,00.html.
3. See Statista, www.statista.com/statistics/454494/china-fortune-500-leading-chinese-real-estate-companies/.
4. Details of CityRE Data Technology Co. can be obtained from www.cityre.cn/en/ or www.cityhouse.cn.
5. See Wu et al. (2012) for a discussion on the homogeneity of China housing.

## REFERENCES

Ahuja, A., L. Cheung, G. Han, N. Porter, and W. Zhang (2010). Are House Prices Rising Too Fast in China. Working paper 08/2010. Hong Kong Monetary Authority.
Baddeley, M. (2005). Housing Bubbles, Herds and Frenzies: Evidence from British Housing Markets. CCEPP Policy Brief No. 02-05, Cambridge Centre for Economic and Public Policy.
Black, A., P. Fraser, and M. Hoesli (2006). House Prices, Fundamental and Bubbles. *Journal of Business Finance and Accounting*, 33, 1535–1555.
Blanchard, O.J., and M. Watson (1982). Bubbles, Rational Expectations and Financial Markets. In P. Wachtel (Ed.), *Crisis in the Economic and Financial Structure*. Lexington, MA: Lexington Books.
Borcard, D. (2002). Multiple and Partial Regression and Correlation Partial $r2$, Contribution and Fraction [a]. http://biol09.biol.umontreal.ca/borcardd/partialr2.pd
Breitung, J. (1999). The Local Power of Some Unit Root Tests for Panel Data. *Discussion Papers, Interdisciplinary Research Project 373: Quantification and Simulation of Economic Processes*, No. 1999, 69, http://nbn-resolving.de/urn:nbn:de:kobv:11-10046584

Breitung, J. and S. Das (2005). Panel Unit Root Tests under Cross-Sectional Dependence. *Statistica Neerlandica*, 59(4), 414–433.

Brunnermeier, M.K., and C. Julliard (2008). Money Illusion and Housing Frenzies. *Review of Financial Studies*, 21(1), 135–180.

Capozza, D, P. Hendershott, and C. Mack (2004). An Anatomy of Price Dynamics in Illiquid Markets: Analysis and Evidence from Local Housing Markets. *Real Estate Economics*, 32, 1–21.

Case, K.E., and R.J. Shiller (1989). The Efficiency of the Market for Single Family Homes. *American Economic Review*, 79(1), 125–137.

Case, K.E., and R.J. Shiller (2003). Is There a Bubble in the Housing Market? *Brookings Papers on Economic Activity*, 2, 299–362.

Case, K.E., J. Cotter, and S. Gabriel (2011). Housing Risk and Return: Evidence from a Housing Asset-Pricing Model. *Journal of Portfolio Management*, Special Real Estate Issue, 37(5), 89–109.

Chan, I.C., S.K. Lee, and K.Y. Woo (2001). Detecting Rational Bubbles in the Residential Housing Markets in Hong Kong. *Economic Modelling*, 18, 61–73.

Chang, Y., A.C. Cutts, and R.K. Green (2005). Did Changing Rents Explain Changing House Prices during the 1990s? Working Paper. Washington, DC: George Washington University School of Business.

Choi, I. (2001). Unit Root Tests for Panel Data. *Journal of International Money and Finance*, 20, 249–272.

Coleman, M. IV, M. LaCour-Little, and K.D. Vandell (2008). Subprime Lending and the Housing Bubble: Tail Wags Dog? Social Science Research Network. http://ssrn.com/abstract=1262365

Cutler, D.M., J.M. Poterba, and L.H. Summers (1991). Speculative Dynamics. *Review of Economic Studies*, 58, 529–546.

DeCoster, G.P., and W.C. Strange (2012). Developers, Herding, and Overbuilding. *Journal of Real Estate Finance and Economics*, 44(1–2), 7–35.

Diba, B.T., and H.I. Grossman (1988). Explosive Rational Bubbles in Stock Prices? *American Economic Review*, 78, 520–528.

Evans, G.W. (1991). Pitfalls in Testing for Explosive Bubbles in Asset Prices. *American Economic Review*, 81(4), 922–930.

Fama, E.F. (1965). The Behavior of Stock-Market Prices. Journal of Business, 38(1), 34–105.

Fama, E.F., and K.R. French (1988). Dividend Yields and Expected Stock Returns. *Journal of Financial Economics*, 22, 3–25.

Garber, P.M. (2000). Famous First Bubbles: The Fundamentals of Early Manias. Cambridge, MA: MIT Press.

Glaeser, E.L., and C.G. Nathanson (2015). Housing Bubbles. In G. Duranton, J. Vernon Henderson, W.C. Strange (Eds), *Handbook of Regional and Urban Economics*, Volume 5. New York: Elsevier, 701–751.

Glaeser, E.L., J. Gyourko, and R. Saks (2005). Why Have Housing Prices Gone Up? *American Economic Review*, 95, 329–333.

Glaeser, E.L., W. Huang, Y. Ma, and A. Shleifer (2017). A Real Estate Boom with Chinese Characteristics, *Journal of Economic Perspectives*, 31(1), 93–116

Hadri, K. (2000). Testing for Stationarity in Heterogeneous Panel Data. *Econometrics Journal*, 3, 148–161.

Hamilton, J.D., and C.H. Whiteman. (1985). The Observable Implications of Self-Fulfilling Expectations. *Journal of Monetary Economics*, 16(3), 353–373.

Harris, R.D.F., and E. Tzavalis (1999). Inference for Unit Roots in Dynamic Panels Where the Time Dimension Is Fixed. *Journal of Econometrics*, 91, 201–226.

Hwang, M., J. Quigley, and J. Son (2006). The Dividend Pricing Model: New Evidence from the Korean Housing Market. *Journal of Real Estate Finance and Economics*, 32, 205–228.

Im, K.S., M.H. Pesaran, and Y. Shin (2003). Testing for Unit Roots in Heterogeneous Panels. *Journal of Econometrics*, 115, 53–74.

Kindleberger, C. and R. Aliber (2005). *Manias, Panics and Crashes: A History of Financial Crises.* Hoboken, NJ: John Wiley and Sons.

Lai, R.N., and R.A. Van Order (2010). Momentum and House Price Growth in the US: Anatomy of a Bubble. *Real Estate Economics*, 38(4), 753–773.

Lai, R.N., and R.A. Van Order (2017). U.S. House Prices over the Last 30 Years: Bubbles, Regime Shifts and Market (In)Efficiency. *Real Estate Economics*, 46(2), 259–300.

Lai, R.N. and R.A. Van Order (2019). A Tale of Two Countries: Comparing the US and Chinese Bubbles Housing Markets. *Journal of Real Estate Finance and Economics*, 61, 507–547.

Lei, V., C.N. Noussair, and C.R. Plott (2001). On Speculative Bubbles in Experimental Asset Markets: Lack of Common Knowledge of Rationality vs. Actual Irrationality. *Econometrica*, 69(4), 831–859.

Levine, S.S., and E.J. Zajac (2007). The Institutional Nature of Price Bubbles. SSRN 960178. https://ssrn.com/abstract=960178

Lin, Z. (2019). Why China's Housing Market Bubble Won't Burst Any Time Soon. *South China Morning Post*, January, 13. www.scmp.com/economy/china-economy/article/2181808/why-chinas-housing-market-bubble-wont-burst-any-time-soon

Ling, D.C., J.T.L. Ooi, and T.T.T. Le (2015). Explaining House Price Dynamics: Isolating the Role of Nonfundamentals. *Journal of Money, Credit, and Banking*, 47(S1), 87–125.

Loayza, N.V., and R. Rancière (2006). Financial Development, Financial Fragility, and Growth. *Journal of Money, Credit and Banking*, 38, 1051–1076.

Nneji, O., C. Brooks, and C. Ward (2013). Intrinsic and Rational Speculative Bubbles in the US Housing Market: 1960–2011. *Journal of Real Estate Research*, 35(2), 121–151.

Pesaran, H.M., and Y. Shin (1999). An Autoregressive Distributed Lag Modelling Approach to Cointegration Analysis. In S. Strom (Ed.), *Econometrics and Economic Theory in the 20th Century: The Ragnar Frisch Centennial Symposium*. Cambridge: Cambridge University Press.

Pesaran, H.M., Y. Shin, and R. Smith (1997). Pooled Estimation of Long-Run Relationships in Dynamic heterogeneous Panels. Working Paper.

Pesaran, H.M., Y. Shin, and R. Smith (1999). Pooled Mean Group Estimation of Dynamic Heterogeneous Panels. *Journal of the American Statistical Association*, 94, 621–634.

Poterba, J.M. (1984). Tax Subsidies to Owner-Occupied Housing: An Asset-Market Approach. *Quarterly Journal of Economics*, 99, 729–751.

Saiz, A. (2010). The Geographic Determinants of Housing Supply. *Quarterly Journal of Economics*, 125(3), 1253–1296.

Shiller, R.J. (2019). *How Stories Go Viral and Drive Major Economic Events*. Princeton, NJ: Princeton University Press.

Smith, V.L., Suchanek, G.L., and Williams, A.W. (1988). Bubbles, Crashes, and Endogenous Expectations in Experimental Spot Asset Markets. *Econometrica*, 56(5), 1119–1151.

Summers, L. (1986). Does the Stock Market Rationally Reflect Fundamental Values? *Journal of Finance*, 41(3), 591–601.

Taipalus, K. (2006). A Global House Price Bubble? Evaluation Based on a New Rent-Price Approach. Bank of Finland Discussion Papers, 29.

Van Norden, S. (1996). Regime Switching as a Test for Exchange Rate Bubbles. *Journal of Applied Econometrics*, 11, 219–251.

Van Norden, S., and H. Schaller (1993). The Predictability of Stock Market Regime: Evidence from the Toronto Stock Exchange. *Review of Economics and Statistics*, 75(3), 505–510.

Van Norden, S., and H. Schaller (1996). Speculative Behavior, Regime-Switching, and Stock Market Crashes. Working paper No. 96-13, Bank of Canada.

Van Order, R., and A. Dougherty (1991). Housing Demand and Real Interest Rates. *Journal of Urban Economics*, 29(2), 191–201.

Wang, S., S. Han Chan, and B. Xu. (2012). The Estimation and Determinants of the Price Elasticity of Housing Supply: Evidence from China, *Journal of Real Estate Research*, 34(3), 311–344.

Westerlund, J. (2007). Testing for Error Correction in Panel Data. *Oxford Bulletin of Economics and Statistics*, 69(6), 709–748.

Wheaton, William C. (2015). The Volatility of Real Estate Markets: A Decomposition, *Journal of Portfolio Management*, Special Real Estate Issue, 41(6), 140–150. DOI: https://doi.org/10.3905/jpm.2015.41.6.140.

Wheaton, W., and G. Nechayev (2008). The 1998–2005 Housing "Bubble" and the Current "Correction": What's Different This Time? *Journal of Real Estate Research*, 30, 1–26.

Wu, J., J. Gyourko, and Y. Deng (2012). Evaluating Conditions in Major Chinese Housing Markets. *Regional Science and Urban Economics*, 42, 531–543.

Yang, Z., and J. Chen (2014). Housing Affordability and Housing Policy in Urban China. Berlin: Springer.

Zhi, T., Z. Li, Z. Jiang, L. Wei, and D. Sornette (2019). Is There a Housing Bubble in China? *Emerging Markets Review*, 39, 120–132.

# 8. The effect of macroeconomic uncertainty on housing returns and volatility: evidence from US state-level data

*Reneé van Eyden, Rangan Gupta, Christophe André and Xin Sheng*

## 1    INTRODUCTION

A collapse in United States (US) house prices, following a prolonged boom, is associated with the global economic and financial crisis of 2007–2009 and the "Great Recession" (Leamer, 2007, 2015; Nyakabawo et al., 2015; Emirmahmutoglu et al., 2016). The period was also characterized by high levels of financial and macroeconomic volatility, after a sustained period of macroeconomic stability, known as the "Great Moderation" (Mumtaz, 2018; Mumtaz et al., 2018; Mumtaz and Musso, 2021). Understanding the role of uncertainty in driving housing market movements is of paramount importance in order to avoid a repeat of the catastrophic effects observed under the Great Recession, not only at the aggregate, but also at the individual state level. Moreover, predicting housing returns and volatility would assist investors in making timely portfolio allocation decisions (Nyakabawo et al., 2018; Gupta et al., 2020a; Segnon et al., 2020). Residential real estate has a major impact on household finances, as it represents about 84 percent of total household non-financial assets, 31 percent of total household net worth and 27 percent of household total assets (Financial Accounts of the US, Fourth Quarter, 2020).[1]

A growing number of studies, which we discuss in detail in the literature review segment of this chapter, have highlighted the role of uncertainty in predicting (primarily) US aggregate and regional housing returns and (to some extent) aggregate volatility (see for example Antonakakis et al., 2015, 2016; André et al., 2017; Christou et al., 2017, 2019; Christidou and Fountas, 2018; Aye et al., 2019; Nguyen Thanh et al., 2020; Strobel et al., 2020; Bouri et al., Forthcoming). At the same time, some studies have indicated that heightened uncertainty can explain herding and co-movement (i.e. synchronicity) of regional housing returns and volatility (Ngene et al., 2017; Gupta et al., 2021), and even decisions to buy or rent (Aye and Gupta, 2019).

Against this backdrop, the objective of our study is to add to the above line of research by providing a comprehensive analysis of the effect of state-level uncertainty on housing returns and volatility in the 50 US states and the District of Columbia (DC), based on a panel data approach. State-level uncertainty is estimated using the average (*n*-period-ahead) forecast error variance of a range of regional variables derived from a factor-augmented forecasting regression with stochastic volatility in the regression residuals and the error term for the factor dynamics. The estimation periods are 1977Q2 to 2015Q3 and 1991Q1 to 2015Q3, contingent on the usage of small (eight) and large (21) numbers of state-level financial and macroeconomic variables, respectively, in the factor regressions, besides 248 aggregate country-level variables. Using a panel-based approach with heterogeneous responses of housing market movements to uncertainty, instead of a time series analysis involving each unit considered separately, allows us to model the underlying interdependence as well as the heterogeneity across US state housing markets (see Gabauer et al., 2020 and Marfatia, 2021 for detailed analyses). At this stage, we need to emphasize that given that the common or national component of housing returns and volatility tends to play an important role in driving the corresponding regional and/or state-level values (Del Negro and Otrok, 2007; Fairchild et al., 2015), analyzing the effect of state-level uncertainty requires disentangling the national from the state- or local-level factors driving housing returns and volatility. Concentrating on the state-level component of housing returns and volatility after filtering out the national factor prevents us from underestimating the impact of state-level uncertainty. Note that the national common factor is understandably driven by aggregate-level US variables, i.e. shocks that are common to the entire economy. To estimate the factors driving house prices, we follow Gupta et al. (2020b) in using a dynamic factor model with time-varying loadings and stochastic volatility (DFM-TV-SV), estimated using Bayesian methods. The generalized DFM-TV-SV model does not only capture changing co-movements among house price returns in the 50 states and DC by allowing for their dependence on a common national factor to evolve over time, but also allows for stochastic volatility in the innovations to the processes followed by the national and idiosyncratic (i.e. state-level) components.

In this regard, we must highlight that Gorodnichenko and Ng (2017) suggest a simple methodology that can separate the level from the volatility factors without directly estimating the volatility processes. The authors make this possible by exploiting features in the second-order approximation of equilibrium models and using information in a large panel of primarily aggregate macroeconomic data to estimate the factors. Then, by augmenting vector autoregression (VAR) with the factors, Gorodnichenko and Ng (2017) shed light on the effects of the level and volatility shocks and their relative importance in business cycle analysis. However, in our case, we are using state-level house prices, i.e. regional data. Unlike the approach of Gorodnichenko and Ng (2017), we need to decompose the aggregate housing market movements in terms of their first and second moments into a national factor and local factors, which is only possible via the usage of the DFM-TV-SV model, before analyzing the impact of corresponding state-level uncertainty. This avoids underestimating the effect of state-level uncertainty by keeping the national factor component within the regional housing prices. We could have followed the approaches of Mumtaz (2018) and Mumtaz et al. (2018), whereby uncertainty is recovered and its effect on the variables used to obtain the metric of uncertainty is analyzed simultaneously. However, then we would not have been able to filter out the national factor and also would not have been able to obtain second moment effects on house price volatility.[2]

Theoretically, the effect of uncertainty on economic decisions, like consumption and investment, is generally explained by the real option theory (see, for example, Bernanke, 1983; Pindyck, 1991; Dixit and Pindyck, 1994; and more recently Bloom, 2009), which suggests that decision-making is affected by uncertainty because it raises the option value of waiting. In other words, given that the costs associated with wrong investment decisions are very high, uncertainty makes investors and consumers of durable goods more cautious. As a result, economic agents postpone investment and consumption decisions to periods of lower uncertainty. Buying a dwelling is for many households the biggest single investment in their lifetime and hence has serious implications for their finances. Hence, uncertainty is bound to lower housing demand and prices. Moreover, as uncertainty is basically associated with second-moment movements of macroeconomic and financial variables, the existence of significant spillover effects from the real and financial segments of the economy to the real estate sector (Gabauer and Gupta, 2020) is likely to raise the volatility of housing returns. In other words, we expect housing returns to decrease and their volatility to increase in episodes of heightened uncertainty.

To the best of our knowledge, this is the first study analyzing the effect of state-level uncertainty on corresponding real housing returns and volatility in the US. The remainder of the chapter is organized as follows: Section 2 presents a review of the literature that has thus far dealt with uncertainty and housing market movements in the US. Section 3 outlines the data and explains the econometric methodologies adopted in this chapter. Section 4 discusses the empirical results and Section 5 concludes.

## 2 LITERATURE REVIEW

To set the contribution of our analysis into perspective, we discuss below in a chronological order the existing literature that has related movements in housing returns and volatility in the US to uncertainty.

Antonakakis et al. (2015) investigate the co-movements between housing market returns and economic policy uncertainty (EPU) and find negative correlations throughout 1987 to 2014. These correlations are time-varying and tend to increase rapidly during high uncertainty times, specifically around US recessions. This implies that tail risks are significant, as also shown in André et al. (2017).

Antonakakis et al. (2016), investigating dynamic spillovers between the housing market, stock market and a news-based measure of EPU, find that US economic fluctuations are significantly impacted by the transmission of various types of shocks and that these spillovers vary considerably over time. They also find that the spillovers during the global financial crisis were exceptionally high from a historical perspective. Large spillovers run from EPU and stock and housing markets to inflation, industrial production and the federal funds rate in particular. The strong policy reaction to the crisis can be seen from the results.

André et al. (2017) find that EPU is useful for predicting future returns on housing-related investments, with EPU improving forecasts of the first and second moments (level and volatility) of real housing returns, both in-sample and out-of-sample. They also find that EPU not only has an indirect impact through the broader economy and financial markets, but also a direct impact on real housing returns and their volatility. André et al. (2017) find evidence of nonlinearity and structural breaks, and that large uncertainty shocks lead to disproportional falls in housing returns. This implies there are significant tail risks for investors during periods of high uncertainty.

Christou et al. (2017) investigate whether including EPU in the set of predictors can improve forecasting performance for real housing returns in ten Organisation for Economic Co-operation and Development (OECD) countries, including the US. Their out-of-sample period is 2008Q2–2014Q4, with an in-sample period of 2003Q1–2008Q1. Using a combination of time series and panel data-based VAR models (which account for heterogeneity and static and dynamic interdependence), they find that EPU does improve forecasting performance, regardless of the model used. They also find that models pooling information (from panel data models, in particular the Bayesian variants which allow for parameter shrinkage) perform better than the time series autoregressive models.

Christidou and Fountas (2018) use bivariate generalized autoregressive conditional heteroskedasticity models for each of the 48 US states in their sample to obtain proxies for house price uncertainty and housing investment (from house price index and housing permits, respectively) to investigate the effect of uncertainty on the housing market. They also use EPU as an alternative measure for uncertainty. They find that the effects are heterogeneous across states and that in most states uncertainty increases housing investment, while it decreases house price inflation.

Christou et al. (2019) find time-varying impacts of uncertainty shocks on the US housing market, with longer-run uncertainties (two- to three-years-ahead horizons) having a negative impact on the housing variables (sales, permits and starts). They use a time-varying factor-augmented vector autoregression (TVP-FAVAR) model, with quarterly data from 1963Q1 to 2014Q3, and control for economic activity, prices and financial variables.

Aye et al. (2019) investigate economic uncertainty spillover effects on the duration of housing booms, busts and normal times using quarterly data from 1985 to 2012 for 12 OECD countries in a discrete-time (hazard) model. They find that higher economic uncertainty significantly increases the probability of exiting housing market busts, while it does not significantly impact the probability of leaving booms and normal times. Thus, housing could serve as a possible hedge against uncertainty.

Strobel et al. (2020) show that macroeconomic uncertainty affects the housing market in two significant ways. First, controlling for a broad set of variables in fixed-effects regressions for US states, economy-wide uncertainty shocks, as developed by Jurado et al. (2015), adversely affect house prices but not the quantities that are traded. Second, when both uncertainty and local demand shocks are introduced, the effect of uncertainty on house prices, median sale prices, the share of houses selling for a loss and transactions dominates that of local labor demand shocks. The aforementioned effects are largest for the states that exhibit relatively high house price volatility, suggesting real options effects in the housing market during times of high uncertainty.

Building on this work to a certain degree, Nguyen Thanh et al. (2020) construct a new measure for uncertainty, specific to the real estate sector (REU). They show that REU accounts for twice as much variation in house prices and starts as aggregate US macro uncertainty (MU), as developed by Jurado et al. (2015). Using VAR and Granger causality analyses, they find that REU affects house prices and starts, whereas MU only affects housing starts.

Finally, Bouri et al. (Forthcoming), confirmed the findings of Christou et al. (2017) using a unique daily dataset of US house prices. They use a $k$-th order nonparametric causality-in-quantiles test, as this allows them to control for misspecification due to nonlinearity and structural breaks, while testing predictability over the whole conditional distribution for returns and volatility, to show that EPU does predict daily housing returns and volatility (barring the extreme upper end of the respective conditional distributions). The results are robust to eight other popular measures of aggregate financial and macroeconomic uncertainty, as well as an alternative dataset involving daily house prices of the ten major metropolitan statistical areas (MSAs), namely Boston, Chicago, Denver, Las Vegas, Los Angeles, Miami, New York, San Diego, San Francisco and Washington, DC.

At this stage, we must also discuss the work by El Montasser et al. (2016). These authors examine the causal linkages between EPU and house prices in a panel of seven advanced countries including the US, based on a bootstrap panel causality test, which allows them to circumvent data limitations, as observations are pooled across countries. They find evidence of a bidirectional causality between real house prices and EPU, suggesting that high uncertainty related to future economic fundamentals and policies increases house price volatility, which in turn may amplify financial and business cycles. This finding is consistent with individual results for France and Spain, while contrasting with the unidirectional causality reported in the remaining countries. Particularly, support for a unidirectional causality running from EPU to real house prices is found in Canada, Germany and Italy, while a unidirectional causality running from real house prices to EPU prevails in the United Kingdom and the US. In other words, El Montasser et al. (2016), unlike the abovementioned papers, could not find evidence of predictability from uncertainty to real house prices in the US.

As can be seen from the discussion of the literature above, the analysis of effects of uncertainty on housing returns and volatility at the regional level is limited. Even if it exists to some extent, for instance in the case of Christidou and Fountas (2018), Strobel et al. (2020) and Bouri et al. (Forthcoming), no attempt has been made to disentangle the national and local factors driving house price movements. In any event, Christidou and Fountas (2018) are more concerned with housing investment than house prices. Moreover, analyses have only been conducted using aggregate and not state-level measures of uncertainty. Our study provides novel information on the relationship between state-level housing returns and volatility, and corresponding uncertainty, which is undoubtedly useful to households, mortgage lenders and investors in making their respective buying, lending and investment decisions.

## 3     DATA AND METHODOLOGIES

### 3.1    Data Series Used

We use the Federal Housing Finance Agency's seasonally adjusted house price indices for the 50 US states and DC to obtain our national and local factors from the Bayesian DFM-TV-SV for both housing returns and the corresponding stochastic volatility. These house price indices provide a broad measure of the movement of single-family house prices. They use weighted, repeat-sales data, i.e. they measure average price changes in repeat sales or refinancing on the same properties. This information is obtained by reviewing repeat mortgage transactions on single-family properties whose mortgages have been purchased or securitized by Fannie Mae or Freddie Mac since January 1975. In particular, we use the quarterly "All-Transactions Indexes."[3] To create a real version of house prices, we deflate the indices by the (seasonally adjusted) US Consumer Price Index (CPI), derived from the FRED database of the Federal Reserve Bank of St. Louis. We use quarter-on-quarter changes in the real house price indices, as the DFM-TV-SV requires stationary data. The details of the model are discussed in the next section.

Uncertainty is a latent variable, and hence implies measurement choices. In this regard, besides the various alternative metrics of aggregate uncertainty associated with financial markets (such as the implied-volatility indices (popularly called the VIX), realized volatility, idiosyncratic volatility of equity returns, corporate spreads), there are primarily three broad approaches to quantifying uncertainty (Gupta et al., 2018): (1) a news-based approach, whose main idea is to perform searches of major newspapers for terms related to economic and policy uncertainty, and then to use the results to construct uncertainty indices; (2) deriving measures of uncertainty from stochastic-volatility estimates through various types of small- and large-scale structural models related to macroeconomics and finance; and (3) uncertainty obtained from disagreements among professional forecasters (dispersion of forecasts).

As far as our metric of state-level uncertainty is concerned, we rely on the second approach, whereby overall measures of state-level economic uncertainty (at forecasting horizons of one to four quarters) are derived from Mumtaz (2018), which thus far is the only publicly available data source on US state-level uncertainty.[4] Mumtaz (2018) obtains these measures by extending the data-rich environment used by Jurado et al. (2015) to derive uncertainty indices for the overall US. It must be pointed out that, while the Jurado et al. (2015)-based measure of uncertainty is the average time-varying variance in the unpredictable component of the real and financial time series, Mumtaz (2018) refines the estimates by filtering out the effects of idiosyncratic uncertainty and measurement error. Note that besides 248 aggregate US-level data series from the FRED-QD database, the state-level uncertainty measures covering 1977Q2 to 2015Q3 use eight macroeconomic and financial data series,[5] while a broader estimate of uncertainty at the four horizons uses 21 variables[6] over the shorter period of 1991Q1 to 2015Q3. These periods constitute our short and long samples for the panel data analyses.

Technically speaking, state-level uncertainty is derived using a factor-augmented econometric model. Let $W_{it,j}$ denote the $j$ th data time series for state $i$. Uncertainty for $W_{it,j}$ is estimated using the $n$-period ahead forecast error variance of a factor augmented forecasting regression with stochastic volatility in the regression residuals and the error term for the factor dynamics. The measure thus depends on uncertainty in $W_{it,j}$ and the factors. State-level uncertainty $u_{it}$ is defined as the average of the uncertainty measures for the $j=1,2,...,J$ series for state $i$. We consider state-specific uncertainty measures for horizons one-, two-, three- and four-quarter ahead. $W_{it}$ includes the 8 or 21 variables mentioned above. The factors in the forecasting regression $F_{it}$ for state $i$ are extracted using data for the remaining states and the US-wide panel of 248 sets of financial and macroeconomic data series, i.e. the FRED-QD database.

## 3.2 Methodologies

In this section, we outline the econometric methodologies associated with the DFM-TV-SV model used to obtain our state-level factors of housing returns and volatility, and the subsequent panel data estimation, whereby we relate these factors to the measures of uncertainty.

### 3.2.1 The DFM-TV-SV model

In this section, we present a generalized dynamic factor model (DFM) that is employed to decompose the real housing returns in each state into a common (or national) factor and an idiosyncratic (or state-specific) factor, following Gupta et al. (2020b). The DFM is often used to tease out the common movements among multiple time series, and has become a standard tool since the work by Stock and Watson (1989). We generalize the standard DFM with constant parameters to DFM-TV-SV. As such, the generalized DFM-TV-SV captures important time-varying co-movements among multiple time series. Formally, our model specification closely follows Del Negro and Otrok (2008), and can be written as follows:

$$r_{i,t} = \beta_{i,t} \cdot f_t + e_{i,t} \tag{8.1}$$

Here, $r_{i,t}$ is the first difference of the natural log of the real house price for state $i$ at time $t$. $f_t$ is the national factor that affects all house prices at time $t$, and $\beta_{i,t}$ is the time-varying loading parameter of this national factor in state $i$. $e_{i,t}$ is the idiosyncratic factor.

The common factor and the idiosyncratic factors are assumed to be independent from each other. Therefore, the variance decomposition of our model is given by:

$$Var(r_{i,t}) = \beta_{i,t}^2 \cdot Var(f_t) + Var(e_{i,t}). \tag{8.2}$$

Note that both the time-varying loading parameters and the stochastic volatility of the factors enable the factors' contribution to the total variance of each variable to vary over time.

Following the standard practice in this literature, we model the common factor $f_t$ as a stationary AR(p) process:

$$f_t = \phi_1^f f_{t-1} + \phi_2^f f_{t-2} + \ldots + \phi_p^f f_{t-p} + \exp(h_t^f) \cdot \varepsilon_t^f. \tag{8.3}$$

where $\varepsilon_t^f \sim i.i.d.N(0, \sigma_f^2)$. Therefore, the shock to the factor has a stochastic volatility, and its time-varying volatility is governed by $\exp(h_t^f)$.

To keep the model parsimonious, we employ a driftless random walk process to capture the time variation of the volatility:

$$h_t^f = h_{t-1}^f + \sigma_f^h \cdot \xi_t^f, \quad \xi_t^f \sim i.i.d.N(0,1). \tag{8.4}$$

The factor loading $\beta_{i,t}$ varies over time and is also assumed to follow a random walk process:

$$\beta_{i,t} = \beta_{i,t-1} + \sigma_i^\beta \cdot \eta_{i,t}, \quad \eta_{i,t} \sim i.i.d.N(0,1). \tag{8.5}$$

Here shocks to the loading parameters in different series are assumed to be orthogonal to each other.[7]

The idiosyncratic factor follows a stationary AR(q) process:

$$e_{i,t} = \phi_{(i,1)} e_{i,t-1} + \phi_{i,2} e_{i,t-2} + \ldots + \phi_{i,q} e_{i,t-q} + \exp(h_{i,t}) \cdot \varepsilon_{i,t} \tag{8.6}$$

where $\varepsilon_{i,t} \sim i.i.d.N(0, \sigma_i^2)$. The stochastic volatility of the idiosyncratic factor follows a random walk process:

$$h_{i,t} = h_{i,t-1} + \sigma_i^h \cdot \xi_{i,t}, \quad \xi_{i,t} \sim i.i.d.N(0,1). \tag{8.7}$$

Here we assume that the shocks to the stochastic volatility in different factors are independent from each other. This assumption simplifies the estimation algorithm.

As usual, some normalizations of the factor rotations are needed before the model can be identified and estimated. The loading parameters and the variance of the shock to the common factor are not separately identifiable. We choose to set $\sigma_f^2 = 1$ to achieve the identification. Following Del Negro and Otrok (2008), we also impose time-varying volatility all starting from zero, for the same identification purpose. We demean each series before the estimation since the means of factors are not separately identifiable. Finally, following work such as Neely and Rapach (2011) and Bhatt et al. (2017), we set $p = q = 2$ to keep the model parsimonious.

We estimate this DFM-TV-SV model using the Monte Carlo Markov Chain Bayesian estimation method. Specifically, we employ the well-established Gibbs sampling algorithm by breaking the model into several blocks and sampling sequentially from posterior conditional densities. The idea of the Gibbs sampling algorithm is that when the algorithm converges after the initial burn-in draws, these random draws from the conditional densities altogether constitute a good approximation of the underlying joint densities. Applying the law of large numbers, the numerical integration can be easily performed to obtain the marginal densities of the parameters and the state variables of interest. Most blocks in the model are linear and Gaussian, and as a result the standard algorithms in Kim and Nelson (1999) are readily applicable. The stochastic volatility introduces a non-Gaussian feature into the model. We apply the procedure proposed in Kim et al. (1998) that utilizes a mixture of normal densities to approximate the underlying non-Gaussian distribution in order to simulate the stochastic volatility. This procedure has been widely used in the literature (e.g. Stock and Watson, 2007; Primiceri, 2005). For further details on the Gibbs sampling estimation algorithm, the reader is referred to Gupta et al. (2020b).

### 3.2.2 The panel data model specification

Given the evidence of US state heterogeneity (Mumtaz et al., 2018) we consider a panel estimator that will appropriately address heterogeneity concerns, while allowing for cross-sectional dependence. Fixed- and random-effects models incorporate panel-specific heterogeneity by including a set of nuisance parameters that essentially provide each panel with its own constant term. However, all panels share common slope parameters, which is undesirable in the current context. Random-coefficients models (Swamy, 1970) are more general in that they allow each panel to have its own vector of slopes randomly drawn from a distribution common to all panels. Implementation of the estimator ensures the best linear unbiased predictors of the panel-specific draws from said distribution (Poi, 2003).

Consider a random-coefficients model of the form:

$$y_i = X_i \beta_i + \epsilon_i \tag{8.8}$$

where $i = 1...51$ denotes the 50 US states and DC, $y_i$ is a $T_i \times 1$ vector of median value of the state-level real house price returns factor and stochastic volatility observations (i.e. either *fmed* or *svmed*, respectively) for the $i$ th panel (derived from the DFM-TV-SV), $X_i$ is a $T_i \times 1$ vector of uncertainty measures according to the Mumtaz (2018) or Jurado et al. (2015) methods, for the one- to four-period forecasting horizons (*u1*, *u2*, *u3* and *u4*). $\beta_i$ is a parameter specific to panel $i$, measuring the impact of uncertainty on the relevant real house price returns factor or stochastic volatility. The error term vector $\epsilon_i$ is distributed with mean zero and variance $\sigma_{ii} I$.

The useful contribution of Swamy's (1970) random coefficients estimator is that state-specific slope parameters can be estimated in addition to state-specific intercept parameters, an improvement over fixed-effects or random-effects models, which only allow for state-specific intercept parameters.

In the case of random-coefficients, each panel-specific $\beta_i$ is related to an underlying common parameter vector $\beta$ :

$$\beta_i = \beta + v_i \tag{8.9}$$

where $E\{v_i\} = 0, E\{v_i v_i'\} = \Sigma, E\{v_i v_j'\} = 0$ for $j \neq i$, and $E\{v_i \epsilon_j'\} = 0$ for all $i$ and $j$.

Parameters in Equation 8.9 are estimated with generalized least squares (GLS). The resulting $\hat{\beta}$ for the overall (national) result is therefore a weighted average of the state-specific ordinary least squares estimates. For further detail on Swamy's (1970) random-coefficients estimator, refer to Appendix A.

Given our interest in the state-specific impact of macroeconomic uncertainty on housing market outcomes, in the next section we present the empirical results for the US at the national level as well as the state level, applying the random-coefficients estimator to the datasets discussed in Section 3.1.

## 4   EMPIRICAL RESULTS

We start by analyzing the univariate properties of the housing factor series, as well as pairwise correlations present in the dataset, for both the longer Mumtaz uncertainty dataset (1977Q2–2015Q3), based on eight underlying economic and financial series, and the shorter dataset (1991Q1–2015Q3), based on 21 series.

### 4.1   Unit Root Test Results

We apply three unit root tests to the house price factor series and uncertainty measures, namely those of Levin, Lin and Chu (LLC) (2002); Im, Pesaran and Shin (IPS) (2003); and Pesaran (CIPS) (2007). The unit root tests differ in that LLC assumes a common unit root process across the different cross-sections, while IPS assumes a cross-sectional-specific unit root process, which is better suited to account for state heterogeneity. CIPS accounts for cross-sectional dependence in addition to cross-section heterogeneity, thereby also allowing for potential spillover effects between cross-sections. Results are presented in Table 8.1. In all instances, a maximum lag of eight is allowed in the augmentation of the test regression. All unit root tests confirm that both house price factors and uncertainty are stationary, $I(0)$ processes, rejecting the null of a unit root in all instances.

*Table 8.1    Unit root test results*

| | LLC | IPS | CIPS |
|---|---|---|---|
| *Uncertainty dataset: Mumtaz (2018), 1977Q2–2015Q3* | | | |
| fmed | Adj t* = −4.13***<br>p=0.0000 | W-t-bar = −12.68***<br>p=0.0000 | CIPS = −3.190***<br>Crit 10% −2.01; 5% −2.06; 1% −2.14 |
| svmed | Adj t* = −2.83***<br>p=0.0023 | W-t-bar = −7.22***<br>p=0.0000 | CIPS = −2.019*<br>Crit 10% −2.01; 5% −2.06; 1% −2.14 |
| u1 | Adj t* = −12.26***<br>p=0.0000 | W-t-bar = −18.54***<br>p=0.0000 | CIPS = −4.431***<br>Crit 10% −2.01; 5% −2.06; 1% −2.14 |
| u2 | Adj t* = −8.91***<br>p=0.0000 | W-t-bar = −16.02***<br>p=0.0000 | CIPS = −4.058***<br>Crit 10% −2.01; 5% −2.06; 1% −2.14 |
| u3 | Adj t* = −5.73***<br>p=0.0000 | W-t-bar = −13.92***<br>p=0.0000 | CIPS = −3.720***<br>Crit 10% −2.01; 5% −2.06; 1% −2.14 |
| u4 | Adj t* = −5.73***<br>p=0.0000 | W-t-bar = −13.75***<br>p=0.0000 | CIPS = −3.411***<br>Crit 10% −2.01; 5% −2.06; 1% −2.14 |
| *Uncertainty dataset: Mumtaz (2018), 1991Q1–2015Q3* | | | |
| | LLC | IPS | CIPS |
| fmed | Adj t* = −2.61***<br>p=0.0046 | W-t-bar = −8.28***<br>p=0.0000 | CIPS = −3.543***<br>Crit 10% −2.01; 5% −2.06; 1% −2.14 |
| svmed | Adj t* = −4.50***<br>p=0.0020 | W-t-bar = −1.98**<br>p=0.0240 | CIPS = −2.081**<br>Crit 10% −2.01; 5% −2.06; 1% −2.14 |
| u1 | Adj t* = −15.82***<br>p=0.0000 | W-t-bar = −22.39***<br>p=0.0000 | CIPS = −4.760***<br>Crit 10% −2.01; 5% −2.06; 1% −2.14 |
| u2 | Adj t* = −13.97***<br>p=0.0000 | W-t-bar = −20.65***<br>p=0.0000 | CIPS = −4.524***<br>Crit 10% −2.01; 5% −2.06; 1% −2.14 |
| u3 | Adj t* = −12.97***<br>p=0.0000 | W-t-bar = −20.511***<br>p=0.0000 | CIPS = −4.116***<br>Crit 10% −2.01; 5% −2.06; 1% −2.14 |
| u4 | Adj t* = −11.06***<br>p=0.0000 | W-t-bar = −18.24***<br>p=0.0000 | CIPS = −3.695***<br>Crit 10% −2.01; 5% −2.06; 1% −2.14 |

Note: * $p < 0.10$, ** $p < 0.05$, *** $p < 0.01$.

*Table 8.2    Pairwise correlation coefficients*

| | fmed | svmed | u1 | u2 | u3 | u4 |
|---|---|---|---|---|---|---|
| *Uncertainty dataset: Mumtaz (2018), 1977Q2–2015Q3* | | | | | | |
| fmed | 1.0000 | | | | | |
| svmed | −0.0830***<br>0.0000 | 1.0000 | | | | |
| u1 | −0.0056<br>0.6189 | 0.0243**<br>0.0312 | 1.0000 | | | |
| u2 | −0.0060<br>0.5958 | 0.0237**<br>0.0357 | 0.9995***<br>0.0000 | 1.0000 | | |
| u3 | −0.0056<br>0.6211 | 0.0218*<br>0.0531 | 0.9989***<br>0.0000 | 0.9998***<br>0.0000 | 1.0000 | |
| u4 | −0.0052<br>0.6436 | 0.0219*<br>0.0524 | 0.9981***<br>0.0000 | 0.9992***<br>0.0000 | 0.9998***<br>0.0000 | 1.0000 |
| *Uncertainty dataset: Mumtaz (2018), 1991Q1–2015Q3* | | | | | | |
| | fmed | svmed | u1 | u2 | u3 | u4 |
| fmed | 1.0000 | | | | | |
| svmed | 0.0077<br>0.5858 | 1.0000 | | | | |
| u1 | −0.0046<br>0.7476 | 0.1205**<br>0.0000 | 1.0000 | | | |
| u2 | −0.0042<br>0.7694 | 0.1221***<br>0.0000 | 0.9996***<br>0.0000 | 1.0000 | | |
| u3 | −0.0046<br>0.7470 | 0.1247***<br>0.0000 | 0.9996***<br>0.0000 | 0.9997***<br>0.0000 | 1.0000 | |
| u4 | −0.0048<br>0.7376 | 0.1227***<br>0.0000 | 0.9995***<br>0.0000 | 0.9995***<br>0.0000 | 0.9998***<br>0.0000 | 1.0000 |

Note: * $p < 0.10$, ** $p < 0.05$, *** $p < 0.01$.

## 4.2 Pairwise Correlation Analysis

The overall correlation results are presented in Table 8.2, with correlation coefficients supplemented by *p*-values. There is a clear indication of a positive and statistically significant correlation between uncertainty and the house price stochastic volatility measure. The correlation between increased volatility and housing returns is negative as expected in the longer sample, but there is no statistically significant overall correlation between uncertainty and housing returns. In subsequent analysis, the case for individual states will be explored.

## 4.3 Regression Analysis

The random-coefficient (Swamy, 1970; Poi, 2003) estimator is used to obtain an overall combined (national) result for the impact of uncertainty on housing returns and the stochastic volatility measure. The result for the longer Mumtaz (2018) dataset is reported in Table 8.3, while the state-specific results are presented in Tables 8.4 to 8.7, which display the coefficient $\beta_i$ in Equation 8.8. Results for the shorter sample are included in Tables 8B.1 to 8B.5 in Appendix B. The overall results for the Jurado et al. (2015) dataset are presented in Table 8B.6 in Appendix B.

Table 8.3   Estimation results for overall uncertainty impact, 1977Q2–2015Q3 (horizons 1 to 4)

|  | (1) | (2) | (3) | (4) | (5) | (6) | (7) | (8) |
|---|---|---|---|---|---|---|---|---|
|  | \multicolumn{4}{c}{Dependent: housing returns factor (*fmed*)} | \multicolumn{4}{c}{Dependent: stochastic volatility (*svmed*)} |
| u1 | −0.331 |  |  |  | 1.741*** |  |  |  |
|  | (−1.04) |  |  |  | (7.59) |  |  |  |
| u2 |  | −0.406* |  |  |  | 1.870*** |  |  |
|  |  | (−1.75) |  |  |  | (6.71) |  |  |
| u3 |  |  | −0.486* |  |  |  | 2.229*** |  |
|  |  |  | (−1.83) |  |  |  | (6.15) |  |
| u4 |  |  |  | −0.557* |  |  |  | 2.541*** |
|  |  |  |  | (−1.72) |  |  |  | (5.61) |
| _cons | 0.082 | 0.133 | 0.161 | 0.192 | −0.766*** | −1.098*** | −1.577*** | −2.043*** |
|  | (0.30) | (0.43) | (0.54) | (0.44) | (−4.27) | (−3.57) | (−4.36) | (−4.58) |
| Obs | 7854 | 7854 | 7854 | 7854 | 7854 | 7854 | 7854 | 7854 |
| Groups | 51 | 51 | 51 | 51 | 51 | 51 | 51 | 51 |
| Chi²(100) | 22143*** | 22539*** | 23085*** | 23739*** | 214.83*** | 202.31*** | 198.40*** | 191.06*** |

Note: *t* statistics in parentheses. *t* statistics based on standard errors that are robust to group (bootstrap) heteroscedasticity. * $p < 0.10$, ** $p < 0.05$, *** $p < 0.01$. $\chi^2$ is a test for parameter constancy.

The weighted overall slope coefficient for the relationship between uncertainty at all horizons and the housing returns factor for all 50 states and DC combined is negative as expected, and marginally significant ($p < 0.10$) for horizons 2, 3 and 4. A statistically significant relationship exists between macroeconomic uncertainty and the stochastic volatility measure at all horizons ($p < 0.01$), with a larger impact at longer horizons. The test statistic $T \sim \chi^2$ for the null hypothesis of parameter constancy ($H_0 : \beta_1 = \beta_2 = ... = \beta_P$) is rejected at the 1 percent significance level, supporting the notion of state heterogeneity.

Having established state heterogeneity, before we discuss state-specific results (reported in Tables 8.4 to 8.7 and Figures 8.1 and 8.2), it is worthwhile to pause to consider the possibility of *endogeneity* present in the relationship. According to Poi (2003), the parameters will be unbiased and efficient, assuming that macroeconomic uncertainty is uncorrelated with the error term. Jurado et al. (2015), and Ludvigson et al. (Forthcoming) in particular, however, argue that a significant portion of "measured uncertainty" might not be uncertainty but endogenous responses to some macroeconomic variables.[8] When applying the Hausman (1978) test to the specification, we indeed find that macroeconomic uncertainty is endogenous to the housing market variables,[9] potentially causing bias in the parameters. Judson and Owen (1999) and Bruno (2005) however show that for $T > 30$, the bias due to endogeneity will be less than the bias potentially introduced by an instrumental variable method like the general method of moments (GMM), whose estimator for samples with a sizeable time dimension inevitably suffers from instrument proliferation (weak instrumentation), which in turn also introduces bias in the parameters.[10] Given that $T$, the number of observations per cross-section, is 154 in the case of the analysis for the period 1977Q2–2015Q3, we can assume a bias of negligible proportion. Furthermore, the parameters in the application of Swamy's (1970) random-coefficients estimator and Arellano and Bond's (1991) system-GMM estimator differ by no more than 5.5 percent on average for housing returns and no more than 4.1 percent for

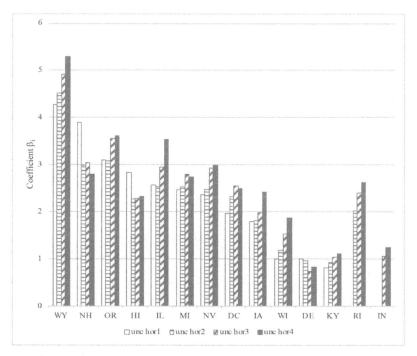

*Note*: unc hor $i$ $(i = 1,2,..4)$ refer to macroeconomic uncertainty taken from Mumtaz (2018), 1977Q2–2015Q3, for horizons of one to four quarters. $\beta_i$ refers to the slope coefficient in the random-coefficients model, Equation 8.8, with the dependent variable housing returns factor (*fmed*).

*Figure 8.1A*   *The lowering impact of macroeconomic uncertainty on housing returns, 1977Q2–2015Q3*

218   *Handbook of real estate and macroeconomics*

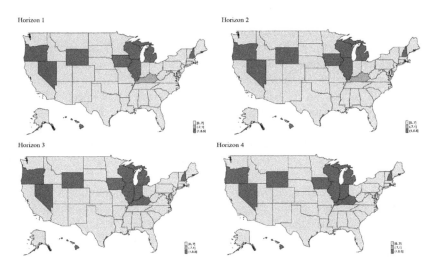

*Source*: Macroeconomic uncertainty data are from Mumtaz (2018), which is available publicly; the visual representations are based on the authors' own estimations.

*Figure 8.1B    The impact of macroeconomic uncertainty on housing returns factor, 1977Q2–2015Q3*

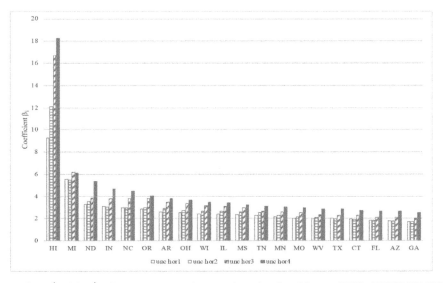

*Note*: unc hor $i$ $(i=1,2,..4)$ refer to macroeconomic uncertainty taken from Mumtaz (2018), 1977Q2–2015Q3, for horizons of 1 to 4 quarters. $\beta_i$ refers to the slope coefficient in the random-coefficients model, Equation 8.8, with the dependent variable stochastic volatility (*svmed*).

*Figure 8.2A    The impact of macroeconomic uncertainty on stochastic volatility, 1977Q2–2015Q3*

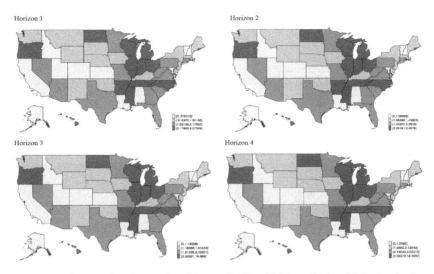

*Source*: Macroeconomic uncertainty data are from Mumtaz (2018), which is available publicly; the visual representations are based on authors' own estimations.

*Figure 8.2B    The impact of macroeconomic uncertainty on stochastic volatility factor, 1977Q2–2015Q3*

housing price volatility for the overall results reported in Table 8.3, across the four horizons. Given that the main purpose of applying Swamy's random-coefficients estimator is to establish the relative impact of state-level macroeconomic uncertainty on the housing market within a state (that is to rank the states from largest and most significant impact to lowest and/or statistically insignificant impact), we can proceed to interpret state-level results, reported in Tables 8.4 to 8.7. Estimation results for the estimated parameters, $\hat{\beta}_i$ in Equation 8.8, are reported in these tables, with dependent variables, *fmed*, representing housing returns and *svmed* representing volatility. Results for uncertainty measures for horizons 1 to 4, namely independent variables $u_1$ to $u_4$, are reported separately in Tables 8.4 to 8.7.

Results contained in Tables 8.1 to 8.4, which are based on our own estimations, are also visually displayed through graphical and spatial depictions in Figures 8.1A and B and 8.2A and B. Figures 8.1A and 8.2A indicate the relative impact of macroeconomic uncertainty on housing returns and volatility, respectively. For housing returns, all states with a non-zero significant impact are displayed, while for volatility, the 20 states with the largest impact are included in the graph. Figures 8.1B and 8.2B display the same results in spatial format, with a darker shade indicative of a more pronounced impact in the specific state. In the spatial depiction, statistically significant coefficients, $\beta_i$, for all states are reflected.

When analyzing state-specific results, it is evident that all states register a positive relationship between macroeconomic uncertainty and the stochastic volatility measure. With the exception of three states, the recorded impact is also statistically significant at the 1 percent level. It is therefore evident that macroeconomic uncertainty also exacerbates uncertainty/volatility in the housing market virtually across all states. Hawaii ranks highest in terms of uncertainty spillover effect, followed by the state of Michigan.

Table 8.4  Estimation results for state-specific uncertainty coefficient, 1977Q2–2015Q3 (horizon 1)

| | Dependent variable: housing returns factor (*fmed*) | | | | Dependent variable: stochastic volatility (*svmed*) | | | |
|---|---|---|---|---|---|---|---|---|
| State | | Coeff | SE | *p*-value | State | | Coeff | SE | *p*-value |
| WY | Wyoming | −4.27*** | 0.75 | 0.0000 | HI | Hawaii | 9.27*** | 0.58 | 0.0000 |
| NH | New Hampshire | −3.90*** | 1.21 | 0.0010 | MI | Michigan | 5.54*** | 0.66 | 0.0000 |
| OR | Oregon | −3.10*** | 1.05 | 0.0030 | ND | North Dakota | 3.28*** | 0.41 | 0.0000 |
| HI | Hawaii | −2.83** | 1.19 | 0.0180 | IN | Indiana | 3.06*** | 0.25 | 0.0000 |
| IL | Illinois | −2.57*** | 0.70 | 0.0000 | NC | North Carolina | 3.00*** | 0.24 | 0.0000 |
| MI | Michigan | −2.47*** | 0.95 | 0.0090 | OR | Oregon | 2.84*** | 0.42 | 0.0000 |
| NV | Nevada | −2.37* | 1.22 | 0.0520 | AR | Arkansas | 2.58*** | 0.33 | 0.0000 |
| DC | Distr. of Columbia | −1.96* | 1.19 | 0.1000 | OH | Ohio | 2.50*** | 0.25 | 0.0000 |
| IA | Iowa | −1.79*** | 0.48 | 0.0000 | WI | Wisconsin | 2.43*** | 0.21 | 0.0000 |
| WI | Wisconsin | −1.00** | 0.45 | 0.0250 | IL | Illinois | 2.42*** | 0.27 | 0.0000 |
| DE | Delaware | −1.00*** | 0.37 | 0.0070 | MS | Mississippi | 2.34*** | 0.25 | 0.0000 |
| KY | Kentucky | −0.81*** | 0.28 | 0.0040 | TN | Tennessee | 2.28*** | 0.30 | 0.0000 |
| AK | Alaska | 0.15 | 1.12 | 0.8960 | MN | Minnesota | 2.18*** | 0.43 | 0.0000 |
| AL | Alabama | −0.43 | 0.26 | 0.1010 | MO | Missouri | 2.05*** | 0.22 | 0.0000 |
| AR | Arkansas | 0.61 | 0.95 | 0.5200 | WV | West Virginia | 2.05*** | 0.51 | 0.0000 |
| AZ | Arizona | 1.76 | 1.13 | 0.1190 | TX | Texas | 2.03*** | 0.29 | 0.0000 |
| CA | California | 0.92 | 1.17 | 0.4330 | CT | Connecticut | 1.98*** | 0.31 | 0.0000 |
| CT | Connecticut | 1.40 | 1.21 | 0.2470 | FL | Florida | 1.84*** | 0.17 | 0.0000 |
| FL | Florida | −0.19 | 0.94 | 0.8430 | AZ | Arizona | 1.78*** | 0.25 | 0.0000 |
| GA | Georgia | 0.46 | 0.67 | 0.4910 | GA | Georgia | 1.74*** | 0.24 | 0.0000 |
| ID | Idaho | −0.24 | 0.80 | 0.7630 | SC | South Carolina | 1.73*** | 0.19 | 0.0000 |
| IN | Indiana | −0.74 | 0.61 | 0.2240 | VA | Virginia | 1.68*** | 0.19 | 0.0000 |
| KS | Kansas | −0.58 | 0.59 | 0.3240 | RI | Rhode Island | 1.61*** | 0.24 | 0.0000 |
| MA | Massachusetts | 1.93 | 1.18 | 0.1010 | NV | Nevada | 1.55*** | 0.38 | 0.0000 |
| MD | Maryland | 0.41 | 1.13 | 0.7190 | PA | Pennsylvania | 1.55*** | 0.17 | 0.0000 |
| ME | Maine | 0.19 | 1.19 | 0.8740 | WA | Washington | 1.50*** | 0.37 | 0.0000 |
| MN | Minnesota | 0.00 | 0.64 | 0.9990 | KY | Kentucky | 1.37*** | 0.10 | 0.0000 |
| MO | Missouri | −0.49 | 0.58 | 0.3940 | SD | South Dakota | 1.35*** | 0.14 | 0.0000 |
| MS | Mississippi | −0.39 | 0.89 | 0.6590 | NM | New Mexico | 1.32*** | 0.17 | 0.0000 |
| MT | Montana | −0.41 | 0.83 | 0.6250 | MA | Massachusetts | 1.26*** | 0.14 | 0.0000 |
| NC | North Carolina | −0.39 | 0.49 | 0.4290 | OK | Oklahoma | 1.26*** | 0.09 | 0.0000 |
| ND | North Dakota | −0.31 | 1.16 | 0.7910 | NJ | New Jersey | 1.24*** | 0.19 | 0.0000 |
| NE | Nebraska | 0.20 | 0.59 | 0.7390 | IA | Iowa | 1.13*** | 0.15 | 0.0000 |
| NJ | New Jersey | −0.85 | 1.12 | 0.4500 | NE | Nebraska | 1.06*** | 0.18 | 0.0000 |
| NY | New York | −0.15 | 0.65 | 0.8160 | ME | Maine | 1.04*** | 0.35 | 0.0030 |
| OH | Ohio | −0.33 | 0.58 | 0.5720 | WY | Wyoming | 1.02*** | 0.10 | 0.0000 |
| RI | Rhode Island | −1.61 | 1.21 | 0.1820 | NY | New York | 1.01*** | 0.08 | 0.0000 |
| SC | South Carolina | 0.19 | 0.72 | 0.7890 | MT | Montana | 0.92*** | 0.08 | 0.0000 |
| SD | South Dakota | −1.04 | 0.71 | 0.1440 | CO | Colorado | 0.92*** | 0.18 | 0.0000 |
| TN | Tennessee | −0.66 | 0.77 | 0.3930 | UT | Utah | 0.86*** | 0.16 | 0.0000 |
| UT | Utah | 0.28 | 1.06 | 0.7910 | MD | Maryland | 0.83*** | 0.17 | 0.0000 |
| VT | Vermont | −0.60 | 0.87 | 0.4950 | AL | Alabama | 0.82*** | 0.05 | 0.0000 |
| WA | Washington | 1.20 | 1.07 | 0.2640 | DE | Delaware | 0.76*** | 0.15 | 0.0000 |
| WV | West Virginia | −1.16 | 1.02 | 0.2570 | LA | Louisiana | 0.74** | 0.31 | 0.0170 |
| VA | Virginia | 1.23** | 0.55 | 0.0250 | KS | Kansas | 0.67** | 0.30 | 0.0270 |
| NM | New Mexico | 1.28** | 0.58 | 0.0260 | CA | California | 0.67*** | 0.08 | 0.0000 |
| OK | Oklahoma | 1.31** | 0.61 | 0.0320 | DC | Distr. of Columbia | 0.24*** | 0.03 | 0.0000 |
| PA | Pennsylvania | 1.38* | 0.74 | 0.0630 | VT | Vermont | 0.23*** | 0.04 | 0.0000 |
| LA | Louisiana | 1.80*** | 0.51 | 0.0000 | AK | Alaska | 1.03 | 0.78 | 0.1900 |
| TX | Texas | 1.97** | 0.93 | 0.0350 | ID | Idaho | 0.09 | 0.12 | 0.4480 |
| CO | Colorado | 3.06*** | 0.90 | 0.0010 | NH | New Hampshire | 0.12 | 0.21 | 0.5830 |

*Note:* *, **, *** denote 10, 5 and 1 percent significance levels. Standard errors are robust to group (conventional) heteroscedasticity. Uncertainty series from Mumtaz (2018) 1977Q–2015Q3.

Table 8.5    Estimation results for state-specific uncertainty coefficient, 1977Q2–2015Q3 (horizon 2)

| | Dependent variable: housing returns factor (*fmed*) | | | | Dependent variable: stochastic volatility (*svmed*) | | | |
|---|---|---|---|---|---|---|---|---|
| State | | Coeff | SE | p-value | State | | Coeff | SE | p-value |
| WY | Wyoming | −4.52*** | 0.81 | 0.0000 | HI | Hawaii | 12.07*** | 0.72 | 0.0000 |
| OR | Oregon | −3.08*** | 0.96 | 0.0010 | MI | Michigan | 5.51*** | 0.71 | 0.0000 |
| NH | New Hampshire | −2.99** | 1.16 | 0.0100 | NC | North Carolina | 3.54*** | 0.27 | 0.0000 |
| MI | Michigan | −2.53*** | 0.93 | 0.0060 | AR | Arkansas | 3.01*** | 0.34 | 0.0000 |
| IL | Illinois | −2.52*** | 0.66 | 0.0000 | MS | Mississippi | 2.98*** | 0.30 | 0.0000 |
| NV | Nevada | −2.47** | 1.17 | 0.0340 | WI | Wisconsin | 2.97*** | 0.24 | 0.0000 |
| DC | Distr. of Columbia | −2.33** | 1.16 | 0.0450 | TX | Texas | 2.92*** | 0.33 | 0.0000 |
| HI | Hawaii | −2.27** | 1.03 | 0.0280 | IN | Indiana | 2.69*** | 0.25 | 0.0000 |
| RI | Rhode Island | −2.01* | 1.17 | 0.0850 | MO | Missouri | 2.68*** | 0.25 | 0.0000 |
| IA | Iowa | −1.81*** | 0.49 | 0.0000 | ND | North Dakota | 2.67*** | 0.32 | 0.0000 |
| WI | Wisconsin | −1.19** | 0.51 | 0.0190 | MN | Minnesota | 2.61*** | 0.50 | 0.0000 |
| DE | Delaware | −0.97** | 0.41 | 0.0170 | OR | Oregon | 2.56*** | 0.37 | 0.0000 |
| KY | Kentucky | −0.92*** | 0.33 | 0.0050 | FL | Florida | 2.29*** | 0.18 | 0.0000 |
| AK | Alaska | 0.34 | 1.13 | 0.7630 | IL | Illinois | 2.13*** | 0.26 | 0.0000 |
| AL | Alabama | −0.48 | 0.31 | 0.1230 | GA | Georgia | 2.10*** | 0.26 | 0.0000 |
| AR | Arkansas | 0.54 | 0.96 | 0.5740 | VA | Virginia | 1.95*** | 0.21 | 0.0000 |
| AZ | Arizona | 0.65 | 1.07 | 0.5450 | WV | West Virginia | 1.87*** | 0.47 | 0.0000 |
| CA | California | 0.40 | 1.15 | 0.7300 | NV | Nevada | 1.85*** | 0.37 | 0.0000 |
| CT | Connecticut | 0.98 | 1.17 | 0.4000 | OH | Ohio | 1.80*** | 0.20 | 0.0000 |
| FL | Florida | −0.39 | 0.99 | 0.6940 | AZ | Arizona | 1.72*** | 0.23 | 0.0000 |
| GA | Georgia | 0.40 | 0.71 | 0.5740 | NM | New Mexico | 1.69*** | 0.17 | 0.0000 |
| ID | Idaho | −0.33 | 0.87 | 0.7050 | PA | Pennsylvania | 1.67*** | 0.19 | 0.0000 |
| IN | Indiana | −0.87 | 0.56 | 0.1220 | CT | Connecticut | 1.66*** | 0.31 | 0.0000 |
| KS | Kansas | −0.39 | 0.63 | 0.5290 | OK | Oklahoma | 1.62*** | 0.11 | 0.0000 |
| MA | Massachusetts | 1.46 | 1.15 | 0.2050 | KY | Kentucky | 1.53*** | 0.12 | 0.0000 |
| MD | Maryland | −0.13 | 1.12 | 0.9070 | CO | Colorado | 1.44*** | 0.19 | 0.0000 |
| ME | Maine | −0.16 | 1.15 | 0.8880 | NJ | New Jersey | 1.43*** | 0.22 | 0.0000 |
| MN | Minnesota | 0.13 | 0.71 | 0.8590 | WA | Washington | 1.42*** | 0.33 | 0.0000 |
| MO | Missouri | −0.59 | 0.67 | 0.3760 | SC | South Carolina | 1.41*** | 0.17 | 0.0000 |
| MS | Mississippi | −0.55 | 0.99 | 0.5740 | DE | Delaware | 1.37*** | 0.19 | 0.0000 |
| MT | Montana | −0.81 | 0.81 | 0.3170 | SD | South Dakota | 1.29*** | 0.14 | 0.0000 |
| NC | North Carolina | −0.52 | 0.55 | 0.3480 | TN | Tennessee | 1.27*** | 0.21 | 0.0000 |
| ND | North Dakota | −0.12 | 1.04 | 0.9050 | MA | Massachusetts | 1.25*** | 0.15 | 0.0000 |
| NE | Nebraska | 0.54 | 0.60 | 0.3670 | RI | Rhode Island | 1.19*** | 0.23 | 0.0000 |
| NJ | New Jersey | −0.83 | 1.14 | 0.4690 | NY | New York | 1.18*** | 0.09 | 0.0000 |
| NY | New York | 0.01 | 0.73 | 0.9890 | IA | Iowa | 1.14*** | 0.15 | 0.0000 |
| OH | Ohio | −0.42 | 0.45 | 0.3520 | WY | Wyoming | 1.10*** | 0.11 | 0.0000 |
| PA | Pennsylvania | 1.28 | 0.80 | 0.1110 | LA | Louisiana | 1.08*** | 0.40 | 0.0070 |
| SC | South Carolina | 0.13 | 0.64 | 0.8340 | ME | Maine | 1.07*** | 0.33 | 0.0010 |
| SD | South Dakota | −1.05 | 0.71 | 0.1400 | UT | Utah | 1.06*** | 0.20 | 0.0000 |
| TN | Tennessee | −0.71 | 0.53 | 0.1770 | AL | Alabama | 0.98*** | 0.06 | 0.0000 |
| UT | Utah | −0.18 | 1.16 | 0.8760 | MD | Maryland | 0.97*** | 0.18 | 0.0000 |
| VA | Virginia | 0.98 | 0.65 | 0.1340 | CA | California | 0.89*** | 0.09 | 0.0000 |
| VT | Vermont | −0.54 | 0.84 | 0.5180 | KS | Kansas | 0.80** | 0.33 | 0.0150 |
| WA | Washington | 0.42 | 0.98 | 0.6690 | MT | Montana | 0.79*** | 0.08 | 0.0000 |
| WV | West Virginia | −0.66 | 0.95 | 0.4830 | NE | Nebraska | 0.64*** | 0.16 | 0.0000 |
| NM | New Mexico | 1.57** | 0.65 | 0.0170 | DC | Dist. of Columbia | 0.25*** | 0.03 | 0.0000 |
| OK | Oklahoma | 1.98*** | 0.76 | 0.0090 | VT | Vermont | 0.19*** | 0.04 | 0.0000 |
| TX | Texas | 2.03** | 1.02 | 0.0470 | AK | Alaska | 0.83 | 0.92 | 0.3690 |
| LA | Louisiana | 2.18*** | 0.65 | 0.0010 | ID | Idaho | 0.10 | 0.14 | 0.4590 |
| CO | Colorado | 2.63*** | 0.97 | 0.0070 | NH | New Hampshire | 0.17 | 0.20 | 0.4190 |

Note: *, **, *** denote 10, 5 and 1 percent significance levels. Standard errors are robust to group (conventional) heteroscedasticity. Uncertainty series from Mumtaz (2018) 1977Q2–2015Q3.

Table 8.6    Estimation results for state-specific uncertainty coefficient, 1977Q2–2015Q3 (horizon 3)

| Dependent variable: housing returns factor (fmed) |||||  Dependent variable: stochastic volatility (svmed) |||||
|---|---|---|---|---|---|---|---|---|---|
| State | | Coeff | SE | p-value | State | | Coeff | SE | p-value |
| WY | Wyoming | −4.91*** | 0.92 | 0.0000 | HI | Hawaii | 16.69*** | 0.92 | 0.0000 |
| OR | Oregon | −3.56*** | 1.07 | 0.0010 | MI | Michigan | 6.21*** | 0.80 | 0.0000 |
| NH | New Hampshire | −3.03** | 1.32 | 0.0220 | MO | Missouri | 3.86*** | 0.30 | 0.0000 |
| IL | Illinois | −2.95*** | 0.78 | 0.0000 | WI | Wisconsin | 3.81*** | 0.29 | 0.0000 |
| NV | Nevada | −2.93** | 1.30 | 0.0250 | NC | North Carolina | 3.80*** | 0.31 | 0.0000 |
| MI | Michigan | −2.79*** | 1.02 | 0.0060 | MS | Mississippi | 3.76*** | 0.36 | 0.0000 |
| DC | Distr. of Columbia | −2.55** | 1.31 | 0.0520 | AR | Arkansas | 3.47*** | 0.38 | 0.0000 |
| RI | Rhode Island | −2.40** | 1.33 | 0.0710 | TX | Texas | 3.37*** | 0.37 | 0.0000 |
| HI | Hawaii | −2.28** | 1.07 | 0.0340 | MN | Minnesota | 3.14*** | 0.59 | 0.0000 |
| IA | Iowa | −1.99*** | 0.53 | 0.0000 | OR | Oregon | 3.08*** | 0.41 | 0.0000 |
| WI | Wisconsin | −1.52** | 0.63 | 0.0150 | IN | Indiana | 2.97*** | 0.28 | 0.0000 |
| IN | Indiana | −1.05* | 0.63 | 0.0920 | ND | North Dakota | 2.64*** | 0.32 | 0.0000 |
| KY | Kentucky | −1.03*** | 0.38 | 0.0070 | IL | Illinois | 2.59*** | 0.31 | 0.0000 |
| DE | Delaware | −0.74* | 0.38 | 0.0510 | FL | Florida | 2.55*** | 0.19 | 0.0000 |
| AK | Alaska | 0.61 | 1.30 | 0.6390 | VA | Virginia | 2.37*** | 0.25 | 0.0000 |
| AL | Alabama | −0.57 | 0.38 | 0.1320 | GA | Georgia | 2.30*** | 0.28 | 0.0000 |
| AR | Arkansas | 0.33 | 1.08 | 0.7610 | NM | New Mexico | 2.28*** | 0.18 | 0.0000 |
| AZ | Arizona | 0.54 | 1.21 | 0.6570 | WV | West Virginia | 2.09*** | 0.55 | 0.0000 |
| CA | California | 0.32 | 1.29 | 0.8070 | CT | Connecticut | 2.07*** | 0.36 | 0.0000 |
| CT | Connecticut | 1.19 | 1.32 | 0.3710 | OH | Ohio | 2.04*** | 0.23 | 0.0000 |
| FL | Florida | −0.63 | 1.10 | 0.5670 | NV | Nevada | 2.00*** | 0.38 | 0.0000 |
| GA | Georgia | 0.43 | 0.78 | 0.5810 | OK | Oklahoma | 1.99*** | 0.14 | 0.0000 |
| ID | Idaho | −0.41 | 0.99 | 0.6770 | AZ | Arizona | 1.95*** | 0.26 | 0.0000 |
| KS | Kansas | −0.41 | 0.77 | 0.5950 | DE | Delaware | 1.93*** | 0.22 | 0.0000 |
| MA | Massachusetts | 1.78 | 1.31 | 0.1750 | WA | Washington | 1.91*** | 0.39 | 0.0000 |
| MD | Maryland | −0.64 | 1.16 | 0.5810 | PA | Pennsylvania | 1.82*** | 0.22 | 0.0000 |
| ME | Maine | −0.37 | 1.30 | 0.7750 | KY | Kentucky | 1.76*** | 0.14 | 0.0000 |
| MN | Minnesota | 0.12 | 0.83 | 0.8830 | CO | Colorado | 1.70*** | 0.20 | 0.0000 |
| MO | Missouri | −0.85 | 0.85 | 0.3150 | SC | South Carolina | 1.62*** | 0.19 | 0.0000 |
| MS | Mississippi | −0.61 | 1.16 | 0.5970 | LA | Louisiana | 1.59*** | 0.52 | 0.0020 |
| MT | Montana | −1.04 | 0.93 | 0.2650 | NJ | New Jersey | 1.45*** | 0.23 | 0.0000 |
| NC | North Carolina | −0.64 | 0.61 | 0.2900 | MA | Massachusetts | 1.44*** | 0.18 | 0.0000 |
| ND | North Dakota | −0.12 | 1.09 | 0.9150 | SD | South Dakota | 1.41*** | 0.15 | 0.0000 |
| NE | Nebraska | 0.57 | 0.58 | 0.3230 | NY | New York | 1.38*** | 0.11 | 0.0000 |
| NJ | New Jersey | −0.93 | 1.27 | 0.4630 | UT | Utah | 1.36*** | 0.25 | 0.0000 |
| NY | New York | 0.15 | 0.85 | 0.8570 | TN | Tennessee | 1.36*** | 0.22 | 0.0000 |
| OH | Ohio | −0.49 | 0.50 | 0.3270 | IA | Iowa | 1.26*** | 0.16 | 0.0000 |
| PA | Pennsylvania | 1.08 | 0.91 | 0.2390 | AL | Alabama | 1.21*** | 0.08 | 0.0000 |
| SC | South Carolina | 0.08 | 0.72 | 0.9130 | ME | Maine | 1.18*** | 0.35 | 0.0010 |
| SD | South Dakota | −1.20 | 0.77 | 0.1210 | WY | Wyoming | 1.18*** | 0.13 | 0.0000 |
| TN | Tennessee | −0.84 | 0.55 | 0.1290 | CA | California | 1.17*** | 0.11 | 0.0000 |
| UT | Utah | −0.48 | 1.36 | 0.7250 | KS | Kansas | 1.12*** | 0.41 | 0.0060 |
| VA | Virginia | 0.88 | 0.66 | 0.1810 | RI | Rhode Island | 1.06*** | 0.24 | 0.0000 |
| VT | Vermont | −0.75 | 0.97 | 0.4420 | MT | Montana | 0.92*** | 0.10 | 0.0000 |
| WA | Washington | 0.47 | 1.14 | 0.6800 | MD | Maryland | 0.75*** | 0.16 | 0.0000 |
| WV | West Virginia | −0.74 | 1.08 | 0.4950 | NE | Nebraska | 0.53*** | 0.16 | 0.0010 |
| NM | New Mexico | 1.99*** | 0.70 | 0.0040 | DC | Distr. of Columbia | 0.29*** | 0.03 | 0.0000 |
| OK | Oklahoma | 2.46*** | 0.88 | 0.0050 | VT | Vermont | 0.21*** | 0.05 | 0.0000 |
| TX | Texas | 2.50** | 1.15 | 0.0290 | AK | Alaska | 0.66 | 1.17 | 0.5710 |
| LA | Louisiana | 2.52*** | 0.82 | 0.0020 | ID | Idaho | 0.15 | 0.16 | 0.3430 |
| CO | Colorado | 2.67** | 1.08 | 0.0130 | NH | New Hampshire | 0.24 | 0.23 | 0.2940 |

*Note:* *, **, *** denote 10, 5 and 1 percent significance levels. Standard errors are robust to group (conventional) heteroscedasticity. Uncertainty series from Mumtaz (2018) 1977Q2–2015Q3.

Table 8.7  Estimation results for state-specific uncertainty coefficient, 1977Q2–2015Q3 (horizon 4)

| Dependent variable: housing returns factor (*fmed*) |||||  Dependent variable: stochastic volatility (*svmed*) |||||
|---|---|---|---|---|---|---|---|---|---|
| State || Coeff | SE | *p*-value | State || Coeff | SE | *p*-value |
| WY | Wyoming | −5.30*** | 1.02 | 0.0000 | HI | Hawaii | 18.26*** | 1.10 | 0.0000 |
| OR | Oregon | −3.61*** | 1.09 | 0.0010 | MI | Michigan | 6.09*** | 0.82 | 0.0000 |
| IL | Illinois | −3.53*** | 0.93 | 0.0000 | MO | Missouri | 5.36*** | 0.36 | 0.0000 |
| NV | Nevada | −2.98** | 1.39 | 0.0310 | WI | Wisconsin | 4.68*** | 0.34 | 0.0000 |
| NH | New Hampshire | −2.80** | 1.41 | 0.0470 | NC | North Carolina | 4.46*** | 0.35 | 0.0000 |
| MI | Michigan | −2.73*** | 1.05 | 0.0090 | AR | Arkansas | 4.06*** | 0.40 | 0.0000 |
| RI | Rhode Island | −2.61* | 1.42 | 0.0650 | TX | Texas | 3.80*** | 0.40 | 0.0000 |
| DC | Distr. of Columbia | −2.49* | 1.39 | 0.0740 | MS | Mississippi | 3.68*** | 0.39 | 0.0000 |
| IA | Iowa | −2.41*** | 0.62 | 0.0000 | MN | Minnesota | 3.49*** | 0.65 | 0.0000 |
| HI | Hawaii | −2.32** | 1.09 | 0.0340 | IN | Indiana | 3.43*** | 0.32 | 0.0000 |
| WI | Wisconsin | −1.88** | 0.75 | 0.0120 | IL | Illinois | 3.23*** | 0.38 | 0.0000 |
| IN | Indiana | −1.25* | 0.72 | 0.0820 | OR | Oregon | 3.10*** | 0.40 | 0.0000 |
| KY | Kentucky | −1.11*** | 0.43 | 0.0100 | VA | Virginia | 3.03*** | 0.31 | 0.0000 |
| DE | Delaware | −0.83* | 0.45 | 0.0650 | FL | Florida | 2.96*** | 0.21 | 0.0000 |
| AK | Alaska | 0.90 | 1.39 | 0.5180 | GA | Georgia | 2.82*** | 0.33 | 0.0000 |
| AL | Alabama | −0.65 | 0.44 | 0.1440 | NM | New Mexico | 2.82*** | 0.19 | 0.0000 |
| AR | Arkansas | 0.25 | 1.17 | 0.8330 | ND | North Dakota | 2.72*** | 0.31 | 0.0000 |
| AZ | Arizona | 0.44 | 1.30 | 0.7330 | DE | Delaware | 2.63*** | 0.27 | 0.0000 |
| CA | California | 0.20 | 1.38 | 0.8840 | OH | Ohio | 2.63*** | 0.28 | 0.0000 |
| CT | Connecticut | 1.08 | 1.42 | 0.4470 | WA | Washington | 2.56*** | 0.45 | 0.0000 |
| FL | Florida | −0.76 | 1.21 | 0.5270 | WV | West Virginia | 2.36*** | 0.63 | 0.0000 |
| GA | Georgia | 0.51 | 0.90 | 0.5710 | OK | Oklahoma | 2.27*** | 0.15 | 0.0000 |
| ID | Idaho | −0.50 | 1.05 | 0.6360 | LA | Louisiana | 2.27*** | 0.65 | 0.0000 |
| KS | Kansas | −0.40 | 0.87 | 0.6410 | CT | Connecticut | 2.25*** | 0.37 | 0.0000 |
| MA | Massachusetts | 1.89 | 1.40 | 0.1760 | AZ | Arizona | 2.15*** | 0.28 | 0.0000 |
| MD | Maryland | −0.98 | 1.28 | 0.4450 | NV | Nevada | 2.14*** | 0.40 | 0.0000 |
| ME | Maine | −0.47 | 1.39 | 0.7350 | KY | Kentucky | 1.96*** | 0.16 | 0.0000 |
| MN | Minnesota | 0.12 | 0.90 | 0.8950 | CO | Colorado | 1.95*** | 0.21 | 0.0000 |
| MO | Missouri | −1.05 | 1.04 | 0.3140 | MA | Massachusetts | 1.75*** | 0.21 | 0.0000 |
| MS | Mississippi | −0.71 | 1.22 | 0.5620 | UT | Utah | 1.75*** | 0.32 | 0.0000 |
| MT | Montana | −1.30 | 1.06 | 0.2200 | PA | Pennsylvania | 1.74*** | 0.24 | 0.0000 |
| NC | North Carolina | −0.76 | 0.70 | 0.2770 | NJ | New Jersey | 1.73*** | 0.26 | 0.0000 |
| ND | North Dakota | −0.20 | 1.12 | 0.8560 | SD | South Dakota | 1.73*** | 0.17 | 0.0000 |
| NE | Nebraska | 0.60 | 0.62 | 0.3270 | TN | Tennessee | 1.66*** | 0.25 | 0.0000 |
| NJ | New Jersey | −0.88 | 1.37 | 0.5210 | NY | New York | 1.58*** | 0.12 | 0.0000 |
| NY | New York | 0.26 | 0.96 | 0.7840 | IA | Iowa | 1.55*** | 0.19 | 0.0000 |
| OH | Ohio | −0.63 | 0.63 | 0.3150 | SC | South Carolina | 1.53*** | 0.19 | 0.0000 |
| PA | Pennsylvania | 0.58 | 0.95 | 0.5390 | AL | Alabama | 1.43*** | 0.09 | 0.0000 |
| SC | South Carolina | −0.03 | 0.71 | 0.9610 | WY | Wyoming | 1.30*** | 0.15 | 0.0000 |
| SD | South Dakota | −1.37 | 0.88 | 0.1180 | KS | Kansas | 1.28*** | 0.47 | 0.0060 |
| TN | Tennessee | −1.03 | 0.64 | 0.1070 | CA | California | 1.27*** | 0.12 | 0.0000 |
| UT | Utah | −0.68 | 1.49 | 0.6480 | ME | Maine | 1.25*** | 0.35 | 0.0000 |
| VA | Virginia | 0.95 | 0.81 | 0.2390 | RI | Rhode Island | 1.14*** | 0.25 | 0.0000 |
| VT | Vermont | −0.93 | 1.06 | 0.3810 | MT | Montana | 1.08*** | 0.11 | 0.0000 |
| WA | Washington | 0.66 | 1.29 | 0.6100 | MD | Maryland | 0.83*** | 0.19 | 0.0000 |
| WV | West Virginia | −0.90 | 1.20 | 0.4530 | NE | Nebraska | 0.52*** | 0.16 | 0.0010 |
| CO | Colorado | 2.56** | 1.16 | 0.0280 | DC | Distr. of Columbia | 0.32*** | 0.03 | 0.0000 |
| NM | New Mexico | 2.61*** | 0.82 | 0.0010 | VT | Vermont | 0.23*** | 0.05 | 0.0000 |
| OK | Oklahoma | 2.63*** | 1.00 | 0.0080 | AK | Alaska | 0.21 | 1.28 | 0.8730 |
| TX | Texas | 2.69** | 1.24 | 0.0300 | ID | Idaho | 0.21 | 0.17 | 0.2100 |
| LA | Louisiana | 2.77*** | 1.00 | 0.0050 | NH | New Hampshire | 0.33 | 0.23 | 0.1530 |

*Note*: *, **, *** denote 10, 5 and 1 percent significance levels. Standard errors are robust to group (conventional) heteroscedasticity. Uncertainty series from Mumtaz (2018) 1977Q2–2015Q3.

The negative impact of increased uncertainty on the housing returns factor is markedly less severe, with only between 12 and 14 states recording a statistically significant negative impact, across the different horizons. Wyoming ranks at the top of the list with the largest negative impact.

An interesting observation is that 6 out of the top 12 states experiencing a positive spillover between macroeconomic uncertainty and house price stochastic volatility are from the Great Lakes/Midwest region, namely Michigan, Indiana, Ohio, Wisconsin, Illinois and Minnesota. Of the states in this region, Michigan, Illinois, Iowa, Wisconsin and Indiana also recorded a negative and significant relationship between uncertainty and housing returns. This result is also visually evident from the graphical and spatial depictions in Figures 8.1A and B and 8.2A and B.

From Figure 8.2, it can be observed that apart from the Midwest, the southern states, most notably Arkansas, Mississippi, Tennessee, North Carolina, South Carolina and Florida, and the southwestern states of Texas, Arizona and Nevada, together with Oregon on the west coast, are all recording large and significant positive links between macroeconomic uncertainty and housing market volatility.

Apart from the Midwestern states mentioned above, other states that registered a significant negative link between macroeconomic uncertainty and housing returns include Wyoming, Oregon and Nevada. It appears that at longer horizons, the impact increases marginally for all states.

When considering the shorter sample period from 1991Q1 onwards, and using the broader measure of uncertainty, we note that all states in the west, with the exception of Washington, are also affected by large spillover effects from macroeconomic uncertainty to house price volatility, especially at three- and four-quarter horizons. In addition, states in the Midwest and southeastern regions are persistent in recording large spillover effects (refer to Tables 8B.1 to 8B.4 and Figures 8B.1A and B and 8B.2A and B in Appendix B). For the macroeconomic uncertainty measure constructed by Jurado et al. (2015), the causal link between macroeconomic uncertainty and housing market is less pronounced. Whereas, the negative relationship between macroeconomic uncertainty and house price returns is confirmed, the earlier positive and significant relationship between macroeconomic uncertainty and the stochastic volatility measure does not find support (refer to Table 8B.6 in Appendix B).

Overall, there is a marked correspondence between the results obtained in this analysis and those of Mumtaz et al. (2018) (refer to Figures 8.1 and 8.4). Mumtaz et al. (2018) find that, in the regions mentioned above, the magnitude of the decline in income is largest, while these are also the states with a larger share of manufacturing and construction industries. Hence, uncertainty shocks seem to have the greatest impact on income and house prices broadly in the same states. A number of factors could explain this parallel. First, regions with a large manufacturing sector, like those of the Great Lakes/Midwest region, are vulnerable to external shocks. A fall in activity can result in sizeable job losses, with a clear impact on demand for dwellings. Second, house prices affect consumption through wealth and collateral effects. Mian et al. (2013), investigating the impact of the US subprime crisis on consumption, find that areas with poorer and more levered households have a significantly higher marginal propensity to consume out of housing wealth. Higher uncertainty will lead indebted households to increase precautionary savings. Furthermore, low-income households may face more difficulty in accessing credit, as lenders may tighten credit conditions, because both collateral values and household income become more uncertain. This will in turn depress consumption and income.

A fall in housing transactions is also likely to impact the consumption of durable goods, which is often closely related to house purchases. Third, a reduction in consumption following house price falls disproportionately hits employment in the non-tradable sector, which depends on local demand. Mian and Sufi (2014) find that this mechanism played a significant role in the decline in US employment between 2007 and 2009. Finally, as uncertainty affects both house prices and residential investment, states with a large construction sector are likely to suffer most from high uncertainty.

## 5  CONCLUSION

In this chapter, we aim to analyze the state-level impact of uncertainty on first- and second-moment movements in real housing returns. For this purpose, we begin by estimating DFM-TV-SV using Bayesian methods to disentangle the national and local factors affecting real housing returns and volatility in the 50 US states and DC. As the common components of housing returns and volatility tend to play an important role in driving the corresponding state-level values, failing to filter them out would result in an underestimation of the impact of state-level uncertainty. We then use panel data methods with heterogeneous coefficients to relate the first and second moments of the local factors with corresponding state-level uncertainty. The latter is estimated using the average forecast error variance from a factor augmented forecasting regression with stochastic volatility in the regression residuals and the error term for the factor dynamics. The model incorporates a large set of regional variables and 248 US-level data series. In our analysis, we use a narrower measure of uncertainty at one- to four-quarter forecast horizons, incorporating eight financial and macroeconomic state-level variables, besides the overall US data used in the factor regressions, over the 1977Q2 to 2015Q3 period, and a broader measure incorporating 21 financial and macroeconomic state-level variables over the period 1991Q1 to 2015Q3. We find that, when considering the narrower uncertainty measure, all but three states register a positive and highly significant relationship between macroeconomic uncertainty and the stochastic volatility measure. Hawaii, followed by Michigan, ranks highest in terms of the uncertainty spillover effect. At the same time, the negative impact of increased uncertainty on the housing returns factor is less severe, with only 12 to 14 states recording a statistically significant negative impact across the different horizons. Amongst the 12 states most affected by increased uncertainty are six states from the Great Lakes/Midwest region, namely Michigan, Indiana, Ohio, Wisconsin, Illinois and Minnesota. Of the states in this region, Michigan, Illinois, Iowa, Wisconsin and Indiana also record a negative and significant relationship between uncertainty and housing returns. Apart from the Midwest, a number of southern states, known to be lower-income states, also record large and significant positive spillover effects from macroeconomic uncertainty to housing market volatility. Lower-income households have fewer recourse options in the face of uncertainty and are often impacted more severely. The southwestern states of Texas, Arizona and Nevada, together with Oregon on the west coast, also count amongst the states with large spillover effects. When considering the shorter sample period from 1991Q1 onwards, and using the broader measure of uncertainty, we note that now all states in the west, with the exception of Washington, are also affected by large spillover effects from macroeconomic uncertainty to house price volatility, especially at three- and four-quarter horizons. In addition, states in the Midwest and southeastern regions are persistent in recording large spillover effects.

Our results have important implications for households, mortgage lenders and investors. As indicated at the onset, the housing market plays an important role in the US economy, since it constitutes a significant share of many households' asset holding and net worth. Therefore, the risk or volatility of house prices is among the largest personal economic risks faced by households. In the event of falling house prices and borrower financial difficulties, mortgage lenders may face defaults on their loans. Housing market turmoil and uncertainty may also create financing difficulties, especially for lenders relying on short-term funding. Investors are affected by shocks to returns, but also, depending on their investment horizon, by house price volatility. Understanding the sensitivity of house prices to uncertainty relative to that of other assets is also essential for portfolio diversification. The fact that uncertainty primarily impacts real housing returns volatility implies that investors need to pay close attention to the movements in state-level variability of a range of macroeconomic and financial variables when taking their housing market-related decisions. At the same time, our results tend to suggest that in the majority of states, households and mortgage lenders should be more worried about heightened second-moment effects of uncertainty on the housing market than about the negative effect on real returns. Both are likely to have a recessionary impact on the regional economy, but of varying degree.

As part of future research, it would be interesting to extend our analysis to a nonlinear set-up, given that the literature has shown that the effect of uncertainty on the housing market (and the economy in general) could be nonlinear, i.e. state-contingent. Preliminary evidence, based on the symbolic transfer entropy causality test for panel data presented by Camacho et al. (2021), which is robust in the presence of cross-sectional heterogeneity, structural breaks, nonlinearity and outliers, is reported in Table 8B.7 in Appendix B of this chapter. It suggests that our linear model-based overall results showing a stronger influence of uncertainty on second-moment movements in real housing returns continue to hold even in a nonlinear context. Nevertheless, more detailed state-level analysis could be of high value to households, mortgage lenders and investors, given the existence of heterogeneity. At the same time, given that in-sample predictability does not guarantee out-of-sample gains, conducting a real-time forecasting analysis could also be an area of further investigation.

## ACKNOWLEDGMENTS

We would like to thank an anonymous referee for many helpful comments. However, any remaining errors are solely ours. In addition, the views expressed in this chapter are those of the authors and do not necessarily reflect those of the Organisation for Economic Co-operation and Development or the governments of its member countries.

## NOTES

1. The reader is referred to www.federalreserve.gov/releases/z1/20210311/html/b101h.htm for further details.
2. We would like to thank the anonymous referee for motivating us to include this discussion.
3. The data can be downloaded from www.fhfa.gov/DataTools/Downloads/Pages/House-Price-Index .aspx.

4. The reader is referred to the computer codes to obtain the measures of uncertainty available at https://sites.google.com/site/hmumtaz77/research-papers?authuser=0.
5. The variables considered are: total personal income divided by population and deflated by CPI; benefit income divided by population and deflated by CPI; dividend income divided by population and deflated by CPI; contributions for social insurance divided by population and deflated by CPI; other income divided by population and deflated by CPI; seasonally adjusted employment rate; seasonally adjusted unemployment rate; seasonally adjusted house prices divided by CPI.
6. The variables include: real personal income and its components (social insurance, dividends, benefits and other income), overall employment, unemployment rate, real house prices, i.e. the eight variables above plus non-performing loans and net assets of banks, leading indicator, coincident indicator, all employees in health and education, financial services, government, information, leisure and hospitality, manufacturing, non-farm, professional and business services, and other services.
7. It is straightforward to see that potential co-movements in the factor loadings across all series can be captured by the common factor volatility. This was pointed out by Del Negro and Otrok (2008).
8. We would like to thank the anonymous referee for alerting us to this issue.
9. When performing the Hausman test with null hypothesis $E(X_{it}|u_{it}) = 0$, that is exogeneity of the $X$-regressors, we reject the null of exogeneity at the 1 percent level of significance. For Model 1 in Table 8.3, the test statistic is $m_1 \sim \chi^2(1) = 12.98$ [p=0.0003], and for Model 5, the test statistic is $m_1 \sim \chi^2(1) = 791.56$ [p=0.0000]. Test results for other horizons also yield rejections of the null.
10. When applying a one-step system GMM estimator to Model 1 in Table 8.3, the Sargan test of overidentifying restrictions is rejected at the 1 percent level of significance ($\chi^2(153) = 695.57$ [p=0.000]), while the $p$-value for the Hansen test takes the implausible value of 1 – indicative of instrument proliferation ($\chi^2(153) = 47.68$ [p=1.000]). The same inference holds true for all other models in Table 8.3.

# REFERENCES

André, C., L. Bonga-Bonga, R. Gupta and J.W.M. Mwamba (2017), "Economic policy uncertainty, US real housing returns and their volatility: A nonparametric approach," *Journal of Real Estate Research*, 39 (4), 493–513.

Antonakakis, N., R. Gupta and C. André (2015), "Dynamic co-movements between economic policy uncertainty and housing market returns," *Journal of Real Estate Portfolio Management*, 21 (1), 53–60.

Antonakakis, N., C. André and R. Gupta (2016), "Dynamic spillovers in the United States: Stock market, housing, uncertainty and the macroeconomy," *Southern Economics Journal*, 83 (2), 609–624.

Arellano, M. and S. Bond (1991), "Some tests of specification for panel data: Monte Carlo evidence and an application to employment equations," *Review of Economic Studies*, 58 (2), 277–297.

Aye, G.C. and R. Gupta (2019), "Macroeconomic uncertainty and the comovement in buying versus renting in the United States," *Advances in Decision Sciences*, 23 (3), 93–121.

Aye, G.C., M.W. Clance and R. Gupta (2019), "The effect of economic uncertainty on the housing market cycle," *Journal of Real Estate Portfolio Management*, 25 (1), 67–75.

Bernanke, B. (1983), "Irreversibility, uncertainty, and cyclical investment," *Quarterly Journal of Economics*, 98, 85–106.

Bhatt, V., N.K. Kishor and J. Ma (2017), "The impact of EMU on bond yield convergence: Evidence from a time-varying dynamic factor model," *Journal of Economic Dynamics and Control*, 82, 206–222.

Bloom, N.A. (2009), "The impact of uncertainty shocks," *Econometrica*, 77 (3), 623–685.

Bouri, E., R. Gupta, C.K. Kyei and R. Shivambu (Forthcoming), "Uncertainty and daily predictability of housing returns and volatility of the United States: Evidence from a higher-order nonparametric causality-in-quantiles test," *Quarterly Review of Economics and Finance*.

Bruno, G. (2005), "Approximating the bias of the LSDV estimator for dynamic unbalanced panel data models," *Economic Letters*, 87 (3), 361–366.

Camacho, M., A. Romeu and M. Ruiz (2021), "Symbolic transfer entropy test for causality in longitudinal data," *Economic Modelling*, 94, 649–661.

Christidou, M. and S. Fountas (2018), "Uncertainty in the housing market: Evidence from US states," *Studies in Nonlinear Dynamics and Econometrics*, 22 (2), 20160064.

Christou, C., R. Gupta and C. Hassapis (2017), "Does economic policy uncertainty forecast real housing returns in a panel of OECD countries? A Bayesian approach," *Quarterly Review of Economics and Finance*, 65, 50–60.

Christou, C., R. Gupta and W. Nyakabawo (2019), "Time-varying impact of uncertainty shocks on the US housing market," *Economics Letters*, 180, 15–20.

Del Negro, M. and C. Otrok (2007), "99 luftballons: Monetary policy and the house price boom across US states," *Journal of Monetary Economics*, 54 (7), 1962–1985.

Del Negro, M. and C. Otrok (2008), "Dynamic factor models with time-varying parameters: Measuring changes in international business cycles," *FRB of New York Staff Report*, 326, May.

Dixit, A.K. and R.S. Pindyck (1994), *Investment under uncertainty*, Princeton, NJ: Princeton University Press.

El Montasser, G., A.N. Ajmi, T. Chang, B.D. Simo-Kengne, C. Andre and R. Gupta (2016), "Cross-country evidence on the causal relationship between policy uncertainty and house prices," *Journal of Housing Research*, 25 (2), 195–211.

Emirmahmutoglu, F., M. Balcilar, N. Apergis, B.D. Simo-Kengne, T. Chang and R. Gupta (2016), "Causal relationship between asset prices and output in the US: Evidence from state-level panel Granger causality test," *Regional Studies*, 50 (10), 1728–1741.

Fairchild, J., S. Wu and J. Ma (2015), "Understanding housing market volatility," *Journal of Money, Credit and Banking*, 47 (7), 1309–1337.

Gabauer, G. and R. Gupta (2020), "Spillovers across macroeconomic, financial and real estate uncertainties: A time-varying approach?" *Structural Change and Economic Dynamics*, 52, 167–173.

Gabauer, D., R. Gupta, H.A. Marfatia and S.M. Miller (2020), "Estimating US housing price network connectedness: Evidence from dynamic elastic net, lasso, and ridge vector autoregressive models," Working Paper No. 2020-08, University of Connecticut, Department of Economics, August.

Gorodnichenko, Y. and S. Ng (2017), "Level and volatility factors in macroeconomic data," *Journal of Monetary Economics*, 91, 52–68.

Greene, W.H. (1997), *Econometric Analysis* (3rd ed.), Upper Saddle River, NJ: Prentice Hall.

Gupta, R., J. Ma, M. Risse and M.E. Wohar (2018), "Common business cycles and volatilities in US states and MSAs: The role of economic uncertainty," *Journal of Macroeconomics*, 57, 317–337.

Gupta, R., C.K.M. Lau and W. Nyakabawo (2020a), "Predicting aggregate and state-level US house price volatility: The role of sentiment," *Journal of Reviews on Global Economics*, 9, 30–46.

Gupta, R., J. Ma, K. Theodoridis and M. Wohar (2020b), "Is there a national housing market bubble brewing in the United States?" Working Paper No. 202023, University of Pretoria, Department of Economics, March.

Gupta, R., H.A. Marfatia, C. Pierdzioch and A.A. Salisu (2021), "Machine learning predictions of housing market synchronization across US states: The role of uncertainty," *Journal of Real Estate Finance and Economics*. DOI: https://doi.org/10.1007/s11146-020-09813-1.

Hausman, J.A. (1978), "Specification tests in econometrics," *Econometrica*, 46 (6), 1251–1271.

Im, K., H. Pesaran and Y. Shin (2003), "Testing for unit roots in heterogeneous panels," *Journal of Econometrics*, 115, 53–74.

Judge, G.G., R.C. Hill, W.E. Griffiths, H. Lütkepohl and T.C. Lee (1985), *The theory and practice of econometrics* (2nd ed.), New York: John Wiley and Sons.

Judson, R.A. and A.L. Owen (1999), "Estimating dynamic panel data models: A guide for macroeconomists," *Economics Letters*, 65 (1), 9–15.

Jurado, K., S.C. Ludvigson and S. Ng (2015), "Measuring uncertainty," *American Economic Review*, 105 (3), 1177–1216.

Kim, C.-J. and C.R. Nelson (1999), *State-space models with regime switching*, Cambridge, MA: MIT Press.

Kim, S., N. Shephard and S. Chib (1998), "Stochastic volatility: Likelihood inference and comparison with ARCH models," *Review of Economic Studies*, 65 (3), 361–393.

Leamer, E.E. (2007), "Housing is the business cycle," Paper presented at the Economic Policy Symposium, Jackson Hole, Federal Reserve Bank of Kansas City, August 30–September 1, 149–233.

Leamer, E.E. (2015), "Housing really is the business cycle: What survives the lessons of 2008–2009?" *Journal of Money, Credit and Banking*, 47 (S1), 43–50.

Levin, A., F. Lin and C. Chu (2002), "Unit root tests in panel data: Asymptomatic and finite sample properties," *Journal of Econometrics*, 108, 1–24.

Ludvigson, S.C., S. Ma and S. Ng (Forthcoming), "Uncertainty and business cycles: Exogenous impulse or endogenous response?" *American Economic Journal: Macroeconomics*.

Marfatia, H.A. (2021), "Modeling house price synchronization across the US states and their time-varying macroeconomic linkages," *Journal of Time Series Econometrics*, 13 (1), 73–117.

Mian, A. and A. Sufi (2014), "What explains the 2007–2009 drop in employment?" *Econometrica*, 82, 2197–2223.

Mian, A., K. Rao and A. Sufi (2013), "Household balance sheets, consumption, and the economic slump," *Quarterly Journal of Economics*, 128 (4), 1687–1726.

Mumtaz, H. (2018), "Does uncertainty affect real activity? Evidence from state-level data," *Economics Letters*, 167, 127–130.

Mumtaz, H. and A. Musso (2021), "The evolving impact of global, region-specific, and country-specific uncertainty," *Journal of Business and Economic Statistics*, 39 (2), 466–481.

Mumtaz, H., L. Sunder-Plassmann and A. Theophilopoulou (2018), "The state-level impact of uncertainty shocks," *Journal of Money, Credit and Banking*, 50 (8), 1879–1899.

Neely, C.J. and D.E. Rapach (2011), "International comovements in inflation rates and country characteristics," *Journal of International Money and Finance*, 30 (7), 1471–1490.

Ngene, G.M., D.P. Sohn and M.K. Hassan (2017), "Time-varying and spatial herding behavior in the US housing market: Evidence from direct housing prices," *Journal of Real Estate Finance and Economics*, 54 (4), 482–514.

Nguyen Thanh, B., J. Strobel and G. Lee (2020), "A new measure of real estate uncertainty shocks," *Real Estate Economics*, 48 (3), 744–771.

Nyakabawo, W.V., S.M. Miller, M. Balcilar, S. Das and R. Gupta (2015), "Temporal causality between house prices and output in the US: A Bootstrap Rolling window approach," *North American Journal of Economics and Finance*, 33 (1), 55–73.

Nyakabawo, W.V., R. Gupta and H.A. Marfatia (2018), "High frequency impact of monetary policy and macroeconomic surprises on US MSAs, aggregate US housing returns and asymmetric volatility," *Advances in Decision Sciences*, 22 (1), 204–229.

Pesaran, M.H. (2007), "A simple panel unit root test in the presence of cross-section dependence," *Journal of Applied Econometrics*, 22, 265–312.

Pindyck, R.S. (1991), "Irreversibility, uncertainty, and investment," *Journal of Economic Literature*, 24, 1110–1148.

Poi, B.P. (2003), "From the help desk: Swamy's random coefficients model," *The Stata Journal*, 3 (3), 302–308.

Primiceri, G.E. (2005), "Time varying structural vector autoregressions and monetary policy," *Review of Economic Studies*, 72 (3), 821–852.

Segnon, M., R. Gupta, K. Lesame and M.E. Wohar (2020), "High-frequency volatility forecasting of US housing markets," *Journal of Real Estate Finance and Economics*. https://doi.org/10.1007/s11146-020-09745-w.

Stock, J.H. and M.W. Watson (1989), "New indexes of coincident and leading economic indicators," *NBER Macroeconomics Annual*, 4, 351–394.

Stock, J.H. and M.W. Watson (2007), "Why has US inflation become harder to forecast?" *Journal of Money, Credit and Banking*, 39, 3–33.

Strobel, J., B. Nguyen Thanh and G. Lee (2020), "Effects of macroeconomic uncertainty and labor demand shocks on the housing market," *Real Estate Economics*, 48 (2), 345–372.

Swamy, P.A.V. (1970), "Efficient inference in a random coefficient regression model," *Econometrica*, 38, 311–323.

## APPENDIX A: TECHNICAL DISCUSSION OF THE RANDOM-COEFFICIENTS ESTIMATOR

Swamy's (1970) random-coefficients estimator allows for the estimation of cross-section specific slope and intercept parameters.

We may combine Equations 8.8 and 8.9 from Section 3.2.2 to get:

$$y_i = X_i(\beta + v_i) + \epsilon_i$$
$$= X_i\beta + u_i$$

with $u_i \equiv X_i v_i + \epsilon_i$. Furthermore,

$$E\{u_i u_i'\} = E\{(X_i v_i + \epsilon_i)(X_i v_i + \epsilon_i)'\}$$
$$= X_i \Sigma X_i' + \sigma_{ii} I$$
$$\equiv \Pi_i.$$

We can stack the $P$ panels,

$$y = X\beta + u \tag{8A.1}$$

where

$$\Pi \equiv E\{u_i u_i'\} = \begin{bmatrix} \Pi_1 & 0 & \cdots & 0 \\ 0 & \Pi_2 & \cdots & 0 \\ \vdots & \vdots & \ddots & \vdots \\ 0 & 0 & \cdots & \Pi_P \end{bmatrix}.$$

Estimating the parameters in Equation 8.9, described in Section 3.2.2, is a standard problem, which can be solved with GLS,

$$\hat{\beta} = (X'\Pi^{-1}X)^{-1} X'\Pi^{-1} y$$
$$= \left(\sum_i X_i' \Pi_i^{-1} X_i\right)^{-1} \sum_i X_i' \Pi_i^{-1} y_i$$
$$= \sum_i W_i b_i \tag{8A.2}$$

with $W_i$ the GLS weight and $b_i = (X_i' X_i)^{-1} X_i' y$. The resulting $\hat{\beta}$ for the overall (national) result is therefore a weighted average of the state-specific OLS estimates. For more detail on GLS weight and $\hat{\beta}$ variance specification, refer to Poi (2003).

In order to obtain the state-specific $\beta_i$ vectors, Judge et al. (1985) suggest that if attention is restricted to the class of estimators $\{\beta_i^*\}$ for which $E\{\beta_i^* | \beta_i\} = \beta_i$, then the state-specific OLS estimator $b_i$ is appropriate. Following Green's (1997) suggested method to obtain the variance of $\hat{\beta}_i$, it follows that $\beta$ is both consistent and efficient; and although inefficient, $b_i$ is also a consistent estimator of $\beta$.

Poi (2003) also suggests a test to determine whether the panel-specific $\beta_i$ are significantly different from one another. The null hypothesis is stated as:

$$H_0 : \beta_1 = \beta_2 = \cdots = \beta_P \tag{8A.3}$$

and the test statistic is defined as:

$$T \equiv \sum_{t=1}^{P} \left(b_i - \beta^{\maltese}\right)' \left\{\hat{\sigma}_{ii}^{-1}(X_i X_i)\right\} \left(b_i - \beta^{\maltese}\right) \tag{8A.4}$$

where

$$\beta^{\maltese} = \left\{\sum_{t=1}^{P} \hat{\sigma}_{ii}^{-1}(X_i X_i)\right\}^{-1} \sum_{t=1}^{P} \hat{\sigma}_{ii}^{-1}(X_i X_i) b_i.$$

The test statistic $T$ is distributed as $\chi^2$ with $k(P-1)$ degrees of freedom.

# APPENDIX B

Table 8B.1   Estimation results for overall uncertainty impact, 1991Q1–2015Q3 (horizons 1 to 4)

|  | (1) | (2) | (3) | (4) | (5) | (6) | (7) | (8) |
|---|---|---|---|---|---|---|---|---|
|  | Dependent: housing returns factor (fmed) | | | | Dependent: stochastic volatility (svmed) | | | |
| u1 | −0.068 |  |  |  | 0.052*** |  |  |  |
|  | (−0.51) |  |  |  | (2.05) |  |  |  |
| u2 |  | −0.0032 |  |  |  | 0.103*** |  |  |
|  |  | (−0.03) |  |  |  | (4.02) |  |  |
| u3 |  |  | −0.038 |  |  |  | 0.127*** |  |
|  |  |  | (−0.30) |  |  |  | (3.99) |  |
| u4 |  |  |  | −0.116 |  |  |  | 0.134*** |
|  |  |  |  | (−0.96) |  |  |  | (4.19) |
| _cons | −0.540 | 1.650 | 5.510 | 12.29 | −0.731 | −2.322** | −3.153* | −3.811** |
|  | (0.20) | (0.35) | (0.88) | (1.33) | (−1.33) | (−2.38) | (−1.85) | (−2.02) |
| Obs | 4950 | 4950 | 4950 | 4950 | 4950 | 4950 | 4950 | 4950 |
| Groups | 50 | 50 | 50 | 50 | 50 | 50 | 50 | 50 |
| Chi²(100) | 512.57*** | 500.66*** | 462.90*** | 449.98*** | 93768*** | 94053*** | 92448*** | 90853*** |

Note: $t$ statistics in parentheses. $t$ statistics based on standard errors that are robust to group (bootstrap) heteroscedasticity. * $p < 0.10$, ** $p < 0.05$, *** $p < 0.01$. $\chi^2$ is a test for parameter constancy.

## 232   Handbook of real estate and macroeconomics

Table 8B.2   Estimation results for state-specific uncertainty coefficient, 1991Q1–2015Q3 (horizon 1)

| \multicolumn{4}{c}{Dependent variable: housing returns factor (fmed)} | \multicolumn{4}{c}{Dependent variable: stochastic volatility (svmed)} |
|---|---|---|---|---|---|---|---|
| State | | Coeff | SE | p-value | State | | Coeff | SE | p-value |
|---|---|---|---|---|---|---|---|---|---|
| FL | Florida | −3.86*** | 0.74 | 0.0000 | ID | Idaho | 0.49*** | 0.06 | 0.0000 |
| ND | North Dakota | −1.81** | 0.66 | 0.0060 | NC | North Carolina | 0.40*** | 0.07 | 0.0000 |
| WA | Washington | −0.86*** | 0.33 | 0.0100 | CA | California | 0.38*** | 0.07 | 0.0000 |
| TN | Tennessee | −0.81** | 0.39 | 0.0370 | LA | Louisiana | 0.33*** | 0.09 | 0.0000 |
| GA | Georgia | −0.71** | 0.30 | 0.0210 | AK | Alaska | 0.24** | 0.10 | 0.0170 |
| NC | North Carolina | −0.63*** | 0.24 | 0.0090 | AZ | Arizona | 0.21*** | 0.06 | 0.0010 |
| UT | Utah | −0.47* | 0.28 | 0.0890 | TN | Tennessee | 0.21*** | 0.03 | 0.0000 |
| NM | New Mexico | −0.35* | 0.19 | 0.0660 | MS | Mississippi | 0.21*** | 0.06 | 0.0000 |
| AK | Alaska | 0.80 | 0.50 | 0.1080 | OK | Oklahoma | 0.19*** | 0.07 | 0.0100 |
| AL | Alabama | −0.02 | 0.20 | 0.9270 | OR | Oregon | 0.16*** | 0.04 | 0.0000 |
| AR | Arkansas | 0.39 | 0.54 | 0.4660 | NE | Nebraska | 0.15*** | 0.05 | 0.0030 |
| AZ | Arizona | −0.26 | 0.32 | 0.4120 | IL | Illinois | 0.15** | 0.06 | 0.0200 |
| CA | California | 0.52 | 0.72 | 0.4730 | MN | Minnesota | 0.12* | 0.06 | 0.0570 |
| CT | Connecticut | −0.08 | 0.25 | 0.7450 | CT | Connecticut | 0.12*** | 0.04 | 0.0010 |
| HI | Hawaii | 0.03 | 0.61 | 0.9630 | UT | Utah | 0.10*** | 0.04 | 0.0030 |
| IA | Iowa | −0.08 | 0.07 | 0.2460 | VA | Virginia | 0.10*** | 0.02 | 0.0000 |
| ID | Idaho | −0.42 | 0.70 | 0.5550 | MT | Montana | 0.08*** | 0.01 | 0.0000 |
| IL | Illinois | −0.04 | 0.32 | 0.8950 | PA | Pennsylvania | 0.07** | 0.04 | 0.0560 |
| KS | Kansas | −0.13 | 0.17 | 0.4690 | RI | Rhode Island | 0.06*** | 0.01 | 0.0000 |
| KY | Kentucky | 0.25 | 0.16 | 0.1100 | MI | Michigan | 0.02* | 0.01 | 0.0880 |
| MA | Massachusetts | 0.12 | 0.32 | 0.7010 | MD | Maryland | 0.0* | 0.01 | 0.0560 |
| MD | Maryland | −0.02 | 0.19 | 0.9130 | NJ | New Jersey | 0.01** | 0.00 | 0.0240 |
| ME | Maine | 0.12 | 0.21 | 0.5920 | FL | Florida | 0.17 | 0.13 | 0.1830 |
| MI | Michigan | −0.08 | 0.10 | 0.4540 | HI | Hawaii | 0.13 | 0.09 | 0.1640 |
| MN | Minnesota | 0.20 | 0.30 | 0.5100 | GA | Georgia | 0.04 | 0.06 | 0.5550 |
| MO | Missouri | −0.27 | 0.45 | 0.5530 | AL | Alabama | 0.02 | 0.04 | 0.6410 |
| MS | Mississippi | −0.37 | 0.38 | 0.3210 | SC | South Carolina | 0.02 | 0.03 | 0.6400 |
| NE | Nebraska | 0.18 | 0.24 | 0.4500 | NV | Nevada | 0.01 | 0.02 | 0.4700 |
| NH | New Hampshire | 0.19 | 0.20 | 0.3570 | KS | Kansas | 0.01 | 0.03 | 0.7010 |
| NJ | New Jersey | −0.05 | 0.15 | 0.7480 | CO | Colorado | 0.01 | 0.03 | 0.7590 |
| NV | Nevada | 0.02 | 0.09 | 0.8270 | WA | Washington | 0.01 | 0.06 | 0.8740 |
| NY | New York | −0.20 | 0.24 | 0.3970 | SD | South Dakota | 0.01 | 0.03 | 0.8510 |
| OH | Ohio | 0.33 | 0.23 | 0.1460 | WY | Wyoming | −0.01 | 0.01 | 0.1450 |
| OK | Oklahoma | −0.01 | 0.41 | 0.9760 | MA | Massachusetts | −0.01 | 0.02 | 0.5330 |
| OR | Oregon | 0.10 | 0.20 | 0.6360 | ME | Maine | −0.01 | 0.01 | 0.2410 |
| PA | Pennsylvania | 0.86 | 0.56 | 0.1210 | NY | New York | −0.02 | 0.02 | 0.3150 |
| RI | Rhode Island | −0.40 | 0.32 | 0.2040 | NH | New Hampshire | −0.02 | 0.03 | 0.4310 |
| SC | South Carolina | −0.15 | 0.26 | 0.5680 | NM | New Mexico | −0.02 | 0.01 | 0.1070 |
| SD | South Dakota | 0.15 | 0.19 | 0.4240 | KY | Kentucky | −0.04 | 0.04 | 0.3330 |
| TX | Texas | 0.44 | 0.27 | 0.1060 | AR | Arkansas | −0.05 | 0.07 | 0.4870 |
| VA | Virginia | 0.18 | 0.19 | 0.3320 | WV | West Virginia | −0.12 | 0.13 | 0.3570 |
| WV | West Virginia | −0.81 | 0.60 | 0.1790 | VT | Vermont | −0.01 | 0.00 | 0.0010 |
| WY | Wyoming | −0.01 | 0.10 | 0.9600 | DE | Delaware | −0.02 | 0.01 | 0.0010 |
| DE | Delaware | 0.32*** | 0.11 | 0.0050 | WI | Wisconsin | −0.06 | 0.03 | 0.0690 |
| VT | Vermont | 0.32* | 0.17 | 0.0650 | IA | Iowa | −0.06 | 0.01 | 0.0000 |
| MT | Montana | 0.49*** | 0.17 | 0.0050 | TX | Texas | −0.11 | 0.03 | 0.0000 |
| WI | Wisconsin | 0.61*** | 0.12 | 0.0000 | MO | Missouri | −0.15 | 0.09 | 0.0950 |
| CO | Colorado | 0.69** | 0.28 | 0.0130 | IN | Indiana | −0.29 | 0.06 | 0.0000 |
| IN | Indiana | 1.08*** | 0.25 | 0.0000 | OH | Ohio | −0.30 | 0.08 | 0.0000 |
| LA | Louisiana | 1.10*** | 0.17 | 0.0000 | ND | North Dakota | −0.33 | 0.11 | 0.0020 |

*Note:* *, **, *** denote 10, 5 and 1 percent significance levels. Standard errors are robust to group (conventional) heteroscedasticity. Uncertainty series from Mumtaz (2018), 1991Q1–2015Q3.

Table 8B.3  Estimation results for state-specific uncertainty coefficient, 1991Q1–2015Q3 (horizon 2)

| | Dependent variable: housing returns factor (*fmed*) | | | | Dependent variable: stochastic volatility (*svmed*) | | | |
|---|---|---|---|---|---|---|---|---|
| State | | Coeff | SE | *p*-value | State | | Coeff | SE | *p*-value |
| FL | Florida | −3.86*** | 0.74 | 0.0000 | ID | Idaho | 0.49*** | 0.06 | 0.0000 |
| ND | North Dakota | −1.81** | 0.66 | 0.0060 | NC | North Carolina | 0.40*** | 0.07 | 0.0000 |
| WA | Washington | −0.86** | 0.33 | 0.0100 | CA | California | 0.38*** | 0.07 | 0.0000 |
| TN | Tennessee | −0.81** | 0.39 | 0.0370 | LA | Louisiana | 0.33*** | 0.09 | 0.0000 |
| GA | Georgia | −0.71** | 0.30 | 0.0210 | AK | Alaska | 0.24** | 0.10 | 0.0170 |
| NC | North Carolina | −0.63*** | 0.24 | 0.0090 | AZ | Arizona | 0.21*** | 0.06 | 0.0010 |
| UT | Utah | −0.47* | 0.28 | 0.0890 | TN | Tennessee | 0.21*** | 0.03 | 0.0000 |
| NM | New Mexico | −0.35* | 0.19 | 0.0660 | MS | Mississippi | 0.21*** | 0.06 | 0.0000 |
| AK | Alaska | 0.80 | 0.50 | 0.1080 | OK | Oklahoma | 0.19*** | 0.07 | 0.0100 |
| AL | Alabama | −0.02 | 0.20 | 0.9270 | OR | Oregon | 0.16*** | 0.04 | 0.0000 |
| AR | Arkansas | 0.39 | 0.54 | 0.4660 | NE | Nebraska | 0.15*** | 0.05 | 0.0030 |
| AZ | Arizona | −0.26 | 0.32 | 0.4120 | IL | Illinois | 0.15** | 0.06 | 0.0200 |
| CA | California | 0.52 | 0.72 | 0.4730 | MN | Minnesota | 0.12* | 0.06 | 0.0570 |
| CT | Connecticut | −0.08 | 0.25 | 0.7450 | CT | Connecticut | 0.12*** | 0.04 | 0.0010 |
| HI | Hawaii | 0.03 | 0.61 | 0.9630 | UT | Utah | 0.10*** | 0.04 | 0.0030 |
| IA | Iowa | −0.08 | 0.07 | 0.2460 | VA | Virginia | 0.10*** | 0.02 | 0.0000 |
| ID | Idaho | −0.42 | 0.70 | 0.5550 | MT | Montana | 0.08*** | 0.01 | 0.0000 |
| IL | Illinois | −0.04 | 0.32 | 0.8950 | PA | Pennsylvania | 0.07** | 0.04 | 0.0560 |
| KS | Kansas | −0.13 | 0.17 | 0.4690 | RI | Rhode Island | 0.06*** | 0.01 | 0.0000 |
| KY | Kentucky | 0.25 | 0.16 | 0.1100 | MI | Michigan | 0.02* | 0.01 | 0.0880 |
| MA | Massachusetts | 0.12 | 0.32 | 0.7010 | MD | Maryland | 0.0* | 0.01 | 0.0560 |
| MD | Maryland | −0.02 | 0.19 | 0.9130 | NJ | New Jersey | 0.01** | 0.00 | 0.0240 |
| ME | Maine | 0.12 | 0.21 | 0.5920 | FL | Florida | 0.17 | 0.13 | 0.1830 |
| MI | Michigan | −0.08 | 0.10 | 0.4540 | HI | Hawaii | 0.13 | 0.09 | 0.1640 |
| MN | Minnesota | 0.20 | 0.30 | 0.5100 | GA | Georgia | 0.04 | 0.06 | 0.5550 |
| MO | Missouri | −0.27 | 0.45 | 0.5530 | AL | Alabama | 0.02 | 0.04 | 0.6410 |
| MS | Mississippi | −0.37 | 0.38 | 0.3210 | SC | South Carolina | 0.02 | 0.03 | 0.6400 |
| NE | Nebraska | 0.18 | 0.24 | 0.4500 | NV | Nevada | 0.01 | 0.02 | 0.4700 |
| NH | New Hampshire | 0.19 | 0.20 | 0.3570 | KS | Kansas | 0.01 | 0.03 | 0.7010 |
| NJ | New Jersey | −0.05 | 0.15 | 0.7480 | CO | Colorado | 0.01 | 0.03 | 0.7590 |
| NV | Nevada | 0.02 | 0.09 | 0.8270 | WA | Washington | 0.01 | 0.06 | 0.8740 |
| NY | New York | −0.20 | 0.24 | 0.3970 | SD | South Dakota | 0.01 | 0.03 | 0.8510 |
| OH | Ohio | 0.33 | 0.23 | 0.1460 | WY | Wyoming | −0.01 | 0.01 | 0.1450 |
| OK | Oklahoma | −0.01 | 0.41 | 0.9760 | MA | Massachusetts | −0.01 | 0.02 | 0.5330 |
| OR | Oregon | 0.10 | 0.20 | 0.6360 | ME | Maine | −0.01 | 0.01 | 0.2410 |
| PA | Pennsylvania | 0.86 | 0.56 | 0.1210 | NY | New York | −0.02 | 0.02 | 0.3150 |
| RI | Rhode Island | −0.40 | 0.32 | 0.2040 | NH | New Hampshire | −0.02 | 0.03 | 0.4310 |
| SC | South Carolina | −0.15 | 0.26 | 0.5680 | NM | New Mexico | −0.02 | 0.01 | 0.1070 |
| SD | South Dakota | 0.15 | 0.19 | 0.4240 | KY | Kentucky | −0.04 | 0.04 | 0.3330 |
| TX | Texas | 0.44 | 0.27 | 0.1060 | AR | Arkansas | −0.05 | 0.07 | 0.4870 |
| VA | Virginia | 0.18 | 0.19 | 0.3320 | WV | West Virginia | −0.12 | 0.13 | 0.3570 |
| WV | West Virginia | −0.81 | 0.60 | 0.1790 | VT | Vermont | −0.01 | 0.00 | 0.0010 |
| WY | Wyoming | −0.01 | 0.10 | 0.9600 | DE | Delaware | −0.02 | 0.01 | 0.0010 |
| DE | Delaware | 0.32*** | 0.11 | 0.0050 | WI | Wisconsin | −0.06 | 0.03 | 0.0690 |
| VT | Vermont | 0.32* | 0.17 | 0.0650 | IA | Iowa | −0.06 | 0.01 | 0.0000 |
| MT | Montana | 0.49*** | 0.17 | 0.0050 | TX | Texas | −0.11 | 0.03 | 0.0000 |
| WI | Wisconsin | 0.61*** | 0.12 | 0.0000 | MO | Missouri | −0.15 | 0.09 | 0.0950 |
| CO | Colorado | 0.69** | 0.28 | 0.0130 | IN | Indiana | −0.29 | 0.06 | 0.0000 |
| IN | Indiana | 1.08*** | 0.25 | 0.0000 | OH | Ohio | −0.30 | 0.08 | 0.0000 |
| LA | Louisiana | 1.10*** | 0.17 | 0.0000 | ND | North Dakota | −0.33 | 0.11 | 0.0020 |

*Note:* *, **, *** denote 10, 5 and 1 percent significance levels. Standard errors are robust to group (conventional) heteroscedasticity. Uncertainty series from Mumtaz (2018), 1991Q1–2015Q3.

Table 8B.4  Estimation results for state-specific uncertainty coefficient, 1991Q1–2015Q3 (horizon 3)

| \multicolumn{5}{|c|}{Dependent variable: housing returns factor (fmed)} | \multicolumn{5}{|c|}{Dependent variable: stochastic volatility (svmed)} |
|---|---|---|---|---|---|---|---|---|
| State | | Coeff | SE | p-value | State | | Coeff | SE | p-value |
| FL | Florida | −1.90*** | 0.42 | 0.0000 | AZ | Arizona | 0.56*** | 0.12 | 0.0000 |
| AZ | Arizona | −1.60*** | 0.62 | 0.0100 | NC | North Carolina | 0.52*** | 0.06 | 0.0000 |
| UT | Utah | −1.44** | 0.63 | 0.0220 | CT | Connecticut | 0.50*** | 0.10 | 0.0000 |
| MI | Michigan | −1.20*** | 0.41 | 0.0030 | OK | Oklahoma | 0.46*** | 0.10 | 0.0000 |
| WA | Washington | −1.05** | 0.43 | 0.0140 | MN | Minnesota | 0.45*** | 0.12 | 0.0000 |
| GA | Georgia | −0.65* | 0.34 | 0.0590 | ID | Idaho | 0.44*** | 0.08 | 0.0000 |
| NC | North Carolina | −0.55** | 0.25 | 0.0280 | LA | Louisiana | 0.40*** | 0.11 | 0.0000 |
| NV | Nevada | −0.42** | 0.21 | 0.0490 | CA | California | 0.37*** | 0.06 | 0.0000 |
| AK | Alaska | 0.14 | 0.14 | 0.3270 | OH | Ohio | 0.29*** | 0.10 | 0.0040 |
| AL | Alabama | −0.18 | 0.51 | 0.7280 | FL | Florida | 0.28*** | 0.08 | 0.0000 |
| AR | Arkansas | 0.10 | 0.27 | 0.6960 | VA | Virginia | 0.27*** | 0.04 | 0.0000 |
| CA | California | 0.06 | 0.33 | 0.8500 | OR | Oregon | 0.27*** | 0.05 | 0.0000 |
| CT | Connecticut | −0.71 | 0.62 | 0.2470 | MS | Mississippi | 0.26*** | 0.06 | 0.0000 |
| HI | Hawaii | 0.17 | 0.35 | 0.6260 | IL | Illinois | 0.24*** | 0.08 | 0.0020 |
| IA | Iowa | −0.17 | 0.15 | 0.2780 | AL | Alabama | 0.22** | 0.11 | 0.0440 |
| ID | Idaho | −0.40 | 0.39 | 0.3010 | MI | Michigan | 0.22*** | 0.07 | 0.0030 |
| IL | Illinois | −0.38 | 0.35 | 0.2760 | GA | Georgia | 0.17** | 0.08 | 0.0330 |
| KS | Kansas | −0.12 | 0.39 | 0.7540 | SC | South Carolina | 0.13** | 0.05 | 0.0120 |
| KY | Kentucky | 0.45 | 0.34 | 0.1860 | IN | Indiana | 0.13* | 0.08 | 0.0920 |
| MA | Massachusetts | 0.09 | 0.44 | 0.8340 | TN | Tennessee | 0.11*** | 0.02 | 0.0000 |
| MD | Maryland | −0.24 | 0.41 | 0.5570 | MT | Montana | 0.10*** | 0.03 | 0.0000 |
| ME | Maine | 0.28 | 0.49 | 0.5610 | UT | Utah | 0.10*** | 0.04 | 0.0080 |
| MN | Minnesota | 0.15 | 0.39 | 0.7000 | NV | Nevada | 0.07* | 0.04 | 0.0840 |
| MO | Missouri | 0.03 | 0.41 | 0.9390 | ND | North Dakota | 0.06** | 0.03 | 0.0330 |
| MS | Mississippi | −0.48 | 0.36 | 0.1830 | PA | Pennsylvania | 0.05** | 0.02 | 0.0210 |
| MT | Montana | 0.27 | 0.37 | 0.4710 | MD | Maryland | 0.04** | 0.02 | 0.0150 |
| ND | North Dakota | 0.05 | 0.18 | 0.7870 | NJ | New Jersey | 0.04** | 0.01 | 0.0110 |
| NE | Nebraska | 0.11 | 0.24 | 0.6490 | RI | Rhode Island | 0.02*** | 0.01 | 0.0080 |
| NH | New Hampshire | 0.24 | 0.53 | 0.6540 | HI | Hawaii | 0.10 | 0.11 | 0.3610 |
| NJ | New Jersey | −0.41 | 0.41 | 0.3200 | CO | Colorado | 0.08 | 0.07 | 0.2920 |
| NM | New Mexico | −0.75 | 0.51 | 0.1420 | WV | West Virginia | 0.07 | 0.06 | 0.2710 |
| OK | Oklahoma | 0.34 | 0.43 | 0.4270 | WA | Washington | 0.05 | 0.09 | 0.5610 |
| OR | Oregon | −0.39 | 0.27 | 0.1390 | AK | Alaska | 0.03 | 0.10 | 0.7300 |
| RI | Rhode Island | −0.33 | 0.28 | 0.2340 | AR | Arkansas | 0.01 | 0.04 | 0.7550 |
| SC | South Carolina | −0.36 | 0.40 | 0.3650 | WI | Wisconsin | 0.01 | 0.09 | 0.8990 |
| SD | South Dakota | 0.26 | 0.47 | 0.5790 | KS | Kansas | 0.01 | 0.08 | 0.9370 |
| TN | Tennessee | −0.33 | 0.28 | 0.2320 | TX | Texas | 0.00 | 0.06 | 0.9390 |
| TX | Texas | 0.47 | 0.42 | 0.2730 | SD | South Dakota | −0.01 | 0.08 | 0.8680 |
| VA | Virginia | 0.45 | 0.47 | 0.3410 | MA | Massachusetts | −0.01 | 0.07 | 0.8270 |
| WV | West Virginia | −0.03 | 0.18 | 0.8750 | NE | Nebraska | −0.02 | 0.06 | 0.7290 |
| WY | Wyoming | −0.05 | 0.25 | 0.8400 | KY | Kentucky | −0.02 | 0.09 | 0.7860 |
| PA | Pennsylvania | 0.55* | 0.31 | 0.0760 | NH | New Hampshire | −0.04 | 0.05 | 0.3850 |
| DE | Delaware | 0.56* | 0.30 | 0.0640 | VT | Vermont | −0.04*** | 0.01 | 0.0000 |
| NY | New York | 0.62* | 0.34 | 0.0690 | WY | Wyoming | −0.05** | 0.02 | 0.0140 |
| OH | Ohio | 0.70** | 0.29 | 0.0170 | NM | New Mexico | −0.06* | 0.04 | 0.0680 |
| IN | Indiana | 0.76*** | 0.30 | 0.0100 | ME | Maine | −0.07* | 0.04 | 0.0880 |
| VT | Vermont | 0.84** | 0.39 | 0.0300 | NY | New York | −0.07*** | 0.02 | 0.0000 |
| WI | Wisconsin | 1.26*** | 0.33 | 0.0000 | DE | Delaware | −0.08*** | 0.02 | 0.0010 |
| CO | Colorado | 1.58*** | 0.56 | 0.0050 | IA | Iowa | −0.12*** | 0.03 | 0.0000 |
| LA | Louisiana | 1.71*** | 0.32 | 0.0000 | MO | Missouri | −0.19** | 0.10 | 0.0530 |

*Note:* *, **, *** denote 10, 5 and 1 percent significance levels. Standard errors are robust to group (conventional) heteroscedasticity. Uncertainty series from Mumtaz (2018), 1991Q1–2015Q3.

*The effect of uncertainty on housing returns and volatility* 235

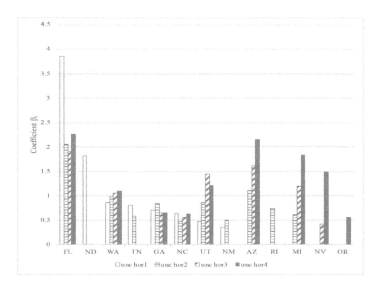

*Note*: *unc hor i* $(i=1,2,..4)$ refer to macroeconomic uncertainty taken from Mumtaz (2018), 1991Q1–2015Q3, for horizons of one to four quarters. $\beta_i$ refers to the slope coefficient in the random-coefficients model, Equation 8.8, with the dependent variable housing returns factor (*fmed*).

*Figure 8B.1A    The impact of macroeconomic uncertainty on housing returns factor, 1991Q1–2015Q3*

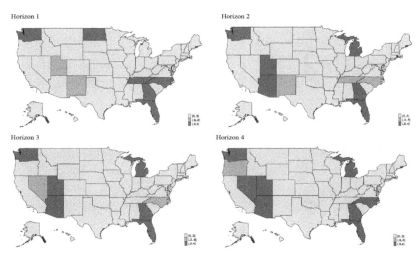

*Source*: Macroeconomic uncertainty data is from Mumtaz (2018), which is available publicly; the visual representations are based on authors' own estimations.

*Figure 8B.1B    The impact of macroeconomic uncertainty on housing returns factor, 1991Q1–2015Q3*

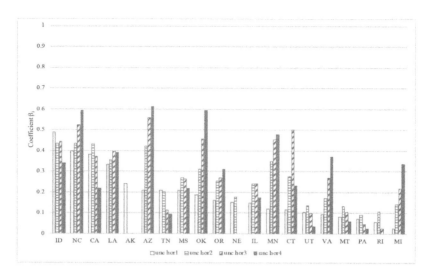

Note: *unc hor i* $(i=1,2,..4)$ refer to macroeconomic uncertainty taken from Mumtaz (2018), 1991Q1–2015Q3, for horizons of one to four quarters. $\beta_i$ refers to the slope coefficient in the random-coefficients model, Equation 8.8, with the dependent variable stochastic volatility (*fmed*).

*Figure 8B.2A*    The impact of macroeconomic uncertainty on stochastic volatility factor, 1991Q1–2015Q3

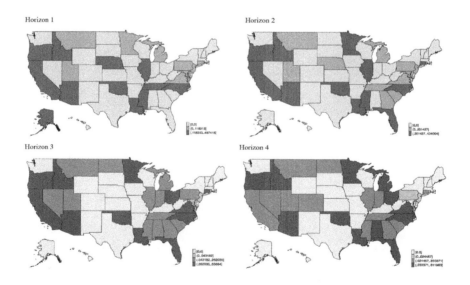

*Source*: Macroeconomic uncertainty data are from Mumtaz (2018), which is available publicly; the visual representations are based on authors' own estimations.

*Figure 8B.2B*    The impact of macroeconomic uncertainty on stochastic volatility factor, 1991Q1–2015Q3

Table 8B.5  Estimation results for state-specific uncertainty coefficient, 1991Q1–2015Q3 (horizon 4)

| | Dependent variable: housing returns factor (*fmed*) | | | | Dependent variable: stochastic volatility (*svmed*) | | | |
|---|---|---|---|---|---|---|---|---|
| State | | Coeff | SE | *p*-value | State | | Coeff | SE | *p*-value |
| FL | Florida | −2.26*** | 0.49 | 0.0000 | AZ | Arizona | 0.61*** | 0.14 | 0.0000 |
| AZ | Arizona | −2.15*** | 0.74 | 0.0040 | NC | North Carolina | 0.59*** | 0.07 | 0.0000 |
| MI | Michigan | −1.83*** | 0.58 | 0.0020 | OK | Oklahoma | 0.59*** | 0.12 | 0.0000 |
| NV | Nevada | −1.49*** | 0.44 | 0.0010 | MN | Minnesota | 0.48*** | 0.13 | 0.0000 |
| UT | Utah | −1.20** | 0.51 | 0.0190 | LA | Louisiana | 0.39*** | 0.12 | 0.0010 |
| WA | Washington | −1.09** | 0.44 | 0.0130 | AL | Alabama | 0.38*** | 0.12 | 0.0020 |
| GA | Georgia | −0.66* | 0.38 | 0.0860 | VA | Virginia | 0.37*** | 0.06 | 0.0000 |
| NC | North Carolina | −0.62** | 0.29 | 0.0310 | OH | Ohio | 0.34*** | 0.11 | 0.0030 |
| OR | Oregon | −0.55* | 0.30 | 0.0680 | ID | Idaho | 0.34*** | 0.08 | 0.0000 |
| AK | Alaska | 0.12 | 0.13 | 0.3310 | MI | Michigan | 0.34*** | 0.11 | 0.0030 |
| AL | Alabama | −0.37 | 0.57 | 0.5130 | FL | Florida | 0.33*** | 0.09 | 0.0000 |
| AR | Arkansas | 0.07 | 0.24 | 0.7680 | OR | Oregon | 0.31*** | 0.05 | 0.0000 |
| CA | California | 0.03 | 0.49 | 0.9480 | CT | Connecticut | 0.23** | 0.10 | 0.0220 |
| CT | Connecticut | −0.38 | 0.70 | 0.5820 | CA | California | 0.22*** | 0.04 | 0.0000 |
| DE | Delaware | 0.30 | 0.46 | 0.5050 | MS | Mississippi | 0.22*** | 0.05 | 0.0000 |
| HI | Hawaii | 0.25 | 0.37 | 0.4920 | NV | Nevada | 0.21*** | 0.08 | 0.0050 |
| IA | Iowa | −0.22 | 0.20 | 0.2790 | GA | Georgia | 0.21** | 0.09 | 0.0200 |
| ID | Idaho | −0.66 | 0.47 | 0.1670 | IN | Indiana | 0.18*** | 0.05 | 0.0010 |
| IL | Illinois | −0.40 | 0.27 | 0.1350 | IL | Illinois | 0.17*** | 0.06 | 0.0050 |
| IN | Indiana | 0.28 | 0.22 | 0.1940 | CO | Colorado | 0.15** | 0.08 | 0.0470 |
| KS | Kansas | −0.13 | 0.53 | 0.8110 | SC | South Carolina | 0.14*** | 0.05 | 0.0080 |
| KY | Kentucky | 0.10 | 0.25 | 0.6900 | TN | Tennessee | 0.09*** | 0.02 | 0.0000 |
| MA | Massachusetts | 0.04 | 0.46 | 0.9270 | MT | Montana | 0.06** | 0.03 | 0.0380 |
| MD | Maryland | −0.22 | 0.39 | 0.5690 | ND | North Dakota | 0.04** | 0.02 | 0.0150 |
| ME | Maine | 0.25 | 0.58 | 0.6640 | UT | Utah | 0.04** | 0.02 | 0.0480 |
| MN | Minnesota | 0.11 | 0.38 | 0.7730 | PA | Pennsylvania | 0.02** | 0.01 | 0.0260 |
| MO | Missouri | 0.22 | 0.44 | 0.6160 | NJ | New Jersey | 0.02* | 0.01 | 0.0980 |
| MS | Mississippi | −0.46 | 0.35 | 0.1880 | HI | Hawaii | 0.07 | 0.11 | 0.5250 |
| MT | Montana | −0.12 | 0.39 | 0.7510 | KY | Kentucky | 0.07 | 0.07 | 0.3390 |
| ND | North Dakota | 0.06 | 0.12 | 0.6250 | WI | Wisconsin | 0.06 | 0.11 | 0.5560 |
| NE | Nebraska | 0.07 | 0.21 | 0.7260 | WA | Washington | 0.06 | 0.09 | 0.4810 |
| NH | New Hampshire | 0.15 | 0.71 | 0.8340 | TX | Texas | 0.06 | 0.06 | 0.3330 |
| NJ | New Jersey | −0.39 | 0.42 | 0.3560 | WV | West Virginia | 0.04 | 0.04 | 0.2740 |
| NM | New Mexico | −0.94 | 0.70 | 0.1820 | MD | Maryland | 0.02 | 0.01 | 0.1030 |
| OK | Oklahoma | 0.48 | 0.49 | 0.3310 | AK | Alaska | 0.02 | 0.10 | 0.8400 |
| PA | Pennsylvania | 0.30 | 0.19 | 0.1180 | AR | Arkansas | 0.01 | 0.03 | 0.7250 |
| RI | Rhode Island | −0.16 | 0.17 | 0.3610 | RI | Rhode Island | 0.01 | 0.01 | 0.1230 |
| SC | South Carolina | −0.38 | 0.43 | 0.3770 | MA | Massachusetts | 0.00 | 0.09 | 0.9860 |
| SD | South Dakota | 0.25 | 0.63 | 0.6940 | KS | Kansas | −0.01 | 0.12 | 0.9220 |
| TN | Tennessee | −0.32 | 0.27 | 0.2460 | SD | South Dakota | −0.02 | 0.11 | 0.8800 |
| TX | Texas | 0.35 | 0.44 | 0.4300 | NE | Nebraska | −0.05 | 0.05 | 0.3450 |
| VA | Virginia | 0.50 | 0.67 | 0.4520 | NH | New Hampshire | −0.05 | 0.05 | 0.3500 |
| WV | West Virginia | −0.01 | 0.12 | 0.9300 | MO | Missouri | −0.08 | 0.10 | 0.4270 |
| WY | Wyoming | −0.23 | 0.37 | 0.5260 | VT | Vermont | −0.05 | 0.02 | 0.0010 |
| NY | New York | 0.79** | 0.33 | 0.0170 | DE | Delaware | −0.06 | 0.03 | 0.0250 |
| OH | Ohio | 0.83** | 0.35 | 0.0190 | NM | New Mexico | −0.07* | 0.04 | 0.0900 |
| VT | Vermont | 1.09** | 0.49 | 0.0260 | NY | New York | −0.08*** | 0.02 | 0.0000 |
| WI | Wisconsin | 1.39*** | 0.43 | 0.0010 | WY | Wyoming | −0.09*** | 0.03 | 0.0050 |
| CO | Colorado | 1.58** | 0.63 | 0.0130 | ME | Maine | −0.13** | 0.06 | 0.0270 |
| LA | Louisiana | 1.81*** | 0.42 | 0.0000 | IA | Iowa | −0.16*** | 0.04 | 0.0000 |

*Note:* *, **, *** denote 10, 5 and 1 percent significance levels. Standard errors are robust to group (conventional) heteroscedasticity. Uncertainty series from Mumtaz (2018), 1991Q1–2015Q3.

Table 8B.6  Estimation results for overall uncertainty impact, using the Jurado et al. (2015) dataset, 1977Q2–2015Q3 (horizons 1 to 4)

|  | (1) | (2) | (3) | (4) | (5) | (6) | (7) | (8) |
|---|---|---|---|---|---|---|---|---|
|  | \multicolumn{4}{c}{Dependent: housing returns factor (*fmed*)} | \multicolumn{4}{c}{Dependent: stochastic volatility (*svmed*)} |
| u1 | −0.406 |  |  |  | −0.386*** |  |  |  |
|  | (−1.26) |  |  |  | (−3.28) |  |  |  |
| u2 |  | −0.740*** |  |  |  | 0.044 |  |  |
|  |  | (−3.15) |  |  |  | (0.21) |  |  |
| u3 |  |  | −0.765** |  |  |  | 0.318 |  |
|  |  |  | (−2.08) |  |  |  | (1.06) |  |
| u4 |  |  |  | −0.894** |  |  |  | 0.475 |
|  |  |  |  | (−2.40) |  |  |  | (1.25) |
| cons | 0.298 | 0.687* | 0.562 | 1.056** | 0.990*** | 0.774*** | 0.463 | 3.74 |
|  | (1.17) | (1.59) | (1.11) | (1.85) | (8.57) | (5.07) | (1.95) | (1.09) |
| Obs | 7854 | 7854 | 7854 | 7854 | 7854 | 7854 | 7854 | 7854 |
| Groups | 51 | 51 | 51 | 51 | 51 | 51 | 51 | 51 |
| $Chi^2(100)$ | 197.51*** | 209.05*** | 208.85*** | 202.37*** | 13009*** | 13105*** | 13238*** | 12977*** |

Note: $t$ statistics in parentheses. $t$ statistics based on standard errors that are robust to group (bootstrap) heteroscedasticity. * $p < 0.10$, ** $p < 0.05$, *** $p < 0.01$. $\chi^2$ is a test for parameter constancy.

Table 8B.7  The Symbolic Transfer Entropy test

| \multicolumn{3}{c}{Panel A Mumtaz (2018) uncertainty data: 1977Q2–2015Q3} |
|---|---|---|
| Direction of causality |  |  |
| $x \to y$ | Test statistic | $p$-value |
| u1 → fmed | 0.0002 | 0.2400 |
| u2 → fmed | 0.0003 | 0.0900 |
| u3 → fmed | 0.0001 | 0.4700 |
| u4 → fmed | 0.0001 | 0.4100 |
| u1 → svmed | 0.0005 | 0.0100 |
| u2 → svmed | 0.0010 | 0.0000 |
| u3 → svmed | 0.0011 | 0.0000 |
| u4 → svmed | 0.0015 | 0.0000 |
| \multicolumn{3}{c}{Panel B Mumtaz (2018) uncertainty data: 1991Q1–2015Q3} |
| Direction of causality |  |  |
| $x \to y$ | Test statistic | $p$-value |
| u1 → fmed | 0.0002 | 0.4200 |
| u2 → fmed | 0.0002 | 0.4100 |
| u3 → fmed | 0.0002 | 0.3600 |
| u4 → fmed | 0.0000 | 0.9100 |
| u1 → svmed | 0.0004 | 0.0600 |
| u2 → svmed | 0.0004 | 0.2100 |
| u3 → svmed | 0.0014 | 0.0000 |
| u4 → svmed | 0.0021 | 0.0000 |
| \multicolumn{3}{c}{Panel C Jurado et al. (2015) uncertainty data: 1977Q2–2015Q3} |
| Direction of causality |  |  |
| $x \to y$ | Test statistic | $p$-value |
| u1 → fmed | 0.0004 | 0.0600 |
| u2 → fmed | 0.0000 | 0.9400 |
| u3 → fmed | 0.0001 | 0.4300 |
| u4 → fmed | 0.0000 | 0.9100 |
| u1 → svmed | 0.0003 | 0.0900 |
| u2 → svmed | 0.0005 | 0.0100 |
| u3 → svmed | 0.0008 | 0.0000 |
| u4 → svmed | 0.0010 | 0.0000 |

Note: $x$ is the independent variable and $y$ is the dependent variable.

# PART III

# FINANCIAL CRISIS AND STRUCTURAL CHANGE

# 9. Financial crisis and the U.S. mortgage markets – a review

*Sumit Agarwal and Sandeep Varshneya*

## 1   INTRODUCTION

The 2007–2008 financial crisis was a severe economic crisis, which affected particularly the United States (U.S.) and, by extension, other parts of the world. In magnitude, many consider it the most severe economic crisis after the Great Depression of the 1930s. In the years leading to the buildup of the financial crisis (hereinafter referred to as 'the financial crisis' or 'the crisis'), the mortgage markets played a large part. In the boom phase, the financial sector extended credit for buying homes to Americans, these mortgages were bundled and sold to investors (securitization), house prices increased and people with weak credit scores also found themselves able to get mortgages (subprime mortgages). Banks and intermediaries indulged in shadow banking and regulatory arbitrage, resulting in their imperfect regulation and buildup of risk in the financial system. Easily available mortgage credit caused home prices to increase and, for a few years, all was well. Then, the bubble burst, with a decline in home prices, defaults in the subprime mortgage sector, and the subsequent collapse of Lehman Brothers. Soon other financial institutions were also affected and then the regulators and the U.S. government stepped in with a series of relief measures and acts aimed at stabilizing the financial system.

In the past 13 years, researchers have studied all aspects of the crisis, beginning with causes of the crisis, its effects on the economy, the efficacy of government interventions and remedies that were introduced to contain the crisis, and finally prescriptions to prevent its recurrence in the future and ways and means to deal with the financial crisis if it recurs. We conduct a selective review to see what the extant literature says about the crisis, with special emphasis on the mortgage markets. Since the U.S. was the epicenter of the crisis and bore the brunt of it, so to speak, and because a large volume of literature deals with the cause and effect of the financial crisis in the U.S. and uses U.S. data, we also focus on the crisis's effect in the U.S. Researchers have gone to great lengths to get the right data and conduct extensive analysis, to reach the right conclusions. This is different from speculation and reporting in the media, which is often based on incomplete analysis and facts. The peer-review process inherent in research ensures that every paper is analyzed and questioned, and only what passes peer muster is accepted and published.

The rest of the chapter is divided as follows. Section 2 details what the extant literature has to say about the causes of the crisis. Section 3 talks about the consequences and effects of the crisis and Section 4 looks at the efficacy of government interventions and policies that were introduced to contain the crisis. Section 5 details economists' views on how to prevent future crises and, if they recur, how to deal with them. Section 6 concludes.

## 2 CAUSES OF THE FINANCIAL CRISIS

The biggest cause of the crisis was probably the inclination of the players in the financial market to make the most of the ongoing trend of increased lending in the mortgage market with the help of securitization, without adequate safeguards for the risks involved. Others also played a role – the regulators, as they were slow to regulate the phenomenon of shadow banking, the credit rating agencies (CRAs) who gave ratings to structured financial products that were perhaps not fully justified, and the consumers themselves who took mortgage loans that they were probably not in a condition to pay back in the long run. Everybody wanted to make the most of the easy credit that was available in the mortgage market. This caused the classic boom-bust scenario. All was well until defaults started happening in the mortgage market and the financial intermediaries most exposed to securitized mortgage lending started facing liquidity problems. With the collapse of Lehman Brothers, the bust truly set in. We look at the various reasons that caused the financial crisis, as mentioned in the extant literature.

### 2.1 Increased and Predatory Lending to Subprime Borrowers

Increased and predatory lending to subprime borrowers is considered to have played a substantial role in the crisis. Mian and Sufi (2009) show that subprime zip codes (zip codes with a large share of subprime borrowers in 1996) had a significantly higher number of mortgage defaults in 2007. In the years 2002 to 2005, these zip codes experienced relatively high growth of mortgage credit and this growth happened despite declining relative income growth in these zip codes. They say that the years 2002 to 2005 were the only period in the past 18 years that showed an increase in mortgage credit despite declining relative income growth. They go on to establish a correlation between the increase in mortgage credit to subprime zip codes and the increase in the securitization of subprime mortgages. Agarwal et al. (2014a) specifically test for predatory lending to subprime borrowers. They make use of a 2006 anti-predatory pilot program in Chicago, where risky mortgage contracts caused counseling and review sessions to happen and the counselors made their findings known to the regulator. This had a significant effect on market activity, reducing it by half. The risky mortgage lenders left the market and the share of the subprime borrowers in the overall mortgage market declined. Their results indicate that predatory lending to subprime borrowers played a role in an increase in their default rates, an increase of approximately one-third.

Both Mian and Sufi (2009) and Agarwal et al. (2014a) show that increased lending to subprime borrowers was accompanied by an increase in their default rates after the onset of the financial crisis. For this to happen, the quality of the subprime mortgages must have been suspect. Demyanyk and Van Hemert (2011) find that this was indeed so. For six years before the financial crisis, the quality of subprime mortgages was declining and the securitizers cannot claim total unawareness of this phenomenon. They further show that the rise and fall of the subprime mortgage market are similar to the boom and bust market scenario, where the uncontrolled rise of the market is followed by its downfall. They say that the problems with the subprime mortgage market could have been uncovered earlier, had it not been for the continuous rise in housing prices from 2003 to 2005.

## 2.2 Securitization of Loans by Banks Led to Reduced Incentives to Screen Borrowers, Increased Foreclosure Probability, and Exacerbated the Crisis

With the onset of securitization, the banks that originated the loans no longer held all of them in their books. Arguably, if the mortgage-originating bank holds the mortgage in its books for the entire period of the mortgage, it would screen the borrower properly, taking into account all hard and soft information about the borrower, and continue to monitor the borrower for the entire period of the mortgage. This is because their default would directly affect the profits of the bank. However, with securitization, this safeguard was diluted. The mortgage-originating bank held only a small portion of the mortgages originated by them in their books. A large portion of these loans was sold to other investors, diluting the responsibility of the originating bank for the quality of these loans, and hence their incentive to properly screen the borrowers was attenuated. In the prime market, where the loans were first sold to government-sponsored enterprises (GSEs) Freddie Mac and Fannie Mae, who further packaged and sold them to investors, this trend was still arrested. That was because the GSEs guaranteed these loans against default, hence their underwriting standards took care of this aspect. However, in the subprime loan market, with no GSEs in between, the investors depended largely on the credit ratings given by the rating agencies. These no longer proved to be adequate safeguards. Brunnermeier (2009) corroborates the above. He says that in the years before the financial crisis, the banking system went through a major changeover. The banks which so far had kept the loans issued by them in their books until repayment started to follow the originate to distribute (OTD) model, where they pooled the loans, divided these pools into tranches, and sold these tranches to other investors, or in other words, securitized them. This practice helped them in getting more funds and in a faster rotation of their funds. However, this also resulted in the slackening of lending standards, as the risk was no longer borne by those who were most capable of bearing it. This also caused a major expansion of credit that supported the growth of housing prices.

In the above chain of events, to begin with, there has to be a relationship between the increase in subprime credit and the securitization of subprime mortgages. Nadauld and Sherlund (2013) find evidence in favor of this. The background for their study is the increase in subprime mortgages in the years 2003 to 2005 and the simultaneous increase in the securitization of subprime mortgages during the same time, especially by the five largest investment banks. They say that this increase in securitization activity by the investment banks was caused by factors not correlated to factors that drive mortgage lending in the primary market and this resulted in growth in subprime loans and the subsequent high defaults. They also show that increased securitization by investment banks diluted their incentives to properly screen subprime borrowers. In keeping with the above trend, one would suspect that with banks that were more active in the securitization market, the quality of their mortgages would be more affected. Purnanandam (2011) finds evidence in favor of this. He shows that banks that were very active in the OTD market, i.e. were originating loans with the primary purpose of securitizing them and getting them off their balance sheets, during the period before the financial crisis severely compromised on the quality of these mortgages. His evidence supports the explanation that this poor quality of mortgages happened because they did not screen their borrowers properly. He finds a stronger effect for those banks that were capital constrained. Thus, his findings support the view that banks especially active in the OTD market compromised on the quality of their mortgages and passed on the related risk to other institutions through securitization. In a related paper, Keys et al. (2010) provide further evidence in this regard.

They compare portfolios with differing ease of securitization with the same risk profile. They find that subject to being securitized, the portfolio with more ease of securitization defaults 10 to 25 percent more than the portfolio with less ease of securitization. However, this is true only for those loans where the soft information about the borrowers played a role in their getting the loan, thus the screening effort expended by the intermediary while evaluating the borrower was important. This evidence points towards intermediaries not putting in enough screening effort when the ease of securitization was high.

FICO scores have played a role in whether a loan will be securitized or not. For historical reasons, loans with a FICO score above 620 had a better probability of being securitized compared to loans with a FICO score below 620. Keys et al. (2012) exploit this fact and establish the channels by which securitization affects screening effort. First, they establish that for low-documentation, non-agency loans, 620+ loans are indeed more likely to be securitized compared to 620− loans. They also find that 620− subprime loans stay on the balance sheet of the lenders for nearly two months longer compared to 620+ loans. They say that this illiquidity may affect the screening effort of the lenders for such loans. They go on to show that low documentation non-agency loans with more ease of securitization default around 20 percent more than loans with less ease of securitization. Their findings are limited to the low documentation part of the subprime market and do not apply to the full documentation part of the subprime market as well as GSE-operated prime markets. Thus, they show that securitization may affect the screening effort of subprime lenders through two channels – the securitization rate (i.e. probability of securitization subject to origination) and time taken to securitize the loan.

Another channel through which securitization could have affected mortgage defaults is inaccurate predictions by statistical models regarding mortgage default risk. The question arises about the accuracy of these models to predict defaults, especially if the assumptions behind the model change drastically, such as during the financial crisis. Rajan et al. (2015) specifically investigate this question. They say statistical models that worked well during the low securitization period may not make the right predictions regarding default risk when the regime changes to a high securitization period, especially for those loans for whom soft information is important. Using data on subprime mortgages between 1997 and 2006, they show that a statistical model fitted on past data predictably understates defaults. They explain this phenomenon by saying that because lenders want to securitize the loan, they are motivated to originate loans that rate high on characteristics reported to investors while not paying enough attention to other characteristics that, though important and affecting loan quality, are not reported to investors. As a result, over a period, the objective of securitizing the loan causes the loan quality to deteriorate, largely with regard to the aspect of unreported information. They go on to show that as securitization increases, the interest rate on a loan is no longer a good predictor of default.

The securitization literature also talks about how securitization of loans resulted in decreased modification probability and increased foreclosure probability, resulting in many Americans losing their homes. Agarwal et al. (2011) explicitly study whether securitization had any effect on the possibility of modification of distressed residential mortgages vis-à-vis their foreclosure, in the context of the financial crisis. They use a database that observes lenders' renegotiation actions and covers 60 percent of the U.S. mortgage market. They compare the renegotiation rates of the bank-held loans vis-à-vis securitized loans and find that bank-held loans are 26–36 percent more likely to be renegotiated, in relative terms. They also find that the modified bank-held loans are 9 percent less likely to default (in relative terms) compared to similar securitized loans. Their results thus suggest that securitized loans are less likely to be modified and, even if modified, are more likely to default compared to similar bank-held loans, thus pointing towards frictions induced by securitization. In a related paper, Piskorski et al. (2010) study the foreclosure rates of bank-held loans as measured against securitized loans. They find that for delinquent loans, the foreclosure rate for bank-held loans is 13 to 32 percent less in relative terms, and this result holds for various specifications and vintages. They also find some heterogeneity in their results – the effect is large for good-quality borrowers and small for poor-quality borrowers. In another paper on this subject, Kruger (2018) uses the unexpected freeze in the securitization of private mortgages in 2007 to study the effect of securitization on foreclosure probability versus modification probability. He finds evidence in favor of foreclosure probability and says that these effects are large even after the Home Affordable Modification Program (HAMP) implementation in 2009. He then studies the contractual terms of service agreements and finds that while servicers can modify loans, their incentives favor foreclosure.

While the above-mentioned papers talk about how securitization of loans resulted in decreased modification probability and increased foreclosure probability, Maturana (2017) goes on to establish that modification of loans helped reduce loan losses. He quantifies the effect of modification on loan performance and finds that compared to the average loss, modification lowered the losses by about 36 percent, which suggests that the marginal benefit of modification is likely more than the marginal cost. He further finds that modifications are more beneficial for borrowers with larger loans, which indicates that modifications are more helpful to borrowers with higher incomes.

Interestingly, Adelino et al. (2013) disagree with the findings of the above papers. They find that securitization did not affect modification probability. They say that modification rates are not much different between securitized and unsecuritized loans, and that the differences are economically small and statistically insignificant for the 2005 to 2011 period. However, overall, they do find a low number of renegotiations during that period. They say that in the year after the first delinquency, lenders reduced monthly payments for about 10 percent of the borrowers and in the initial stages of the financial crisis these numbers are even smaller. They compare their results with Agarwal et al. (2011), saying that paper looked only at 2008 and 2009 data, and when they do the same, their results are comparable with the results of Agarwal et al. (2011).

Securitization affected the mortgage market in other ways. It stands to reason in the years leading to the financial crisis, with securitization being the flavor of the season, that the mortgage contracts that had a high probability of being securitized would abound over those that had a lower probability of being securitized. In this regard, Fuster and Vickery (2015) find securitization affected the origination of fixed-rate mortgages (FRMs). They say that when conditions for the securitization of mortgages are not conducive, the market share of FRMs drop. They link this with the intermediaries not wanting to retain prepayment and interest rate risk, which are an integral part of FRMs. They find that when the private securitization markets are functioning well, the origination of FRMs is not affected. Thus, securitization seems to have played a role in the design of mortgage contracts and allocation and sharing of risk between the players in the mortgage market. This brings us to an interesting question – did the institutions that bought these FRMs during the height of the securitization boom understand the inherent risks of FRMs and were they better equipped to deal with them?

## 2.3 Disclosure of False Information by Intermediaries

Did search for quick profits and the desire to make the most of an ongoing trend lead to false information disclosure by intermediaries and subsequent losses? Given human nature, this was certainly possible. However, did it happen? Evidence points in that direction. Many papers talk about false information disclosure by intermediaries. One way of falsifying information was misrepresenting borrowers' second lien on the property. Piskorski et al. (2015) find that false information disclosure by financial intermediaries regarding borrowers' second lien in the contract documents affected 7 to 14 percent of total loans. They say that loan default for these loans was 70 percent higher than other comparable loans. They find that securities sold by reputable intermediaries also contain these misrepresentations. They go on to say that this caused huge losses, even to large institutions, due to subsequent defaults, reductions in prices, and lowering of ratings; and that pools of loans containing misrepresentations were not sold at a price lower than other comparable pools. In a related paper, Griffin and Maturana (2016a) also investigate the second lien misreporting and find that zip codes that had a high concentration of originators who falsified information regarding the second lien underwent a house price increase from 2003 to 2006 that was 75 percent larger vis-à-vis other zip codes. These zip codes subsequently underwent a house price decrease from 2007 to 2012 which was 90 percent larger when compared to other zip codes. Thus, zip codes with a high concentration of untrustworthy originators underwent huge fluctuations in house prices. This resulted in borrowers with dubious credentials getting mortgage loans and, through their subsequent behavior, causing regional variations in the house prices. Griffin and Maturana (2016b) specifically look at various categories of fraud. They identify three categories within securitized non-agency loans – unreported second charge on the property, wrongly reporting occupancy by the owner, and overappraisal of the property. Astonishingly, they find that as many as 48 percent of the total loans are afflicted by at least one of the above falsifications. They do not find any difference in this misreporting between full-documentation and low-documentation loans. They say that these falsifications increase the probability of delinquency by 51 percent. Interestingly, for unreported second charges on properties, in about two-thirds of the cases, the same originator had issued both first and second charges on the property. They thus provide evidence of apparent fraud by mortgage underwriters and loan originators.

Another line of misinformation was a false declaration about the income of the borrower. Jiang et al. (2014a) highlight two problems that happened during the mortgage crisis – one was reliance on mortgage brokers who originated loans of questionable quality; and the other was a large volume of low-documentation loans, which they say are known in the industry as liar's loans, as the borrower information furnished in these loans is not trustworthy. They find that half the difference in delinquency between the full-documentation loans and low-documentation loans is potentially due to a declaration of false income in the documents.

## 2.4 Lax Ratings by Credit Rating Agencies

No discussion of the causes of the financial crisis is complete without mentioning the role played by CRAs. CRAs have been held responsible for playing a role in the subprime crisis by giving lenient ratings to many securitized structured products during the pre-crisis boom period. A question that arises is what could cause CRAs to compromise their rating integrity, given that that very integrity if compromised can also jeopardize their business model.

Researchers have looked at this aspect theoretically and come up with a couple of reasons. One is the source of their income, i.e. does it depend heavily on issuers vis-à-vis investors; and the other arises out of the intensity of competition, i.e. the desire to get more business may lead to lax ratings. Mathis et al. (2009) say that the business model of CRAs could be at fault, as a major source of their income was issuers rather than investors. In response, CRAs have long argued that since this approach puts their reputation at risk, it is not conducive for them to do so. They test this very hypothesis through a model – do rating agencies care enough about their reputation so as not to compromise their rating integrity? They show that this depends on whether a major part of their income comes from rating complex products or other sources. If it comes from rating complex products, then there is a large probability that they will compromise their rating integrity by inflating their ratings, especially when they have a good reputation. This finally results in the house of cards crumbling down, when a single default can tarnish their reputation. Griffin and Tang (2012) provide empirical evidence that is consistent with the above theory. They analyze 916 collateralized debt obligations (CDOs) and find that a top CRA often made adjustments beyond their model. As a result, the AAA tranche sizes of CDOs were increased although CRAs' model implied a smaller AAA tranche size. CDOs that underwent larger adjustments were subsequently downgraded more severely. Additionally, before April 2007, while 91.2 percent of the CDOs that were rated AAA, as far as CRAs' default rate standard is concerned, they measured only up to their AA rating. Accounting for both of the above, this implied that AAA tranches were structured to BBB support levels, on average.

Bolton et al. (2012) examine competition theory. They say that the conflict of interest within CRAs was magnified by the defaults of AAA-rated securitized structured products in 2007 and 2008. They create a competition model where they look at three sources of conflict: (1) CRAs understating risk to get more business; (2) issuers' ability to buy favorable ratings; and (3) investors trusting the CRAs to give the right rating. They get two results: (1) since the issuer can go shopping for a good rating, competition between CRAs can result in a less than optimal ratings; and (2) especially during boom periods with trusting investors, the integrity of ratings is more likely to be compromised. Becker and Millbourn (2011) provide empirical evidence in favor of competition theory. They find that when Fitch entered the rating market, in what was earlier a duopoly (the rating market was dominated by Moody's and Standard & Poor's), this increased competition resulted in the incumbents compromising on their rating quality. Incumbents started giving higher ratings, market yields were no longer as well correlated with ratings as earlier, and the ratings were relatively worse off in predicting defaults. Ironically, before Fitch's entry, regulators and lawmakers had been calling for more competition in the rating industry. On the subject of competition, Griffin et al. (2013) examine the subject of rating catering, as compared to rating shopping. They look at CDO tranches rated AAA by both Moody's and Standard & Poor's. They find that the AAA-rated tranches rated by both agencies default more frequently when compared to AAA-rated tranches rated by only one of the agencies. They find that when one of the agencies has more lenient assumptions, other agencies makes an upward revision to their model's implied rating. Finally, they look at rating agency interactions and find that when there is disagreement/adjustment between the two agencies regarding the rating, this is reflected in subsequent rating downgrades. This implies that it was not just rating shopping by issuers that was going on. CRAs were also "catering" to their clients, especially in cases of tranches that were rated AAA by both agencies.

After looking at the above papers where it seems that the CRAs have taken advantage of naive investors, He et al. (2012) provide some evidence that investors were not completely naive. They look at mortgage-backed security (MBS) tranches sold by large issuers and small issuers. They find that for both AAA and non-AAA rated MBS tranches, the initial yields on large issuer backed-MBS tranches were higher than similar small issuer-backed MBS tranches during the period 2004 to 2006. They also find that large issuer-backed MBS tranches issued in the period 2004 to 2006 suffered a bigger fall in price compared to small issuer-backed MBS tranches. This indicates that investors were perceptive enough to understand that large issuers received more inflated ratings than small issuers did, especially during the boom period of 2004 to 2006, and they accordingly priced that risk.

## 2.5 Investor Panic, Runs, and Fire Sales Aggravated the Financial Crisis

In the financial sector, the asset–liability maturity mismatch can sometimes prove fatal. In boom times, financial intermediaries tend to expand their asset base taking advantage of the conducive conditions, and this often gets funded by liabilities whose maturity is shorter term compared to asset maturity. Given the boom time, financial intermediaries assume that they are able to roll over their liabilities and they often succeed in doing so. Problems may start occurring in the bust scenario. When the intermediaries are faced with defaults on the asset side, they start finding it difficult to roll over their short-term liabilities. Investors begin to panic and this may cause runs, and if the intermediaries do not have other options, they may resort to fire sales and this may bring the house of cards crumbling down, thus endangering not just the financial sector, but also the real economy.

Shleifer and Vishny (2010) explore a financial market driven by investor sentiment. They propose a theory in which financial intermediaries operate in a market in which investor sentiment plays a major role. In their model, the banks are shown to cater to investor sentiment. When sentiment is high, the banks use their scarce capital to co-invest in securitized loans, and when sentiment is low, they try to either hold on to securities despite falling prices or, if they have funds, they buy the fire sale securities. However, in times of high investor sentiment, the banks borrow short term and invest relatively long term, thus causing an asset–liability mismatch. This carries the risk of fire sales or the need to sell securities prematurely at inefficient prices if the short-term loans taken by them are not renewed. Also, by stretching their balance sheets to the limit at a time of high investor sentiment, the banks forgo the opportunity to buy distressed assets during lower investor sentiment times. Thus, the banking system is subject to some instability because of the inherent investor sentiment-influenced behavior exhibited by the banks. In a related paper, Shleifer and Vishny (2011) emphasize the importance of government interventions, saying that it is important that governments intervene in fire sales in order to prevent them because not doing so can cause severe harm to the financial system. As the banks do not have the ability to access capital and buy fire sale assets, either the government can lend to banks against collateral that seems risky because of falling prices or it can directly buy the assets on fire sale. They support the government helping market participants in buying fire sale securities or directly participating in a fire sale, in preference to governments propping up weak or failing financial institutions. They say that models of fire sales can account for many phenomena observed in the financial crisis, including the shrinking of the banking system and the fact that there was a substantial difference in the prices of similar securities, suggesting that arbitrage did not work in the financial markets.

Some investor panic and runs were perhaps inevitable, given the nature of the financial crisis. Covitz et al. (2013) find that in the last five months of 2007, the asset-backed commercial paper market shrank by $350 billion and this was largely due to runs by investors. They say that within weeks of the start of the asset-backed commercial paper crisis, one-third of the programs experienced a run. There was a higher probability of these runs for weaker programs, such as programs with poorer ratings and weaker liquidity support, and the runs increased as the macro-financial risks increased.

## 2.6 Role of Investors/Flippers/Speculative Buyers

The role of investors and flippers/speculative buyers has also come under scrutiny while enumerating the causes of the financial crisis. Multiple studies document the role of investors and speculators during the financial crisis. Haughwout et al. (2014) document that investor participation in the housing market increased in the buildup to the financial crisis, especially in the states that experienced the largest housing boom-bust cycle. They find evidence of apparent misreporting by investor buyers of their intent to occupy the property. They establish that such misreporting investors bid more aggressively during the boom, paying a margin above the listing price that was 4–8 and 9–16 percentage points higher compared to non-investors and declared investors respectively. They also find that investors defaulted at a much higher rate than owner-occupants after home prices started declining. Bhutta (2015) finds that during the housing boom period leading to the financial crisis, the mortgage inflows from investors tripled and far exceeded the inflows from other segments such as first-time homebuyers, and during the bust, the overall mortgage inflows collapsed and their effect in mortgage debt decline was far greater than expansion in defaults. Agarwal et al. (2016) study the condominium loan market. This market was a significant portion of the total residential market, with 15 percent of the total residential loan originations between 2001 and 2007 and a 15-fold rise in originations during that period. This market also experienced a rise in defaults, with the two-year default rate increasing by 30 times between 2003 and 2007. They find that condominium defaults grew at a faster rate compared to single-family loan defaults, with a default rate that was 12 percent higher than even subprime single-family loan defaults, and the borrowers who were primarily investors defaulted more, particularly when house prices started their declining trend.

Coming to the role of speculation in the financial crisis, Gao et al. (2020) find that housing speculation was responsible for price appreciation and economic expansion witnessed in the 2004–2006 boom period, and it also led to a more severe economic downturn during the subsequent 2007–2009 bust period. Leung and Tse (2017) model the role of flippers (investors who attempt to profit from buying and selling) in the housing market to examine how they contribute to housing price volatility and whether they serve any useful purpose. They model flippers being able to enter and exit en masse in response to interest rate shocks and find that this increases housing price volatility. They find that flipping in a sluggish and illiquid market to increase turnover can be socially beneficial, while flipping in a tight and liquid market can be wasteful due to efficiency gain from faster turnover being unable to offset the loss from more vacant houses in the hands of flippers. Depken II et al. (2009), examining flipping activity in Las Vegas from 2004 to mid-2007, find that as the residential property market in Las Vegas began to flourish, the percentage of flip homes in total sales increased. By 2004, when the housing boom was near its peak, a typical flip produced economic profits of 20 percent, which reduced to zero by 2007. Using data for the Los Angeles area for the period 1988 to 2012, Bayer et al. (2020) document that speculators entered the housing market during the boom phase, bought and sold properties at market prices, and did not anticipate the bust. The sheer magnitude of their activity suggested that these speculators played a non-negligible role in the market. The authors find no indication that speculators who entered the market late in the boom in large numbers had access to superior information.

A couple of studies document the role of private-label mortgage securitization/out-of-town second house buyers in the financial crisis. Mian and Sufi (2018) find that an increase in private-label mortgage securitization in 2003 led to growth in mortgage credit supply by lenders financed with non-core deposits. This resulted in increased transaction volume in areas more exposed to these lenders. A small group of speculators drove this increase, and these areas experienced an amplified housing boom and bust. In another study, Chinco and Mayer (2016), using data for 21 U.S. cities from 2000 to 2007, find that demand from out-of-town second house buyers predicted house price appreciation rates as well as implied to actual rent ratio appreciation (mispricing proxy) rates. They also provide evidence for out-of-town second house buyers buying around the peak of the market and earning lower capital gains compared to local second house buyers.

Finally, Liebowitz (2009) points at the role of speculative buyers during not only the boom but also the bust phase of the housing bubble. He comments that in attempting to increase homeownership in the U.S., many branches of the government encouraged a decline in mortgage underwriting standards, praising it as innovation. While this helped increase homeownership in the U.S., it also led to a housing price bubble and allowed speculators to buy homes without putting their own money at risk. He says that the increase in home prices peaked in the second quarter of 2006 and foreclosures began to rise in the very next quarter. Further, nominal housing prices dropped only by 1.4 percent in the six months from the second quarter of 2006 to the fourth quarter of 2006, yet foreclosure start rates (rates of loans entering the foreclosure process) increased by 43 percent. He further says that this increase in foreclosures was not due to economic recession or a large price drop in homes; with nominal housing prices beginning to decline, speculative buyers found the opportunity for quick profit drying up and, hence, began to default.

## 2.7   Diversification of Risk

In the financial lexicon, diversification of risk has always been an important consideration. Traditionally, investors do not like putting too many eggs in one basket. However, if the investor understands a single investment well enough, that is sometimes better than making multiple but less well-understood investments. Some studies find that diversification reduces risk, at least during normal times. Akhigbe and Whyte (2003) find that after the passage of the Riegle–Neal Act of 1994 (which set the stage for full nationwide interstate banking to become a reality in the U.S.), banks with assets in multiple states experienced a significant reduction in risk while banks with assets in one state experienced no significant change in risk. Deng and Elyasiani (2008) find that geographic diversification is associated with bank holding companies' (BHCs) value enhancement and risk reduction. Goetz et al. (2016) find that geographic expansion of BHCs across U.S. metropolitan statistical areas reduces risk. Their results support the argument that geographic expansion lowers exposure to local risks, resulting in overall reduced risk, and is inconsistent with the argument that geographical expansion enhances overall risk by reducing the ability of BHCs to monitor loans and manage risks. Levine et al. (2020) find that banks' funding costs decrease with increased geographic diversification across U.S. states, which is consistent with geographic diversification facilitating risk diversification.

In contrast, two studies find that in normal times, diversification has an ambiguous effect on risk. Demsetz and Strahan (1997) find that diversification by BHCs does not result in reduced risk due to their lower capital ratios and riskier, potentially more profitable loan portfolios. Chong (1991) finds that interstate banking in the U.S. increases both banks' profitability and their exposure to market risk.

Even during times of financial crisis, it is not clear whether diversification helps reduce risk. In this context, Doerr and Schaz (2020) find that geographically diversified banks maintain a higher loan supply in borrower countries during banking crises and they have a stabilizing effect due to their ability to raise additional funds during times of distress. However, they also show that the positive effects of diversification on loan supply are significantly lower during episodes of global distress, i.e. when a significant share of banks' global portfolio is subject to shocks. In the context of the financial crisis, Loutskina and Strahan (2011) find that geographically concentrated lenders performed better than geographically diversified lenders. They investigate the role of geographical diversification on screening by lenders and find that it led to less screening. Their argument is as follows. Lenders are of two types – concentrated lenders and diversified lenders. Concentrated lenders focus on a few markets and invest more in understanding those markets, obtaining private information, and properly screening their borrowers. Thus, they understand the risk profile of their borrowers better. Diversified lenders operate in many markets, but do not invest much in obtaining private information – their lending decisions are based on publicly available information. They find that concentrated lenders were more profitable, had less variation in their profits, and their stock prices showed less decline during the 2007–2008 financial crisis, as compared to diversified lenders.

To summarize, the relationship between the financial crisis and the diversification of risk is not clear. While diversification of risk may help reduce risk during normal times, during crises times, this relationship may not hold.

## 2.8 Other Causes

In addition to the causes mentioned above, economists have found some other factors that played a role in causing this crisis. Foremost amongst them are the demand-side factors, i.e. the role played by consumers in this crisis. Given the easily available mortgage credit and increasing property prices, it would have been natural for them to avail of it, even if they did not have the long-term ability to repay their mortgage loan, especially when faced with an economic downturn. Mian and Sufi (2011) find that existing homeowners used the opportunity of an increase in home equity to increase their borrowings and that this borrowing explains much of the increase in U.S. household borrowings between 2002 and 2006 and subsequent increase in defaults that happened between 2006 and 2008. They show for every $1 increase in home equity, U.S. households extracted 25 cents and that low credit score households and younger households did more of these borrowings against increased home equity. They say that this borrowing against increased home equity was responsible for an additional $1.25 trillion of household debt between 2002 and 2008 and 39 percent of additional defaults between 2006 and 2008.

Traditionally, banks have depended on deposits from consumers as a source of their funds. The years leading to the financial crisis changed that to a certain extent. Banks also started relying on wholesale funding which typically has shorter maturity but is perhaps easier to roll over in good times. However, wholesale funds arguably have a riskier profile, given their short-term nature. In accordance with the above, Dagher and Kazimov (2015), using data on millions of mortgage loan applications from 1992 to 2010, show that banks that relied more on wholesale funding reduced their credit supply more during the financial crisis as compared to banks that relied more on retail funding. This effect was particularly strong during 2008 and 2009 when market liquidity was significantly affected.

Banks also indulged in regulatory arbitrage, i.e. used off-balance sheet financing to get around the risk-based capital requirements of the regulators. Acharya et al. (2013) investigate asset-backed commercial paper conduits that experienced runs in the early phases of the financial crisis. They show that commercial banks set up conduits to securitize assets worth $1.3 trillion but retained the risk of default as they guaranteed the repayment of these loans. This was done to get around the regulatory requirements of risk-based capital. As a result, they find that banks with more exposure to conduits retained the losses from these conduits instead of the investors and these banks also experienced lower stock returns.

Sanders (2008) examines the role of sophisticated risk management models. He finds a strong relationship between falling housing prices and an increase in seriously delinquent subprime mortgage rates after the year 2005, but not before it, thus implying that sophisticated risk management models based on historical data can be misleading when they do not take care of paradigm shifts. In this context, as mentioned earlier, Rajan et al. (2015) also say statistical models that work well during the low securitization period may not make the right predictions regarding default risk when the regime changes to a high securitization period, especially for those loans for which soft information is important.

Chen and Leung (2008) study the role of land supply elasticity and land use on the financial crisis with the help of a model. They say that sufficiently adverse shocks can cause constrained entrepreneurs to liquidate their assets for debt repayment and this effect can spill over to the residential property market with households also defaulting on their mortgages. Their model establishes that both converting costs and land use regulation tend to enhance the effect of unfavorable shock, with the former affecting positive and negative shock asymmetrically, and the latter raising the threshold value of liquidation and thus increasing the crisis probability.

Finally, since mortgage defaults played a role in the crisis, researchers have studied the factors that cause borrowers to default on their mortgages. Elul et al. (2010) investigate the impact of two factors for mortgage defaults – negative equity and illiquidity – and find that both factors play a significant role in mortgage defaults. They also find that county-level unemployment shocks are correlated with higher default risk and so is having a second mortgage, especially for those mortgage holders for whom the loan to value ratio of the first mortgage is close to 100 percent. Guiso et al. (2013) use survey data to specifically investigate strategic defaults, especially when home equity is negative, i.e. the value of the mortgage is more than the value of the house. They find that as the absolute and relative value of negative home equity increases, the willingness to default increases. Interestingly, they also find that this willingness is influenced by qualitative factors such as fairness and morality. Another interesting finding is that exposure to people who have already strategically defaulted increases the proclivity to do the same because now they have information on how probable it is that they will be sued by their lender. However, Bhutta et al. (2017) have a different take on this subject. They do a detailed investigation of house prices and mortgage data and find that the strategic default behavior of homeowners was much less compared to predictions by traditional models – they did not default unless they were majorly in trouble and unable to pay. They argue that this result could be driven by emotional and behavioral reasons and also find that this behavior was not driven by lender recourse.

## 2.9 Why Did the Housing Bubble Keep Getting Bigger?

A question arises as to what caused the housing price bubble to keep inflating. Why was it not nipped in the bud? Many factors combined to cause the housing bubble to get bigger. According to Holt (2009), a combination of four causes – low mortgage interest rates, low short-term interest rates, relaxed standards for mortgage loans, and irrational exuberance – caused the housing bubble to be more extreme and the resulting credit crisis to be more severe. According to Duca et al. (2010), structured financial innovations like securitized financing of subprime mortgages and overoptimism due to misjudgment of the probability of subprime mortgage defaults, and loss given defaults, in addition to low interest rates and a major easing of mortgage credit standards contributed to the housing price bubble. Brunnermeier (2009) further says that by early 2007, many observers were already concerned about the risk of a bubble but were reluctant to bet against it. He also quotes Citigroup's former chief executive officer, Chuck Prince: "When the music stops, in terms of liquidity, things will be complicated. But as long as the music is playing, you've got to get up and dance. We're still dancing."

Here, it is also relevant to explore what triggered the bust of the housing bubble. As also mentioned before, Liebowitz (2009) points at the possible role of speculative buyers – when nominal housing prices began to decline, speculative buyers found the opportunity for quick profit drying up and began to default.

## 2.10 Causes That Were Not

Any discussion of the causes of the crisis needs to account for all possible causes. Some of these, as mentioned above, find support in the literature. However, there are also some other possible causes that have been investigated by researchers and found wanting.

*Theory 1: Homebuilders contributed to the formation of the housing bubble and the ensuing foreclosure crisis by extending unconventional mortgage products to borrowers with less than stellar credit histories.*

Agarwal et al. (2014b), using loan-level data from 2001 to 2008, show that homebuilders financing affiliates do give loans to borrowers with a riskier profile and a bigger share of their loans have risky characteristics. However, their 12 month and 24 month delinquency rates are lower when compared to other lenders. Some of the potential explanations that they offer for this surprising phenomenon are that homebuilders have more information about their borrowers; a better understanding of the collateral; self-selection of borrowers that stems from the sometimes lengthy period between downpayment by the borrower and their getting possession of the property; better management of risk in their loan underwriting, which can be attributed to dependence on capital markets for their funding requirements; and the nature of their housing projects, which are often multi-stage.

*Theory 2: Lenders could have incentives to take advantage of their unobservable private information about borrowers and retain higher-quality loans on their balance sheets while selling inferior-quality loans.*

Now, the above-mentioned reason would hold only if the investors were naive and unaware of this moral hazard problem. It turns out that they were very much aware of this problem and took steps to defend themselves against it, but could not completely safeguard themselves. Using data from a major national mortgage lender, Jiang et al. (2014b) find that loans kept by banks on their balance sheets ex post show higher delinquency rates as compared to loans sold by them. They also find that this gap is wider for those loans that are perceived to be easier to resell. They model this seemingly counter-intuitive result by saying that this is mostly a result of information about the loans that is revealed to the investors after loan origination but prior to the sale. Thus, in their model, the investors have an information advantage over the bank, because they can take advantage of the information that was revealed after the loan origination. In a similar vein, Agarwal et al. (2012) look at the prime mortgage market and find that banks kept higher default risk loans on their balance sheet and sold the lower default risk loans to investors. However, their reason for this differs from Jiang et al. (2014b). They say that prime lenders typically sold their loans to GSEs, Freddie Mac and Fannie Mae, who in turn sold it to investors. GSEs guarantee their investors against default risk. As a result, their underwriting standards could be expected to guard against loans with high default risks.

However, this did not prevent the banks from playing this another way. Agarwal et al. (2012) also find that the same banks kept loans with low prepayment risk on their books while selling loans with high prepayment risks to investors. They say that in the pre-crisis boom years, this would have been a profitable strategy because prepayment risk was a bigger concern compared to default risk. However, closer to the financial crisis, when defaults became a bigger concern, the banks became less inclined to trade prepayment risk for default risk. Interestingly, in the subprime loan market, when the retained loans and securitized loans are compared, they do not find a significant difference in default risk and prepayment risk.

## 3  CONSEQUENCES OF THE CRISIS

The consequences of the financial crisis have been extensive, especially for the U.S. It caused a decrease in employment, reduction in consumer credit leading to a drop in consumer spending, diminishing investment, and foreclosure-induced increase in crime and deteriorating mental health for Americans. Reduction in house values resulted in loss of wealth, and for many Americans it led to the loss of their homes. It also affected the lending practices of the banks, with a decrease in cross-border lending.

### 3.1   Increase in Unemployment

In the immediate aftermath of the financial crisis, unemployment in the U.S. increased. Mian and Sufi (2014) find a strong relationship between the decline in housing net worth and the sharp decline in U.S. employment in the years 2007 to 2009. They divide job losses into job losses in the tradable sector (industries with significant exports/imports) and non-tradable sector (retail sector and restaurants). They find that counties that suffered a large decline in housing net worth also suffered significantly higher job losses in the non-tradable sector. They find a 3.7 percent decline in non-tradable employment for every 10 percent decline in housing net worth. They conjecture that since the tradable sector depends largely on national and international demand, the relationship between the decline in housing net worth and job losses in the tradable sector should be significantly weaker, and they find that indeed this is so. They find zero correlation between the two. They do not find much evidence of labor wage decline in relation to the housing net worth shock. They also test for labor mobility from counties affected by large housing net worth decline to those that are less affected and do not find evidence in its favor.

In this context, Kehoe et al. (2019) build a model where credit tightening raises the cost of investing in new job vacancies, resulting in the reduction of job-finding rates and employment. In the quantified version of their model, human capital accumulation on the job increases the duration of the benefit flows from posting vacancies, which amplifies the drop in employment from credit contraction by a factor of ten relative to the standard model. This is consistent with the financial crisis phenomenon of U.S. regions that experienced large declines in household debt also experiencing large drops in consumption, employment, and wages. On a related note, Chodorow-Reich (2014) examines unemployment at firms that took credit from less healthy lenders. He finds that post-Lehman Brothers bankruptcy, such firms had less probability of getting credit, and even if they did, it was at higher interest rates and they cut employment more compared to firms that were clients of healthy lenders pre-crisis. They say that this effect can explain one-third to one-half of the drop in employment in small and medium firms in the year after Lehman's bankruptcy. However, they also find that this effect is limited to small and medium firms and do not find any effect on large or highly transparent firms.

## 3.2  Decrease in Consumer Credit and Consumer Spending

Not surprisingly, the financial crisis affected credit availability to consumers. It appears to have affected the most vulnerable households the most. Mian et al. (2013) find that zip codes that have poorer households and households with larger debt burdens have a significantly greater tendency to consume more out of their housing wealth. They also find that zip codes that experienced a larger decrease in wealth, especially those with poorer and larger debt burden households, sustained a greater cut in credit limits and credit scores, and had more difficulty in refinancing their debt. Thus, their findings show why a reduction in consumer credit between 2006 and 2009 varied across the geography of the U.S. Ramcharan et al. (2016) show that the slump of the asset-backed securities market between 2007 and 2009 resulted in a decrease in credit to consumers, more so amidst credit unions that were weakly capitalized before the start of the crisis. This market slump also caused a decline in consumer credit for mortgages and automobiles.

Given that the U.S. is a consumer debt-driven economy, a decline in consumer credit was bound to affect consumer spending. Mian and Sufi (2010) show that U.S. counties with a greater rise in household leverage between 2002 and 2006 exhibited a large relative decrease in consumption of durables from the third quarter of 2006, more than a year before the start of the recession in the fourth quarter of 2007. They also find that counties with the largest credit card borrowings showed a larger relative decrease in consumption of durables after the onset of the financial crisis. In a related paper, Dynan et al. (2012) also find a link between household leverage and consumer spending during the years of the financial crisis. They say that house owners with higher leverage exhibited a greater decrease in consumer spending in the 2007 to 2009 period, despite their net worth changes being small. They thus say that wealth effects alone cannot explain the decline in consumer spending and household leverage had a role to play beyond the wealth effects. They further show that the decrease in household leverage over the years has been limited and say that decreasing it to norms prevalent before the crisis could be a time-consuming affair.

### 3.3    Decreased Investment in Future Housing

Given that house prices decreased during the financial crisis, this was bound to affect future investment in housing. Melzer (2017) finds a downward effect on home improvement spending. He finds that homeowners with negative home equity and those at risk of default reduce home improvements significantly and also cut back on mortgage principal payments, even when they do not appear to have financial constraints. He says that this happens because, in cases of default and possession of the property by the bank, a good portion of home improvement benefit may accrue to the bank. He also finds that homeowners at risk of default do not stop buying home appliances, furniture, and automobiles, as these would stay with them even after foreclosure.

### 3.4    The Foreclosures Contagion Effect

With the onset of the financial crisis, as housing prices declined, homeowners defaulted on their mortgages and foreclosures increased. This increase in foreclosures depressed property prices and also affected neighborhood crime rates and the mental health of Americans, especially those who lost their homes to the foreclosure process or were in imminent danger of doing so. In this section, we review the literature on the foreclosure contagion effect.

#### 3.4.1    Effect of foreclosures on market price and additional defaults in the neighborhood

Many papers document the effect of foreclosures in lowering the market price of houses in the neighborhood, especially during the time of the financial crisis. Mian et al. (2015) show that foreclosures led to a large decline in house prices, residential investment, and consumer demand from 2007 to 2009 in the U.S. Using data for St. Louis County, Missouri for the period 1998 to 2007, Rogers and Winter (2009) study the impact of foreclosures on nearby housing sales and find a decline in prices of neighboring sales. Using U.S. data for the period 1989 to 2007, Harding et al. (2009) find that foreclosures reduce the prices of nearby non-distressed sales through a contagion effect. The peak discount is roughly 1 percent per nearby foreclosed property and they associate the reduction in price for immediate neighbors with deferred maintenance and neglect of foreclosed properties.

The following three papers study the effect of foreclosure on market prices of houses in the neighborhood in different parts of the U.S. and find that foreclosure at a distance of 0.05/0.10 miles lowers the price of a house by about 1 percent or so. Using data for Massachusetts for the period 1987 to 2009, Campbell et al. (2011a) find that foreclosed houses or those houses that are sold around the time of death/bankruptcy of the seller are sold at prices 27 percent lower than other comparable properties, on average. They also find that foreclosures taking place in the neighborhood of a house lower the price at which it is sold – a distance of 0.05 miles lowers the price of a house by about 1 percent. Using data for 15 large metropolitan statistical areas in the U.S. for the period 2001 to 2010, Gerardi et al. (2015) find that properties with seriously delinquent loans within 0.1 miles decrease transaction prices of non-distressed properties by approximately 1 percent on average. Using data for Chicago for the period 2000 to 2011, Hartley (2014) estimates that each extra unit of the supply of foreclosed property decreases prices within 0.05 miles by about 1.2 percent.

Anenberg and Kung (2014) go a step further and examine the mechanism behind how foreclosures caused a drop in property prices. Using a dataset on residential properties listed for sale in the San Francisco, Washington, DC, Chicago, and Phoenix metro areas from January 2007 to June 2009, first, they provide evidence that foreclosures have a negative causal effect on home prices. They then divide this effect into two: (1) competition, meaning foreclosures increase salable properties in the market and thus have a downward impact on prices; and (2) disamenities, meaning since foreclosed properties are poorly maintained and subject to vandalism, they may become an eyesore causing nearby properties to become less attractive to buyers. They identify the causal effect by showing the response of sellers to real estate-owned (foreclosed-upon real estate in a lender's portfolio) listings in the same week of the listing. They find that competition effects are important in all neighborhoods, but the disamenities effect is important in less affluent neighborhoods with a high density of homes.

Finally, Towe and Lawley (2013) find that foreclosures can also play a role in causing more foreclosures in the neighborhood. Using data for Maryland for the period 2006 to 2009, they find that a neighboring foreclosure increases the hazard of additional defaults by 18 percent.

### 3.4.2 Effect of foreclosures on crime

Theoretically, foreclosures may affect crime rates as vacant or abandoned properties may not be adequately protected and are thus prone to vandalism. To the extent that foreclosures affect disadvantaged sections of the society, this may cause them to indulge in crime, either to vent their frustration or just to tackle their newly enhanced poverty due to the loss of their homes because of foreclosures. Using data from different cities in the U.S., the following five papers investigate the link between foreclosures and crime rates during the time of financial crisis.

Using data for 5517 census tracts within 50 large U.S. cities for the period 2007 to 2009, Baumer et al. (2012) find that high neighborhood foreclosure rates yield elevated robbery rates, primarily in cities with relatively low foreclosure rates and high levels of socioeconomic disadvantage. Using data for Chicago for the period 1998 to 2009, Williams et al. (2014) find that completed foreclosures temporally lead to property crimes and not vice versa, and further, more completed foreclosures during a year both increase the level of property crime and slow its decline subsequently. Using data for Indianapolis for the period 2003 to 2008, Stucky et al. (2012) find that foreclosures are a robust predictor of crime and exhibit consistent positive effects on indices of overall, property, rape, aggravated assault, and burglary counts. Using data for New York City for the period 2003 to 2010, Ellen et al. (2013) find that additional foreclosures on a block face lead to additional total crimes, violent crimes, and public order crimes. On a different note, Cui and Walsh (2015), using data for Pittsburgh, Pennsylvania for the period 2005 to 2009, find that while foreclosure alone does not affect crime, violent crime rates increase by roughly 19 percent once the foreclosed home becomes vacant – an effect that increases with length of vacancy.

### 3.4.3   Effect of foreclosures on health

Past literature has also linked foreclosures with deteriorating mental health for Americans. We quote here four studies that link foreclosures during the time of financial crisis in the U.S. to depression, psychological distress, and increased hospital visits, two studies that link foreclosures to increased suicide rate, and one study that synthesizes the evidence regarding the effect of foreclosure on health from 40 other studies.

Using data from Detroit, Michigan, for the period 2008 to 2010, McLaughlin et al. (2012) find that foreclosures were associated with an increased rate of symptoms of major depression, suggesting that the foreclosure crisis may have had adverse effects on the mental health of the U.S. population. In a similar vein, Yilmazer et al. (2015) use data from the Panel Study of Income Dynamics for 2007–2011 and find that the decline in housing wealth is associated with a small but statistically significant increase in psychological distress. Houle (2014), using data from 2245 counties in 50 U.S. states for the period 2006 to 2011, finds that not only is the rise in a county's foreclosure rate associated with a decline in residents' mental health, but this association is also especially pronounced in counties with a high concentration of low socioeconomic status and minority residents. Currie and Tekin (2015) link foreclosures with hospital visits. Using data for the states of Arizona, California, Florida, and New Jersey for the period 2005 to 2009, they find that living in a neighborhood with a spike in foreclosures is associated with significant increases in urgent unscheduled visits to hospitals, including increases in visits for preventable conditions.

Regarding the link between foreclosures and suicide rates, Houle and Light (2014), using data from all 50 U.S. states and Washington, DC, for the period 2005 to 2010, find that the foreclosure crisis has likely contributed to increased suicides, independent of other economic factors associated with the recession. In a similar vein, using data from 16 U.S. states for the period 2005 to 2010, Fowler et al. (2015) find that foreclosure-related suicides increased 253 percent from 2005 to 2010.

Finally, Downing (2016), synthesizing evidence from 40 studies, finds that experiencing foreclosure and living near foreclosures is associated with poor psychological and behavioral morbidities, namely anxiety and violent behavior, and declining health utilization. She cautions, however, that evidence is sparse on suicide, substance abuse, somatic morbidities, and mortality.

### 3.5   Dip in Homeownership

Homeownership is deep-seated and is viewed as a symbol of economic achievement in the American culture. Homeownership in the U.S. has traditionally been encouraged through many federal and state policies. However, the loss of homes for many Americans because of the financial crisis had a deep-rooted impact. It affected future homeownership, which touched new lows and was somewhat indicative of skepticism regarding future homeownership.

According to Gabriel and Rosenthal (2015), from 1970 to the mid-1990s, U.S. homeownership rates varied between 64 and 65 percent, were flat at 64 percent between 1985 and 1995, and then rose to a historic high of over 69 percent in late 2006. However, after the financial crisis in 2007, homeownership rates fell to 65 percent in early 2013. They further investigate and find that the dampening effect of local house price volatility on homeownership decreased between 2000 and 2005 and increased following the financial crisis. They argue that this is suggestive of households becoming more risk-loving during the boom and more risk-averse during the subsequent market downturn. Acolin et al. (2016) examine the impact of borrowing constraints on homeownership in the U.S. after the 2008 financial crisis and estimate that the homeownership rate in the 2010 to 2013 period was 2.3 percentage points lower than if the borrowing constraints were set at the 2001 level. Lindblad et al. (2017) specifically examine the impact on low-income renters. They use U.S. panel data for the period 2004 to 2014 and find that the financial crisis is negatively associated with home-buying intentions and home purchases. They further find that the negative shift in home-buying intentions is magnified for older low-income renters aged 35+ years. Younger low-income renters report the highest level of home-buying intentions pre- and post-crisis, yet their home-buying intentions also decline.

### 3.6 Changes in Banking Practices Consequent to the Financial Crisis

The financial crisis was bound to affect the lending practices and capital levels of the financial institutions globally. It had a decreasing effect on cross-border lending and the regulatory changes caused the banks to hold more capital and arguably improved aggregate bank stability.

Cerutti and Claessens (2017) find that international banks greatly reduced direct cross-border and local affiliates' lending as the financial crisis strained their balance sheets, lowered borrower demand and altered government policies, and that these reductions were largely in line with markets' assessments of banks' vulnerabilities. On similar lines, Bremus and Fratzscher (2015) find that cross-border bank lending decreased and the home bias in the credit portfolio of banks rose sharply after the financial crisis, especially among banks in the euro area. While Claessens and van Horen (2015) also find that cross-border lending has fallen sharply since the crisis, foreign bank presence, i.e. "brick-and-mortar" operations, declined to a lesser extent. Documenting the impact of the financial crisis on banking globalization, they find that banks in the Organisation for Economic Co-operation and Development (OECD) reduced their presence (though still controlling 89 percent of foreign banks' assets), while non-OECD banks more than doubled theirs. Banks from countries facing systemic crises exited markets that are more distant and curtailed their subsidiaries' growth. Banks were more likely to sell smaller, more recent investments and enter closer and more important trading partners, shunning crisis and euro area countries. McCauley et al. (2019) find that decline in cross-border banking since 2007 was not a broad-based reduction in international lending. They show that this supposedly global shrinkage of bank positions was actually driven by European banks. Global footprints of other banking systems, especially Japanese, Canadian, and U.S. banks, actually increased after 2007.

Regulatory changes caused banks to hold more capital and arguably improved their ability to withstand financial stress. Adrian et al. (2018) find that after the financial crisis, the total balance sheet capacity of U.S. banks as measured by total balance sheet size declined, regulatory reforms increased the quantity and quality of regulatory capital held by banks, and liquidity requirements enhanced the liquidity profile of banks and improved their ability to withstand liquidity shocks arising from financial and economic stress. Schoenmaker (2017) examined capital levels of global systemically important banks after the financial crisis and found a substantial increase in capital levels but with uneven distribution. China and the U.S. led with leverage ratios (Tier 1 capital divided by total assets) of around 7 percent for their large banks, whereas Europe and Japan trailed with ratios between 4 and 5 percent.

Vallascas et al. (2017) examine the effect of board independence on bank risk-taking after the financial crisis. Using global data on large banks for the period 2004–2014, they find that after 2009, an increase in board independence led to more prudent bank risk-taking compared to the rest of the sample period, but only for the group of banks who benefited from a government bailout during the financial crisis.

Finally, Fratzscher et al. (2016) analyze the effect of post-crisis tightening in supervision and regulation on bank stability and credit growth. Using data for 50 advanced and emerging market economies for the period 2003 to 2013, they find that higher capital buffers improved aggregate bank stability after the financial crisis, and strengthening of supervisory independence helped reduce the decline in domestic credit and improved bank stability.

## 4 REMEDIES

To tackle the financial crisis, the U.S. government introduced several measures. Chief amongst them were the Home Affordable Refinance Program (HARP), HAMP, Dodd–Frank Act, Cash for Clunkers program, Economic Stimulus Act of 2008, and Troubled Asset Relief Program (TARP). Economists have looked at the efficacy of these programs and their success in meeting the stated policy objectives. The general findings are that while most programs were successful in meeting their objective to some extent, many of them were not able to reach out to their entire targeted constituency.

The 2009 HAMP incentivized servicers financially to renegotiate mortgages with homeowners. This was done to reduce foreclosures and provide relief to homeowners. Agarwal et al. (2017b) examine the efficacy of HAMP and find that while HAMP did increase renegotiations and prevented many foreclosures, it was able to reach only one-third of the intended recipients. This was largely because some intermediaries, due to factors that were specific to them, did not implement the program fully. Factors such as organizational capacity and poor infrastructure hampered their efforts. However, overall, HAMP resulted in fewer foreclosures, delinquencies, and increased spending on consumer durables. The U.S. government also launched HARP in 2009, to make the mortgage market more accessible to borrowers. This program gave government credit guarantees on new loans to eligible borrowers with insufficient home equity to enable them to refinance their agency mortgages. Agarwal et al. (2015) examine the efficacy of this program and find that HARP resulted in a significant increase in refinancing. More than 3 million borrowers made use of this program, reducing their interest rate by 1.4 percent on average, resulting in average annual savings of $3500. Borrowers also increased their spending on durables, with the effect stronger for borrowers with more debt. Regions where HARP was implemented in a better manner experienced a higher increase in consumer spending, better house price improvements, and fewer foreclosures. However, competitive frictions played a role in reducing the program's impact, resulting in the reduction of take-up rate by 10 to 20 percent and a reduction in annual savings by $400 to $800 amidst those who refinanced. The borrowers with the highest debt were affected the most by these frictions. Agarwal and Zhang (2018) study the effect of the Capital Purchase Program of the year 2008 TARP that invested $205 billion in the financial system. They say that when faced with liquidity constraints, the design of the servicing agreement causes the mortgage servicers to choose foreclosure over modification. They theorize that increase in liquidity should reverse this phenomenon. They find that TARP helped increase modification rates by about 50 percent. Hsu et al. (2018) examine the effect of unemployment insurance (UI) on house prices and find that UI helped in preventing mortgage default by the unemployed. They quantify this effect and say that 1.3 million foreclosures were prevented in the period 2008 to 2013 by UI and this effect was two-thirds more than HAMP and HARP combined. They also find that the effect was strongest for single- and zero-savings households. UI had a direct stabilizing influence on house prices, especially in areas with increasing unemployment. Also, to the extent that UI prevented deadweight losses associated with foreclosures like undermaintenance and vandalism, UI had an indirect stabilizing influence on house prices. Campbell et al. (2011b) study the Term Asset-Backed Securities Loan Facility, created by the Federal Reserve in 2008, which offered loans to investors to purchase certain newly issued AAA-rated asset-backed securities that were non-recourse and collateralized only by securities being purchased. They find that this program did not affect the prices of individual securities. However, it did decrease the interest rate spread for certain classes of securities. Thus, the program had some positive impact on the financial markets. They also find that due to the program structure that included the rejection of riskiest securities, the probability of loss to the U.S. government was limited.

For some of the programs, the effect was not long-lasting. Probably, the design of the program itself introduced that possibility. Two such programs were the economic stimulus payments (ESPs) of 2008 and the 2009 Cash for Clunkers program. Parker et al. (2013) study the effect of ESPs on household spending. There was variation in ESPs received by various households, in timing, in the method of disbursement, and amount. Single individuals received between $300 and $600, while couples received between $600 and $1200, and couples with children qualifying for child tax credit received $300 more. They find that households spend 50 to 90 percent of the ESPs received by them within three months, out of which 12 to 30 percent was on consumer non-durables. In terms of heterogeneity of response, the effects were stronger for lower-income, older, and homeowning households. They also find some spending response in the subsequent three-month period. Mian and Sufi (2012) study the effect of the 2009 Cash for Clunkers program on auto purchases. Under this program, car dealers were paid $3500 to $4500 by the government for every old, less fuel-efficient vehicle traded in by customers and replaced by a newer, more fuel-efficient vehicle. They find that the program caused an additional 370,000 cars to be sold in July and August 2009. However, this effect was largely reversed in the 10 months after the expiry of the program, with high clunker counties making fewer auto purchases. They also find that the Cash for Clunkers program did not influence house prices, household default rates, or employment in the cities more exposed to the program.

Sometimes, government policies may not have the desired effect. Agarwal et al. (2018a) find that banks pass on credit expansions least to those who want to borrow the most, thus limiting the efficacy of government policies that involve banks as an intermediary in credit expansions. They estimate the banks' marginal propensity to lend (MPL) and the borrowers' marginal propensity to borrow (MPB) in the credit card market. They find that the borrowers' MPB declines with credit score, while for the banks, for the lowest FICO score customers, increasing credit limits majorly limits banks' profit from lending. Now since these two effects are at odds with each other, using banks to pass on credit expansions may not result in the benefits reaching the intended recipients, i.e. those with low credit scores who need to borrow the most.

There is some evidence that homeowners took undue advantage of some government policies. Mayer et al. (2014) examine whether the announcement of mortgage modification programs influenced strategic defaults by homeowners. They use the setting of the 2008 settlement of U.S. government lawsuits against Countrywide Financial Corporation, which agreed to offer modifications to delinquent mortgage holders. They find that immediately after the settlement's announcement, Countrywide's monthly delinquency rate increased relatively by 10 percent. They also find that a large part of this increase was by those mortgage holders who were otherwise not likely to default.

Researchers have also looked at the interplay of legislative actions by politicians and their constituents and strategic action by financial institutions to curry political favor. Agarwal et al. (2018b) look at the politics of foreclosure. They use the setting of the U.S. House of Representatives Financial Services Committee considering important banking reforms from 2009 to 2010. They find that during this period foreclosure starts were delayed in the districts of the committee members by half a month relative to the 12-month average. This was despite there being no difference in delinquency rates between the districts of committee members vis-à-vis non-committee members. They also estimate the cost of this delay and find that it exceeds the campaign contributions to the committee members by the largest mortgage servicing banks. In a similar vein, Mian et al. (2010) study the effect of constituents, ideology, and special interests on congress voting on two important legislations in the U.S., in the context of the financial crisis. These two acts were the American Housing Rescue and Foreclosure Prevention Act of 2008 (FPA) and the Emergency Economic Stabilization Act of 2008 (EESA). The FPA provided up to $300 billion in Federal Housing Administration insurance for renegotiated mortgages and unlimited support for Freddie Mac and Fannie Mae. The EESA enabled the Treasury to capitalize troubled banks by directly investing in their new equity; and in severely distressed MBSs, to the tune of $700 billion. They find that U.S. representatives whose constituencies saw major growth in mortgage defaults were more likely to support the FPA, especially if the defaulters belonged to their party. They also find that higher campaign contributions from the financial industry increased the probability of the representatives supporting the EESA. However, ideologically conservative representatives were less likely to be swayed by these factors.

## 5  TACKLING THE FUTURE CRISIS

Economists have explored ways and means of preventing and tackling the future crisis. Some researchers have explored optimal mortgage design. Others talk about optimal government policy to prevent and solve crisis situations. Some others emphasize the advantages of financial education.

Piskorski and Tchistyi (2010) study optimal mortgage design in a setting where the market interest rate has a random probability distribution, individual income is not publicly visible, foreclosure is a costly option for the borrower, and the borrower is risky and has to be incentivized to repay their debt. They show that under these conditions, the optimal contract has features that are consistent with the option adjustable-rate mortgage. Under this contract, the borrower can increase their debt by not paying interest, however, only up to a certain limit. After that, they are considered to be in default and the lender forecloses, which is costly for the borrower. As a result, the borrower finds it optimal to use their excess income to make interest payments and loan repayments. Thus, this contract takes care of the income variability of the borrower. Piskorski and Tchistyi (2011) further assume that the house price is stochastic. The terms of the optimal contract now also depend on economic conditions. In boom time, when house prices and interest rates are both increasing, the credit limit (the maximum borrowing against the house) increases along with the house price, and the least credit-worthy borrowers are given an interest rate cut. In bust time, mortgages get modified, with interest rate reduction, balance write-offs, and lowering of the credit limit; and foreclosures for the least credit-worthy borrowers. The terms of the modification depend on borrowers' income and loan balance. Fuster and Willen (2017) provide empirical evidence that reducing monthly payments can indeed help in reducing defaults, by showing that reducing the monthly required payment by half can reduce the default hazard by 55 percent; the effects are larger for borrowers who have large negative home equity, and these effects are slightly stronger for borrowers with low credit scores. They also find that cutting monthly payments increases the probability of curing a default. Piskorski and Seru (2018) look at a combination of ex ante and ex post solutions, to account for both booms and bust. They say that the optimal contract will be an automatically indexed mortgage with features that enable quick implementation of debt relief in a crisis. The mortgage terms would be linked to local indicators, as economic conditions are not the same across all geographies.

While the above papers focus on mortgage design, optimum contracts, and the effect of reducing monthly mortgage payments in a crisis, Eberly and Krishnamurthy (2014) and Diamond and Rajan (2011) talk about government policies that would be effective in handling a financial crisis. Eberly and Krishnamurthy (2014) develop a policy framework to guide government policy in response to a distressed mortgage-induced financial crisis. They talk about three aspects of mortgage modification to support distressed mortgages in a bust situation. First, government resources should support liquidity in a crisis, in the sense that monthly mortgage payments should get reduced for the period of the crisis rather than the whole life of the mortgage. Second, financial institutions should voluntarily reduce the debt of the borrowers, as this would be in their long-term best interests and would reduce strategic default. Finally, a well-designed mortgage contract should automatically reduce payments during recessions and reduce debt when home prices fall. Diamond and Rajan (2011) model the financial system. They say that there would be financial institutions (banks) with substantial short-term liabilities and they would have significant assets with a limited potential buyer pool. Also, with some probability, the banks would need liquidity in the future, which may be due to the liquidity needs of bank customers. There may be a run on the banks and this may result in fire sales, which the banks may try to avoid. Thus, in any financial crisis, there is some probability of adverse feedback and that is why the role of the government in a financial crisis becomes important. The authorities may need to stabilize the system by making liquidity available to potential buyers, or by moving distressed assets into safer hands. They could also recapitalize distressed banks and provide liquidity to them to meet their liquidity needs.

In addition to optimum mortgage design and effective government policies, yet another way to prevent/tackle the crisis is the financial education of potential mortgage holders. Agarwal et al. (2010) study the effect of a voluntary financial education program on default rates within program graduates. The program studied by them was run by the Indianapolis Neighborhood Housing Partnership, designed to assist low- and moderate-income households in their effort to own a home sustainably and also to improve their financial literacy, and involved a series of one-on-one counseling sessions, over two years. They find lower default rates amongst program graduates and this effect was stronger for graduates with low credit scores and income, but who were granted loans based on soft information gathered during counseling sessions. Finally, they find that the effects of counseling tended to persist over time, showing that preparing low-income households for homeownership through financial counseling pays dividends and sustains them through economic shocks. On a related note, Agarwal et al. (2017a) find that finance professionals are 16 percent less likely to default on their subprime mortgages, compared to non-finance professionals.

## 6 CONCLUSION

The objective of this study was to look at various aspects of the financial crisis with special emphasis on the mortgage markets that have played a major role in this crisis. We have conducted a selective survey of the extant literature and presented the views and findings of economists and researchers who have examined various aspects of the crisis. We hope that this chapter will throw light on various aspects of the financial crisis and present a picture grounded in data, thorough data analysis, and intensive peer review, as opposed to media reports and internet articles. We also hope that this chapter gives researchers a glimpse of the financial crisis through the lens of economists and encourages them to conduct further research on this subject.

Regarding directions for future research, 13 years have passed since the onset of the financial crisis and many papers have already been written about it. The time has now come to see whether this entire analysis of the financial crisis actually made an impact in the real world. Have the governments/regulators incorporated the lessons learned through research and are they better equipped to prevent/deal with a new crisis? Have all the papers on optimal mortgage design made an impression on actual mortgage design, in the aftermath of the financial crisis, and are the current mortgage contracts better equipped to deal with future crises? Are the consumers of today better educated financially and able to fully understand the risks involved in their mortgage contracts? This evaluation of financial crisis research's impact on the real world is one possible direction for future research. Another direction for future research is making the right predictions. There is a need to periodically evaluate the current state of risk buildup in various parts of the financial system and its ability to engender another financial crisis/economic downturn. Given the current state of technology, i.e. machine learning and artificial intelligence, we are probably better prepared than before to be able to predict the next crisis or even the next downturn in the world economy.

## REFERENCES

Acharya, Viral V., Philipp Schnabl, and Gustavo Suarez, 2013, "Securitization without risk transfer," *Journal of Financial Economics*, Volume 107, Issue 3, pp. 515–536.

Acolin, Arthur, Jesse Bricker, Paul Calem, and Susan Wachter, 2016, "Borrowing constraints and homeownership," *American Economic Review*, Volume 106, Issue 5, pp. 625–629.

Adelino, Manuel, Kristopher Gerardi, and Paul S. Willen, 2013, "Why don't lenders renegotiate more home mortgages? Redefaults, self-cures and securitization," *Journal of Monetary Economics*, Volume 60, Issue 7, pp. 835–853.

Adrian, Tobias, John Kiff, and Hyun Song Shin, 2018, "Liquidity, leverage, and regulation 10 years after the Global Financial Crisis," *Annual Review of Financial Economics*, Volume 10, pp. 1–24.

Agarwal, Sumit, and Yunqi Zhang, 2018, "Effects of government bailouts on mortgage modification," *Journal of Banking and Finance*, Volume 93, pp. 54–70.

Agarwal, Sumit, Gene Amromin, Itzhak Ben-David, Souphala Chomsisengphet, and Douglas D. Evanoff, 2010, "Learning to cope: Voluntary financial education and loan performance during a housing crisis," *American Economic Review*, Volume 100, Issue 2, pp. 495–500.

Agarwal, Sumit, Gene Amromin, Itzhak Ben-David, Souphala Chomsisengphet, and Douglas D. Evanoff, 2011, "The role of securitization in mortgage renegotiation," *Journal of Financial Economics*, Volume 102, Issue 3, pp. 559–578.

Agarwal, Sumit, Yan Chang, and Abdullah Yavas, 2012, "Adverse selection in mortgage securitization," *Journal of Financial Economics*, Volume 105, Issue 3, pp. 640–660.

Agarwal, Sumit, Gene Amromin, Itzhak Ben-David, Souphala Chomsisengphet, and Douglas D. Evanoff, 2014a, "Predatory lending and the subprime crisis," *Journal of Financial Economics*, Volume 113, Issue 1, pp. 29–52.

Agarwal, Sumit, Gene Amromin, Claudine Gartenberg, Anna Paulson, and Sriram Villupuram, 2014b, "Homebuilders, affiliated financing arms, and the mortgage crisis," *Economic Perspectives*, Volume 38, Issue 2, pp. 38–51.

Agarwal, Sumit, Gene Amromin, Souphala Chomsisengphet, Tim Landvoigt, Tomasz Piskorski, Amit Seru, and Vincent Yao, 2015, "Mortgage refinancing, consumer spending, and competition: Evidence from the Home Affordable Refinancing program," NBER working paper 21512.

Agarwal, Sumit, Yongheng Deng, Chenxi Luo, and Wenlan Qian, 2016, "The hidden peril: The role of the condo loan market in the recent financial crisis," *Review of Finance*, Volume 20, Issue 2, pp. 467–500.

Agarwal, Sumit, Souphala Chomsisengphet, and Yunqi Zhang, 2017a, "How does working in a finance profession affect mortgage delinquency?" *Journal of Banking and Finance*, Volume 78, pp. 1–13.

Agarwal, Sumit, Gene Amromin, Itzhak Ben-David, Souphala Chomsisengphet, Tomasz Piskorski, and Amit Seru, 2017b, "Policy intervention in debt renegotiation: Evidence from the Home Affordable Modification Program," *Journal of Political Economy*, Volume 125, Issue 3, pp. 654–712.

Agarwal, Sumit, Souphala Chomsisengphet, Neale Mahoney, and Johannes Stroebel, 2018a, "Do banks pass through credit expansions to consumers who want to borrow?" *Quarterly Journal of Economics*, Volume 133, Issue 1, pp. 129–190.

Agarwal, Sumit, Gene Amromin, Itzhak Ben-David, and Serdar Dinc, 2018b, "The politics of foreclosures," *Journal of Finance*, Volume 73, Issue 6, pp. 2677–2717.

Akhigbe, Aigbe, and Ann Marie Whyte, 2003, "Changes in market assessments of bank risk following the Riegle–Neal Act of 1994," *Journal of Banking and Finance*, Volume 27, Issue 1, pp. 87–102.

Anenberg, Elliot, and Edward Kung, 2014, "Estimates of the size and source of price declines due to nearby foreclosures," *American Economic Review*, Volume 104, Issue 8, pp. 2527–2551.

Baumer, Eric P., Kevin T. Wolff, and Ashley N. Arnio, 2012, "A multicity neighborhood analysis of foreclosure and crime," *Social Science Quarterly*, Volume 93, Issue 3, pp. 577–601.

Bayer, Patrick, Christopher Geissler, Kyle Mangum, and James W. Roberts, 2020, "Speculators and middlemen: The strategy and performance of investors in the housing market," *Review of Financial Studies*, Volume 33, Issue 11, pp. 5212–5247.

Becker, Bo, and Todd Milbourn, 2011, "How did increased competition affect credit ratings?" *Journal of Financial Economics*, Volume 101, Issue 3, pp. 493–514.

Bhutta, Neil, 2015, "The ins and outs of mortgage debt during the housing boom and bust," *Journal of Monetary Economics*, Volume 76, pp. 284–298.

Bhutta, Neil, Jane Dokko, and Hui Shan, 2017, "Consumer ruthlessness and mortgage default during the 2007 to 2009 housing bust," *Journal of Finance*, Volume 72, Issue 6, pp. 2433–2466.

Bolton, Patrick, Xavier Freixas, and Joel Shapiro, 2012, "The credit ratings game," *Journal of Finance*, Volume 67, Issue 1, pp. 85–111.

Bremus, Franziska, and Marcel Fratzscher, 2015, "Drivers of structural change in cross-border banking since the global financial crisis," *Journal of International Money and Finance*, Volume 52, pp. 32–59.

Brunnermeier, Markus K., 2009, "Deciphering the liquidity and credit crunch 2007–2008," *Journal of Economic Perspectives*, Volume 23, Issue 1, pp. 77–100.

Campbell, John Y., Stefano Giglio, and Parag Pathak, 2011a, "Forced sales and house prices," *American Economic Review*, Volume 101, Issue 5, pp. 2108–2131.

Campbell, Sean, Daniel Covitz, William Nelson, and Karen Pence, 2011b, "Securitization markets and central banking: An evaluation of the term asset-backed securities loan facility," *Journal of Monetary Economics*, Volume 58, Issue 5, pp. 518–531.

Cerutti, Eugenio, and Stijn Claessens, 2017, "The great cross-border bank deleveraging: Supply constraints and intra-group frictions," *Review of Finance*, Volume 21, Issue 1, pp. 201–236.

Chen, Nan-Kuang, and Charles Ka Yui Leung, 2008, "Asset price spillover, collateral and crises: With an application to property market policy," *Journal of Real Estate Finance and Economics*, Volume 37, pp. 351–385.

Chinco, Alex, and Christopher Mayer, 2016, "Misinformed speculators and mispricing in the housing market," *Review of Financial Studies*, Volume 29, Issue 2, pp. 486–522.

Chodorow-Reich, Gabriel, 2014, "The employment effects of credit market disruptions: Firm-level evidence from the 2008–9 financial crisis," *Quarterly Journal Of Economics*, Volume 129, Issue 1, pp. 1–59.

Chong, Beng Soon, 1991, "The effects of interstate banking on commercial banks' risk and profitability," *Review of Economics and Statistics*, Volume 73, Issue 1, pp. 78–84.

Claessens, Stijn, and Neeltje van Horen, 2015, "The impact of the Global Financial Crisis on banking globalization," *IMF Economic Review*, Volume 63, Issue 4, pp. 868–918.

Covitz, Daniel, Nellie Liang, and Gustavo A. Suarez, 2013, "The evolution of a financial crisis: Collapse of the asset-backed commercial paper market," *Journal of Finance*, Volume 68, Issue 3, pp. 815–848.

Cui, Lin, and Randall Walsh, 2015, "Foreclosure, vacancy and crime," *Journal of Urban Economics*, Volume 87, pp. 72–84.

Currie, Janet, and Erdal Tekin, 2015, "Is there a link between foreclosure and health?" *American Economic Journal: Economic Policy*, Volume 7, Issue 1, pp. 63–94.

Dagher, Jihad, and Kazim Kazimov, 2015, "Banks' liability structure and mortgage lending during the financial crisis," *Journal of Financial Economics*, Volume 116, Issue 3, pp. 565–582.

Demsetz, Rebecca S, and Philip E. Strahan, 1997, "Diversification, size, and risk at bank holding companies," *Journal of Money, Credit and Banking*, Volume 29, Issue 3, pp. 300–313.

Demyanyk, Yuliya, and Otto Van Hemert, 2011, "Understanding the subprime mortgage crisis," *Review of Financial Studies*, Volume 24, Issue 6, pp. 1848–1880.

Deng, Saiying, and Elyas Elyasiani, 2008, "Geographic diversification, bank holding company value, and risk," *Journal of Money, Credit and Banking*, Volume 40, Issue 6, pp. 1217–1238.

Depken II, Craig A., Harris Hollans, and Steve Swidler, 2009, "An empirical analysis of residential property flipping," *Journal of Real Estate Finance and Economics*, Volume 39, pp. 248–263.

Diamond, Douglas W., and Raghuram G. Rajan, 2011, "Fear of fire sales, illiquidity seeking, and credit freezes," *Quarterly Journal of Economics*, Volume 126, Issue 2, pp. 557–591.

Doerr, Sebastian, and Philipp Schaz, 2020, "Geographic diversification and bank lending during crises," *Journal of Financial Economics*, https://ssrn.com/abstract=3082945.

Downing, Janelle, 2016, "The health effects of the foreclosure crisis and unaffordable housing: A systematic review and explanation of evidence," *Social Science and Medicine*, Volume 162, pp. 88–96.

Duca, John V., John Muellbauer, and Anthony Murphy, 2010, "Housing markets and the financial crisis of 2007–2009: Lessons for the future," *Journal of Financial Stability*, Volume 6, Issue 4, pp. 203–217.

Dynan, Karen, Atif Mian, and Karen M. Pence, 2012, "Is a household debt overhang holding back consumption? [With comments and discussion]," *Brookings Papers on Economic Activity*, Spring, pp. 299–362.

Eberly, Janice, and Arvind Krishnamurthy, 2014, "Efficient credit policies in a housing debt crisis," *Brookings Papers on Economic Activity*, Fall, pp. 73–136.

Ellen, Ingrid Gould, Johanna Lacoe, and Claudia Ayanna Sharygin, 2013, "Do foreclosures cause crime," *Journal of Urban Economics*, Volume 74, pp. 59–70.

Elul, Ronel, Nicholas S. Souleles, Souphala Chomsisengphet, Dennis Glennon, and Robert Hunt, 2010, "What 'triggers' mortgage default?" *American Economic Review*, Volume 100, Issue 2, pp. 490–494.

Fowler, Katherine A., R. Matthew Gladden, Kevin J. Vagi, Jamar Barnes, and Leroy Frazier, 2015, "Increase in suicides associated with home eviction and foreclosure during the U.S. housing crisis: Findings from 16 national violent death reporting system states, 2005–2010," *American Journal of Public Health*, Volume 105, Issue 2, pp. 311–316.

Fratzscher, Marcel, Philipp Johann Konig, and Claudia Lambert, 2016, "Credit provision and banking stability after the Great Financial Crisis: The role of bank regulation and the quality of governance," *Journal of International Money and Finance*, Volume 66, pp. 113–135.

Fuster, Andreas, and James Vickery, 2015, "Securitization and the fixed-rate mortgage," *Review of Financial Studies*, Volume 28, Issue 1, pp. 176–211.

Fuster, Andreas, and Paul S. Willen, 2017, "Payment size, negative equity, and mortgage default," *American Economic Journal: Economic Policy*, Volume 9, Issue 4, pp. 167–191.

Gabriel, Stuart A., and Stuart S. Rosenthal, 2015, "The boom, the bust and the future of homeownership," *Real Estate Economics*, Volume 43, Issue 2, pp. 334–374.

Gao, Zhenyu, Michael Sockin, and Wei Xiong, 2020, "Economic consequences of housing speculation," *Review of Financial Studies*, Volume 33, Issue 11, pp. 5248–5287.

Gerardi, Kristopher, Eric Rosenblatt, Paul S. Willen, and Vincent Yao, 2015, "Foreclosure externalities: New evidence," *Journal of Urban Economics*, Volume 87, pp. 42–56.

Goetz, Martin R., Luc Laeven, and Ross Levine, 2016, "Does the geographic expansion of banks reduce risk?" *Journal of Financial Economics*, Volume 120, Issue 2, pp. 346–362.

Griffin, John M., and Gonzalo Maturana, 2016a, "Did dubious mortgage origination practices distort house prices?" *Review of Financial Studies*, Volume 29, Issue 7, pp. 1671–1708.

Griffin, John M., and Gonzalo Maturana, 2016b, "Who facilitated misreporting in securitized loans?" *Review of Financial Studies*, Volume 29, Issue 2, pp. 384–419.

Griffin, John M., and Dragon Yongjun Tang, 2012, "Did subjectivity play a role in CDO credit ratings?" *Journal of Finance*, Volume 67, Issue 4, pp. 1293–1328.

Griffin, John M., Jordan Nickerson, and Dragon Yongjun Tang, 2013, "Rating shopping or catering? An examination of the response to competitive pressure for CDO credit ratings," *Review of Financial Studies*, Volume 26, Issue 9, pp. 2270–2310.

Guiso, Luigi, Paola Sapienza, and Luigi Zingales, 2013, "The determinants of attitudes toward strategic default on mortgages," *Journal of Finance*, Volume 68, Issue 4, pp. 1473–1515.

Harding, John P., Eric Rosenblatt, and Vincent W. Yao, 2009, "The contagion effect of foreclosed properties," *Journal of Urban Economics*, Volume 66, Issue 3, pp. 164–178.

Hartley, Daniel, 2014, "The effect of foreclosures on nearby housing prices: Supply or dis-amenity?" *Regional Science and Urban Economics*, Volume 49, pp. 108–117.

Haughwout, Andrew, Donghoon Lee, Joseph Tracy, and Wilbert van der Klaau, 2014, "Real estate investors and the housing market crisis," Federal Reserve Bank of New York.

He, Jie, Jun Qian, and Philip E. Strahan, 2012, "Are all ratings created equal? The impact of issuer size on the pricing of mortgage-backed securities," *Journal of Finance*, Volume 67, Issue 6, pp. 2097–2137.

Holt, Jeff, 2009, "A summary of the primary causes of the housing bubble and the resulting credit crisis: A non-technical paper," *Journal of Business Inquiry*, Volume 8, Issue 1, pp. 120–129.

Houle, Jason N., 2014, "Mental health in the foreclosure crisis," *Social Science and Medicine*, Volume 118, pp. 1–8.

Houle, Jason N., and Michael T. Light, 2014, "The home foreclosure crisis and rising suicide rates, 2005 to 2010," *American Journal of Public Health*, Volume 104, Issue 6, pp. 1073–1079.

Hsu, Joanne W., David A. Matsa, and Brian T. Melzer, 2018, "Unemployment Insurance as a housing market stabilizer," *American Economic Review*, Volume 108, Issue 1, pp. 49–81.

Jiang, Wei, Ashlyn Aiko Nelson, and Edward Vytlacil, 2014a, "Liar's loan? Effects of origination channel and information falsification on mortgage delinquency," *Review of Economics and Statistics*, Volume 96, Issue 1, pp. 1–18.

Jiang, Wei, Ashlyn Aiko Nelson, and Edward Vytlacil, 2014b, "Securitization and loan performance: Ex ante and ex post relations in the mortgage market," *Review of Financial Studies*, Volume 27, Issue 2, pp. 454–483.

Kehoe, Patrick J., Virgiliu Midrigan, and Elena Pastorino, 2019, "Debt constraints and employment," *Journal of Political Economy*, Volume 127, Issue 4, pp. 1926–1991.

Keys, Benjamin J., Tanmoy Mukherjee, Amit Seru, and Vikrant Vig, 2010, "Did securitization lead to lax screening? Evidence from subprime loans," *Quarterly Journal of Economics*, Volume 125, Issue 1, pp. 307–362.

Keys, Benjamin J., Amit Seru, and Vikrant Vig, 2012, "Lender screening and the role of securitization: Evidence from prime and subprime mortgage markets," *Review of Financial Studies*, Volume 25, Issue 7, pp. 2071–2108.

Kruger, Samuel, 2018, "The effect of mortgage securitization on foreclosure and modification," *Journal of Financial Economics*, Volume 129, Issue 3, pp. 586–607.

Leung, Charles Ka Yui, and Chung-Yi Tse, 2017, "Flipping in the housing market," *Journal of Economic Dynamics and Control*, Volume 76, pp. 232–263.

Levine, Ross, Chen Lin, and Wensi Xie, 2020, "Geographic diversification and banks' funding costs," *Management Science*, pp. 1–22.

Liebowitz, Stan J., 2009, "Anatomy of a train wreck: Causes of the mortgage meltdown," in Randall G. Holcombe and Benjamin Powell (eds), *Housing America: Building out of a Crisis*. Oakland, CA: Independent Institute.

Lindblad, Mark R., Hye-Sung Han, Siyun Yu, and William M. Rohe, 2017, "First-time homebuying: Attitudes and behaviors of low-income renters through the financial crisis," *Housing Studies*, Volume 32, Issue 8, pp. 1127–1155.

Loutskina, Elena, and Philip E. Strahan, 2011, "Informed and uninformed investment in housing: The downside of diversification," *Review of Financial Studies*, Volume 24, Issue 5, pp. 1447–1480.

Mathis, Jerome, James McAndrews, and Jean-Charles Rochet, 2009, "Rating the raters: Are reputation concerns powerful enough to discipline rating agencies?" *Journal of Monetary Economics*, Volume 56, Issue 5, pp. 657–674.

Maturana, Gonzalo, 2017, "When are modifications of securitized loans beneficial to investors?" *Review of Financial Studies*, Volume 30, Issue 11, pp. 3824–3857.

Mayer, Christopher, Edward Morrison, Tomasz Piskorski, and Arpit Gupta, 2014, "Mortgage modification and strategic behavior: Evidence from a legal settlement with Countrywide," *American Economic Review*, Volume 104, Issue 9, pp. 2830–2857.

McCauley, Robert N., Agustín S. Benetrix, Patrick M. McGuire, and Goetz von Peter, 2019, "Financial deglobalisation in banking?" *Journal of International Money and Finance*, Volume 94, pp. 116–131.

McLaughlin, K.A., A. Nandi, K.M. Keyes, M. Uddin, A.E. Aiello, S. Galea, and K.C. Koenen, 2012, "Home foreclosure and risk of psychiatric morbidity during the recent financial crisis," *Psychological Medicine*, Volume 42, Issue 7, pp. 1441–1448.

Melzer, Brian T., 2017, "Mortgage debt overhang: Reduced investment by homeowners at risk of default," *Journal of Finance*, Volume 72, Issue 2, pp. 575–612.

Mian, Atif, and Amir Sufi, 2009, "The consequences of mortgage credit expansion: Evidence from the U.S. mortgage default crisis," *Quarterly Journal of Economics*, Volume 124, Issue 4, pp. 1449–1496.

Mian, Atif, and Amir Sufi, 2010, "Household leverage and the recession of 2007–09," *IMF Economic Review*, Volume 58, Issue 1, pp. 74–117.

Mian, Atif, and Amir Sufi, 2011, "House prices, home equity-based borrowing, and the U.S. household leverage crisis," *American Economic Review*, Volume 101, Issue 5, pp. 2132–2156.

Mian, Atif, and Amir Sufi, 2012, "The effects of fiscal stimulus: Evidence from the 2009 Cash for Clunkers program," *Quarterly Journal of Economics*, Volume 127, Issue 3, pp. 1107–1142.

Mian, Atif, and Amir Sufi, 2014, "What explains the 2007–2009 drop in employment?" *Econometrica*, Volume 82, Issue 6, pp. 2197–2223.

Mian, Atif, and Amir Sufi, 2018, "Credit supply and housing speculation," NBER working no. paper 24823.

Mian, Atif, Amir Sufi, and Francesco Trebbi, 2010, "The political economy of the U.S. mortgage default crisis," *American Economic Review*, Volume 100, Issue 5, pp. 1967–1998.

Mian, Atif, Kamalesh Rao, and Amir Sufi, 2013, "Household balance sheets, consumption, and the economic slump," *Quarterly Journal of Economics*, Volume 128, Issue 4, pp. 1687–1726.

Mian, Atif, Amir Sufi, and Francesco Trebbi, 2015, "Foreclosures, house prices, and the real economy," *Journal of Finance*, Volume 70, Issue 6, pp. 2587–2634.

Nadauld, Taylor D., and Shane M. Sherlund, 2013, "The impact of securitization on the expansion of subprime credit," *Journal of Financial Economics*, Volume 107, Issue 2, pp. 454–476.

Parker, Jonathan A., Nicholas S. Souleles, David S. Johnson, and Robert McClelland, 2013, "Consumer spending and the economic stimulus payments of 2008," *American Economic Review*, Volume 103, Issue 6, pp. 2530–2553.

Piskorski, Tomasz, and Amit Seru, 2018, "Mortgage market design: Lessons from the Great Recession," Brookings Papers on Economic Activity, Spring, pp. 429–513.

Piskorski, Tomasz, and Alexei Tchistyi, 2010, "Optimal mortgage design," *Review of Financial Studies*, Volume 23, Issue 8, pp. 3098–3140.

Piskorski, Tomasz, and Alexei Tchistyi, 2011, "Stochastic house appreciation and optimal mortgage lending," *Review of Financial Studies*, Volume 24, Issue 5, pp. 1407–1446.

Piskorski, Tomasz, Amit Seru, and Vikrant Vig, 2010, "Securitization and distressed loan renegotiation: Evidence from the subprime mortgage crisis," *Journal of Financial Economics*, Volume 97, Issue 3, pp. 369–397.

Piskorski, Tomasz, Amit Seru, and James Witkin, 2015, "Asset quality misrepresentation by financial intermediaries: Evidence from the RMBS market," *Journal of Finance*, Volume 70, Issue 6, pp. 2635–2678.

Purnanandam, Amiyatosh, 2011, "Originate-to-distribute model and the subprime mortgage crisis," *Review of Financial Studies*, Volume 24, Issue 6, pp. 1881–1915.

Rajan, Uday, Amit Seru, and Vikrant Vig, 2015, "The failure of models that predict failure: Distance, incentives, and defaults," *Journal of Financial Economics*, Volume 115, Issue 2, pp. 237–260.

Ramcharan, Rodney, Skander J. van den Heuvel, and Stephane Verani, 2016, "From Wall Street to Main Street: The impact of the financial crisis on consumer credit supply," *Journal of Finance*, Volume 71, Issue 3, pp. 1323–1356.

Rogers, William H., and William Winter, 2009, "The impact of foreclosures on neighboring housing sales," *Journal of Real Estate Research*, Volume 31, Issue 4, pp. 455–479.

Sanders, Anthony, 2008, "The subprime crisis and its role in the financial crisis," *Journal of Housing Economics*, Volume 17, Issue 4, pp. 254–261.

Schoenmaker, Dirk, 2017, "What happened to global banking after the crisis," *Journal of Financial Regulation and Compliance*, Volume 25, Issue 3, pp. 241–252.

Shleifer, Andrei, and Robert Vishny, 2010, "Unstable banking," *Journal of Financial Economics*, Volume 97, Issue 3, pp. 306–318.

Shleifer, Andrei, and Robert Vishny, 2011. "Fire sales in finance and macroeconomics," *Journal of Economic Perspectives*, Volume 25, Issue 1, pp. 29–48.

Stucky, Thomas D., John R. Ottensmann, and Seth B. Payton, 2012, "The effect of foreclosures on crime in Indianapolis, 2003–2008," *Social Science Quarterly*, Volume 93, Issue 3, pp. 602–624.

Towe, Charles, and Chad Lawley, 2013, "The contagion effect of neighboring foreclosures," *American Economic Journal: Economic Policy*, Volume 5, Issue 2, pp. 313–335.

Vallascas, Francesco, Sabur Mollah, and Kevin Keasey, 2017, "Does the impact of board independence on large bank risks change after the global financial crisis?" *Journal of Corporate Finance*, Volume 44, pp. 149–166.

Williams, Sonya, George Galster, and Nandita Verma, 2014, "Home foreclosures and neighborhood crime dynamics," *Housing Studies*, Volume 29, Issue 3, pp. 380–406.

Yilmazer, Tansel, Patryk Babiarz, and Fen Liu, 2015, "The impact of diminished housing wealth on health in the United States: Evidence from the Great Recession," *Social Science and Medicine*, Volume 130, pp. 234–241.

# 10. Is housing still the business cycle? Perhaps not.
*Richard K. Green*

## 1    INTRODUCTION

Twenty-three years ago, as of this writing, I published a paper on real estate economics (Green, 1997), on residential investment's remarkable track record for predicting subsequent gross domestic product (GDP). The paper used a straightforward time series technique—Granger causality—across a variety of specifications and found that while detrended residential investment Granger caused detrended GDP, non-residential investment did not. Moreover, residential investment was, at that time, orthogonal with respect to GDP—that is, adding GDP to a vector autoregression explaining residential investment did not improve the ability to forecast residential investment.

The fact that Granger causation went in one direction—from housing to GDP—was important to identify the forecasting parameters from housing to GDP. The paper made no claims about causation, but it did argue that following residential investment was useful for those making economic forecasts. This was followed by papers by Coulson and Kim (2000), Davis and Heathcote (2005), and Leamer (2007); the last of these was titled "Housing is the business cycle." The papers, all using different methods from mine, confirmed what I found—that residential investment led the broader economy, without being led by it.

Enough time and enough events have passed that it is worth revisiting whether the empirical regularities found in the research cited above remain. In particular, the economy has since 2007—the end of a housing boom—seen a housing bust, a housing price, but not investment, recovery, and, of course, a pandemic. In light of these shocks, it would be reasonable to ask whether the relationship between housing investment and economic activity remains.

As such, this chapter will take the techniques used in Green and Coulson and Kim to update the results. It finds that housing continues to lead the business cycle, but that the business cycle, to a limited extent, leads housing. Coulson and Kim recommend a decomposition of GDP to determine the mechanisms through which housing influences and is influenced by the housing market, and this chapter will consequently update their results.

The chapter is organized as follows. It begins with a brief review of the techniques used in the papers listed above and their findings. It then presents descriptive evidence of how housing has changed relative to the business cycle beginning with and subsequent to the great financial crises. It then presents pretests of the data we use to update the findings of past papers. It then runs a series of bivariate and multivariate tests examining how housing leads and is led by the business cycle and individual components of that cycle. The chapter finishes with some forecasts and implications.

## 2 LITERATURE REVIEW

A number of papers over the past 20 years have looked at the relationship between housing and the business cycle. One interesting takeaway is that in the United States (US), housing investment is an unusually strong leading indicator (Leung, 2004). For this chapter, I will focus on three papers listed in the introduction, as they are the foundation for updating past findings.

Green (1997) uses simple Granger causality tests using a variety of specifications. The purpose of a Granger test is to take a stationary time series and find whether the lagged values of one variable may improve the ability to forecast another variable, taking into account the lagged value of that other variable. In other words, one begins by estimating the equation:

$$y_t = \alpha + \sum_{i=1}^{I} \beta_{t-i} y_{t-i} + \sum_{i=1}^{I} \gamma_{t-i} x_{t-i} + \varepsilon \qquad (10.1)$$

where $y$ is the variable to be forecast, $x$ is the variable contributing to the forecast, and $\varepsilon$ is an error term. The next step is an F-test of whether the $\gamma_{t-i}$ coefficients are jointly different from zero at customary levels of significance (Granger, 1980). If they are jointly different from zero, we say that $x$ Granger causes $y$.

Green (1997) used residential and non-residential investment as x variables in separate regressions and found that residential investment Granger caused GDP, while non-residential investment did not. At the same time, when the regressions were reversed, GDP Granger caused non-residential investment but did not Granger cause residential investment, suggesting that changes in residential investment were a function of exogenous shocks rather than embeddedness in the broader economy.

These results were consistent through a variety of specifications, including models with different lag lengths. The results were also subject to the Brown et al. (1975) CUSUM test for coefficient stability. The paper found that there was a structural break in the coefficients in the year 1980, but that running separate, stable regressions before and after that break had no impact on the qualitative results: in both periods, residential investment Granger caused GDP, non-residential investment did not, and GDP Granger caused non-residential investment, while it did not Grange cause residential investment. We shall revisit those results with the benefit of an added 28 years of data.

Coulson and Kim (2000) went a step further by investigating the effect of residential investment on various components of GDP: consumption, non-residential investment, and government spending. They then used a technique that allowed them to uncover the channels through which non-residential investment operated. In the end, they determined that residential investment had an impact on consumption, and that it did indeed influence GDP.

Leamer (2007) summed up his views on how housing revealed itself to be a leading indicator:

> Of the components of GDP, residential investment offers by far the best early warning sign of an oncoming recession. Since World War II, we have had eight recessions preceded by substantial problems in housing and consumer durables. Housing did not give an early warning of the Department of Defense Downturn after the Korean Armistice in 1953 or the Internet Comeuppance in 2001, nor should it have. By virtue of its prominence in our recessions, it makes sense for housing to play a prominent role in the conduct of monetary policy. A modified Taylor Rule would depend on a long-term

measure of inflation having little to do with the phase in the cycle, and, in place of Taylor's output gap, housing starts and the change in housing starts, which together form the best forward-looking indicator of the cycle of which I am aware. This would create pre-emptive anti-inflation policy in the middle of the expansions when housing is not so sensitive to interest rates, making it less likely that anti-inflation policies would be needed near the ends of expansions when housing is very interest rate sensitive, thus making our recessions less frequent and/or less severe.

Leamer (2007) is thus arguing that housing is an important tool for the transmission of monetary policy.

Leamer's (2007) regressions were similar to Coulson and Kim's (2000), except that he did not use time series techniques (i.e., he did not use first differences to eliminate non-stationarity). Nevertheless, his result was similar to those papers that preceded his—residential investment with a one-quarter lag was the most reliable predictor of the business cycle. The *t*-statistic on lagged residential investment was far larger than that of any other explanatory variable for predicting GDP. Davis and Heathcote (2005) and Leung (2004) also found housing to be a leading indicator.

If we look at what has happened since 2007, however, we see a mixed bag. On the one hand, housing absolutely led the economy into a recession that year—residential investment declined by an extraordinary 57 percent between the first quarter of 2006 and the second quarter of 2009, and the contraction that followed that collapse was, by any measure, the worst since the Great Recession. But then, in the following years, while housing recovered, it did so slowly and has not recovered its share of GDP, which in the first quarter of 2021 is 9.1 percent lower than it was in the fourth quarter of 2006. The fact that residential investment never recovered, while the broader economy arguably reached full employment before the advent of COVID, suggests that perhaps the link between residential investment and the business cycle has broken. This chapter investigates that possibility.

## 3   DESCRIPTIVE DATA

We begin with a depiction of US GDP and gross fixed residential investment relative to the 1946 beginning of the National Income and Products Account series of the US Commerce Department (Figure 10.1). The figure is quite striking in at least three dimensions: (1) it is clear that housing investment is more volatile than the broader economy; (2) up until the Great Financial Crisis, housing investment had a very similar long-term trend to GDP; and (3) from 2007 on, housing investment dropped relative to GDP, and has remained relatively depressed since.

The recovery from the Great Financial Crisis is often characterized as slow: GDP growth in the aftermath of the recession that ended in 2009 was slow relative to growth following previous recessions, although it is worth noting that the expansion of the 2010s was notable for its length and for its ultimate ability to drive unemployment down to sub-4 percent levels before the COVID-induced recession. That said, the labor force participation rate in the US never recovered to its pre-Crisis levels.

One wonders if the slowness of the recovery can be traced to the sluggishness of housing investment. It is also worth noting that the lack of investment in housing comes in the face of two forces that should have encouraged it: rising house prices and low real interest rates.

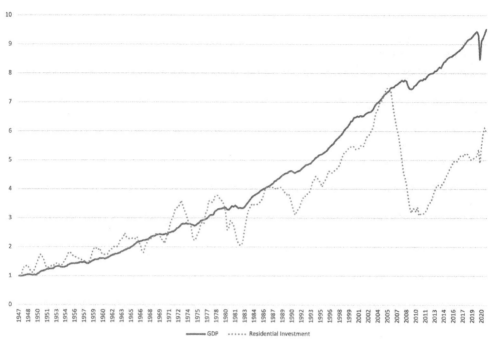

*Note*: 1947 = 1.
*Source*: Bureau of Economic Analysis.

*Figure 10.1    Private residential investment and GDP relative to 1947–2021 in the United States*

Figure 10.2 depicts the real Federal Housing Finance Authority Repeat Sales index, deflected by the GDP deflator, and real gross fixed residential investment from 1975 (the first year of the Federal Housing Finance Authority series) forward. Note that while in 2020 real house prices had returned to their near high point of 2006, residential investment *relative to GDP* remained 9.1 percent below its long-term average—an average that had been pulled down since 2008 (Figure 10.1).

At the same time, as measured by the ten-year Treasury inflation-protected (TIP) rate, real interest rates were negative in 2020, yet, again, housing investment was below trend (Figure 10.3). Indeed, the correlation between TIPs and residential investment from 2002 to 2020 was 0.41. This is perhaps not entirely surprising, as high interest rates are associated with strong economic performance. But suppose we lag TIP rates by two quarters relative to residential investment. In that case, we still get a positive correlation of 0.31, meaning that there is no direct evidence that rising interest rates cool off housing investment, nor that falling interest rates stimulate it. As it turns out, however, the TIP rate is surprisingly not a stationary series, meaning that an appropriate model specification requires differencing TIPs in a vector autoregressive model. We will later show the results of this specification.

This chapter is not about why the expected relationships between prices and investment or real estate rates and investment seem to have broken down—although there is a substantial literature on how availability (as opposed to the cost) of credit has affected homebuilding, as

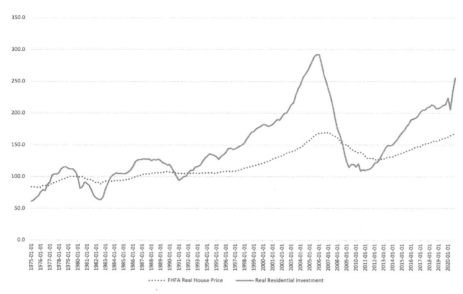

*Note*: 1980 = 100.
*Source*: Bureau of Economic Analysis and Federal Housing Finance Authority.

*Figure 10.2*   *Real house prices and residential investment in the United States (1975–2020)*

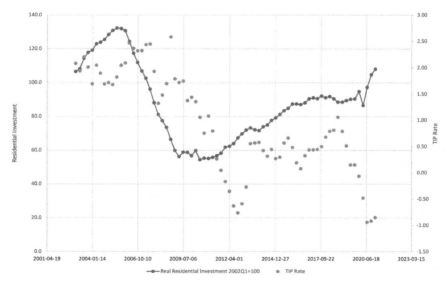

*Source*: Bureau of Economic Analysis and Federal Reserve System.

*Figure 10.3*   *Real interest rates and residential investment: ten-year Treasury inflation indexed security and real residential investment in the United States, 2003–2021*

well as literature on how land use regulation has prevented homebuilding. But it is striking how housing investment has remained at a very low level by historical standards for more than a decade.

Given past results, it is possible that the sluggish performance of residential investment kept the economy from reaching its potential output until just before the COVID-induced recession. But it is also possible that a once stable relationship between housing investment and GDP has ceased to be stable. The remainder of this chapter will test whether the coefficients reported in Green (1997), Coulson and Kim (2000), and Leamer (2007) have remained undisturbed or whether they have changed.

## 4  PRETESTING DATA

Hamilton's (1994) classic text discusses the treatment of time series data necessary to make sure that regression results rooted in such data are not spurious. It involves testing for the stationarity of each individual data series and the cointegration of the various dependent variables. If the data series are individually not stationary, and the dependent variables are not cointegrated, the times series regressions must be in first differences not to be spurious.

Following Coulson and Kim (2000), we are going to investigate the relationships among GDP, residential investment, non-residential investment, consumption, and government spending. Table 10.1 presents the Dickey-Fuller tests for unit root for each of these five series. In all four cases, the series exhibit unit root, indicating non-stationarity.

*Table 10.1*  *Dickey-Fuller tests for unit root with no lags*

| Variable | Test statistic | 5% critical value |
| --- | --- | --- |
| GDP | −2.72 | −2.88 |
| Residential investment | −2.07 | −2.88 |
| Non-residential investment | −0.49 | −2.88 |
| Consumption | −2.23 | −2.88 |
| Government spending | −5.01 | −2.88 |

*Note*: N = 292. All variables are in natural logs.

We then turn to tests of cointegration. Table 10.2 presents Engle-Granger tests of cointegration and finds that residential investment and GDP are not cointegrated, but it is not possible to reject the null hypothesis that non-residential investment, consumption, and government spending are not cointegrated with GDP. Nevertheless, the focus of this chapter is on residential investment, and so it will not contain estimates of error correction models. We, therefore,

*Table 10.2*  *Cointegration tests*

| Variable | Test statistic | 5% critical value |
| --- | --- | --- |
| Residential investment | −1.85 | −2.88 |
| Non-residential investment | −3.22 | −2.88 |
| Consumption | −3.65 | −2.88 |
| Government spending | −3.20 | −2.88 |

*Note*: N = 292. All variables are in natural logs.

will do all our specifications in the first differences in natural logs of each series—we use natural logs so that we may interpret the first differences as growth rates.

## 5    SIMPLE GRANGER TESTS

We begin by updating the results from Green (1997), which tests for Granger causality among GDP, residential investment, and non-residential investment. Table 10.3, column 1 presents Wald Chi-square tests for rejecting the null of Granger causality in a bivariate setting using two lags (we tried other lags as well, and the results were the same). The period for this column is the entire post-Second World War period for the US. As the series themselves have unit roots, we estimate the model in natural log differences.

Table 10.3    Simple Granger tests of residential investment, non-residential investment, and GDP

|         | (1) Δgdp | (2) Δres | (3) Δnonres |
|---------|----------|----------|-------------|
| Δgdp    |          | 4.17     | 2.62        |
| Δres    | 30.7***  |          | 23.4***     |
| Δnonres | 1.13     | 9.49***  |             |
| N       | 292      | 292      | 292         |

Note: p-values in parentheses; $^*p<0.05$, $^{**}p<0.01$, $^{***}p<0.001$.

As in the earlier paper, residential investment Granger causes GDP, and non-residential does not. GDP also continues to Granger cause non-residential investment, but the reverse is not true.

We test for the stability of these results using the Brown et al. (1975) CUSUM test. This is a recursive regression test that may identify breaks in time series regimes. The idea of a CUSUM test is that in the event that the coefficients in a time series are stable, the sum of residuals as one moves forward through time should have an expected value of zero.

To test this proposition, Brown et al. (1975) show that the estimate

$$W_r = \frac{1}{\hat{\sigma}} \sum_{k+1}^{r} w_j \qquad (10.2)$$

where $w_r = \dfrac{y_r - x_r' b_{r-1}}{\sqrt{\left(1 + x_r'(X_{r-1}' X_{r-1})^{-1} x_r\right)^2}}$ , $Y_r$ is a time series of a dependent variable running

from time 1 through r, $X_r$ is a time series of a matrix of explanatory dependent variables running from time 1 through r, and $B_r$ is a vector of estimated coefficients derived from the regression running from time t through r, is distributed Chi-squared. The null hypothesis of coefficient stability implies that the sum of the recursive residuals stays within 95 percent confidence bands, which widen as the time series lengthens.

Surprisingly, the CUSUM test does *not* reveal a structural break (Figure 10.4). Ploberger and Krämer (1992) note that the CUSUM recursive residual test often fails to pick up structural breaks toward the end of a time series and recommend the use of ordinary least squares (OLS) residuals, which should have an expected value of zero throughout the time series period. But when we run CUSUM tests based on OLS residuals, we still fail to find a structural break, even using 90 percent confidence bands.

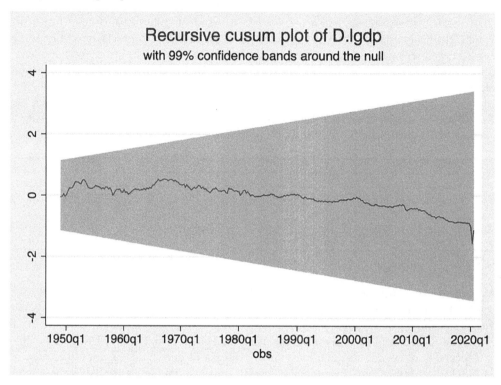

*Figure 10.4*   Coefficient stability test of Granger equation on residential investment "causing" GDP

Yet Figure 10.1 reveals something very strange that happened at the time of the Great Financial Crisis—housing's share of GDP dropped dramatically and has never since recovered. We thus turn to another test of structural stability—the Chow test. This test has us break a combined regression into two pieces, and test whether the coefficients remain stable from one piece to the next. The Chow test statistic is

$$\frac{\dfrac{SSR_c - SSR_1 - SSR_2}{k}}{\dfrac{SSR_1 + SSR_2}{N - 2k}}. \tag{10.3}$$

*Table 10.4*    *Chow test of Granger test between residential investment and GDP*

|  | (1) Δgdp | (2) Δgdp | (3) Δgdp |
| --- | --- | --- | --- |
| Δgdp$_{-1}$ | −0.0822 | 0.080 | −0.220 |
|  | (0.239) | (0.262) | (0.173) |
| Δgdp$_{-2}$ | 0.0750 | 0.111 | −0.258 |
|  | (0.362) | (0.061) | (0.363) |
| Δres$_{-1}$ | 0.0562*** | 0.076*** | −0.047 |
|  | (0.001) | (0.015) | (0.058) |
| Δres$_{-2}$ | 0.0461** | 0.019 | 0.109 |
|  | (0.009) | (0.016) | (0.060) |
| _cons | 0.007*** | 0.006*** | 0.006** |
|  | (0.000) | (0.000) | (0.002) |
| N | 292 | 217 | 75 |
| rss | 0.0397 | 0.022 | 0.0168 |

*Note:* p-values in parentheses: * $p < 0.05$, ** $p < 0.01$, *** $p < 0.001$.

We thus run regressions on two sets of truncated data. Given the lack of guidance from the CUSUM test, we must choose a year to determine whether there was a structural break. We look at two potential years: 2002 and 2008. In the year 2002, mortgage lending changed dramatically, with the private label market and exotic mortgages swelling (Green and Wachter, 2005), while 2008 was the most dramatic year of the Great Financial Crisis. Since we see such a large drop in residential investment in 2008, we will experiment with it as a structural break year.[1]

Table 10.4 shows the results of simple VARs for the total sample period (1947–2020), the first 56 years of that period (1947–2002), and the 18 years since.

Unlike the CUSUM test, the Chow test reveals that a structural break must happen at some point. The test statistic here is $\dfrac{(.0397 - .022 - .0168)/4}{(.022 + .0168)/292} = 26$. The test statistic is distributed F(4284) and has $p < .00001$.

When we limit the data to 2008 forward, we find very different results—there is no evidence that residential investment Granger causes GDP. There is more to this finding than the power of the test—we may use the vector autoregressions that were the foundation of the Granger cause tests to plot impulse response functions (IRFs). Figure 10.5 is an IRF based on estimates from the full sample period, and Figure 10.6 is an IRF based on estimates from 2002 forward.

The contrast between the two is striking. It is clear that a one standard deviation shock in residential investment growth has a meaningful impact on GDP growth—about 30 basis points after two quarters. Given that average GDP growth is about 70 basis points a quarter, this is material. Note also that zero is well outside the confidence interval of the effect of residential investment on GDP.

The IRF based on the past 18 years, though, gives us a different picture. It is not only the case that zero is well within the confidence band (which might simply indicate the weaker power of an estimate based on 18 years of data), but also the predicted impact of residential investment on GDP turns negative.

278  *Handbook of real estate and macroeconomics*

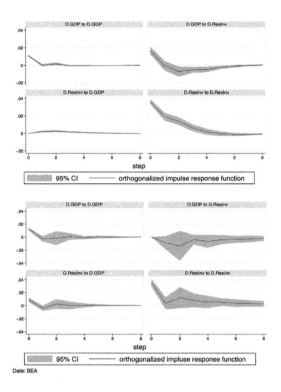

*Figure 10.5*   Impulse response functions based on regressions from 1947 to 2020 (top) and 2002 to 2020 (bottom)

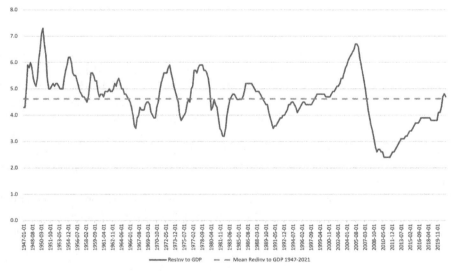

*Source*: National Income and Products Accounts.

*Figure 10.6*   Gross residential investment as a share of GDP, 1947–2021

# 6 GRANGER TESTS ON COMPONENTS OF GDP

*Table 10.5* Granger tests of housing on various components of GDP

|  | (1) Δ consumption | (2) Δ government spending | (3) Δ residential investment | (4) Δ non-residential investment |
|---|---|---|---|---|
| $\Delta c_{-1}$ | −0.124 | −0.0266 | 0.306 | 0.0919 |
|  | (−1.61) | (−0.35) | (1.37) | (0.78) |
| $\Delta c_{-2}$ | 0.183* | 0.00310 | 0.364 | 0.213 |
|  | (2.41) | (0.04) | (1.65) | (1.84) |
| $\Delta rinv_{-1}$ | 0.0430 | −0.0360 | 0.405*** | 0.0876* |
|  | (1.89) | (−1.62) | (6.15) | (2.53) |
| $\Delta rinv_{-2}$ | 0.0621** | 0.0344 | 0.111 | 0.0478 |
|  | (2.80) | (1.59) | (1.73) | (1.41) |
| $\Delta nrinv_{-1}$ | −0.0695 | 0.0613 | −0.508*** | 0.262*** |
|  | (−1.58) | (1.43) | (−3.98) | (3.91) |
| $\Delta nrinv_{-2}$ | −0.0577 | −0.00902 | −0.344** | 0.0346 |
|  | (−1.34) | (−0.21) | (−2.75) | (0.53) |
| $\Delta g_{-1}$ | 0.0534 | 0.474*** | −0.244 | −0.122 |
|  | (0.88) | (8.04) | (−1.39) | (−1.32) |
| $\Delta g_{-2}$ | −0.0795 | 0.167** | 0.0286 | 0.0494 |
|  | (−1.30) | (2.82) | (0.16) | (0.53) |
| _cons | 0.00869*** | 0.00190 | 0.00734* | 0.00467* |
|  | (7.35) | (1.65) | (2.14) | (2.59) |
| N | 292 | 292 | 292 | 292 |

*Note*: t statistics in parentheses; * $p < 0.05$, ** $p < 0.01$, *** $p < 0.001$.

*Table 10.6* Granger tests of housing on various components of GDP

|  | (1) Δ consumption | (2) Δ government spending | (3) Δ residential investment | (4) Δ nonresidential investment |
|---|---|---|---|---|
| $\Delta c_{-1}$ | 0.191 | 0.0630 | 0.985 | 0.675* |
|  | (0.79) | (0.65) | (1.49) | (2.01) |
| $\Delta c_{-2}$ | 0.493 | −0.146 | 1.366 | 0.749* |
|  | (1.87) | (−1.39) | (1.91) | (2.06) |
| $\Delta rinv_{-1}$ | −0.145* | −0.00107 | −0.0133 | −0.248** |
|  | (−2.40) | (−0.04) | (−0.08) | (−2.96) |
| $\Delta rinv_{-2}$ | 0.165** | −0.0158 | 0.409* | 0.102 |
|  | (2.75) | (−0.66) | (2.50) | (1.22) |
| $\Delta nrinv_{-1}$ | −0.225 | −0.00275 | −0.733 | 0.365 |
|  | (−1.63) | (−0.05) | (−1.95) | (1.91) |
| $\Delta nrinv_{-2}$ | −0.120 | 0.0699 | −0.483 | −0.356 |
|  | (−0.90) | (1.31) | (−1.33) | (−1.93) |
| $\Delta g_{-1}$ | 0.0433 | 0.260 | −1.166 | −0.513 |
|  | (0.12) | (1.86) | (−1.22) | (−1.05) |
| $\Delta g_{-2}$ | −0.645 | 0.474** | −2.040* | −1.161* |
|  | (−1.84) | (3.40) | (−2.14) | (−2.40) |
| _cons | 0.00663* | 0.000196 | −0.00130 | 0.00176 |
|  | (2.59) | (0.19) | (−0.19) | (0.50) |
| N | 75 | 75 | 75 | 75 |

*Note*: t statistics in parentheses; * $p < 0.05$, ** $p < 0.01$, *** $p < 0.001$.

We now turn to how residential investment influences or is influenced by the three largest non-investment components of GDP: consumption, government spending, and non-residential investment (Table 10.5). It is clear that consumption was the channel through which residential investment moved GDP—and later through itself (very likely reflecting the long-held view that new construction leads to demand for consumer durables).

As before, we now limit ourselves to observations beginning with the first quarter of 2002. And again, the results change (Table 10.6). Note how the strong relationship between residential investment and consumption becomes attenuated—the sum of the coefficients of the impact of residential investment on consumption drops from 0.105 to 0.02. The impact of residential investment on non-residential investment turns from positive to negative.

## 7 HAS HOUSING CEASED TO BE AN INSTRUMENT OF MONETARY POLICY?

We return to Leamer's (2007) discussion of how housing should be an element of the Taylor rule. Housing investment is easy to measure, and once foretold recessions and recoveries. Under such circumstances, one could imagine a monetary policy rule where interest rates adjusted in response to changes in residential investment.

Yet, we have already seen that the business cycle is not as sensitive (if it is still sensitive at all) to residential investment. This finding undermines the efficacy of housing as an instrument of monetary policy. And under the circumstances, it is worth asking whether the Federal Reserve still has an influence on residential investment.

We turn to three measures of interest rates and examine their effects on residential investment: the ten-year Treasury rate, the ten-year TIP rate, and the Federal Funds rate. We do Granger tests using the full set of data from all three series and then using data from January 2003 on for the ten-year and Federal Funds rates so that their data length matches those of TIPs, which have only been available since that date. The regressions are in first differences so that the time series are stationary.

We find that long-term interest rates, whether protected for inflation or not, predict residential investment, whether we are looking at long time series or the truncated series (Table 10.7). This is also true of Freddie Mac 30-year fixed rate mortgage rates. But the Federal Funds rate has ceased to be a predictor of residential investment activity. Note that the sum of coefficients of the effect of the Federal Funds rate on residential investment was −0.027 for the entire post-1947 period but was only −0.002 for the post-2003 period. While the ten-year Treasury continued to have an impact on housing, it has operated with a longer lag in the post-2003 period than over the entire post-1947 period.

The Federal Reserve's policy of quantitative easing (QE) included the purchase of long-Treasury bonds. Because the Federal Reserve acted directly on long-term interest rates, it is possible that short-term interest rates ceased to have an impact on housing. Housing's durability implies long duration, and so its activity should be more influenced by long-term rates. Moreover, mortgage rates are generally correlated with ten-year Treasury rates (the correlation is .99 over the longer term, although it is slightly lower, at .98, over the post-2013 period). And indeed, when we look at the impact of mortgage rates themselves on residential investment, they are slightly stronger than the impact of the ten-year Treasury notes. Krishnamurthy and Vissing-Jorgensen (2011) found that QE had a strong impact on both ten-year notes and agency mortgage-backed securities rates, and so we have some evidence that the channel through which the Federal Reserve stimulated housing shifted from the traditional Federal Funds rate to longer-term securities. Nevertheless, while monetary policy once had a nearly immediate impact on residential investment, in recent periods, it operates with a lag.

Table 10.7   The impact of interest rates on residential investment

|  | (1) Δ.lrinv 54-20 | (2) Δ.lrinv 03-20 | (3) Δ.lrinv 47-20 | (4) Δ.lrinv 03-20 | (5) Δ.lrinv 03-20 | (6) Δ.lrinv 03-20 | (7) Δ.lrinv 71-20 |
|---|---|---|---|---|---|---|---|
| Δlrinv$_{-1}$ | 0.324*** | 0.0538 | 0.349*** | 0.084 | 0.138 | 0.038 | 0.226** |
|  | (4.82) | (0.46) | (5.61) | (0.67) | (0.99) | (0.33) | (3.09) |
| Δlrinv$_{-2}$ | 0.191** | 0.595*** | 0.253*** | 0.631*** | 0.502*** | 0.696*** | 0.248*** |
|  | (2.98) | (4.91) | (4.09) | (4.90) | (3.51) | (5.69) | (3.66) |
| ΔTENYR$_{-1}$ | −0.029*** |  |  | 0.013 |  |  |  |
|  | (−5.45) |  |  | (0.96) |  |  |  |
| ΔTENYR$_{-2}$ | −0.022*** |  |  | −0.051*** |  |  |  |
|  | (−3.76) |  |  | (−3.83) |  |  |  |
| ΔTIPS$_{-1}$ |  | −0.025 |  |  |  |  |  |
|  |  | (−1.75) |  |  |  |  |  |
| ΔTIPS$_{-2}$ |  | −0.057*** |  |  |  |  |  |
|  |  | (−3.96) |  |  |  |  |  |
| ΔFedFunds$_{-1}$ |  |  | −0.017*** |  | −0.013 |  |  |
|  |  |  | (−6.29) |  | (−0.75) |  |  |
| ΔFedFunds$_{-2}$ |  |  | −0.010*** |  | 0.010 |  |  |
|  |  |  | (−3.39) |  | (0.59) |  |  |
| Δmortgagerates$_{-1}$ |  |  |  |  |  | −0.006 | −0.038*** |
|  |  |  |  |  |  | (−0.41) | (−6.96) |
| Δmortgagerates$_{-2}$ |  |  |  |  |  | −0.074*** | −0.018** |
|  |  |  |  |  |  | (−4.96) | (−2.95) |
| _cons | 0.00159 | −0.00411 | 0.00157 | −0.00259 | −0.00150 | −0.00401 | 0.000302 |
|  | (0.66) | (−1.01) | (0.70) | (−0.62) | (−0.33) | (−1.02) | (0.12) |
| N | 232 | 68 | 262 | 68 | 68 | 68 | 195 |

Note: t statistics in parentheses; * $p < 0.05$, ** $p < 0.01$, *** $p < 0.001$.

## 8   WHY DOES HOUSING MATTER LESS?

A long literature has developed arguing that land use regulation has long had an impact on the production of housing and that regulation has gotten tighter over the years (see Aura and Davidoff, 2008; Gyourko et al., 2008). Morrow (2013) gives a rather spectacular example of this: the city of Los Angeles, through a series of down-zonings, has reduced its zoning capacity from 10 million to slightly more than 4 million people. In city after city, building permits per capita have been falling over time. California's 2020 population loss—the first since it became a state in 1850—was partially the result of the fact that it is not building much housing—barely enough to make up for losses arising from the demolition of old houses. From 2018 to 2019, California only added 10,000 net housing units on a base of 14 million.

The frictions in housing construction are also reflected in the findings here about how interest rates influence residential investment. Rates have become less influential and take more time to exert any influence at all on residential investment. As permitting processes have become more arduous and more stretched out, the ability of monetary policy to influence the business cycle through housing has become attenuated.

At the same time, as the regulatory environment has become more stringent, housing has to some extent become a latent variable. Heckman's series of papers on latent variables may well apply to housing. Regulation increasingly "censors" housing. Such censorship leads to housing appearing to have a smaller influence on GDP than it might if it were permitted to respond more quickly and sensitively to countercyclical policy.

Consider a world where housing limits are so severe that the maximum construction permitted is less than would be constructed at a place in the business cycle where housing demand is at its lowest. The California experience is not far removed from that—note again that it is currently not expanding its housing stock in a period of very low interest rates and very high prices. Under these circumstances, it is impossible to identify the effect of housing on the business cycle because we cannot observe normal fluctuations in the housing market.

Hsieh and Moretti (2019) have shown that zoning as practiced in the US undermines the long-run competitive position of the US economy by creating artificial shortages of housing in places people wish to live. The severing of housing from the business cycle over the past 18 years or so suggests that zoning may also have neutered the ability of the Federal Reserve to do countercyclical monetary policy.

## 9 CONCLUSION

A long series of papers have concluded that in the US, housing has been a reliable predictor of the business cycle. Indeed, an important monetary channel for the Federal Reserve has been new housing construction. For many years, its principal policy lever—the Federal Funds rate—immediately influenced residential construction. If it raised the Federal Funds rate, new construction would fall, leading to a cooling economy in the following quarters. Conversely, the Fed could reduce the Federal Funds rate to stimulate new construction and hence the broader economy.

In the aftermath of the Great Financial Crisis of 2008, these relationships seem to have broken down. Short-term interest rates no longer seem to influence new construction. That said, the Federal Reserve's policy levers did grow in the aftermath of the Great Financial Crisis. One of these new levers—QE—allowed the Federal Reserve to buy securities, such as government-sponsored enterprise-backed mortgage-backed securities, beyond those that had traditionally been part of open market operations. QE allowed the Federal Reserve to influence mortgage rates and other long-term rates.

One could easily imagine that the central bank's new levers attenuated the influence of the more traditional levers. Hence, we see that while short-term rates ceased to influence new construction, long-term rates did so, albeit with a lag.

But even though long-term rates continue to influence new construction, the levels of new construction relative to GDP remain quite low by historical standards. Figure 10.6 demonstrates this point.

This may explain the puzzle of the recent detachment between residential investment and GDP. The continuing below-average levels of new construction between 2007 and 2020 may explain why we cannot identify the previously strong link between residential investment and GDP in recent data. Hsieh and Moretti (2019) showed how regulatory constraints against housing have prevented its construction in the country's best labor markets, thus inhibiting efficient mobility and reducing GDP. Those same constraints may also be inhibiting the ability of housing to take its traditional role as a channel for countercyclical monetary policy.

## NOTE

1. Leung and Ng (2019) use 2006 as a breakpoint, and find correlations between residential investment and GDP are muted from 2006 to 2017 relative to 1991 to 2017.

## REFERENCES

Aura, Saku, and Thomas Davidoff. "Supply constraints and housing prices." *Economics Letters* 99.2 (2008): 275–277.

Brown, Robert L., James Durbin, and James M. Evans. "Techniques for testing the constancy of regression relationships over time." *Journal of the Royal Statistical Society: Series B* (Methodological) 37.2 (1975): 149–163.

Coulson, N. Edward, and Myeong-Soo Kim. "Residential investment, non-residential investment, and GDP." *Real Estate Economics* 28.2 (2000): 233–247.

Davis, Morris A., and Jonathan Heathcote. "Housing and the business cycle." *International Economic Review* 46.3 (2005): 751–784.

Granger, Clive W.J. "Testing for causality: A personal viewpoint." *Journal of Economic Dynamics and Control* 2 (1980): 329–352.

Green, Richard K. "Follow the leader: How changes in residential and non-residential investment predict changes in GDP." *Real Estate Economics* 25.2 (1997): 253–270.

Green, Richard K., and Susan M. Wachter. "The American mortgage in historical and international context." *Journal of Economic Perspectives* 19.4 (2005): 93–114.

Gyourko, Joseph, Albert Saiz, and Anita Summers. "A new measure of the local regulatory environment for housing markets: The Wharton Residential Land Use Regulatory Index." *Urban Studies* 45.3 (2008): 693–729.

Hamilton, James Douglas. *Time series analysis*. Princeton, NJ: Princeton University Press, 1994.

Hsieh, Chang-Tai, and Enrico Moretti. "Housing constraints and spatial misallocation." *American Economic Journal: Macroeconomics* 11.2 (2019): 1–39.

Krishnamurthy, Arvind, and Annette Vissing-Jorgensen. "The effects of quantitative easing on interest rates: Channels and implications for policy." No. w17555. National Bureau of Economic Research, 2011.

Leamer, Edward E. "Housing is the business cycle." No. w13428. National Bureau of Economic Research, 2007.

Leung, Charles Ka Yui. "Macroeconomics and housing: A review of the literature." *Journal of Housing Economics* 13.4 (2004): 249–267.

Leung, Charles Ka Yui, and Cho Yiu Joe Ng. "Macroeconomic aspects of housing." *Oxford Research Encyclopedia of Economics and Finance* (2019).

Morrow, Greg. *The homeowner revolution: Democracy, land use and the Los Angeles slow-growth movement, 1965–1992*. Los Angeles: University of California, 2013.

Ploberger, Werner, and Walter Krämer. "The CUSUM test with OLS residuals." *Econometrica: Journal of the Econometric Society* (1992): 271–285.

# 11. International macroeconomic aspect of housing
## Joe Cho Yiu Ng

## 1 INTRODUCTION

For decades, economists have sought to establish stylized facts among aggregate variables and provide theories to explain those facts (Cooley 1995). Among others, Leung and Ng (2018) recently show that the relationships among housing market variables and macro-finance variables in the United States significantly changed after the 2008 Global Financial Crisis (GFC). This chapter extends their analysis to 22 Organisation for Economic Co-operation and Development (OECD) member countries. The focus is to investigate the relationships among the business cycle components of housing prices and macroeconomic variables in each country.[1] I separate the pre-crisis from the post-crisis sub-samples and examine whether the correlations have changed since the GFC.

This chapter focuses on business cycle (a periodical fluctuation between 6–32 quarters) correlations. Most economic and financial variables are non-stationary, either containing a trend, a unit root, or both. Taking the first difference is a typical way to remove the unit root.[2] A natural question arises: what should we do if some variables are trend-stationary, but some are difference-stationary?[3] One may take the first difference on all the variables because growth rates are easier to compare and interpret. However, by doing so, we only study the short-run components or the fast-moving components of the variables. How about the lower frequency components? It is well known that relationships could exist only in lower-frequency bands of variables (Baxter 1994). For instance, Kishor and Marfatia (2017) find that in 10 out of 15 OECD countries, short-run movements in house prices are independent of the movements in income and interest rates, and only their permanent movements are associated with each other. Therefore, to complement studies that focus on growth rates, this chapter compares variables at a lower frequency band, i.e., the business cycle frequency.

Leung (2004) indicates that traditional macroeconomics did not include housing. However, much has changed in recent decades.[4] In the following, I will first provide a literature review on why housing markets are important for the propagation of shocks and how they are related to business cycles. Then, Section 3 will show that housing prices and macroeconomic variables are correlated, and their relationships have changed since the GFC. The last section concludes.

## 2 LITERATURE REVIEW

As mentioned by Leung (2004), "Conventional housing economics and urban economics research for its part virtually ignores interactions with the macroeconomy. At best, some of the theoretical and empirical analyses for urban and housing economics include macroeconomic variables (such as the inflation, the economic growth, gross domestic product (GDP), the unemployment rate, etc.) as exogenous control variables." In recent decades, much attention has been paid to a bidirectional causality between housing variables and macroeconomic variables. Many studies show that housing market fluctuations can propagate shocks and even generate aggregate volatility. In this section, I will provide a literature review on why housing markets are important for the propagation of shocks and how they are related to business cycles. Since these topics are too broad to review here, I only highlight a few related studies. Interested readers can find more complete discussions in Leung and Ng (2018) and Duca et al. (2020), among others.

## 2.1  Shock Propagation

The literature finds that frictions in credit markets are important for propagating the effects of shocks. What will happen in an economy where credit limits are endogenously determined? In the model proposed by Kiyotaki and Moore (1997), durable assets, such as land, buildings, and machinery, can serve as collateral for loans. Therefore, the prices of collateral affect borrowers' credit limits. The dynamic interaction between credit limits and asset prices generates a powerful transmission mechanism. Suppose there is a temporary adverse productivity shock that reduces net worth at time t. Firms who are credit-constrained and have borrowed heavily against the value of their durable assets are unable to borrow more. Those firms are forced to reduce their investment expenditure. In the next period, since they earn less, their net worth falls, and again, they reduce investment. Such knock-on effects will continue, so the effects of the temporary shock persist.

Aoki et al. (2004) study the impact of housing prices on consumption when houses are served as collateral to lower the borrowing cost. In their model, homeowners face an external finance premium due to imperfections in credit markets. The endogenous developments in credit markets, such as variations in net worth or collateral, will amplify and propagate shocks to the economy. Suppose an economy receives a positive shock to economic activity, causing an increase in demand for housing. A rise in housing prices will lead to an increase in homeowners' net worth and hence lower the external finance premium. It will lead to a further rise in housing demand and spill over into consumption demand. Aoki et al. (2004) also consider the implications for monetary policy when home equity becomes easier and cheaper to access. They find that the response of consumption to an unanticipated change in interest rates will be amplified because when housing prices increase, and more borrowing will be devoted to consumption relative to housing investment. Therefore, the response of house prices and housing investment will be smaller.

Iacoviello (2005) focuses on how a general equilibrium model with financial frictions can explain the aggregate time series evidence and be used for monetary policy analysis. In the model, collateral constraints are tied to real estate values for firms as in Kiyotaki and Moore (1997), and nominal debts for a sub-set of households. The transmission mechanism is as follows. Suppose a positive demand shock leads to an increase in consumer and asset prices. Borrowers are less constrained and willing to spend and invest more. Furthermore, the increase in consumer prices will benefit the borrowers and hurt the lenders. So, the borrowers have a higher propensity to spend than lenders, and the net effect on demand is positive. Given that, demand shocks move housing and nominal prices in the same direction and are amplified and propagated over time.

Iacoviello and Neri (2010) study the dynamics of residential investment and housing prices and the spillover effect of the housing market. In the model, they introduce sectoral heterogeneity as in Davis and Heathcote (2005). Also, housing can be used as collateral for loans, like

Kiyotaki and Moore (1997) and Iacoviello (2005). In the model, fluctuations in house prices affect the borrowing constraint of a fraction of households and the relative profitability of producing new homes. These generate feedback effects for the expenditure of households and firms. The authors find that the housing market spillovers are non-negligible and concentrated on consumption rather than business investment.

## 2.2 Business Cycle

Leamer (2007, 2015) mentions that housing is the most critical part of the United States business cycle. Although it may be unimportant during normal periods, weakness in housing is a critical part of the United States economic recessions.[5] Indeed, the literature finds durable assets are important for the generation and propagation of business cycles.

Baxter (1996) develops a two-sector model (consumption goods and durable goods) to simulate empirical patterns of cross-sector volatility and co-movement and attempts to investigate whether consumer durables are important for the generation and propagation of business cycles. He finds roughly half of the higher volatility in the durable goods industry is due to the higher volatility of productivity shocks in that industry, with the remaining half due to the endogenous accelerator mechanism. The model also correctly predicts positive cross-sectoral co-movement of outputs, investments, and labor input. Unfortunately, compared to a one-sector model, incorporating durable consumer goods does not have much effect on the behavior of other macroeconomic variables.

Different from Baxter (1996), Jin and Zeng (2004) consider a three-sector dynamic stochastic general equilibrium to distinguish residential investment goods production, non-residential investment goods production, and consumption goods production. The model introduces monetary frictions and credit market activities. Households need to finance residential investment out of their nominal wealth. Under this framework, fluctuations in the nominal interest rate affect the financing cost of firms' working capital and households' residential investment. Therefore, both residential investment and house prices are sensitive to fluctuations in the nominal interest rate. The model also generates the procyclicality of house prices and the high volatility of residential investment and hours worked in the house investment goods-producing sector.

Davis and Heathcote (2005) construct a multisector growth model with two final goods sectors. One sector produces the consumption or business investment goods. The other one produces residential structures that are combined with newly available land to produce houses. The model succeeds in reproducing two facts: GDP, consumption, residential investment, and non-residential investment co-move positively; and the volatility of the residential investment is more than twice that of the non-residential investment.

Iacoviello and Pavan (2013) study housing and mortgage debt in a general equilibrium model in which a house can be owned or rented and can be used as collateral for loans. The model matches the cyclicality and volatility of housing investment and the procyclicality of debt. Also, the reduced volatility of housing investment and the reduced procyclicality of debt can be explained by higher individual income risk and lower down payments.

## 3 STYLIZED FACTS

The literature review indicates that housing variables are not only affected by but also interact with the macroeconomy. To establish some stylized facts on the macro-housing relationship, this section provides contemporaneous, as well as lead-lag, correlations between the business cycle frequency of real housing prices and macroeconomic variables in 22 OECD countries: Australia, Austria, Belgium, Canada, Denmark, Finland, France, Germany, Iceland, Ireland, Israel, Italy, Japan, Korea, Lithuania, the Netherlands, New Zealand, Norway, Spain, Sweden, Switzerland, and the United Kingdom. I use the band-pass filter developed by Christiano and Fitzgerald (2003) to extract the business cycle frequency. Studies on a large group of countries are subject to data availability. Here, I only study a sub-set of macroeconomic variables as in Leung and Ng (2018). Table 11.1 summarizes the sample size. To study whether there is a structural change following the 2008 GFC, as suggested by some studies, I compare two sampling periods: (1) from 1997Q1 to 2006Q4, which will be referred to as the pre-crisis sub-sample, and (2) from 2010 Q1 to 2019 Q4, which will be referred to as the post-crisis sub-sample. In the following, we may find that some correlations are "counter-intuitive." This is not uncommon when we study the same relationships across countries with different economic structures, institutions, and government policies. I will conjecture some possible reasons. Hopefully, this may perhaps encourage more in-depth research.

*Table 11.1   Sample size, all the variables from 1997Q1 to 2019Q4 except the following*

| Real housing prices | | Unemployment rate | | Current account balance | |
|---|---|---|---|---|---|
| Austria | 2000Q1–2019Q4 | Ireland | 2003Q1–2019Q4 | Belgium | 2003Q1–2019Q4 |
| Ireland | 2000Q1–2019Q4 | Switzerland | Not available | Denmark | Not available |
| Lithuania | 1998Q4–2019Q4 | | | France | 1999Q1–2019Q4 |
| | | | | Ireland | 2002Q1–2019Q4 |
| | | | | Lithuania | Not available |
| | | | | Netherlands | 2003Q2–2019Q4 |
| | | | | Switzerland | 2000Q1–2019Q4 |
| **Real short-term interest rate** | | **Real credit to households** | | | |
| Japan | 2002Q2–2019Q4 | Iceland | Not available | | |
| Lithuania | 1999Q1–2019Q4 | Ireland | 2002Q1–2019Q4 | | |
| | | Lithuania | Not available | | |
| | | Switzerland | 1999Q4–2019Q4 | | |

Figure 11.1 shows the contemporaneous correlations between real housing prices and macroeconomic variables in different countries. The lead-lag correlations and the descriptive statistics are provided in the Appendix in the interest of space. The x-axis and the y-axis are respectively the pre-crisis and the post-crisis correlation. The 45-degree line indicates the following: (1) if the observation stays close to the 45-degree line, no substantial change in the relationship is observed after the GFC; (2) when the observation stays at the first (third) quadrant, the relationship is *numerically* positive (negative); (3) if the observation at the first and the third quadrants stays above (below) the 45-degree line, the relationship is *numerically* strengthened

288  *Handbook of real estate and macroeconomics*

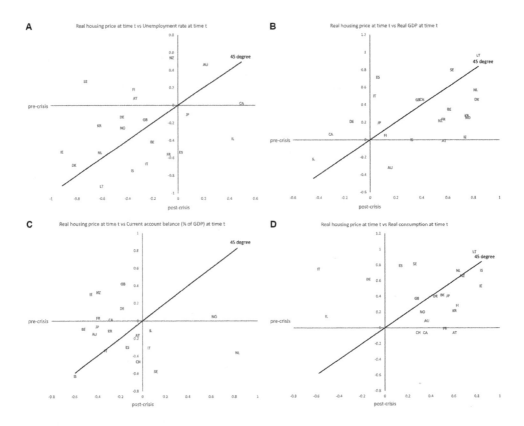

*Figure 11.1A–D  Contemporaneous correlation between real housing prices and macroeconomic variables*

(weakened) after the GFC; (4) if the observation falls into the second and the fourth quadrants, the relationship is *numerically* reversed after the GFC. Table 11.2 shows the abbreviations. Table 11.3 provides statistical tests on whether the correlations and the difference in correlations are significant. Readers are suggested to read the figures together with Table 11.3 since a numerical difference does not imply a statistically significant difference. Several observations are in order. First, the correlations in most of the countries do not close to the 45-degree line (Figure 11.1 and the Appendix). A z-test is provided in Table 11.3 to test whether the correlations are statistically different before and after the crisis.[6] It shows that many pre-crisis and post-crisis correlations are indeed significantly different from each other. It suggests that the GFC has an impact on the macro-housing relationship.

Second, many observations lie on the third quadrant in Figure 11.1A, while most lie on the first quadrant in Figure 11.1B. In other words, in both the pre-crisis and post-crisis sub-samples, the real housing prices are negatively and positively correlated with the unemployment rate and the real GDP, respectively, in general. These correlations are intuitive. For instance, when an economy receives a positive productivity shock, it produces more goods and services for the same relative work. Firms hire more workers, and people are more willing to buy housing units, resulting in an increase in the real output and a decrease in the unemployment rate. However, the correlations in some countries, like Australia, Canada, and Israel, are

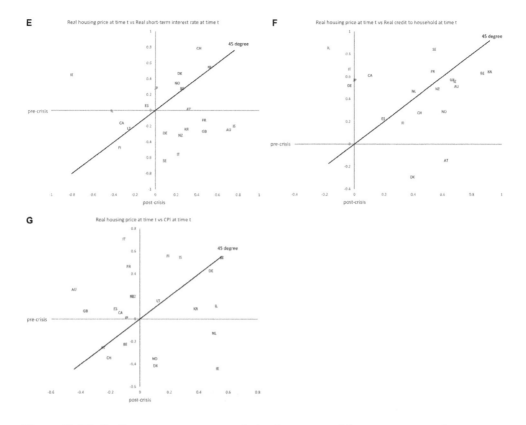

*Figure 11.1E–G* Contemporaneous correlation between real housing prices and macroeconomic variables

Table 11.2  Abbreviations

| Country | Abbreviation | Country | Abbreviation | Country | Abbreviation |
|---|---|---|---|---|---|
| Australia | AU | Iceland | IS | Netherlands | NL |
| Austria | AT | Ireland | IE | New Zealand | NZ |
| Belgium | BE | Israel | IL | Norway | NO |
| Canada | CA | Italy | IT | Netherlands | NL |
| Denmark | DK | Japan | JP | Spain | ES |
| Finland | FI | Korea | KR | Sweden | SE |
| France | FR | Lithuania | LT | Switzerland | CH |
| Germany | DE | | | United Kingdom | GB |

not consistent with these theoretical predictions. The most interesting case is Australia. The unemployment rate at time t-1 is significantly and positively correlated with the housing price at time t in the pre-crisis and post-crisis periods. Also, the output at time t-1 is significantly and negatively correlated with the housing price at time t in the post-crisis period (Table 11.3). It suggests the real output and the unemployment rate drive the real housing price in Australia. A conjecture is that it is a supply-driven housing market. Suppose in an economy the demand for housing is inelastic. Also, the construction industry hires a large portion of the labor force.

Table 11.3  Business cycle correlations

### Australia real housing price

| Macro variable at time t | t-1 Pre-crisis | t-1 Post-crisis | t-1 z statistic | t Pre-crisis | t Post-crisis | t z statistic | t+1 Pre-crisis | t+1 Post-crisis | t+1 z statistic |
|---|---|---|---|---|---|---|---|---|---|
| Unemployment rate | 0.02 | 0.27 | -1.1 | 0.22 | 0.47*** | -1.23 | 0.37** | 0.64*** | -1.59 |
| Real GDP | 0.28 | -0.28 | 2.47** | 0.15 | -0.32** | 2.08** | 0.02 | -0.42*** | 2.01** |
| Current account balance | -0.53*** | -0.23 | -1.53 | -0.42*** | -0.15 | -1.28 | -0.29 | -0.09 | -0.9 |
| Real consumption | 0.48*** | 0 | 2.25** | 0.37** | 0.09 | 1.28 | 0.26 | 0.11 | 0.67 |
| Real short-term interest rate | 0.71*** | -0.08 | 4.16*** | 0.71*** | -0.24 | 4.87*** | 0.61*** | -0.39** | 4.82*** |
| Real credit to household | 0.84*** | 0.67*** | 1.77 | 0.7*** | 0.51*** | 1.31 | 0.47*** | 0.28 | 0.96 |
| CPI | -0.32** | 0.16 | -2.12** | -0.44*** | 0.26 | -3.18*** | -0.58*** | 0.33** | -4.32*** |

### Austria real housing price

| Macro variable at time t | t-1 Pre-crisis | t-1 Post-crisis | t-1 z statistic | t Pre-crisis | t Post-crisis | t z statistic | t+1 Pre-crisis | t+1 Post-crisis | t+1 z statistic |
|---|---|---|---|---|---|---|---|---|---|
| Unemployment rate | -0.44** | 0.11 | -2.25** | -0.34 | 0.08 | -1.68 | -0.13 | -0.11 | -0.08 |
| Real GDP | 0.57*** | -0.11 | 2.93*** | 0.57*** | -0.01 | 2.54** | 0.48*** | 0.1 | 1.63 |
| Current account balance | 0.05 | -0.07 | 0.46 | -0.04 | -0.16 | 0.47 | -0.15 | -0.25 | 0.4 |
| Real consumption | 0.55*** | -0.17 | 3.05*** | 0.61*** | -0.06 | 2.97*** | 0.56*** | 0.09 | 2.1** |
| Real short-term interest rate | 0.5*** | 0 | 2.12** | 0.32 | 0.02 | 1.2 | 0.07 | -0.02 | 0.35 |
| Real credit to household | 0.62*** | -0.26 | 3.83*** | 0.62*** | -0.15 | 3.38*** | 0.57*** | -0.01 | 2.54** |
| CPI | -0.27 | -0.12 | -0.6 | -0.25 | -0.25 | 0 | -0.17 | -0.3 | 0.53 |

### Belgium real housing price

| Macro variable at time t | t-1 Pre-crisis | t-1 Post-crisis | t-1 z statistic | t Pre-crisis | t Post-crisis | t z statistic | t+1 Pre-crisis | t+1 Post-crisis | t+1 z statistic |
|---|---|---|---|---|---|---|---|---|---|
| Unemployment rate | -0.38** | -0.47*** | 0.47 | -0.2 | -0.41*** | 1 | -0.04 | -0.44*** | 1.86 |
| Real GDP | 0.65*** | 0.31 | 1.96** | 0.61*** | 0.35** | 1.48 | 0.44*** | 0.29 | 0.75 |
| Current account balance | -0.52*** | -0.06 | -1.6 | -0.52** | -0.09 | -1.51 | -0.71*** | -0.35** | -1.62 |
| Real consumption | 0.54*** | 0.45*** | 0.51 | 0.5*** | 0.42*** | 0.44 | 0.38** | 0.18 | 0.94 |
| Real short-term interest rate | 0.36** | 0.27 | 0.43 | 0.26 | 0.28 | -0.09 | 0.02 | 0.09 | -0.3 |
| Real credit to household | 0.83*** | 0.52*** | 2.63*** | 0.87*** | 0.63*** | 2.54** | 0.82*** | 0.55*** | 2.32** |
| CPI | 0.03 | -0.16 | 0.82 | -0.1 | -0.22 | 0.53 | -0.05 | -0.18 | 0.57 |

## Canada real housing price

| Macro variable at time t | t-1 Pre-crisis | t-1 Post-crisis | z statistic | t Pre-crisis | t Post-crisis | z statistic | t+1 Pre-crisis | t+1 Post-crisis | z statistic |
|---|---|---|---|---|---|---|---|---|---|
| Unemployment rate | 0.54*** | -0.21 | 3.52*** | 0.49*** | 0.02 | 2.22** | 0.42*** | 0.2 | 1.05 |
| Real GDP | -0.29 | 0.23 | -2.29** | -0.31 | 0.06 | -1.64 | -0.35** | -0.11 | -1.1 |
| Current account balance | -0.38** | 0.03 | -1.85 | -0.28 | 0.01 | -1.28 | -0.2 | -0.01 | -0.83 |
| Real consumption | 0.46*** | 0 | 2.14** | 0.35** | -0.06 | 1.83 | 0.16 | -0.14 | 1.3 |
| Real short-term interest rate | -0.36** | -0.03 | -1.49 | -0.32** | -0.16 | -0.73 | -0.33** | -0.26 | -0.33 |
| Real credit to household | 0.31 | 0.42** | -0.55 | 0.1 | 0.61*** | -2.62*** | -0.12 | 0.68*** | -4.08*** |
| CPI | 0 | 0.16 | -0.69 | -0.13 | 0.06 | -0.82 | -0.22 | -0.04 | -0.79 |

## Denmark real housing price

| Macro variable at time t | t-1 Pre-crisis | t-1 Post-crisis | z statistic | t Pre-crisis | t Post-crisis | z statistic | t+1 Pre-crisis | t+1 Post-crisis | z statistic |
|---|---|---|---|---|---|---|---|---|---|
| Unemployment rate | -0.86*** | -0.79*** | -0.95 | -0.82*** | -0.68*** | -1.41 | -0.72*** | -0.57*** | -1.12 |
| Real GDP | 0.75*** | 0.45*** | 2.1** | 0.83*** | 0.46*** | 2.97*** | 0.83*** | 0.59*** | 2.2** |
| Current account balance | - | - | - | - | - | - | - | - | - |
| Real consumption | 0.24 | 0.44*** | -0.98 | 0.44*** | 0.4*** | 0.21 | 0.6*** | 0.44*** | 0.95 |
| Real short-term interest rate | 0.32** | 0.6*** | -1.55 | 0.23 | 0.47*** | -1.19 | 0.1 | 0.21 | -0.49 |
| Real credit to household | 0.46*** | -0.32** | 3.57*** | 0.39** | -0.29 | 3.06*** | 0.3 | -0.31** | 2.71*** |
| CPI | 0.04 | -0.32** | 1.6 | 0.11 | -0.41*** | 2.35** | 0.27 | -0.27 | 2.38** |

## Finland real housing price

| Macro variable at time t | t-1 Pre-crisis | t-1 Post-crisis | z statistic | t Pre-crisis | t Post-crisis | z statistic | t+1 Pre-crisis | t+1 Post-crisis | z statistic |
|---|---|---|---|---|---|---|---|---|---|
| Unemployment rate | -0.4** | -0.12 | -1.3 | -0.35** | 0.18 | -2.35** | -0.25 | 0.37** | -2.77*** |
| Real GDP | 0.12 | 0.33** | -0.96 | 0.12 | 0.05 | 0.3 | 0.04 | -0.17 | 0.91 |
| Current account balance | -0.16 | -0.43*** | 1.28 | -0.33** | -0.34** | 0.05 | -0.51*** | -0.24 | -1.37 |
| Real consumption | 0.43*** | 0.38** | 0.26 | 0.63*** | 0.28 | 1.95 | 0.76*** | 0.18 | 3.5*** |
| Real short-term interest rate | -0.27 | -0.66*** | 2.22** | -0.34** | -0.47*** | 0.67 | -0.39** | -0.27 | -0.58 |
| Real credit to household | 0.54*** | -0.02 | 2.68*** | 0.33** | 0.19 | 0.65 | 0.12 | 0.28 | -0.72 |
| CPI | 0.4** | 0.77*** | -2.57** | 0.19 | 0.56*** | -1.89 | -0.05 | 0.24 | -1.27 |

## France real housing price

| Macro variable at time t | t-1 Pre-crisis | t-1 Post-crisis | z statistic | t Pre-crisis | t Post-crisis | z statistic | t+1 Pre-crisis | t+1 Post-crisis | z statistic |
|---|---|---|---|---|---|---|---|---|---|
| Unemployment rate | -0.24 | -0.66*** | 2.36** | -0.07 | -0.56*** | 2.42** | 0.11 | -0.52*** | 2.95*** |
| Real GDP | 0.71*** | 0.22 | 2.85*** | 0.57*** | 0.23 | 1.78 | 0.35** | 0.38** | -0.15 |
| Current account balance | -0.38** | 0.04 | -1.77 | -0.39** | 0.03 | -1.78 | -0.47*** | 0 | -2.06** |
| Real consumption | 0.67*** | -0.1 | 3.92*** | 0.52*** | -0.01 | 2.52** | 0.36** | 0.21 | 0.7 |

## Germany real housing price

| Macro variable at time t | t-1 | | | t | | | t+1 | | |
|---|---|---|---|---|---|---|---|---|---|
| | Pre-crisis | Post-crisis | z statistic | Pre-crisis | Post-crisis | z statistic | Pre-crisis | Post-crisis | z statistic |
| Real short-term interest rate | 0.64*** | 0.04 | 3.09*** | 0.47*** | -0.12 | 2.71*** | 0.22 | -0.25 | 2.06** |
| Real credit to household | 0.66*** | 0.63*** | 0.22 | 0.53*** | 0.65*** | -0.8 | 0.34** | 0.61*** | -1.53 |
| CPI | -0.07 | 0.34** | -1.82 | -0.08 | 0.47*** | -2.54** | 0.06 | 0.5*** | -2.1** |

| Macro variable at time t | Pre-crisis | Post-crisis | z statistic | Pre-crisis | Post-crisis | z statistic | Pre-crisis | Post-crisis | z statistic |
|---|---|---|---|---|---|---|---|---|---|
| Unemployment rate | -0.33** | -0.23 | -0.47 | -0.44*** | -0.13 | -1.47 | -0.5*** | -0.14 | -1.76 |
| Real GDP | 0.09 | 0.14 | -0.22 | -0.14 | 0.21 | -1.52 | -0.34** | 0.25 | -2.62*** |
| Current account balance | -0.07 | -0.12 | 0.22 | -0.18 | 0.14 | -1.39 | -0.26 | 0.29 | -2.43** |
| Real consumption | 0.03 | 0.51*** | -2.29** | -0.14 | 0.62*** | -3.72*** | -0.32** | 0.57*** | -4.21*** |
| Real short-term interest rate | -0.03 | -0.44*** | 1.9 | 0.09 | -0.29 | 1.67 | 0.2 | -0.24 | 1.92 |
| Real credit to household | -0.18 | 0.16 | -1.48 | -0.03 | 0.52*** | -2.61*** | 0.15 | 0.66*** | -2.76*** |
| CPI | 0.37** | 0.51*** | -0.75 | 0.48*** | 0.43*** | 0.27 | 0.53*** | 0.36** | 0.92 |

## Iceland real housing price

| Macro variable at time t | t-1 | | | t | | | t+1 | | |
|---|---|---|---|---|---|---|---|---|---|
| | Pre-crisis | Post-crisis | z statistic | Pre-crisis | Post-crisis | z statistic | Pre-crisis | Post-crisis | z statistic |
| Unemployment rate | -0.33 | -0.77*** | 2.91*** | -0.36 | -0.74*** | 2.47** | -0.39 | -0.73*** | 2.22** |
| Real GDP | 0.49** | 0.04 | 2.13** | 0.32 | 0 | 1.43 | 0.18 | 0.09 | 0.39 |
| Current account balance | -0.57*** | -0.62*** | 0.33 | -0.59*** | -0.63*** | 0.27 | -0.58*** | -0.63*** | 0.34 |
| Real consumption | 0.72*** | 0.8*** | -0.82 | 0.84*** | 0.73*** | 1.26 | 0.88*** | 0.67*** | 2.43** |
| Real short-term interest rate | 0.72*** | -0.15 | 4.55*** | 0.76*** | -0.2 | 5.16*** | 0.71*** | -0.01 | 3.86*** |
| Real credit to household | - | - | - | - | - | - | - | - | - |
| CPI | 0.43** | 0.65*** | -1.36 | 0.27 | 0.55*** | -1.47 | 0.16 | 0.41*** | -1.18 |

## Ireland real housing price

| Macro variable at time t | t-1 | | | t | | | t+1 | | |
|---|---|---|---|---|---|---|---|---|---|
| | Pre-crisis | Post-crisis | z statistic | Pre-crisis | Post-crisis | z statistic | Pre-crisis | Post-crisis | z statistic |
| Unemployment rate | -0.94*** | -0.48*** | -3.77*** | -0.91*** | -0.53*** | -2.91*** | -0.83*** | -0.55*** | -1.77 |
| Real GDP | 0.71*** | 0.27 | 2.36** | 0.73*** | 0.03 | 3.47*** | 0.69*** | -0.19 | 4.02*** |
| Current account balance | -0.35 | 0.2 | -1.94 | -0.45*** | 0.3 | -2.71*** | -0.59*** | 0.29 | -3.33*** |
| Real consumption | 0.81*** | 0.58*** | 1.79 | 0.83*** | 0.53*** | 2.31** | 0.79*** | 0.45*** | 2.27** |
| Real short-term interest rate | -0.7*** | 0.34*** | -4.72*** | -0.8*** | 0.45*** | -6.12*** | -0.84*** | 0.37*** | -6.22*** |
| Real credit to household | 0.52** | 0.42*** | 0.44 | 0.69*** | 0.56*** | 0.73 | 0.8*** | 0.59*** | 1.44 |
| CPI | 0.43*** | -0.36** | 3.23*** | 0.53*** | -0.44*** | 4.1*** | 0.55*** | -0.39** | 3.98*** |

International macroeconomic aspect of housing 293

### Israel real housing price

| Macro variable at time t | t-1 Pre-crisis | t-1 Post-crisis | z statistic | t Pre-crisis | t Post-crisis | z statistic | t+1 Pre-crisis | t+1 Post-crisis | z statistic |
|---|---|---|---|---|---|---|---|---|---|
| Unemployment rate | 0.35** | −0.5*** | 3.93*** | 0.43*** | −0.38** | 3.7*** | 0.44*** | −0.11 | 2.51*** |
| Real GDP | −0.32** | −0.33** | 0.05 | −0.44*** | −0.22 | −1.07 | −0.55*** | −0.11 | −2.18** |
| Current account balance | 0.2 | −0.33** | 2.35** | 0.07 | −0.11 | 0.78 | 0.08 | 0.15 | −0.31 |
| Real consumption | −0.57*** | 0.08 | −3.13*** | −0.51*** | 0.15 | −3.07*** | −0.41** | 0.07 | −2.18** |
| Real short-term interest rate | −0.3 | 0.07 | −1.63 | −0.42*** | 0 | −1.93 | −0.37*** | −0.1 | −1.24 |
| Real credit to household | −0.24 | 0.77*** | −5.44*** | −0.17 | 0.86*** | −6.3*** | −0.22 | 0.83*** | −6.07*** |
| CPI | 0.27 | 0.2 | 0.32 | 0.52*** | 0.12 | 1.96** | 0.49*** | −0.01 | 2.35** |

### Italy real housing price

| Macro variable at time t | t-1 Pre-crisis | t-1 Post-crisis | z statistic | t Pre-crisis | t Post-crisis | z statistic | t+1 Pre-crisis | t+1 Post-crisis | z statistic |
|---|---|---|---|---|---|---|---|---|---|
| Unemployment rate | −0.05 | −0.4** | 1.61 | −0.25 | −0.67*** | 2.39** | −0.43*** | −0.85*** | 3.42*** |
| Real GDP | 0.06 | 0.28 | −0.98 | 0.04 | 0.5*** | −2.19** | 0.06 | 0.65*** | −3.08*** |
| Current account balance | −0.18 | −0.03 | −0.65 | 0.06 | −0.31 | 1.64 | 0.29 | −0.6*** | 4.27*** |
| Real consumption | −0.44*** | 0.52*** | −4.51*** | −0.58*** | 0.75*** | −7.03*** | −0.68*** | 0.89*** | −9.68*** |
| Real short-term interest rate | 0.06 | −0.7*** | 3.99*** | 0.22 | −0.56*** | 3.68*** | 0.32** | −0.41*** | 3.3*** |
| Real credit to household | −0.24 | 0.42*** | −2.98*** | −0.03 | 0.67*** | −3.62*** | 0.15 | 0.84*** | −4.6*** |
| CPI | 0.06 | 0.8*** | −4.47*** | −0.11 | 0.71*** | −4.29*** | −0.2 | 0.58*** | −3.72*** |

### Japan real housing price

| Macro variable at time t | t-1 Pre-crisis | t-1 Post-crisis | z statistic | t Pre-crisis | t Post-crisis | z statistic | t+1 Pre-crisis | t+1 Post-crisis | z statistic |
|---|---|---|---|---|---|---|---|---|---|
| Unemployment rate | 0.17 | −0.36** | 2.36** | 0.08 | −0.1 | 0.78 | −0.02 | 0.03 | −0.22 |
| Real GDP | −0.03 | 0.11 | −0.6 | 0.07 | 0.2 | −0.57 | 0.18 | 0.19 | −0.04 |
| Current account balance | −0.26 | −0.35** | 0.43 | −0.4** | −0.06 | −1.56 | −0.52*** | 0.17 | −3.22*** |
| Real consumption | 0.35** | 0.39*** | −0.2 | 0.55*** | 0.41*** | 0.79 | 0.68*** | 0.26 | 2.42** |
| Real short-term interest rate | 0 | −0.03 | 0.1 | 0.01 | 0.28 | −0.95 | 0.04 | 0.45*** | −1.52 |
| Real credit to household | 0.11 | 0.4** | −1.35 | 0 | 0.57*** | −2.79*** | −0.1 | 0.56*** | −3.15*** |
| CPI | 0.16 | 0.32** | −0.73 | −0.09 | 0.01 | −0.43 | −0.3 | −0.3 | 0 |

### Korea real housing price

| Macro variable at time t | t-1 Pre-crisis | t-1 Post-crisis | z statistic | t Pre-crisis | t Post-crisis | z statistic | t+1 Pre-crisis | t+1 Post-crisis | z statistic |
|---|---|---|---|---|---|---|---|---|---|
| Unemployment rate | −0.5*** | −0.38** | −0.64 | −0.62*** | −0.23 | −2.11** | −0.61*** | −0.06 | −2.79*** |
| Real GDP | 0.71*** | 0.23 | 2.81*** | 0.75*** | 0.28 | 2.95*** | 0.62*** | 0.31 | 1.74 |
| Current account balance | 0.05 | −0.03 | 0.34 | −0.29 | −0.11 | −0.81 | −0.5*** | −0.2 | −1.49 |
| Real consumption | 0.34** | 0.15 | 0.87 | 0.61*** | 0.22 | 2.09** | 0.73*** | 0.29 | 2.71*** |

| | t-1 | | | t | | | t+1 | | |
|---|---|---|---|---|---|---|---|---|---|
| | Pre-crisis | Post-crisis | z statistic | Pre-crisis | Post-crisis | z statistic | Pre-crisis | Post-crisis | z statistic |
| Real short-term interest rate | 0.44*** | −0.13 | 2.59*** | 0.3 | −0.24 | 2.38** | 0.1 | −0.38** | 2.15** |
| Real credit to household | 0.88*** | 0.69*** | 2.27** | 0.92*** | 0.65*** | 3.5*** | 0.85*** | 0.53*** | 2.86*** |
| CPI | 0.64*** | 0.05 | 3.05*** | 0.38** | 0.09 | 1.33 | 0.13 | 0.19 | −0.26 |

**Lithuania real housing price**

| | t-1 | | | t | | | t+1 | | |
|---|---|---|---|---|---|---|---|---|---|
| | Pre-crisis | Post-crisis | z statistic | Pre-crisis | Post-crisis | z statistic | Pre-crisis | Post-crisis | z statistic |
| Macro variable at time t | | | | | | | | | |
| Unemployment rate | −0.68*** | −0.9*** | 2.69*** | −0.6*** | −0.92*** | 3.74*** | −0.47*** | −0.91*** | 4.25*** |
| Real GDP | 0.88*** | 0.92*** | −0.89 | 0.84*** | 0.97*** | −3.64*** | 0.69*** | 0.98*** | −6.05*** |
| Current account balance | - | - | - | - | - | - | - | - | - |
| Real consumption | 0.84*** | 0.97*** | −3.64*** | 0.78*** | 0.97*** | −4.37*** | 0.66*** | 0.94*** | −3.95*** |
| Real short-term interest rate | −0.14 | −0.17 | 0.13 | −0.25 | −0.23 | −0.09 | −0.35 | −0.48*** | 0.66 |
| Real credit to household | - | - | - | - | - | - | - | - | - |
| CPI | 0.15 | 0.14 | 0.04 | 0.13 | 0.16 | −0.13 | 0.2 | 0.41*** | −0.97 |

**Netherlands real housing price**

| | t-1 | | | t | | | t+1 | | |
|---|---|---|---|---|---|---|---|---|---|
| | Pre-crisis | Post-crisis | z statistic | Pre-crisis | Post-crisis | z statistic | Pre-crisis | Post-crisis | z statistic |
| Macro variable at time t | | | | | | | | | |
| Unemployment rate | −0.69*** | −0.78*** | 0.85 | −0.62*** | −0.54*** | −0.52 | −0.53*** | −0.27 | −1.35 |
| Real GDP | 0.81*** | 0.54*** | 2.25** | 0.82*** | 0.57*** | 2.19** | 0.77*** | 0.51*** | 1.97** |
| Current account balance | 0.76*** | −0.18 | 3.65*** | 0.83*** | −0.36** | 4.85*** | 0.87*** | −0.45*** | 5.64*** |
| Real consumption | 0.47*** | 0.72*** | −1.71 | 0.64*** | 0.73*** | −0.73 | 0.78*** | 0.61*** | 1.45 |
| Real short-term interest rate | 0.44*** | 0.35** | 0.46 | 0.52*** | 0.55*** | −0.18 | 0.53*** | 0.63*** | −0.65 |
| Real credit to household | 0.18 | 0.44*** | −1.25 | 0.4*** | 0.47*** | −0.37 | 0.59*** | 0.41*** | 1.04 |
| CPI | 0.64*** | 0.13 | 2.7*** | 0.5*** | −0.12 | 2.88*** | 0.34** | −0.26 | 2.67*** |

**New Zealand real housing price**

| | t-1 | | | t | | | t+1 | | |
|---|---|---|---|---|---|---|---|---|---|
| | Pre-crisis | Post-crisis | z statistic | Pre-crisis | Post-crisis | z statistic | Pre-crisis | Post-crisis | z statistic |
| Macro variable at time t | | | | | | | | | |
| Unemployment rate | −0.21 | 0.4** | −2.74*** | −0.05 | 0.54*** | −2.81*** | 0.18 | 0.59*** | −2.13** |
| Real GDP | 0.58*** | 0.31 | 1.47 | 0.54*** | 0.22 | 1.64 | 0.31 | 0.06 | 1.12 |
| Current account balance | −0.4** | 0.25 | −2.92*** | −0.39** | 0.32** | −3.2*** | −0.29 | 0.38** | −3*** |
| Real consumption | 0.56*** | 0.6*** | −0.26 | 0.68*** | 0.67*** | 0.08 | 0.68*** | 0.58*** | 0.72 |
| Real short-term interest rate | 0.27 | −0.44*** | 3.22*** | 0.24 | −0.31** | 2.43** | 0.14 | −0.2 | 1.48 |
| Real credit to household | 0.64*** | 0.46*** | 1.12 | 0.57*** | 0.49*** | 0.48 | 0.34*** | 0.4*** | −0.3 |
| CPI | 0.37** | 0.37** | 0 | −0.05 | 0.2 | −1.09 | −0.45*** | −0.01 | −2.04** |

## Norway real housing price

| Macro variable at time t | Pre-crisis | t-1 Post-crisis | z statistic | Pre-crisis | t Post-crisis | z statistic | Pre-crisis | t+1 Post-crisis | z statistic |
|---|---|---|---|---|---|---|---|---|---|
| Unemployment rate | -0.45*** | -0.38** | -0.36 | -0.44*** | -0.26 | -0.89 | -0.3 | -0.18 | -0.55 |
| Real GDP | 0.69*** | 0.43*** | 1.67 | 0.76*** | 0.25 | 3.19*** | 0.79*** | 0.13 | 4.05*** |
| Current account balance | 0.57*** | 0.13 | 2.22** | 0.63*** | 0.05 | 2.97*** | 0.7*** | -0.04 | 3.9*** |
| Real consumption | 0.17 | 0.29 | -0.55 | 0.33** | 0.2 | 0.6 | 0.34** | 0.11 | 1.05 |
| Real short-term interest rate | 0.36** | 0.41*** | -0.25 | 0.21 | 0.35** | -0.65 | 0 | 0.34** | -1.52 |
| Real credit to household | 0.74*** | 0.52*** | 1.61 | 0.61*** | 0.29 | 1.77 | 0.38** | 0.09 | 1.33 |
| CPI | 0.29 | -0.31 | 2.66*** | 0.1 | -0.35** | 2** | 0.11 | -0.34** | 2** |

## Spain real housing price

| Macro variable at time t | Pre-crisis | t-1 Post-crisis | z statistic | Pre-crisis | t Post-crisis | z statistic | Pre-crisis | t+1 Post-crisis | z statistic |
|---|---|---|---|---|---|---|---|---|---|
| Unemployment rate | 0.02 | -0.72*** | 3.99*** | 0.02 | -0.53*** | 2.62*** | 0.07 | -0.22 | 1.26 |
| Real GDP | -0.11 | 0.71*** | -4.29*** | 0.06 | 0.72*** | -3.65*** | 0.08 | 0.65*** | -2.99*** |
| Current account balance | -0.16 | -0.35** | 0.88 | -0.14 | -0.3 | 0.73 | -0.09 | -0.17 | 0.35 |
| Real consumption | 0.14 | 0.83*** | -4.5*** | 0.14 | 0.79*** | -4*** | 0.09 | 0.65*** | -2.95*** |
| Real short-term interest rate | -0.12 | -0.04 | -0.35 | -0.08 | 0.06 | -0.6 | -0.18 | 0.15 | -1.43 |
| Real credit to household | 0.09 | 0.21 | -0.53 | 0.19 | 0.23 | -0.18 | 0.17 | 0.22 | -0.22 |
| CPI | 0.25 | 0.23 | 0.09 | -0.17 | 0.09 | -1.13 | -0.34** | -0.03 | -1.39 |

## Sweden real housing price

| Macro variable at time t | Pre-crisis | t-1 Post-crisis | z statistic | Pre-crisis | t Post-crisis | z statistic | Pre-crisis | t+1 Post-crisis | z statistic |
|---|---|---|---|---|---|---|---|---|---|
| Unemployment rate | -0.62*** | 0.12 | -3.64*** | -0.73*** | 0.27 | -5.19*** | -0.81*** | 0.41*** | -6.72*** |
| Real GDP | 0.41*** | 0.74*** | -2.21** | 0.63*** | 0.8*** | -1.54 | 0.79*** | 0.73*** | 0.61 |
| Current account balance | 0.12 | -0.65*** | 3.85*** | 0.12 | -0.58*** | 3.37*** | 0.14 | -0.53*** | 3.14*** |
| Real consumption | 0.01 | 0.74*** | -4.05*** | 0.26 | 0.82*** | -3.83*** | 0.48*** | 0.84*** | -3*** |
| Real short-term interest rate | -0.11 | -0.76*** | 3.81*** | 0.09 | -0.64*** | 3.65*** | 0.2 | -0.45*** | 2.96*** |
| Real credit to household | 0.56*** | 0.9*** | -3.61*** | 0.54*** | 0.84*** | -2.65*** | 0.49*** | 0.73*** | -1.69 |
| CPI | 0.69*** | 0.67*** | 0.16 | 0.56*** | 0.54*** | 0.12 | 0.35** | 0.32** | 0.15 |

## Switzerland real housing price

| | t-1 | | | t | | | t+1 | | |
|---|---|---|---|---|---|---|---|---|---|
| Macro variable at time t | Pre-crisis | Post-crisis | z statistic | Pre-crisis | Post-crisis | z statistic | Pre-crisis | Post-crisis | z statistic |
| Unemployment rate | - | - | - | - | - | - | - | - | - |
| Real GDP | 0.42*** | 0.59*** | -0.99 | 0.4*** | 0.46*** | -0.32 | 0.31 | 0.39** | -0.39 |
| Current account balance | -0.27 | -0.45*** | 0.8 | -0.04 | -0.47*** | 1.82 | 0.04 | -0.51*** | 2.33** |
| Real consumption | 0.3 | 0.13 | 0.77 | 0.29 | -0.06 | 1.54 | 0.31 | -0.23 | 2.39** |
| Real short-term interest rate | 0.32** | 0.83*** | -3.68*** | 0.42*** | 0.79*** | -2.68*** | 0.33** | 0.61*** | -1.57 |
| Real credit to household | 0.21 | 0.33** | -0.51 | 0.44** | 0.28 | 0.72 | 0.51*** | 0.18 | 1.49 |
| CPI | 0.09 | -0.31 | 1.77 | -0.21 | -0.34** | 0.61 | -0.1 | -0.35** | 1.14 |

## United Kingdom real housing price

| | t-1 | | | t | | | t+1 | | |
|---|---|---|---|---|---|---|---|---|---|
| Macro variable at time t | Pre-crisis | Post-crisis | z statistic | Pre-crisis | Post-crisis | z statistic | Pre-crisis | Post-crisis | z statistic |
| Unemployment rate | -0.52*** | -0.13 | -1.92 | -0.26 | -0.16 | -0.45 | 0.01 | -0.11 | 0.52 |
| Real GDP | 0.33** | 0.36** | -0.15 | 0.37** | 0.46*** | -0.47 | 0.35** | 0.43*** | -0.41 |
| Current account balance | 0 | 0.44*** | -2.03** | -0.17 | 0.42*** | -2.66*** | -0.4** | 0.47*** | -4.02*** |
| Real consumption | 0.34** | 0.37** | -0.15 | 0.28 | 0.37** | -0.43 | 0.19 | 0.29 | -0.46 |
| Real short-term interest rate | 0.48*** | -0.38** | 3.97*** | 0.47*** | -0.26 | 3.34*** | 0.32 | -0.13 | 1.99** |
| Real credit to household | 0.69*** | 0.49*** | 1.34 | 0.67*** | 0.57*** | 0.7 | 0.55*** | 0.56*** | -0.06 |
| CPI | -0.29 | 0.33** | -2.76*** | -0.37** | 0.07 | -1.97** | -0.43*** | -0.17 | -1.24 |

*Note:* ** and *** indicate 5 and 1 percent level of significance, respectively. The null hypothesis of the z-test: the pre-crisis and post-crisis correlations are not significantly different. Statistical significance indicates the null hypothesis is rejected.

When an adverse productivity shock hits the economy, the unemployment rate rises, and the real output drops. Many workers in the construction industry become unemployed, leading to a decrease in housing prices. Since the demand for housing is inelastic, the housing price, which mainly reflects the movements in housing supply, increases. In fact, the Australian construction industry hired 9.3 percent of the labor force in 2019. The inelastic housing demand might be caused by strong foreign demand for Australian real estate, especially the demand from Chinese investors.

Another set of important correlations is related to the current account balance. On the one hand, a current account surplus (deficit) indicates the capital account is in deficit (surplus), suggesting that there is an outflow (inflow) of capital. If foreign capital is an important driver of real housing prices, real housing prices will be negatively correlated with the current account balance. On the other hand, their relationship could be positive in a trade-dependent economy. For instance, if the demand for export of a trade-dependent economy shrinks after a global crisis, the current account deficit increases, and the real income decreases, resulting in a decrease in the real housing prices. Table 11.3 shows that the negative correlations between current account balance and real housing prices in some countries become statistically insignificant after the GFC. This may be a result of shrinking demand for exports.

The housing wealth effect indicates a positive relationship between real housing prices and real consumption. After the GFC, while the positive relationship between real housing prices and real consumption has weakened in many countries, some countries exhibit a stronger positive correlation (Figure 11.1D). This adds to the evidence that the correlations between real housing prices and macroeconomic variables have changed since the GFC. It is not surprising that some countries, like Israel, Italy, and the United Kingdom, show a negative correlation. The relationship between real housing prices and real consumption also depends on other factors, such as the size of the rental market and the down-payment requirement. For instance, the Bank of Israel sets a minimum down-payment requirement of 25 percent for a mortgage. In practice, the banks demand closer to 40 percent.[7] With a large amount of down payment, people may save more when real housing prices increase, leading to a decrease in consumption.

In the relationship between short-term interest rates and real housing prices, the observations in Figure 11.1E are quite dispersed. They mainly lie on the first, third, and fourth quadrants. In many countries, the relationship changes from positive in the pre-crisis period to negative in the post-crisis period. The idea for a positive correlation is simple. Short-term interest rates are mainly driven by the central bank policy rate. During an economic boom, housing prices increase, and inflation rises above the targeted level. The central bank raises the (targeted) policy rate in response, resulting in an increase in short-term interest rates. On the other hand, a negative relationship could be explained by a reduction in the cost of borrowing. In the post-crisis period, real short-term interest rates drop below zero in many countries. If a large majority of the population tends to borrow money to purchase property, a lower cost of borrowing will stimulate the demand for housing.

There is every reason to expect that credit to households is correlated with housing prices since houses may serve as collateral. Credit is also an endogenous variable that responds to macroeconomic factors and expectations. Therefore, its relationship with real housing prices could be complicated across countries with different economic conditions. A simple economic intuition is that when the demand for housing increases, the demand for mortgages and housing prices will also increase. Therefore, a positive relationship exists between the two variables. In general, countries with insignificant correlations between real housing prices and credit to households in the pre-crisis period tend to have positive and significant correlations after the GFC (Figure 11.1F and Table 11.3). Denmark is an exception. The correlations turn from positive in the pre-crisis period to negative after the GFC. This evidence, again, shows that the GFC has an impact on the macro-housing relationship.

Lastly, the consumer price index (CPI) and inflation are important variables in macroeconomics since central banks around the world widely adopt inflation targeting. In many countries, the relationship between CPI and real housing prices is positive and significant but has either weakened or strengthened after the GFC. Australia shows negative correlations between CPI and real housing prices (Figure 11.1G). As discussed earlier, in a supply-driven housing market, the relationship between real housing prices and real output could be negative. As CPI and real output tend to move in the same direction, correlations between CPI and real housing prices will also be negative. Furthermore, Denmark, Ireland, and Norway exhibit a negative relationship in the post-crisis period. A conjecture is that the housing market has still not fully recovered since the GFC while quantitative easing adopted by central banks has already pushed up the price level.

## 4 CONCLUSION

Housing variables are not only affected by but also interact with the macroeconomy. Much prior literature shows that housing market fluctuations can propagate shocks or even generate aggregate volatility. This chapter studies whether the relationships between housing prices and macroeconomic variables have changed since the 2008 GFC in 22 OECD countries. In general, macroeconomic variables exhibited a strong association with housing prices. Since the GFC, the strength of the linear association between housing prices and many macroeconomic variables has changed. For instance, measuring in real terms, the correlations between housing prices and GDP have weakened in Austria, Belgium, Denmark, France, Iceland, Ireland, Israel, Korea, Netherlands, and Norway. At the same time, the correlations between housing prices and unemployment rate have strengthened in France, Iceland, Italy, and Lithuania. The direction of some correlations has even reversed. For instance, the directions of correlations between housing prices and short-term interest rate have reversed in Australia, Ireland, New Zealand, and the United Kingdom. Therefore, we should pay more attention to the stylized facts in macro-housing, especially after the GFC. Hopefully, this chapter will inspire new research on the macro-housing relationship.

## NOTES

1. Some prior literature studies how housing bubbles in an economy would transmit to other economies. For example, see Gomez-Gonzalez et al. (2017).
2. Some series require taking the second difference or even more.
3. Trend-stationary means once the deterministic trend is estimated and removed from the data, the residual series is a stationary stochastic process. Difference-stationary means the trend is stochastic, and differencing the series n times yields a stationary stochastic process.
4. See, for example, Chang (2000), Favilukis et al. (2017), Ghent and Owyang (2010), Justiniano et al. (2015), Kan et al. (2004), Kwong and Leung (2000), Leung (1999, 2003, 2014), Leung and Feng

(2005), Leung et al. (2002a, 2002b), Lin et al. (2004), Ortalo-Magné and Rady (2006), Pataracchia et al. (2013), and Tse and Leung (2002).
5. On the other hand, Green (2021) finds that residential investment is a much weaker leading indicator than before.
6. The correlation coefficients are transformed into z-scores through the Fisher Z-Transformation before calculating the z-test statistics.
7. See: www.ogen.org/en/loans-for-homes/.

# REFERENCES

Aoki, K., J. Proudman, and G. Vlieghe (2004), "House Prices, Consumption, and Monetary Policy: A Financial Accelerator Approach," *Journal of Financial Intermediation* 13 (4), 414–435.

Baxter, M. (1994), "Real Exchange Rates and Real Interest Differentials: Have We Missed the Business-Cycle Relationship?" *Journal of Monetary Economics* 33 (1), 5–37.

Baxter, M. (1996), "Are Consumer Durables Important for Business Cycles," *Review of Economics and Statistics* 78 (1), 147–155.

Chang, Y. (2000), "Comovement, Excess Volatility, and Home Production," *Journal of Monetary Economics* 46 (2), 385–396.

Christiano, L. and T. Fitzgerald (2003), "The Band Pass Filter," *International Economic Review* 44 (2), 435–465.

Cooley, T.F. (ed.) (1995), *Frontiers of Business Cycle Research*, Princeton, NJ: Princeton University Press.

Davis, M. and J. Heathcote (2005), "Housing and the Business Cycle," *International Economic Review* 46 (3), 751–784.

Duca, J., J. Muellbauer, and A. Murphy (2020), "What Drives House Price Cycles? International Experience and Policy Issues," *Journal of Economic Literature* 59 (3), 773–864.

Favilukis, J., S. Ludvigson, and Van S. Nieuwerburgh (2017), "The Macroeconomic Effects of Housing Wealth, Housing Finance and Limited Risk Sharing in General Equilibrium," *Journal of Political Economy* 125 (1), 140–222.

Ghent, A. and T. Owyang (2010), "Is Housing the Business Cycle? Evidence from US Cities," *Journal of Urban Economics* 67, 336–351.

Gomez-Gonzalez, J.E., J. Gamboa-Arbeláez, J. Hirs-Garzón, and A. Pinchao-Rosero (2017), "When Bubble Meets Bubble: Contagion in OECD Countries," *Journal of Real Estate Finance and Economics* 56, 546–566.

Green, R.K. (2021), "Is Housing Still the Business Cycle? Perhaps Not," https://lusk.usc.edu/research/working-papers/housing-still-business-cycle-perhaps-not.

Iacoviello, M. (2005), "House Prices, Borrowing Constraints, and Monetary Policy in the Business Cycle," *American Economic Review* 95 (3), 739–764.

Iacoviello, M. and S. Neri (2010), "Housing Market Spillovers: Evidence from an Estimated DSGE Model," *American Economic Journal: Macroeconomics* 2 (2), 125–164.

Iacoviello, M. and M. Pavan (2013), "Housing and Debt over the Life Cycle and over the Business Cycle," *Journal of Monetary Economics* 60 (2), 221–238.

Jin, Y. and Z. Zeng (2004), "Residential Investment and House Prices in a Multi-Sector Monetary Business Cycle Model," *Journal of Housing Economics* 13 (4), 268–286.

Justiniano, A., G. Primiceri, and A. Tambalotti (2015), "Credit Supply and the Housing Boom," *Journal of Political Economy* 127 (3), 1317–1350.

Kan, K., S.K.S. Kwong, and C. Leung (2004), "The Dynamics and Volatility of Commercial and Residential Property Prices: Theory and Evidence," *Journal of Regional Science* 44 (1), 95–123.

Kishor, N.K. and H.A. Marfatia (2017), "The Dynamic Relationship Between Housing Prices and the Macroeconomy: Evidence from OECD Countries," *Journal of Real Estate Finance and Economics* 54, 237–268.

Kiyotaki, N. and J. Moore (1997), "Credit Cycles," *Journal of Political Economy* 105 (2), 211–248.

Kwong, S.K.S. and C.K.Y. Leung (2000), "Price Volatility of Commercial and Residential Property," *Journal of Real Estate Finance and Economics* 20 (1), 25–36.
Leamer, E. (2007), "Housing Is the Business Cycle," NBER Working Paper 13428.
Leamer, E. (2015), "Housing Really Is the Business Cycle," *Journal of Money, Credit and Banking* 47 (S1), 43–50.
Leung, C. (1999), "Income Tax, Property Tax, and Tariff in a Small Open Economy," *Review of International Economics* 7 (3), 541–554.
Leung, C. (2003), "Economic Growth and Increasing House Price," *Pacific Economic Review* 8 (2), 183–190.
Leung, C. (2004), "Macroeconomics and Housing: A Review of the Literature," *Journal of Housing Economics* 13 (4), 249–267.
Leung, C. (2014), "Error Correction Dynamics of House Price: An Equilibrium Benchmark," *Journal of Housing Economics* 25, 75–95.
Leung, C. and D. Feng (2005), "What Drives the Property Price-Trading Volume Correlation: Evidence from a Commercial Real Estate Market," *Journal of Real Estate Finance and Economics* 31 (2), 241–255.
Leung, C. and J.C.Y. Ng (2018), "Macroeconomic Aspects of Housing," *Oxford Research Encyclopedia of Economics and Finance*, https://doi.org/10.1093/acrefore/9780190625979.013.294.
Leung, C., C.K.G. Lau, and C.F.Y. Leong (2002a), "Testing Alternative Theories of the Property Price-Trading Volume Correlation," *Journal of Real Estate Research* 23 (3), 253–263.
Leung, C., Y.C.F. Leong, and I.Y.S. Chan (2002b), "TOM: Why Isn't Price Enough?" *International Real Estate Review* 5 (1), 91–115.
Lin, C.C., C.C. Mai, and P. Wang (2004), "Urban Land Policy and Housing in an Endogenously Growing Monocentric City," *Regional Science and Urban Economics* 34 (3), 241–261.
Ortalo-Magné, F. and S. Rady (2006), "Housing Market Dynamics: On the Contribution of Income Shocks and Credit Constraints," *Review of Economic Studies* 73 (2), 459–485.
Pataracchia, B., R. Raciborski, M. Ratto, and W. Roeger (2013), "Endogenous Housing Risk in an Estimated DSGE Model of the Euro Area," European Commission Economic Papers 505.
Tse, C.Y. and C. Leung (2002), "Increasing Wealth and Increasing Instability: The Role of Collateral," *Review of International Economics* 10 (1), 45–52.

# APPENDIX

This appendix provides lead-lag correlations between real housing prices and macro variables and the descriptive statistics of the variables.

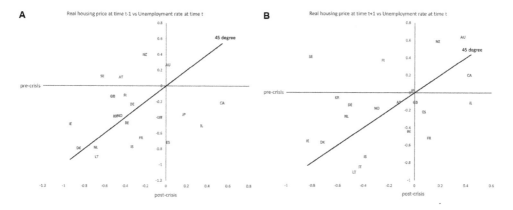

*Figure 11A.1   Lead-lag correlations between real housing prices and unemployment rate*

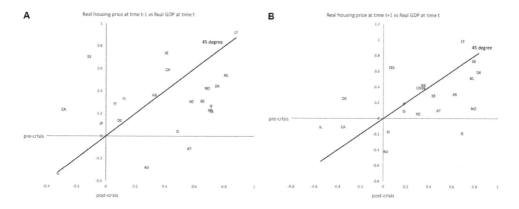

*Figure 11A.2   Lead-lag correlations between real housing prices and real GDP*

302  *Handbook of real estate and macroeconomics*

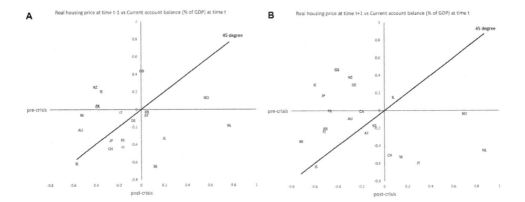

*Figure 11A.3   Lead-lag correlations between real housing prices and current account balance*

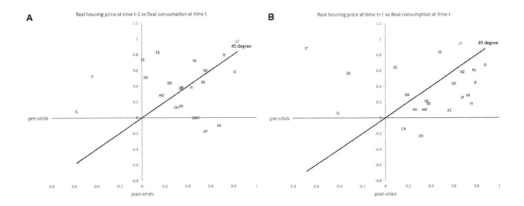

*Figure 11A.4   Lead-lag correlations between real housing prices and real consumption*

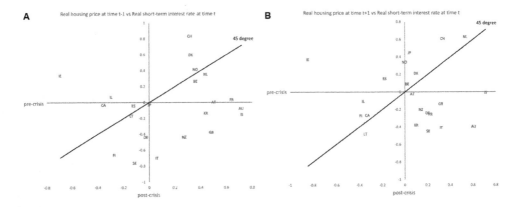

*Figure 11A.5   Lead-lag correlations between real housing prices and real short-term interest rate*

*International macroeconomic aspect of housing* 303

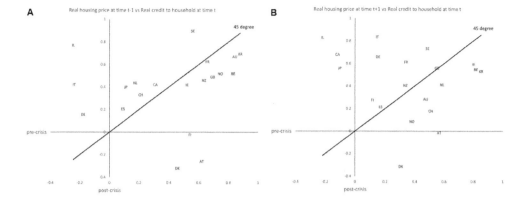

*Figure 11A.6    Lead-lag correlations between real housing prices and real credit to household*

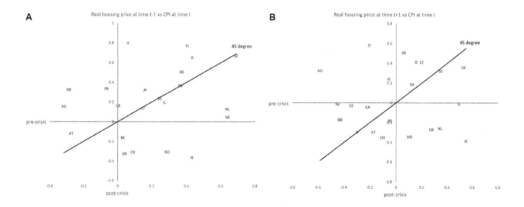

*Figure 11A.7    Lead-lag correlations between real housing prices and CPI*

Table 11A.1  Descriptive statistics

**Real housing price index (2010 = 100)**

**Pre-crisis sample**

| | Austria | Australia | Belgium | Canada | Denmark | Finland | France | Germany | Iceland | Ireland | Israel |
|---|---|---|---|---|---|---|---|---|---|---|---|
| Mean | 91.8 | 66.22 | 72.37 | 66.61 | 82.45 | 76.35 | 68.93 | 113.55 | 103.74 | 104.76 | 88.01 |
| Median | 91.78 | 63.46 | 68.68 | 62.4 | 76.99 | 74.26 | 63.42 | 114.62 | 95.84 | 101.44 | 86.52 |
| Maximum | 98.24 | 85.73 | 96.26 | 91.1 | 126.7 | 95.28 | 103.14 | 123.64 | 139.39 | 153.2 | 99.99 |
| Minimum | 84.68 | 46.59 | 55.47 | 56.29 | 63 | 59.23 | 49.52 | 102.59 | 85.07 | 59.12 | 77.33 |
| Std. dev. | 2.75 | 13.77 | 11.24 | 10.31 | 17.26 | 10.03 | 16.52 | 6.43 | 20.08 | 24.62 | 7.68 |
| Skewness | 0.02 | 0.08 | 0.63 | 0.92 | 1.43 | 0.34 | 0.71 | −0.29 | 0.82 | 0.13 | 0.26 |
| Kurtosis | 3.79 | 1.34 | 2.38 | 2.62 | 4.03 | 2.16 | 2.23 | 1.71 | 2.02 | 2.32 | 1.54 |
| Obs. | 28 | 40 | 40 | 40 | 40 | 40 | 40 | 40 | 28 | 40 | 40 |

| | Italy | Japan | Korea | Lithuania | Netherlands | New Zealand | Norway | Spain | Sweden | Switzerland | United Kingdom |
|---|---|---|---|---|---|---|---|---|---|---|---|
| Mean | 85.25 | 129.06 | 90.92 | 69.6 | 88.88 | 74.39 | 67.11 | 74.35 | 61.02 | 79.38 | 78.46 |
| Median | 83.1 | 131.68 | 93.8 | 57.39 | 95.26 | 63.83 | 67.38 | 66.71 | 59.54 | 78.42 | 72.71 |
| Maximum | 102.77 | 154.59 | 101.65 | 154.64 | 107.44 | 108.11 | 91.52 | 113.41 | 85.55 | 90.89 | 113.58 |
| Minimum | 75.71 | 103.8 | 79.62 | 36.24 | 59.47 | 59.81 | 45.89 | 51.38 | 41.26 | 75.37 | 46.74 |
| Std. dev. | 9.25 | 16.32 | 7.32 | 32.9 | 15.17 | 16.2 | 12.03 | 20.37 | 12.62 | 3.44 | 22.14 |
| Skewness | 0.5 | −0.16 | −0.23 | 1.23 | −0.72 | 0.84 | 0.17 | 0.53 | 0.31 | 1.54 | 0.11 |
| Kurtosis | 1.78 | 1.63 | 1.47 | 3.36 | 2.07 | 2.08 | 2.36 | 1.82 | 2.22 | 5.05 | 1.55 |
| Obs. | 40 | 40 | 40 | 33 | 40 | 40 | 40 | 40 | 40 | 40 | 40 |

**Post-crisis sample**

| | Austria | Australia | Belgium | Canada | Denmark | Finland | France | Germany | Iceland | Ireland | Israel |
|---|---|---|---|---|---|---|---|---|---|---|---|
| Mean | 118.98 | 106.39 | 101.14 | 116.98 | 103.25 | 98.94 | 98.66 | 111.92 | 123.7 | 92.99 | 126.65 |
| Median | 117.12 | 105.63 | 100.71 | 110.26 | 100.75 | 99.09 | 98.35 | 106.7 | 115.2 | 93.51 | 126.55 |
| Maximum | 138.86 | 123.12 | 107.72 | 141.64 | 118.67 | 100.94 | 105.4 | 137.13 | 162.14 | 119.84 | 148.89 |
| Minimum | 97.7 | 91.57 | 97.41 | 98.65 | 90.41 | 96.93 | 93.95 | 99.14 | 99.22 | 66.75 | 96.77 |
| Std. dev. | 12.88 | 10.18 | 2.2 | 15.91 | 9.15 | 0.86 | 2.84 | 12 | 23.53 | 17.85 | 17.43 |
| Skewness | −0.02 | 0.12 | 1.18 | 0.44 | 0.24 | −0.1 | 0.35 | 0.63 | 0.56 | 0.05 | −0.17 |
| Kurtosis | 1.84 | 1.65 | 4.47 | 1.5 | 1.69 | 2.8 | 2.3 | 1.93 | 1.65 | 1.74 | 1.5 |
| Obs. | 40 | 40 | 40 | 40 | 40 | 40 | 40 | 40 | 40 | 40 | 40 |

| | Italy | Japan | Korea | Lithuania | Netherlands | New Zealand | Norway | Spain | Sweden | Switzerland | United Kingdom |
|---|---|---|---|---|---|---|---|---|---|---|---|
| Mean | 84.64 | 102.54 | 102.59 | 111.13 | 90.33 | 124.98 | 117.76 | 78.04 | 122.28 | 120.75 | 102.89 |
| Median | 79.88 | 101.08 | 102.35 | 108.28 | 89.69 | 119.25 | 118.01 | 75.61 | 121.88 | 124.75 | 101.15 |
| Maximum | 100.28 | 109.5 | 106.44 | 133.25 | 104.28 | 159.03 | 130.73 | 101.31 | 148.64 | 134.47 | 114.31 |
| Minimum | 75.01 | 98.79 | 99.51 | 98.05 | 79.26 | 96.17 | 97.86 | 65.86 | 97.21 | 98.35 | 90.29 |
| Std. dev. | 9.09 | 3.16 | 2.2 | 11.68 | 8.31 | 23.42 | 9.22 | 10.34 | 19.5 | 10.34 | 8.48 |
| Skewness | 0.68 | 0.64 | 0.1 | 0.54 | 0.11 | 0.15 | −0.52 | 0.88 | −0.01 | −0.78 | −0.02 |
| Kurtosis | 1.86 | 2.03 | 1.58 | 1.86 | 1.54 | 1.33 | 2.28 | 2.84 | 1.24 | 2.51 | 1.39 |
| Obs. | 40 | 40 | 40 | 40 | 40 | 40 | 40 | 40 | 40 | 40 | 40 |

## International macroeconomic aspect of housing 305

### Unemployment rate

#### Pre-crisis sample

| | Austria | Australia | Belgium | Canada | Denmark | Finland | France | Germany | Iceland | Ireland | Israel |
|---|---|---|---|---|---|---|---|---|---|---|---|
| Mean | 4.71 | 6.35 | 8.12 | 7.45 | 4.84 | 9.62 | 9.77 | 9.3 | 3.26 | 5.57 | 9.19 |
| Median | 4.68 | 6.29 | 8.25 | 7.37 | 4.9 | 9.12 | 8.9 | 9.52 | 3.3 | 4.77 | 8.88 |
| Maximum | 5.73 | 8.62 | 9.43 | 9.43 | 5.77 | 13.4 | 12.5 | 11.2 | 3.6 | 10.63 | 10.92 |
| Minimum | 3.63 | 4.52 | 6.07 | 6.17 | 3.63 | 7.37 | 8.3 | 7.67 | 2.9 | 3.97 | 7.22 |
| Std. dev. | 0.61 | 1.11 | 0.92 | 0.8 | 0.54 | 1.45 | 1.48 | 1.03 | 0.22 | 1.76 | 0.97 |
| Skewness | 0.16 | 0.31 | -0.48 | 0.71 | -0.35 | 0.92 | 0.85 | 0 | -0.22 | 1.64 | 0.22 |
| Kurtosis | 2.03 | 2.27 | 2.35 | 3.01 | 2.38 | 3.24 | 1.96 | 1.95 | 1.79 | 4.55 | 2.14 |
| Obs. | 40 | 40 | 40 | 40 | 40 | 40 | 40 | 40 | 16 | 40 | 40 |

| | Italy | Japan | Korea | Lithuania | Netherlands | New Zealand | Norway | Spain | Sweden | Switzerland | United Kingdom |
|---|---|---|---|---|---|---|---|---|---|---|---|
| Mean | 9.24 | 4.58 | 4.23 | 12.5 | 4.77 | 5.5 | 3.69 | 12.24 | 7.08 | - | 5.5 |
| Median | 8.85 | 4.68 | 3.73 | 12.9 | 4.77 | 5.4 | 3.63 | 11.43 | 6.98 | - | 5.23 |
| Maximum | 11.5 | 5.43 | 8.13 | 17.73 | 6.9 | 7.9 | 4.6 | 18.7 | 10.3 | - | 7.32 |
| Minimum | 6.47 | 3.33 | 2.43 | 5.1 | 3.1 | 3.7 | 2.77 | 8.27 | 5.1 | - | 4.68 |
| Std. dev. | 1.53 | 0.59 | 1.46 | 3.68 | 1.06 | 1.37 | 0.55 | 3 | 1.27 | - | 0.69 |
| Skewness | 0.09 | -0.52 | 1.46 | -0.46 | 0 | 0.22 | 0.09 | 0.84 | 0.9 | - | 0.99 |
| Kurtosis | 1.72 | 2.64 | 4.13 | 2.27 | 1.94 | 1.75 | 1.82 | 2.75 | 3.38 | - | 3.17 |
| Obs. | 40 | 40 | 40 | 35 | 40 | 40 | 40 | 40 | 40 | - | 40 |

#### Post-crisis sample

| | Austria | Australia | Belgium | Canada | Denmark | Finland | France | Germany | Iceland | Ireland | Israel |
|---|---|---|---|---|---|---|---|---|---|---|---|
| Mean | 5.2 | 5.5 | 7.48 | 6.91 | 6.58 | 8.15 | 9.61 | 4.75 | 5.22 | 10.7 | 5.34 |
| Median | 5.18 | 5.47 | 7.72 | 7.05 | 6.6 | 8.23 | 9.57 | 4.85 | 4.93 | 10.78 | 5.43 |
| Maximum | 6.2 | 6.26 | 8.7 | 8.3 | 8.1 | 9.47 | 10.5 | 7.33 | 8.4 | 15.93 | 7.13 |
| Minimum | 4.13 | 4.96 | 5.2 | 5.6 | 4.83 | 6.57 | 8.23 | 3.03 | 3.1 | 4.7 | 3.58 |
| Std. dev. | 0.53 | 0.37 | 1.1 | 0.71 | 1.05 | 0.8 | 0.63 | 1.14 | 1.84 | 3.95 | 1.08 |
| Skewness | 0.01 | 0.39 | -0.72 | -0.24 | -0.19 | -0.4 | -0.31 | 0.35 | 0.42 | -0.12 | -0.02 |
| Kurtosis | 2.08 | 2.07 | 2.27 | 2.33 | 1.64 | 2.43 | 2.02 | 2.41 | 1.8 | 1.48 | 1.72 |
| Obs. | 40 | 40 | 40 | 40 | 40 | 40 | 40 | 40 | 40 | 40 | 40 |

| | Italy | Japan | Korea | Lithuania | Netherlands | New Zealand | Norway | Spain | Sweden | Switzerland | United Kingdom |
|---|---|---|---|---|---|---|---|---|---|---|---|
| Mean | 10.9 | 3.57 | 3.55 | 10.58 | 5.55 | 5.37 | 3.89 | 20.5 | 7.44 | - | 6.03 |
| Median | 11.2 | 3.48 | 3.6 | 9.77 | 5.42 | 5.5 | 3.78 | 20.43 | 7.68 | - | 5.65 |
| Maximum | 12.93 | 5.13 | 4.1 | 18.2 | 7.83 | 6.7 | 5.03 | 26.23 | 8.93 | - | 8.39 |
| Minimum | 8.13 | 2.3 | 3.07 | 6 | 3.33 | 4 | 3.17 | 13.83 | 6.13 | - | 3.77 |
| Std. dev. | 1.46 | 0.89 | 0.27 | 3.88 | 1.35 | 0.78 | 0.47 | 3.96 | 0.72 | - | 1.68 |
| Skewness | -0.52 | 0.19 | -0.1 | 0.55 | -0.02 | -0.24 | 0.68 | -0.18 | -0.01 | - | 0.06 |
| Kurtosis | 2.13 | 1.84 | 2.38 | 2.11 | 1.88 | 1.95 | 2.67 | 1.86 | 2.01 | - | 1.35 |
| Obs. | 40 | 40 | 40 | 40 | 40 | 40 | 40 | 40 | 40 | - | 40 |

### Real GDP (domestic currency)

#### Pre-crisis sample

|  | Austria | Australia | Belgium | Canada | Denmark | Finland | France | Germany | Iceland | Ireland | Israel |
|---|---|---|---|---|---|---|---|---|---|---|---|
| Mean | 65477.1 | 243881.2 | 80082.77 | 344726 | 411407.4 | 40786.13 | 445565.8 | 614658.4 | 344813.4 | 37152.14 | 165288.6 |
| Median | 65259.05 | 237966.1 | 79845.57 | 345115.1 | 407545.2 | 40795.36 | 450210.9 | 614853.8 | 345062.6 | 38305.7 | 167008.9 |
| Maximum | 76216.25 | 311686.9 | 93365.4 | 410818.3 | 470915.3 | 49498.77 | 508069.6 | 661388.1 | 437619.9 | 48139.6 | 194047.3 |
| Minimum | 56016.57 | 190966.9 | 69332.34 | 277267.4 | 363967 | 30913.84 | 386333.7 | 561785.6 | 257467.9 | 22760 | 134814.6 |
| Std. dev. | 4279.15 | 28494.09 | 5591.56 | 35743.69 | 27041.49 | 4176.93 | 30153.29 | 19651.62 | 46487.57 | 7482.04 | 16213.89 |
| Skewness | 0.19 | 0.4 | 0.2 | 0.02 | 0.42 | −0.11 | −0.22 | −0.23 | 0.16 | −0.29 | −0.19 |
| Kurtosis | 3.01 | 2.48 | 2.54 | 2.19 | 2.48 | 2.6 | 2.32 | 3.21 | 2.45 | 1.97 | 2.21 |
| Obs. | 40 | 40 | 40 | 40 | 40 | 40 | 40 | 40 | 40 | 40 | 40 |

|  | Italy | Japan | Korea | Lithuania | Netherlands | New Zealand | Norway | Spain | Sweden | Switzerland | United Kingdom |
|---|---|---|---|---|---|---|---|---|---|---|---|
| Mean | 390927.6 | 131000000 | 240000000 | 5296.17 | 139002 | 40814.11 | 465944.4 | 227047.6 | 714434.2 | 129691.1 | 353085.9 |
| Median | 391780.2 | 129000000 | 240000000 | 4875.52 | 140955.6 | 40545.78 | 459660.3 | 225441.6 | 715281.7 | 129661.1 | 347965.3 |
| Maximum | 449170.8 | 140000000 | 302000000 | 8155.39 | 162030.1 | 50703.61 | 632196.3 | 286635.9 | 872143.7 | 149365.1 | 411826.4 |
| Minimum | 335888.3 | 124000000 | 185000000 | 3587.98 | 115432.3 | 33274.53 | 358049 | 174144.4 | 570936.3 | 114627.3 | 302271.4 |
| Std. dev. | 27234.46 | 4475260 | 33861243 | 1168.05 | 10910.31 | 4580.06 | 74405.67 | 29050.83 | 73276.4 | 7433.31 | 33473.22 |
| Skewness | 0.16 | 0.88 | −0.04 | 0.89 | −0.28 | 0.13 | 0.48 | 0.06 | 0.02 | 0.39 | 0.2 |
| Kurtosis | 2.48 | 2.52 | 1.87 | 2.89 | 2.57 | 2.01 | 2.49 | 2.08 | 2.44 | 3.14 | 1.83 |
| Obs. | 40 | 40 | 40 | 40 | 40 | 40 | 40 | 40 | 40 | 40 | 40 |

#### Post-crisis sample

|  | Austria | Australia | Belgium | Canada | Denmark | Finland | France | Germany | Iceland | Ireland | Israel |
|---|---|---|---|---|---|---|---|---|---|---|---|
| Mean | 78093.7 | 373659.7 | 94931.21 | 457606 | 478526.9 | 49273.56 | 519688.6 | 700753.5 | 486123 | 57463.57 | 268050.4 |
| Median | 77960.88 | 369695.7 | 94873.33 | 453265.1 | 469377.6 | 49087.29 | 515757.6 | 692900.8 | 475191.7 | 53983.98 | 269341.8 |
| Maximum | 87088.12 | 430654.5 | 107787.7 | 514292.9 | 546078.5 | 55405.14 | 564484.3 | 781675.6 | 618260.8 | 87082.2 | 335871.2 |
| Minimum | 69854.88 | 316981.6 | 87475.63 | 395202.4 | 434299.1 | 44086.22 | 490782.5 | 620052.2 | 406213 | 40708.33 | 212676.3 |
| Std. dev. | 4178.18 | 25677.37 | 5232.51 | 30355.84 | 30405 | 2808.49 | 20385.42 | 44921.05 | 66671.4 | 15968.16 | 35799.64 |
| Skewness | 0.22 | 0.32 | 0.46 | 0.03 | 0.53 | 0.37 | 0.41 | 0.1 | 0.48 | 0.4 | 0.15 |
| Kurtosis | 2.34 | 2.72 | 2.52 | 2.23 | 2.19 | 2.35 | 2.14 | 1.76 | 1.88 | 1.63 | 1.77 |
| Obs. | 40 | 40 | 40 | 40 | 40 | 40 | 40 | 40 | 40 | 40 | 40 |

|  | Italy | Japan | Korea | Lithuania | Netherlands | New Zealand | Norway | Spain | Sweden | Switzerland | United Kingdom |
|---|---|---|---|---|---|---|---|---|---|---|---|
| Mean | 392835.3 | 129000000 | 372000000 | 8592.63 | 161457.6 | 58359.91 | 716022 | 258490.6 | 999947.3 | 170006.7 | 427883.5 |
| Median | 395249 | 129000000 | 369000000 | 8504.02 | 159902.4 | 57523.56 | 721956.9 | 260648.1 | 991059 | 170618.7 | 428131.2 |
| Maximum | 429793.2 | 139000000 | 430000000 | 11026.33 | 178493.4 | 73896.88 | 786223.7 | 290494.7 | 1180481 | 186810.5 | 472810 |
| Minimum | 355670.5 | 121000000 | 311000000 | 6341.5 | 149273.5 | 48263 | 628357.9 | 231771.4 | 847252.4 | 152167.8 | 393359.7 |
| Std. dev. | 18395.65 | 4516746 | 34774703 | 1165.36 | 7710.23 | 7256.89 | 38220.37 | 15179.26 | 98633.89 | 8980.88 | 24046.14 |
| Skewness | 0.21 | 0.18 | 0.12 | 0.22 | 0.56 | 0.38 | −0.51 | 0.06 | 0.26 | −0.05 | 0.12 |
| Kurtosis | 2.61 | 2.2 | 1.74 | 2.27 | 2.53 | 1.96 | 2.82 | 2.11 | 1.81 | 2.05 | 1.6 |
| Obs. | 40 | 40 | 40 | 40 | 40 | 40 | 40 | 40 | 40 | 40 | 40 |

## Current account balance (% of GDP)

### Pre-crisis sample

| | Austria | Australia | Belgium | Canada | Denmark | Finland | France | Germany | Iceland | Ireland | Israel |
|---|---|---|---|---|---|---|---|---|---|---|---|
| Mean | 0.31 | -4.7 | 2.71 | 1.09 | - | 5.66 | 1.12 | 1.35 | -8.35 | -1.66 | -0.01 |
| Median | 0.43 | -5.02 | 3.03 | 1.36 | - | 5.39 | 0.85 | 0.62 | -7.37 | -0.99 | -0.5 |
| Maximum | 4.54 | -1.74 | 4.83 | 3.72 | - | 8.85 | 4.85 | 7.05 | 4.18 | 2.08 | 5.09 |
| Minimum | -3.09 | -7.27 | 0.37 | -2.45 | - | 1.13 | -0.31 | -2.33 | -26.35 | -6.96 | -4.26 |
| Std. dev. | 2.18 | 1.43 | 1.35 | 1.52 | - | 1.91 | 1.15 | 2.71 | 7.24 | 2.86 | 2.37 |
| Skewness | 0.02 | 0.52 | -0.33 | -0.58 | - | -0.04 | 1.72 | 0.45 | -0.62 | -0.68 | 0.41 |
| Kurtosis | 1.65 | 2.25 | 2.02 | 2.53 | - | 2.29 | 6.23 | 1.82 | 2.95 | 2.28 | 2.51 |
| Obs. | 40 | 40 | 16 | 40 | - | 40 | 32 | 40 | 40 | 20 | 40 |

| | Italy | Japan | Korea | Lithuania | Netherlands | New Zealand | Norway | Spain | Sweden | Switzerland | United Kingdom |
|---|---|---|---|---|---|---|---|---|---|---|---|
| Mean | 0.16 | 2.87 | 2.28 | - | 7.48 | -4.02 | 11.12 | -4.35 | 5.02 | 11.03 | -1.88 |
| Median | -0.22 | 2.77 | 1.38 | - | 7.24 | -3.33 | 12.2 | -4.13 | 4.77 | 11.05 | -2.21 |
| Maximum | 3.07 | 4.33 | 15.52 | - | 9.74 | 0.14 | 18.92 | -0.32 | 9.17 | 16.68 | 0.8 |
| Minimum | -1.95 | 1.48 | -3.99 | - | 5.2 | -8.92 | -2.65 | -9.29 | 2.89 | 5.39 | -3.25 |
| Std. dev. | 1.4 | 0.67 | 3.54 | - | 1.42 | 2.34 | 5.68 | 2.34 | 1.56 | 3.06 | 1.04 |
| Skewness | 0.74 | 0.1 | 1.65 | - | 0.08 | -0.3 | -0.86 | -0.38 | 0.7 | -0.17 | 0.93 |
| Kurtosis | 2.5 | 2.32 | 6.72 | - | 1.82 | 2.06 | 2.87 | 2.61 | 2.81 | 2.59 | 3.07 |
| Obs. | 40 | 40 | 40 | - | 15 | 40 | 40 | 40 | 40 | 28 | 40 |

### Post-crisis sample

| | Austria | Australia | Belgium | Canada | Denmark | Finland | France | Germany | Iceland | Ireland | Israel |
|---|---|---|---|---|---|---|---|---|---|---|---|
| Mean | 2.03 | -2.95 | 0.35 | -2.91 | 7.6 | -1.1 | -0.68 | 7.31 | 2.41 | -0.87 | 3.02 |
| Median | 2 | -3.18 | 0.47 | -2.95 | 7.53 | -1.14 | -0.63 | 7.34 | 3.9 | 0.44 | 3.14 |
| Maximum | 5.34 | 1.59 | 4.19 | -1.61 | 10.1 | 2.27 | 1.36 | 10.2 | 10.12 | 21.69 | 6.13 |
| Minimum | -0.53 | -5.66 | -4.33 | -4.81 | 4.75 | -4.44 | -2.06 | 5.34 | -11.09 | -45.37 | -2.62 |
| Std. dev. | 1.17 | 1.59 | 2.19 | 0.71 | 1.33 | 1.35 | 0.7 | 1.08 | 5.61 | 12.43 | 1.7 |
| Skewness | 0.4 | 0.99 | -0.22 | -0.05 | -0.01 | 0.36 | 0.36 | 0.48 | -0.87 | -1.96 | -0.82 |
| Kurtosis | 3.62 | 4.18 | 2.59 | 2.92 | 2.49 | 3.54 | 3.54 | 3.05 | 2.81 | 8.54 | 4.6 |
| Obs. | 40 | 40 | 40 | 40 | 40 | 40 | 40 | 40 | 40 | 40 | 40 |

| | Italy | Japan | Korea | Lithuania | Netherlands | New Zealand | Norway | Spain | Sweden | Switzerland | United Kingdom |
|---|---|---|---|---|---|---|---|---|---|---|---|
| Mean | 0.9 | 2.68 | 4.53 | -0.04 | 9 | -3.06 | 8.46 | 0.95 | 4.27 | 9.27 | -3.92 |
| Median | 1.61 | 3.27 | 4.76 | 0.03 | 9.43 | -3.26 | 9.24 | 1.82 | 4.46 | 8.89 | -3.63 |
| Maximum | 3.72 | 4.52 | 8.54 | 6.51 | 14.86 | -0.99 | 14.44 | 3.65 | 6.79 | 17.06 | 0.29 |
| Minimum | -4.18 | -0.71 | -0.64 | -6.22 | -6.97 | -4.65 | 1.63 | -4.29 | 1.99 | 4.38 | -6.5 |
| Std. dev. | 2.25 | 1.39 | 2.06 | 2.83 | 3.22 | 0.93 | 3.68 | 2.31 | 1.36 | 3.4 | 1.51 |
| Skewness | -0.96 | -0.67 | -0.51 | -0.01 | -2.97 | 0.37 | -0.28 | -1.08 | -0.1 | 0.39 | 0.37 |
| Kurtosis | 2.57 | 2.16 | 3.09 | 2.95 | 16.39 | 2.3 | 1.93 | 2.69 | 1.83 | 2.22 | 3.44 |
| Obs. | 40 | 40 | 40 | 40 | 40 | 40 | 40 | 40 | 40 | 40 | 40 |

308  Handbook of real estate and macroeconomics

### Real consumption (domestic currency)

#### Pre-crisis sample

| | Austria | Australia | Belgium | Canada | Denmark | Finland | France | Germany | Iceland | Ireland | Israel |
|---|---|---|---|---|---|---|---|---|---|---|---|
| Mean | 35291.66 | 140970.7 | 41240.54 | 191023.1 | 197182.8 | 19992.96 | 240893 | 345050.2 | 196067.9 | 16893.4 | 89881.54 |
| Median | 35231.09 | 139456.3 | 41179.3 | 190290.7 | 191165.8 | 19689.12 | 243069.5 | 345513.4 | 191846.5 | 17274.16 | 90370.17 |
| Maximum | 40274.45 | 176546.2 | 46410.84 | 225754.4 | 226308.5 | 24107.12 | 273808.9 | 368887.6 | 248868.9 | 22381.67 | 111231.1 |
| Minimum | 30732.91 | 110305.3 | 36424.88 | 155012.3 | 180820.9 | 15908.93 | 209954.9 | 318802.2 | 140041.5 | 11327.67 | 71479.42 |
| Std. dev. | 2324.67 | 15697.99 | 2180.92 | 17680.18 | 11508.89 | 2069.45 | 16878.75 | 12404.54 | 26430.27 | 2803.99 | 10423.86 |
| Skewness | 0.17 | 0.18 | 0.01 | 0.02 | 0.93 | 0.16 | −0.18 | −0.09 | 0.24 | −0.23 | −0.06 |
| Kurtosis | 2.27 | 2.37 | 2.83 | 2.24 | 3 | 2.18 | 2.14 | 2.39 | 2.59 | 2.29 | 2.22 |
| Obs. | 40 | 40 | 40 | 40 | 40 | 40 | 40 | 40 | 40 | 40 | 40 |

| | Italy | Japan | Korea | Lithuania | Netherlands | New Zealand | Norway | Spain | Sweden | Switzerland | United Kingdom |
|---|---|---|---|---|---|---|---|---|---|---|---|
| Mean | 232802.2 | 70865606 | 128000000 | 3392.39 | 68902.77 | 23712.07 | 205600 | 133561.1 | 335092.1 | 73382.32 | 2320060.7 |
| Median | 234918 | 70920005 | 136000000 | 3155.92 | 70513.03 | 23334.04 | 201630.4 | 133201.1 | 338132 | 73803.17 | 2306904 |
| Maximum | 251831.1 | 75242330 | 157000000 | 5173.22 | 74438.41 | 29417.73 | 256595.6 | 161629.5 | 392779 | 79151.45 | 269847.2 |
| Minimum | 206168.5 | 67096106 | 92065761 | 2398.34 | 58303.36 | 19288.16 | 162966.5 | 167021.7 | 273730.9 | 67750.01 | 193169.6 |
| Std. dev. | 10817.82 | 1907065 | 18117133 | 756.5 | 4354.39 | 2549.17 | 23827.11 | 15142.04 | 29844.8 | 2741.74 | 20715.3 |
| Skewness | −0.51 | −0.02 | −0.45 | 0.83 | −1.02 | 0.34 | 0.33 | 0.01 | −0.19 | −0.16 | 0.03 |
| Kurtosis | 2.66 | 2.77 | 1.99 | 2.73 | 2.91 | 2.24 | 2.25 | 2.05 | 2.34 | 2.48 | 2.02 |
| Obs. | 40 | 40 | 40 | 40 | 40 | 40 | 40 | 40 | 40 | 40 | 40 |

#### Post-crisis sample

| | Austria | Australia | Belgium | Canada | Denmark | Finland | France | Germany | Iceland | Ireland | Israel |
|---|---|---|---|---|---|---|---|---|---|---|---|
| Mean | 41245.53 | 209368.2 | 49019.77 | 261262.3 | 225405.3 | 26397.14 | 282587.8 | 374494.8 | 247653.4 | 20965.28 | 147824.8 |
| Median | 41172.51 | 208620 | 49173.17 | 261359.8 | 224115.2 | 26446.1 | 281320.2 | 371051.4 | 240157.6 | 20428.79 | 144842.5 |
| Maximum | 44811.53 | 239101.5 | 55208.4 | 294835.1 | 255000.2 | 28905.68 | 303491 | 408259.5 | 306013.6 | 25758.07 | 184093.9 |
| Minimum | 37075.7 | 179362.2 | 44662 | 222902.7 | 209917.2 | 23275.12 | 268814.5 | 338012.4 | 208616 | 18263.88 | 119952.1 |
| Std. dev. | 1904.19 | 14893.65 | 2651.36 | 18979.09 | 12089.51 | 1343.27 | 8992.73 | 17870.76 | 29214.72 | 2018.99 | 18173.49 |
| Skewness | −0.13 | 0.02 | 0.32 | −0.01 | 0.6 | −0.04 | 0.41 | 0.06 | 0.53 | 0.58 | 0.26 |
| Kurtosis | 2.52 | 2.22 | 2.39 | 2.06 | 2.35 | 2.49 | 2.22 | 2.09 | 2.07 | 2.26 | 1.85 |
| Obs. | 40 | 40 | 40 | 40 | 40 | 40 | 40 | 40 | 40 | 40 | 40 |

| | Italy | Japan | Korea | Lithuania | Netherlands | New Zealand | Norway | Spain | Sweden | Switzerland | United Kingdom |
|---|---|---|---|---|---|---|---|---|---|---|---|
| Mean | 238034.8 | 72432799 | 183000000 | 5344.93 | 72502.73 | 33754.63 | 303703.1 | 151169.9 | 462193.2 | 88924.2 | 275579.5 |
| Median | 238651 | 72115159 | 182000000 | 5315.46 | 72008.87 | 32888.38 | 304662.6 | 151197.2 | 463434.4 | 88869.58 | 273989.9 |
| Maximum | 250448.3 | 75605761 | 208000000 | 6464.47 | 77362.41 | 42944.63 | 343396.9 | 164969 | 528467.7 | 96059.47 | 305802.2 |
| Minimum | 225219.8 | 69578104 | 163000000 | 4144.19 | 69027.71 | 27944.13 | 261221.3 | 137315.7 | 402063.3 | 81626.35 | 247610 |
| Std. dev. | 6640.55 | 1416239 | 12162471 | 622.42 | 2287.95 | 4192.34 | 21233.22 | 7398.11 | 38357.3 | 4159.48 | 16962.12 |
| Skewness | −0.09 | 0.16 | 0.31 | 0.08 | 0.55 | 0.47 | −0.19 | −0.11 | 0.12 | −0.05 | 0.12 |
| Kurtosis | 2.24 | 2.61 | 1.99 | 2.03 | 2.4 | 2.08 | 2.37 | 2.01 | 1.71 | 1.77 | 1.77 |
| Obs. | 40 | 40 | 40 | 40 | 40 | 40 | 40 | 40 | 40 | 40 | 40 |

## Real short-term interest rate

### Pre-crisis sample

| | Austria | Australia | Belgium | Canada | Denmark | Finland | France | Germany | Iceland | Ireland | Israel |
|---|---|---|---|---|---|---|---|---|---|---|---|
| Mean | 1.5 | 2.75 | 1.3 | 1.74 | 1.35 | 1.72 | 1.64 | 1.74 | 5 | 0.34 | 4.93 |
| Median | 1.65 | 2.93 | 1.72 | 1.42 | 1.25 | 1.63 | 1.97 | 1.76 | 5.18 | -0.46 | 5.22 |
| Maximum | 3.06 | 5.45 | 2.83 | 4.47 | 3.12 | 2.56 | 3.44 | 3.36 | 7.91 | 4.84 | 9.55 |
| Minimum | -0.76 | -1.22 | -1.01 | -1.48 | -0.09 | 0.81 | -0.31 | 0.16 | 2.55 | -2.23 | 0.51 |
| Std. dev. | 0.97 | 1.48 | 1.03 | 1.45 | 0.85 | 0.38 | 1.12 | 0.89 | 1.4 | 1.98 | 2.28 |
| Skewness | -0.65 | -0.42 | -0.59 | 0.05 | 0.45 | 0.41 | -0.23 | 0.04 | 0.04 | 1.13 | -0.08 |
| Kurtosis | 2.73 | 3.47 | 2.35 | 2.33 | 2.34 | 3.19 | 1.65 | 2.13 | 2.15 | 3.03 | 2.13 |
| Obs. | 40 | 40 | 40 | 40 | 40 | 40 | 40 | 40 | 40 | 40 | 40 |

| | Italy | Japan | Korea | Lithuania | Netherlands | New Zealand | Norway | Spain | Sweden | Switzerland | United Kingdom |
|---|---|---|---|---|---|---|---|---|---|---|---|
| Mean | 1.41 | 0.32 | 3.49 | 4.18 | 0.93 | 4.33 | 2.7 | 0.51 | 2.22 | 0.67 | 3.58 |
| Median | 1.11 | 0.32 | 2.14 | 3.51 | 0.87 | 4 | 2.36 | 0.54 | 2.01 | 0.59 | 3.3 |
| Maximum | 5.06 | 1 | 13.79 | 20.58 | 2.79 | 7.65 | 6.46 | 3.78 | 4.91 | 2.37 | 6.01 |
| Minimum | -0.6 | -0.42 | -0.62 | -0.67 | -0.56 | 2.45 | 0.35 | -1.4 | 0.57 | -0.65 | 2.22 |
| Std. dev. | 1.54 | 0.35 | 3.41 | 4.7 | 0.77 | 1.29 | 1.84 | 1.49 | 1.18 | 0.88 | 1.18 |
| Skewness | 1.01 | 0.14 | 1.2 | 1.45 | 0.31 | 1.09 | 0.33 | 0.57 | 0.63 | 0.08 | 0.52 |
| Kurtosis | 3.26 | 3.12 | 3.74 | 5.7 | 2.55 | 3.64 | 1.75 | 2.38 | 2.45 | 1.71 | 1.92 |
| Obs. | 40 | 19 | 40 | 32 | 40 | 40 | 40 | 40 | 40 | 40 | 40 |

### Post-crisis sample

| | Austria | Australia | Belgium | Canada | Denmark | Finland | France | Germany | Iceland | Ireland | Israel |
|---|---|---|---|---|---|---|---|---|---|---|---|
| Mean | -1.67 | 0.68 | -1.63 | -0.56 | -0.96 | -1.1 | -0.93 | -1.14 | 2.38 | -0.36 | -0.14 |
| Median | -1.68 | 0.53 | -2.01 | -0.51 | -1.01 | -1.13 | -0.76 | -1.1 | 2.18 | -0.46 | -0.18 |
| Maximum | -0.74 | 2.78 | 0.53 | 0.4 | -0.17 | 0.5 | 0.29 | 0.1 | 4.93 | 4.05 | 1.02 |
| Minimum | -2.59 | -0.94 | -2.96 | -2.18 | -2.12 | -2.42 | -2.57 | -2.3 | -1.61 | -1.57 | -2.24 |
| Std. dev. | 0.56 | 0.88 | 0.91 | 0.6 | 0.53 | 0.76 | 0.65 | 0.65 | 1.67 | 1.01 | 0.76 |
| Skewness | 0.04 | 0.46 | 0.74 | -0.56 | -0.21 | 0.3 | -0.52 | -0.06 | -0.4 | 2.34 | -0.58 |
| Kurtosis | 1.81 | 2.59 | 2.5 | 3.08 | 2.11 | 2.42 | 2.76 | 1.84 | 2.53 | 10.67 | 2.91 |
| Obs. | 40 | 40 | 40 | 40 | 40 | 40 | 40 | 40 | 40 | 40 | 40 |

| | Italy | Japan | Korea | Lithuania | Netherlands | New Zealand | Norway | Spain | Sweden | Switzerland | United Kingdom |
|---|---|---|---|---|---|---|---|---|---|---|---|
| Mean | -0.98 | -0.28 | 0.55 | -1.44 | -1.43 | 0.98 | -0.42 | -1.04 | -0.92 | -0.36 | -1.42 |
| Median | -0.93 | -0.25 | 0.7 | -1.57 | -1.31 | 1.12 | -0.55 | -1.25 | -0.89 | -0.19 | -1.53 |
| Maximum | 0.29 | 1.36 | 1.61 | 2.67 | -0.12 | 3.39 | 2.26 | 1.06 | 1.21 | 1.12 | 0.25 |
| Minimum | -2.81 | -3.39 | -0.83 | -4.69 | -3.07 | -2.62 | -2.93 | -3.07 | -2.88 | -1.86 | -3.23 |
| Std. dev. | 0.79 | 1.1 | 0.79 | 1.72 | 0.89 | 1.35 | 1.32 | 1.12 | 1.3 | 0.79 | 0.9 |
| Skewness | -0.37 | -1.04 | -0.32 | 0.23 | -0.43 | -0.5 | 0.22 | 0.12 | 0.08 | -0.21 | 0.16 |
| Kurtosis | 2.42 | 4.03 | 1.65 | 2.43 | 1.96 | 3.04 | 2.37 | 1.95 | 1.67 | 2.03 | 2.51 |
| Obs. | 40 | 40 | 40 | 40 | 40 | 40 | 40 | 40 | 40 | 40 | 40 |

## Real credit to household (domestic currency)

### Pre-crisis sample

| | Austria | Australia | Belgium | Canada | Denmark | Finland | France | Germany | Iceland | Ireland | Israel |
|---|---|---|---|---|---|---|---|---|---|---|---|
| Mean | 119.47 | 777.54 | 129.36 | 881.81 | 1508.64 | 57.9 | 639.84 | 1669.01 | - | 114.62 | 241.77 |
| Median | 118.49 | 704.58 | 126.89 | 850.62 | 1444.59 | 52.48 | 619.73 | 1701.35 | - | 109.11 | 250.78 |
| Maximum | 150.47 | 1235.99 | 160.3 | 1199.65 | 2132.62 | 92.06 | 865.35 | 1741.08 | - | 172.04 | 276.72 |
| Minimum | 97.24 | 448.06 | 109.58 | 681.66 | 1130.01 | 40.45 | 513.21 | 1476.1 | - | 75.34 | 188.44 |
| Std. dev. | 14.87 | 239.3 | 11.61 | 141.83 | 274.73 | 15.67 | 98.24 | 75.62 | - | 32.96 | 25.37 |
| Skewness | 0.5 | 0.43 | 1.01 | 0.63 | 0.68 | 0.75 | 0.68 | -1.3 | - | 0.37 | -0.67 |
| Kurtosis | 2.51 | 1.86 | 3.67 | 2.34 | 2.42 | 2.35 | 2.49 | 3.44 | - | 1.74 | 2.27 |
| Obs. | 40 | 40 | 40 | 40 | 40 | 40 | 40 | 40 | - | 20 | 40 |

| | Italy | Japan | Korea | Lithuania | Netherlands | New Zealand | Norway | Spain | Sweden | Switzerland | United Kingdom |
|---|---|---|---|---|---|---|---|---|---|---|---|
| Mean | 386.28 | 348757.9 | 528247.4 | - | 513.1 | 107.78 | 1107.92 | 463.82 | 1443.04 | 550.17 | 995.31 |
| Median | 376.63 | 358562.5 | 522810.2 | - | 508.94 | 99.51 | 1052.74 | 423.69 | 1399.02 | 542.2 | 940.79 |
| Maximum | 594.03 | 367068.2 | 769188.7 | - | 687.15 | 165.18 | 1685.11 | 843.46 | 2076.68 | 612.79 | 1452.52 |
| Minimum | 244.5 | 312453.1 | 348052.5 | - | 334.35 | 70.99 | 763.79 | 228.46 | 1024.27 | 509.52 | 675.09 |
| Std. dev. | 102.86 | 17167.69 | 137022.8 | - | 100.71 | 27.55 | 274.69 | 176.23 | 309.44 | 33.43 | 249.52 |
| Skewness | 0.37 | -1 | 0.07 | - | -0.06 | 0.59 | 0.57 | 0.58 | 0.47 | 0.42 | 0.37 |
| Kurtosis | 2.05 | 2.58 | 1.45 | - | 1.93 | 2.14 | 2.12 | 2.25 | 2.13 | 1.78 | 1.75 |
| Obs. | 40 | 40 | 40 | - | 40 | 40 | 40 | 40 | 40 | 29 | 40 |

### Post-crisis sample

| | Austria | Australia | Belgium | Canada | Denmark | Finland | France | Germany | Iceland | Ireland | Israel |
|---|---|---|---|---|---|---|---|---|---|---|---|
| Mean | 157.04 | 1718.55 | 215.17 | 1764.53 | 2312.5 | 121.84 | 1162.95 | 1526.68 | - | 152.25 | 426.16 |
| Median | 157.66 | 1700.37 | 218.51 | 1752.88 | 2301.14 | 118.98 | 1138.04 | 1515.29 | - | 148.08 | 417.68 |
| Maximum | 164.05 | 1978.06 | 251.14 | 2026.22 | 2416.06 | 140.78 | 1355.3 | 1654.83 | - | 197.91 | 542.91 |
| Minimum | 150.36 | 1460.08 | 185.05 | 1499.7 | 2256.8 | 109.13 | 1030.36 | 1471.92 | - | 125.19 | 324.49 |
| Std. dev. | 3.46 | 170.94 | 18.2 | 162.69 | 37.86 | 9.96 | 86.99 | 51.14 | - | 21.51 | 67.63 |
| Skewness | -0.18 | 0.16 | 0.06 | 0.04 | 1.5 | 0.43 | 0.57 | 0.92 | - | 0.51 | 0.17 |
| Kurtosis | 2.26 | 1.55 | 1.88 | 1.64 | 4.72 | 1.86 | 2.3 | 2.8 | - | 2.01 | 1.65 |
| Obs. | 40 | 40 | 40 | 40 | 40 | 40 | 40 | 40 | - | 40 | 40 |

| | Italy | Japan | Korea | Lithuania | Netherlands | New Zealand | Norway | Spain | Sweden | Switzerland | United Kingdom |
|---|---|---|---|---|---|---|---|---|---|---|---|
| Mean | 660.69 | 302933.4 | 1206960 | - | 725.03 | 205.65 | 2596.16 | 738.08 | 3253 | 792.69 | 1474.01 |
| Median | 652.11 | 301250.3 | 1153788 | - | 717.25 | 197.12 | 2639.41 | 709.08 | 3190.29 | 805.52 | 1474.05 |
| Maximum | 696.23 | 319246.8 | 1582034 | - | 764.14 | 254.8 | 3082.95 | 919.72 | 3997.7 | 911.09 | 1547.86 |
| Minimum | 642.38 | 290068 | 906434.4 | - | 701.16 | 175.41 | 2007.19 | 633.58 | 2583.96 | 649.33 | 1412.11 |
| Std. dev. | 18.25 | 7971.36 | 212922.1 | - | 19.43 | 26.55 | 317.54 | 90.22 | 463.67 | 82.37 | 45.96 |
| Skewness | 0.91 | 0.37 | 0.31 | - | 0.82 | 0.44 | -0.25 | 0.68 | 0.16 | -0.26 | 0.02 |
| Kurtosis | 2.34 | 2.1 | 1.67 | - | 2.2 | 1.69 | 1.93 | 2.13 | 1.55 | 1.69 | 1.45 |
| Obs. | 40 | 40 | 40 | - | 40 | 40 | 40 | 40 | 40 | 40 | 40 |

## CPI (2010 = 100)

### Pre-crisis sample

|  | Austria | Australia | Belgium | Canada | Denmark | Finland | France | Germany | Iceland | Ireland | Israel |
|---|---|---|---|---|---|---|---|---|---|---|---|
| Mean | 85.5 | 78.49 | 84.19 | 85.1 | 84.13 | 87.66 | 87.26 | 88.04 | 59.2 | 83.49 | 82.81 |
| Median | 85.47 | 78.82 | 84.23 | 84.5 | 84.42 | 88.87 | 86.41 | 88.07 | 60.57 | 83.81 | 83.04 |
| Maximum | 92.96 | 90.22 | 92.46 | 94.05 | 92.1 | 93.34 | 94.63 | 94.24 | 73.28 | 98.43 | 90.33 |
| Minimum | 79.28 | 69.3 | 77.39 | 77.33 | 75.26 | 80.64 | 81.76 | 82.77 | 49.14 | 70.77 | 69.78 |
| Std. dev. | 4.55 | 6.82 | 4.81 | 5.53 | 5.22 | 3.85 | 4.29 | 3.58 | 7.21 | 8.73 | 5.61 |
| Skewness | 0.16 | 0.09 | 0.2 | 0.1 | -0.14 | -0.41 | 0.31 | 0.19 | 0.18 | 0 | -0.63 |
| Kurtosis | 1.68 | 1.69 | 1.79 | 1.65 | 1.74 | 1.7 | 1.7 | 1.76 | 1.89 | 1.63 | 2.4 |
| Obs. | 40 | 40 | 40 | 40 | 40 | 40 | 40 | 40 | 40 | 40 | 40 |

|  | Italy | Japan | Korea | Lithuania | Netherlands | New Zealand | Norway | Spain | Sweden | Switzerland | United Kingdom |
|---|---|---|---|---|---|---|---|---|---|---|---|
| Mean | 84.11 | 101.81 | 77.48 | 75.06 | 85.83 | 80.55 | 84.12 | 80.19 | 89.15 | 93.01 | 83.54 |
| Median | 83.84 | 101.25 | 76.87 | 74.8 | 86.75 | 79.97 | 84.93 | 79.38 | 89.14 | 93.07 | 83.19 |
| Maximum | 93.3 | 104.33 | 88.65 | 82.01 | 94 | 90.64 | 92.3 | 92.89 | 94.66 | 97.41 | 91.29 |
| Minimum | 75.46 | 100.25 | 64.91 | 68.2 | 76.12 | 73.86 | 75.5 | 70.02 | 84.55 | 89.75 | 76.9 |
| Std. dev. | 5.7 | 1.29 | 6.99 | 2.83 | 5.97 | 5.25 | 5.04 | 7.19 | 3.38 | 2.43 | 3.89 |
| Skewness | 0.07 | 0.41 | 0.01 | 0.07 | -0.17 | 0.4 | -0.23 | 0.21 | 0.03 | 0.1 | 0.21 |
| Kurtosis | 1.67 | 1.62 | 1.86 | 3.77 | 1.54 | 1.94 | 1.81 | 1.8 | 1.4 | 1.84 | 2.11 |
| Obs. | 40 | 40 | 40 | 40 | 40 | 40 | 40 | 40 | 40 | 40 | 40 |

### Post-crisis sample

|  | Austria | Australia | Belgium | Canada | Denmark | Finland | France | Germany | Iceland | Ireland | Israel |
|---|---|---|---|---|---|---|---|---|---|---|---|
| Mean | 109.75 | 110.54 | 109.08 | 108.25 | 106.37 | 107.81 | 105.39 | 106.69 | 115.69 | 104.34 | 105.75 |
| Median | 110.11 | 111.03 | 108.19 | 107.91 | 106.78 | 108.81 | 105.48 | 106.66 | 116.35 | 104.65 | 106.42 |
| Maximum | 119.05 | 120.92 | 117.26 | 117.34 | 110.53 | 112.71 | 110.49 | 113.72 | 130.17 | 107.05 | 108.6 |
| Minimum | 99.05 | 99.06 | 98.95 | 99.11 | 99.13 | 99.19 | 99.34 | 99.44 | 99.17 | 99.12 | 98.34 |
| Std. dev. | 5.49 | 6.27 | 5.07 | 5.09 | 3.02 | 3.59 | 2.86 | 3.85 | 8.87 | 1.83 | 2.4 |
| Skewness | -0.21 | -0.16 | -0.08 | 0.11 | -0.78 | -0.97 | -0.21 | -0.08 | -0.33 | -1.3 | -1.53 |
| Kurtosis | 2.18 | 1.92 | 2.3 | 2.09 | 2.93 | 3.14 | 2.69 | 2.3 | 2.18 | 4.28 | 4.8 |
| Obs. | 40 | 40 | 40 | 40 | 40 | 40 | 40 | 40 | 40 | 40 | 40 |

|  | Italy | Japan | Korea | Lithuania | Netherlands | New Zealand | Norway | Spain | Sweden | Switzerland | United Kingdom |
|---|---|---|---|---|---|---|---|---|---|---|---|
| Mean | 106.75 | 102.37 | 109.07 | 109.15 | 108.18 | 107.7 | 108.73 | 106.55 | 104.81 | 99.35 | 110.51 |
| Median | 107.43 | 103.31 | 109.46 | 108.36 | 108.62 | 107.79 | 107.23 | 107.02 | 103.88 | 99.53 | 110.86 |
| Maximum | 110.94 | 105.95 | 115.48 | 119.23 | 116.82 | 115.21 | 120.97 | 111.84 | 111.31 | 101.18 | 120.33 |
| Minimum | 99.24 | 99.28 | 99.02 | 99.11 | 99.18 | 98.74 | 99.54 | 98.36 | 99.27 | 97.62 | 98.83 |
| Std. dev. | 3.12 | 2.25 | 4.62 | 5.18 | 4.65 | 4.05 | 6.95 | 3.2 | 2.93 | 0.84 | 5.85 |
| Skewness | -0.97 | -0.09 | -0.47 | 0.16 | -0.18 | -0.23 | 0.33 | -0.63 | 0.53 | -0.2 | -0.17 |
| Kurtosis | 3.16 | 1.41 | 2.45 | 2.63 | 2.39 | 2.75 | 1.73 | 3.12 | 2.93 | 2.48 | 2.29 |
| Obs. | 40 | 40 | 40 | 40 | 40 | 40 | 40 | 40 | 40 | 40 | 40 |

# 12. How did the asset markets change after the Global Financial Crisis?

*Kuang-Liang Chang and Charles Ka Yui Leung*

## 1 INTRODUCTION

This chapter focuses on two crucial aspects of the recent Global Financial Crisis (GFC). First, there is the underestimation and mispricing of risk. Second, investors significantly change their portfolios after the GFC. Shortly after the collapse of Lehman Brothers, J. C. Trichet (2009), then President of the European Central Bank, stated that *"the appropriate identification, assessment and handling of risks in the financial sector are the key issue to be considered most carefully amid the current global financial turmoil"* (italics added). The reassessment of risk then led to a dramatic change in the market. The *Wall Street Journal* (2012) reported,

> *The landscape has changed for the asset management industry in the wake of the global financial crisis.* Investors are skittish after seeing their portfolios shrink in value ... admits Emad Mansour, chief executive officer of the Qatar First Investment Bank. *"There is a general lack of interest by investors—both individuals and institutional—to plow money into markets that are directionless"* (italics added).

Also, central banks and governments responded with significant policy changes, such as adoption of unconventional monetary policies by the major central banks and different "fiscal stimulus packages" (Cochrane et al., 2019). With all these changes, the pre-crisis statistical models for the empirical asset return dynamics may or may not provide a good approximation after the GFC.

Therefore, this chapter first reassesses the risk and risk-adjusted return (or "performance") of major assets, such as stock, equity real estate investment trusts (EREITs), and housing markets, by utilizing different measures of economic risk and performance.[1] Second, this chapter provides a simple method to assess whether statistical models built before the GFC continue to be useful in describing the return dynamics after the GFC. Implicitly, we adopt the statistics literature view that "all models are wrong, but some models are more useful than others."[2] Hence, a model can lose the usefulness after a dramatic event such as the GFC. We devote a separate section to more discussion on this issue.

Risk and performance measurement are not trivial tasks.[3] Since we cannot directly observe risk, there are many different risk measures and, correspondingly, various estimates of risk-adjusted performance—such diversity in measurement matters. For instance, Homm and Pigorsch (2012) investigate performance rankings across 25 hedge funds and find that hedge fund rankings change dramatically when a distinct performance index is used. We choose an economic performance indicator that remains valid for non-normal distribution, as asset returns are typically non-normal.[4]

Economic reasons also drive our concerns for useful statistical models of asset return dynamics. For both academic researchers and practitioners, statistical models summarize the history, guide future forecasts, and quantify our evaluation of risk and performance. For instance, if the asset return is independent and identically distributed, as some previous studies assume, then the current period return would not help us predict future yield. However, if asset return is positively and serially correlated, a high performance observed in the current period would suggest a high return in the next period. It would thus alter our forecast for the near future (Anand et al., 2016). Many "early warning systems" adopted by policymakers also assume some form of intertemporal dependence. Therefore, choosing a model with the "right" type of dependency is essential. This chapter estimates different models, each of which implicitly assumes another form of "intertemporal correlation."

Since housing plays a vital role in the GFC, we include its return dynamics and compare them with other financial assets.[5] Consequently, the highest frequency we can use is monthly data. This study complements previous research, which uses higher-frequency data and focuses only on financial assets (Mondria and Quintana-Domeque, 2013; Lehkonen, 2015; Mollah et al., 2016).

Constrained by the sample size, we proceed with relatively simple models that we can estimate more accurately. These include four commonly used specifications, including the auto-regressive (AR) model, AR-GARCH model, Markov-switching AR model (MS-AR), and Markov-switching AR-ARCH (MS-AR-ARCH) model. While these models may be relatively simple, various authors have adopted these specifications to study asset returns' dynamic behaviors: stock, REIT, and real estate.[6] We therefore adopt these models in this study to facilitate the comparison. We then conduct a formal model comparison to select the "best" model from our set of candidate models for the asset returns in each period (pre-crisis and post-crisis). Our empirical strategy allows for the possibility that, for some asset, the "best" model that describes the return dynamics before the GFC may no longer be so in the post-crisis era. As we have briefly reviewed, many changes have taken place in the asset market, and we cannot rule out such a possibility. We will provide more discussion on this point later.

This chapter builds on several existing lines of literature. Our focus on the risk and performance of different asset classes is related to the research on the "asset return premium," including the "equity premium puzzle" highlighted by Mehra and Prescott (1985) and the "real estate premium puzzle" highlighted by Shilling (2003). In this chapter, we compute different riskiness measures and the risk-adjusted performance of various asset classes before and after the GFC. We therefore contribute to the discussion on those puzzles.

This chapter also builds on emerging literature insights, which compare the dynamic properties of different assets. We depart from these studies by including the possibility that different asset returns could be proxied by various statistical models during different times. This chapter also relates to the "structural change" literature, which assumes that the same statistical model applies, but a change in parameter values has occurred. With some abuse of notations, we may label such parameter change as "structural change in the intensive margin" (SCIM). At the same time, this chapter allows for an additional possibility that even the statistical model has changed, which we may label as "structural change in the extensive margin" (SCEM). Our model selection procedure chooses the "optimal model" and hence differentiates the SCIM from the SCEM.

There is also an ongoing debate on the impacts on the financial market and the real economy of the unconventional monetary policy and large-scale asset purchase that the major central banks have conducted. Our focus is more on the (potential) changes in the asset return distribution and the statistical models that we can use to approximate the asset return dynamics after the GFC, which would include not only the effects of unconventional monetary policy but also other factors. Hence, this chapter is related to that literature but with a different research focus.

The rest of the chapter is organized as follows. Section 2 introduces the indices to measure economic risk and economic performance, the models we use to characterize the return processes, and the Monte Carlo simulation method. Section 3 reports the different models' forecasting performance and explains their classification into different "equivalent predictive power classes" (EPPC). We also discuss empirical findings. The last section concludes the chapter.

## 2 THE ECONOMIC PERFORMANCE MEASURE AND EMPIRICAL SPECIFICATION

This chapter utilizes the economic performance index (EPI) developed by Aumann and Serrano (2008) and Homm and Pigorsch (2012) to reinvestigate financial assets' risk and performance. For each asset during each sampling period, we allow its return dynamics to follow one of the four widely used models, which essentially assumes the returns correlate over time in different ways. They are the AR, AR-GARCH, MS-AR, and MS-AR-ARCH models. We adopt the Monte Carlo simulation method to compute asset returns' economic performance, as no closed-form solutions are available given these choices. Since alternative empirical models and alternative performance indices will be developed in the future, and they are unlikely to have closed-form solutions, this chapter also demonstrates how a performance comparison can be conducted using the Monte Carlo simulation method.

### 2.1 Economic Index of Riskiness and Economic Performance Index

Although the Sharpe ratio is a widely accepted method used to compare financial assets' relative performance and is easily implemented, it lacks monotonic stochastic dominance and axiomatic justifications. Homm and Pigorsch (2012) propose an alternative EPI, which is defined as follows:

$$\text{EPI} = \frac{E(r_t - r_{f,t})}{AS(r_t - r_{f,t})} \tag{12.1}$$

where $r_t$ is the nominal return of a risky asset; $r_{f,t}$ is the return of a risk-free asset; $r_t - r_{f,t}$ is the excess return; $E$ denotes the expectation operator; and $AS(r_t - r_{f,t})$ refers to the economic risk index of Aumann and Serrano (2008). Like the Sharpe ratio, the EPI measure is also a *risk-adjusted* index. Aumann and Serrano (2008, Theorem A) prove that for any given gamble $g$, there is a unique positive number $R(g)$ that satisfies the equation

$$E\left(e^{-g/R(g)}\right) = 1. \tag{12.2}$$

Aumann and Serrano (2008) prove that their index has several desirable properties. However, we refer readers to the original papers for discussion of the EPI and Aumann and Serrano Risk Index indices due to space limitations. Chang and Leung (2021) provide more discussion.

## 2.2 The Time-Series Dynamics of Excess Return

This chapter employs four widely adopted models of the time-series dynamics of excess returns. Our first model is the simple AR model. It is often regarded as an "atheoretical benchmark." Formally, it is given by

$$r_t - r_{f,t} = \theta_0 + \theta_1 \left( r_{t-1} - r_{f,t-1} \right) + \varepsilon_t \tag{12.3a}$$

$$\varepsilon_t = \sqrt{\omega} z_t, z_t \sim N(0,1) \tag{12.3b}$$

where $r_t$ is the return of the asset, $r_{f,t}$ is the risk-free return, $\theta_0$ and $\theta_1$ are parameters that describe the AR process, $\omega$ is the variance, and $z_t$ is a Gaussian random error with a mean of zero and a variance of one.

The second model is the AR-GARCH model, which Bollerslev (1986) developed to capture the fact that the innovation's variance may be time-varying. It is formulated as follows:

$$r_t - r_{f,t} = \theta_0 + \theta_1 \left( r_{t-1} - r_{f,t-1} \right) + \varepsilon_t \tag{12.4a}$$

$$\varepsilon_t = \sqrt{h_t} z_t, z_t \sim N(0,1) \tag{12.4b}$$

$$h_t = \omega + \alpha \varepsilon_{t-1}^2 + \beta h_{t-1} \tag{12.4c}$$

where $\omega$, $\alpha$, and $\beta$ are parameters that describe the conditional variance process and conditional variance $h_t$ is a linear function of $\varepsilon_{t-1}^2$ and $h_{t-1}$. The persistence of conditional variance is captured by the sum of parameters $\alpha$ and $\beta$.

The third model captures the idea that the relationship between the current and previous period returns could change across different regimes. More specifically, the MS-AR model is an AR specification with two different dynamic processes, and can be specified as follows:

$$r_t - r_{f,t} = \theta_{0,s_t} + \theta_{1,s_t} \left( r_{t-1} - r_{f,t-1} \right) + \varepsilon_{t,s_t} \tag{12.5a}$$

$$\varepsilon_{t,s_t} = \sqrt{\omega_{s_t}} z_t, z_t \sim N(0,1) \tag{12.5b}$$

where $s_t$ is a state variable that controls the pattern of regime switches. Constrained by data availability, we assume in this chapter that the state variable has two states: 1 and 2. The evolution specification of $s_t$ is assumed to depend on the last period's state variable. A logistic function is used to ensure that the transition probabilities of the state variable are positive values. The four transition probabilities are given by:

$$P(s_t = 1|s_{t-1} = 1) = P_{11} = \frac{\exp(p)}{1+\exp(p)} \qquad (12.5c)$$

$$P(s_t = 2|s_{t-1} = 1) = P_{12} = \frac{1}{1+\exp(p)} \qquad (12.5d)$$

$$P(s_t = 1|s_{t-1} = 2) = P_{21} = \frac{1}{1+\exp(q)} \qquad (12.5e)$$

$$P(s_t = 2|s_{t-1} = 2) = P_{22} = \frac{\exp(q)}{1+\exp(q)}. \qquad (12.5f)$$

Our fourth model, MS-AR-ARCH, is an extension of the AR-ARCH specification and has the following dynamics:

$$r_t - r_{f,t} = \theta_{0,s_t} + \theta_{1,s_t}\left(r_{t-1} - r_{f,t-1}\right) + \varepsilon_{t,s_t} \qquad (12.6a)$$

$$\varepsilon_{t,s_t} = \sqrt{h_{t,s_t}}\, z_t, z_t \sim N(0,1) \qquad (12.6b)$$

$$h_{t,s_t} = \omega_{s_t} + \alpha_{s_t} \bar{\varepsilon}_{t-1}^2 \qquad (12.6c)$$

where $s_t$ is a state variable, and $\bar{\varepsilon}_{t-1}$ is the conditional mean of $\varepsilon_{t-1}$, given the information set in $\Omega_{t-2}$. The transition probabilities of the state variable are the same as those described in the MS-AR model.

## 2.3 The Monte Carlo Simulation Method

Although the four models of asset return dynamics considered in this chapter are somehow standard, closed-form solutions for the EPI and economic risk index are unavailable. Therefore, we follow the approach of Chen et al. (2014) to compute the EPI and economic risk index. Formally, we consider the following unconstrained minimization problem:

$$\min \left(\frac{1}{N}\sum_{t=1}^{N}\exp\left(-\frac{r_t - r_{f,t}}{AS(r_t - r_{f,t})}\right) - 1\right)^2. \qquad (12.7)$$

The indices can be obtained through the following steps:
Step 1: Estimate the parameters of the time-series model using the quasi-maximum likelihood estimation method.
Step 2: Simulate 100,000 observations of excess returns through a time-series process where the model parameters are estimated from Step 1.

Step 3: Calculate the economic index of riskiness and the sample mean using the last 50,000 observations generated from Step 2.[7] Following Chen et al. (2014), the numerical optimization procedure is implemented using the OPTMUM procedure of the Gauss program.

Step 4: Calculate the EPI through the sample mean and the economic index of riskiness obtained from Step 3.

A merit of this method is that it is simulation-based. Hence, the small sample issue is not a concern in our calculation.

## 3  DATA AND EMPIRICAL FINDINGS

### 3.1  Data

This chapter investigates the economic index of riskiness and several asset market indices' economic performance at a monthly frequency.[8] The indices include Standard & Poor's 500 Stock Index, the Dow Jones Industrial Average Index, the Nasdaq Composite Index, the FTSE NAREIT All Equity REITs Price Index, the Office of Federal Housing Enterprise Oversight (OFHEO) purchase-only index, and the S&P/Case-Shiller U.S. National Home Price Index. As the GFC might have changed the market participants' expectations and investment strategies, we allow for the possibility that a statistical model that works well with a particular asset before the crisis may no longer work well after. In this chapter, the pre-crisis period covers 2000:m1–2006:m6. The post-crisis period covers 2009:m1–2019:m12, and the "in-crisis" period is avoided.[9] We also avoid the Russian financial crisis's potential effect in 1998 by starting our sample in 2000.

Our data come from the usual sources. Standard & Poor's 500 Stock Index and the Dow Jones Industrial Average Index are obtained from Datastream. The OFHEO purchase-only index and the Equity RETIS Index are obtained from the Federal Housing Finance Agency and the REIT.com website. The Nasdaq Composite Index and three-month Treasury Bill interest rate come from the Federal Reserve Bank of St. Louis. The S&P/Case-Shiller Index comes from S&P Dow Jones Indices LLC. The annualized excess return is derived by subtracting the three-month Treasury Bill rate from the annualized return of a given financial asset.

According to the transaction process, transaction time, and transaction cost, the three stock indices and the Equity REITs index are labeled as "high-liquidity assets" in this chapter. In comparison, the two national housing indices are considered as "low-liquidity assets." Figures 12.1 and 12.2 provide the time-series plots of annualized excess returns for the pre- and post-crisis periods. The time-series patterns for the high- and low-liquidity assets are entirely different. In Figure 12.1, the annualized excess returns for high-liquidity assets increase significantly around 2003. However, the counterpart of the low-liquidity assets first increase and then decline sharply before the GFC. Figure 12.2 shows that the high-liquidity assets' returns decrease slightly over time, while the low-liquidity assets' counterparts significantly increase around 2011–2013.

318  *Handbook of real estate and macroeconomics*

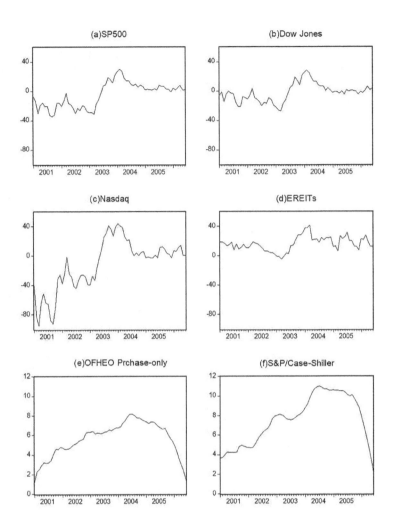

*Figure 12.1    Annualized excess returns for the pre-crisis period, 2000m1–2006m6*

### 3.2    Empirical Findings

Chang and Leung (2021) use the root mean square error (RMSE) to compare the in-sample forecasting performance across four empirical models.[10] They find that the MS-AR model has a smaller RMSE than the other three models in most cases for the pre-crisis period.[11] The MS-AR model seems to be more accurate for return forecasts during the post-crisis period, but it is not always superior for variance forecasts.

While the RMSEs across models are not the same, the difference might not be statistically significant in differentiating their forecast performance. Combining the results in Hansen et al. (2011), Mariano and Preve (2012), Kwan et al. (2015), and Chang et al. (2016) propose a procedure to classify competing models into different EPPCs. Models in the same class have the same predictive power, while models in Class 1 have higher predictive power than the models

*How did the asset markets change after the GFC?* 319

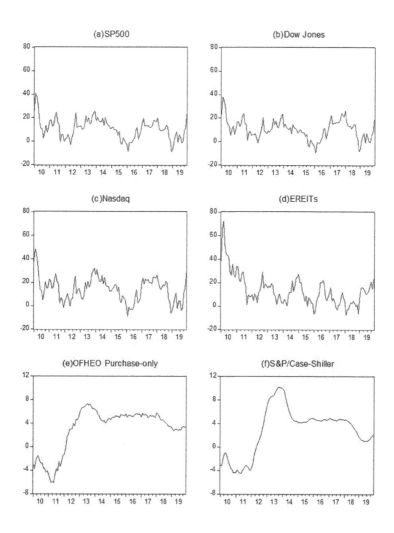

*Figure 12.2    Annualized excess returns for the post-crisis period, 2009m1–2019m12*

in Class 2. The square loss criterion (SLC) is used here to implement the EPPC procedure.[12] Tables 12.1 and 12.2 summarize the relative model performance for the pre- and post-crisis periods, respectively. The predictive power classes in the pre- and post-crisis periods are slightly different. Panel A of Table 12.1 shows that the four models have the same forecasting ability in return forecasts. Panel B of Table 12.1 shows that the four models can be divided into two classes for three different stock returns. For the SP500 stock return, the MS-AR and MS-ARCH models belong to Class 1, and they produce more accurate forecasts than the AR and AR-GARCH models, which are classified as Class 2. However, for the EREITs, OFHEO housing index, and Case-Shiller housing index, the four specifications' variance forecasts are not statistically different. In other words, for stock returns, models differ not in terms of forecasting the performance, but in terms of predicting the risk in the pre-crisis period. For real estate-related assets, there is no difference in terms of return or variance.

*Table 12.1    Summary of equivalent predictive power classes for pre-crisis period in terms of square loss criterion*

|  | Class 1 | Class 2 |
|---|---|---|
| Panel A: return forecasts |  |  |
| SP500 | All models | \ |
| Dow Jones | All models | \ |
| Nasdaq | All models | \ |
| EREITs | All models | \ |
| OFHEO purchase only | All models# | \ |
| S&P/Case-Shiller | All models# | \ |
| Panel B: variance forecasts |  |  |
| SP500 | MS-AR, MS-ARCH | AR, AR-GARCH |
| Dow Jones | AR, AR-GARCH, MS-AR | MS-ARCH |
| Nasdaq | MS-AR, MS-ARCH | AR, AR-GARCH |
| EREITs | All models | \ |
| OFHEO purchase only | All models# | \ |
| S&P/Case-Shiller | All models# | \ |

*Note*: The predictive power of Class 1 is better than that of Class 2. # means that the AR(1)-ARCH(1) model is employed.

*Table 12.2    Summary of equivalent predictive power classes for post-crisis period in terms of square loss criterion*

|  | Class 1 | Class 2 |
|---|---|---|
| Panel A: return forecasts |  |  |
| SP500 | AR, AR-GARCH, MS-AR | MS-ARCH |
| Dow Jones | AR, AR-GARCH, MS-AR | MS-ARCH |
| Nasdaq | All models | \ |
| EREITs | All models | \ |
| OFHEO purchase only | AR, AR-ARCH, MS-ARCH | MS-AR |
| S&P/Case-Shiller | MS-AR, MS-ARCH | AR, AR-ARCH |
| Panel B: variance forecasts |  |  |
| SP500 | All models | \ |
| Dow Jones | All models | \ |
| Nasdaq | All models | \ |
| EREITs | All models | \ |
| OFHEO purchase only | All models# | \ |
| S&P/Case-Shiller | AR, MS-AR, MS-ARCH | AR-ARCH |

*Note*: The predictive power of Class 1 is better than that of Class 2. # means that the AR(1)-ARCH(1) model is employed.

In the post-crisis period, Panel A of Table 12.2 shows that the four models do not have a statistically significant difference in return forecasts for SP500 returns, Dow Jones stock returns, and two housing returns (OFHEO and Case-Shiller). Moreover, the variance forecasts of the four models for three stock returns are not significantly different. Hence, models display no difference in forecasting stock returns in the post-crisis era. For the Case-Shiller return, the MS-AR and MS-ARCH models produce more accurate forecasts in returns (Class 1) than the AR and AR-ARCH models (Class 2). However, for the OFHEO return, the AR, AR-ARCH, and MS-ARCH models predict better than the MS-AR, and the latter is therefore considered Class 2.

We define the "best model" as the model which delivers the smallest RMSE for Class 1 models. We then use the estimated parameters to simulate each of the asset returns.[13] We use the Epanechnikov kernel density to find the empirical distribution based on the simulated data, using Silverman's bandwidth (1992). We simulate it for 100,000 periods and then drop the first half (sometimes regarded as the "training period"), using only the second half to "plot" the empirical distribution and other calculations (such as performance measures). As we use 50,000 periods, "small sample bias" is not a concern.

The empirical distributions of asset returns are plotted in Figure 12.3. The solid (*dotted*) line shows the simulated distribution for the pre-crisis (*post-crisis*) period. The empirical distributions across different asset markets are very different. Furthermore, its empirical distributions before and after the crisis also differ for any given asset market. For instance, in the pre-crisis period, the SP500 stock return and OFHEO housing return have a bimodal distribution, and the remaining asset markets have a unimodal distribution. In the post-crisis period, the OFHEO housing returns have an asymmetric bimodal distribution, while the high-liquidity markets have an asymmetric unimodal distribution.[14]

Compared with the empirical distribution in the pre-crisis period return, the *post-crisis distributions for the three stock market indices shift to the right*. The value ranges of the three stock market indices in the post-crisis period are narrower. It means that there is a *decrease in extreme negative returns* and a *reduction in return variation* for financial asset markets. In contrast, the empirical distributions of the OFHEO and Case-Shiller's housing returns *shift to the left* in the post-crisis period, and the *ranges of the distributions are more extensive* in the post-crisis period than in the pre-crisis period, suggesting an *increase in extreme negative return and growth in return variation*. For the EREITs returns, the empirical distribution is more or less symmetric around the mean in both the pre- and post-crisis periods. The observed distribution in the post-crisis period has a little shorter left tail and a longer right tail than the pre-crisis period, which also suggests a *decrease in extreme negative return* and an *increase in extra-ordinary positive returns*.[15]

Notice that Figure 12.3 is based on the ex post data. When agents need to make economic decisions in real time, they *may not be sure of the proper distribution* and need to *take the uncertainty of variances into consideration*. Figure 12.4 provides such an estimate. The empirical distribution of the (implied) variance for the post-crisis period is *more concentrated around the mean* than that for the pre-crisis period for all asset returns, which means that the uncertainty of variances becomes less severe post-crisis period. For instance, the "best model" for Dow Jones returns in the post-crisis period is an AR specification with constant variance. Hence, Figure 12.4 shows that its distribution of the variance of return collapses to a vertical line during the post-crisis period. One possible explanation is the active participation of the United States government in the asset markets through the Troubled Asset Relief Program and quantitative easing policies which are useful in shortening an otherwise more prolonged recession and reducing the uncertainty of variance (Brookings Institution, 2018; Liang et al., 2018).

Chang and Leung (2021) report that the values of variance and value-at-risk are more substantial for the more liquid assets than the less liquid ones, regardless of the period.[16] Moreover, *according to the variance and value-at-risk, the risk measure for three stock returns dramatically decreases after the financial crisis*. This observation is consistent with Figures 12.3A–C that the range of the stock return empirical distributions falls. The observed distributions also move to the right after the GFC, thus decreasing the risk measures. On the other hand, the variances and value-at-risk measures for two housing markets increase after the

322  *Handbook of real estate and macroeconomics*

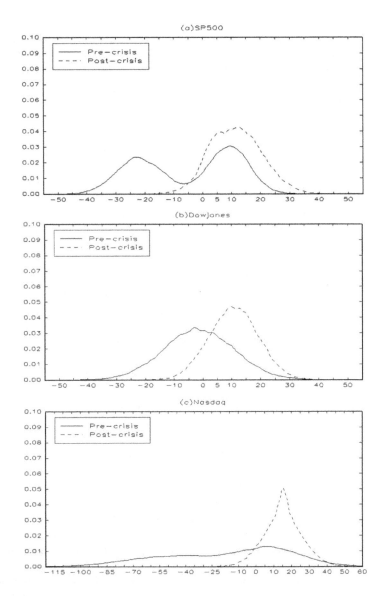

*Note*: The third best model is employed for the S&P/Case-Shiller return in the pre-crisis period because the best and second best models are non-stationary.

*Figure 12.3A–C   Empirical distributions for returns in terms of minimum root mean square error*

*How did the asset markets change after the GFC?* 323

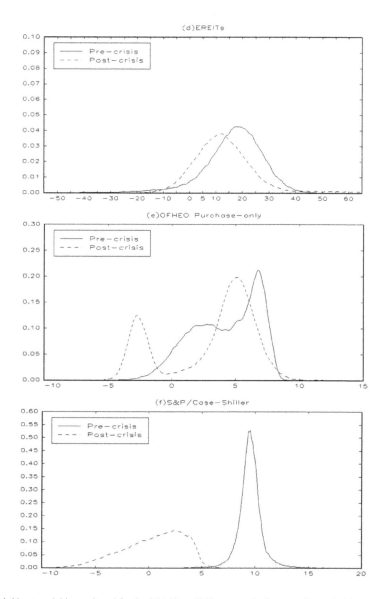

*Note*: The third best model is employed for the S&P/Case-Shiller return in the pre-crisis period because the best and second best models are non-stationary.

*Figure 12.3D–F Empirical distributions for returns in terms of minimum root mean square error*

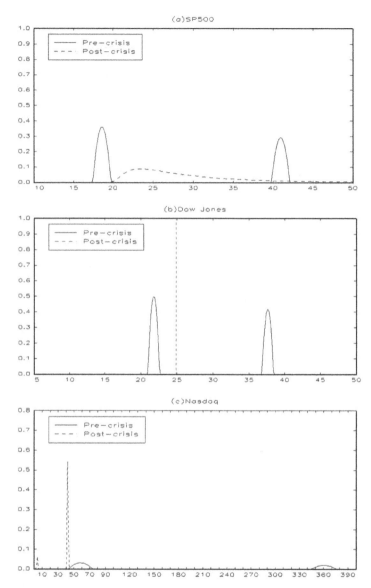

*Note*: The third best model is employed for the S&P/Case-Shiller return in the pre-crisis period because the best and second best models are non-stationary.

*Figure 12.4A–C   Empirical distributions for variances in terms of minimum root mean square error*

How did the asset markets change after the GFC? 325

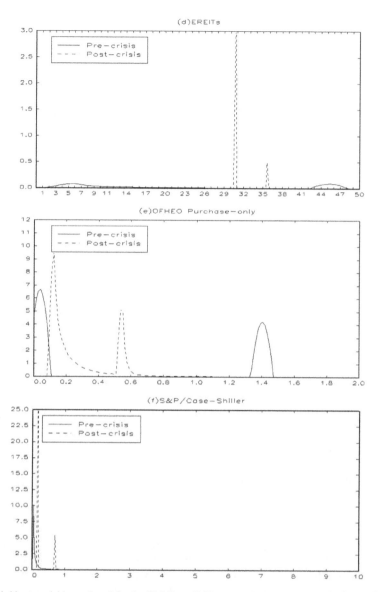

*Note*: The third best model is employed for the S&P/Case-Shiller return in the pre-crisis period because the best and second best models are non-stationary.

*Figure 12.4D–F  Empirical distributions for variances in terms of minimum root mean square error*

Table 12.3  Summary of performance measures for the best specification

|  | Pre-crisis | Post-crisis |
|---|---|---|
| Panel A: Sharpe ratio |  |  |
| SP500 | −0.306 | 1.295 |
| Dow Jones | −0.120 | 1.263 |
| Nasdaq | −0.489 | 1.430 |
| EREITs | 1.452 | 0.805 |
| OFHEO purchase only | 1.629 | 0.835 |
| S&P/Case-Shiller | 7.575# | 0.171 |
| Panel B: $EPI_N$ |  |  |
| SP500 | - | 3.356 |
| Dow Jones | - | 3.192 |
| Nasdaq | - | 4.090 |
| EREITs | 4.218 | 1.295 |
| OFHEO purchase only | 5.310 | 1.395 |
| S&P/Case-Shiller | 114.749# | 0.058 |
| Panel C: EPI |  |  |
| SP500 | - | 3.776 |
| Dow Jones | - | 3.332 |
| Nasdaq | - | 3.788 |
| EREITs | 1.707 | 6.337 |
| OFHEO purchase only | 6.722 | 1.368 |
| S&P/Case-Shiller | 6.576# | 0.052 |

*Note*: - means that the performance measure cannot be calculated. # means that the third best model is employed due to stationarity.

GFC. This observation is consistent with Figures 12.3E–F that the range of the empirical distributions of housing returns increases. The observed distributions of housing returns move to the left after the GFC, thus increasing the risk measures. For the EREITs returns, the variance increases, but the value-at-risk measure decreases after the GFC. Chang and Leung (2021) also employ other measures of risk and reach a similar conclusion.

Table 12.3 summarizes the performance measures for the best specification. The economic performance measures include the Sharpe ratio, $EPI_N$, and EPI. As Panel A of Table 12.3 shows, the Sharpe ratios for the three stock markets are negative before the financial crisis but positive after the financial crisis. The Sharpe ratios of the three real estate-related assets (EREITs, OFHEO purchase only, and S&P/Case-Shiller) decrease after the financial crisis. Panel A of Table 12.3 also shows that in terms of the Sharpe ratio, the housing returns are higher than the more liquid assets (stock and REIT) only in the pre-crisis period. It suggests that the *asset markets do not compensate for the illiquidity of housing in the post-crisis period*. Panels B and C of Table 12.3 further confirm that, during the pre-crisis period, the two housing market indices outperform the EREITs index. However, after the financial crisis, the illiquid housing does not perform as well as the more liquid assets, irrespective of the economic performance measures. In other words, the illiquidity premium for housing vanishes in ex post terms. Furthermore, the high- and low-liquidity assets' performance rankings do not change the Sharpe ratio and $EPI_N$. The $EPI_N$ and EPI measures show a slight difference in performance ranking.[17]

One may wonder how it can be possible that the less liquid assets deliver lower risk-adjusted returns than other investments in equilibrium. We conjecture that several explanations are possible. Unlike financial assets, housing is traded in a lumpy fashion: we either sell the whole housing unit or not. Macroprudential measures also limit the number of mortgage loans and participation in the housing market. At the same time, the Obama government imposed many urban and housing policies, which may have changed the incentives of the housing market participants (Agarwal and Varshneya, 2020; DeFilippis, 2016). This chapter focuses on estimating and comparing the risk and returns across different asset markets before and after the GFC, leaving lower returns in the housing market issue for future research.

## 4    HOW IMPORTANT IS THE MODEL SELECTION PROCEDURE?

We receive a common question from different conferences and seminars: how important is the model selection procedure in the current context? How would it affect our results? To address this question, we conduct the following experiment. Consider an asset $i$, $i = 1, 2, ...$ Assume that the best model to explain the return of asset $i$ during the pre-crisis period is $j(i)$. Notice that if the best model in the pre-crisis period maintains the best model in the post-crisis period, there is no need for model selection. We simply re-estimate the parameters with the post-crisis period data of asset $i$. For future reference, we label this re-estimated model as $j'(i)$. Thus, $j(i)$ and $j'(i)$ differ only in parameter values, but not in functional forms.

On the other hand, we have already selected the best model for asset $i$ during the post-crisis period in the previous section, based on Kwan et al. (2015) and Chang et al. (2016). For future reference, we label that model as $k(i)$. If models $k(i)$ and $j'(i)$ are the same, our model selection procedure simply confirms that the same model maintains its supremacy over the other models. For instance, MS-AR(1) is the best model to explain the SP500, Nasdaq, and EREITs returns for both the pre-crisis and post-crisis periods. On the other hand, in the previous section, we have seen that $k(i)$ and $j'(i)$ can be different models. For instance, while the best model for OFHEO purchase-only return in the pre-crisis period is MS-AR(1), it is replaced by MS-ARCH in the post-crisis period. Notice that we select the "best model" by minimizing the sum of some (conditional) forecast error. In Figure 12.5, we plot the distributions of return of the data, and the counterpart implied by $k(i)$ and $j'(i)$. Here are more detailed remarks.

1. SP500, Nasdaq, and EREITs have the same best model before and after the GFC.
2. The difference between the best pre-crisis model applies to the post-crisis period, and the best post-crisis model is insignificant for Dow Jones.
3. For the S&P/Case-Shiller index, the empirical distribution of actual data is a bimodal distribution. Yet the observed distribution evaluated from the pre-crisis best model applied to the post-crisis period is a single-peak distribution. Hence, if we insist the best model in the pre-crisis period continues to be the best model in the post-crisis period, the bias could be enormous. Now, through the model selection procedure, our best model in the post-crisis period also generates a bimodal distribution, which mimics the distribution of the data.

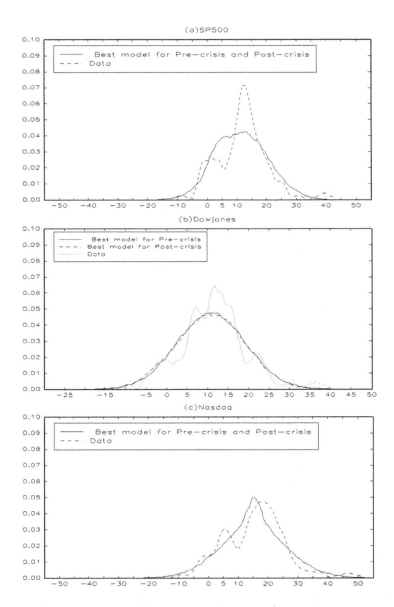

*Figure 12.5A–C   Empirical distributions for returns of the data after the GFC, the best performing models in the pre-crisis period and post-crisis period*

## How did the asset markets change after the GFC? 329

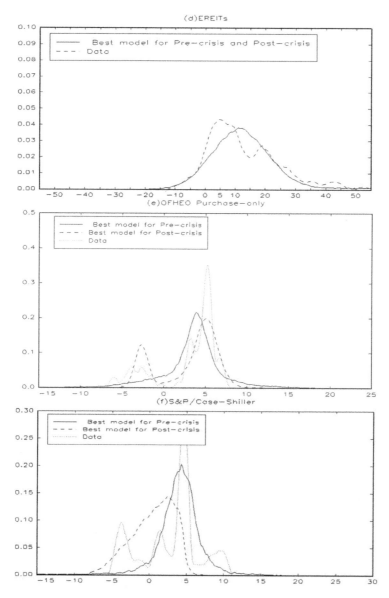

*Figure 12.5D–F* Empirical distributions for returns of the data after the GFC, the best performing models in the pre-crisis period and post-crisis period

330  *Handbook of real estate and macroeconomics*

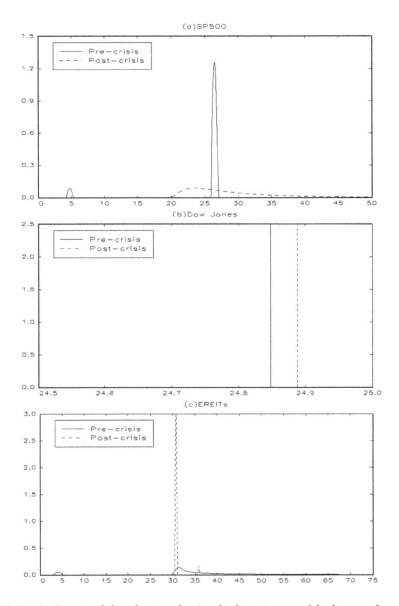

*Figure 12.6A–C  Empirical distributions for (implied) variances of the best performing model in the post-crisis period, and the best pre-crisis model applies to post-crisis period*

*How did the asset markets change after the GFC?* 331

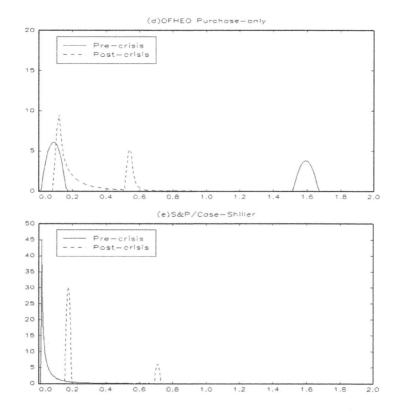

*Figure 12.6D–E Empirical distributions for (implied) variances of the best performing model in the post-crisis period, and the best pre-crisis model applies to post-crisis period*

In Figure 12.6, we apply the same logic to model-implied variance. The distributions generated by $j'(i)$ (i.e. when we assume the same model maintains to be the best before and after the crisis) are, in general, very different from that generated by $k(i)$, the model selected by our model comparison procedure. In many cases, the distribution implied by $k(i)$ appears to be "closer" to that generated by $j'(i)$. Here are more detailed remarks.[18]

1. Notice that the "true variance" is unknown. Only the empirical distributions for variances of the best pre-crisis model apply to the post-crisis period, and the best post-crisis model is plotted.
2. The best model for Nasdaq does not change before and after the GFC.
3. For EREITs, OFHEO purchase-only, and S&P/Case-Shiller, the pre-crisis best model applied to the post-crisis period has a more considerable variance than the post-crisis best model referring to the post-crisis period. If we ignore the structural change and use the same model found in the pre-crisis period, the "uncertainty about variance" will be overestimated.
4. For SP500, the risk is more spread out in the post-crisis best model than the pre-crisis counterpart. Thus, the pre-crisis best model applied to the post-crisis period will underestimate the *"uncertainty about variance."*
5. In Figure 12.6B (Dow Jones), the shape of the empirical distribution of variance generated by the best model in the pre-crisis period and the counterpart in the post-crisis period is very similar. However, the post-crisis best model's empirical distribution applied to the post-crisis period is slightly to the right of that of the pre-crisis best model applied to the post-crisis period. If we ignore the structural change and use the same model found in the pre-crisis period, the "possibility of higher variance occurring" will be underestimated.

In sum, our chapter demonstrates that even for the same asset, there is a need to choose the "best model" in different periods. If the best model selection mechanism is ignored, the return and risk can be significantly mismeasured.

## 5 CONCLUSIONS

This chapter began with an insightful observation by Mr. J. C. Trichet that an inappropriate measure of risk is crucial. An inadequate economic risk measure can lead to suboptimal investment strategies for individuals and governments' misdirected policy. Several authors have made outstanding contributions in this area. For instance, Aumann and Serrano (2008) develop an economic index of riskiness to evaluate an asset's price risk. Homm and Pigorsch (2012) develop a performance index and show that their index is superior to the usually adopted Sharpe ratio. Recently, in a review of the GFC, Malpezzi (2017) also observes that *"Many risks are 'fat in the tails,' and anyway rare events do occur"* (italics added). This chapter compares relative risk and relative performance across housing, REITs, and stock markets in light of these contributions. Our models allow for different forms of "fat tails" in the risk distribution. This chapter selects the "best" model for each asset return before and after the GFC based on the recent econometrics literature. We find that the "best" model does change in some cases.

Furthermore, the risk measures and risk-adjusted performance ranks also significantly change after the GFC. In particular, the empirical distributions of the OFHEO purchase-only housing returns and S&P/Case-Shiller returns shift considerably to the left and become more spread out after the GFC, resulting in an increase in variance and growth in value-at-risk measure. The two housing markets have the same structures of economic riskiness. The economic risk increases for OFHEO purchase-only and S&P/Case-Shiller housing returns after the GFC. The ex post real estate premium virtually *disappears* after the financial crisis.

This chapter can be extended in different directions. We have established that the riskiness and risk-adjusted performance of the major asset markets change significantly after the GFC. However, we have not investigated the causes and mechanisms. Future research should fill the research gap. We should expand the analysis to asset markets outside the United States. One may also explore whether the co-movement among different asset returns changes after the GFC (Leung and Ng, 2019; Riddiough, 2020). Some of these directions are being pursued and will hopefully enrich our understanding of the asset markets and financial crises.

## NOTES

1. Heaton and Lucas (2000) examine several waves of data from the Survey of Consumer Finance. The portfolio weights vary across years and levels of net worth. Stock accounts for 14–33 percent of the portfolio. Real estate accounts for 30–60 percent of the portfolio, cash accounts for 5–16 percent of the portfolio, bonds account for 3–11 percent of the portfolio, and pensions account for less than 10 percent of the portfolio.
2. See Lv and Liu (2014), among others, for more discussion on this point.
3. The Sharpe ratio is a common and widely accepted measure for comparing the relative performance of asset markets. Aumann and Serrano (2008) demonstrate that widely used risk measures such as standard deviation and value-at-risk are inadequate for measuring price risk due to monotonicity failure concerning first-order dominance. Homm and Pigorsch (2012) recommend an economic performance index for estimating a risky asset's performance.
4. For instance, see Homm and Pigorsch (2012) and Schulze (2014) for analytically solvable examples. Note that the analytical solutions of the economic risk and performance indices are not always available. Chen et al. (2014), among others, utilize a numerical method to solve the economic index of riskiness for the Student's t-distribution, left-skewed log-normal distribution, and right-skewed log-normal distribution. They show that the economic index of riskiness is related to the mean, skewness, and kurtosis. Furthermore, Homm and Pigorsch (2012) observe no significant difference in the economic index of riskiness and the economic performance index for parametric specification and non-parametric specification.
5. Many authors have discussed this point. Among others, see Hendershott et al. (2010) and Malpezzi (2017) for a review of the literature.
6. In the interest of space, see Chang and Leung (2021) for a review of the literature.
7. The first 50,000 observations are omitted to remove the possible influence of starting values on simulated data.
8. We do not have access to data that are more frequent than monthly observations. Studies have examined the joint dynamics of different assets at a quarterly rate (e.g., Chang et al., 2011, 2012, 2013). However, the sample size is relatively small in that case, and the estimation of pre-crisis versus post-crisis sub-samples could be difficult. Therefore this study, which is based on monthly data, naturally complements the previous studies.
9. There are different classifications of the pre-crisis versus post-crisis periods. See Dungey et al. (2015) for a detailed analysis. Since we employ monthly data, we cannot divide the sample into

more than two sub-periods. Several studies suggest that lending and trading behaviors during the GFC are very different from those before the crisis. Hence, it may be essential to examine the pre-crisis and post-crisis periods separately. Again, see Chang and Leung (2021) for more discussion of the literature.
10. Chang and Leung (2021) also adopt the mean absolute error and report the corresponding results. Compared to the mean absolute error, the RMSE tends to "punish more" for significant forecast error and hence might be more suitable for the study of risk in this chapter.
11. The AR-ARCH model is selected for two housing returns. For the S&P/Case-Shiller return, the MS-ARCH model does not converge.
12. We also repeat the analysis with the absolute loss criterion. Again, the SLC tends to impose a more massive penalty on "large error" than absolute loss criterion. The results are similar and are reported in Chang and Leung (2021).
13. If the best model is non-stationary, then a second best model is chosen. If the second best model is non-stationary, a third best model is used to simulate the observations. This chapter uses the third best model for the S&P/Case-Shiller housing return during the pre-crisis period.
14. Bimodal distribution or "twin peaks" have been studied in the economics literature. For instance, see Quah (1996).
15. It should be clear that while our sample may be relatively small, the "small sample issue" should apply to both pre-crisis and post-crisis sub-samples. A small sample issue by itself would not make "model switching" more or less likely to happen. For instance, MS-AR(1) is the best model to explain the housing return (S&P/Case-Shiller) for both the pre-crisis and post-crisis periods. A small sample issue would not make models that implied "more risk" be selected. The results of our model selection procedures suggest a decrease in risk in financial asset returns and an increase in housing returns in the post-crisis period at the same time.
16. The value-at-risk measure at ±% is defined as the ±th percentile of the distribution of excess returns multiplied by -1. The larger the value-at-risk, the larger the negative return.
17. Furthermore, the performance rankings of the high- and low-liquidity assets do not change the Sharpe ratio and $EPI_N$. The $EPI_N$ and EPI measures show a slight difference in performance ranking.
18. Notice that as the bandwidth suggested by Silverman (1992) is used, $h = \dfrac{0.9}{(N)^{1/5}} \min\left(\sqrt{V(X)}, \dfrac{Q_3 - Q_1}{1.349}\right)$

, where $Q_3$ is the third quartile and $Q_1$ is the first quartile. For the MS-AR model, there are two different variances. When the $Q_3 - Q_1 = 0$, the maximum variance replaces the $Q_3$, and the minimum variance replaces $Q_1$.

# REFERENCES

Agarwal, S., and Varshneya, S., 2020. Financial crisis and the US mortgage markets: A review, mimeo.
Anand, A., Li, T., Kurosaki, T., and Kim, Y. S., 2016. Foster-Hart risk and the too-big-to-fail banks: An empirical investigation, *Journal of Banking and Finance*, 68, 117–130.
Aumann, R. J., and Serrano, R., 2008. An economic index of riskiness, *Journal of Political Economy*, 116, 810–836.
Bollerslev, T., 1986. Generalized autoregressive conditional heteroscedasticity, *Journal of Econometrics*, 31, 307–327.
Brookings Institution, 2018, Charting the financial crisis: U.S. strategy and outcomes, mimeo.
Chang, K. L., and Leung, C. K. Y., 2021. How did the asset markets change after the Global Financial Crisis, Working paper.
Chang, K. L., Chen, N. K., and Leung, C. K. Y., 2011. Monetary policy, term structure and real estate return: Comparing REIT, housing and stock, *Journal of Real Estate Finance and Economics*, 43, 221–257.

Chang, K. L., Chen, N. K., and Leung, C. K. Y., 2012. The dynamics of housing returns in Singapore: How important are the international transmission mechanisms? *Regional Science and Urban Economics*, 42, 516–530.

Chang, K. L., Chen, N. K., and Leung, C. K. Y., 2013, In the shadow of the United States: The international transmission effect of asset returns, *Pacific Economic Review*, 18(1), 1–40.

Chang, K. L., Chen, N. K., and Leung, C. K. Y., 2016. Losing track of the asset markets: The case of housing and stock, *International Real Estate Review*, 19, 435–492.

Chen, Y. T., Ho, K. Y., and Tzeng, L. Y., 2014. Riskiness-minimizing spot-futures hedge ratio, *Journal of Banking and Finance*, 40, 154–164.

Cochrane, J. H., Taylor, J. B., and Palermo, K., ed., 2019. *Currencies, Capital, and Central Bank Balances*, Stanford, CA: Hoover Institution Press.

DeFilippis, J., ed., 2016. *Urban Policy in the Time of Obama*, Minneapolis, MN: University of Minnesota Press.

Dungey, M., Milunovich, G., Thorp, S., and Yang, M., 2015. Endogenous crisis dating and contagion using smooth transition structural GARCH, *Journal of Banking and Finance*, 58, 71–79.

Hansen, P., Lunde, A., and Nason, J., 2011. The model confidence set, *Econometrica*, 79(2), 453–497.

Heaton, J., and Lucas, D., 2000, Portfolio choice and asset prices: The importance of entrepreneurial risk, *Journal of Finance*, 55, 1163–1198.

Hendershott, P., Hendershott, R., and Shilling, J., 2010. The mortgage finance bubble: Causes and corrections, *Journal of Housing Research*, 19, 1–16.

Homm, U., and Pigorsch, C., 2012. Beyond the Sharpe ratio: An application of the Aumann-Serrano index to performance measurement, *Journal of Banking and Finance*, 36, 2274–2284.

Kwan, Y. K., Leung, C. K. Y., and Dong, J., 2015. Comparing consumption-based asset pricing models: The case of an Asian city, *Journal of Housing Economics*, 28, 18–41.

Lehkonen, H., 2015. Stock market integration and the global financial crisis, *Review of Finance*, 19, 2039–2094.

Leung, C. K. Y., and Ng, C. Y. J., 2019. Macroeconomic aspects of housing. In Hamilton, J., Dixit, A., Edwards, S., and Judd, K. (eds), *Oxford Research Encyclopedia of Economics and Finance*, Oxford: Oxford University Press.

Liang, N., McConnell, M. M., and Swagel, P., 2018. Evidence on outcomes, mimeo, Brookings Institution.

Lv, J., and Liu, J., 2014. Model selection principles in misspecified models, *Journal of the Royal Statistical Society*, Series B, 76, 141–167.

Malpezzi, S., 2017. Residential real estate in the U.S. financial crisis, the Great Recession, and their aftermath, *Taiwan Economic Review*, 45, 5–56.

Mariano, R., and Preve, D., 2012. Statistical tests for multiple forecast comparison, *Journal of Econometrics*, 169, 123–130.

Mehra, R., and Prescott, E. C., 1985. The equity premium: A puzzle, *Journal of Monetary Economics*, 15, 145–161.

Mollah, S., Shahiduzzaman Quoreshi, A. M. M., and Zafirov, G., 2016. Equity market contagion during global financial and Eurozone crises: Evidence from a dynamic correlation analysis, *Journal of International Financial Markets, Institutions and Money*, 41, 151–167.

Mondria, J., and Quintana-Domeque, C., 2013. Financial contagion and attention allocation, *Economic Journal*, 123, 429–454.

Quah, D. T., 1996. Twin peaks: Growth and convergence in models of distribution dynamics, *Economic Journal*, 106, 1045–1055.

Riddiough, T., 2020. Pension funds and private equity real estate: History, performance, pathologies, risks, mimeo.

Schulze, K., 2014. Existence and computation of the Aumann-Serrano index of riskiness and its extension, *Journal of Mathematical Economics*, 50, 219–224.

Shilling, J., 2003. Is there a risk premium puzzle in real estate? *Real Estate Economics*, 31, 501–525.

Silverman, B. W., 1992. *Density Estimation for Statistics and Data Analysis*, London: Chapman and Hall.

Trichet, J. C., 2009. (Under-)pricing of risks in the financial sector, speech, European Central Bank, January.
Wall Street Journal, 2012. Global Financial Crisis spurs evolution in the asset management industry, August 4.

# PART IV

# NON-RESIDENTIAL REAL ESTATE

# 13. From the regional economy to the macroeconomy

*Santiago M. Pinto and Pierre-Daniel G. Sarte*

## 1 INTRODUCTION

The spatial concentration of economic activity produces a number of benefits.[1] Places with higher production and population densities exhibit faster growth in productivity and per capita gross domestic product, resulting in higher wages. These places are also wellsprings of innovation, accounting for a disproportionate share of new patents. The literature in urban and regional economics gives particular importance to the advantages of the spatial concentration of economic activity. These advantages are typically referred to as "agglomeration economies" (AEs). While these forces are certainly relevant at the local level, are they quantitatively important at the aggregate level? Do granular shocks, originated at the local or regional level, simply level out and vanish at the aggregate level, or do they propagate and amplify, affecting the overall economy in a meaningful way? What are the implications on the resource allocation, such as labor, across regions?

This chapter focuses on how and why the spatial distribution of economic activity is relevant for aggregate outcomes. In other words, topics that have traditionally been studied by regional or urban economists are not without implications for questions and concerns pertinent to macroeconomists. Economic activity is not uniformly distributed across regions. The composition of economic activity also varies across space. Some industries locate and operate in certain locations and then trade with other industries located elsewhere. The nature of trade, and factors that influence it such as the distribution of trade costs and productivity across space, then affects aggregate allocations in a way that, in the last decade, has started to be fully fleshed out.

Recent research has focused on understanding not only how the spatial characteristics of an economy determine the economic performance of regions, but also how they explain fluctuations in aggregate outcomes. In general, this research concludes that the effects observed at the aggregate level are not independent of the allocation of resources across space. The transmission and propagation of local and regional shocks, and their economic importance, critically depend on the spatial distribution of resources. To the extent that the existence of spatial spillovers, externalities, and mobility frictions lead to a sub-optimal allocation of factors of productions across locations, it becomes relevant to evaluate the ability of certain policy interventions to correct for those distortions.

The next sections review recent work that examines the connection between the regional allocation of resources and aggregate outcomes, and highlights directions for future research.

## 2  WHY SPACE MATTERS

Consider an economy in which locations are completely homogeneous, transportation is costly, and there are no economies of scale. Then, in a competitive equilibrium, each location is self-sufficient; in other words, regions do not trade (in equilibrium, there are no shipments of goods across regions). The latter is known as the "spatial impossibility theorem" (Starrett, 1978).

However, economic activity tends to be concentrated in a limited number of locations. Regions do not necessarily produce every good and service, so they trade. The clustering of productive activities, firms, and workers gives rise to AEs, which enhances the locational advantages of a specific region. The spatial allocation of economic activity determines how much and the type of trade that takes place across regions (Rossi-Hansberg, 2005).

Locations are heterogeneous, differing in several dimensions, such as endowments, geography, and accessibility, and may have different comparative advantages (Behrens and Robert-Nicoud, 2015). The location of economic activity is the outcome of the interaction of various forces. Individuals and firms are also heterogeneous. They sort themselves across space and decide where to locate themselves, driven by their preferences and productive abilities. These decisions are, however, constrained by spatial frictions, including mobility and transportation costs. As people decide where to reside and firms where to establish their operations, they affect the outcomes of other people and firms.

### 2.1   A Simple Conceptual Framework

Understanding the relative importance of regional attributes and why some locations have certain attributes is key to explain the observed variation of spatial outcomes. What explains the location choices of mobile factors? Are places attracting people by offering high wages or cheap housing or good weather? Why do firms stay in places where they must pay high wages? If all factors are completely mobile, why do some regions perform systematically better than others in terms of economic development and wealth? Moreover, the degree of factor mobility (households, firms) constrains the design of regional policy.

In this section, we briefly describe a simple theoretical framework used by regional economists to explain spatial outcomes. The framework, founded on the seminal work by Roback (1982), is built on three key no-arbitrage conditions:

1. Individuals must be indifferent across space: flows of wages + amenities − housing costs are equal in every location.
2. Firms must be indifferent over space and over hiring new workers: differences in wages must be offset by differences in productivity.
3. Developers must be indifferent about developing land or not and about building new units or not: housing prices cannot rise too far above the total costs of construction.

Different versions and extensions of the basic model developed by Roback (1982) are commonly used as the main analytical tool to predict how wages and land (or housing) prices adjust to differences in amenities across regions. The model has also been used to construct indexes of quality of life and quality of business environment. The main underlying assumption is that firms and households move across cities to attain the highest possible profit (firms) and utility (households). In equilibrium, generally referred to as a spatial equilibrium, there are no incentives to move, i.e., profits and utility levels should be equalized across space. This means that if a region has amenities that makes it a nice place to live, it will attract households until higher housing prices, lower wages, or a combination of both eliminate the incentive to move. A location that offers a good business environment will attract firms into the region until a combination of higher land rents and higher wages makes it no longer desirable to move into that region. In other words, land or housing prices and wages vary to compensate consumers and firms for the interregional differences in the "quality" of locations.

## 2.2 The Model

Consider a system of regions, where each region i is characterized by a level of amenity $A_i$. Households (workers) and firms decide where to locate themselves, and their decisions depend on wages earned and paid at each location (w); the cost of living at each location, driven mostly by land rents and housing prices (r); and the local amenity ($A_i$), which may affect households and firms differently.

### 2.2.1 Households

The utility of a consumer in region i is described by $u(r, w, A_i)$. While a higher r reduces utility, higher levels of w and $A_i$ increase utility. Consider a constant-utility curve for region i, defined as $u(r, w, A_i) = U$. This curve implicitly defines combinations of $\{r, w\}$ that offer the same utility U, given an amenity level $A_i$. As shown in Figure 13.1a, the curve depicts a positive relationship between r and w. If w increases and r remains constant, then utility increases. To restore utility level U, r should therefore increase. Moreover, consider two regions and suppose the amenity level in region 1 is higher than in region 0, i.e., $A_1 > A_0$. Then, the constant-utility curve for region 1 lies above the constant-utility curve for region 0. Consider a given combination of $\{w, r\}$ on the constant-utility curve of region 0. Since the utility increases as $A_i$ rises, the utility evaluated at $\{w, r\}$ and $A_1$ will be higher than the utility evaluated at $\{w, r\}$ and $A_0$. To restore utility U, then r should increase and/or w should decrease.

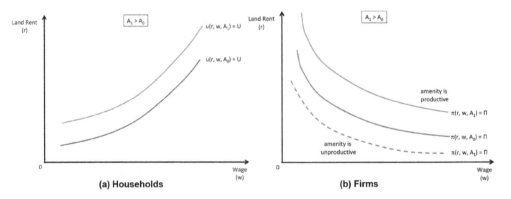

Figure 13.1    Households and firms: A1 > A0

### 2.2.2 Firms

The profit of a firm that operates in region i is given by $\pi(r, w, A_i)$. Both higher land rents r and wages w decrease profits. For firms, the amenity in region i can be productive (reduce production costs or increase productivity), in which case a higher $A_i$ increases profits, or unproductive (increase production costs or reduce productivity), so that a higher $A_i$ decreases profits. An isoprofit curve for region i is defined as combinations of r and w that give the same profit $\Pi$ for a fixed amenity level $A_i$. The curve, shown in Figure 13.1b, depicts an inverse relationship between r and w. If r increases, profits go down. To restore the previous level of profits $\Pi$, w should decrease.

As mentioned earlier, local amenities may affect firms and households differently. For instance, suppose that amenities are productive (*unproductive*) for the firm. Then, if $A_0 > a_0$, the isoprofit curve for region 1 will lie above (*below*) the isoprofit curve of region 0.

### 2.2.3 Spatial equilibrium

Consider an economy with two regions, 0 and 1, with amenity levels $A_0$ and $A_1$. In a spatial equilibrium: (1) consumers should be equally well off in all locations, so that $u(r, w, A_0) = u(r, w, A_1) = U$; and (2) firms should have the same profits at all locations, so $\pi(r, w, A_0) = \pi(r, w, A_1) = \Pi$. In Figure 13.2, the equilibrium wage and land rent at a location with amenity $A_i$ are represented by $\{w_i, r_i\}$ (point $E_i$).

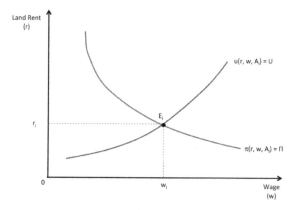

*Figure 13.2    Spatial equilibrium*

How can this framework be used to explain the spatial variation in land rents and wages? Suppose that region 1 is always more attractive than region 0 for consumers, so that $A_1 > A_0$. However, suppose $A_i$ may have different effects on the costs or productivity of firms that produce in 1: (a) $A_i$ may not have an impact, (b) $A_i$ may only have a weak impact, or (c) $A_i$ may have strong impact on local productivity. The three cases are shown in Figure 13.3. From the figures we conclude that land rents are unambiguously higher in region 1 than in region 0. However, wages can either be higher or lower. For instance, if the effect of the amenity on firm productivity is sufficiently small in magnitude (represented by cases (a) and (b)), then a higher level of $A_i$ in region 1 would lead to lower wages at that location. If the effect is sufficiently large (such as in case (c)), then wages may also be higher in region 1.

342  Handbook of real estate and macroeconomics

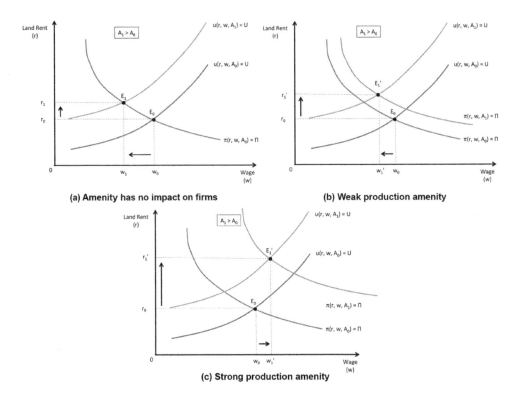

*Figure 13.3  Spatial equilibrium: comparing two regions (A1 > A0)*

The shift from $A_0$ to $A_1$ can also be interpreted as a positive productivity shock that only affects firms that produce in a given region (in other words, suppose the constant-utility curve does not shift). The positive shock will then tend to increase land rents, wages, or a combination of both. The precise outcome will depend on the curvature of the constant-utility curve. For example, if this curve is vertical, then the local productivity shock will be fully capitalized into land values, while if the curve is completely horizontal, it would only increase nominal wages. In general, the shock will tend to increase both land rents and wages.

Several factors explain how much wages and land rents would vary across regions or how they would change when a region experiences a productivity shock. These factors include mobility costs (for instance, mobility costs may be different for households with different skill levels, firms that operate in certain sectors may need to locate close to natural resources or other key inputs, making them less spatially mobile), the elasticity of housing supply (determined by both geographical constraints and local regulations), local taxes, the quality of locally provided goods and services, and the quality of the transportation infrastructure, among others. The main takeaway from this framework is that to the extent that factors of production are spatially mobile, in equilibrium land rents and wages will reflect the region's attributes.

## 2.3 Extensions

The basic Roback model has been extended in several directions to examine and understand the role played by several factors in determining the spatial distribution of factors of production. Modern approaches in regional economics, for instance, build on extended versions of the Roback model to quantify the impact of a variety of policy interventions. Some of the extensions assume that workers are heterogeneous in their skills, the type of work they are best suited for, or in their mobility costs.[2] Firms may be heterogeneous as well: some of them may be more productive than others. Amenities, both in consumption and production, can be assumed to be, at least in part, endogenous. For instance, $A_i$ may depend on the population size, the demographic composition, or the number and types of firms operating in each region. We will review some of this literature in the following sections.

## 3 FROM THE REGION TO THE NATION

Macroeconomists have traditionally looked to aggregate shocks as sources of aggregate economic fluctuation or trends. More recently, however, they have come to increasingly rely on detailed and disaggregated data capturing granular and idiosyncratic shocks as sources of, and to characterize, aggregate changes. Some of the granularity is regional in nature.

### 3.1 Granular Shocks and Macroeconomics

The work by Gabaix (2011) was among the first to establish the importance of granularity to understanding both aggregate fluctuations and aggregate trends (the "granular hypothesis"). The paper claims that when the distribution of firm sizes in an economy has a "fat tail," idiosyncratic shocks affecting large firms do not simply level out and vanish in the aggregate. In fact, these shocks have the potential of generating considerable aggregate fluctuations. The propagation of granular shocks crucially depends on how the economy is organized. Acemoglu et al. (2012) show that granular shocks may trigger aggregate fluctuations when sectors are interrelated through input and output linkages. A shock to a specific sector may be amplified as it triggers a chain reaction to other sectors through the input–output network.

Recent developments in quantitative models that combine calibration and structural estimation techniques with granular data are increasingly used in several fields in economics. This research approach has been widely used in international trade. Costinot and Rodríguez-Clare (2014) offer a thorough review of the work that relies on microfounded gravity models to quantify different counterfactuals, such as the aggregate trade liberalization.

More recent work also follows a granular approach, but within models that explicitly account for the spatial distribution of economic activities. For instance, Giroud and Mueller (2019) uses United States (U.S.) establishment-level data to examine how demand shocks propagate across regions through the firms' internal network. Their analysis uses the regional variation in housing prices observed during the Great Recession as drivers of negative local consumer demand shock. They find that the shock does not only adversely affect establishment-level employment in the local non-tradeable sector (restaurants, retailers, grocery stores), but it also negatively affects employment at locations where the parent firms operate.

A related literature has been emerging in urban and regional economics with the development of a wide range of quantitative spatial models. Many of these models build on the theoretical framework developed by Roback (1982) summarized in the previous section. While the literature is broad, most of the research focuses on examining the broader implications of shocks and policy interventions that take place at the local or regional level, such as changes in amenities, productivity, or the expansion of the transportation network. Redding and Rossi-Hansberg (2017) thoroughly review recent work in these areas.[3]

An analysis based on quantitative models offers several advantages over the traditional reduced-form approach. First, since this methodology is directly founded on theoretical models, it becomes easier to identify the causal effects of policies. Moreover, these models are constructed to explicitly account for the aggregation of granular shocks. Second, quantitative models can be used to construct counterfactual policy evaluation exercises, and characterize, quantify, and compare outcomes under different scenarios. One advantage of this approach over the traditional reduced-form analysis is that it accounts for the general equilibrium of the policy interventions. Third, they can be used to perform a welfare analysis of regional policies, which considers their impact on the entire economy.

Several studies exploit cross-variation to identify the key parameters, and use the structural estimations to do counterfactual analysis. Such an approach complements the quantitative spatial models described above. Among others, the work by Guren et al. (2018) estimates the housing wealth effect by exploiting systematic differences in city-level exposure to regional house price cycles. Greenwald and Guren (2019) estimate the impact of credit expansion on housing prices, rents, and homeownership rates using cross-city variation. They calibrate a quantitative model using these moments to measure the degree of segmentation between owner-occupied and rental units. More recently, Yao (2020) estimates the land shares in producing houses and apartments using cross-city variation. The study finds that the difference in land intensities can largely account for the cross-city variations in housing prices and rents.

## 3.2  Aggregate Effects of Regional Shocks

Granular shocks may have different aggregate implications depending on both the specific sector and region originally affected. Different mechanisms explain how regional shocks propagate and gain importance in the aggregate. Recent work attempts to assess the quantitative impact of some of these mechanisms and evaluate their impact on regional and national economic performance.[4] To explain the transmission and propagation of shocks, Caliendo et al. (2017) construct a quantitative spatial model which assumes regions are endowed with different stocks of immobile factors, the sectoral composition differs across regions, and transportation costs are determined by the geography. Using granular manufacturing data for the U.S., they estimate how regional and sectoral productivity shocks affect total factor productivity (TFP), gross domestic product, and employment at the regional, sectoral, and aggregate levels.

A recent strand of literature focuses on regional fiscal multipliers. This work uses cross-sectional variation as a strategy to identify how fiscal policy may affect the aggregate economy (see Nakamura and Steinsson (2018) for the more general question on identification in macroeconomics). While it is generally understood that the aggregate effect is not simply the sum of the regional effects, this approach has generally been used to assess and compare the effectiveness of different fiscal policies. To account for the aggregate effects of regional policies, it is necessary to develop a general equilibrium model. Nakamura and Steinsson (2014), Chodorow-Reich (2019), and Beraja et al. (2019b), among several others, follow this kind of approach.

Local TFP shocks directly affect cities hit by the shock by increasing local employment, earnings, and purchasing power of workers. However, as the spatial allocation of factors of production changes in response to the shock, other localities will be indirectly affected. The work by Hornbeck and Moretti (2019) quantifies the importance of the direct and indirect effects of local manufacturing TFP shocks. At the local level, they find that homeowners benefit from the positive shock. However, for renters, the increase in earnings is almost perfectly matched by an increase in the local cost of living. Their work also shows that local inequality declines after the local productivity growth in manufacturing, since earnings of local low-skilled workers increase more than those of high-skilled workers. The differential impact on the two groups is partly explained by the fact that low-skill workers tend to move less across space. It follows from their analysis that the indirect effects of local TFP shocks are also important. The local shock may have a small impact on other cities individually, but the aggregate effect is not negligible. In fact, their results indicate that 38 percent of the increase in workers' purchasing power is explained by what happens in cities not directly affected by the shock.

## 3.3 Agglomeration and Aggregate Growth

The notion of AEs is quite broad and it encompasses a wide range of factors (see, for example, Duranton and Puga, 2004). Agglomeration is generally introduced as a shifter of the production function in a Hicks-neutral way. Specifically, establishment i's production function is given by $y_i = A_i f(x_i)$, where $x_i$ is a vector of inputs including labor, capital (physical or human), land, and other materials, and $A_i = g(a_i)$ includes all external factors $a_i$ that may affect the establishment's productivity. Models differ on how they specify the function $g(a_i)$. For instance, $a_i$ may include variables that capture the size of the industry, the size of the city, or the skill composition of the labor force.

A large body of research in urban and regional economics focuses on the impact of AEs on city growth (see, for example, Rosenthal and Strange (2004) and Combes and Gobillon (2015) for a comprehensive review of the literature). But what is the contribution of local AEs to aggregate economic growth? Only a limited number of studies have focused on this specific issue. Rossi-Hansberg and Wright (2007) develop an economic growth model in the context of cities. In their model, knowledge spillovers underlie agglomeration forces. Specifically, the productivity of local firms depends on the total number of workers in the city and on the total stock of human capital. The main challenge is to reconcile increasing returns at the local level with constant returns to scale at the aggregate level, required for a balanced growth path. Rossi-Hansberg and Wright (2007) address this issue by incorporating urban costs (specifically congestion) that balance agglomeration forces. Such interaction ultimately drives the birth, growth, and death of cities.

Davis et al. (2014) quantify the impact of local agglomeration on aggregate growth. The paper develops a dynamic spatial stochastic general equilibrium growth model. The notion of agglomeration used in their analysis assumes a very simple reduced form, based on previous work by Ciccone and Hall (1996). Specifically, output produced at location j is given by

$$y_j = A_j \ell_j^{(1-\phi)} k_j^{\alpha\phi} n^{(1-\alpha)\phi}, \phi \in [0,1], \tag{13.1}$$

where $\ell_j$ is finished land available for production at location j, $k_j$ is capital, $n_j$ is the number of workers, $\alpha$ and $(1-\alpha)$ the factor shares, and $\varphi$ represents a congestion effect in production. TFP at location j is given by

$$A_j = (\tilde{A}_j z_j)^{(1-\alpha)\phi} a_j^{(\lambda-1)/\lambda}, \lambda \geq 1, \tag{13.2}$$

where $\tilde{A}_j$ is the exogenous city-specific productivity, $z_j$ is an exogenous productivity shock, and $a_j$ is city j's output density, defined as total production in j per unit of finished land. The effect of $a_j$ on TFP $A_j$ is determined by $\lambda$. The quantitative exercise confirms the fact that $\lambda$ is significantly greater than one, so agglomeration does affect TFP. Moreover, from their estimations it follows that local agglomeration forces increase the growth rate of aggregate consumption per capita in about 10 percent.

Finally, the urban growth model developed by Duranton and Puga (2019) assumes that AEs are driven by human capital spillovers. These spillovers promote entrepreneurship and ultimately increase local productivity. When the population of a city rises, it increases learning and the accumulation of human capital. From the quantification of their model, it follows that if city population had remained at 1950 levels, the average growth rate of income per capita in the U.S. would have been 0.8 percent instead of 2.1 percent.

### 3.4 Regional Trends: Growth Convergence (Divergence) in the United States

Evidence shows that regions within a country do not necessarily grow at the same rates. In the U.S., the disparity in regional growth rates until approximately the 1980s has contributed to explaining a process of remarkable per capita income convergence across regions. Since then, however, income convergence has slowed down and almost disappeared. Moreover, cities do not always grow at the same pace.[5]

This recent decline in regional income convergence has been observed at different geographical levels, including regions, states, and cities. The work by Ganong and Shoag (2017), for instance, studies regional convergence of per capita incomes across U.S. states. The authors document that from 1880 to 1980, incomes across states converged at a rate of 1.8 percent per year from 1880 until 1980. This relationship weakened dramatically during the period 1990–2010 (the convergence rate declined to less than half the historical values), and there was practically no convergence during the period before the Great Recession. Using city-level (metropolitan statistical area) data, recent work by Giannone (2017) establishes that during the period 1940 and 1980, the wage gap between poorer and richer U.S. cities declined at an annual rate of roughly 1.4 percent. The data show no further regional convergence after 1980 though.

The lack of regional convergence is generally attributed to a variety of factors. For instance, the lower-income convergence coincides with a decline in migration. There is substantial evidence suggesting that labor mobility in the U.S. is not as high as in the past (see Molloy et al., 2016; Austin et al., 2018). However, not only has labor mobility been declining, it has become less directed toward high-income areas. Ganong and Shoag (2017) relate the lack of convergence of state income per capita to the observed decline in directed migration. While before 1980 people were migrating from low- to high-income places, this pattern has declined over the last 30 years. Ganong and Shoag (2017) attribute such decline to changes that have been taking place in the housing markets, specifically in high-income locations. The returns to migration and the resulting migration flows depend in part on housing prices and how they respond to the increase in housing demand. While housing prices have always been higher in higher-income states, Ganong and Shoag (2017) claim that housing supply has become more inelastic in high-income locations due to more stringent land use regulations (LURs). Such changes tend to disproportionately affect more low-skill workers than high-skill workers, reducing their incentives to move.

To explain the lack of convergence, Giannone (2017) focuses on the differential behavior of workers with different skills. A closer look at the data reveals that while prior to 1980 the wage convergence for high- and low-skilled workers was the same, after 1980 wages did not converge for the high skilled, but continued to converge at 1.4 percent annually for low-skill workers.

Using Public Use Microdata Areas data, Austin et al. (2018) show evidence for a number of stylized facts: (1) declining geographic mobility; (2) increasingly inelastic housing supplies in high-income areas; (3) declining income convergence; (4) increased sorting by skills across space; and (5) persistent pockets of non-employment. All this supports the conclusions from the previous papers.

## 4 WHAT EXPLAINS THE INEFFICIENT SPATIAL ALLOCATION OF RESOURCES?

Recent work indicates that the spatial distribution of wages, and consequently productivity differences, across urban areas within the U.S. has been increasing (see, for instance, Hsieh and Moretti (2019) or Fajgelbaum and Gaubert (2020)). The latter suggests that the spatial allocation of resources is inefficient. The spatial misallocation of resources may partly explain the lack of convergence across regions, and could eventually affect aggregate outcomes, as mentioned in the previous section. The literature has considered several factors that may prevent poorer regions from integrating with the more prosperous parts of the national economy and explain the observed inefficient spatial distribution of labor and firms. Some of those factors include spatial spillovers and externalities, LURs, and regional taxes.

### 4.1 Externalities and Spatial Spillovers

Section 3.3 focuses on the effects of AEs on growth. The spatial concentration of economic activity increases local productivity and city growth. These effects eventually percolate across the entire economy and affect aggregate growth. However, AEs generate external effects, which means their presence may induce a sub-optimal spatial allocation of resources. From an efficiency standpoint, the presence of AEs could justify the implementation of policies that target resources to more productive areas. This intervention would only increase aggregate welfare if the net benefits at those locations that attract resources more than compensate for the losses that take place elsewhere. A number of recent papers attempts to quantify these effects.

Greenstone et al. (2010) quantify agglomeration spillovers by estimating the impact of the opening of a large manufacturing plant, the "million-dollar plant" (MDP), on the TFP of incumbent plants in the same county. They compare incumbent plants in the county where the new plant chose to locate (winning county), with incumbent plants in the runner-up county (losing county). The main finding of their research is that five years after the new MDP opening, the TFP of incumbent plants in winning counties is on average 12 percent higher than the TFP of incumbent plants in losing counties. The estimated productivity gains are, however, very heterogeneous, with some incumbent plants even showing a decline in TFP.

The work by Gaubert (2018) explains productivity differences between cities by disentangling agglomeration forces from firm sorting. The paper develops a quantitative spatial model that examines how much of the productivity advantage of a region is driven by the efficiency of the firms it attracts. The model examines the localization choices of heterogeneous firms in an environment where firm productivity is higher in places with larger populations, and characterizes the optimal spatial allocation. Two main conclusions emerge from the analysis. First, the equilibrium is sub-optimal in the sense that firms locate in cities that are too small. The first best solution would entail taxing firms' wages in smaller cities and subsidizing firms' wages in larger cities. Second, as city size increases by 1 percent, firm productivity increases by 4.2 percent, where approximately half of it is attributed to firm sorting (2.3 percent). The model is next used to perform a number of counterfactual exercises in order to evaluate the effectiveness of certain place-based policies. We will revisit the policy implications of these exercises in Section 6.

Fajgelbaum and Gaubert (2020) also examine the welfare impact of spatially targeted policies. The main difference with Gaubert (2018) is that the model includes spillover effects among heterogeneous workers taking place through both the productive and consumption processes. The analysis, which focuses on the U.S. economy, proceeds in three steps. First, it evaluates the observed spatial distribution of economic activity and compares it to the efficient allocation. Second, it examines the kind of policies (transfers) that would restore efficiency. Third, it characterizes the properties of the optimal spatial distribution and compares it to the observed outcome. Specifically, it examines whether an optimal spatial distribution entails stronger or weaker spatial disparities and sorting by skill relative to the observed one. The main conclusion from their analysis is that the U.S. economy shows an excessive concentration of high-skill workers and wage inequality in larger cities relative to efficient outcome.

Rossi-Hansberg et al. (2019) focus on the spillover effects among workers in different occupations, performing different types of tasks. Occupations are generally divided into those that require "cognitive" and "non-routine" tasks, or CNR occupations, and the rest, grouped into non-CNR occupations. Moreover, the spatial distribution of occupations is not uniform: workers in CNR occupations tend to be concentrated in large cities, workers in non-CNR occupations are located in small, generally declining cities. The work by Rossi-Hansberg et al. (2019) presents evidence showing large productivity spillovers among CNR occupations, but none among non-CNR workers. Motivated by this evidence, the paper evaluates next the ability of certain spatially targeted policies to attain optimal allocation resources across regions.

## 4.2 Land Use Regulations

Land and housing can be costly at certain locations or regions for a number of possible reasons. As described in Section 2.1, local amenities attract population and firms, raising the demand for land, and consequently land prices, in those areas. Prices could also be high if land supply is constrained by the geography. In some other areas, however, land prices are high because of stringent LURs, such as zoning laws or minimum lot sizes. While the implementation of LURs could theoretically be justified on the basis that they intend to correct for market imperfections, many researchers have questioned their cost-effectiveness. Regardless of their merits, the use of LURs has become widespread and their intensity has been steadily increasing. Understanding the impact of LURs is important, but at the same time, challenging. Due to the complexity and overlap of a large number of local rules in place, it is not easy to quantify their economic consequences.

Shifts in population from less-productive areas to more-productive ones are desirable since they would tend to increase the overall productivity in a country.[6] LURs, however, make it difficult for local housing markets to respond to growing demand. By reducing land availability and increasing land prices at certain locations, LURs make the process of moving to thriving regions more difficult, beyond the normal costs of changing residential locations. Workers facing these additional hurdles to moving may end up being trapped in less productive areas. Otherwise productive labor migration is discouraged, generating a sub-optimal distribution of labor across the nation and an excessively large dispersion of wages across regions.

Herkenhoff et al. (2018) develop a spatial growth model and estimate the impact of state-level LURs on the spatial allocation of capital and workers, and on aggregate productivity and growth. They conclude that by reducing the intensity of LURs to its 1980 levels in highly productive states (namely California and New York), aggregate productivity could increase by 7 percent and consumption by 5 percent. These gains, they show, are largely explained by the reallocation of capital across states.

The work by Hsieh and Moretti (2019) quantify the aggregate economic importance of LURs in a Roback-type framework. To the extent that these regulations induce a mismatch between workers and regions, they would entail lower aggregate productivity and welfare. Using data from 220 U.S. metropolitan areas, the paper finds that during the period 1964–2009 LURs effectively decreased aggregate economic growth by 36 percent. Moreover, the authors state that LURs in exceptionally productive cities (such as New York City, San Francisco, and San Jose) are particularly responsible for curtailing aggregate economic growth in the U.S. Duranton and Puga (2019) find similar results.[7] In their framework, by alleviating regulations in the three most productive cities in the U.S. to match the level of regulations in the median U.S. city, average real income would increase by 8.2 percent.

While rules and standards are necessary to generate the best possible urban life, there is always the risk of shifting toward an excessively regulated environment in which the cost of the regulations overshadows their intended objectives. The challenge is, of course, to determine what kind of minimal regulations would be necessary to ensure a pleasant and, at the same time, productive environment without imposing unwarranted costs on both the local and the aggregate economy.

### 4.3 Regional Taxes

Regional taxes may also distort the spatial allocation of resources. In general, a heterogeneous regional tax system will generate a distortion that in principle depends on the ability of factors of production to change their locations in response to tax changes. The work by Suárez Serrato and Zidar (2016) quantifies welfare effects of changes in state corporate taxes on workers, firms, and landowners. It is generally believed that corporate taxation in an open economy tends to hurt workers more because companies can be moved to places with lower tax pressure. In other words, firms are more mobile than workers. However, from their analysis, the opposite conclusion follows: higher taxes on businesses do not always seem to push them away. In fact, firm owners bear approximately 40 percent of the tax burden, workers between 30 and 35 percent, and landowners between 25 and 30 percent. Companies do not only consider tax changes when deciding where to operate, but also other factors, such as local productive amenities and worker productivity.

A series of studies (Restuccia and Rogerson, 2008; Albouy, 2009; Hsieh and Klenow, 2009; Desmet and Rossi-Hansberg, 2013; Suárez Serrato and Zidar, 2016; Fajgelbaum et al., 2019; and others) focus on the benefits of tax harmonization. This research agrees with the conclusion that heterogeneity in regional taxes generates aggregate welfare losses. A shift towards a regime with a lower dispersion of regional taxes induces a reallocation of workers and firms and increases welfare. Specifically, the work by Fajgelbaum et al. (2019) finds that if states harmonize their tax systems, aggregate welfare may increase by 0.6 percent if spending remains constant, and 1.2 percent if state spending endogenously responds to the tax changes.[8]

## 5 TRANSPORTATION

The transportation system is a key determinant of the economic performance of regions. To a large extent, the benefits of the spatial concentration of activities can only be exploited if transportation costs are not prohibitively high. Translating the impact of transportation investment or improvements on regional growth is, however, particularly challenging. If, for instance, current transportation investment is driven by expected population growth, then the benefits of the investment will be confounded with other effects. Before reviewing recent work that has dealt with some of these challenges, we first briefly explain how regional economists think about the role of transportation in a spatial setting.

### 5.1 How Do Regional Economists Think about the Role of Transportation in the Economy?

Accessibility, which is in part determined by the transportation system in place, affects the localization decisions of individuals and firms, and how land is used. Accessibility, however, depends on where individuals and firms locate. In other words, transportation and land use interact and influence one another. Economists do not consider transportation in isolation but as one of the components of a more complex and interrelated system that includes cities and regions.

The role of transportation in the context of a spatial equilibrium model is twofold. First, as mentioned earlier, one of the main reasons for the existence of cities refers to the advantage of carrying out economic activities in close proximity, or the presence of AEs. Transportation in this context plays a critical role, since lower transportation costs would allow a higher concentration of production, and larger benefits from agglomeration.

Second, local wages and housing prices adjust at every location so that households and firms do not have an incentive to move (as described in Section 2.1). In other words, wages and land prices will reflect regional differences, making households and firms indifferent across locations. When choosing where to live, individuals consider a wide range of factors, including job opportunities, housing options, social networks, and commuting costs. Within a city, some people might choose to live far away from jobs, possibly accepting a costlier commute, because they would be compensated, in effect, by other factors such as lower housing costs. As a result, a trade-off between commuting costs and land prices emerges in equilibrium: at locations near employment centers, commuting costs are low and land prices are high; at more distant locations, commuting costs are higher and land prices are lower. The different levels of accessibility are explained, in part, by the quality of the local transportation system.

## 5.2 The Economic Importance of Transportation

Research in urban transportation has mainly focused on the effects of transportation on job accessibility and local economic conditions. Estimating those effects is challenging, however, precisely because of the interdependence between transportation and land use explained earlier.

Duranton and Turner (2011) explore the relationship between transportation infrastructure and traffic congestion. Specifically, they estimate the effect of increasing highway capacity on congestion. Their main finding is that people actually drive more when the stock of roads in their city increases. In fact, they find a one-for-one relationship between the two. It follows from this research, then, that an increase in the provision of highways would not alleviate congestion. Their explanation of this outcome is that cities with better roads attract more people. The use of the roads would therefore increase until traffic congestion reaches its pre-existing levels.

In a different paper, Duranton and Turner (2012) examine the effect of increasing highway miles on employment growth in American cities; they find that a 10 percent increase in a city's initial stock of highways caused about a 1.5 percent increase in its employment over a 20-year period.

Between 1950 and 1990, the aggregate population of central cities in the U.S. declined by 17 percent, despite the fact that population increased by 72 percent in metropolitan statistical areas. This process is generally known as suburbanization. Baum-Snow (2007) investigates the extent to which this phenomenon is attributable to the expansion of the highway system, which eventually leads to lower commuting costs. The paper finds a positive relationship between roads and suburbanization. The results show that one additional "ray," or segment, of interstate highway originating from the city center leads to about a 9 percent decline in the central city population. It should be noted, however, that other factors occurring at that time were also inducing residents to move out of downtown areas. Some of these factors include an increase in income, a flight from blight due to crime, the degradation of housing stock, and changes in the school system.

U.S. cities show differing patterns of residential sorting by income. In most U.S. metropolitan statistical areas, the suburbs are of higher income status and the central cities are relatively poor. There are important exceptions, such as Chicago, Philadelphia, and others. To explain this kind of spatial sorting, the literature suggests a variety of different mechanisms. One such explanation focuses on the transportation mode choices made by households with different income levels. Work by Glaeser et al. (2008), for instance, states that transport modes are key for explaining the central location of the poor. The reasons are twofold: first, the larger financial costs associated with owning a car may cause lower-income families to rely on other modes of transportation, such as public transit; and second, public transit is more accessible in central cities than in suburbs.

A different line of research that also focuses on job accessibility is related to the spatial mismatch hypothesis. The spatial mismatch hypothesis pioneered in 1968 by John Kain intends to explain an apparent spatial disconnection between jobs and workers' locations. The suburbanization of jobs observed during the 1960s and 1970s hurt the labor market prospects of minorities. African-American populations, largely concentrated in central urban areas, were unable to relocate closer to the jobs for different reasons. As a result, they end up experiencing either excessive commuting costs or higher and persistent unemployment levels. In Kain's view, the inability of minorities to move and follow the jobs to the suburbs was mainly due to racial discrimination in the suburban housing market.

The spatial mismatch hypothesis motivated a large body of research on job accessibility and transportation. This literature has mainly examined how the lack of connection to job opportunities affects individuals' labor market prospects, especially for low-skilled workers and minorities. Research generally confirms the hypothesis. The main findings can be summarized as follows. First, the effect of spatial mismatch is stronger in large central urban areas, where low-skilled minorities tend to live. Jobs are generally located far away from central areas, and minorities face geographical barriers that prevent them from finding and keeping jobs. Second, the research establishes that better job accessibility significantly decreases the duration of joblessness among lower-paid displaced workers, the result being strongest for non-Hispanic, African-American, female, and older workers.

A corollary of these findings is that improving spatial access to jobs would lead to better labor market outcomes. Investing in transportation infrastructure and improving transportation services (increasing frequency, capacity, and so on) would increase connectivity between high-unemployment neighborhoods and locations with an abundance of jobs and help alleviate the negative consequences of the spatial mismatch.

## 5.3   Aggregate Economic Impact of Transportation Improvements

It is important, however, to distinguish the impact that transportation has on economic activity and growth from its effects on the spatial reorganization of existing activity (see Redding and Turner (2015) for a review of this discussion). As stated earlier, accessibility and localization choices are jointly determined in a spatial equilibrium model. Improvements in transportation infrastructure may simply induce a relocation of resources from one place to another and generate only localized benefits, if any.

Some recent work attempts to quantify the aggregate impact of investment in transportation. This work accounts for all the direct and indirect effects generated and propagated throughout the entire transportation network across space.

Desmet and Rossi-Hansberg (2013) consider an urban equilibrium model within a system of cities and examine how different factors, such as productivity, amenities, and frictions, affect the size distribution of cities and welfare. One of the frictions considered in the analysis is commuting costs, which are assumed to depend on local transportation infrastructure. In their counterfactual exercise, they evaluate the general equilibrium effects of removing differences across cities in any of the three components. They find that for the U.S., eliminating differences in any of these features generates a large redistribution of agents across space, but welfare does not change that much (the redistribution of population can be 40 percent or more, but welfare gains are less than 2 percent). Allen and Arkolakis (2014) develop a structural spatial model that considers trade and labor mobility. They find that the U.S. Interstate Highway System contributed to increasing welfare by about 1.1–1.4 percent. The benefits of this investment are, as a result, substantially larger than its cost. The paper by Donaldson and Hornbeck (2016) focuses on the impact on the agricultural sector of expanding the U.S. railroad system in 1890. Their approach assumes that the expansion of the network increases market access, and its benefits will be capitalized into land values. The authors find that, after accounting for the general equilibrium effects, the removal of the railroad system would have entailed a 60 percent decrease in agricultural land values.

Fajgelbaum and Schaal (2020) study the properties of an optimal transportation network. They use their framework to study the welfare loss of road misallocation in Europe. They find that, on average, such misallocation reduces real consumption by 2 percent. Allen and Arkolakis (2019) develop a spatial general equilibrium model to evaluate how an improvement of the U.S. Highway System would affect aggregate welfare. They find that adding 10 lane-miles would generate large and heterogeneous effects across different highway segments, ranging between $10 and $20 million for most of them. Moreover, the benefits are higher than construction and maintenance costs for all segments.

## 6   POLICY IMPLICATIONS

In light of the importance of the spatial distribution of resources in explaining aggregate economic fluctuations, and given the role of frictions and spatial externalities in determining where individuals and firms locate, is there a rationale for policy interventions? What is the nature of these policies? To what extent should resources and policies be regionally targeted?

In the presence of agglomeration externalities, attracting firms may generate external productivity benefits for existing firms (as shown by Greenstone et al., 2010). So, are spatially targeted, publicly financed subsidies to attract new firms efficiency-enhancing? From the locality's perspective, the subsidies may be designed to internalize externalities and increase efficiency. From an aggregate point of view, overall efficiency gains depend on whether the benefits for the receiving location of attracting news firms are similar everywhere else.

The quantitative model developed by Gaubert (2018) is used to evaluate the aggregate impact of two types of place-based policies: a subsidy targeted to firms that locate in the smallest (and also less productive) cities of the country (local tax incentives); and the relaxation of local LURs. The paper concludes that a subsidy targeted to smaller localities will benefit the local area, but will decrease aggregate TFP. In other words, subsidizing firms to locate in smaller cities may not be welfare-enhancing. However, consistent with other recent research (for example, Hsieh and Moretti, 2019), an overall increase in the housing supply elasticity (through the relaxation of LURs) would lead to an aggregate increase in TFP.

A number of policy implications also emerge from the analysis performed by Fajgelbaum and Gaubert (2020). First, skill heterogeneity along with the presence of spillovers across different types of workers could justify the implementation of place-specific labor subsidies for each labor type. Second, the paper documents that the U.S. economy is characterized by an excessive concentration of high-skill workers and wage inequality in larger cities compared to the efficient allocation. Spatial efficiency would require a redistribution towards low-wage cities and weaker sorting by skill relative to the observed data, leading to lower wage inequality in larger cities. This policy would generate a greater mixing of high- and low-skill workers in low-wage cities, and generate large welfare gains.

# 7 DIRECTIONS FOR FUTURE RESEARCH

The literature offers different explanations on the possible channels through which granular shocks propagate, amplify, and affect the aggregate economy in non-trivial ways. Evidence seems to support some of those explanations. The previous discussion, however, reveals several important areas in the literature that deserve further study and that will drive much of the future research work on the aggregate effects of regional shocks. We focus below on four different areas of interest.

## 7.1 Transportation Investment: Reorganization of Economic Activity versus Economic Growth

Research has found that improvements in transportation systems may increase local employment and local economic growth. But are there positive economic effects explained by the spatial reallocation of economic activity, at the expense of other regions, or do the transportation improvements increase overall productivity? As mentioned earlier, quantifying and distinguishing among the two effects is key in order to evaluate the aggregate implications of investing in transportation infrastructure.

## 7.2 General Equilibrium Effects of Agglomeration Economies

Understanding the general equilibrium implications of AEs is still pending. Several of the policy interventions described earlier rely on the assumption of the existence of such external forces at the local level. While a wide range of papers show that AEs do play an important role in explaining regional growth, a precise quantification of the aggregate effects of these forces is still necessary.

## 7.3 General Equilibrium Effects of Changes in Housing Policy

Another area that has received a lot of attention at the micro level is housing policy. However, the general equilibrium and aggregate implications of changes in the housing policy (see, for example, Davis and Van Nieuwerburgh, 2015), such as the elimination of mortgage interest tax deductions, or incentives for the development of affordable housing, are not completely understood.

## 7.4 Localization Decisions by Both Households and Firms

The original Roback model described in Section 2.1 highlights the importance of combining the simultaneous decisions of households (or workers) and firms to explain variations in prices across space. However, most of the recent quantitative models account for either workers' or firms' localization decisions. In order to understand historical trends and changes in regional economic activity, the quantitative analysis should consider both household and firm mobility.

## NOTES

1. The views expressed herein are those of the authors and are not necessarily those of the Federal Reserve Bank of Richmond or the Federal Reserve System.
2. Diamond (2016), for example, develops a spatial equilibrium model that includes local markets for labor and housing, in addition to amenities.
3. Also see Holmes and Sieg (2015) for a survey on different applications of structural estimation to urban equilibrium.
4. A related strand of literature examines the extent to which aggregate shocks affect regions differently. Different studies (see, for example, Carlino and DeFina (2006) and Leung and Teo (2011)) find that the response of income and housing prices to monetary policy shocks varies across states and regions. The work by Beraja et al. (2019a), for example, shows that the impact of an interest rate cut on mortgage refinancing and spending decisions varies across regions. They state that regional differences in housing equity explain this differential impact. The purpose of this chapter, however, is to review the research work that focuses on the aggregate implications of shocks originated at a granular, regional level.
5. Duranton and Puga (2014) mention that during the period 1920–2010, the average growth rate of an individual city in the U.S., Spain, and France was about the same size as its standard deviation.
6. While excessive levels of LURs at the local level may decrease aggregate productivity, they may not necessarily reduce welfare. For instance, Parkhomenko (2020) shows that residents in high-amenity cities choose stricter regulations. Deregulation, in their analysis, increases labor productivity, but reduces welfare.
7. LURs are essentially taken as exogenous in Hsieh and Moretti (2019). In Duranton and Puga (2019), however, they are endogenously chosen through a local political process. As a result, regulations change as cities change in size due to population mobility.
8. The argument used by Albouy (2009) is somewhat different to that raised by the other authors. The paper claims that a federal tax code that does not account for differences in the cost of living across cities may distort workers' location decisions and lead to an inefficient spatial distribution of labor.

## REFERENCES

Acemoglu, Daron, Vasco M. Carvalho, Asuman Ozdaglar, and Alireza Tahbaz-Salehi (2012). "The network origins of aggregate fluctuations." *Econometrica* 80.5, pp. 1977–2016.

Albouy, David (2009). "The unequal geographic burden of federal taxation." *Journal of Political Economy* 117.4, pp. 635–667.

Allen, Treb and Costas Arkolakis (2014). "Trade and the topography of the spatial economy." *Quarterly Journal of Economics* 129.3, pp. 1085–1140.

Allen, Treb and Costas Arkolakis (2019). *The welfare effects of transportation infrastructure improvements*. Tech. rep. National Bureau of Economic Research.

Austin, Benjamin, Edward Glaeser, and Lawrence Summers H. (2018). "Saving the heartland: Place-based policies in 21st century America." *Brookings Papers on Economic Activity* 8.

Baum-Snow, Nathaniel (2007). "Did highways cause suburbanization?" *Quarterly Journal of Economics* 122.2, pp. 775–805.

Behrens, Kristian and Frédéric Robert-Nicoud (2015). "Agglomeration theory with heterogeneous agents." In Gilles Duranton, J. Vernon Henderson, and William C. Strange (eds), *Handbook of regional and urban economics*. Vol. 5. New York: Elsevier, pp. 171–245.

Beraja, Martin, Andreas Fuster, Erik Hurst, and Joseph Vavra (2019a). "Regional heterogeneity and the refinancing channel of monetary policy." *Quarterly Journal of Economics* 134.1, pp. 109–183.

Beraja, Martin, Erik Hurst, and Juan Ospina (2019b). "The aggregate implications of regional business cycles." *Econometrica* 87.6, pp. 1789–1833.

Caliendo, Lorenzo, Fernando Parro, Esteban Rossi-Hansberg, and Pierre-Daniel Pierre-Daniel Sarte (2017). "The impact of regional and sectoral productivity changes on the US economy." *Review of Economic Studies* 85.4, pp. 2042–2096.

Carlino, Gerald A. and Robert H. DeFina (2006). "Macroeconomic analysis using regional data: An application to monetary policy." In Richard J. Arnott and Daniel P. McMillen (eds), *A companion to urban economics*. Chichester: Wiley, pp. 440–459.

Chodorow-Reich, Gabriel (2019). "Geographic cross-sectional fiscal spending multipliers: What have we learned?" *American Economic Journal: Economic Policy* 11.2, pp. 1–34.

Ciccone, Antonio and Robert E. Hall (1996). "Productivity and the density of economic activity." *American Economic Review* 86.1, pp. 54–70.

Combes, Pierre-Philippe and Laurent Gobillon (2015). "The empirics of agglomeration economies." In Gilles Duranton, J. Vernon Henderson, and William C. Strange (eds), *Handbook of regional and urban economics*. Vol. 5. New York: Elsevier, pp. 247–348.

Costinot, Arnaud and Andrés Rodríguez-Clare (2014). "Trade theory with numbers: Quantifying the consequences of globalization." In Gita Gopinath, Elhanan Helpman, and Kenneth Rogoff (eds), *Handbook of international economics*. Vol. 4. New York: Elsevier, pp. 197–261.

Davis, Morris A. and Stijn Van Nieuwerburgh (2015). "Housing, finance, and the macroeconomy." In Gilles Duranton, J. Vernon Henderson, and William C. Strange (eds), *Handbook of regional and urban economics*. Vol. 5. New York: Elsevier, pp. 753–811.

Davis, Morris A., Jonas D.M. Fisher, and Toni M. Whited (2014). "Macroeconomic implications of agglomeration." *Econometrica* 82.2, pp. 731–764.

Desmet, Klaus and Esteban Rossi-Hansberg (2013). "Urban accounting and welfare." *American Economic Review* 103.6, pp. 2296–2327.

Diamond, Rebecca (2016). "The determinants and welfare implications of U.S. workers' diverging location choices by skill: 1980–2000." *American Economic Review* 106.3, pp. 479–524.

Donaldson, Dave and Richard Hornbeck (2016). "Railroads and American economic growth: A 'market access' approach." *Quarterly Journal of Economics* 131.2, pp. 799–858.

Duranton, Gilles and Diego Puga (2004). "Chapter 48: Micro-foundations of urban agglomeration economies." In J. Vernon Henderson and Jacques-Francois Thisse (eds), *Handbook of regional and urban economics*. Vol. 4. New York: Elsevier, pp. 2063–2117.

Duranton, Gilles and Diego Puga (2014). "The growth of cities." In Philippe Aghion and Steven N. Durlauf (eds), *Handbook of economic growth*. Vol. 2. New York: Elsevier, pp. 781–853.

Duranton, Gilles and Diego Puga (2019). "Urban growth and its aggregate implications." *National Bureau of Economic Research* 26591.

Duranton, Gilles and Matthew A. Turner (2011). "The fundamental law of road congestion: Evidence from U.S. cities." *American Economic Review* 101.6, pp. 2616–2652.

Duranton, Gilles and Matthew A. Turner (2012). "Urban growth and transportation." *Review of Economic Studies* 79.4, pp. 1407–1440.

Fajgelbaum, Pablo D. and Cecile Gaubert (2020). "Optimal spatial policies, geography, and sorting." *Quarterly Journal of Economics* 135.2, pp. 959–1036.

Fajgelbaum, Pablo D. and Edouard Schaal (2020). "Optimal transport networks in spatial equilibrium." *Econometrica* 88.4, pp. 1411–1452.

Fajgelbaum, Pablo D., Eduardo Morales, Juan Carlos Suárez Serrato, and Owen Zidar (2019). "State taxes and spatial misallocation." *Review of Economic Studies* 86.1, pp. 333–376.

Gabaix, Xavier (2011). "The granular origins of aggregate fluctuations." *Econometrica* 79.3, pp. 733–772.

Ganong, Peter and Daniel Shoag (2017). "Why has regional income convergence in the U.S. declined?" *Journal of Urban Economics* 102, pp. 76–90.

Gaubert, Cecile (2018). "Firm sorting and agglomeration." *American Economic Review* 108.11, pp. 3117–53.

Giannone, Elisa (2017). "Skilled-biased technical change and regional convergence." University of Chicago. Unpublished manuscript.

Giroud, Xavier and Holger M. Mueller (2019). "Firms' internal networks and local economic shocks." *American Economic Review* 109.10, October, pp. 3617–3649.

Glaeser, Edward L., Matthew E. Kahn, and Jordan Rappaport (2008). "Why do the poor live in cities? The role of public transportation." *Journal of Urban Economics* 63, pp. 1–24.

Greenstone, Michael, Richard Hornbeck, and Enrico Moretti (2010). "Identifying agglomeration spillovers: Evidence from winners and losers of large plant openings." *Journal of Political Economy* 118.3, pp. 536–598.

Greenwald, Daniel L. and Adam Guren (2019). *Do credit conditions move house prices?* Cambridge, MA: MIT Press.

Guren, Adam M., Alisdair McKay, Emi Nakamura, and Jón Steinsson (2018). "Housing wealth effects: The long view." *Review of Economic Studies*, 88.2, pp. 669–707.

Herkenhoff, Kyle F., Lee E. Ohanian, and Edward C. Prescott (2018). "Tarnishing the golden and empire states: Land-use restrictions and the U.S. economic slowdown." *Journal of Monetary Economics* 93, pp. 89–109.

Holmes, Thomas J. and Holger Sieg (2015). "Structural estimation in urban economics." In Gilles Duranton, J. Vernon Henderson, and William C. Strange (eds), *Handbook of regional and urban economics*. Vol. 5. New York: Elsevier, pp. 69–114.

Hornbeck, Richard and Enrico Moretti (2019). "Estimating who benefits from productivity growth: Direct and indirect effects of city manufacturing TFP growth on wages, rents, and inequality." Institute of Labor Economics, https://ftp.iza.org/dp12277.pdf.

Hsieh, Chang-Tai and Peter J. Klenow (2009). "Misallocation and manufacturing TFP in China and India." *Quarterly Journal of Economics* 124.4, pp. 1403–1448.

Hsieh, Chang-Tai and Enrico Moretti (2019). "Housing constraints and spatial misallocation." *American Economic Journal: Macroeconomics*, 11.2, pp. 1–39.

Kain, J.F. (1968). "Housing segregation, negro employment, and metropolitan decentralization." *Quarterly Journal of Economics*, 82.2, pp. 175–197.

Leung, Charles Ka Yui and Wing Leong Teo (2011). "Should the optimal portfolio be region-specific? A multi-region model with monetary policy and asset price co-movements." *Regional Science and Urban Economics* 41.3, pp. 293–304.

Molloy, Raven, Riccardo Trezzi, Christopher L. Smith, and Abigail Wozniak (2016). "Understanding declining fluidity in the U.S. labor market." *Brookings Papers on Economic Activity* 1, pp. 183–259.

Nakamura, Emi and Jón Steinsson (2014). "Fiscal stimulus in a monetary union: Evidence from U.S. regions." *American Economic Review* 104.3, pp. 753–792.

Nakamura, Emi and Jón Steinsson (2018). "Identification in macroeconomics." *Journal of Economic Perspectives* 32.3, pp. 59–86.

Parkhomenko, Andrii (2020). "Local causes and aggregate implications of land use regulation." SSRN, January 29, https://papers.ssrn.com/sol3/papers.cfm?abstract_id=3739183.

Redding, Stephen J. and Esteban Rossi-Hansberg (2017). "Quantitative spatial economics." *Annual Review of Economics* 9.1, pp. 21–58.

Redding, Stephen J. and Matthew A. Turner (2015). "Transportation costs and the spatial organization of economic activity." In Gilles Duranton, J. Vernon Henderson, and William C. Strange (eds), *Handbook of regional and urban economics*. Vol. 5. New York: Elsevier, pp. 1339–1398.

Restuccia, Diego and Richard Rogerson (2008). "Policy distortions and aggregate productivity with heterogeneous establishments." *Review of Economic dynamics* 11.4, pp. 707–720.

Roback, Jennifer (1982). "Wages, rents, and the quality of life." *Journal of Political Economy*, 90.6, pp. 1257–1278.

Rosenthal, Stuart S. and William C. Strange (2004). "Evidence on the nature and sources of agglomeration economies." In J. Vernon Henderson and Jacques-François Thisse (eds), *Handbook of regional and urban economics*. Vol. 4. New York: Elsevier, pp. 2119–2171.

Rossi-Hansberg, Esteban (2005). "A spatial theory of trade." *American Economic Review* 95.5, pp. 1464–1491.

Rossi-Hansberg, Esteban and Mark L.J. Wright (2007). "Urban structure and growth." *Review of Economic Studies* 74.2, pp. 597–624.

Rossi-Hansberg, Esteban, Pierre-Daniel Sarte, and Felipe Schwartzman (2019). *Cognitive hubs and spatial redistribution.* Tech. rep. National Bureau of Economic Research.

Starrett, David (1978). "Market allocations of location choice in a model with free mobility." *Journal of Economic Theory* 17.1, pp. 21–37.

Suárez Serrato, Juan Carlos and Owen Zidar (2016). "Who benefits from state corporate tax cuts? A local labor markets approach with heterogeneous firms." *American Economic Review* 106.9, pp. 2582–2624.

Yao, Yuxi (2020). "Land and the rise in the dispersion of house prices and rents across U.S. cities." https://lusk.usc.edu/sites/default/files/attachments/02_Slides_YuxiYao.pdf.

# 14. Industrial parks and urban growth: a political economy story in China
*Matthew E. Kahn, Jianfeng Wu, Weizeng Sun and Siqi Zheng*

## 1 INTRODUCTION

China has achieved rapid urbanization and economic growth over the past four decades, and thousands of industrial parks are the key engine for such remarkable development.[1] Industrial parks attract firms to cluster spatially, generating strong agglomeration economies through input sharing, labor pooling, and knowledge spillovers. More importantly, these industrial parks have been built up as experiments for governments at different levels to test out market economy mechanisms and new institutions. However, an industrial park is not cost-free as huge amounts of upfront investment, assembling and development of a large parcel of land, and economic incentives including tax and tariff reductions and regulatory relaxation are required. The past decades of experience of building industrial parks have illustrated a mixed picture: some industrial parks have been successful in creating industrial agglomerations and contributed to local gross domestic product (GDP), employment, exports, and foreign direct investment (Alder et al., 2016; Wang, 2013). Others, however, have fizzled and even become "ghost towns."

In this chapter, we explain such huge differences in the returns to industrial parks' investment by relating them to the initial city selection. Particularly, we discuss the role played by political connection in the placement of industrial parks and the consequent urban growth effect. Our analysis is based on national and provincial industrial parks built since the beginning of the 1980s. These higher-ranked parks enjoy a higher level of political autonomy in designing and experimenting with new institutions and policies (Alder et al., 2016). Anticipating these policy privileges and consequent economic gains, local governments have strong incentives to establish an industrial park with national or provincial-level status to compete for external investment and increase local economic growth (Wu et al., 2013). All of these national and provincial industrial parks went through a formal approval process, allowing us to explore leaders' priorities in placing these huge capital investments. We explore how provincial leaders allocate industrial parks' investment across cities within their jurisdictions, as they have the major decision-making power in determining where national and provincial-level industrial parks are built in their province. Another innovation that we discuss below is our creation of a detailed social network database that allows us to track the long-term connections between provincial leaders and city leaders at different points in time.

We start by showing that industrial parks are one major type of place-based policy with general characteristics, and many governments in this world are fans of building industrial parks. Then we briefly review the history of industrial parks initiated by governments at different levels in China, including policy objectives, types of industrial parks, the number of high-ranked industrial parks, and their spatial distribution since the beginning of the 1980s.

We also provide the macro evidence that industrial parks have made a great contribution to China's urban economic growth.

Next, we turn to a political economy framework to explain Chinese provincial leaders' priorities in selecting initial park site locations. In China, the placement of an industrial park is attributed to both economic and political factors. Firstly, realizing the policy privilege and huge economic gains induced by industrial parks, local leaders have strong incentives to invest in such large capital investment for urban growth and competition as economic performance raises the probability of their being promoted in the Chinese Communist Party (CCP). Secondly, rising income inequality in China in recent years has been viewed as a threat to social stability. Since Hu Jintao became China's president in 2002, the CCP has sought to promote the "balanced development" strategy, and thus has also rewarded political leaders who have successfully reduced their area's income inequality. Thirdly, a political leader also has a willingness to play favorites and allocate industrial parks to his/her connected subordinates, as a way to reward his/her friends and cultivate their loyalty. Thus, we assume each leader has a revealed preference in allocating industrial parks over three attributes: expected economic growth, expected inequality reduction, and rewarding a political connection. The leader would trade-off among these three factors to achieve their highest utility. Economic loss would occur when a political leader allocates an industrial park to a connected city with weak economic fundamentals and lower expected economic gain.

In the third section, we use city-level data since the 1980s and estimate park site selection models to test for the marginal effects of a city's growth potential, expected inequality reduction, and social connections on the probability that a park is sited in a given city. We measure how much economic growth a provincial leader is willing to sacrifice in order to help a subordinate friend. Our empirical results indicate that the misallocation of capital in China represents a tradeoff and thus has an "economic price" (the lost economic growth as an opportunity cost). We conclude in the last section.

## 2 INDUSTRIAL PARKS: ENGINES OF URBAN GROWTH

### 2.1 What Are Industrial Parks?

Industrial parks are a typical type of place-based policy and have been increasingly noticeable in developing countries where manufacturing has a large share of the GDP. Industrial parks are built to act as a catalyst to enhance industrial development by providing public service and the accompanying policy interventions in support of investment. Industrial parks contribute to economic performance by attracting foreign investors and promoting exports. In general, an industrial park includes several characteristics: (1) it is a geographically delimited area designated, planned, and zoned for the purpose of industrial development; (2) it offers incentives in tax, tariffs, and regulator rules for firms based on physical location within a park; and (3) it has a single management and administrator (Zeng, 2010).

Many governments embrace the idea of setting up industrial parks to generate agglomeration economies as firms cluster spatially. Such agglomeration benefits may enhance a firm's productivity through input sharing, labor market pooling, and knowledge spillovers (Zheng and Tan, 2020). The past experiences of building industrial parks in East Asian economies provide examples of success. However, establishing an industrial park is very expensive and may create distortions inside the economy. Some industrial parks in Africa, for example, failed entirely (Zeng, 2016).

## 2.2    China's Experience with Industrial Parks

In China, industrial parks are typically established to achieve the following policy objectives (Zeng 2016): (1) attracting capital investment and generating job opportunities; (2) experimenting with economic reform strategies that Chinese leaders were fearful of rolling out nationwide in one go; and (3) creating economic engines for the local economy and learning technologies from foreign investors.

Given China's enormous population and economic geography, industrial park policies have been implemented using a broad range of industrial parks at different administration levels.[2] At the national level, beside citywide special economic zones (SEZs), other types of industrial parks include economic and technological development zones, high-tech industrial development zones (HIDZs), bonded zones, export-processing zones (EPZs), border economic cooperation zones (BECZs), and others. They share favorable policies but have different focuses. For example, HIDZs are to provide incentives stimulating the development of domestic high-tech firms, while the goals of EPZs and BECZs are to promote foreign direct investment and foster growth in export-oriented sectors. The success of national-level industrial parks led local governments to set up industrial parks within their jurisdictions to boost local industrialization. According to the Bulletin List for the Official Boundaries of Chinese Industrial Parks provided by the Ministry of National Resource (Ministry of Land and Resource of China prior to 2018), there were 1,568 national-level and provincial-level industrial parks in more than 270 Chinese cities between 1980 and 2009.[3] Figure 14.1 presents the spatial distribution of national- and provincial-level industrial parks across cities over time in China. The provincial-level industrial parks far outnumber the state-level ones. In terms of geography, the cities in the eastern area of China account for more than half of the parks and most of them were built before 2003.[4] As shown in Figure 14.2, we also observe a substantial growth in the number of SEZs over time, especially those established by provincial governments.

These national and provincial-level industrial parks only occupy 0.1 percent of China's total land area, but they contain 40 percent of the nation's manufacturing jobs and accommodate 33 percent of foreign direct investment. These industrial parks have played a crucial role in transforming China from an agricultural economy toward a manufacturing powerhouse. Several studies have provided macro evidence that establishing industrial parks in China has positive impacts on urban economies (Alder et al., 2016; Schminke and Biesebroeck, 2013; Wang, 2013). On the other hand, there is great heterogeneity in the return of these parks' investment. Around 30 percent of national and provincial industrial parks built in eight large cities in China during the period of 1998–2007 are found to fail to generate productivity spillovers (Zheng et al., 2017).

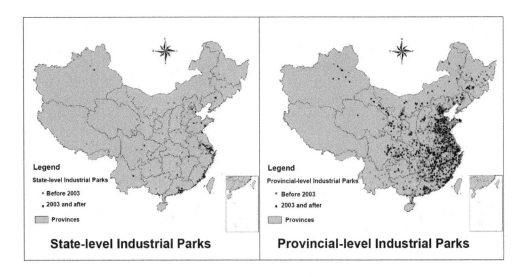

*Figure 14.1    China's industrial parks from 1988 to 2009*

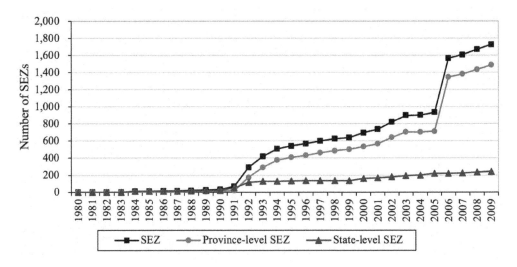

*Figure 14.2    The trends in the number of special economic zones, 1980–2009*

## 3    ALLOCATION OF INDUSTRIAL PARKS ACROSS CITIES: A POLITICAL ECONOMY FRAMEWORK

The ex post different returns on industrial park investment raises questions about the initial location selection problem. Industrial parks feature necessary infrastructure investment and huge opportunity cost of developing large parcels of land as well as regulation privileges. Such huge park investment is always geographically allocated in a top-down approach in China. Take the national-level industrial parks as an example. There are normally two distinct ways through which an industrial park acquires national-level status. One is that industrial parks are directly initiated by the central government before any construction or business activities are promoted. The other is that the local governments first set up industrial parks and then submit proposals to be granted national-level status some years later. The process through which industrial parks are granted provincial-level titles is similar to that for national-level industrial parks in two ways. One is a type of local implementation of provincially initiated projects whereas the other is considered to be locally initiated projects.

A benevolent planner would invest in those areas offering the highest marginal productivity of investment as a leader with political career concerns who seeks to rise in the CCP and has an incentive to invest in projects that contribute to economic growth (Li and Zhou, 2005). Local economic performance, measured as real GDP growth, is considered to be the main performance measure for judging a provincial leader (Maskin et al., 2000). On the other side, rising income inequality in China in recent years has been viewed as a threat to social stability. Since Hu Jintao became China's president in 2002, the CCP has sought to promote the "balanced development" strategy, and thus has also rewarded political leaders who have successfully reduced their area's income inequality. This suggests that a leader would trade-off efficiency gains versus equity considerations when choosing where to locate place-based policies such as a new industrial park.

An alternative theory is that such top-down approaches in placing industrial parks, especially those with high-level status, would provide incentives for a leader to play favorites. Allocating large sums of capital investment such as industrial parks to the closet followers is helpful in strengthening the loyalty of subordinates to the political leader, thus increasing the probability of the latter to survive in office. Dittmer (1995) and Jia et al. (2015) argue that building a network of loyal subordinates is very important for political leaders to reduce the uncertainty of their political survival in the context of China.

We posit that there is a huge heterogeneity in the growth outcomes of placing industrial parks across cities as Chinese leaders' priorities in selecting initial park site locations are different. To test this hypothesis, a revealed preference framework for Chinese leaders in allocating industrial parks across cities is employed. We assume that each provincial leader has the same objective function defined over three attributes: expected economic growth, expected inequality reduction, and rewarding a political connection.

The provincial leader's expected utility from building a park in city $j$ is expressed as follows:

$$U_{ij}^* = f\left(\overline{\Delta GDP_{ij}}, \overline{\Delta GINI_{GDP_{ij}}}, CONNECTION_j\right).$$

The expected economic gain is measured as the expected increase in the value-added GDP that park i will bring to city j, $\overline{\Delta GDP}$. The expected inequality reduction is measured as the expected decrease in the within-province city-level Gini coefficient (based on GDP per capita) attributed to the growth generated by this park, $\overline{\Delta GINI\_GDP}$. Expected economic growth and expected inequality reductions will directly increase a provincial leader's likelihood of promotion.

The connection measure, CONNECTION, is to represent whether the provincial leader is politically connected to a city leader within his/her jurisdiction. It is a dummy variable as we are unable to quantify a dollar value of these personal benefits.

We assume that provincial leaders are aware that they face a counter-factual treatment effect problem because they do not know what the GDP growth caused by a new park will be for each city in the choice set. We model the provincial leaders as econometricians who use all available information to impute this counter-factual expectation. Intuitively, a leader must predict what the GDP growth in each city would be if he/she assigns a park there. One of the key assumptions in such a framework is a symmetry in solving this prediction problem between the econometrician and the decision maker. Under our assumption of symmetry, we are able to recreate the provincial leader's perceived tradeoff at the time he/she makes the allocation decision. Provincial leaders will recognize that they may sacrifice significant expected economic growth by helping a political connection.[5] This is an "economic price" because there is a direct connection between local economic growth and being promoted within the CCP.

## 4 ECONOMIC COST OF POLITICALLY DRIVEN DISTRIBUTION OF INDUSTRIAL PARKS: ESTIMATION AND CALCULATION

### 4.1 Measuring Political Connection

Testing for the role of political connections as a cause of capital misallocation requires measures of the political connections between local officials (city mayor or party secretary) and the upper-level government leaders (provincial-level governor or party secretary). Past research on the political economy of such connections has emphasized two criteria (Xu, 2018). One is that this political tie measure should be objective. The other is that such measures can solve the issue of endogenous social network information. To meet these criteria, we measure political connections between city leaders and provincial leaders along four dimensions: workplace, birthplace, university/college, and political faction.

The first measure defines a city leader and a provincial leader as connected if they once worked in the same workplace, based on the assumption that politicians are more likely to be friends with those who share a workplace. Jia et al. (2015) measure political connections for provincial governors with top leaders in the central government using this shared work experience approach. The second measure is based on the geographic location where politicians were born. The underlying assumption is that politicians are more likely to keep close relations with others who come from the same birthplace. Do et al. (2017) provide evidence for favoritism towards one's hometown among government officials in Vietnam. The third measure defines social connections between city leaders and provincial leaders when they share the study experience in the same university or college. This is based on the assumption that politicians are more likely to form social ties in their alumni network. Fourth, we define city leaders and provincial leaders as connected through their political factions. The underlying assumption is that politicians tend to be allies when they belong to the same faction (Francois et al., 2016). We highlight two main factions within the CCP, *tuanpai* (Communist Youth League of China) and non-*tuanpai*.

To build these political connections, we construct a data set on the city and provincial leaders in China between 1980 and 2008 by undertaking a large-scale data collection from *Duxiu*, a local Scholar Search Engine with millions of digitized literatures, newspapers, journalists, and books in Chinese provided by China's CNKI. This data set contains extensive biographic information on each official including name, birth year, birth place, education record, list of positions held in the party or in the government in the past along with the period

*Table 14.1  Summary statistics for political connections*

|  | Provincial party secretary | | Provincial governor | |
| --- | --- | --- | --- | --- |
|  | (1) | (2) | (3) | (4) |
|  | City-level party secretary | City mayors | City-level party secretary | City mayors |
| Workplace | 24.3% | 14.0% | 27.0% | 17.7% |
| Birthplace | 4.3% | 4.0% | 3.6% | 5.5% |
| Alumni | 0.7% | 0.4% | 1.7% | 1.7% |
| Faction | 2.7% | 3.0% | 4.5% | 3.8% |
| No. of provincial officials | 107 | | 136 | |

*Note*: The percentages in this table are the share of city-level leaders (city party secretaries or mayors) with political connections with the corresponding provincial government leaders (provincial party secretaries or provincial governors) in all the same-type city leaders.

in which each position was held, and the record of whether they have received training in China's Central Party School.

We mainly use the workplace-based social connections measure between city and provincial CCP party secretaries (Jia et al. (2015) employ a similar strategy). In China's bureaucratic hierarchy, party secretary has a higher ranking than the governor at the same administrative level (province or prefecture city). Table 14.1 summarizes the shares of city-level top officials who are politically connected to the corresponding provincial-level key leaders. As shown in column 1, roughly one quarter of the 107 provincial-level party secretaries are politically connected with his/her city-level subordinates (party secretaries) if they have worked in the same workplace, based on the assumption that politicians are more likely to befriend others who share a similar working experience in the same place.

### 4.2  Predicting Economic Growth and Income Inequality Dynamics Induced by Industrial Parks

Another task for recovering a provincial leader's objective utility from placing an industrial park within his/her jurisdiction is predicting the growth effect and income inequality dynamics induced by new parks. We collect city-level data from the China city statistical yearbooks. We use GIS to calculate a city's straight-line distance to the nearest highway entrance, airport, railway station, and main seaport. We cover 276 prefecture-level cities during the period 1988–2008.[6]

Similar to Wang (2013) and Alder et al. (2016), we first estimate the park treatment effect. Then we decompose such treatment effect as a function of city–park–year attributes, including natural endowment, economic fundamentals, park attributes, and year dummies. Based on such a decomposition, we calculate the heterogenous ex post growth effect of receiving a park in terms of GDP across cities and in different years. With these expected GDP increases after receiving a park, we further calculate the expected Gini coefficient in a province and its change over time based on the expected GDP per capita at the city level.

Figure 14.3 shows the descriptive statistics of the one-year GDP increase and three-year Gini coefficient change due to the introduction of a real or hypothetical park by region and by time period. We present the data at a broader regional unit: eastern, central, and western regions. Our study period was split into two regimes under two Chinese presidents – Jiang Zemin (1989–2002) and Hu Jintao (2003–2008). On average, the expected city GDP increases

366  Handbook of real estate and macroeconomics

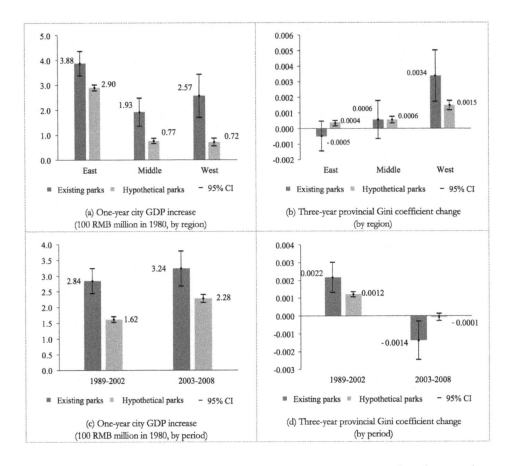

Figure 14.3  Estimated GDP increase and Gini coefficient change attributed to a real or a hypothetical park in a city

generated by parks are larger in the east region, and in the latter period. At the same time, we can see that such expected GDP increase generated by an average industrial park is significantly larger than the counterfactual effect when placing this park in other cities. This indicates that provincial leaders do choose to place parks in the cities where those parks can generate higher expected economic gains. This preference (measured in the gap between real and hypothetical parks) is stronger in middle and western regions, and in the earlier period. When looking at how industrial parks change the expected income inequality in a province (Gini coefficient of GDP per capita), real parks in the east and middle regions do not have a significant effect on the Gini coefficient, but those in the west region significantly deteriorate income inequality. The regime change is clear – in the earlier period, the placement of industrial parks significantly deteriorates income inequality, while this pattern reverses in the latter period.

## 4.3 Economic Loss of Placing a Park Generated by Political Connection

One of the key assumptions in our analysis is that provincial leaders have a career incentive to pursue economic growth in the political system of current China. To test for this assumption, we regress a dummy variable of whether a provincial leader is promoted on GDP growth, income inequality measured by Gini coefficient of GDP per capita across cities, and connection with top leaders in the central government. The estimation results show a highly positive effect of provincial GDP growth on provincial leaders' promotion likelihood. Reducing within-province inequality is found to be positively related to provincial leaders' promotion when we use the party secretary sample. Not surprisingly, these provincial leaders' social ties with top leaders in the central government also help them to get promoted. These results confirm the argument that economic performance is complementary to political connections in affecting political leaders' promotions (Jia et al., 2015).

Next, following our analytical framework of the provincial leader's expected utility function, we recover a provincial leader's preference in allocating an industrial park within their jurisdiction. We assume that a provincial leader would maximize their utility from choosing a city to place a park through a tradeoff of the expected GDP growth induced by the new park, the expected income inequality reduction, and rewarding political connections. We estimate a model for parks' location choice by regressing a dummy variable of whether a park is placed in a city in one year on the expected GDP growth and the corresponding income inequality induced by this park as well as the variable measuring the connection between provincial- and city-level leaders.[7] We consider the short-, medium-, and long-run growth effect of receiving a park and its consequent within-province income inequality reductions as new parks create a cumulative growth process (Zheng et al., 2017).

Table 14.2 reports the baseline results. New parks create a cumulative growth process as a new agglomeration takes root. This means that the long-run growth effects are larger than the short-run effects. Across columns 1 to 4, we consider the short-, medium- and long-run impacts, from 1 year to 10 years after the opening of a park. Here $\overline{\Delta GDP}$ is the expected accumulated GDP increase over that period, and $\overline{\Delta GINI\_GDP}$ is the expected change in the Gini coefficient of GDP per capita between the start and end years of that period. The dummy CONNECTION equals 1 if the provincial leader and city leader in the park's city in the opening year are socially connected. In this baseline model we use the workplace-based connection measure between the city and provincial CCP secretaries.[8] For each time horizon, $\overline{\Delta GDP}$ and CONNECTION both have a statistically significant effect on the likelihood of site selection. When a provincial leader decides where to place a park, he/she considers both short-run and long-run growth effects. For the short-run (one year) effects, if a park is expected to generate a 100 million RMB GDP increase in a given city, this city will enjoy a 0.76 percentage point increase in the likelihood of receiving the park. Since $\overline{\Delta GDP}$ is the expected accumulated GDP increase, its coefficient shrinks from column 1 to 4 but the size of its effect is stable.

Controlling for the effects of a new park on economic growth and regional cross-city income inequality, we find that social connections influence the siting of a park. This connection variable is statistically significant at the 1 percent level in each of the four regressions. As shown in column 1, the probability that a park is placed in a given city increases by 6.6 percentage points when the local leader is connected.

Table 14.2  Conditional Logit Estimates of the Industrial Park Locational Choice Decision

|  | (1) 1 year | (2) 3 years | (3) 5 years | (4) 10 years |
|---|---|---|---|---|
| $\overline{\Delta GDP}$ | 0.00759 | 0.00264 | 0.00158 | 0.000796 |
|  | (0.00347) | (0.000995) | (0.000587) | (0.000316) |
| $\overline{\Delta GINI\_GDP}$ | 1.765 | -0.452 | -0.408 | -0.323 |
|  | (4.739) | (0.812) | (0.464) | (0.387) |
| CONNECTION | 0.0663 | 0.0694 | 0.0667 | 0.0686 |
|  | (0.0219) | (0.0214) | (0.0216) | (0.0215) |
| N | 16543 | 16386 | 16166 | 16130 |
| Pseudo R2 | 0.013 | 0.013 | 0.014 | 0.013 |
| Total cost of social connections GDP (100 million RMB) | 8.74 | 26.29 | 42.22 | 86.18 |
| Annualized cost of social connections GDP (100 million RMB) | 8.74 | 8.76 | 8.44 | 8.62 |
| Annualized cost of social connections as a share of provincial GDP | 1.62% | 1.62% | 1.56% | 1.60% |

*Note*: Top number in cell is marginal effect df/dx. Robust standard errors are reported in parentheses, which are clustered at province year level.

For the whole sample, income inequality is not a major consideration for provincial leaders' park placement decision. The coefficient of $\overline{\Delta GINI\_GDP}$ is insignificant for all time horizons. It has a positive sign in the first year and turns negative from the third year. This is suggestive evidence that the inequality concern only matters when provincial leaders consider a park's long-term impact.

We are interested in what economic cost in terms of GDP growth a provincial leader would sacrifice to place an industrial park in the city where his/her friend sits in office. The last three rows of Table 14.2 show the calculations of the misallocation costs induced by political connection based on the estimates of a provincial leader's allocating an industrial park across cities within his/her jurisdiction. The annualized cost of social connections is quite stable for short and long time horizons – about 850 to 875 million RMB, around 1.5–1.6 percent of that province's annual GDP.

## 5    CONCLUSION

This chapter has contributed to the political economy literature by studying the choices of Chinese provincial leaders in allocating industrial parks, engines for urban economic growth. We present a revealed preference analysis of provincial leaders' placing such huge capital investment, in which he/she maximizes the utility through a tradeoff among expected economic growth, the dynamic income inequality, and rewarded connection. By creating a new social connections database, we show that Chinese provincial leaders are willing to sacrifice some urban economic growth in order to help a local leader with whom they have a social connection. Political connections are a cause of capital misallocation. Such decisions do impose some costs for the decision maker. In the CCP, provincial leaders are more likely to be promoted if their province's GDP is growing faster. Our estimates suggest that a leader reduces his/her own promotion chances by about 1.8 percentage points when he/she assigns a park to a connected friend.

# NOTES

1. A longer version of this study with complete models and empirical results was published earlier: Kahn et al. (2018).
2. Industrial parks are authorized by different level governments: state, provincial, or prefecture (or below) government. Those parks authorized by the state and provincial governments enjoy more favorable policies, such as lower interest rate loans and larger tax, land price, and utility price discounts. We only focus on those parks because many of the lower-level industrial parks did not obtain formal approval from the central and provincial governments and violated the relevant laws and regulations.
3. We choose 2008 as the ending year of our study period for two reasons. First, in response to the 2008 global financial crisis, the Chinese government rolled out a RMB 4 trillion ($586 billion) stimulus program that ramped up expenditures on affordable housing, transportation infrastructure (highways, railways, and airports), and education, environment, and technology innovation, making it difficult for us to disentangle the urban growth effect of industrial parks from that of other place-based policies associated with this stimulus program. Second, China's president Xi Jinping launched an anticorruption campaign after he took power in 2012. The greater intensity of this campaign and the strengthening of Xi's personal leadership have led to local governments' various other incentives, which is hard to analyze using our analytical framework on the tradeoff among efficiency, equity, and cronyism.
4. We divide China into three greater regions: the eastern region including Beijing, Tianjin, Shanghai, Liaoning, Hebei, Jiangsu, Zhejiang, Fujian, Shandong, and Guangdong, Hainan, and Guangxi; the central region including Inner Mongolia, Jilin, Heilongjiang, Shanxi, Anhui, Jiangxi, Henan, Hubei, and Hunan; and the western region covering Shananxi, Gansu, Qinghai, Ningxia, Xinjiang, Choingqing, Sichuan, Guizhou, and Yunnan Guangxi (Tibet is excluded due to missing data).
5. We acknowledge that we ignore province-level general equilibrium effects triggered by the park. We are implicitly assuming that a new park located in city $j$ generates new activity or attracts firms from outside the province and does not lead to a significant reshuffling of economic activity (such as population migration) within the province. We are also assuming away any cross-city spillover effects. Alder et al. (2016) directly test for park spillovers and find some evidence of positive spillovers for cities close to the treated city. In the main results, we assume the Stable Unit Treatment Value Assumption condition holds.
6. We exclude four municipal cities and those in Qinghai, Tibet, and Ningxia. There were no new national- or provincial-level parks built after 2008.
7. The provincial leader's expected utility from building a park in city j is expressed as follows:

$S_{ij} = \beta_1 \overline{\Delta GDP}_{ij} + \beta_2 \overline{\Delta GINI\_GDP}_{ij} + \beta_3 CONNECTION_j + \varepsilon_{ij}$,

where we model the provincial leader as choosing the expected utility-maximizing location for the park. $S_{ij}$ is an indicator variable, which is 1 if a park i is placed in city j by a provincial leader, and 0 otherwise. Under the assumption that $\varepsilon_{ij}$ is a random variable from a standard Type 1 extreme value distribution, this yields the standard conditional logit formula.
8. We rely on a workplace-based connection measure for two reasons. One is that two leaders with experience of working together in the same government agency in an overlapped period should be more effective in reducing this information cost compared with connections based on other dimensions. The other is related to a measurement error. The workplace connection measure in this chapter is more accurate than those based on college, birthplace, and faction as the time dimension for the workplace connection is considered.

# REFERENCES

Alder, S., L. Shao, and F. Zilibotti (2016), "Economic reforms and industrial policy in a panel of Chinese cities," *Journal of Economic Growth*, 21(4), 305–349.

Dittmer, L. (1995), "Chinese informal politics," *The China Journal*, 34, 1–34.

Do, Q., K. Nguyen, and A. Tran (2017), "One mandarin benefits the whole clan: Hometown favoritism in an authoritarian regime," *American Economic Journal: Applied Economics*, 9(4), 1–29.

Francois, P., F. Trebbi, and K. Xiao (2016), "Factions in nondemocracies: Theory and evidence from the Chinese Communist Party," NBER Working Paper 22775.

Jia, R., M. Kudamatsu, and D. Seim (2015), "Political selection in China: The complementary role of connections and performance," *Journal of the European Economic Association*, 13(4), 631–668.

Kahn, M., W. Sun, J. Wu, and S. Zheng (2018), "The revealed preference of the Chinese Communist Party leadership: Investing in local economic development versus rewarding social connections," NBER working paper 24457.

Li, H. and L. Zhou (2005), "Political turnover and economic performance: The incentive role of personnel control in China," *Journal of Public Economics*, 89(9–10), 1743–1762.

Maskin, E., Y. Qian, and C. Xu (2000), "Incentives, information, and organizational form," *Review of Economic Studies*, 67(2), 359–378.

Schminke, A., and J. Biesebroeck (2013), "Using export market performance to evaluate regional preferential policies in China," *Review of World Economics*, 149(2), 343–367.

Wang, J. (2013), "The economic impact of special economic zones: Evidence from Chinese municipalities," *Journal of Development Economics*, 101, 133–147.

Wu, J., Y. Deng, J. Huang, R. Morck, and B. Yeung (2013), "Incentives and outcomes: China's environmental policy," NBER Working Paper 18754.

Xu, G. (2018), "The cost of patronage: Evidence from the British Empire," *American Economic Review*, 108(11), 3170–3198.

Zeng, D. Z. (2010), *Building Engines for Growth and Competitiveness in China: Experience with Special Economic Zones and Industrial Clusters*, Washington, DC: World Bank.

Zeng, D. Z. (2016), "Global experiences with special economic zones: Focus on China and Africa," World Bank Policy Research Working Paper 7240.

Zheng, S. and Z. Tan (ed.) (2020), *Toward Urban Economic Vibrancy: Patterns and Practices in Asia's New Cities*, Cambridge, MA: MIT Press.

Zheng, S., W. Sun, J. Wu, and M. Kahn (2017), "The birth of edge cities in China: Measuring the effects of industrial parks policy," *Journal of Urban Economics*, 100, 80–103.

# 15. Pension funds and private equity real estate: history, performance, pathologies, risks
*Timothy J. Riddiough*

## 1 INTRODUCTION AND OVERVIEW

There is an estimated $60–100 trillion of commercial property in use worldwide, $12–16 trillion of which is located in the United States (US) (LaSalle Investment Management, 2018; Ghent et al., 2019).[1] Commercial real estate (CRE) as an asset class is, in the US, larger than both the Treasury and corporate bond markets, and about half the size of both the listed stock market and the stock of residential real estate. Not all CRE is "investable," however. Ghent et al. (2019) estimate that approximately two-thirds of all CRE is owned by firms and other organizations to be deployed as a factor of their own production.

Organisation for Economic Co-operation and Development (OECD) data show that as of year-end 2018 there are $16 trillion of assets held by all US pension plans. Of this, approximately $9 trillion belong to defined benefit (DB) plans. Portfolio allocations of DB plan assets to CRE in the US are now in excess of 9 percent, implying that DB pension funds own approximately 20 percent of all investable CRE in the US.[2]

CRE is clearly a big and important asset class, and pension funds are clearly big and important investors. Moreover, they overlap with one another in important ways, having had a long and sometimes rocky relationship. Yet, although pension funds and CRE have been much studied on their own, they have been little studied in combination, particularly from historical, macroeconomic and policy perspectives.[3]

Pension funds and CRE are co-dependent. CRE that sits inside private equity (PE) fund investment vehicles has become increasingly important to pension funds as many struggle with underfunding problems. These underfunding problems – which emerged in the early 2000s, largely caused by a combination of generous retirement benefit promises and mediocre investment performance – have created incentives for plan sponsors to reach for return. They do so by targeting investments with high promised returns, but with less focus on the risks of investment. PE has been the favored alternative investment vehicle for plan sponsors, and real estate has for over 40 years been the favored category of investment within PE.

Within private equity real estate (PERE), the favored strategies in recent years have been so-called value-add and opportunity funds.[4,5] These funds purchase risky CRE assets – either ground-up development or projects requiring significant redevelopment or repositioning. Moreover, these funds typically deploy leverage in the 50 to 75 percent range, with general partners' (GPs) targeting net-of-fee internal rate of returns (IRRs) at the time of fund marketing of 13.5 to 18.0 percent.

To date these funds have not delivered returns that were targeted at the time of investment. PERE value-add and opportunity funds delivered 3.8 and 4.5 percent IRRs on average, respectively, for fund vintage years 2001 to 2008. To-date performance for vintage years 2009 through 2017 has improved to 14.7 and 14.0 percent, respectively. But the combination of downward net asset value (NAV) drift and COVID-19's negative impact on retail, office and hotel property types will undoubtedly cause declines in measured performance over the next few years. After accounting for risk adjustments Bollinger and Pagliari (2019) estimate that, over their 2000–2017 sample period, value-add and opportunity funds underperform on a risk-adjusted basis by about 3 percent a year. In analyzing data over the same time frame, but using different data sources and methods, Gupta and Van Nieuwerburgh (2021) similarly estimate that PERE funds underperform by 3–4 percent a year.

Perhaps most informative is a simple comparison of returns to owning the NFI-ODCE (private open-end core CRE fund investment) versus Nareit (the public market CRE investment alternative) indices. Although there are some structural and compositional differences in the two indices, both have been available to pension funds for 42 years now, providing broad and highly similar exposure to CRE.[6] From 1978 to 2019, NFI-ODCE has returned 7.57 percent per year on average while Nareit has returned 12.45 percent. This is almost a 5.0 percent difference per year, where, over a 42-year time period, holding the Nareit index would have generated nearly *seven times* the wealth of holding the NFI-ODCE index. Over a truncated 27-year time period, 1993–2019, during which real estate investment trust (REIT) shares were more easily held by pension funds, the NFI-ODCE returned 7.89 versus 10.91 percent for Nareit – still a 3.0 percent per annum performance differential.

Evidence from several sources thus indicates that pension funds are willing to accept a 3 to 4 percent *discount* in their rate of return for the PE fund investment vehicle wrapper – a wrapper that hinders price discovery and veils true asset volatility. This apparent willingness by pension funds to pay a premium for CRE assets held in opaque investment vehicles is anomalous. Paying such prices for PERE investment has failed to help close pension underfunding gaps, while increasing the pension funds' overall risk exposure.

Why would plan sponsors continue to invest in PERE – much less increase their allocations over time – when PERE investment performance is well below target? I document a process where GPs' target returns of 13.5 to 18.0 percent on value-add and opportunity funds, but then deliver returns in the 10.0 to 13.0 percent range. All the while, plan sponsors benchmark their performance to the NFI-ODCE index that returns 7.0 to 8.0 percent on average. Thus, it appears to me that plan sponsors are engaging in what I call *Lake Wobegon benchmarking*, where plan sponsors give themselves As and Bs for C and D work. In doing so, they perpetuate a cycle of increased risk taking and inferior investment performance relative to the readily available public market alternative – listed REITs.

I also document several concentration risks that exist with pension funds and their investment in CRE. First, there is increasing concentration in PE fundraising among fewer GP sponsors, the most prominent of which are Blackstone and Brookfield. Second, I estimate a DB pension plan ownership share in PERE funds that is in the 50 percent range. This compares to an approximately 10 percent pension fund ownership share in non-PERE and hedge funds (HFs). Third, there is surprisingly high institutional investor ownership shares of CRE assets concentrated in top 10 gateway-superstar cities located around the world. As evidence from Ling et al. (2020) and industry sources such as Green Street Advisors indicate, these densely populated urban areas have been particularly vulnerable to the negative CRE asset pricing shocks following the COVID-19 pandemic. I argue that the cumulative effect of these concentration risks, combined with the significant leverage employed in PERE and PE more broadly, pose underappreciated threats to economic and financial stability.

This chapter is organized as follows. In Section 2, I start with a short history of pension funds and CRE that covers the 1974 to 1992 time period. Here, I focus on the implications of the Employee Retirement Income Security Act (ERISA) on pension plan sponsor investment behavior. I also document the early performance of CRE investment fund vehicles, as well as some puzzling economic relationships. Section 3 covers the 1993 to 2008 time period. Here, I document the emergence of the public markets as capital sources to fund CRE investments. Growth in alternative investments is also considered. I further describe early academic studies that revealed the extent of the structural pension plan underfunding problem. Section 4 contains many of the chapter's main findings. I analyze pension fund portfolio allocations to PERE as well as realized investment performance, focusing on the 2001 to 2019 time period. I combine my own analysis with that of existing studies to establish PERE underperformance. The critical distinction between alpha and beta is addressed, as well as the apparent negative illiquidity risk premia that exist with private CRE fund investment. Section 5 concludes by documenting the ownership concentrations noted above, with arguments that the structural pension underfunding problem presents some very real risks to economic and financial stability.

## 2    1974–1992: ERISA AND THE REAL ESTATE ALTERNATIVE

### 2.1    ERISA and the Great Inflation

The emergence of real estate investment by US pension funds can be traced back to 1974 with the passage of the landmark ERISA. ERISA set legal standards for participation, vesting, benefit accrual and the funding of DB retirement plans.[7] Among other things, the legislation identified pension plan sponsors as fiduciaries with legal duties to act in the best interests of their plan participants.

Analogous to the better-known business judgment rule, ERISA's *prudent person rule* allowed plan sponsors to take investment risks on behalf of plan participants, with the potential of incurring investment losses, as long as they acted prudently and in the best interests of plan participants given the information available at the time. Given these new and yet untested legal requirements, plan sponsors had strong incentives to elevate compliance over risk taking in asset portfolio management. This in turn caused plan sponsors to establish investment processes and compliance standards, with everything blessed by third-party consultants.

Indeed, these processes and standards caused a strong initial focus on wealth preservation and conservative risk management, which almost immediately led plan sponsors to mimic one another's investment approaches. They could, in other words, reduce their risks of breaching fiduciary duty by herding with respect to their investment processes and asset allocation decisions. Given the new legal-regulatory landscape, it was far better to fail with a great deal of company than to go it alone, acting as a renegade in search of alpha through some exotic investment strategy.

In addition to encouraging conformance amongst plan sponsors, there was an almost religious adherence to the application of classical portfolio theory. As well as the benefits associated with prudent diversification, conformity to this orthodoxy generated additional legal cover for the plan sponsors, having the advantage of looking formal and scientific in the context of complying with established investment practices.

Prior to the late 1970s pension plan sponsors allocated the vast majority of fund assets to public equities and traditional fixed-income securities. But the oil supply shocks and the Great Inflation of the 1970s changed that mindset. With inflation and treasury rates running into double digits, stock and bond portfolios were simultaneously devastated.

This caused plan sponsors to consider alternative asset classes that might supply some insurance against broad economic shocks. Just such an alternative seemed to exist in the form of real estate, which performed marvelously during these dark times. As Leombroni et al. (2020) have recently documented, and as many observers recognized at the time, relative wealth shifted significantly from stocks to real estate during the mid-1970s. The shift was substantial and fairly permanent. The clear implication was that prudent investment management demanded exposure to real estate in the pension fund asset portfolio.

## 2.2 Putting the Pieces in Place

Although there seemed to be a lot of real estate available for investment, nobody really knew how much. Moreover, there were important differences between owner-occupied housing, which at the time was not investable, and income-producing CRE, which was. Nor were there any studies of longer-run investment performance of real estate, which would be necessary to document portfolio investment relations and to assess the robustness of recent performance. There was also the issue of what sort of investment vehicle would be required to accommodate private asset ownership. Finally, there was the question of how to measure relative investment performance. Although well-known indices such as the Dow Jones Industrial Average existed to benchmark listed equity performance, no industry-specific benchmarks existed for private real estate investment.

The first two questions of how much real estate there was and how it performed were tackled together in a study authored by Ibbotson and Siegel (1984). The authors show that over a 36-year time period covering 1947 to 1982, the share of real estate in the US was approximately that of all stocks, bonds and Treasury securities combined. Even if all of this real estate was not actually investable, a meaningful percentage had to be.[8]

*Table 15.1A    Risk and return to stocks, bonds and real estate: 1947–1982: means and standard deviations of returns*

| Investment category | Mean return (%) | S.D. return (%) |
|---|---|---|
| Stocks | 11.00 | 17.52 |
| Long-term bonds | 2.99 | 9.71 |
| Treasury bills | 4.44 | 3.29 |
| Real estate | 8.03 | 3.78 |

Moreover, as seen in Table 15.1A, investment performance of real estate over the longer run was quite respectable. Average annual returns of 8 percent were smack dab in-between returns to stocks and bonds. In addition, real estate showed remarkable stability in returns over time, attributable in part to stable operating income streams. And perhaps most importantly, as seen in Table 15.1B, the data showed that real estate returns were essentially uncorrelated with stock and bond returns. This latter relation seemed to confirm the insurance-like qualities displayed by real estate during the Great Inflation of the 1970s. The impact of this study was immediate and widespread, stoking an already burning interest in real estate investment.

*Table 15.1B   Risk and return to stocks, bonds and real estate: 1947–1982: correlations of returns*

| Investment category | Stocks | Long-term bonds | Treasury bills | Real estate |
|---|---|---|---|---|
| Stocks | 1.0 | | | |
| Long-term bonds | .14 | 1.0 | | |
| Treasury bills | −.25 | .15 | 1.0 | |
| Real estate | −.06 | −.08 | .44 | 1.0 |

*Note*: Data derived from tables 1 and 3 in Ibbotson and Siegel (1984).

Ironically, in light of ERISA's prudent man fiduciary rule, it was the Prudential Insurance Company that led the way in developing vehicles that facilitated investment in CRE. The company had its own portfolio of CRE, from which it took its better-located, newer, higher-quality office, retail and apartment properties (later labeled as *core assets*) and placed them into what was then referred to as an *open-end commingled real estate fund*.[9] Prudential would manage the fund as the GP that earned fees as a percentage of assets under management (AUM), with plan sponsors investing as limited partners (LPs). Prudential's early offerings of core commingled CRE funds are one of the earliest known GP-LP structured PE investment vehicles marketed to institutional investors.

The last piece of the CRE investment puzzle was to create an index with which to benchmark relative performance. The Russell-NCREIF index (now simply known as the NCREIF index, with a number of variations) was publicly introduced in 1983, with performance dating back to 1978.[10] The index was immediately deemed an acceptable industry performance benchmark and remains widely used to this day.

## 2.3   Early Performance

In the early 1980s, with green lights flashing go, and plenty of consultants and processes put into place to demonstrate fiduciary duty, plan sponsors began dipping their toes into CRE investment through the open-end commingled fund vehicle. Coincidently they did so right at the front end of what was the biggest CRE development boom of the twentieth century. This building boom, which shaped the skylines of many major US cities for decades to come, ended badly and became known as the savings and loan crisis. Fortunately for most pension funds, there was not yet much CRE exposure. The building boom and bust did, however, reveal a dark side of the industry that shook plan sponsor confidence regarding the stability of CRE cash flows and asset prices.

Using annual return data, Figure 15.1 displays the NCREIF (NFI-ODCE) index versus the FTSE-Nareit all-equity index from 1978 through 1992. The Nareit index is composed of publicly listed firms (REITs) that own income-producing CRE (so-called equity REITs). Both indices reflect returns to the CRE sector, thus having similar factor exposures.

Table 15.2 shows that the performance differential on a net-of-fee basis over this 15-year period is significant: 7.54 percent for NCREIF versus 15.28 percent for Nareit. This is a differential that exceeds 7.5 percent per year. As highlighted by Riddiough et al. (2005), adjusting for property type and leverage differences do not fully account for the return differential. Furthermore, equity REIT ownership interests are generally liquid, since shares are exchange-traded, whereas LP interests in commingled CRE funds are much less so.[11]

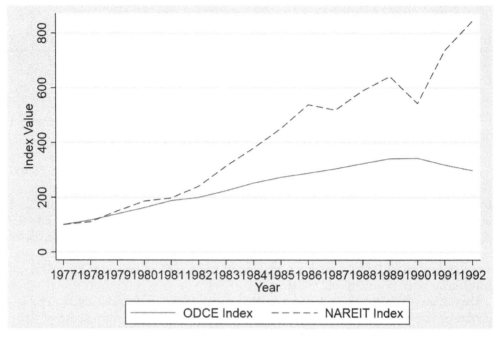

*Note*: Index values for NCREIF and Nareit from the inception of NCREIF in 1978. NCREIF data are obtained via membership access to their website, www.ncreif.org/. Nareit data are from www.reit.com/.

*Figure 15.1   NFI-ODCE versus Nareit index: 1978–1992*

*Table 15.2   Summary performance measures: 1978–1992*

| Return statistic | NFI-ODCE index | Nareit index |
|---|---|---|
| Mean | 7.54% | 15.28% |
| Standard deviation | 8.01% | 13.89% |
| Autocorrelation | .859 | −.121 |
| Contemporaneous cross-correlation | .174 | |
| Lagged cross-correlation | .376 | |

*Note*: Based on annual return data used to construct Figure 15.3. Mean return is a geometric average. Lagged cross-correlation is calculated using the time $t$ NFI-ODCE return and the time $t-1$ Nareit return.

## 2.4   Puzzling Relations

Differences in investment performance are not the only interesting feature of the data. As seen in Table 15.2, the standard deviation of returns to the NFI-ODCE Index are significantly less than that of the Nareit index. Differences in the autocorrelation of returns are striking – near 1 for NCREIF and near 0 for Nareit. The cross-correlations are also eye-catching. On a contemporaneous basis the correlation between NCREIF and Nareit returns is only .174, suggesting very little relation between listed firms and private funds that hold highly similar assets. However, when quarterly returns from NCREIF are correlated with the prior quarter's returns from Nareit, the cross-correlation increases to .376. Correlations between current returns to

NCREIF and lagged returns to Nareit increase further with additional lags. Clearly there is something peculiar about the data.

It turns out that most of the puzzling relations found in Table 15.1, as well as those seen in Figure 15.2 and Table 15.2, can be attributed to *appraisal smoothing*. Seminal studies authored by Geltner (1991) and Ross and Zisler (1991) highlight the fact that CRE assets are sold infrequently, with updates coming primarily through appraisals. They document that appraisers exhibit valuation behavior at odds with the forward-looking approach with which investors take in informationally efficient stock markets. Rather than engage in price discovery as described by Fama (1970), appraisers heavily anchor on recent historical appraised values. The resulting updated valuation estimates are smoothed relative to their "full information" values, leading to significant lags in prices. In other words, appraisal smoothing artificially depresses return volatility and correlations by imposing an autoregressive return structure on the available valuation data.[12]

Insights gained from appraisal smoothing can explain most but not quite all of the puzzling relations documented in Table 15.2. The long-run return differential – which has narrowed over time but remains to this day a robust relation – indicates that institutional investors are willing to accept net-of-fee returns on their core CRE investments that are significantly less than those realized from holding a diversified portfolio of REIT stocks.[13] This does not include compensation for illiquidity risk, which some have estimated to be on the order of about 3 percent per year (see, e.g., Franzoni et al., 2012).

## 3 1993–2008: SHIFTING CAPITAL SOURCES, THE RISE OF ALTERNATIVES AND THE EMERGING PENSION UNDERFUNDING PROBLEM

Within the 16-year window from 1993 to year-end 2008, there are three distinctive sub-periods worth highlighting: 1993–1998, 1999–2003 and 2004–2008. I will consider each in turn.

### 3.1   1993–1998: Wall Street to the Rescue

Traditional debt and equity capital suppliers to the CRE sector were crippled by the S&L crisis.[14] Private capital sources had previously dominated both sides of the market. On the debt side, S&L, a significant source of CRE debt capital in the 1980s, were gone forever. Commercial banks, which had supplied much of the short-term construction finance during the building boom of the 1980s, faced large losses due to the bust. Insurance companies were traditional sources of long-term mortgage loans on income-producing CRE, and they too faced large losses related to high default and foreclosure rates. On the equity side, outside capital often came from LPs. But these capital sources were mostly *not* institutional. Rather, because of tax laws that allowed individuals to offset personal income with depreciation-based accounting losses, outside equity capital sources were primarily higher-earning individual investors. This critical source of capital dried up when tax laws changed in 1986 to eliminate the favorable tax treatment.

With traditional capital sources sidelined or gone forever, the entire CRE sector was severely financially distressed in the early 1990s. Furthermore, opportunity and distress funds set up to swoop in with liquidity and turn-around expertise were only just forming in the early 1990s in response to the S&L crisis and had very little early impact.

Importantly, in sharp contrast with the Global Financial Crisis (GFC) of 2007–2008, Wall Street was mostly unscathed by the S&L crisis. Smelling a big opportunity, and with nowhere else for the CRE sector to turn, Wall Street entered the fray. What emerged was a permanent and significant redirection of capital from private to public market sources.

The commercial mortgage-backed securities (CMBS) market – structured by combining elements of the residential mortgage-backed security and the corporate junk bond – emerged in 1991 as a mechanism to package and sell distressed CRE mortgage loans. It then quickly morphed into a source of permanent mortgage loan financing – known as the "conduit" CMBS market – taking the place of S&L and some insurance companies. Figure 15.2 displays CMBS issuance volume from 1993 through 2008. Note that CMBS outstanding prior to 1993 was only in the order of $10 billion. Issuance volume from 1993 through 1998 was, in contrast, nearly $200 billion, with 50 percent of all new CRE mortgage originations occurring through the CMBS market during that time. This novel source of mortgage debt capital achieved more than a 15-fold market expansion in only a five-year time period.

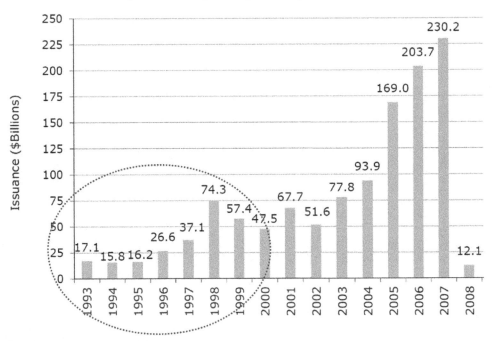

*Source*: Morgan Stanley CRE market research.

*Figure 15.2    Commercial mortgage-backed securities issuance volume: 1993–2008*

On the equity side, Wall Street took an existing investment vehicle off the shelf in the form of the publicly listed equity REIT. Portfolios of privately held distressed CRE assets with fundamentally sound physical and locational attributes were parachuted into tax-efficient REIT investment vehicles, which were then taken public. A REIT initial public offering boom

*Pension funds and private equity real estate* 379

ensued as these firms were valued well above the value of the in-place CRE assets.[15] Figure 15.3 displays equity capitalization of publicly listed REITs from 1978 through 2008. This figure shows that total capitalization was about $10 billion in 1990, growing to $40 billion by 1993 and to over $150 billion by 1998. Similar to growth rates realized in the CMBS market, equity market capitalization of REITs increased by 15 times in the span of only seven or eight years.

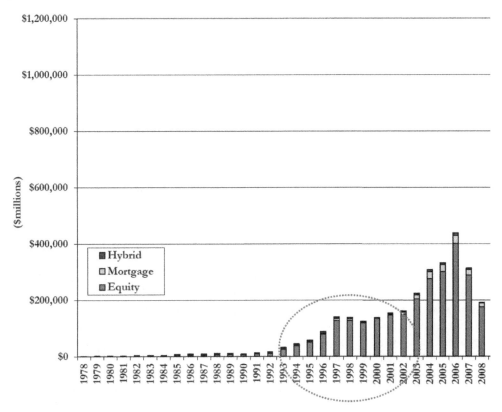

*Source*: Morgan Stanley CRE market research.

*Figure 15.3   REIT market equity capitalization*

Where were pension funds during this 1993–1998 time period? Largely on the sidelines, still shell-shocked by the aftermath of the S&L debacle and the new dynamics of capital allocation. They were, in fact, as measured by NCREIF data, net sellers of CRE during this period. Table 15.3 provides a comparison of net acquisition-disposition activity from 1993–998 to the earlier 1978–1992 time period. During the earlier, formative period, the number of net acquisitions increased at an annual rate of 16.3 percent. Net acquisitions as measured in nominal dollar terms increased by 30.1 percent annually.[16] In contrast, over the six-year 1993–1998 time period that coincided with the introduction of CRE public capital markets, nominal net pension fund investment actually shrunk by about 1 percent per year.

*Table 15.3    Growth in NCREIF assets*

| Time interval | Change in # assets | Total % increase | Annual growth rate (%) | Net new investments | Total % increase | Annual growth rate (%) |
|---|---|---|---|---|---|---|
| 1980–1992 | 2,000 | 858.4 | 16.3 | $29,555 | 5,086.9 | 30.1 |
| 1993–1998 | 207 | 9.3 | 1.5 | ($2,102) | (5.3) | (0.9) |

*Note*: Net new investment is in millions of dollars. Change in total number of assets is reported assets held in the index at the end of the time interval less reported assets held in the index at the start of the time interval. Total percentage increase in the number of assets is calculated by dividing the change in number of assets by total number of assets at the start of the time interval, and multiplying by 100. Annual percentage growth rate in the number of assets is calculated by first dividing end of interval total assets by beginning of interval total assets. This quantity is then taken to the power of 1 divided by the total number of years in the time interval. Finally, 1 is subtracted from the latter quantity, which is then multiplied by 100. Net new investment in NCREIF assets is estimated by first taking the market value (MV) of index assets at the beginning of a given year included in the time interval and multiplying it by 1 plus the total return for that year. That quantity is the estimated "same-store" value of NCREIF assets at the end of the year. Then, in a second step, the year-end same-store MV is subtracted from the total MV of index assets at the end of the year. The latter quantity incorporates the net value of asset acquisitions and dispositions that occurred during the year. The difference of the year-end total MV and same-store MV produces our estimate of net new investment in a given year. Net new investment in all years in a given time interval are summed up to produce net new investment. Total percentage increase in new investment is calculated by dividing new investment by the MV of all NCREIF assets at the start of the time interval, multiplied by 100. Annual percentage growth rate in new investment is calculated by first dividing the sum of new investment and the MV of all NCREIF assets at the start of the time interval by the MV of all NCREIF assets at the start of the time interval. This quantity is then taken to the power of 1 divided by the total number of years in the time interval. Finally, 1 is subtracted from the latter quantity, which is then multiplied by 100.

### 3.2    1999–2003: The End of the Beginning, Growth in Alternative Investments

The 1999–2003 sub-period marked the "end of the beginning" for many DB pension funds. By the end of 2003, the earlier era, characterized by a "prudent man" investment approach that stressed wealth preservation over risk taking, gave way to a new era shaped by an increasing gap between plan sponsor assets and retirement payout liabilities. Secular declines in nominal interest rates and yields on fixed-income investments combined with disappointing returns to public equities to negatively impact pension fund asset values. This then combined with generous retirement promises made to plan participants to create a structural underfunding problem. The underfunding problem had begun to emerge by 2003, but few realized it at the time.

I will provide a detailed analysis of the underfunding problem in the next section. For now it is worth briefly documenting the rise of alternative investments, which broadly coincided with the emergence of the pension underfunding problem. Alternatives are at a high level classified as liquid or illiquid. Liquid alternatives generally refer to HFs, while illiquid alternatives generally refer to PE. Within PE there are several types of funds, including buyout, venture capital and real assets. PERE has historically dominated the real asset category.[17]

Figure 15.4 displays assets under management for HFs from 1990 to 2010. From 1999 to the end of 2003, HF AUM roughly doubled from $0.5 trillion to $1.0 trillion. Figure 15.5 shows the aggregated NAV for non-PERE and PERE funds from 1990 to 2019. Fund growth is also seen to ramp up starting in the late 1990s.

A comparison of fund sizes in Figures 15.4 and 15.5, together with pension fund allocations to these three categories of investment, reveals an important fact regarding pension fund investment in CRE. Taking the year 2001 as a baseline, according to the Public Plans Database (PPD), aggregate plan sponsor allocations to CRE were 4.4 percent, with a 3.6 percent allocation to PE and a .34 percent allocation to HFs. At the time, pension funds were the dominant

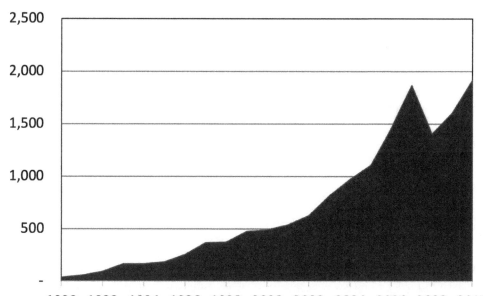

Source: Data are from HHF.

Figure 15.4    Hedge fund assets under management, 1990–2019

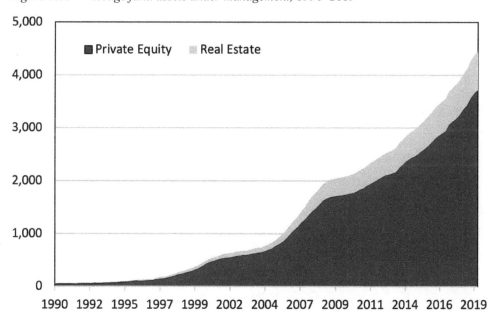

Source: Data are from Burgiss.

Figure 15.5    Aggregated private equity fund net asset value

investor in CRE funds, with an LP investor share estimated to be in excess of 80 percent.[18] In contrast, as a result of their large aggregated fund sizes, along with lower allocation percentages, pension fund investment shares to PE and HFs are much smaller – 13.8 percent to non-PERE and 1.3 percent to HFs.[19] The implication: at 80 percent, the share of pension fund investment in PERE is much more meaningful than it is in non-PERE and HFs.

### 3.3    2004–2008: The Underfunding Problem Emerges

Figure 15.6 displays NFI-ODCE versus Nareit indexed performance over the 1993 to 2010 time frame. During the 2004–2008 window, Nareit eked out a small positive annualized return of just under 1 percent, while NCREIF delivered a robust performance of 9.73 percent annually.[20] The broader equity markets were not so fortunate. Figure 15.7 shows a long time series of the S&P 500 index through 2010, with red lines demarcating the three sub-periods – 1993–1998, 1998–2003, 2004–2008 – considered in this section. As summarized in Table 15.4, annualized public equity returns are negative in both the 1998–2003 and 2004–2008 sub-periods. Also reported in Table 15.4 are 10-year Treasury bond yields as of beginning-year 1993, 1999, 2004 and 2009, respectively, with a longer time series of 10-year Treasury rates displayed in Figure 15.8 (red lines again demarcate sub-periods considered in this section). As buy-and-hold investors, in the short-run pension funds were partially protected against declining interest rates. They were, however, exposed to the declining rates as bonds matured and because retirement fund inflows were extremely high at the time.

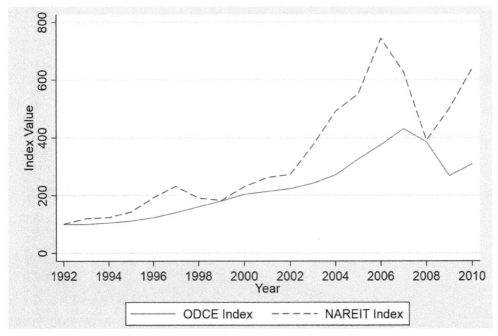

*Source*: Morgan Stanley CRE market research.

*Figure 15.6*    NCREIF versus Nareit index, 1993–2010

*Pension funds and private equity real estate* 383

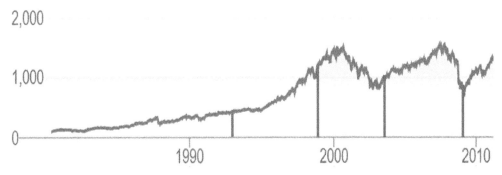

*Note*: Vertical lines demarcate the sub-periods considered in Section 3, corresponding to year-end 1992, 1998, 2003, and 2008.

*Figure 15.7    S&P 500 Index*

*Note*: Vertical lines demarcate the sub-periods considered in Section 3, corresponding to year-end 1992, 1998, 2003, and 2008.

*Figure 15.8    10-year Treasury security yields*

*Table 15.4    Annual stock returns and 10-year Treasury rates, 1993–2008*

| Index/Interest Rate | 1/93 | 1993–1998 | 1/99 | 1999–2003 | 1/04 | 2004–2008 | 1/09 |
|---|---|---|---|---|---|---|---|
| S&P 500 | | 19.6% | | −2.7% | | −4.3% | |
| 10-year Treasury | 6.57% | | 4.64% | | 4.04% | | 2.36% |

DB pension plan sponsors were allocating over 90 percent of their portfolios to public equities and traditional fixed income in the early 2000s. At the same time they targeted overall returns of 8.0 percent to meet funding requirements. Given declining interest rates and poor equity market performance, gaps began to appear in the balance sheets of plan sponsors. These gaps – measured by the difference between pension fund assets (the market value of investment portfolio) and accumulated benefit obligations to plan participants (the present value of the forecasted liability stream) – became large enough by 2008 to begin to draw the notice of researchers. The seminal work on the topic belongs to Brown and Wilcox (2009) and Novy-Marx and Rauh (2009) (henceforth B-W and NM-R), which I will now summarize.

Focusing on public DB pension funds, both papers expose an accounting device that served to mask the underfunding problem. Pension fund liabilities are estimated as a series of actuarially determined payout obligations to plan participants based on contributions and payout formulas, expected and realized retirement timing and life expectancy. These obligations can be forecasted with reasonable accuracy, providing the numerator for a present value calculation of pension fund liabilities. But what are known as GASB 25 and ASOP 27 provide public plan sponsors discretion to choose discount rates on the liability stream that reflect the risks of the invested assets. In particular, GASB 25 states that the discount rate "should be based on an estimated long-term investment yield for the plan, with consideration given to the nature and mix of current and expected plan investments" (Brown and Wilcox, 2009). From 2000 to 2008, the vast majority of public DB pension funds chose a discount rate of 8.0 percent. Based on that discount rate the estimated value of liabilities was such that, prior to 2008, no meaningful underfunding problem appeared to exist.

B-W and NM-R argued there is no necessary connection between the risk-adjusted discount rate appropriate for the asset portfolio and the discount rate applied to value pension liabilities. This is because the liability stream – retirement payout promises made to public employees and backed by the taxing and bond issuance authority of the states or localities sponsoring these plans – more resembled riskless cash flows than risky ones.

By using discount rates that better reflect the low-risk nature of the liability streams, NM-R estimate a funding gap as of year-end 2008 at $3.23 trillion if liabilities are discounted at Treasury rates and at $1.31 trillion if liabilities are discounted at taxable municipal bond rates. These estimates compare to just under $2 trillion in state-level pension assets, indicating a rather massive gap. Using the underfunding upper bound of $3.23 trillion, NM-R assign a liability of $21,500 for each and every household in the US. The authors further estimate an additional $1 trillion funding gap for local public pension plans. Finally, they go on to show that, although the funding gap grew significantly in 2008 because of the effects of the GFC, large shortfalls existed even in 2005 and 2006.

These two papers have spawned a robust literature over the last 10-plus years that has sought to refine underfunding estimates and examine more subtle incentive effects. For example, according to the World Economic Forum, across major economies the underfunding gap is forecast to be $224 trillion by 2050. Pagliari (2019) shows that the state of Illinois pension fund, as of 2018, is by itself underfunded by at least $131 billion. He further calculates that accrued pension liabilities from 2003 to 2016 grew at three times the growth rate of state gross domestic product. There is also research that shows that plan sponsor board composition affects investment choices, with poorer results corresponding with more politically connected board members (Andonov et al., 2017). Importantly, research now shows that more underfunded pension funds: (1) hold riskier asset portfolios that realize lower relative returns,

(2) apply higher discount rates to their liability streams and (3) pay higher investment management fees (Franzoni and Marin, 2006; Andonov et al., 2017; Aubry and Crawford, 2019).

B-W and NM-R raise several moral hazard problems that accompany GASB 25 and ASOP 27. First, by decreasing liabilities with an artificially high discount rate, incentives for plan sponsors and governments to address funding gaps are reduced. Second, when retirement funding shortfalls can no longer can be ignored, there are incentives for states and localities to issue "Pension Obligation Bonds" that shift underfunding costs to future generations.[21] And third, by linking liability discount rates to the risk of the investment portfolio, incentives exist for plan sponsors to increase portfolio risk in order to apply a higher discount rate to their liabilities.[22] I note that a related but slightly different rationale for increasing investment risk is to "gamble for resurrection."[23] This gamble may not be quite as urgent for pension funds today as it is for firms on the brink of bankruptcy and potential liquidation, but the incentive exists nonetheless, suggesting a gradual shift towards higher-returning (in expectation) but riskier investments as plan sponsors reach for yield.[24]

Another way to express the incentive issue is that, starting in the early 2000s, many plan sponsors found themselves beginning to live a life of quiet desperation. Quiet desperation, a symptom of addressing a pension underfunding overhang problem along with having to meet aggressive portfolio return objectives in a low-yielding investment environment, manifests itself in the distorted choices that plan sponsors make in response and the outcomes that they actually realize.

A particularly revealing choice is the plan sponsor portfolio allocation decision. In 2001, according to PPD, pension fund allocations to alternative investments (including commodities) were 8.8 percent, implying that over 90 percent of the DB plan sponsor portfolio was allocated to traditional investment categories public equities and fixed income (including a small percentage of cash). Fast-forward to 2008 and allocations to alternatives almost doubled to 16.9 percent, with 6.9 percent going to PERE, 6.6 percent to non-PERE, and 2.0 percent to HFs. Allocations to traditional investment categories had decreased to just over 83 percent.

Is such an allocation increase meaningful? Suppose a plan sponsor is asked to generate an 8.0 percent return on its portfolio over the next year. Further suppose that, based on low interest rates and market risk premia, public equities and traditional fixed income together are expected to generate a 6.0 percent return. A 100 percent allocation to those two asset classes will obviously fail to produce the required 8.0 percent expected return, so a higher-yielding – and riskier – category of investments is required. Introducing alternatives, including PERE, we can suppose alternatives are expected to produce a 16.0 percent return. An 8.8 percent allocation to alternatives (which existed in 2001) generates a 6.9 percent expected portfolio return. Not enough. Now increase the allocation to alternatives to 16.9 percent (that existed in 2008), and a 7.69 percent overall return is anticipated. Close, but not quite there. Go to the 20 percent allocation and, voilà, an 8.0 percent expected return is generated. The 20 percent allocation mark for alternative investments was, in fact, crossed in 2011.

This simple investment calculus, known as *return targeting*, accurately describes the thinking and general approach that many plan sponsors make when living a life of quiet desperation. In other words, investors that target returns put more focus on absolute performance than risk-adjusted returns, implying violations to the usual assumptions underlying classical finance theory (see Gompers et al., 2016). There is further evidence that institutional investors display loss-averse behavior – another violation of classical finance theory (Bodnaruk and Simonov, 2016). Loss-averse preferences on the part of underfunded plan sponsors may have particularly deleterious effects. These plan sponsors will naturally reference their retirement liability estimate in relation to total portfolio asset value. The more underfunded the plan sponsor is, the more it "hurts" from a utility perspective, implying *risk-seeking behavior* as plan sponsors attempt to recoup pain-inducing losses caused by historical underperformance and generous retirement benefit promises.[25]

## 4  2001–2019: CRE ALLOCATIONS AND PERE INVESTMENT PERFORMANCE

In the previous section I documented how persistently low interest rates and market risk premia combined with generous retirement benefit promises to create a structural pension underfunding problem. The underfunding problem goes a long way in explaining increasing allocations to PERE funds, as well as other forms of alternatives, under the theory that alternatives can deliver high absolute returns over sustained periods of time.

In this section I detail how pension fund portfolio allocations have changed over time and how PERE funds have actually performed since 2001. I also address related issues of whether alpha can, from a normative perspective, exist with PERE fund investment and pension funds' revealed preference for illiquid PERE fund investment vehicles that are apparently priced at a *premium* to liquid alternatives. Finally, I consider how it is that pension fund allocations continue to increase when PERE funds in aggregate consistently underperform GP-specified return targets.

### 4.1  Allocations to CRE, PERE Investment Performance

Table 15.5 summarizes CRE allocations and PERE fund performance over the 2001 through 2019 time period. There are two sub-period groupings: 2001–2008 (pre-GFC) and 2009–2019 (post-GFC). Within each grouping public pension fund allocations to CRE are reported based on data from PPD, housed at Boston College. Preqin data are used to measure investment performance at the fund level. Fund IRRs are weighted by fund size and aggregated to obtain weighted means. Funds are grouped by vintage year, which is the first year that the fund reports receive a non-zero cash flow. Only funds that invest in North America and with GP-sponsor addresses located in the US are included in my sample. Further, only funds categorized as core, core-plus, value-add and opportunistic are considered. Sample sizes are the total number of distinct funds included in a vintage year. The sample size in parentheses is the number of funds categorized as value-add or opportunistic. Finally, Δ-IRR measures relative investment performance. It is defined as the IRR of a fund minus the IRR of a hypothetical investment in the US FTSE-Nareit all-equity index over the exact same time frame over which the PERE fund IRR is calculated. Thus, PERE fund performance is measured relative to the public market investment alternative.[26]

Public pension fund allocations to CRE are seen to increase steadily over the full sample period, more than doubling from 4.4 percent in 2001 to 9.1 percent in 2019. Did investment performance justify the increased allocations? During the pre-GFC sample period, the answer supplied by the Preqin data is no. Although performance is solid for funds with vintage years 2001–2003, the adverse effects of the GFC severely impacted post-2003 performance on an absolute as well as a relative basis. Over the entire pre-GFC sample period, PERE funds

Table 15.5    PERE allocation and investment performance, 2001–2019

| Year | Allocation Percent (%) | Sample Size (N) | Vintage IRR (%) | Vintage Δ-IRR (%) |
|---|---|---|---|---|
| 2001 | 4.4 | 24 (20) | 16.6 | 5.7 |
| 2002 | 4.6 | 21 (21) | 10.1 | 0.9 |
| 2003 | 4.4 | 26 (23) | 21.3 | 10.7 |
| 2004 | 4.2 | 44 (40) | 5.6 | (4.4) |
| 2005 | 4.4 | 55 (49) | 0.5 | (7.2) |
| 2006 | 5.0 | 68 (60) | (0.7) | (7.9) |
| 2007 | 5.5 | 65 (57) | 4.9 | (1.7) |
| 2008 | 6.9 | 46 (38) | 3.9 | (5.1) |
| Total | | 349 (308) | 4.3 | (3.7) |
| | | | | |
| 2009 | 6.3 | 18 (14) | 15.2 | (1.7) |
| 2010 | 6.0 | 38 (31) | 14.2 | 1.0 |
| 2011 | 6.7 | 65 (55) | 18.7 | 8.1 |
| 2012 | 7.9 | 59 (50) | 14.9 | 4.5 |
| 2013 | 7.9 | 75 (67) | 14.8 | 4.4 |
| 2014 | 7.7 | 62 (56) | 15.8 | 5.7 |
| 2015 | 8.2 | 82 (68) | 10.7 | (0.3) |
| 2016 | 8.8 | 49 (39) | 10.4 | 2.9 |
| 2017 | 8.4 | 46 (40) | 11.9 | (3.3) |
| 2018 | 8.4 | | | |
| 2019 | 9.1 | | | |
| Total | | 494 (420) | 14.1 | 3.4 |

*Note*: Allocation percentages are from PPD. PERE sample size and IRR data are from Preqin. Only core, core-plus, value-add and opportunity fund categories are analyzed. Sample size covers all four categories, while sample size in parentheses is value-add and opportunity funds only. Vintage year is the first year in which a fund generates a cash flow. Δ-IRR is obtained by first calculating the IRR obtained from investing in the all-equity FTSE-Nareit index over the sample period, and subtracting this quantity from the fund IRR. IRR and Δ-IRR as reported in the table are means-weighted by fund size.

returned only 4.3 percent and underperformed the public market benchmark by 3.7 percent. Furthermore, 308 of the 349 funds in the sample are value-add and opportunistic funds. These funds are advertised as higher risk, targeting returns in the 13.5 to 18.0 percent range on a net-of-fee basis. They clearly did not come close to meeting their return targets (as can be specifically seen in Table 15.6).

With these less than stellar results, what happened to pension fund allocations to CRE in the post-GFC sub-sample period? They decrease somewhat in 2009 and 2010, and then resume their upward trend. This outcome may at first seem surprising given the poor showing of the 2004–2008 PERE fund vintages, but it highlights two important aspects of the PE fund business model. First, because neither LP fund ownership interests nor the underlying assets generally trade while the fund is active, there are typically significant lags in accurately assessing fund performance.[27] These lags can create allocation persistence. Second, although the GFC hammered the performance of 2004–2008 vintage funds, it also created opportunities for newly formed funds. Market turmoil thus cuts both ways, creating a valuable hedge for GP sponsors who selectively highlight the future over the past when fundraising from pension funds and other institutional investors.

## 388  Handbook of real estate and macroeconomics

Table 15.6A    PERE allocation and investment performance, 2001–2019

| Line item | Core | Core-plus | Value-add | Opportunistic |
|---|---|---|---|---|
| Working definition | Higher-quality income-producing assets without any major problems to fix | Income-producing assets with one problem to fix, such as leasing vacant space or doing minor renovations | Assets requiring increased asset management, like repositioning and refurbishing, with more vacancy risk | Assets that require taking significant risk for planning, full development and leasing; perhaps operating risk as well |
| Fund target IRR (net) | 8.0–8.5% | 11.0–12.5% | 13.5–16.0% | 16.0–18.0% |
| Fund target leverage | 20–40% | 50–60% | 50–65% | 50–70% |

Table 15.6B    PERE allocation and investment performance, 2001–2019

| Year | Core IRR (%) | Core Δ-IRR (%) | Core-P IRR (%) | Core-P Δ-IRR (%) | Val-Ad IRR (%) | Val-ad Δ-IRR (%) | Opp IRR (%) | Opp Δ-IRR (%) |
|---|---|---|---|---|---|---|---|---|
| 2001 | 19.0 | 9.1 | 13.8 | 3.0 | 15.4 | 4.4 | 19.9 | 9.1 |
| 2002 | - | - | - | - | 17.6 | 9.0 | (4.4) | (14.7) |
| 2003 | 6.6 | (4.5) | 17.5 | 6.6 | 13.7 | 3.5 | 33.0 | 21.9 |
| 2004 | 31.7 | 22.3 | - | - | 8.0 | (2.1) | (0.6) | (10.4) |
| 2005 | 4.5 | (3.0) | 3.9 | (4.0) | 1.8 | (5.8) | (1.2) | (9.0) |
| 2006 | (10.5) | (17.3) | 8.0 | 0.6 | (5.4) | (12.4) | 4.1 | (3.1) |
| 2007 | (37.5) | (42.3) | 9.3 | 2.1 | 2.9 | (3.4) | 6.7 | (0.0) |
| 2008 | 8.0 | (1.2) | 10.4 | 2.2 | 6.4 | (2.5) | 0.4 | (8.6) |
| Total | 0.1 | (7.6) | 9.0 | 0.8 | 3.8 | (4.2) | 4.5 | (3.4) |
| 2009 | 11.5 | (5.0) | 21.5 | 1.1 | 18.0 | 1.1 | 5.1 | (11.7) |
| 2010 | 12.9 | 0.1 | 12.9 | (0.3) | 13.7 | 0.1 | 15.5 | 2.5 |
| 2011 | 11.8 | 1.6 | 18.9 | 8.3 | 20.0 | 9.4 | 18.8 | 8.2 |
| 2012 | 12.4 | 2.0 | 18.4 | 8.7 | 16.2 | 5.8 | 13.8 | 3.2 |
| 2013 | 12.9 | 3.6 | 10.2 | 0.8 | 17.2 | 6.7 | 11.8 | 1.2 |
| 2014 | 15.9 | 5.4 | 10.5 | 1.0 | 14.9 | 5.0 | 17.1 | 6.8 |
| 2015 | 5.4 | (5.4) | 13.3 | 2.6 | 13.4 | 2.2 | 9.3 | (1.7) |
| 2016 | 11.6 | 4.0 | 10.5 | 3.1 | 8.8 | 1.0 | 12.5 | 5.7 |
| 2017 | 15.9 | 5.6 | 16.6 | 4.0 | 11.5 | (0.4) | 11.2 | (0.6) |
| Total | 11.5 | 0.8 | 13.2 | 3.1 | 14.7 | 3.9 | 14.0 | 3.3 |

*Note*: Performance data are broken down by fund category by vintage year and are split into pre-GFC and post-GFC sample periods. Fund target IRR and target leverage are obtained from PREA survey results and my own analysis of Preqin fund data. IRR and Δ-IRR are calculated as reported in the notes to Table 15.5.

Are the more recent allocation increases justified by performance in the post-GFC sample period? At first blush, the answer appears to be yes. Absolute performance to date is consistently strong, with IRRs ranging from 10.4 to 18.7 percent on average across all vintages in the post-GFC sample. To provide a more detailed look at PERE fund performance, panel B of Table 15.6B reports absolute and relative performance for funds categorized as core, core-plus, value-add and opportunistic. Panel A of Table 15.6A provides working definitions for the four fund categories, ranges of GP-specified net-of-fee IRR targets and ranges of fund leverage targets. Data to establish target IRR and leverage ranges come from PREA's 2016 Management Fees and Terms Study and my own analysis of Preqin PERE fund-level data. Figure 15.9 visually displays IRRs by fund category over the 2001–2019 sample period.[28]

*Pension funds and private equity real estate* 389

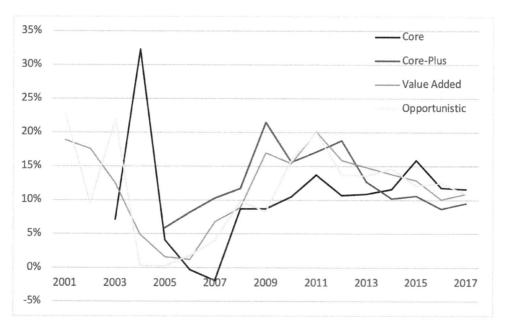

*Note*: Preqin data are used to construct non-weighted average IRRs by vintage and fund category.

*Figure 15.9    PERE fund IRRs by vintage year and category*

Focusing on the post-GFC sample period, Table 15.6 indicates that investment performance is consistently strong by category on an absolute basis. Performance is also good overall relative to the Nareit public market benchmark. But, performance is mixed relative to target IRRs seen in Table 15.6A. Core and core-plus performance is above target, while value-add is at target. Opportunistic, on the other hand, is below target.

There are several reasons to question whether this more recent performance will hold up over time. First, there is likely some upward bias in reported fund IRRs. All IRRs are self-reported to Preqin by participating GP sponsors. GPs may have incentives to bias their reported IRRs upward by cherry-picking the best performing LPs from within a fund.[29]

Second, there is a well-known upward bias in self-reported NAVs of non-liquidated funds, which generally declines over time as funds get closer to liquidation. This bias is enhanced by the fact that high-performing funds generally liquidate sooner than mediocre or poorly performing funds. Approximately 10 percent of funds (48 out of 494) in the post-GFC sub-sample period liquidated by year-end 2019, with a 22.8 percent weighted average IRR versus 13.7 percent to date for non-liquidated funds. As time goes on, as the currently active funds liquidate and NAVs decline, average performance should trend lower.

Third and most important is that we have faced another major economic shock – the COVID-19 pandemic. The ultimate economic impact of this episode on PERE performance is still in question, but will likely be negative. The most vulnerable funds in our sample are, given their risky operating and financial leverage characteristics, value-add and opportunity funds, especially those holding office, retail and hotel property types. Importantly, 382 out of the 494 funds in our post-GFC sub-period sample are non-liquidated and classified as value-add or opportunistic.

## 4.2 Does PERE Fund Alpha Exist? Positive and Normative Perspectives

What does other research have to say about PERE investment performance? Using a combination of Burgiss, Cambridge Associates and NCREIF data over a sample period covering 2000–2017, Bollinger and Pagliari (2019) measure PERE fund performance under a classical mean-variance framework.[30] They find that value-add and opportunity funds underperform by about 3 percent per year on a risk-adjusted basis.

Gupta and Van Nieuwerburgh (2021) use Preqin data covering the same 2000–2017 sample period to empirically analyze PE fund performance using a cash flow-based asset pricing approach. To do so, they match PE fund cash flow strips with cash flow strips implied by available bonds and publicly listed equity securities over matching time horizons. This generates a replicating portfolio of publicly available securities with which to assess PERE fund (as well as other PE fund) returns. After considering a large set of possible pricing factors, they find that PERE fund strip returns load primarily on returns to REIT dividends and capital gains. For every $1 of capital committed to PERE, they find the LP loses 17 cents on the dollar on average on a present value risk-adjusted basis. Given an average fund duration of five to seven years, underperformance is on the order to 3–4 percent per year.

Riddiough and Wiley (2021) use both Preqin and Burgiss data to analyze fund performance based on the public market equivalent (PME) measure developed by Kaplan and Schoar (2005).[31] Over their 1992–2016 sample period they find an average PME of 1.0 using Preqin data (indicating break-even performance) and 0.93 using Burgiss data (indicating underperformance of between 1.5 to 2.0 percent per year).[32] Based on vintage year results reported in their paper, and mapping these results into the same 2001–2008 and 2009–2017 sub-sample periods used in this study, their findings indicate PMEs of 0.79/0.78 to Preqin/Burgiss over the pre-GFC sample period (indicating underperformance of 3–4 percent per year) and 1.09/1.06 to Preqin/Burgiss over the post-GFC sample period (indicating outperformance of 2–3 percent per year).

Thus, in summary, Bollinger and Pagliari (2019) and Gupta and Van Nieuwerburgh (2019) find inferior risk-adjusted performance of 3–4 percent per year.[33] My results along with those of Riddiough and Wiley (2021) indicate significant underperformance for vintages 2001 through 2008, with much-improved performance for 2009 and later vintages. But, as discussed, more recent vintage performance is very much up in the air with the aftershocks anticipated from COVID-19.

In general, I am skeptical that, across the sector as a whole, PERE funds are capable of generating positive alpha. To do so, PERE GP sponsors would have to have access to capital and/or possess skills in capital allocation – buying, selling, owning, operating and developing CRE – that don't exist and are not replicable in other parts of the CRE market. Are there other investors such as REITs or private non-PERE enterprises that can do what, say, Blackstone does with CRE? I believe the answer is yes, certainly with respect to income-producing assets. I believe this to be true even with very large-scale transactions. Some may argue that REITs are not well suited to do development. But neither are large PERE sponsors, as real estate development generally requires a strong local presence to identify and successfully execute opportunities. Can REITs manage CRE assets more cheaply than PERE fund sponsors? The answer again seems to be yes, as REIT fees in the form of G&A expenses average 0.90 percent of equity value. In comparison, PERE fees roughly match those of REITs for core/core-plus funds, but equal approximately 3 percent for value-add and 4 percent for opportunistic funds.

Even though PERE performance may be questionable across the sector as a whole, it could be that certain GPs deliver persistently strong performance while other GPs generate persistently mediocre or poor returns for their investors. In recent work with Da Li (Li and Riddiough, 2020), we address this question, focusing on fully liquidated PERE value-add and opportunity funds. In doing so, Li and I analyze Preqin data and apply the method of Korteweg and Sorensen (2017) to distinguish between noise, true long-term persistence and overlapping fund effects. We do find evidence of long-term persistence in investment performance. But we also find that it is hard to act on performance information in real time because it takes a number of years before GP outperformance can be pinned on skill rather than luck. We also find the better and more persistently performing GPs tend to be smaller and have fewer funds. In contrast, brand name GPs that offer multiple, large funds such as Blackstone, AEW and Carlyle Group generate middling performance of 10.4, 10.3 and 9.1 percent, respectively. This places all three GPs in the third quartile of performance, ranked 111, 113 and 123, respectively, out of 200 GPs in our sample. The only GP with five or more funds to place in the first quartile of performance is Waterton, with eight funds and a 21.1 percent average return (ranked 37). But its average fund size is only about one-tenth that of the previously identified GPs. All of this implies that, although alpha may exist with certain GPs, it is hard to act on. Moreover, scale seems to be the enemy of alpha.

### 4.3    The Illiquidity Price Premium

Standard economic reasoning suggests that investors should discount the acquisition price of assets that are less liquid than otherwise equivalent assets (see, among many others, Brunnermeier and Pedersen, 2009). This price discount maps into an illiquidity premium in the risk-adjusted rate of return required on investment. Consequently, conventional thinking would suggest shareholders of CRE held in a REIT investment vehicle would require lower returns than otherwise equivalent CRE held in an illiquid PERE fund vehicle.

Comparisons of NFI-ODCE versus Nareit investment performance indicates the opposite in fact seems to hold. Figure 15.10 graphs the NFI-ODCE versus Nareit indices over the full 1978 to 2019 time frame covered in this chapter. NFI-ODCE generates a 7.57 percent average annual return, whereas Nareit produces a 12.45 percent average return.[34] This is almost a 5.0 percent return differential realized over a 42-year time period.[35] To put this difference in perspective, as seen in the figure a pension fund that held the Nareit index over this time period would be nearly seven times better off than a pension fund that held the NCREIF index.[36, 37]

Berk and Green (2004) provide an internally consistent framework that predicts fund investors will earn zero alpha after fees. This happens because fund managers internalize any surplus they create so as to make investors indifferent to the public market alternative.[38] Applying this logic, the greater than 3 percent differential we identify can be attributed to illiquidity, but not in the expected direction. In other words, pension funds, which are by far the largest single class of investors in PERE, seem to have revealed a strong preference for *illiquidity* in CRE investment relative to liquid alternatives. At a rate that may exceed 3 percent per year, this is a remarkable relationship, particularly considering that Franzoni et al. (2012) and Sorensen et al. (2014) estimate a diametrically opposite 3 percent illiquidity risk premia

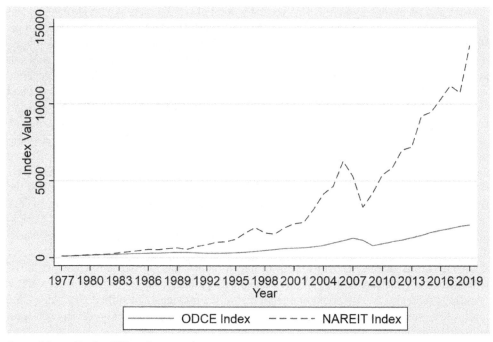

*Source*: Morgan Stanley CRE market research.

*Figure 15.10   NFI-ODCE versus Nareit index, 1978–2019*

required on PE investment. Accounting for liquidity risk in the usual direction thus represents a 6 percent return differential *per annum*.

I am not the first to comment on this unusual relationship. Gupta and Van Nieuwerburgh (2021) state that:

> To the best of our knowledge there is no hard evidence of the existence of an illiquidity premium [included in the discount rate]. Many institutional investors such as pension funds value the fact that PE investments do not have to be marked to market. Given that public pensions make up the largest asset allocator to PE, then the illiquidity premium could in fact be negative.

Asness (2019) in his discussion of a possible illiquidity rate discount in PE fund investment makes the following observations:

> pricing opacity may actually be a feature [of PE fund investment] not a bug. Liquid, accurately priced investments let you know precisely how volatile they are and they smack you in the face with it ... What if illiquid, very infrequently and inaccurately priced investments made them better investors as essentially it allows them to ignore such investments given low measured volatility and very modest paper drawdowns? ... So, I think its entirely possible that investors are accepting a discounted expected net return ... for the privilege of not being told prices.

Green Street Advisors, a highly respected independent CRE industry and REIT analyst, is more circumspect:

> The excuse given [by pension funds] for avoiding listed REITs is their high volatility ... Claims that the public [investment vehicle] wrapper somehow changes the nature of a property portfolio's investment merits are not only non-sensical – they're demonstrably false. ("If It Looks Like a Duck ...," December 20, 2018)

The price premium paid by pension funds for PERE fund investment thus seems to originate from inhibiting the observation of return volatility. But the low measured return volatility of NFI-ODCE (9.14 versus 16.64 percent for Nareit over the entire 1978–2019 time period) and the low contemporaneous cross-correlation of NFI-ODCE with Nareit (.05 over the same time period, which increases to .615 if Nareit returns are lagged one year) are simply an artifact of appraisal smoothing – nothing more. Pension funds are in essence paying for a veil – the PERE fund vehicle wrapper – that hinders price discovery.

Some argue that, well, the smoothed numbers are the numbers. If a tree falls in a forest and nobody is there to see or hear it, it never happened. In that case, to be logically and behaviorally consistent, the same individuals should simply cover their eyes and ears most of the time to filter out stock market noise. Not trusting exchange-traded stock prices, they should also look back at historical returns to infer current returns. To be more precise, I suggest the following: purchase the public market alternative with factor exposure that matches the PERE investment (i.e., the Nareit index), self-impose a no-trade constraint and ignore daily returns with observation only occurring on a once-a-quarter basis. Then take the observed quarterly returns and input them into a regression-based filtering model to create smoothed returns that mirror those generated by PERE investment.

This is precisely what I do in panels A through C in Figure 15.11. In panel A, I plot actual index values to holding Nareit versus the NPI from 1982 through 2020. Here, Nareit is clearly more volatile than the NPI on a quarterly return basis. Is that volatility, which is veiled in the NPI, so problematic that it is worth giving up an annual 5.0 percent return differential? To generate the smoothed Nareit index seen in panel B, I simply regress NPI returns on the current and past 16 quarters worth of Nareit returns. This filtering formula can be applied to update Nareit returns. The fit from this model mostly eliminates the return differential, while also eliminating much of the quarterly variation in the Nareit index. In panel C, I impose a constraint on the regression coefficients. The constraint requires the coefficients to sum to a constant such that the geometric return equals that actually realized over the sample period by the Nareit index. Doing so recaptures the superior returns generated by Nareit over this time period, while filtering out the stock price volatility that seems to bother plan sponsors so much. In the end, the only difference in the Nareit index series when moving from panel A to panel C is the imposition of a fiction – the same fiction that generates smoothed returns to PERE investment.

In sum, the essential problem is that pension funds pay very high prices to gain broad-based CRE exposure through the PERE investment vehicle relative to what they could pay for similar exposure through share ownership in publicly listed firms. These high PERE prices create a drag on pension fund investment performance, defeating the purpose for allocating to these high-risk investment vehicles to begin with.

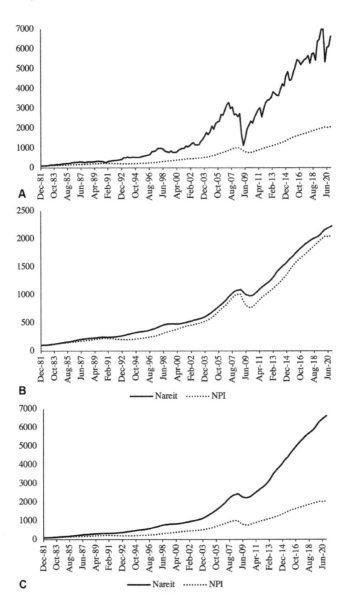

*Figure 15.11   Quarterly value index: Nareit versus the NPI; panel A: Nareit versus NPI – based on actual Nareit returns; panel B: Nareit versus NPI – based on best fit filtered Nareit returns; panel C: Nareit versus NPI – based on filtered Nareit returns with return differences preserved*

### 4.4   Lake Wobegon Benchmarking of the Marvelous Kind

Value-add and opportunity funds now attract more than 70 percent of total funds raised in PERE. As seen in Table 15.6A, fund sponsors target returns for their investors of between 13.5 and 18.0 percent. Yet, as seen in Table 15.6B, performance overall has been below target, with gaps in targeted versus actual performance in the order of 10.0 percent or more in the pre-GFC time period. Given that GPs regularly miss hitting promised return targets, with poor risk-adjusted returns as documented in recent academic studies, how is it that pension funds continue to allocate to value-add and opportunity PERE funds? One might expect this kind of performance to discourage rather than encourage fund flows.

An important piece of evidence that helps explain this is internal pension fund performance benchmarking. Although limited, the available evidence indicates that internal benchmarks are set well below return targets advertised by GPs at the beginning of fund lives.

Based on 2015 data I obtained from Hewitt-EnnisKnupp, of the 30 largest public pension funds in the US, 20 benchmark directly to the NCREIF NPI or NFI-ODCE indices with no adjustment, 8 add a premium of between 50 and 200 basis points to the chosen index and 2 actually subtract 25–130 basis points from the NPI index (presumably to account for the NPI being reported on a gross-of-fee basis). Separately, MacKinnon (2019) surveyed 29 US-based institutional investors (presumably pension funds). Here the use of the NCREIF NFI-ODCE as a benchmark is at 50 percent. An eye-opening statistic is that out of 16 investors that identify themselves as deploying value-add and/or opportunistic strategies, only four, or 25 percent, add a premium to NCREIF when benchmarking. Most investors simply benchmark off the NFI-ODCE index, which generates a 7.0 to 8.0 percent return on average. This is more than 5.0 percent, and up to 10.0 percent, below GP-advertised target returns to value-add and opportunity funds.

My own review of PPD data, which incorporate a broader cross-section of public pension funds, shows similar variation in the chosen internal index benchmark. NPI and NFI-ODCE are by far the most popular benchmarks for PERE investors, including those with generous allocations to value-add and opportunity PERE funds. Thus, it appears to be common practice for public pension funds to take GP return targets and mark them down internally to bring them more in line with their own expected returns.

Benchmarking to the NFI-ODCE may not be inappropriate for pension fund portfolios that contain only low-levered core investment, but it certainly seems inappropriate for riskier PERE portfolios.[39] A differential of approximately 5.0 to 10.0 percent between returns targeted at the start of the fund's life and the internal benchmarks applied to assess realized investment performance is both meaningful and surprising. It particularly strikes me as highly distortionary from a resource allocation perspective, and analogous to Lake Wobegon self-assessment where below-average performance results in increasing funds flow for the GP sponsor and an above-average performance evaluation for the LP investor.

How can plan sponsors get away with this kind of thing? I am not really sure. It does not appear to be a violation of ERISA, and I am not aware of any fund sponsor that has been sued by plan beneficiaries for this benchmarking approach. Setting internal benchmarks at or somewhat above current overall portfolio return targets of 7.0 to 7.5 percent does not seem outrageous, until one considers the investment risks involved and that target returns promised by GPs are 5.0 to 10.0 percent higher than those referenced through internal benchmarks. The real issue here is that, unfortunately, it does not appear that increased allocations to PERE and other alternatives are solving pension fund underfunding problems. The problems in fact keeps getting worse, while increased allocations to alternatives further increase portfolio investment risk.[40]

## 5 CONCLUDING REMARKS: DO PENSION FUNDS POSE RISKS TO ECONOMIC AND FINANCIAL STABILITY?

### 5.1 Some General Observations

From a classical financial economics perspective, plan sponsors exhibit pathological investment behaviors. They tend to herd, making it harder for them to exploit truly valuable investment platforms; they display loss aversion, seeking out riskier investment opportunities to mitigate the "pain" associated with underfunding; they focus on absolute returns (IRR) rather than evaluating investment on a risk-adjusted, net present value basis; they seem indifferent to whether targeted returns are due to alpha or beta; they show a special aversion to having to observe asset price volatility; they engage in delusional benchmarking, giving themselves As and Bs for C and D work. All of these behaviors seem to be influenced by agency concerns and conflicts of interest that exist up and down the pension fund investment chain.

A few more words about alpha versus beta. The distinction between the two is crucially important, with significant macro and political economy implications. Alpha in PE is about earning extra-normal returns, typically as a result of superior GP skill. Alpha is not a priced risk of investment; rather, for an LP, it is about hooking up with a GP that is skillful at locating and creating value when nobody else can, and that then shares some of the gains with the LP. Evidence suggests, however, that true alpha in PERE fund investment is very hard to find.[41] In fact, based on their realized relative investment performance over the last 20-plus years, pension funds seem content to underperform on the order of 3–4 percent per year on average.

Without alpha, the only thing left to help meet aggressive return targets is beta. And beta is about systematic risk. Although pension funds may not seem to care about the distinction between alpha and beta, society should. Why? Pension funds are a big and important investor category, particularly in PE and especially in PERE. They are capable of and in fact do move CRE markets (Ghent, 2021). If pension funds systematically take large risks when trying to hit high portfolio return targets, some underfunded pension funds will "fail."[42, 43] Perhaps many will fail, and they may all fail at the same time.

It has been well established that underfunded pension funds pose a threat to local economic stability (see, e.g., Pagliari (2019) for a detailed analysis of Illinois and the city of Chicago). A recently released study by the Pew Charitable Trust documents the broader geographical risks, showing an increasing public pension liability funding gap. On average across all states, public pension liabilities are only 71 percent funded, having returned only 5.2 percent on average for the past 20 years (according to Wilshire Trust data). New Jersey and Illinoi are less than 40 percent funded, two other states are less than 50 percent funded and there are nine states overall that are less than 60 percent funded.

Should public pension funds be unable to meet their funding obligations, they will certainly seek and will inevitably obtain government bailouts. Bailouts will create big local economic problems, as costs will be borne by taxpayers and perhaps retirees who vote in elections. But are pension funds a systemic risk as well – a threat to financial stability? Many would answer no, as pension funds have historically not used much of their own leverage to finance asset ownership (they didn't need to give their ample funding sources). This is rapidly changing, however, as persistent and increasing underfunding problems are causing plan sponsors to "juice" their returns with debt.[44] Furthermore, investment in equities and especially PE and HFs are themselves levered. To the extent this leverage contributes to financial system risks, the concern is whether pension funds are enabling the firms and funds they invest in to deploy excessive amounts of debt.

A related concern is that we don't know enough about the interconnectedness of pension funds in the financial system (at least I don't). For example, it is estimated that shadow banks now originate more than 50 percent of residential mortgage loans in the US (Buchak et al., 2018), and that they have made major inroads on the commercial lending side. Many shadow banks are privately owned. For example, Burgiss data indicate that PE debt funds alone are valued in excess of $800 billion as of year-end 2019, growing by 11 times since year-end 2005. Pension funds and other institutional investors own those debt funds because they provide almost all of the funds' equity capital.[45] Are debt PE funds making loans to equity PE funds to finance their activities? If so, it sounds like a potential problem to me.[46]

Consider specifically the following "circle of life" that currently exists in the world of PERE. As described previously in Table 15.6, value-add and opportunity PERE funds invest in projects that often require significant renovation or ground-up development. These are risky projects and, as we know, pension funds are the largest investor class in these funds. These funds are often financed, as advertised in their offering documents, with mortgage debt or development loans at 50 to 75 percent loan to value or cost. Where do these PERE funds obtain their financing? In recent years a significant proportion has come from mortgage REITs (which are also a type of shadow bank). The mortgage REITs then place these risky mortgage/development loans into collateralized loan obligations (CLOs) and sell tranches to outside investors (more shadow banking).

Who purchases those tranches? Debt PERE funds are reportedly major investors in CRE-CLOs. Who owns those debt PERE funds? Pension funds and other institutional investors. Do the very same LPs that invest in the value-add or opportunity PERE funds (that own the CRE asset) also own the debt PERE funds (that purchase the CLOs issued by the mortgage REITs) that debt finance the CRE owned by the value-add or opportunity funds? In other words, are pension funds, possibly the very same pension funds, lending to themselves when they invest in both PERE debt and PERE equity funds? I don't yet know, but from a systemic financial risk perspective it would be good to find out.[47]

## 5.2    Concentration Risks

Pension fund concentration risks may serve to increase risks of economic and financial instability. Herding instincts among plan sponsors are the primary cause of concentration risk, which takes on several different forms.

One manifestation of herding-based concentration risk is a preference to invest with larger, more reputable GP sponsors. Blackstone is the behemoth and gold standard in the PE and especially the PERE fund world. Table 15.7 shows the top-10 PERE fundraisers over the past five years. Blackstone has raised approximately $65 billion in capital, more than double second-place Brookfield Asset Management. Blackstone and Brookfield together have nearly a 20 percent market share, with the top-10 firms showing a 40 percent market share. According to *Fortune* and other sources, Blackstone and Brookfield are the largest publicly traded CRE firms in the world.

Expect increasing GP concentration as a result of the pandemic. This happened after the GFC, with greater uncertainty causing capital to flow to the more reputable brand name firms. In the first half of 2020 alone, Blackstone raised $11.0 billion in PERE capital, three times as

Table 15.7  Top-10 GP sponsors in institutional capital raised, 2015–2019

| Rank | Manager | Headquarters | Capital raised ($ billion) | % share | Cum % share |
|---|---|---|---|---|---|
| 1 | Blackstone | New York | 64.93 | 13.1 | 13.1 |
| 2 | Brookfield Asset Management | Toronto | 29.01 | 5.9 | 19.0 |
| 3 | Starwood Capital Group | Miami | 16.86 | 3.4 | 22.4 |
| 4 | GLP | Singapore | 16.44 | 3.3 | 25.7 |
| 5 | Lone Star Funds | Dallas | 16.20 | 3.3 | 29.0 |
| 6 | AEW | Boston | 12.23 | 2.5 | 31.5 |
| 7 | The Carlyle Group | Washington, DC | 10.86 | 2.2 | 33.7 |
| 8 | Rockpoint Group | Boston | 10.74 | 2.2 | 35.8 |
| 9 | BentallGreenOak | New York | 9.71 | 2.0 | 37.8 |
| 10 | Angelo Gordon | New York | 9.45 | 1.9 | 39.7 |

*Note*: Data from PERE's listing of the top-100 PERE firms ranked by capital raised in the last five years.

much as the second-place firm. Together with Brookfield Asset Management, these two firms chalked up a 40 percent market share in 2020.

A concentration perspective begs the next question of how much investment in PERE originates from pension funds. Earlier I did back-of-the-envelope calculations showing that, as of 2001, pension funds had a significantly greater share of total PERE investment than they did in non-PERE and HF investment. How have pension fund investment shares in PERE evolved in more recent years, and has ownership concentration remained high?

In Table 15.8, I combine data from several sources to provide estimates of the US share of pension fund investment in PERE, non-PERE and HFs for years 2005 through 2019. PPD data are used to provide total public pension assets by year (PPD assets) and percentage allocations to PERE, non-PERE and HFs, respectively (PERE all, PE all, HF all). Burgiss data are used to generate annual aggregated fund capitalization for PERE and non-PERE (PERE NAV, PE NAV), while HF data are used to generate HF AUM by year. To obtain investment shares for PERE, PE and HFs, respectively, I multiply total public plan assets in a given year by the respective allocation percentage to obtain total investment by category. This number is then divided by the respective NAV or AUM for that year to obtain the share percentage (PERE share, PE share, HF share).

These percentages (in italic) indicate substantial pension fund investor shares in PERE since 2009, generally in the 40 to low 50 percent range. Pension fund investor shares in non-PERE and HFs are, in contrast, much lower. They are consistently in the 10 percent range for non-PERE while the HF shares are seen to increase over the past 15 years to the point where they now exceed 8 percent. These data therefore indicate substantial concentration of pension fund investment in PERE. At the same time there is increasing concentration of GP sponsors within PERE.[48]

With these significant pension fund investor share estimates in mind, I turn to yet another type of concentration risk: geographical. Where do Blackstone and the other major PERE fund sponsors like to focus their CRE investments? Core funds have typically focused on gateway "superstar" city markets – i.e., the largest most densely populated markets in the world, which also often serve as financial hubs – with increasing focus in those same markets coming from riskier fund types. Why the interest? These markets are touted as low risk due to their

Table 15.8  Pension fund investment shares in PERE, PE and HFs

| Year | PPD assets ($ trillion) | PERE all (%) | PERE NAV ($b) | PERE share (%) | PE all (%) | PE NAV ($b) | PE share (%) | HF all (%) | HF AUM ($b) | HF share (%) |
|---|---|---|---|---|---|---|---|---|---|---|
| 2005 | 2.442 | 4.4 | 143 | 75.1 | 3.9 | 851 | 11.2 | 0.5 | 1105 | 1.0 |
| 2006 | 2.630 | 5.0 | 190 | 68.7 | 4.1 | 1125 | 9.6 | 0.5 | 1465 | 0.9 |
| 2007 | 2.997 | 5.5 | 281 | 59.0 | 4.8 | 1422 | 10.1 | 1.3 | 1868 | 2.1 |
| 2008 | 2.713 | 6.9 | 322 | 57.8 | 6.6 | 1665 | 10.8 | 2.0 | 1407 | 3.9 |
| 2009 | 2.218 | 6.3 | 342 | 41.0 | 7.4 | 1724 | 9.6 | 2.8 | 1600 | 3.9 |
| 2010 | 2.450 | 6.0 | 356 | 41.4 | 8.3 | 1790 | 11.3 | 3.2 | 1917 | 4.1 |
| 2011 | 2.784 | 6.7 | 393 | 47.7 | 8.7 | 1945 | 12.4 | 3.7 | 2008 | 5.2 |
| 2012 | 2.791 | 7.9 | 414 | 53.5 | 9.2 | 2104 | 12.2 | 4.4 | 2252 | 5.4 |
| 2013 | 3.041 | 7.9 | 464 | 51.8 | 8.8 | 2253 | 11.8 | 5.4 | 2628 | 6.2 |
| 2014 | 3.404 | 7.7 | 500 | 52.2 | 8.5 | 2456 | 11.7 | 6.3 | 2845 | 7.6 |
| 2015 | 3.405 | 8.2 | 557 | 49.9 | 8.4 | 2658 | 10.8 | 6.7 | 2897 | 7.9 |
| 2016 | 3.375 | 8.8 | 603 | 49.5 | 8.5 | 2898 | 9.9 | 6.9 | 2971 | 7.8 |
| 2017 | 3.701 | 8.4 | 650 | 47.7 | 8.4 | 3178 | 9.8 | 7.0 | 3210 | 8.1 |
| 2018 | 3.859 | 8.4 | 707 | 45.7 | 9.0 | 3567 | 9.7 | 7.0 | 3102 | 8.7 |
| 2019 | 4.002 | 9.1 | 741 | 48.9 | 9.3 | 3867 | 9.6 | 6.8 | 3291 | 8.2 |

*Note*: PPD assets are in trillions of dollars, while NAV and AUM are in billions of dollars. Public pension asset and allocation data are from PPD. PERE and PE NAV data are from Burgiss. HF data are from HHF. Share percentages are calculated by first multiplying PPD assets by the allocation percentage, which is then divided by the NAV or AUM, whichever is applicable.

diversified economic bases, their educated workforce that is well positioned to compete in an evolving global marketplace and because of their enhanced liquidity at the asset level.

How concentrated is institutional investment in the largest CRE asset markets in the world and the US? Data from LaSalle Investment Management (2018) provide some estimates. In Table 15.9A the top-10 global CRE markets are listed together with institutional investor ownership share. The top-10 US markets are displayed in Table 15.9B. Three columns are shown: (1) total CRE available for investment; (2) total CRE that is institutionally owned; and (3) the percentage of total CRE available for investment that is owned by institutional investors. Office, retail and warehouse property are considered. Institutional owner-investors include pension funds, endowments, sovereign wealth funds, insurance companies and listed REITs. Breakdowns of individual institutional investor-owner categories are not available.

The ownership concentrations displayed in the tables are significant. As seen in Table 15.9A, Tokyo, which has the largest dollar amount of available CRE in the world, is two-thirds institutionally owned. London comes in at 75 percent and Hong Kong at 70 percent. Only Seoul and Shanghai have less than 40 percent institutional ownership. Institutional ownership percentages for top-10 US cities vary between 40 and 70 percent, with Washington, DC, showing the highest concentration of institutional ownership.

Ghent (2021) documents "delegated investor" shares that are disproportionately concentrated in the top-10 US markets. By combining her estimates with my previous estimates of pension fund investment shares in PERE funds, a back-of-the-envelope calculation indicates total pension fund investor shares in CRE in the top-10 US markets to be in the 20 percent range. The only other investor category that rivals this ownership concentration is publicly listed REITs, which have investor shares of 10 to 20 percent in the larger markets (see Ghent, 2021).

Table 15.9A  Institutional ownership of CRE in 10 largest markets – 2017: global

| City | Total CRE available ($ billion) | Institutionally owned CRE ($ billion) | Percentage institutionally owned (%) |
|---|---|---|---|
| 1 Tokyo | $800 | $528 | 66.0 |
| 2 New York City | $631 | $302 | 47.9 |
| 3 Los Angeles | $457 | $219 | 47.9 |
| 4 Hong Kong | $443 | $308 | 69.5 |
| 5 Paris | $419 | $281 | 67.1 |
| 6 London | $410 | $305 | 74.4 |
| 7 Seoul | $399 | $156 | 39.1 |
| 8 Singapore | $263 | $155 | 58.9 |
| 9 San Francisco | $256 | $164 | 64.1 |
| 10 Shanghai | *$228* | *$77* | *33.8* |
| Total | $4,305 | $2,495 | 58.0 |

Table 15.9B  Institutional ownership of CRE in 10 largest markets, 2017: US only

| City | Total CRE available ($ billion) | Institutionally owned CRE ($ billion) | Percentage institutionally owned (%) |
|---|---|---|---|
| 1 New York City | $631 | $302 | 47.9 |
| 2 Los Angeles | $457 | $219 | 47.9 |
| 3 San Francisco | $256 | $164 | 64.1 |
| 4 Chicago | $211 | $94 | 44.5 |
| 5 Washington, DC | $201 | $142 | 70.6 |
| 6 Boston | $178 | $92 | 51.7 |
| 7 Houston | $146 | $59 | 40.4 |
| 8 Dallas | $143 | $65 | 45.5 |
| 9 Miami | $139 | $67 | 48.2 |
| 10 Atlanta | *$116* | *$46* | *39.7* |
| Total | $2,478 | $1,250 | 50.4 |

*Note*: Data are from LaSalle Investment Management (2018).

As highlighted by Green Street Advisors ("Risky Misperceptions," July 16, 2018; "If It Looks Like a Duck," December 20, 2018; "Calculated Risk," January 10, 2019), CRE located in top-10 US cities have lower cap rates (higher transaction prices) and higher betas (price co-movement with the broader economy) than cities outside the top 10.[49] Green Street further argue that the cap rate-beta relation is due to risk misperceptions of institutional investors. Interestingly, Ghent (2021) documents the same low cap rate phenomenon in top-10 cities, implying that delegated investors move CRE prices in major markets. She argues that there are compensating liquidity benefits, however, as measured by increased CRE asset transaction volumes.

My previous analysis indicated that pension funds do not value liquidity in the PERE fund vehicles in which they invest. As LPs, why would they value liquidity in the CRE assets owned by the PERE funds they invest in and not in the funds themselves? It may be because asset-level liquidity provides fund sponsors the necessary (anticipated) flexibility to sell assets and close out funds early (or even on time) when market conditions warrant it. In support of this conjecture, Ghent (2021) finds that CRE assets owned by delegated investors have shorter ownership hold periods than assets held by other investor types.

Ling et al. (2020) present evidence that, over a sample period spanning January 21 through April 15 2020, as measured by REIT share prices, CRE properties located in densely populated gateway superstar cities in the US have experienced disproportionally larger negative price drops. Green Street Advisors show that "old economy" REITs owning multi-family, health care, net lease and office property delivered only 25 percent cumulative returns over the five-year period ending December 2020, whereas "new economy" REITs owning data centers, industrial, life science and cell tower property returned 135 percent ("Déjà vu," January 18, 2021). In another series of recent articles, Green Street Advisors highlight negative price and liquidity effects that have followed from the COVID-19 pandemic (e.g., "Unrequited Love," July 14, 2020, and "Urban Flight," August 19, 2020). High taxes and strict regulation, together with increases in crime and remote work in large urban markets, are combining to change the conventional wisdom about gateway markets.

In summary, there are several layers of risks associated with the concentrated levels of pension fund ownership in CRE. These include: (1) GP sponsor concentration risks, with increasingly concentrated fundraising in PERE by a handful of GP sponsors; (2) LP concentration risks, with high LP ownership shares in PERE by pension funds; and (3) geographical concentration risks, with high ownership of CRE assets by pension funds in the largest cities in the US and across the globe. Given the sheer quantity of pension assets, estimated at more than $40 trillion globally, along with the leverage baked into their increasingly prominent alternative investment platforms, and given the underfunded pension problems that are forecasted to get worse, it seems hard not to conclude that pension funds pose some real risks to economic and financial stability.

### 5.3    Will the Pension Fund-Real Estate Marriage Last?

One might summarize this chapter as documenting a shotgun marriage between pension funds and real estate that looked good on paper and seemed ripe with possibilities. But soon after there were bumps in the road and then a mid-life crisis of sorts. After that, things became a bit dysfunctional, with money issues at the center of things. But will the marriage end in divorce? Unlikely, unless beneficiaries start challenging prudent person investor rules and regulators intervene, deciding that in the interests of everyone involved that one of the partners (pension funds) requires protection from the other.

The truth is that there is a strong co-dependency between pension funds and PERE that will be hard to break, suggesting that the marriage will continue for the foreseeable future.[50] PERE without pension fund capital would be disruptive, particularly in larger gateway-superstar city markets. REITs could, however, and probably would, step in and pick up a lot of the ownership slack in the US. Pension funds without the PERE investment alternative would be less disruptive, as there is no shortage of investment opportunities – traditional or alternative – available to investors.

The wildcard at the moment is, of course, what will happen as a result of the COVID-19 pandemic. Pension underfunding problems will likely get worse. PERE and PE funds more broadly have already taken some significant write-downs. With a crisis comes opportunity, but as it did in response to the GFC, the Fed is operating as a giant HF. These operations may be valuable for society, but they limit opportunity for HFs and PE to exploit market imbalances. Structural changes to the global and US economies in response to the pandemic are already well under way. CRE will look and act differently by the time we come out the other side of this crisis. It will be particularly interesting to see how the large densely populated gateway-superstar cities evolve, and how PERE funds perform in response.

## ACKNOWLEDGMENTS

I wish to thank Da Li for his excellence research assistance. I also want to thank Mitch Bollinger, Greg Brown, John Cochrane, Jeff Fisher, Andra Ghent, Jacques Gordon, Mike Kirby, Charles Leung, David Ling, Greg MacKinnon, Jacob Sagi, Calvin Schnure, David Shulman and an anonymous referee for their helpful input and suggestions. I am particularly grateful to Joe Pagliari, who has provided detailed commentary and guidance throughout this project, and who brought several of the prominent issues addressed herein to my attention. This, however, is not meant to implicate anyone, as all views, opinions, mistakes and other shortcomings are mine alone.

## NOTES

1. For additional background and analysis on commercial property from a macro perspective, see, among others, Gort et al. (1999), Kan et al. (2004) and Ng et al. (2020).
2. The 20 percent market share comes from $4 trillion of investable CRE in the US, with a bit over $0.8 trillion of pension fund assets allocated to CRE. Pension fund assets and DB shares for many countries in the OECD data are either missing or unreliable, so I omit a global analysis. But given pension fund interest in CRE located around the world (primarily in gateway-superstar city markets, where much of the value is concentrated), global ownership percentages are likely similar to those of the US.
3. Private CRE fund performance has been much studied, using primarily NCREIF data. But pension fund motives and investment objectives are generally either taken for granted or ignored. Ghent (2021) is a recent exception. I will emphasize the influence that pension fund investment has had on investment vehicle fund structure and performance, which has received little attention. There are some good articles from a macro-historical perspective that were written in the 1990s and early 2000s, but not much to my knowledge has been done since; see, e.g., Winograd (2004).
4. According to a recent article published in the *PREA Quarterly* ("Leveraging History," Spring 2020), 60 percent of PERE fund investors favor value-add funds and 23 percent favor opportunistic. My own data from Preqin indicates that 85 percent of PERE funds with vintage dates from 2009 to 2019 are classified as value-add or opportunistic.
5. Throughout this chapter, I am going to abuse standard terminology by taking PERE to mean any type of CRE private equity fund that pension funds will consider for investment. This includes open-end core funds as well as closed-end value-add and opportunity funds. I will specifically refer to the NCREIF and the NFI-ODCE indices when I am primarily thinking of open-end core investment funds.
6. I will get into those structural and compositional differences later in the chapter. For now I note that, contrary to frequent assertions by industry participants, it is not clear, particularly in light of the COVID-19 pandemic that has revealed stark performance differences between people-centric core CRE and tech-centric CRE such as cell towers and data centers, that investment in the Nareit index poses greater risk than investing in core CRE that comprise the NFI-ODCE index.
7. For more on ERISA, see, among other possible sources, www.investopedia.com/terms/e/erisa .asp. Defined benefit retirement plans are distinct from defined contribution retirement plans. With defined benefit plans, investments are made by the plan sponsor on behalf of plan participants.

There are pre-specified formulas that determine retirement benefits to be paid to retirees. Defined contribution plans are, in contrast, participant self-directed and are often chosen from a menu of investment alternatives provided by the employer. No preset formulas are applied, nor are there promises of payouts made to the participant in advance. See, among many others, Novy-Marx and Rauh (2009) for more on this distinction.

8. The real estate data included residential, commercial and farmland. Interestingly, the size weights of the three components are never disclosed, so one does not know the relative share of commercial property within the index. Also, the commercial return data do not start until 1960, whereas both the residential and farmland data go back to 1947.

9. Prudential formed the first commingled real estate fund vehicle in 1970, called the Prudential Property Investment Separate Account, or PRISA. Note that PRISA conveniently rhymes with ERISA, suggesting not only prudence but compliance.

10. NCREIF stands for the National Council of Real Estate Investment Fiduciaries. For additional information, see www.ncreif.org.

11. Open-end commingle funds did advertise redemption on a quarterly basis, suggesting a certain degree of liquidity. But the S&L crisis revealed that LP share liquidity was largely illusory. This followed because, when investors demanded liquidity as a result of the industry downturn, redemptions were often denied because LPs were all requesting redemptions at the same time and in a depressed asset market that itself was highly illiquid.

12. Ibbotson and Siegel (1984) recognize that value estimates are largely appraisal-based and that returns in their index were smoothed. But they do not address the implications of smoothing for variance and covariance calculations.

13. For more recent estimates at the low end of the difference range, see Ling and Naranjo (2015). They carefully match by property type and location to control for risk differences. I will note that compositional differences between the NFI-ODCE and the FTSE-Nareit Equity indices have increased over time based on property type. Nareit is increasingly comprised of "tech-oriented" CRE such as life sciences, infrastructure (e.g., cell towers) and data centers. This is clearly not traditional people-centric core real estate exposure, but it does reflect the shifting role of CRE in the modern economy. There are also leverage differences between NCREIF and Nareit, but these have narrowed significantly over the last 15 years. Moreover, Giambona et al. (2017) and Riddiough and Steiner (2019) find that lower-levered REITs deliver higher stock returns than higher-levered REITs, even in bull markets. In the end, despite their differences, given the difficulties in accurately measuring true return variances and covariances to private direct CRE investment, it is not clear to me whether investment in the Nareit index is any riskier than investment in NFI-ODCE. As will be discussed in greater detail later in this chapter, recent events indicate that core investment concentrated in urban gateway markets (as reflected in NCREIF) is actually riskier than investment in the better diversified Nareit index.

14. The S&L crisis along with Japan's banking-real estate problems of the early to middle 1990s spurred a large macro literature on credit cycles. See Kiyotaki and Moore (1997) for the seminal work on the topic. Also see Chen and Leung (2007) for an analysis of property market spillover effects.

15. An underappreciated outcome of the REIT initial public offering boom in the US is the migration of top managerial talent from the private to the public side of the market. This shift in the balance of talent persists to this day. For additional analysis on talent migration into the REIT sector, see Packer et al. (2014).

16. Early growth was also spurred by new NCREIF members that added their assets into the data-tracking pool.

17. As noted earlier, I use PERE to encompass everything from core to opportunistic investment strategies, with a focus on equity funds. PERE therefore refers to all forms of institutional (primarily pension fund) investment in private CRE equity funds.

18. Allocations to CRE will be discussed in detail in Section 4.

19. The 13.8 percent non-PERE share derives from a 3.62 percent pension fund allocation to PE multiplied by $2.075 billion of pension assets reported in 2001. The resulting number is divided by the aggregated PE NAV of $543.5 billion to produce the 13.8 percent share. The HF share follows

404  *Handbook of real estate and macroeconomics*

a similar method based on a .342 percent pension fund allocation and $539 billion in HF AUM in 2001.
20. As seen in Figure 15.8, the Nareit index recovered quickly after Q1 2009 while NFI-ODCE displayed its usual subdued and lagged response to changing market conditions. If returns to NCREIF versus Nareit are instead calculated over 2004–2009, NCREIF returned 1.71 percent while Nareit returned 4.99 percent.
21. Novy-Marx and Rauh (2009) comment on Ricardian equivalence, emphasizing that full information is required for equivalence to obtain. They state, "without public knowledge about the extent of the pension underfunding, individuals do not know how much to set aside for their children to help them pay off this debt" (p. 206).
22. See Andonov et al. (2017) for evidence.
23. "Gambling for resurrection" was a term commonly used during the S&L crisis of the 1980s to describe S&L behavior when it had little or no net worth. Standard corporate finance refers to this as the "risk-shifting problem," whereby financial distress causes equity holders to instruct managers to take on risky, negative NPV projects, hoping to realize upside gains if things go better than expected and disproportionately shift the losses to bondholders if things don't.
24. See, e.g., Rauh (2016), who states, "In order to target such returns [of 7.5–8.0 percent per year], [pension] systems have taken increased investment positions in the stock market and other risky asset classes such as private equity, hedge funds, and real estate." See Andonov et al. (2017) for additional detailed evidence. For evidence on incentives to reach for yield in a low inflationary and interest rate environment, see Becker and Ivashina (2015) and Choi and Kronlund (2017).
25. The canonical citation on loss aversion is Tversky and Kahneman (1979). For additional background, see Kahneman et al. (1991).
26. A shortcoming of the Δ-IRR approach when measuring relative returns is that cash flows used to generate the IRR for the benchmark portfolio do not exactly match cash flows to the fund in terms of timing and duration. A better method in that regard is the direct alpha method of Gredil et al. (2014). However, this method requires detailed cash flows, which are mostly unavailable in the Preqin data.
27. There is in fact limited liquidity in closed-end fund LP shares, but there are no pricing indices based on secondary market trades with which to benchmark fund performance. It is generally known that LP shares will typically sell at substantial discounts to current fund NAVs, in the range of 10–25 percent. See "Secondaries Gather Strength to Navigate the Crisis," *Private Equity International*, June 17, 2020, www.prviateequityinternational.com/. Funds of funds are known to purchase LP interests. The GP may also make a market for the shares to better control the identity of the LP interest holder. See also "A Guide to Limited Partner Secondary Sales for Real Estate Private Equity Investors," *PREA Quarterly*, Winter 2020.
28. To construct this figure I use average IRR by vintage year instead of weighted average IRR as reported in Table 15.6.
29. LP performance can vary within a fund because of differences in fees or how distributions are calculated.
30. Pagliari (2020) is a companion paper published after the 2019 paper, but written prior to the 2019 paper. Its sample period ends in 2012, with findings that are generally consistent with the 2019 paper.
31. PME is defined as the PV of net-of-fee LP cash inflows divided by the PV of net-of-fee cash outflows. Discount rates are time-varying realized rates of return to an appropriate benchmark index over the relevant fund-holding period.
32. Riddiough and Wiley (2021) use the all-equity FTSE-Nareit index as the benchmark index. They also use LP cash flow data to calculate PMEs, whereas in this study I use IRRs provided by GPs to Preqin.
33. Also see Arnold et al. (2019). Using data from Cambridge Associates they document performance of value-add and opportunity funds with vintage dates ranging from 2000 to 2013 in the 7.0 to 9.0 percent return range. This is consistent with other findings, if not on the lower end of the performance range.
34. Some have argued that part of the illiquidity premium paid by LPs is actually a control premium, whereby the large LP fund investors (often pension funds) can influence initial fund structure and

*Pension funds and private equity real estate* 405

fees, as well as have input on certain operating decisions when the fund is active. It is an open empirical question whether control is real and whether it generates tangible benefits for the LP investor.
35. Again, some readers may object to my failure to adjust for perceived risk differences between the two indices. I stand by my earlier commentary, noting further that recent events have revealed significant geographical concentration risks embedded in the core-based NCREIF index. Which category of investment is, for example, riskier in light of COVID-19: retail malls and office property located in New York City or cell towers and data centers dispersed throughout the US and the rest of the world?
36. Some have argued that Nareit was not investable prior to the REIT initial public offering boom of the early and mid-1990s due to the small scale of the sector and the five or fewer rule that did not contain a look-through provision at the time. If instead the 27-year period ranging from 1993 to 2019 is considered, NFI-ODCE returns increase to 7.89 percent while Nareit returns decrease to 10.91 percent. This narrows the outperformance gap from almost 5.0 to 3.0 percent, which is probably more representative of actual longer-run differences. The performance differential is clearly substantial nonetheless.
37. That said, one must be cognizant that 27 or even 42 years of quarterly observations do not, statistically speaking, generate a whole lot of power. Even a century's worth of higher frequency stock return data cannot definitively indicate whether there is a positive relation between risk and return – see Lundblad (2007).
38. For a thorough empirical analysis of after-fee private equity returns that conform closely to predictions of Berk and Green (2004), as well as for estimates of carried interest fees paid in PE, see Phalippou (2020).
39. According to an article published in the Winter 2020 edition of the *PREA Quarterly* ("Real Estate Benchmarks: Challenges and Implications for Performance Measurement"): "While non-core fund indices do exist, they remain in their infancy ... until better options are established, investors should be aware of the shortcomings of existing benchmarks and understand the limitations of benchmarking and performance evaluation ... no truly satisfactory benchmark is currently available to [non-core] investors."
40. Many argue that diversification benefits to alternatives more than offset liquidity and other investment risks. It is important to keep in mind the distinction between genuine diversification and illusory benefits reflected by stale prices that are correlated with public market alternatives. In short, I am dubious of the advertised diversification benefits, particularly given the close substitute that exists with REITs in CRE investment.
41. In ongoing work with Da Li, we are finding no evidence that PERE LPs exhibit investment persistence of their own by systematically matching with high-performing GPs.
42. I use failure here to mean failure to meet retirement funding obligations. Pension funds won't fail in the usual sense, they will be bailed out.
43. An often overlooked fact about reaching for return by taking greater risk is that it can be self-defeating due to the standard convexity correction involved when converting arithmetic returns into geometric returns (also referred to as *volatility drag*). For example, take two assets that are identical in value at 100 but differ in risk. One asset's standard deviation of return is 10 percent and the other is 30 percent. A one standard deviation increase and then decrease in return to the first asset over two periods results in an asset valued 99, resulting in a 1 percent decline in value (and a 0 percent arithmetic return). The other asset experiences the same one standard deviation increase and then decrease in return over two periods. It is worth 91, experiencing a 9 percent reduction in value (and a 0 percent arithmetic return). The general formula for the convexity correction with normally distributed returns is $r_{Geometric} = r_{Arithmetic} - \sigma^2/2$.
44. In June 2020 CALPERS announced it would begin to use leverage much more systematically, at about 20 percent of assets on average, stating "There is no alternative" (see "Calpers CIO Eyes More Private Equity, Leverage to Hit Target," and "For CalPERS CIO, Revolution is Now," *Pensions and Investment*). More recently, the chief information officer of CalSTERs was quoted as saying, "We have found we may have to accept the higher loan-to-value ratios in order to achieve the core returns we're promising the teachers of California" (*PREA Quarterly*, Winter 2021).
45. For example, during the mid-2000s I was on the board of a private "b-piece" CMBS buyer. It was essentially a shadow bank that purchased the risky securities carved out of securitized CRE mort-

gage pools. Our equity investors were public pension funds and PE sponsors whose equity money was sourced from public pension funds.
46. See also Pagliari (2017).
47. One might argue that gains or losses from lending to oneself are simply a transfer. This ignores misallocations, deadweight losses and transaction costs incurred from the transfers, however. Such arrangements usually end badly for all involved, including the innocent, due to the severe resource misallocations that can occur.
48. There is measurement error in calculating these share percentages. The dollar allocations into alternative investment categories derive from US-based DB public pension plans only. There are other types of DB pension plans, such as corporate, as well as non-US DB pension plans that invest in CRE in the US. Thus the numerator in our investor share calculation is biased towards the low side. On the other hand, the Burgiss and HHF data used to calculate the denominator in the investor share percentage do not contain the universe of all fund activity. They contain only activity associated with funds that contribute data to Burgiss and HHF. This biases the share percentage upwards. Finally, Burgiss and HHF data are for global funds, not just US funds, which biases fund sizes upward and the share percentage downward.
49. Also see Gang et al. (2020).
50. In a Salomon Brothers report written 30 years ago in 1990, David Shulman recognized this co-dependency, stating: "Favoring this [appraisal as a means to maintain the 'illusion of value'] approach is the 'iron triangle' of investment managers, plan sponsor staff and consultants, each of whom has a vested interest in keeping reported values high. Simply put, the investment manager sold the deal, the plan sponsor staff bought it and the consultant blessed it."

# REFERENCES

Andonov, A., R. Bauer and M. Cremers (2017), "Pension fund asset allocation and liability discount rates," *Review of Financial Studies*, 30, 2555–2595.
Arnold, T., D. Ling and A. Naranjo (2019), "Private equity real estate funds: Returns, risk exposures and persistence," *Journal of Portfolio Management*, 24–42.
Asness, C. (2019), "The illiquidity discount?" *AQR Perspective*, December 19.
Aubry, J-P and C. Crawford (2019), "Impact of public sector assumed returns on investment choices," *Center for Retirement Research*, January.
Becker, B. and V. Ivashina (2015), "Reaching for yield in the bond market," *Journal of Finance*, 70, 863–902.
Berk, J. and R. Green (2004), "Mutual fund flows and performance in rational markets," *Journal of Political Economy*, 112, 1269–1295.
Bodnaruk, A. and A. Siminov (2016), "Loss-averse preference, performance, and career success of institutional investors," *Review of Financial Studies*, 29, 3140–3176.
Bollinger, M. and J. Pagliari, Jr. (2019), "Another look at private real estate returns by strategy," *Journal of Portfolio Management*, 45, 1–18.
Brown, J. and D. Wilcox (2009), "Discounting state and local pension liabilities," *American Economic Review: Papers and Proceedings*, 99, 538–542.
Brunnermeier, M. and L.H. Pedersen (2009), "Market liquidity and funding liquidity," *Review of Financial Studies*, 22, 2201–2238.
Buchak, G., G. Matvos, T. Piskorski and A. Seru (2018), "Fintech, regulatory arbitrage, and the rise of shadow banks," *Journal of Financial Economics*, 130, 453–492.
Chen, N.-K. and C.K.Y. Leung (2007), "Asset spillover, collateral and crises: with an application to property market policy," *Journal of Real Estate Finance and Economics*, 37, 351–385.
Choi, J. and M. Kronlund (2017), "Reaching for yield in corporate bond mutual funds," *Review of Financial Studies*, 31, 1930–1965.
Fama, E. (1970), "Efficient capital markets: a review of theory and empirical work," *Journal of Finance*, 25, 383–417.

Franzoni, F. and J. Marin (2006), "Pension plan funding and stock market efficiency," *Journal of Finance*, 61, 921–956.

Franzoni, F., E. Nowak and L. Phalippou (2012), "Private equity performance and liquidity risk," *Journal of Finance*, 67, 2341–2373.

Gang, J., L. Peng and T. Thibodeau (2020), "Risk and returns of income producing properties: Core versus non-core," *Real Estate Economics*, 48, 476–503.

Geltner, D. (1991), "Smoothing in appraisal-based returns," *Journal of Real Estate Finance and Economics*, 4, 327–345.

Ghent, A. (2021), "What's wrong with Pittsburgh? Delegated investors and liquidity concentration," *Journal of Financial Economics*, 139(2), 337–358.

Ghent, A., W. Torous and R. Valkanov (2019), "Commercial real estate as an asset class," *Annual Review of Financial Economics*, 11, 53–71.

Giambona, E., S. M. Antonio and T. J. Riddiough (2017), "Real Assets, Collateral and the Limits of Debt Capacity," *Real Estate Economics*, 46, 836–886.

Gompers, P., S. Kaplan and V. Mukharlyamov (2016), "What do private equity firms say they do?" *Journal of Financial Economics*, 121, 449–476.

Gort, M., J. Greenwood and P. Rupert (1999), "Measuring the rate of technological progress in structures," *Review of Economic Dynamics*, 2, 207–230.

Gredil, O., B. Griffiths and R. Stucke (2014), "Benchmarking private equity: The direct alpha method," Unpublished manuscript, SSRN.

Gupta, A. and S. Van Nieuwerburgh (2021), "Valuing private equity strip by strip," *Journal of Finance*, 76(6), 3255–3307.

Ibbotson, R. and L. Siegel (1984), "Real estate returns: A comparison with other investments," *Real Estate Economics*, 12, 219–242.

Kahneman, D., J. Knetsch and R. Thaler (1991), "Anomalies: The endowment effect, loss aversion, and status quo bias," *Journal of Economic Perspectives*, 5, 193–206.

Kan, K., S.K.-S. Kwong and C.K.-Y. Leung (2004), "The dynamics and volatility of commercial and residential property prices: Theory and evidence," *Journal of Regional Science*, 44, 95–123.

Kaplan, S. and A. Schoar (2005), "Private equity returns: Persistence and capital flows," *Journal of Finance*, 60, 1791–1823.

Kiyotaki, N. and J. Moore (1997), "Credit cycles," *Journal of Political Economy*, 105, 211–248.

Korteweg, Arthur and Morten Sorensen (2017), "Skill and Luck in Private Equity Performance," *Journal of Financial Economics*, 124, 535–562.

LaSalle Investment Management (2018), "The real estate investment universe," March.

Leombroni, M., M. Piazzesi, M. Schneider and C. Rogers (2020), "Inflation and the price of real assets," NBER working paper.

Li, D. and T. Riddiough (2020), "GP performance and investable persistence in private equity real estate," Unpublished manuscript, University of Wisconsin – Madison.

Ling, D. and A. Naranjo (2015), "Returns and information transmission dynamics in public and private real estate markets," *Real Estate Economics*, 43, 163–208.

Ling, D., C. Wang and T. Zhou (2020), "A first look at the impact of COVID-19 on commercial real estate prices: Asset level evidence," *Review of Asset Pricing Studies*, 10, 669–704.

Lundblad, C. (2007), "The risk-return tradeoff in the long run: 1836–2003," *Journal of Financial Economics*, 85, 123–150.

MacKinnon, G. (2019), "The state of benchmarking in commercial real estate," *PREA Quarterly*, Spring, 24–26.

Ng, J.C.Y., C.K.Y. Leung and S. Chen (2020), "Corporate real estate holding and stock returns: International evidence," Unpublished manuscript, City University of Hong Kong.

Novy-Marx, R. and J. Rauh (2009), "The liabilities and risks of state-sponsored pension plans," *Journal of Economic Perspectives*, 23, 191–210.

Packer, F., T. Riddiough and J. Shek (2014), "A global tour of commercial property and reit markets," *International Real Estate Review*, 17, 241–274.

Pagliari, J. (2017), "High-yield lending: It's good until it's not," *Journal of Portfolio Management*.

Pagliari, J. (2019), "Thoughts on the looming pension problems facing Chicago, Cook County and Illinois," Unpublished manuscript, University of Chicago.

Pagliari, J. (2020), "Real estate returns by strategy: Have value-added and opportunistic funds pulled their weight?" *Real Estate Economics*, 48, 89–134.

Phalippou, L. (2020), "An inconvenient fact: Private equity returns and the billionaire factory," *Journal of Investing*, 30, 11–39.

Rauh, J. (2016), "Hidden debt, hidden deficits," Hoover Institute.

Riddiough, T. and E. Steiner (2019), "Financial Flexibility and Manager-Shareholder Conflict: Evidence from REITs," *Real Estate Economics*, 48, 200–239.

Riddiough, T. and J. Wiley (2021), "Private funds for ordinary people: Fees, fund flows and performance," *Journal of Financial and Quantitative Analysis*, April 7.

Riddiough, T., M. Moriarty and P.J. Yeatman (2005), "Private versus publicly held asset investment performance," *Real Estate Economics*, 33, 121–146.

Ross, S. and R. Zisler (1991), "Risk and return in real estate," *Journal of Real Estate Finance and Economics*, 4, 175–190.

Sorensen, M., N. Wang and J. Yang (2014), "Valuing private equity," *Review of Financial Economics*, 27, 1977–2021.

Tversky, A. and D. Kahneman (1979), "Prospect theory: An analysis of decision under risk," *Econometrica*, 47, 263–292.

Winograd, B. (2004), "US pension funds and real estate: Still crazy after all these years," in W. Seabrooke, P. Kent and H. H.-H. How (eds), *International Real Estate: An Institutional Approach*, Oxford: Blackwell.

# APPENDIX: GLOSSARY OF TERMS, ABBREVIATIONS AND ACRONYMS

| | |
|---|---|
| alpha | A measure of investment performance that functions independently of systematic and idiosyncratic risk effects. In PE, positive alpha is often attributed to GP skill and typically measured on a net-of-fee basis. |
| alternative investment | Refers to non-traditional investments that fall outside of the tradition set that includes listed equity, corporate bonds and Treasury securities. Private equity and hedge funds are the most prominent alternatives held by pension funds. |
| appraisal smoothing | The act of creating an autoregressive relation in return measurement. Typically attributed to the fact that appraisers anchor on prior period asset values when updating current asset values. Appraisal smoothing artificially lowers return volatility and return correlation in relation to securities traded in informationally efficient markets. |
| AUM | Assets under management. Often used to measure the size of hedge funds. |
| BO | Buyout fund. A category of PE, often referred to as an LBO due to the prominent use of leverage. |
| Burgiss | Data provider of PE fund performance and related information. |
| CLO | Collateralized loan obligation. Short-term loans used to finance assets purchased by value-add and opportunity PERE funds. Loans often get pooled together and sold as part of a CLO transaction. |
| CMBS | Commercial mortgage-backed security. Commercial mortgages that are pooled, securitized and sold to investors. |
| conduit loan | A newly originated CRE mortgage loan that is placed into a CMBS. |
| consultant | An agent hired by a pension fund plan sponsor to assist in making investment and portfolio allocation decisions. Often used to help ensure compliance with ERISA and other relevant regulations. |
| core fund | See Table 15.6A. |
| core-plus fund | See Table 15.6A. |
| CRE | Commercial real estate, generally indicating income-producing, investor-owned property. |
| DB plan | Defined benefit pension fund, whereby plan participants are promised certain retirement benefits, calculated according to predefined formulas, regardless of how fund investments actually perform. |
| ERISA | Employee Retirement Income Security Act of 1974. Regulation that set standards for participation, vesting, benefit accrual and funding of retirement benefits for plan participants. Established the plan sponsor as a fiduciary with a duty to work in the best interests of retirement plan participants. |
| FTSE-Nareit index | Index of publicly traded US equity REIT stocks that provides broad exposure to the CRE investment market. See www.reit.org for additional information. |

| | |
|---|---|
| GASB 25 | A pension fund accounting standard that provides pension funds discretion to choose their discount rate when determining the present value of fund liabilities. Many argue that the chosen discount rates are too high, and liability estimates are too low, given the true risks associated with the liability stream. |
| GFC | Global Financial Crisis, 2007–2009. |
| GP | General partner of a PE fund. GPs exert day-to-day control of the fund, earning fees for their services that can include, among other services, the provision of investment, financing, operational and governance expertise. |
| HF | Hedge fund. Generally invests in liquid securities, looking for market inefficiencies that provide opportunities to generate superior risk-adjusted returns. |
| illiquidity premium | The apparent price *premium* paid by pension funds for illiquid PERE funds. The premium results because the fund investment vehicle inhibits price discovery to create the illusion of low return volatility. *See also* appraisal smoothing, volatility veil. |
| institutional investor | Often used to indicate a broad set of entities that invest other people's money. Can include mutual funds and other intermediaries. In a PE setting, institutional investors are typically a subset of investors that includes pension funds, endowments and sovereign wealth funds. |
| Lake Wobegon effect | Idea introduced by Garrison Keiller on his US radio show that, in Lake Wobegon, everyone is above average. This very notion contradicts the definition of a population distribution and the average, indicating an intentional or unintentional bias. Sometimes used to refer to grade inflation at universities, among other things. |
| LP | Limited partner. In PE, the LP is an equity investor in a fund offered by a GP sponsor. LPs earn returns on their investment and pay GPs fees for their management services. |
| Nareit index | See the FTSE-Nareit index reference. |
| NAV | Net asset value. In PE, an estimate, typically provided by the GP, of the equity value of the fund prior to liquidation. NAV is known to be subject to appraisal bias, among other possible biases, that also include a consistent upward bias that dissipates as the fund converges towards its liquidation date. |
| NAV smoothing | *See* appraisal smoothing, NAV. |
| NCREIF index | National Council of Real Estate Investment Fiduciaries. Members contribute private investment data used to create index benchmarks. For more, see www.ncreif.org. |
| NFI-ODCE index | NCREIF Fund index, composed of open-end, diversified core equity funds. These funds are typically levered, with returns reported on a net-of-fee basis. |
| NPI index | NCREIF property index. The original index of unlevered core open-end funds. Index returns are reported prior to fees and on an unlevered basis. |
| OECD | Organisation for Economic Co-operation and Development. Among other things, a broad-based data provider, including the provision of information on pension funds across the world. |

| | |
|---|---|
| opportunity fund | See Table 15.6A. |
| PE | Private equity. An illiquid form of investment that typically relies on the GP-LP ownership and control structure. Under the PE umbrella are buyout, venture capital and private equity real estate funds. Newer categories have emerged in recent years, including prominently infrastructure funds. |
| PERE | Private equity real estate. As used in this chapter, refers to all forms of private investment vehicles available to pension funds and other institutional investors, including open- and closed-end funds. A more common usage is for closed-end funds only, which include value-add and opportunity funds. |
| persistence | The notion that, if GPs are skilled at creating value for their investors on a risk-adjusted basis, skill and therefore investment performance should persist over time. |
| plan sponsor | Entity designated as a fiduciary whose duty it is to act in the best interests of pension plan participants. |
| PPD | Public Plan Database, housed at Boston College. |
| PREA | Pension Real Estate Association, the trade group for pension funds and their agents that invest in all forms of real estate. See www.prea.org for more. |
| Preqin | Data provider of PE fund information that includes performance measures. |
| prudent man rule | Part of ERISA legislation, and analogous to the business judgment rule whereby plan sponsors are allowed to take risks and actions on behalf of pension plan participants as long as the risk taking and actions are deemed to be reasonable and prudent, and in the best interests of the plan participants. |
| REIT | Real estate investment trust. An investment vehicle that holds equity or debt interests in real estate assets. It does not pay taxes at the entity level as long as it satisfies certain operating, investing and financing criteria. REITs come in a number of different forms. In this chapter I focus primarily on listed REITs that hold ownership (equity) positions in CRE assets. |
| return targeting | Refers specifically to one of two alternative practices. The first is the practice of GPs establishing *ex ante* net-of-fee fund return estimates for LPs at the time of fundraising. The second is the practice of pension funds to establish investment return goals or targets in order to satisfy overall portfolio return objectives or to attempt to close underfunding gaps. Return targeting emphasizes investment return over investment risk, often revealed through the use of IRR in assessing investment performance. |
| S&L crisis | The widespread failures of savings and loans in the US in the late 1980s and early 1990s. CRE loans were at the center of the crisis. The resolution of the crisis resulted in the introduction of new ways to intermediate capital for CRE, the most prominent of which were REITs, CMBs and opportunity-vulture fund investing. |
| shadow bank | An entity that intermediates debt in one form or another, and that operates outside the established formal commercial banking system. |

| | |
|---|---|
| sponsor | The parent organization of the GP. |
| value-add fund | See Table 15.6A. |
| venture capital | A type of PE fund that focuses on nurturing start-up firms, with a goal of creating viable products and sustainable management teams that can survive as going concerns. |
| volatility drag | Refers to the fact that actual returns as measured by the geometric mean differ from, and are typically lower than, arithmetic mean returns. Greater volatility in returns increases the drag in realized geometric returns due to an asymmetry in changes to investment value as a result of +/− changes in return. |
| volatility veil | Refers to illiquid private fund vehicles whose reported values and returns are smoothed and lagged over time. Some investors such as pension funds apparently find the veil to be beneficial, and are willing to pay a premium to own assets held by those fund vehicles. |

# 16. A mayor's perspective on tackling air pollution
*Shihe Fu and V. Brian Viard*

## 1  INTRODUCTION

Suppose you are the recently elected mayor of Model City, a large city facing severe air pollution. You ran on a platform promising voters that you will improve the city's air quality. How would you fulfill your promise? What are the sources and social costs of air pollution? What policies can you use to reduce the pollution levels your constituents face? How should you decide how much to spend reducing the pollution levels in your city?

First of all, you should know that you are not alone. The World Health Organization (WHO) estimates that in 2012, 90 percent of people living in urban areas experienced air pollution that exceeded the WHO's recommended limits and that air quality was generally declining (WHO, 2016). If you are a mayor in a lower-income country then your task is likely even more difficult. Pollution is worse in low- and middle-income countries, with 98 percent of cities not meeting guidelines compared to 56 percent in high-income countries (WHO, 2016). The consequences of such high levels of pollution are dire. The WHO estimates that in 2012 ambient air pollution caused 3 million deaths, 87 percent of which were in low- and middle-income countries, and associated health complications caused 85 million disability-adjusted life years (DALYs) (WHO, 2016).[1]

This chapter's goal is to provide useful advice on these questions for mayors based on high-quality academic economic studies. What do these economic studies offer to help mayors better understand the sources of air pollution, the costs it imposes on cities, and policies that are effective in reducing it? Section 2 describes the local and imported sources of air pollution in cities. Section 3 explores the economic costs that air pollution imposes on cities via its impact on health, mortality, psychological well-being, labor productivity, labor mobility, and out-migration. Section 4 discusses the effectiveness of pollution-reduction policies that cities around the world have implemented – a possible tool box for mayors. Section 5 discusses whether pollution policy design and implementation is compatible with mayors' incentives, including the role of information. The last section summarizes how mayors can use the insights from the studies reviewed in this chapter and proposes future research directions.

There are earlier economic review articles on air pollution and cities that take different perspectives. Kahn (2006) reviews the supply and demand of city air pollution and provides a conceptual framework for government policy interventions. Kahn and Walsh (2015) survey theoretical and empirical work on the relationship between environmental amenities (including air pollution) and urban growth. In contrast to these papers, we focus on recent empirical work that measures the economic costs of air pollution and evaluates city government interventions to reduce these costs. Wherever possible, we focus on papers that provide causal quantification and provide theoretical background only where necessary to interpret the empirical results. We consider articles examining all countries, although empirical work thus far has focused predominantly on the United States (US) and China.

This is not a comprehensive survey of city air pollution, the scope of which would require a book rather than a chapter. We focus on topics that are prevalent in empirical economics. In doing so, we benefit from a recent surge in empirical studies using careful identification methods and micro data that examine these issues. We impose some boundaries on what we discuss. We look at only ambient, not indoor, air pollution and consider sources largely within a mayor's control. Although we try to include studies on a variety of ambient pollutants, more results relate to particulate matter (PM) as it has been studied most extensively and is a common proxy for pollution exposure more generally (WHO, 2016: 19). One gray area that we choose not to cover is power plants. While mayors may influence the location of power plants, this is largely out of their control. Power plants are extremely difficult to move once constructed and the initial location of power plants is based primarily on engineering considerations (see Chen (2021) for a discussion).[2]

## 2 SOURCES OF AMBIENT AIR POLLUTION IN CITIES

Ambient air pollutants include the six criteria pollutants: PM, sulfur dioxide ($SO_2$), ozone ($O_3$), carbon monoxide (CO), nitrogen dioxide ($NO_2$), and lead.[3] Of these, the most pernicious is typically PM – small particles that are usually measured as either smaller than 10 micrometers in diameter ($PM_{10}$) or smaller than 2.5 micrometers in diameter ($PM_{2.5}$). Globally, 25 percent of ambient $PM_{2.5}$ in urban areas originates from vehicular traffic, 15 percent from industrial activities, 20 percent from household fuel burning, 22 percent from unspecified human activity, and 18 percent from natural dust and salt, although these compositions differ considerably across cities (Karagulian et al., 2015).

Mayors must also contend with pollution imported from neighboring cities. Although larger particles do not travel as far, $PM_{2.5}$ can travel hundreds of miles, making its importation an issue for mayors (EPA, 2021). There are a few empirical papers that quantify pollution spillover effects across or within cities. Transboundary air pollution has been shown to significantly affect housing prices across Chinese cities (Zheng et al., 2014b), mortality across census blocks within Los Angeles county (Anderson, 2019), and manufacturing productivity across major Chinese cities (Fu et al., 2022). Kahn (1999) estimates industry-specific spillovers across US counties of manufacturing activity on total suspended particulates (TSP)[4] and compares them to locally generated manufacturing pollution. For primary metals manufacturing, which declined the most during the sample period, the elasticity of TSP with respect to local value shipped was 3.5 versus 1.1 percent for value shipped in an adjacent county. Thus, spillovers are a significant concern for mayors.

## 3 ECONOMIC IMPACTS OF AMBIENT URBAN AIR POLLUTION

Mayors need a comprehensive understanding of the economic costs that air pollution imposes on city residents. Understanding of the scope of pollution's economic costs on cities has broadened recently due to novel empirical economic research. Traditionally, studies focused on two main areas, each of which generated a large literature. The first quantified the health and mortality costs of air pollution. The second measured willingness to pay for air quality via its effect on local property values.[5] We will only summarize these two well-developed areas and instead focus primarily on emerging areas. Recent empirical economics work has quantified new sources of air pollution's costs including effects on mental health, labor productivity, and avoidance behavior. Avoidance behavior, which in the extreme includes out-migration, not only imposes costs but also introduces error in traditional measures of air pollution's costs.

### 3.1 Physical Health and Mortality

Short-run exposure to air pollution can lead to decreased lung function, irregular heartbeat, increased respiratory problems, non-fatal heart attacks, and angina, while long-run exposure can lead to cardiopulmonary diseases, respiratory infections, lung cancer (EPA, 2004), and obesity (Deschênes et al., 2020). The medical literature has long estimated the health and mortality effects of pollution using exposure-response (ER) functions. Worldwide, Cohen et al. (2017) estimate that $PM_{2.5}$ was the fifth-ranked mortality risk factor in 2015, causing 4.2 million deaths with 59 percent occurring in East and South Asia and 103.1 million DALYs. To convert these ER relationships into economic costs, the DALYs can be multiplied by the value of a statistical life (VSL) which is an estimate of the marginal rate of substitution between income and mortality risk (the OECD (2012) provide a meta-analysis of VSL estimates). Matus et al. (2008) provide a more sophisticated methodology (an integrated assessment model) for estimating costs by incorporating ER effects into a computable, general-equilibrium model of the economy. This allows for effects on leisure time and separately estimates medical expenditures as these are resources diverted from other, productive sectors.

These studies rely on a statistical relationship between pollution exposure and health effects. This creates two issues. First, these are not necessarily causal effects due to omitted variable bias, measurement error, and correlations between different pollutants. Chen et al. (2013) and Ebenstein et al. (2017) address these issues using a spatial discontinuity design method. Due to central planning, residents north of China's Huai River burned coal for winter heating while residents on the south side did not. Using this discontinuity, the authors find that particulate concentrations on the north are substantially higher and that this reduces life expectancies by 3.1 to 5.5 years. Deryugina et al. (2019) address these issues using high-frequency changes in wind direction as an instrumental variable (proxying for imported pollution). The authors find larger effects on mortality, health-care use, and medical costs when instrumenting, consistent with a downward bias in traditional estimates. Cheung et al. (2020) use air pollution blowing from mainland China as an instrument to estimate air pollution's effect on cardio-respiratory mortality in Hong Kong. Second, ER studies include the effect of any avoidance behavior and spatial sorting.[6] Therefore, these models generally understate air pollution's true health costs. Recent work on avoidance behavior, summarized below, attempts to quantify this.

### 3.2 Mental and Psychological Health

An emerging empirical literature provides convincing evidence that air pollution adversely affects cognitive and psychological health. Being exposed to air pollution during an exam period or a school year lowered students' contemporaneous test scores in California (Ham et al., 2011), Israel (Ebenstein et al., 2016), and China (Graff Zivin et al., 2020). Long-term cumulative exposure to air pollution reduced students' academic performance (Kweon et al., 2018; Bharadwaj et al., 2017; Heissel et al., 2020), adults' cognitive performance (Zhang et al., 2018), and caused dementia (Bishop et al., 2018). As a countermeasure, installing air filters in classrooms improved students' academic performance (Gilraine, 2020).

Decision-making skills are also adversely affected by air pollution. CO and $PM_{2.5}$ caused US baseball umpires to make more incorrect calls (Archsmith et al., 2018). $PM_{2.5}$ caused United Kingdom drivers to have more accidents (Sager, 2019) and degraded quality of political speeches in Ottawa (Heyes et al., 2016b). In an experimental setting, air pollution affected subjects' decision making, increased their risk and ambiguity aversion and made them less prosocial and reciprocal (Chew et al., 2021). These laboratory findings are consistent with investor behavior in financial markets: $PM_{2.5}$ levels lowered New York City investors' returns as measured by a New York Stock Exchange index (Heyes et al., 2016a); investors in the Chinese stock market performed worse on hazy days (Huang et al., 2020) as did mutual fund investors (Li et al., 2021); and investment analysts in China were more likely to provide pessimistic forecasting on severely polluted days (Dong et al., 2021).

Psychologically, air pollution reduced self-reported happiness or life satisfaction in Germany (Luechinger, 2009), the US (Levinson, 2012), and China (X. Zhang et al., 2017). Extensive public health and medical studies demonstrate that air pollution is associated with annoyance, anxiety, mental disorders, self-harm, and unethical behavior (see review by Lu, 2020). Recently, economists have begun to provide causal evidence of these effects. Air pollution negatively affected self-reported mental health in China (S. Chen et al., 2018a) and increased the rate of depressive symptoms (X. Zhang et al., 2017). Air pollution also increased violent crime in Chicago (Herrnstadt et al., 2021) and London (Bondy et al., 2020).

### 3.3 Labor Productivity and Supply

Historically, pollution reduction efforts have been viewed as purely a tax on city output. Pollution abatement either increases firms' costs per unit of output (e.g., purchasing pollution reduction equipment or hiring compliance personnel) or requires direct reductions in output. However, recent work has shown that air pollution reductions can enhance physical and human capital, increasing labor productivity and labor supply. Given labor markets are local, mayoral efforts to reduce local air pollution will bring benefits in increased output and therefore property values and tax revenue that may countervail pollution reduction costs.

The physical and cognitive impairments caused by pollution can reduce labor productivity due to reduced physical or mental effort while at work and the death of older, more experienced workers who are replaced by younger, less experienced workers. Labor supply may also fall due to sick days from impaired health of workers or because workers stay home to care for family members – particularly infants and the elderly who are more vulnerable to air pollution. Empirical studies have quantified both labor productivity (output per hour worked) and labor supply effects. The latter is measured as hours worked, days worked, or number of workers depending on the study's time frame.

Recent studies measure the relationship between pollution and output carefully, addressing simultaneity and omitted variable biases. Regions with more output will have more pollution, leading to a downward bias, while if pollution lowers output, this will in turn lower pollution, leading to an upward bias. In addition, confounding factors may affect both pollution and output, in particular the sorting of firms, workers, or regulatory changes in response to pollution. Hanna and Oliva (2015) utilize an exogenous shock (the closing of a single factory in Mexico City) as an instrumental variable to address these endogeneity issues and find an elasticity of −0.18 of hours worked with respect to $SO_2$ pollution.[7] Graff Zivin and Neidell (2012) estimate an output elasticity with respect to ozone of −0.26 for California fruit pickers. Since the fruit pickers represent a small fraction of total output, simultaneity bias is not an issue. The authors are able to directly confirm that number of workers and hours worked remained the same so that these are per hour productivity effects.

Do these effects on productivity extend to indoor workers? This is relevant because $PM_{2.5}$ pollution is small enough that it can permeate buildings in the absence of preventative measures. Chang et al. (2016) find significant but more modest effects for indoor pear packers – an output elasticity of −0.062 or one-fourth the effects on outdoor fruit pickers. However, He et al. (2019) find that cumulative effects may be greater in examining indoor textile workers in China. Cumulative (over 25 to 30 days) exposure to $PM_{2.5}$ results in output elasticities ranging from −0.035 to −0.30.

These studies combined with evidence that pollution affects mental and psychological well-being suggest that knowledge workers may be affected. A number of studies across different professions find such evidence. Chang et al. (2019) find an elasticity of −0.023 in productivity of call center workers in China with respect to the Air Pollution Index (API).[8] These are per hour productivity effects as the authors find no effect on hours worked or number of workers. These effects extend to high-skilled indoor workers. Kahn and Li (2020) find that decision times of judges in China increased in response to the average Air Quality Index (AQI)[9] over the duration of cases. Meyer and Pagel (2017) find that $PM_{10}$ reduces the likelihood that individual investors in Germany sit down, log in, and trade in their brokerage accounts.

To control for endogeneity, these papers focus on a single firm or type of worker whose output is a small part of aggregate output. While these results are useful for targeted environmental policies, more comprehensive estimates are necessary to evaluate broad-based policies. Doing so also requires moving from partial equilibrium estimates that ignore the feedback of output on pollution to general equilibrium estimates. Fu et al. (2021) address this by identifying causal effects of pollution on output and output on pollution and simulating an integrated assessment model to estimate the general equilibrium effects. The authors find an output elasticity of −0.28 with respect to $PM_{2.5}$ including both productivity and labor supply effects. The authors also find greater effects for high- than low-skilled workers. Consistent with this, Adhvaryu et al. (2019) find pollution affects productivity more for workers performing more complex tasks.

These results suggest that mayors should be aware that air pollution has significant effects on productivity and labor supply and that these effects apply outdoors, to a lesser extent indoors, and to both low- and high-skilled workers. There is much that is still unknown. Little is known about the underlying reasons for reduced productivity. An exception is the work of Aragón et al. (2017) which finds that moderate $PM_{2.5}$ levels affect work hours for households with small children and elderly members disproportionately while high levels affect all households equally. The appropriate policy response depends on the underlying cause. For example, if lost productivity is due to reduced worker stamina then better workplace air filtration is warranted; while if work is missed to take care of children better school air filtration is in order. More work is needed on the services sector. The evidence for call centers and investors is suggestive but more comprehensive evidence would be useful.

While the firm- and industry-specific studies can test for avoidance behavior, the aggregate estimates in Fu et al. (2021) are inclusive of avoidance behavior. This could be material. Using detailed task data for Indian garment workers, Adhvaryu et al. (2019) show that managers are more likely to reassign workers away from tasks most degraded by pollution. Results so far indicate greater effects for highly skilled, highly complex work. More work is needed to confirm this but, if so, there is an added urgency for mayors to reduce pollution because these workers contribute disproportionately to output.

### 3.4 Avoidance Behavior

Understanding avoidance behavior is important for mayors for three reasons: increased information disclosure may lead to defensive actions that better protect citizens, estimates of pollution's costs that do not account for avoidance behavior may be understated, and the most extreme form of avoidance behavior, migration, may reduce the city's productive work force and long-run growth.

Pollution information disclosures such as smog alerts can help people take action to reduce exposure. Even absent public air quality information, people can identify, with error, pollution severity based on visibility, haze, or respiratory reactions. There are three types of avoidance behavior: reducing outdoor activities, buying protective equipment, and traveling or moving to locations with better air quality.

When air pollution is moderate (AQI between 200 and 300), the elderly and people with respiratory diseases are recommended to stay indoors, while when it is above 300 even healthy people are recommended to do so. Research indicates that many people follow these guidelines at least partially. In southern California, the first day of a smog alert caused attendance at a public zoo and an observatory to drop by 15 and 8 percent, respectively; however, decreased attendance diminished dramatically on the second consecutive alert day and disappeared on the third (Graff Zivin and Neidell, 2009). Children and the elderly responded more to alerts than non-elderly adults (Graff Zivin and Neidell, 2009; Neidell, 2009). In Texas, school absences were more likely during bad air pollution, which could be due to students becoming sick or parents keeping them home to avoid exposure (Currie et al., 2009). In China, international students (Liu and Salvo, 2018) and Chinese students in big cities (S. Chen et al., 2018b) were more likely to be absent on polluting days and movie attendance declined with pollution (He et al., 2020).

Purchasing defensive equipment is another way to avoid pollution. Chinese households' expenditures on face masks increased by 55 percent when air quality moved from slightly to heavily polluted (AQI increase of 100) (Zhang and Mu, 2018). Runners even wore face masks during the 34th Beijing International Marathon held in 2014 because of severe pollution on the race day (Guo and Fu, 2019). People buy home-use air purifiers to reduce indoor air pollution (Ito and Zhang, 2020). High-income households are more likely to do so (Sun et al., 2017), suggesting income inequality may play a role in defensive expenditures.

The most extreme forms of avoidance behavior are traveling and migration. On severe pollution days, online searches related to international emigration increased in China (Qin and Zhu, 2018). Chen et al. (2020a) find that between March 2008 and April 2010, a degradation in Beijing's air quality relative to another city increased air travel from Beijing to that city. The increase was greater for first-class flyers, again suggesting income inequality. Similarly, cell phone data for 25 Chinese cities in 2016 indicate that the difference in air quality between two cities led to increased population flow to the city with cleaner air (Chen et al., 2020b). Over a longer horizon, people can relocate to cities with better air quality. Using three waves of population census data in China from 1996 to 2010, Chen et al. (2022) find that a 10 percent increase in $PM_{2.5}$ in a county causes 27 people per 1000 inhabitants to move out, with greater effects for college-educated residents.

These empirical results suggest that citizens engage in significant avoidance behavior and defensive expenditures. This is good news in that pollution damage is mitigated, although there is some evidence that poor citizens are at a disadvantage in defensive investments. However, it is bad news in that estimated pollution damages are understated to the extent this avoidance behavior is unaccounted for. Mayors should be most concerned about the evidence on permanent migration. High pollution levels may reduce a city's labor force and tax base with greater effects for high-skilled workers, which are the main driver of long-run urban growth (Shapiro, 2006). More evidence is needed on long-run avoidance behavior and the inequality in avoidance behavior.

## 3.5 Willingness to Pay for Air Quality

It is important for a mayor to know residents' willingness to pay for air quality so that it can be compared to pollution reduction costs. However, since air quality is a non-market good, marginal willingness to pay (MWTP) for air quality must be deduced through indirect methods. Although there are many approaches,[10] we focus on the three approaches most intuitively understandable to mayors.

The first regresses self-reported happiness or life satisfaction ratings on individual characteristics including income, air quality, and residential location. The MWTP for air quality is inferred from the marginal rate of substitution between income and air quality that keeps individuals equally happy. Using the US General Social Survey data from 1984 to 1996, Levinson (2012) estimates a MWTP of 459 to 891 USD for a one µg/m³ annual reduction in $PM_{10}$. Luechinger (2009) uses the installation of power plant scrubbers and wind direction as an instrument to control for endogeneity and estimates a MWTP of EUR 313 for a one µg/m³ annual reduction in $SO_2$ using the German Socio-Economic Panel data from 1985 to 2003.

The second approach is the quality of life literature which utilizes hedonic models. Good air quality is an urban amenity specific to a location. As more people move to a location with good air quality, housing demand there will increase and MWTP for air quality will be reflected in the increased housing costs. At the same time, workers may tolerate lower wages in locations with good air quality. Thus, housing and wage hedonic models together, controlling for urban amenities, can recover MWTP for air quality (Blomquist, 2006). Chay and Greenstone (2005) use non-attainment status under the US Clean Air Act as an instrumental variable to estimate an elasticity of −0.20 to −0.32 for median property values with respect to TSP using data from 1972 to 1983 (a one µg/m³ decrease in TSP increases property values by 240 in 2001 USD). Using data for 85 Chinese cities from 2006 to 2009 and imported pollution as an instrument, Zheng et al. (2014b) estimate a much smaller elasticity: −0.08 for home prices with respect to $PM_{10}$. Bayer et al. (2009) incorporate moving costs in a locational discrete choice model and find hedonic models that ignore this underestimate MWTP for air quality. The authors estimate that the median household is willing to pay USD 149–185 (in 1982–1984 USD) for a one µg/m³ decrease in $PM_{10}$ – three times larger than estimates without moving costs.[11] Causal estimates of MWTP in wages are lacking, perhaps because the quality-of-life literature emerged in urban rather than environmental economics. Since recent work has shown that air pollution may affect labor productivity and labor supply both directly and through migration, wage hedonic estimates would need to be adjusted for these.

The third approach uses expenditures to reduce pollution exposure or treat its effects. For non-marginal air quality improvements, these can approximate willingness to pay (WTP) for air quality (Bartik, 1988). Zhang and Mu (2018) estimate that face mask expenditures in China increased CNY 610,000 per severely polluted day (AQI above 300) during 2013 to 2014. Ito and Zhang (2020) estimate that a Chinese household is willing to pay USD 1.34 annually to remove one µg/m³ of $PM_{10}$ based on scanner data for air purifier sales. Deschênes et al. (2017) estimate that the US Nitrogen Oxides Budget Program from 2003 to 2008 reduced air pollution and pharmaceutical expenditures to address respiratory and cardiovascular problems by USD 800 million (1.6 percent) in participating states. The authors estimate this represents over one-third of overall WTP for pollution reductions. Using data tracking asthmatics' use of rescue medication, Williams et al. (2019) estimate that a 4.5 µg/m³ increase in $PM_{2.5}$ is associated with a 3.6 percent increase in rescue medication use. Converting this to WTP and extrapolating to all US asthmatics, a one µg/m³ reduction in $PM_{2.5}$ nationwide would save USD 350 million annually.

These estimates provide mayors with a few estimates of WTP for air quality but primarily for the US and China. More work is needed on estimates for other countries. Most notably lacking are causal estimates for effects on wages.

## 3.6    Long-Term Impacts

Air pollution can have very long-term impacts on individuals who are exposed early in life. Isen et al. (2017) find that US cohorts born in years with more pollution have lower labor force participation and earnings at age 30. In China, childhood exposure to higher air pollution causes fewer schooling years and lower earned income in adulthood (Ebenstein and Greenstone, 2020). Air pollution can also had very long-term impacts on neighborhood stratification and land use due to spatial sorting of city residents. Lin (2018) finds that US census tracts located downwind of 1970 industrial sites had lower housing prices, lower skilled employment shares, and lower wages in 2000; they also had lower growth rates in all these outcomes from 1980 to 2000. Heblich et al. (2021) geocode industrial chimneys in 70 English cities as of 1880 and recreate the spatial distribution of air pollution at that time using an atmospheric dispersion model. Using the 1881 census data, the authors find that highly polluted locations attract a higher share of low-skilled workers. Most striking, a location's pollution level in 1880 increases the share of low-skilled workers in 1971, 1981, 1991, 2001, and 2011, suggesting very persistent effects. The authors show that once a neighborhood passes a pollution threshold, it develops low amenities and continues to attract low-skilled, low-income residents long after the historical pollution has waned.

These studies suggest that very high pollution levels in some city neighborhoods may permanently trap those areas, where low income and racial minority residents disproportionally concentrate, in disadvantage.[12] Understanding the causal relationship between air pollution and the spatial distribution of different demographics can help mayors design policies to increase environmental justice.

## 4 POLICIES TO ALLEVIATE AMBIENT URBAN AIR POLLUTION

### 4.1 Information Disclosure

Monitoring and announcing real-time and future projected air quality information is helpful for residents to make informed decisions about avoidance behavior. The US Environmental Protection Agency (EPA) issues Air Quality Alerts at times when ground-level ozone or particle concentrations reach, or are approaching, unhealthy levels in an area and also in the late afternoon when either is predicted to be elevated on the following day.[13] People respond to these alerts by taking action to avoid exposure such as reducing outdoor activities (Graff Zivin and Neidell, 2009; Neidell, 2009). Awareness of severe pollution may lead residents to buy face masks and air filters to protect themselves or show a greater interest in relocation (see Section 3.4). Another potential upside of information disclosure is that citizens may take actions to reduce pollution on severe days such as by taking public transit instead of driving (Cutter and Neidell, 2009). Disclosure is also important for timing large gatherings such as sports events when the air quality is good.

Although most cities in developed countries monitor and publicize daily and sometimes even hourly air quality information, many cities in developing countries lag behind. Chinese cities started to roll out automated monitoring stations in 2012 for both $PM_{10}$ and $PM_{2.5}$ (previously only $PM_{10}$ data were collected and only manually). Greenstone et al. (2020) find that the $PM_{10}$ concentrations reported by the automated monitoring network were significantly higher than previous readings, suggesting that automation significantly reduced underreporting, data manipulation, or both. The introduction of automated collection also increased online searches for face masks and air filters when air quality was bad, suggesting that more precise information and better access helped residents make more informed decisions.

In the absence of $PM_{2.5}$ concentration information, urban residents in China are often confused as to whether severe pollution is fog or smog since they must judge based on visibility. Barwick et al. (2019) find that $PM_{2.5}$ disclosure increased media coverage about air pollution, increased defensive expenditures on air purifiers, and reduced outdoor activities on highly polluted days with a resulting reduction in pollution-related mortality. Interestingly, the housing price discount of pollution also increased. Importantly for mayors, the authors conclude that improving access to air pollution information is a low-cost, high-return policy for alleviating pollution's effects.

### 4.2 Auto License and Driving Restrictions

While not a new idea – it goes back to at least the times of ancient Rome (Matthews, 1960) – driving restrictions are increasingly used around the world as urban air pollution has deteriorated. These policies usually restrict cars from driving one or more days per week during certain hours based on the last digit of their license plate number. This is one of the few policies that may address road dust, which contributes to $PM_{2.5}$.[14] Driving restrictions will not necessarily reduce pollution due to purchases of second vehicles, intertemporal substitution to non-restricted periods, and substitution to dirtier forms of transport (W. Zhang et al., 2017). There is probably no other city-level pollution policy that has more mixed evidence than driving restrictions.

The first systematic and rigorous analysis of driving restrictions (Davis, 2008) finds no improvement in air quality from Mexico City's Hoy No Circula policy implemented in 1989 due to an increase in the number of vehicles on the road, especially higher-polluting used vehicles. Consistent with this, Gallego et al. (2013) use hourly CO emissions as a proxy for vehicle use and find more vehicles on the road in response to the policy. Blackman et al. (2018) use a contingent valuation approach to estimate the cost of the Hoy No Circula program in 2013 at USD 130 per vehicle per year conditional on vehicle and location choice.

However, these policies have been found to be effective in other contexts. Viard and Fu (2015) find that Beijing's driving restrictions implemented in 2008 improved air quality, perhaps because China's rapid growth meant that few used cars were available. However, the policy also reduced work time for those with discretionary work hours. Consistent with reduced car usage in response to the policy, Xu et al. (2015) find that housing prices increased near subway stations and relatively more for those with better commute times. Zhong et al. (2017) exploit variation in the number of vehicles restricted each day due to superstitions in China about the last digit on license plate numbers. The authors find that days with more allowed vehicles have higher pollution levels and more ambulance calls. Blackman et al. (2020) estimate that the Beijing restrictions imposed costs of USD 54 to 107 per vehicle per year, which are below the benefits of pollution reduction identified in Viard and Fu (2015).

In contrast to the mixed evidence for vintage-agnostic restrictions, studies have found vintage-specific restrictions to be generally effective. Theoretically, such restrictions may induce drivers to upgrade to cleaner vehicles but may also induce drivers of non-qualifying vehicles to travel further to avoid restricted zones so that the effects are indeterminate. Santiago's vintage-specific driving restrictions implemented in 1992 were effective in reducing pollution because they induced drivers to adopt cleaner vehicles (Barahona et al., 2020). Wolff (2014) finds that Germany's Low Emissions Zones (LEZs), allowing only vehicles with low $PM_{10}$ emissions in certain zones, are effective at lowering pollution. These German LEZs are also effective in reducing $PM_{10}$ across a broader set of zones and cities (Malina and Scheffler, 2015), improving infant health (Gehrsitz, 2017), and reducing cardiovascular disease (Margaryan, 2021). In contrast to these favorable outcomes, Bento et al. (2014) find that allowing single-occupant, low-emissions vehicles into high-occupancy vehicle lanes lowers welfare due to increased congestion for carpoolers.

Episodic driving restrictions are sometimes used to address acute, temporary pollution spikes. These are less likely to result in long-run avoidance behavior such as purchasing a second vehicle. De Grange and Troncoso (2011) find that temporary, rush-hour bans on all cars decreased pollution and increased subway but not bus ridership. Han et al. (2020) investigate a temporary, 16-day driving restriction policy in Jinan in 2009 and find significant reductions in CO and $PM_{10}$.

An alternative policy for reducing the number of cars on the road is restricting automobile licenses. Their use has increased in China as the stock of cars has risen along with increased wealth. The two primary methods have been auctions and lotteries, although some cities use hybrids (Xiao et al., 2017). Using the random outcomes to compare winners and losers, Yang et al. (2020a) find that Beijing's lottery reduced the total stock of cars by 14 percent and vehicle kilometers traveled by 15 percent.[15] Using a structural model, Xiao et al. (2017) find that Shanghai's auction increased welfare because the benefit from reduced externalities exceeded the loss from reduced vehicle transactions given reasonable assumptions about vehicle life, license prices, and externalities. Li (2018) compares the welfare effects of Beijing's lottery to the counterfactual of a uniform-price auction similar to Shanghai's. While the lottery is more effective at reducing automobile externalities (because externalities increase in willingness to pay for a car), overall welfare is much higher under the auction because of the allocative inefficiencies in car usage under the lottery.

Barahona et al. (2020) construct a structural model that allows for vintage-specific driving restrictions with a uniform program as a limiting case. Using data from a Santiago driving restrictions program that exempted cars with catalytic converters beginning in 1992, the authors show that vintage-based restrictions that affect choice of cars driven (extensive margin) are preferable to uniform restrictions that affect car usage (intensive margin). Placing more onerous limits on older, dirtier vehicles encourages drivers to upgrade to newer, cleaner vehicles in contrast to uniform restrictions which encourage the adoption of a second (possibly dirtier) vehicle.

Theoretically, scrappage programs induce car owners to replace older, dirtier vehicles with newer, cleaner vehicles. However, empirical studies have generally found them to be ineffective due to adverse selection. Li et al. (2013) find that a one-month program in the US in 2009 resulted in limited pollution reductions in part because 45 percent of the subsidies went to consumers who would have purchased a new vehicle absent the program. Similarly, Sandler (2012) finds that in a long-running California program (from 1996 to 2010) owners were more likely to scrap vehicles with few remaining miles to be traveled and therefore a short time for pollution production. Jacobsen and van Benthem (2015) quantify the reduced effectiveness of these programs due to the resulting increase in used car prices, estimating a scrappage elasticity of $-0.7$ with respect to used vehicle prices for the US between 1993 and 2009.

Barahona et al. (2020) extend their analysis to compare driving restrictions to license-restriction and scrappage policies. Vintage-based driving restrictions compare favorably to scrappage policies because the latter do not allow older cars to relocate to less polluted settings where they remain valuable. A gasoline tax (discussed below) outperforms vintage-based restrictions in the short run by deterring car usage[16] but is disadvantageous in the long run as it does not induce a move toward cleaner (per gallon) vehicles. Vintage-based registration fees outperform vintage-based driving restrictions because they allow a full menu of prices that reflect the marginal social cost of using each vintage.

What do these results mean for mayors? Vintage-specific registration fees are likely the most effective means to reduce auto emissions but may be infeasible to implement. If infeasible, vintage-specific driving restrictions would be the next most effective and would be preferable to scrappage programs which suffer from unintended consequences.

## 4.3    Congestion Tolls

Congestion tolls have been extensively discussed theoretically and have been implemented in several cities. Although the primary goal of these tools is to reduce traffic congestion, as a byproduct they reduce air pollution (Parry et al., 2007). As a mayor, how should a congestion toll be calculated and is it practically feasible to levy these tolls in urban areas? If so, how effective are they in reducing pollution?

When traffic on a road exceeds its capacity, congestion occurs and each additional driver slows down all other drivers, increasing their travel costs for gasoline and vehicle maintenance and opportunity cost of time. The marginal increase in all others' travel costs is the "congestion externality" imposed by the additional driver. The optimal toll charged to each driver should equal this congestion externality to ensure socially optimal usage of the road (Arnott and Kraus, 2003). Incorporating the pollution externality into this calculation requires estimating the increased pollution costs that occur from all vehicles when an additional driver joins the road. Since congestion varies across time (e.g., rush versus non-rush hours) and roads (e.g., downtown versus suburban areas), optimal congestion tolls should be time- and road-specific (Arnott et al., 1993).

Historically, setting and implementing optimal congestion tolls has been difficult. Setting a congestion toll, even approximately close to the optimal, requires real-time data on traffic flows. This is only recently feasible with the advent of sophisticated communication and GPS technologies. Moreover, in the past collecting tolls required stopping vehicles to collect physical currency. Recent technologies, such as "smart" cards that are installed in vehicles and scanned while passing a toll collection point, have automated this process.

Although technological hurdles for implementing congestion tolls have diminished, mayors still face political, economic, and social constraints that limit their effectiveness in reducing pollution. Congestion tolls are regressive and may be opposed on this basis. Drivers may avoid tolled areas by driving around them thereby increasing pollution. Drivers may be concerned about the privacy of their travels and avoid using tolls or oppose them politically. Although congestion tolls have not yet been widely adopted, Singapore, London, Stockholm, Milan, San Diego, Houston, Toronto, Seoul, and some Norwegian cities have implemented them (Small and Verhoef, 2007; Lindsey et al., 2008; Anas and Lindsey, 2011).

For mayors, what do economic studies have to say about congestion tolls and how they influence pollution? A few papers have estimated optimal congestion tolls. The main difficulty in doing so is obtaining an exogenous shift in traffic density to identify the increased travel costs. A good example of how to overcome this is Yang et al. (2020b) who use exogenous shifts in daily traffic density due to plate number rotations under Beijing's driving restrictions (some digits are favored over others and therefore in greater use). The authors estimate optimal congestion tolls of CNY 0.15 per vehicle kilometer for peak hours and CNY 0.10 for off-peak hours using 2014 data.

We are not aware of any empirical estimates of optimal congestion tolls inclusive of the pollution externality. However, there are a few empirical studies that estimate how imposing congestion tolls affect pollution. Using a differences-in-differences (DD) approach with other UK cities as a control group, Green et al. (2020) find that London's congestion pricing program implemented in 2003 reduced $PM_{10}$ by 5.6 to 7.7 percent and CO by 6 to 9 percent depending on the controls employed but increased $NO_2$ by 14 to 17 percent.[17] $NO_2$ may have increased because diesel vehicles (buses and taxis), which produce more $NO_2$, were exempted and increased their driving due to reduced congestion brought about by the tolls. Simeonova et al. (2019) use a DD approach with other Swedish cities as a control group to examine Stockholm's congestion pricing program implemented in 2007.[18] The authors find that the toll reduced $PM_{10}$ by 10 to 15 percent depending on the controls employed and $NO_2$ by 15 to 20 percent. Milan suspended its congestion pricing program for about two months in mid-2012 due to a lawsuit.[19] Gibson and Carnovale (2015) take advantage of this unexpected policy change and estimate the suspension increased CO by 6 percent and $PM_{10}$ by 17 percent.

Chinese cities charge highway tolls to finance road construction rather than to reduce congestion (Beijing and Guangzhou are currently discussing implementation of the first urban center congestion programs in China). Beginning on October 1, 2012, the central government waved highway tolls on four nationwide holidays. Fu and Gu (2017) use a regression discontinuity design combined with a DD estimate using the previous years as a control group to estimate pollution effects during the first National Day holiday to be exempted (October 1–7, 2012). The authors find that air pollution, predominately $PM_{10}$, increased by 20 percent. Based on average toll data, the elasticity of urban air pollution with respect to tolls is −0.15.

Economic studies confirm that congestion tolls can be effective in reducing auto pollution. However, they do not offer much guidance on setting the optimal toll that takes account of pollution externalities. Future work on this would be useful. In implementing congestion tolls, mayors must consider the practical technological, political, and social constraints.

## 4.4 Public Transit Infrastructure

Many cities invest in public transit (subway, light rail, bus rapid transit) to reduce congestion and pollution. Theoretically, public transit may or may not be effective in doing so. On the one hand, drivers may substitute to public transit and reduce vehicle kilometers traveled (Adler and van Ommeren, 2016; Bento et al., 2005; Liu and Li, 2020). On the other hand, if latent demand for automobile trips exists, reduced road congestion from expanded public transit can be offset by new drivers – the "fundamental law of highway congestion" (Duranton and Turner, 2011). In addition, urban sprawl can reduce public transit ridership (Baum-Snow et al., 2005). Whether public transit reduces pollution is therefore an empirical matter. The small amount of evidence thus far indicates that public transit is effective in reducing pollution for heavily polluted cities but the effects are highly local.

Chen and Whalley (2012) use hourly pollution data and a regression discontinuity design to estimate the effect of opening the Taipei Metro's first line in 1996. The authors find a 5 to 15 percent reduction, depending on the specification, in CO but little effect on ozone. Between 2008 and 2016, Beijing built 14 subway lines and 252 stations. Using this setting and historical subway planning as an instrument, Li et al. (2019) find that a one standard deviation increase in subway network density improved city air quality by 2 percent and that air quality within 2 kilometers of a new subway line improved by 7.7 percent relative to areas more than 20 kilometers away, suggesting a highly local effect. Bauernschuster et al. (2017) use DD estimates applied to 71 one-day strikes in the public transportation sector in five German cities between 2002 and 2011. The authors find that the absence of public transit during morning rush hours increased $PM_{10}$ by 14 percent and $NO_2$ by 4 percent.

Gendron-Carrier et al. (2021) provide more comprehensive evidence using a large sample of subway stations from 58 world cities that opened between August 2001 and July 2016. The authors employ an event study approach based on monthly pollution data before and after subway openings and find no average effect on $PM_{2.5}$. However, there is substantial heterogeneity: $PM_{2.5}$ fell in 26 cities, increased in 20, and did not change in 12. The cities with declines are overwhelmingly above the median in initial pollution levels and $PM_{2.5}$ fell by 4 percent for all cities above the median. Similar to Li et al. (2019), the authors find larger pollution reductions near city centers where subway ridership is concentrated and little effect beyond 25 kilometers. Gu et al. (2021) provide complementary evidence for 45 newly opened subway lines in 25 Chinese cities between August 2016 and December 2017. Opening lines increases rush hour speed by 4 percent on roads near subway lines, with effects declining with distance from the lines.

Empirical evidence so far suggests that public transit likely reduces air pollution in locations that have high population density, are close to the access points, and have high pollution levels.

Improving access to public transit to ensure ridership is also important. For example, many Chinese cities have introduced shared bicycles to help solve this "last mile problem."[20]

## 4.5 Emissions Standards and Controls

Emissions standards are generally set at the supra-city level but implemented at the local level and therefore relevant for a mayor. Economic studies have found emissions targets to be effective locally in both the US and China. The studies generally do not identify the mechanisms used to reduce pollution but show that the targets themselves are useful, at least if set in the right way. The US Clean Air Act implemented in 1990 provides evidence that emissions standards are an effective city-level tool for reducing pollution. Although a federal law, US counties were responsible for implementation and those in non-compliance faced sanctions. Bento et al. (2015) show that $PM_{10}$ reductions from the Act were highly localized by examining changes in housing prices in close proximity to a monitoring station (all monitors had to be in compliance to avoid sanctions).

A similar policy in China – the Air Pollution Prevention and Control Law – has been shown to be effective in reducing air pollution. One iteration of this law implemented in 1998 as the Two Control Zone (TCZ) policy designated 175 of 333 prefectures that exceeded nationally mandated thresholds for $SO_2$ and faced more stringent regulations.[21] Tanaka (2015) finds that the TCZ policy reduced infant mortality in prefectures subject to it relative to those that were not.

Mayors must be careful in setting emissions targets to avoid incentive misalignment. The US Clean Air Act Amendment of 1977 specified that a county was in attainment as long as the highest hourly reading over all hours and days of the year did not exceed a certain limit.[22] In response, local regulators relocated polluting industries from more- to less-polluted counties to avoid triggering non-attainment in the dirtier counties (Henderson, 1996) and shifted pollution from monitored to non-monitored days (Zou, 2021). While not necessarily detrimental to improving air pollution, these actions were inconsistent with the law's intention which was to reduce source emissions.

Vehicle smog checks are a tool that mayors may use, although type I and type II errors have both been shown to plague them.[23] Oliva (2015) finds widespread cheating in Mexico City through the use of substitute "donor" cars to pass the test for vehicles that would otherwise fail. As the author points out, requiring pollution-reduction equipment on new vehicles is easier to enforce given the smaller number of manufacturers to monitor.[24] Jacobsen et al. (2021) find that new-car emissions standards are effective in reducing vehicle air pollution but are not cost-effective because they exempt or impose more lax standards on older, dirtier vehicles. Hubbard (1998) finds evidence of type I errors in California's smog checks – inspectors use their discretion to avoid passing vehicles in order to sell repairs for failed vehicles. Sanders and Sandler (2020) find that California emissions checks were effective in reducing ambient air pollution but only from vehicles utilizing older emissions control technologies. This suggests that improvements in engine technology over time may render these tests less effective.

Both general emissions standards and smog checks appear to be useful tools that mayors can use to reduce pollution but they must be cognizant of incentive alignment and unintended consequences for both.

### 4.6 Gasoline Taxes

Theoretically, a mayor could employ gasoline taxes as they have been shown effective in reducing auto emissions (Fullerton and Li, 2005). However, implementing gas taxes is not a viable option for most cities except large or geographically isolated ones that can prevent diversion of gas purchases to neighboring cities. This is consistent with the empirical evidence. Only one out of five of the largest cities in each US state have either an excise tax or a sales tax on gasoline or both (Michael, 2017).[25] Presumably, smaller cities would be even less likely to have a gasoline tax. In China, there is a separate fuel tax although, consistent with preventing arbitrage across cities, it is a uniform national rate.

### 4.7 Transboundary Air Pollution

Pollution that drifts from neighboring cities is outside of a mayor's direct control. These externalities can be internalized at a higher political level by exerting centralized control as shown by Yang and Chou (2018). The US Clean Air Act allows for such a procedure. Its Section 126 allows a downwind state to petition the federal-level EPA to take action against an upwind state that impedes its ability to comply with pollution standards.[26] Transboundary pollution can also be resolved through merging two jurisdictions (Wang and Wang, 2020) or through negotiations between two or more cities, although this requires clear assignment of property rights (Coase, 1960). For example, in 2012 Hong Kong SAR and Guangdong province in China agreed on joint pollution reduction targets for the region.[27] As the central government was not involved in the negotiations of this agreement, this is an interesting example of Coasian bargaining at work.[28]

Regardless of the approach used, a quantification of imported pollution's costs as a function of distance is required for the higher political authority to set damages or for cities to negotiate prices amongst themselves. Chemical transport models quantify imported pollution via simulation (e.g., Seigneur and Dennis, 2011) but not its costs upon arrival. These would need to be combined with causal damage estimates. Fu et al. (2022) provide a method for estimating costs as a function of distance using daily pollution and weather data.

In the absence of such solutions, neighboring mayors are caught in a Prisoner's Dilemma in which there is an incentive to produce socially excessive levels of pollution and to locate pollution sources close to and upwind of adjacent cities – phenomena that have been documented empirically (Helland and Whitford, 2003; Bošković, 2015). Such free-riding can sometimes be subtle. For example, electric vehicle subsidies initiated by one city can increase air pollution in other cities through increased electric generation (Holland et al., 2016).

## 5 INCENTIVES

US mayors' incentives revolve around the electoral process. In the short run, voters exert pressure via whether a mayor gets re-elected (see evidence in List and Sturm (2006) for state governors who face similar electoral pressures as mayors). Consistent with this, the incentives of governors to experiment are affected by whether they are eligible for re-election and their chances of being re-elected (Bernecker et al., 2021). In the long run, citizens subject mayors to inter-jurisdictional competition and Tiebout sorting (Tiebout, 1956). Mayors face a tradeoff which can lead to either a "race to the bottom" or a "race to the top." On the one hand, they have an incentive to attract capital (inter-jurisdictional competition) to generate more local economic activity which increases pollution levels (Oates and Schwab, 1988). On the other hand, cities compete in urban amenities and quality of life, including air quality, which gives mayors an incentive to reduce pollution levels. This Tiebout sorting arises from residents' ability to move (i.e., "vote with their feet"). Which effect dominates depends crucially on the applicability of these models' assumptions.

Millimet (2014) summarizes these theoretical models and the empirical evidence concerning their underlying assumptions and concludes that the evidence is not yet conclusive as to whether there is a race to the top or bottom. A few papers directly test how moving from a centralized to a decentralized system of governance affects pollution levels. The results are consistent with a race to the top or at least the avoidance of a race to the bottom. List and Gerking (2000) find that environmental quality either continues to improve or did not decline after US environmental regulation was decentralized to the states in the early 1980s while Millimet (2003) finds no significant change using different econometric techniques. As Millimet (2014) notes these results do not necessarily mean that the decentralized outcome is more efficient than the centralized.

China's central government employs a "tournament competition" to promote local government officials. Before 2005, the promotion criteria were based mainly on local GDP growth (Li and Zhou, 2005; Yu et al., 2016), giving local officials an incentive to sacrifice environmental quality for growth (Wu et al., 2013; Jia, 2017). In 2005, environmental quality and protection were added to the promotion criteria including reducing $SO_2$ emissions in targeted cities through the TCZ program. J. Y. Chen et al. (2018) use a DD approach with non-TCZ cities as a control and find that cities subjected to TCZ reduced $SO_2$ emissions more but at the cost of reduced GDP growth. Consistent with this, city mayors and party secretaries whose regions reduced pollution more were more likely to be promoted (Zheng et al., 2014a; Wu and Cao, 2021).

An unintended consequence of environmental-based performance evaluation is that local officials have an incentive to manipulate environmental data. Many Chinese cities are required to reach the goal of 85 percent "blue-sky days" (API less than 100) in a year. Ghanem and Zhang (2014) find evidence of sharp discontinuities at the blue-sky day threshold for 50 percent of the 113 cities in their data and that such manipulation is more likely to occur on days with high visibility when manipulation is hardest to detect. Such manipulation is also effective as it is correlated with future promotions of officials (Ghanem et al., 2020). Nonetheless, the API is highly correlated with two alternative measures of air pollution: visibility and Aerosol Optical Depth, suggesting that the API contains useful information (Chen et al., 2012).

## 6    CONCLUSION

Recently, high-quality empirical economic research that is relevant for mayors in tackling air pollution has blossomed. However, because the baseline of research that examines "micro" policy issues relevant to mayors was previously small, there remains much work to be done. The most glaring omission is estimates of the costs of reducing pollution. Empirical work overwhelmingly focuses on the benefits of reduction. For example, what decline in economic activity is necessary to achieve pollution reductions? As it stands, there are few results that would allow mayors to know whether policies are cost-effective or not.

More research is also needed for mayors outside of China and the US, especially in India – a large and populous country with relatively bad air quality. Institutional differences such as the ability and opportunity to migrate away from pollution or enforcement of policies may differ dramatically across countries and affect policy outcomes.[29] As the work on driving restrictions has shown, historical antecedents such as the stock of used cars may affect outcomes and these antecedents will differ across countries.

Nonetheless, extant work has provided extensive evidence of a wide range of costs created by pollution going well beyond the traditional health and mortality costs that were historically examined. It has also identified numerous policies that are effective in reducing pollution: some forms of driving restrictions, appropriately set congestion tolls, targeted public transit infrastructure, and incentive-aligned emissions standards. Mayors will also undoubtedly develop new policies, such as promoting active commuting (walking or biking to work), subsidizing green vehicles, increasing the percentage of pre-fabricated materials in construction, and using water-canon trucks to suppress road dust, that will require evaluation.

## ACKNOWLEDGMENTS

We thank the editor Charles Leung for inviting us to write this chapter. We thank the referee, Junjie Zhang, and Peng Zhang for very helpful comments and thank Jessie Qin, Tie Shi, and Yinlong Wang for providing excellent research support. Shihe Fu acknowledges financial support by the National Natural Science Foundation of China (Grant #71773096).

## NOTES

1. Deaths resulting from particulate matter ($PM_{2.5}$ and $PM_{10}$) only. Morbidity effects include acute lower respiratory disease, chronic obstructive pulmonary disease, stroke, ischemic heart disease, and lung cancer.
2. There is a large literature examining national efforts to reduce sulfur dioxide emissions through allowance markets (Goulder, 2013).
3. Criteria pollutants are the only air pollutants for which the US EPA has established national standards. All of these are directly emitted except for ozone which forms from chemical reactions between nitrogen oxides and volatile organic compounds triggered by sunlight.
4. "Total suspended particulates" is an older measure of PM pollution.
5. Many of the papers in the property values strand used ordinary least squares hedonic models rather than causal estimates of the effects.
6. People may change residence to avoid air pollution. Not correcting for this will result in an underestimate of pollution's effects. Firms may respond to air pollution by sorting to low-pollution regions (to increase productivity, see Section 3.3) or to high-pollution regions (the "pollution haven" effect – see Becker and Henderson, 2000; Greenstone, 2002; Levinson and Taylor, 2008), resulting in either an under- or over-statement of pollution's effects.
7. Since a single plant is closed, aggregate goods and labor demand are relatively unaffected. The authors also test for evidence of migration and find none.
8. The API provides a scaled measure of the worst pollutant for each day based on $SO_2$, $NO_2$, CO, $PM_{10}$, and ozone. The value ranges between 0 and 500 with higher values indicating higher pollution concentrations and more harmful health effects.

9. The AQI replaced the API in China in 2012. The AQI also provides a scaled measure of the worst pollutant for each day but is based on six pollutants: $SO_2$, $NO_2$, CO, $PM_{2.5}$, $PM_{10}$, and ozone.
10. These include the contingent valuation method, stated preference method, and recreation demand model.
11. Freeman et al. (2019) apply the same method in China.
12. Banzhaf et al. (2019) provide a survey of the economics of race, place, and environmental pollution.
13. A description is available at www3.epa.gov/region1/airquality/smogalrt.html (accessed April 14, 2021).
14. Road-watering policies also reduce road dust but we know of no economics research on these.
15. These are partial equilibrium effects – holding congestion and other factors affecting car adoption fixed at the time of the lottery.
16. Tan et al. (2019) show that a fuel tax outperforms a license auction in the short run due to these usage reductions.
17. The program, introduced in 2003, charged GBP 5 initially, increasing to GBP 8 in 2005 and GBP 10 in 2011.
18. The toll varied by time of day but did not exceed USD 2.60.
19. Before this the charge was EUR 5.
20. For example, see "Bike-Sharing Data and Cities: Lessons from China's Experience," Global Environment Facility, January 17, 2018, available at www.thegef.org/blog/bike-sharing-data-and-cities-lessons-chinas-experience (accessed April 14, 2021).
21. Although the law imposed some specific measures that must be taken by non-compliant prefectures, local regulators had significant discretion over how to meet the targets.
22. The first day with the highest annual hourly reading was exempted.
23. A type I error is a "false positive" ("an innocent person is convicted") and a type II error is a "false negative" ("a guilty person is not convicted").
24. Although the Volkswagen emissions cheating scandal in 2015 shows that this is not foolproof either. "Volkswagen: The Scandal Explained," *BBC News*, December 10, 2015.
25. Sales taxes on gasoline do not necessarily differ from sales taxes on other items and therefore are not specifically targeted at reducing vehicular miles traveled and therefore pollution.
26. This is described at www.epa.gov/ground-level-ozone-pollution/ozone-national-ambient-air-quality-standards-naaqs-section-126 (accessed April 14, 2021).
27. "A Clean Air Plan for Hong Kong," Environment Bureau of Hong Kong, March 2013.
28. See "Legislative Council Panel on Environmental Affairs: Report on the Cleaner Production Partnership Programme," Legislative Council Paper No. CB(1)869/19-20(01), www.legco.gov.hk/yr19-20/english/panels/ea/papers/eacb1-869-1-e.pdf (accessed April 14, 2021).
29. Karplus et al. (2021) review the development of China's complex and unique environmental regulations over the past half century.

# REFERENCES

Adhvaryu, A., Kala, N., and Nyshadham, A. (2019). "Management and Shocks to Worker Productivity," NBER Working Paper #25865.

Adler, M., and van Ommeren, J. N. (2016). "Does Public Transit Reduce Car Travel Externalities? Quasi-Natural Experiments' Evidence from Transit Strikes," *Journal of Urban Economics*, 92, 106–119.

Anas, A., and Lindsey, R. (2011). "Reducing Urban Road Transportation Externalities: Road Pricing in Theory and in Practice," *Review of Environmental Economics and Policies*, 5 (1), 66–88.

Anderson, M. L. (2019). "As the Wind Blows: The Effects of Long-Term Exposure to Air Pollution on Mortality," *Journal of the European Economic Association*, 18(4), 1886–1927.

Aragón, F. M., Miranda, J. J., and Oliva, P. (2017). "Particulate Matter and Labor Supply: The Role of Caregiving and Non-Linearities," *Journal of Environmental Economics and Management*, 86, 295–309.

Archsmith, J., Heyes, A., and Saberian, S. (2018). "Air Quality and Error Quantity: Pollution and Performance in a High-Skilled, Quality-Focused Occupation," *Journal of the Association of Environmental and Resource Economists*, 5(4), 827–863.

Arnott, R., and Kraus, M. (2003). "Transport Economics," in Hall, R. (Ed.), *Handbook of Transportation Science*, New York: Springer, 689–726.

Arnott, R., de Palma, A., and Lindsey, R. (1993). "A Structural Model of Peak-Period Congestion: A Traffic Bottleneck with Elastic Demand," *American Economic Review*, 83, 161–179.

Banzhaf, S., Ma, L., and Timmins, C. (2019). "Environmental Justice: The Economics of Race, Place, and Pollution," *Journal of Economic Perspectives*, 33(1), 185–208.

Barahona, N., Gallego, F., and Montero, J. P. (2020). "Vintage-Specific Driving Restrictions," *Review of Economic Studies*, 87, 1646–1682.

Bartik, T. J. (1988). "Evaluating the Benefits of Non-Marginal Reductions in Pollution Using Information on Defensive Expenditures," *Journal of Environmental Economics and Management*, 15(1), 111–127.

Barwick, P. J., Li, S., Lin, L., and Zou, E. (2019). "From Fog to Smog:.The Value of Pollution Information," NBER Working Paper #26541.

Bauernschuster, S., Hener, T., and Rainer, H. (2017). "When Labor Disputes Bring Cities to a Standstill: The Impact of Public Transit Strikes on Traffic, Accidents, Air Pollution, and Health," *American Economic Journal: Economic Policy*, 9(1), 1–37.

Baum-Snow, N., Kahn, M., and Voith, R. (2005). "Effects of Urban Rail Transit Expansions: Evidence from Sixteen Cities, 1970–2000," *Brookings-Wharton Papers on Urban Affairs*, 147–206.

Bayer, P., Keohane, N., and Timmins, C. (2009). "Migration and Hedonic Valuation: The Case of Air Quality," *Journal of Environmental Economics and Management*, 58(1), 1–14.

Becker, R., and Henderson, J. (2000). "Effects of Air Quality Regulations on Polluting Industries," *Journal of Political Economy*, 108, 379–421.

Bento, A., Cropper, M., Mobarak, A. M., and Vinha, K. (2005). "The Effects of Urban Spatial Structure on Travel Demand in the United States," *Review of Economics and Statistics*, 87(3): 466–478.

Bento, A., Kaffine, D., Roth, K., and Zaragoza-Watkins, M. (2014). "The Effects of Regulation in the Presence of Multiple Unpriced Externalities: Evidence from the Transportation Sector," *American Economic Journal: Economic Policy*, 6(3), 1–29.

Bento, A., Freedman, M., and Lang, C. (2015). "Who Benefits from Environmental Regulation? Evidence from the Clean Air Act Amendments," *Review of Economics and Statistics*, 97(3), 610–622.

Bernecker, A., Boyer, P. C., and Gathmann, C. (2021). "The Role of Electoral Incentives for Policy Innovation: Evidence from the US Welfare Reform," *American Economic Journal: Economic Policy*, 13(2): 26–57.

Bharadwaj, P., Gibson, M., Graff Zivin, J., and Neilson, C. (2017). "Gray Matters: Fetal Pollution Exposure and Human Capital Formation," *Journal of the Association of Environmental and Resource Economists*, 4(2), 505–542.

Bishop, K., Ketcham, J. D., and Kuminoff, N. V. (2018). "Hazed and Confused: The Effect of Air Pollution on Dementia," NBER Working Paper #24970.

Blackman, A., Alpízar, F., Carlsson, F., and Planter, M. R. (2018). "A Contingent Valuation Approach to Estimating Regulatory Costs: Mexico's Day without Driving Program," *Journal of the Association of Environmental and Resource Economists*, 5(3), 607–641.

Blackman, A, Qin, P., and Yang, J. (2020). "How Costly Are Driving Restrictions? Contingent Valuation Evidence from Beijing," *Journal of Environmental Economics and Management*, 104, 102366.

Blomquist, G. (2006). "Measuring Quality of Life," in Arnott, R. and McMillen, D. (Eds), *A Companion to Urban Economics*, Malden, MA: Blackwell Publishing, 483–501.

Bondy, M., Roth, S., and Sager, L. (2020). "Crime Is in the Air: The Contemporaneous Relationship between Air Pollution and Crime," *Journal of the Association of Environmental and Resource Economists*, 7(3), 555–585.

Bošković, B. (2015). "Air Pollution, Externalities, and Decentralized Environmental Regulation," Working Paper.

Chang, T., Graff Zivin, J., Gross, T., and Neidell, M. (2016). "Particulate Pollution and the Productivity of Pear Packers," *American Economic Journal: Economic Policy*, 8(3), 141–169.

Chang, T., Graff Zivin, J., Gross, T., and Neidell, M. (2019). "The Effect of Pollution on Worker Productivity: Evidence from Call-Center Workers in China," *American Economic Journal: Applied Economics*, 11, 151–172.

Chay, K., and Greenstone, M. (2005). "Does Air Quality Matter? Evidence from the Housing Market," *Journal of Political Economy*, 113(2), 376–424.

Chen, J. Y., Li, P., and Lu, Y. (2018). "Career Concerns and Multitasking Local Bureaucrats: Evidence of a Target-Based Performance Evaluation System in China," *Journal of Development Economics*, 133, 84–101.

Chen, S., Oliva, P., and Zhang, P. (2022). "The Effect of Air Pollution on Migration: Evidence from China," *Journal of Development Economics*, 156, 102833.

Chen, S., Oliva, P., and Zhang, P. (2018a). "Air Pollution and Mental Health: Evidence from China," NBER Working Paper #24686.

Chen, S., Guo, C., and Huang, X. (2018b). "Air Pollution, Student Health, and School Absences: Evidence from China," *Journal of Environmental Economics and Management*, 92, 465–497.

Chen, S., Chen, Y., Lei, Z., and Tan-Soo, J. (2020a). "Impact of Air Pollution on Short-Term Movements: Evidence from Air Travels in China," *Journal of Economic Geography*, 20, 939–968.

Chen, S., Chen, Y., Lei, Z., and Tan-Soo, J. (2020b). "Chasing Clean Air: Pollution-Induced Travels in China," *Journal of the Association of Environmental and Resource Economists*, 8(1), 59–89.

Chen, Y., Ebenstein, A., Greenstone, M., and Li, H. (2013). "Evidence on the Impact of Sustained Exposure to Air Pollution on Life Expectancy from China's Huai River Policy," *Proceedings of the National Academy of Sciences*, 110(32), 12936–12941.

Chen, Y. (2021). "Pollution Regulations, Local Labor Markets, and Skill Heterogeneity," Working Paper.

Chen, Y., and Whalley, A. (2012). "Green Infrastructure: The Effects of Urban Rail Transit on Air Quality," *American Economic Journal: Economic Policy*, 4(1): 58–97.

Chen, Y., Zhe, J. G., Naresh, K., and Shi, G. (2012). "Gaming in Air Pollution Data? Lessons from China," *B. E. Journal of Economic Analysis and Policy*, 13, 1–43.

Cheung, C., He, G., and Pan, Y. (2020). "Mitigating the Air Pollution Effect? The Remarkable Decline in the Pollution-Mortality Relationship in Hong Kong," *Journal of Environmental Economics and Management*, 102316.

Chew, S. H., Huang, W., and Li, X. (2021). "Does Haze Cloud Decision Making? A Natural Laboratory Experiment," *Journal of Economic Behavior and Organization*, 182, 132–161.

Coase, R. H. (1960). "The Problem of Social Costs," *Journal of Law and Economics*, 3, 1–44.

Cohen, A., Brauer, M., Burnett, R. et al. (2017). "Estimates and 25-Year Trends of the Global Burden of Disease Attributable to Ambient Air Pollution: An analysis of Data from the Global Burden of Diseases Study 2015," *Lancet*, 389, 1907–1918.

Currie, J., Hanushek, E. A., Kahn, E. M., Neidell, and M., Rivkin, S. G. (2009). "Does Pollution Increase School Absences?" *Review of Economics and Statistics*, 91(4), 682–694.

Cutter, B., and Neidell, M. (2009). "Voluntary Information Programs and Environmental Regulation: Evidence from 'Spare the Air,'" *Journal of Environmental Economics and Management*, 58, 253–265.

Davis, L. W. (2008). "The Effects of Driving Restrictions on Air Quality in Mexico City," *Journal of Political Economy*, 116(1), 38–81.

de Grange, L., and Troncoso, R. (2011). "Impacts of Vehicle Restrictions on Urban Transport Flows: The Case of Santiago, Chile," *Transport Policy*, 18(6), 862–869.

Deryugina, T., Heutel, G., Miller, N. H., Molitor, D., and Reif, J. (2019). "The Mortality and Medical Costs of Air Pollution: Evidence from Changes in Wind Direction," *American Economic Review*, 109, 4178–4219.

Deschênes, O., Greenstone, M., and Shapiro, J. S. (2017). "Defensive Investments and the Demand for Air Quality: Evidence from the NOx Budget Program," *American Economic Review*, 107(10), 2958–2989.

Deschênes, O., Wang, H., Wang, S., and Zhang, P. (2020). "The Effect of Air Pollution on Body Weight and Obesity: Evidence from China," *Journal of Development Economics*, 145, 102461.

Dong, R., Fisman, R., Wang, Y., and Xu, N. (2021). "Air Pollution, Affect, and Forecasting Bias: Evidence from Chinese Financial Analysts." *Journal of Financial Economics*, 139, 971–984.

Duranton, G., and Turner, M. A. (2011). "The Fundamental Law of Road Congestion: Evidence from US Cities," *American Economic Review*, 101(6), 2616–2652.

Ebenstein, A., and Greenstone, M. (2020). "Childhood Exposure to Particulate Air Pollution, Human Capital Accumulation, and Income: Evidence from China," Working Paper.

Ebenstein, A., Lavy, V., and Roth, S. (2016). "The Long-Run Economic Consequences of High-Stakes Examinations: Evidence from Transitory Variation in Pollution," *American Economic Journal: Applied Economics*, 8(4): 36–65.

Ebenstein, A., Fan, M., Greenstone, M., He, G., and Zhou, M. (2017). "New Evidence on the Impact of Sustained Exposure to Air Pollution on Life Expectancy from China's Huai River Policy," *Proceedings of the National Academy of Sciences*, 114(39), 10384–10389.

EPA (US Environmental Protection Agency) (2004). "Air Quality Criteria for Particulate Matter."

EPA (US Environmental Protection Agency) (2021). "Report on the Environment: Particulate Matter Emissions," www.epa.gov/roe.

Freeman, R., Liang, W., Song, R., and Timmins, C. (2019). "Willingness to Pay for Clean Air in China," *Journal of Environmental Economics and Management*, 94, 188–216.

Fu, S., and Gu, Y. (2017). "Highway Toll and Air Pollution: Evidence from Chinese Cities," *Journal of Environmental Economics and Management*, 83, 32–49.

Fu, S., Viard, V. B., and Zhang, P. (2022). "Trans-Boundary Air Pollution Spillovers: Physical Transport and Economic Costs by Distance," *Journal of Development Economics*, 155, 102808.

Fu, S., Viard, V. B., and Zhang, P. (2021). "Air Pollution and Manufacturing Firm Productivity: Nationwide Estimates for China," *Economic Journal*, 131(640), 3241–3273.

Fullerton, D., and Li, G. (2005). "Cost-Effective Policies to Reduce Vehicle Emissions," *American Economic Review*, 95, 300–304.

Gallego, F., Montero, J., and Salas, C. (2013). "The Effect of Transport Policies on Car Use: Evidence from Latin American Cities," *Journal of Public Economics*, 107(C), 47–62.

Gehrsitz, M. (2017). "The Effect of Low Emission Zones on Air Pollution and Infant Health," *Journal of Environmental Economics and Management*, 83, 121–144.

Gendron-Carrier, N., Gonzalez-Navarro, M., Polloni, S., and Turner, M. A. (2021). "Subways and Urban Air Pollution," *American Economic Journal: Applied Economics*, 14(1), 164–196.

Ghanem, D., and Zhang, J. (2014). "'Effortless Perfection': Do Chinese Cities Manipulate Air Pollution Data?" *Journal of Environmental Economics and Management*, 68, 203–225.

Ghanem, D., Shen, S., and Zhang, J. (2020). "A Censored Maximum Likelihood Approach to Quantifying Manipulation in China's Air Pollution Data," *Journal of the Association of Environmental and Resource Economists*, 7(5).

Gibson, M., and Carnovale, M. (2015). "The Effects of Road Pricing on Driver Behavior and Air Pollution," *Journal of Urban Economics*, 89, 62–73.

Gilraine, M. (2020). "Air Filters, Pollution, and Student Achievement," Working Paper, New York University.

Goulder, L. H. (2013). "Markets for Pollution Allowances: What Are the (New) Lessons?" *Journal of Economic Perspectives*, 27(1), 87–102.

Graff Zivin, J., and Neidell, M. (2009). "Days of Haze: Environmental Information Disclosure and Intertemporal Avoidance Behavior," *Journal of Environmental Economics and Management*, 58, 119–128.

Graff Zivin, J., and Neidell, M. (2012). "The Impact of Pollution on Worker Productivity," *American Economic Review*, 102, 3652–3673.

Graff Zivin, J., Liu, T., Song, Y., Tang, Q., and Zhang, P. (2020). "The Unintended Impacts of Agricultural Fires: Human Capital in China," *Journal of Development Economics*, 147, 102560.

Green, C., Heywood, J., and Paniagua, M. N. (2020). "Did the London Congestion Charge Reduce Pollution?" *Regional Science and Urban Economics*, 84(C), 103573.

Greenstone, M. (2002). "The Impacts of Environmental Regulations on Industrial Activity: Evidence from the 1970 and 1977 Clean Air Act Amendments and Census of Manufactures," *Journal of Political Economy*, 110, 1175–219.

Greenstone, M., He, G., Jia, R., and Liu, T. (2020). "Can Technology Solve the Principal-Agent Problem? Evidence from China's War on Air Pollution," NBER Working Paper #27502.

Gu, Y., Jiang, C., Zhang, J., and Zou, B. (2021). "Subways and Road Congestion," *American Economic Journal: Applied Economics*, 13(2), 83–115.

Guo, M., and Fu, S. (2019). "Running with a Mask? The Effect of Air Pollution on Marathon Runners' Performance," *Journal of Sports Economics*, 20(7), 903–928.

Ham, J., Zweig, J. S., and Avol, E. (2011). "Pollution, Test Scores and the Distribution of Academic Achievement: Evidence from California Schools 2002–2008," Working Paper.

Han, Q., Liu, Y., and Lu, Z. (2020). "Temporary Driving Restrictions, Air Pollution, and Contemporaneous Health: Evidence from China," *Regional Science and Urban Economics*, 84, 103572.

Hanna, R., and Oliva, P. (2015). "The Effect of Pollution on Labor Supply: Evidence from a Natural Experiment in Mexico," *Journal of Public Economics*, 122, 68–79.

He, J., Liu, H., and Salvo, A. (2019). "Severe Air Pollution and Labor Productivity: Evidence from Industrial Towns in China," *American Economic Journal: Applied Economics*, 11(1), 173–201.

He, X., Luo, Z., and Zhang, J. (2020). "The Impact of Air Pollution on Movie Theater Admissions," SSRN Working Paper.

Heblich, S., Trew, A., and Zylberberg, Y. (2021). "East Side Story: Historical Pollution and Persistent Neighborhood Sorting," *Journal of Political Economy*, 129(5), 1508–1552.

Heissel, J., Persico, C., and Simon, D. (2020). "Does Pollution Drive Achievement? The Effect of Traffic Pollution on Academic Performance," *Journal of Human Resources*, 57(1).

Helland, E., and Whitford, A. B. (2003). "Pollution Incidence and Political Jurisdiction: Evidence from the TRI," *Journal of Environmental Economics and Management*, 46, 403–424.

Henderson, J. V. (1996). "Effects of Air Quality Regulation," *American Economic Review*, 86(4), 789–813.

Herrnstadt, E., Heyes, A., Muehlegger, E., and Saberian, S. (2021). "Air Pollution and Criminal Activity: Microgeographic Evidence from Chicago," *American Economic Journal: Applied Economics*, 13(4), 70–100.

Heyes, A., Neidell, M., and Saberian, S. (2016a). "The Effect of Air Pollution on Investor Behavior: Evidence from the S&P 500," NBER Working Paper #22753.

Heyes, A., Rivers, N., and Schaufele, B. (2016b). "Politicians, Pollution and Performance in the Workplace: The Effect of PM on MPs," SSRN Working Paper.

Holland, S. P., Mansur, E. T., Muller, N. Z., and Yates, A. J. (2016). "Are There Environmental Benefits from Driving Electric Vehicles? The Importance of Local Factors," *American Economic Review*, 106(12), 3700–3729.

Huang, J., Xu, N., and Yu, H. (2020). "Pollution and Performance: Do Investors Make Worse Trades on Hazy Days?" *Management Science*, 66(10), 4455–4476.

Hubbard, T. A. (1998). "An Empirical Examination of Moral Hazard in the Vehicle Inspections Market," *RAND Journal of Economics*, 29(2), 406–426.

Isen, A., Rossin-Slater M., and Walker, W. R. (2017). "Every Breath You Take-Every Dollar You'll Make: The Long-Term Consequences of the Clean Air Act of 1970," *Journal of Political Economy*, 125(3), 849–909.

Ito, K., and Zhang, S. (2020). "Willingness to Pay for Clean Air: Evidence from Air Purifier Markets in China," *Journal of Political Economy*, 128(5), 1627–1672.

Jacobsen, M. R., and van Benthem, A. A. (2015). "Vehicle Scrappage and Gasoline Policy," *American Economic Review*, 105, 1312–1338.

Jacobsen, M. R., Sallee, J. M., Shapiro, J. S., and van Benthem, A. A. (2021). "Regulating Untaxable Externalities: Are Vehicle Air Pollution Standards Effective and Efficient?" Working Paper.

Jia, R. (2017). "Pollution for Promotion," Working Paper.

Kahn, M. E. (1999). "The Silver Lining of Rust Belt Manufacturing Decline," *Journal of Urban Economics*, 46(3), 360–376.

Kahn, M. E. (2006). "Air Pollution in Cities," in Arnott, R. J. and McMillen, D. P. (Eds), *A Companion to Urban Economics*, Malden, MA: Blackwell Publishing.

Kahn, M. E., and Li, P. (2020). "Air Pollution Lowers High Skill Public Sector Worker Productivity in China," *Environmental Research Letters*, 15, 084003.

Kahn, M. E., and Walsh, R. (2015). "Cities and the Environment," in Duranton, G., Henderson, V. and Strange, W. (Eds), *Handbook of Regional and Urban Economics*, Vol. 5A, Amsterdam: Elsevier B.V.

Karagulian, F., C. Belis, C. Dora et al. (2015). "Contributions to Cities' Ambient Particulate Matter (PM): A Systematic Review of Local Source Contributions at Global Level," *Atmospheric Environment*, 120, 475–483.

Karplus, V. J., Zhang, J., and Zhao, J. (2021). "Navigating and Evaluating the Labyrinth of Environmental Regulation in China," *Review of Environmental Economics and Policy*, 15(2).

Kweon, B.-S., Mohai, P., Lee, S., and Sametshaw, A. (2018). "Proximity of Public Schools to Major Highways and Industrial Facilities, and Students' School Performance and Health Hazards," *Environment and Planning B: Planning and Design*, 45(2), 312–329.

Levinson, A. (2012). "Valuing Public Goods Using Happiness Data: The Case of Air Quality," *Journal of Public Economics*, 96, 869–880.

Levinson, A., and Taylor, M. S. (2008). "Unmasking the Pollution Haven Effect," *International Economic Review*, 49(1), 223–254.

Li, H., and Zhou, L. (2005). "Political Turnover and Economic Performance: The Incentive Role of Personnel Control in China," *Journal of Public Economics*, 89, 1743–1762.

Li, J., Massa, M., Zhang, H., and Zhang, J. (2021). "Air Pollution, Behavioral Bias, and the Disposition Effect in China," *Journal of Financial Economics*, 142(2), 641–673.

Li, S. (2018). "Better Lucky Than Rich? Welfare Analysis of Automobile License Allocations in Beijing and Shanghai," *Review of Economic Studies*, 85, 2389–2428.

Li, S., Linn, J., and Spiller, E. (2013). "Evaluating 'Cash-for-Clunkers': Program Effects on Auto Sales and the Environment," *Journal of Environmental Economics and Management*, 65, 175–193.

Li, S., Liu, Y., Purevjav, A., and Yang, L. (2019). "Does Subway Expansion Improve Air Quality?" *Journal of Environmental Economics and Management*, 96, 213–235.

Lin, Y. (2018). "The Hidden Cost of Industrial Pollution: Environmental Amenities and the Location of Service Jobs," HKUST Working Paper.

Lindsey, R., Zhang, A., and Gómez-Ibáñez, J. A. (2008). "Prospects for Urban Road Pricing in Canada," *Brookings-Wharton Papers on Urban Affairs*, 235–293.

List, J. A., and Gerking, S. (2000). "Regulatory Federalism and Environmental Protection in the United States," *Journal of Regional Science*, 40(3), 453–471.

List, J. A., and Sturm, D. M. (2006). "How Elections Matter: Theory and Evidence from Environmental Policy," *Quarterly Journal of Economics*, 121(4), 1249–1281.

Liu, C., and Li, L. (2020). "How do Subways Affect Urban Passenger Transport Modes? Evidence from China," *Economics of Transportation*, 23, 100181.

Liu, H., and Salvo, A. (2018). "Severe Air Pollution and Child Absences When Schools and Parents Respond," *Journal of Environmental Economics and Management*, 92, 300–330.

Lu, J. G. (2020). "Air Pollution: A Systematic Review of Its Psychological, Economic, and Social Effects," *Current Opinion in Psychology*, 32, 52–65.

Luechinger, S. (2009). "Valuing Air Quality Using the Life Satisfaction Approach," *Economic Journal*, 119(536), 482–515.

Malina, C., and Scheffler, F. (2015). "The Impact of Low Emission Zones on Particulate Matter Concentration and Public Health," *Transportation Research Part A*, 77, 372–385.

Margaryan, S. (2021). "Low Emission Zones and Population Health," *Journal of Health Economics*, 76, 102402.

Matthews, K. D. (1960). "The Embattled Driver in Ancient Rome," *Expedition Magazine*, 2(3), 135.

Matus, K., Yang, T., Paltsev et al. (2008). "Toward Integrated Assessment of Environmental Change: Air Pollution Health Effects in the USA," *Climatic Change*, 88, 59–92.

Meyer, S., and Pagel, M. (2017). "Fresh Air Eases Work: The Effect of Air Quality on Individual Investor Activity," NBER Working Paper #24048.

Michael, J. (2017). "Survey of State and Local Gasoline Taxes," House Research Department, State of Minnesota. www.house.mn/hrd/hrd.htm

Millimet, D. L. (2003). "Assessing the Empirical Impact of Environmental Federalism," *Journal of Regional Science*, 43(4), 711–733.

Millimet, D. L. (2014). "Environmental Federalism: A Survey of the Empirical Literature," *Case Western Reserve Law Review*, 64(4), 1669–1757.

Neidell, M. (2009). "Information, Avoidance Behavior, and Health," *Journal of Human Resources*, 44(2), 450–478.

Oates, W. E., and Schwab, R. M. (1988). "Economic Competition among Jurisdictions: Efficiency Enhancing or Distortion Inducing?" *Journal of Public Economics*, 35(3), 333–354.

OECD (2012). *Mortality Risk Valuation in Environment, Health and Transport Policies*. Paris: OECD Publishing.

Oliva, P. (2015). "Environmental Regulations and Corruption: Automobile Emissions in Mexico City," *Journal of Political Economy*, 123(3), 686–724.

Parry, I., Walls, M., and Harrington, W. (2007). "Automobile Externalities and Policies," *Journal of Economic Literature*, 45(2), 373–399.

Qin, Y., and Zhu, H. (2018). "Run Away? Air Pollution and Emigration Interests in China," *Journal of Population Economics*, 31, 235–266.

Sager, L. (2019). "Estimating the Effect of Air Pollution on Road Safety Using Atmospheric Temperature Inversions," *Journal of Environmental Economics and Management*, 98, 102250.

Sanders, N. J., and Sandler, R. (2020). "Technology and the Effectiveness of Regulatory Programs over Time: Vehicle Emissions and Smog Checks with a Changing Fleet," *Journal of the Association of Environmental and Resource Economists*, 7(3), 587–618.

Sandler, R. (2012). "Clunkers or Junkers? Adverse Selection in a Vehicle Retirement Program," *American Economic Journal: Economic Policy*, 4, 253–281.

Seigneur, C., and Dennis, R. (2011). "Atmospheric Modeling" in *Technical Challenges of Multipollutant Air Quality Management*, Dordrecht: Springer.

Shapiro, J. M. (2006). "Smart Cities: Quality of Life, Productivity, and the Growth Effects of Human Capital," *Review of Economics and Statistics*, 88(2), 324–335.

Simeonova, E., Currie, J., Nilsson, P., and Walker, R. (2019). "Congestion Pricing, Air Pollution, and Children's Health," *Journal of Human Resources*, 57(1).

Small, K., and Verhoef, E. (2007). *The Economics of Urban Transportation*, London: Routledge.

Sun, C., Kahn, M., and Zheng, S. (2017). "Self-Protection Investment Exacerbates Air Pollution Exposure Inequality in Urban China," *Ecological Economics*, 131, 468–474.

Tan, J., Xiao, J., and Zhou, X. (2019). "Market Equilibrium and Welfare Effects of a Fuel Tax in China: The Impact of Consumers' Response through Driving Patterns," *Journal of Environmental Economics and Management*, 93, 20–43.

Tanaka, S. (2015). "Environmental Regulations on Air Pollution in China and Their Impact on Infant Mortality," *Journal of Health Economics*, 42, 90–103.

Tiebout, C. M. (1956). "A Pure Theory of Local Expenditures," *Journal of Political Economy*, 64(5), 416–424.

Viard, V. B., and Fu, S. (2015). "The Effect of Beijing's Driving Restrictions on Pollution and Economic Activity," *Journal of Public Economics*, 125, 98–115.

Wang, S., and Wang, Z. (2020). "The Environmental and Economic Consequences of Internalizing Border Spillovers," Working Paper.

WHO (World Health Organization) (2016). *Ambient Air Pollution: A Global Assessment of Exposure and Burden of Disease*. Washington, DC: WHO.

Williams, A., Phaneufa, D. J., Barrett, M. A., and Su, J. G. (2019). "Short-Term Impact of $PM_{2.5}$ on Contemporaneous Asthma Medication Use: Behavior and the Value of Pollution Reductions," *Proceedings of the National Academy of Sciences*, 116(12), 5246–5253.

Wolff, H. (2014). "Keep Your Clunker in the Suburb: Low-Emission Zones and Adoption of Green Vehicles," *Economic Journal*, 124(578), 481–512.

Wu, J., Deng, Y., Huang, J., Morck, R., and Yeung, B. (2013). "Incentives and Outcomes: China's Environmental Policy," NBER Working Paper #18754.

Wu, M., and Cao, X. (2021). "Greening the Career Incentive Structure for Local Officials in China: Does Less Pollution Increase the Chances of Promotion for Chinese Local Leaders?" *Journal of Environmental Economics and Management*, 107, 102440.

Xiao, J., Zhou, X., and Hu, W. (2017). "Welfare Analysis of the Vehicle Quota System in China," *International Economic Review*, 58(2), 617–650.

Xu, Y., Zhang, Q., and Zheng, S. (2015). "The Rising Demand for Subway after Private Driving Restriction: Evidence from Beijing's Housing Market," *Regional Science and Urban Economics*, 54, 28–37.

Yang, J., Liu, A. A., Qin, P., and Linn, J. (2020a). "The Effect of Vehicle Ownership Restrictions on Travel Behavior: Evidence from the Beijing License Plate Lottery," *Journal of Environmental Economics and Management*, 99, 114–133.

Yang, J., Purevjav, A., and Li, S. (2020b). "The Marginal Cost of Traffic Congestion and Road Pricing: Evidence from a Natural Experiment in Beijing," *American Economic Journal: Economic Policy*, 12(1), 418–453.

Yang, M., and Chou, S. Y. (2018). "The Impact of Environmental Regulation on Fetal Health: Evidence from the Shutdown of a Coal-Fired Power Plant Located Upwind of New Jersey," *Journal of Environmental Economics and Management*, 90, 269–293.

Yu, J., Zhou, L., and Zhu, G. (2016). "Strategic Interaction in Political Competition: Evidence from Spatial Effects across Chinese Cities," *Regional Science and Urban Economics*, 57, 23–37.

Zhang, J., and Mu, Q. (2018). "Air Pollution and Defensive Expenditures: Evidence from Particulate-Filtering Facemasks," *Journal of Environmental Economics and Management*, 92, 517–536.

Zhang, W., Lin Lawell, C.-Y. C., and Umanskaya, V. I. (2017). "The Effects of License Plate-Based Driving Restrictions on Air Quality: Theory and Empirical Evidence," *Journal of Environmental Economics and Management*, 82, 181–220.

Zhang, X., Zhang, X., and Chen, X. (2017). "Happiness in the Air: How Does a Dirty Sky Affect Subjective Well-Being?" *Journal of Environmental Economics and Management*, 85, 81–94.

Zhang, X., Chen, X., and Zhang, X. (2018). "The Impact of Exposure to Air Pollution on Cognitive Performance," *Proceedings of the National Academy of Sciences*, 115(37), 9193–9197.

Zheng, S., Kahn, M. E., Sun, W., and Luo, D. (2014a). "Incentives for China's Urban Mayors to Mitigate Pollution Externalities: The Role of the Central Government and Public Environmentalism," *Regional Science and Urban Economics*, 47, 61–71.

Zheng, S., Cao, J., Kahn, M., and Sun, C. (2014b). "Real Estate Valuation and Cross-Boundary Air Pollution Externalities: Evidence from Chinese Cities," *Journal of Real Estate Finance and Economics*, 48, 398–414.

Zhong, N., Cao, J., and Wang, Y. (2017). "Traffic Congestion, Ambient Air Pollution, and Health: Evidence from Driving Restrictions in Beijing," *Journal of the Association of Environmental and Resource Economists*, 4(3), 821–856.

Zou, E. Y. (2021). "Unwatched Pollution: The Effect of Intermittent Monitoring on Air Quality," *American Economic Review*, 111(7), 2101–2126.

# Index

Acemoglu, D. 45, 343
Acharya, Viral V. 251
Acolin, Arthur 258
Act on Investment Trusts and Investment Corporations 24
Adamopoulos, T. 43
Adelino, Manuel 244
adequacy cases 117–19
Adhvaryu, A. 417, 418
Adrian, Tobias 258
affordability, regional dimension of 92–5
affordable housing conundrum in India 83
    literature 85–7
    macro context for housing in India 87–91
    regional dimension of affordability and housing inadequacies 92–5
    regional disparity in economic growth 92
    regional variation in access to finance 95–7
    regional variation in local governance 98–9
    regional variations in implementation of PMAY 99–101
Agarwal, Sumit 241, 243, 244, 248, 252, 253, 259–62
agency-based models 143
agglomeration economies (AEs) 338, 347, 354
aggregate economic impact of transportation improvements 352–3
aggregated private equity fund net asset value 381
agricultural farmland prices 66
agricultural production 52
agricultural productivity 42
agriculture and aggregate productivity 43
Ahuja, A. 175
air pollution 413, 420
    in cities, sources of ambient 414
    economic impacts of ambient urban 414–20
    incentives 427–8
    policies to alleviate ambient urban 421–7
Air Pollution Index (API) 417
Air Pollution Prevention and Control Law 426
air quality, pay for 419–20
Air Quality Index (AQI) 417
Akhigbe, Aigbe 249
Albouy, David 355
Alder, S. 365, 369
Aliber, R. 169
Allen, Treb 353
Alonso, W. 107
Alonso-Muth model 108

ambient urban air pollution
    economic impacts of 414–20
    policies to alleviate 421–7
American Housing Rescue and Foreclosure Prevention Act of 2008 (FPA) 261
André, C. 208
Anenberg, Elliot 256
Antonakakis, N. 208
Aoki, K. 285
Aragón, F. M. 417
AR-ARCH model 334
Arellano, M. 217
AR-GARCH model 315
Arkolakis, Costas 353
Arnot, C.D. 42
Aron, J. 5
Ascari, G. 158
Asness, C. 392
asset-backed commercial paper market 248, 251
asset-backed securities market 254
asset–liability maturity 247
"asset return premium" 313
assets under management (AUM) 375
"atheoretical benchmark" 315
Augmented Dickey–Fuller (ADF) test 148
Aumann, R. J. 314, 315, 332, 333
Austin, Benjamin 347
auto license and driving restrictions 421–3
autoregressive distributed lag (ARDL) model 179–81
avoidance behavior 415, 418–19
Aye, G.C. 209

Baddeley, M. 169
"balanced development" strategy 360, 363
Ban, S.H. 42
bank holding companies (BHCs) 249, 250
Bank of Israel 297
Bank of Japan (BOJ) 21, 157
    cox hazard model with time-dependent covariates 29–30
    data 26–7
    Japanese REIT market 24–6
    linear probability model 28–9
    REIT purchase behavior 30–34
    REIT share prices, effect on 34–5
    unconventional monetary policy 22–4
Banzhaf, S. 430
Barahona, N. 423

Barwick, P. J. 421
baseline model 52–3
basic regression results 182
Basile, A. 158
Bauernschuster, S. 425
Baumer, Eric P. 256
Baum-Snow, Nathaniel 351
Baxter, M. 286
Bayer, Patrick 110, 112, 126, 249, 419
Bayesian methods 207
Becker, Bo 246
beneficiary-led construction scheme 100
Bento, A. 422, 426
Beraja, Martin 345, 355
Berk, J. 391, 405
Bernanke, B.S. 142
Bertrand, M. 52
Besley, T. 42
Bezemer, D. 41
Bhalotra, S. 52
Bhatt, V. 213
Bhattacharya, P.S. 40, 41, 46, 47, 49, 53, 66, 67
Bhutta, Neil 248, 251
Binswanger-Mkhize, H.P. 63
Black, A. 179
Black, Sandra E. 126
Blackman, A. 422
Blanchard, O.J. 169
Boadway, Robin 110
Bollerslev, T. 315
Bollinger, M. 372, 390
Bolton, Patrick 246
Bond, S. 217
bootstrap panel causality test 210
Borcard, D. 191
border economic cooperation zones (BECZs) 361
Borland, Melvin V. 114
Bouri, E. 209, 210
Boustan, Leah P. 109
Breitung, J. 138, 148, 181
Bremus, Franziska 258
"brick-and-mortar" operations 258
Brooks, Leah 109
Brown, J. 384
Brown, Robert L. 270, 275
*Brown v. Board of Education of Topeka* 119, 123
Brueckner, Jan K. 109
Brulhart, Marius 110
Brunnermeier, Markus K. 144, 242, 252
Bruno, G. 217
bubbles
 on filtered price, testing for 149–50
 fundamentals and 145–7
 and present-value model 144
 in price-to-rent ratio, testing for 148–9

 test on log price-to-rent ratio 151–3
 types 143–4
 typology 142–7
business cycle 286
 correlations 290–296

Caceres, C. 19
Caetano, Gregorio 112
Calabrese, Stephen 126
Caldera, A. 153
Caliendo, Lorenzo 344
CALPERS 405
Camacho, M. 226
Campbell, J.Y. 6, 145, 255
Campbell, S.D. 139, 149
Campbell, Sean 260
Capozza, D. 143, 179
Card, David 119
Carnovale, M. 424
Case, K.E. 166
Case-Shiller return 320
Cash for Clunkers program 260
Cerutti, Eugenio 258
*ceteris paribus* 45, 46
Chambers, M. 83
Chan, I.C. 179
Chang, K. L. 315, 318, 321, 326, 334
Chang, T. 318, 417
Chang, Y. 179
charter schools 124–5
Chay, K. 419
chemical transport models 427
Chen, J. Y. 428
Chen, N.K. 18, 19, 143, 251
Chen, S. 418, 419
Chen, Y. 415, 425
Chen, Y. T. 316, 317, 333
Cheung, C. 415
China, political economy in 359
 allocation of industrial parks across cities 362–4
 economic cost of politically driven distribution of industrial parks 364–8
 industrial parks 360–362
Chinco, Alex 249
Chinese Communist Party (CCP) 360, 363
Chinese housing markets 171, 193, 195
Chinese housing price dynamics 192–201
 disaggregation 195–201
 long-/short-term mechanisms 193–5
 sample data 192–3
Chodorow-Reich, Gabriel 254, 345
Choi, I. 181
Chong, Beng Soon 250
Chou, S. Y. 427

Chow test 276, 277
Christiano, L. 287
Christidou, M. 209, 210
Christou, C. 208–9
Chu, C. 214
Ciccone, Antonio 346
Civil Rights Act of 1964 119
Claessens, Stijn 258
Clark, Melissa 118
coastal and inland MSAs 196
Cocco, J.F. 6
Cohen, A. 415
cointegration tests 274
Coleman, M. IV 179
collateral channel 4
collateralized debt obligations (CDOs) 246
collateralized loan obligations (CLOs) 397
combined end user motives land reform
    implementation 65
  on manufacturing 79
  on nominal farmland price index 76
combined end user rights motives land reform
    implementation
  on urbanization 73
combined land ceiling 75, 81
commercial bank branches 96
commercial mortgage-backed securities (CMBS) 379
  issuance volume 378
  market 378
commercial real estate (CRE) 371, 375, 380
  allocations 386–95
community choice models 107, 109–12, 114
"conduit" CMBS market 378
confidence interval (CI) 71
congestion 90
"congestion externality" 423
congestion tolls 423–5
consolidation motive land reform implementation 55, 65, 71, 75, 77
consolidation-type reforms 57
consumer borrowings 7
  variance decomposition of 8
consumer credit 254–5
consumer debt-driven economy 254
consumer price index (CPI) 298
consumer spending 254–5
consumption function by panel data 16
control variables 49
conventional social housing policy research 83
Coons, John E. 127
Cooper, D. 19
corporate junk bond 378
Costinot, Arnaud 343
Coulson, N. Edward 269–71, 274

Couture, Victor 109
Covitz, Daniel 248
cox hazard model 21
  of starting decisions 34
  of stopping decisions 34
  with time-dependent covariates 29–30
credit-linked subsidy scheme 91
credit rating agencies (CRAs) 241, 245–7
crime, foreclosures on 256
Cui, Lin 256
cumulative housing shortage 90
Currie, Janet 257
customary/indigenous/community/religious/
    traditional (CICRT)
  land rights 48
  recognition 60, 63, 74, 80
CUSUM test 275–7
Cutler, D.M. 178

Dagher, Jihad 251
Das, S. 181
data sources 164
Davidoff, Thomas 126
Davis, M.A. 40, 44, 269, 271, 285, 286, 345
de Bartolome, Charles A.M. 110, 111
decision-making process 112
decision-making skills 416
DeCoster, G.P. 168
defined benefit (DB) plans 371
de Grange, L. 422
Deininger, K. 58, 63
"delegated investor" 399
Del Negro, M. 211, 213
DeLong, J.B. 45
demand-side policies 102
Demsetz, Rebecca S. 250
Demyanyk, Yuliya 241
Deng, Saiying 249
dependent variable 46
Depken II, Craig A. 248
Deryugina, T. 415
Deschênes, O. 420
descriptive statistics 50–51
Desmet, Klaus 352
developed countries, nominal farmland price
    index in 75
DFM-TV-SV model 207, 211–13
Diamond, Douglas W. 262
Diamond, Rebecca 355
Diba, B.T. 169
Dickey-Fuller tests 274
Dickey–Fuller unit root test 7
differences-in-differences (DiD) technique 41, 66, 424
disability-adjusted life years (DALYs) 413, 415

disaggregation 195–201
  in policies 176
disposable income 6, 7
distributive land reform implementation 63
distributive motive land reform implementation 55, 71, 77
Dittmer, L. 363
diversification of risk 249–50
diversified lenders 250
Djankov, S. 44, 66
Do, Q. 364
Doerr, Sebastian 250
Donaldson, Dave 353
Dougherty, A. 179
Downing, Janelle 257
dual nature of real estate markets 141
Duca, J. 285
Duca, John V. 252
Duranton, Gilles 346, 349, 351, 355
Dynan, Karen 254

"early warning systems" 313
East Asian crisis 137
Ebenstein, A. 415
Eberly, Janice 262
econometric models 169
economic activity *versus* economic growth 354
economic importance of transportation 351–2
economic index of riskiness 314–15
economic performance index (EPI) 314–15
economic policy uncertainty (EPU) 208
economic stimulus payments (ESPs) 260
economic theory of land market 40
economically weaker sections (EWSs) 85, 86, 102
education in the U.S. 106
education production function 111
Education Reform Act 118
electric vehicle subsidies 427
Elementary and Secondary Education Act of 1965 119
Ellen, Ingrid Gould 256
Ellickson, Bryan 109
El Montasser, G. 209
Elul, Ronel 251
Elyasiani, Elyas 249
Emergency Economic Stabilization Act of 2008 (EESA) 261
emissions standards and controls 426
Employee Retirement Income Security Act (ERISA) 373–7
end user rights-focused land reforms 66
end user rights land reform implementation 64
end user rights motives land reform implementation 73

endogenous supply 140
Engle-Granger tests 274
Engsted, T. 151
environmental-based performance evaluation 428
Epanechnikov kernel density 321
episodic driving restrictions 422
Epple, Dennis 110, 112, 126
equity cases 117
"equity premium puzzle" 313
equity real estate investment trusts (EREITs) 312, 321, 326
"equivalent predictive power classes" (EPPC) 314
error equation, sums of coefficients of 183
Evans, A.W. 40
Evans, G.W. 138
exchange-traded funds (ETFs) 21, 22
explanatory power of various models 200
explanatory variables 46–9
export-processing zones (EPZs) 361
exposure-response (ER) functions 415
external finance premium 4
externalities 347–8

Fahey, T. 83
Fajgelbaum, Pablo D. 348, 350, 353, 354
Fama, E. 377
Fama, E.F. 144, 178
Fane, G. 42
Feder, G. 63
federal funding of schools 115
Federal Funds 280, 282
Fernández, Raquel 110, 126
Ferreyra, Maria Marta 110, 112
FICO 243, 260
Figlio, David N. 113
Filardo, A. 143
financial assets, homogeneity of 141
financial crisis
  causes of 241–53
  consequences of 253–9
"fiscal stimulus packages" 312
Fischel, William A. 118
Fisher Z-Transformation 299
Fitzgerald, T. 287
fixed-rate mortgages (FRMs) 244
Food and Agricultural Organization statistical database 49
foreclosures contagion effect 255–7
foreign capital 297
Fountas, S. 209, 210
Fowler, Katherine A. 257
Franzoni, F. 391
Fratzscher, Marcel 258, 259
Freeman, R. 430
French, K.R. 178

Freyaldenhoven, S. 52
Friedman, Milton 122
Fu, S. 417, 422, 424, 427
"fundamental law of highway congestion" 425
Fuster, Andreas 244, 262
future housing, investment in 255

Gabaix, Xavier 343
Gabriel, Stuart A. 257
Gallego, F. 422
"gambling for resurrection" 404
Gan, J. 18
Ganong, Peter 346, 347
Gao, Zhenyu 248
Gardner, B.L. 42
gasoline taxes 427
Gaubert, Cecile 348, 353, 354
Gauss program 317
Geltner, D. 377
Gendron-Carrier, N. 425
general method of moments (GMM) 217
generalized dynamic factor model (DFM) 211
generalized least squares (GLS) 214
Gerardi, Kristopher 256
Gerking, S. 428
German Socio-Economic Panel 419
Ghanem, D., 428
Ghent, A. 371, 399–402
Giambona, E. 403
Giannone, Elisa 346, 347
Gibbs sampling algorithm 213
Gibson, M. 424
Gini coefficient 366, 367
Giroud, Xavier 343
Glaeser, E.L. 44, 63, 108, 137, 138, 158, 168, 169, 175, 179, 181, 352
Glaeser, G.L. 176
Global Financial Crisis (GFC) 137, 141, 168, 170, 171, 175, 201, 284, 288, 298, 312, 333, 378
  data and empirical findings 317–27
  "early warning systems" 313
  economic performance measure and empirical specification 314–17
  model selection procedure 327–32
Glomm, Gerhard 110, 112
Goetz, Martin R. 249
Goldfeld–Quandt test 184, 191
Goldstein, M. 42
Gomes, S. 158
Gomez-Gonzalez, J.E. 151
Gong, Yifan 127
Gordon Dividend Discount model 165
Gordon growth model 146, 177
Gordon model 180

Gorodnichenko, Y. 207
governmental appropriation decisions 115
government-sponsored enterprises (GSEs) 242
Graff Zivin, J. 417
Graham, James 112
granger tests on components of GDP 279–80
granular shocks and macroeconomics 343–4
Great Depression 240
Great Financial Crisis 271, 276, 277
"Great Moderation" 206
"Great Recession" 206
Gredil, O. 404
Green, C. 424
Green, R. 270, 274, 275, 391, 405
Green, R.K. 299
*Green v. County School Board of New Kent County* 119
Greenstone, M. 348, 419, 421
Greenwald, Daniel L. 344
Griffin, John M. 245, 246
gross domestic product (GDP) 42, 269
  granger tests on components of 279–80
Grossman, H.I. 169
growth convergence (divergence) in the United States 346–7
Gu, Y. 424, 425
Guiso, Luigi 251
Gupta, A. 372, 390, 392
Gupta, R. 207, 211, 213
Guren, Adam M. 344
Gurkanyak, R.S. 138
Gyourko, J. 44

Hadri, K. 181
Hall, Robert E. 346
Hamilton, J.D. 169, 274
Han, Q. 422
Handbury, Jessie 109
Hanna, R. 416
Hannan–Quinn information criteria 7
Hansen, P. 318
Hanushek, Eric A. 111, 119, 125–7
Harding, John P. 255
Harish, S. 86
Harris, R.D.F. 181
Hartley, Daniel 256
Harvey, D.I. 148
Hashimoto, Y. 154
Haughwout, Andrew 248
Hausman, J.A. 217
Hausman test 227
Hayami, Y. 39
Hazama, M. 18
He, J. 247, 417
Headet, D. 41

health, foreclosures on 257
Heathcote, J. 40, 44, 269, 271, 285, 286
Heaton, J. 333
Heblich, S. 420
Heckman 282
hedge funds (HFs) 372, 381
herding-based concentration risk 397
Herkenhoff, Kyle F. 349
heterogeneities 51
high-income households 94
"high-liquidity assets" 317
high-tech industrial development zones (HIDZs) 361
Himmelberg, C. 146
Hirono, K.N. 158
Holt, Jeff 252
Home Affordable Modification Program (HAMP) implementation 244
Home Affordable Refinance Program (HARP) 259
homeownership 87, 257–8
homeschooling 123
Homm, U. 138, 148, 312, 314, 332, 333
Hori, M. 5, 6
Hornbeck, Richard 345, 353
Hott, G. 153
Houle, Jason N. 257
house price dynamics 165
    Chinese housing price dynamics 192–201
    housing bubbles 166–76
    model of fundamentals 176–8
    pooled mean group model 179–81
    pricing dynamics 178–9
    United States housing price dynamics 181–92
house price index 90
house price *versus* the cost of ownership 144–5
households 340
    and firms, localization decisions by 355
    in slums 87
houses/apartments in India 88
housing
    affordability 89, 93
    bubbles 166–76
    construction projects 99
    inadequacies 84, 92–5, 101
    in India 87–91
    non-fundamental bubble detection for Japan 150–157
    ownership 83
    policies 83
    shortage 90
    variables 298
    wealth 14, 17, 297
housing finance institutions (HFIs) 95

housing market
    bubbles 167, 168
    and institutional reforms 102
    movements 206, 207
    returns 208
    turmoil and uncertainty 226
housing policy 102
    general equilibrium effects of changes in 354
    welfare implications of 83
housing returns and volatility 206–7
    data series used 210–211
    literature review 208–10
    methodologies 211–14
    pairwise correlation analysis 215–16
    regression analysis 216–25
    unit root test results 214–15
housing returns factor 218
    macroeconomic uncertainty on 235
housing units 165
    heterogeneity 141–2
Howsen, Roy M. 114
Hoxby, Caroline M. 114, 118
Hoy No Circula policy 422
Hsieh, Chang-Tai 282, 349, 355
Hsu, Joanne W. 259
Hu, Y. 151
Hu Jintao 365
Hubbard, T. A. 426
Hwang, M. 179
hybrid residential choice models 110–111

Iacoviello, M. 142, 285–6
Ibbotson, R. 374, 403
illiquidity price premium 391–4
Im, K. 181, 214
impulse response functions (IRFs) 9, 10, 12, 13, 277, 278
incentives 427–8
income-based approach 94
India, housing in 87–91
Indianapolis Neighborhood Housing Partnership 262
Indian housing market 83
industrial parks 360–362
    across cities 362–4
    economic cost of politically driven distribution of 364–8
    locational choice decision 368
inefficient spatial allocation of resources 347–50
Inman, Robert P. 110
institutional owner-investors 399
institutional ownership of CRE 400
instrumental variable method (IVX) 139, 149
integration/cointegration-based tests 138
interdistrict open enrollment 124

intermediaries, false information by 245
International Labour Organization 86
international macroeconomic aspect of housing 284
    business cycle 286
    shock propagation 285–6
    stylized facts 287–98
"intertemporal correlation" 313
intradistrict open enrollment 123
investors/flippers/speculative buyers, role of 248–9
Isen, A. 420
Ito, K. 420
Ito, T. 153, 158
Iwaisako, T. 153
Iwata, S. 19

Jackson, C. Kirabo 119
Jacobi, H.G. 42
Jacobsen, M. R. 423, 426
Jacobson, L.S. 52
Japan Household Panel Survey (KHPS/JHPS) 4, 14
Japanese Family Income and Expenditure Survey (FIES) 6
Japanese Government Bonds (JGBs) 21
Japanese Panel Survey of Consumption 5
Japanese REIT market 24–6
Jia, R. 363, 364
Jiang, Wei 245, 253
Jiang Zemin 365
Jin, Y. 286
Johansson, A. 153
Johnston, B.F. 42
Joyce, J.P. 158
Judson, R.A. 217
Jurado, K. 209, 211, 213, 216, 217, 224, 238

Kahn, M. 369
Kahn, M. E. 413, 414, 417
Kain, John F. 107
Karplus, V. J. 430
Kazimov, Kazim 251
Keelery, S. 89, 90
Kehoe, Patrick J. 254
*Keyes* v. *School District No. 1* 120
Keys, Benjamin J. 242
Kholodilin, K. 151
Kim, C.-J. 213
Kim, Myeong-Soo 269–71, 274
Kim, S. 213
Kindleberger, C. 169
King, R. 18
Kishor, N.K. 284
Kitasaka, S. 18

Kiyotaki, N. 285, 286
Knoll, K. 40, 41, 44, 46, 54, 64, 66
Korteweg, Arthur 391
Kostakis, A. 139, 149
Krainer, J. 158
Krämer, Walter 276
Krishnamurthy, Arvind 262, 280
Kruger, Samuel 244
Kuang, P. 143
Kung, Edward 256
Kwan, Y. K. 318

labor productivity and supply 416–18
Lafortune, Julien 119
Lai, Rose Neng 166, 169, 178, 179, 181, 186, 191, 192, 201
Lake Wobegon benchmarking 372, 394–5
Lambertini, L. 142
land, agricultural productivity and growth 41–2
land and macroeconomics 39
    agriculture and aggregate productivity 43
    control variables 49
    dependent variable 46
    descriptive statistics 50–51
    empirical strategy 51–4
    end user rights motives for land reform implementation on urbanization 55–60
    explanatory variables 46–9
    land, agricultural productivity and growth 41–2
    land and urban macroeconomic concepts 40
    land price variable as dependent variables 64–6
    land reforms with end user rights 44–6
    land tenure security and its impact on growth and development 42–3
    non-end user rights motives land reform implementation on urbanization 60–62
    two-way differences-in-differences estimation 62–4
    urban connections 43–4
land and urban macroeconomic concepts 40
land-holding ceiling imposition 49
land market development 41
land market-oriented transactions 41
land market recognition activities 63
land market-related transactions 55
*Land Market Value Publication* 6
land price variable as dependent variables 64–6
land reforms 51, 55, 63
    with end user rights 44–6
    motives 66
    on urbanization 55–60

land tenure security and its impact on growth and development 42–3
land use regulations (LURs) 347, 349, 353, 355
land wealth of household sector 3
large-scale asset purchase (LSAP) programs 21
LaSalle Investment Management 399
Lawley, Chad 256
lax ratings by credit rating agencies 245–7
Lead-lag correlations 301–3
Leamer, E. 269–71, 274, 280, 286
Leombroni, M. 374
LeRoy, Stephen F. 108, 109, 138
Leung, Charles Ka Yui 18, 40, 127, 143, 248, 251, 271, 283–5, 287, 315, 318, 321, 326, 334
Levin, A. 214
Levine, Ross 250
Li, P. 417
Li, S. 422, 423, 425
Liebowitz, Stan J. 249, 252
life cycle permanent income hypothesis of consumption (LCY-PIH) 4, 5
Light, Michael T. 257
limited partners (LPs) 375
Lin, F. 214
Lin, Y. 420
Lindblad, Mark R. 258
Lindseth, Alfred A. 127
linear asset pricing model 145
linear probability model (LPM) 21, 28–32, 38
Ling, D. 372, 401
liquid wealth 6, 7
List, J. A. 428
Liu, Z. 40, 44
localization decisions by households and firms 355
log price-to-rent ratio, bubble test on 151–3
long-/short-term mechanisms 193–5
   Chinese housing price dynamics 193–5
   United States housing price dynamics 186–92
Loutskina, Elena 250
Low Emissions Zones (LEZs) 422
low-income group (LIG) 86, 102
low-income households 87, 90, 102, 224
Lucas, D. 333
Lucas, Maurice E. 113
Luechinger, S. 419
Lutz, Byron 109, 120

Machin, Stephen 113
MacKinnon, G. 395
'macroeconomic' asset price bubbles 137, 143
macroeconomic uncertainty 219
   on housing returns factor 235
   on stochastic volatility 218
   on stochastic volatility factor 219, 236
macroeconomic variables 289
Magdalinos, T. 139, 149
Malpezzi, S. 143, 332
Mansuri, G. 42
Marfatia, H.A. 284
marginal propensity to borrow (MPB) 260
marginal propensity to consume (MPC) 4, 6
marginal propensity to lend (MPL) 260
marginal willingness to pay (MWTP) 419–20
Margo, Robert A. 109
Mariano, R. 318
market-oriented land transactions 45–6
market price, foreclosures on 255–6
Markov-switching model 147
Mastromonaco, Ralph 112
Mathis, Jerome 246
Maturana, Gonzalo 244, 245
Matus, K. 415
Mayer, Christopher 249, 260
McCauley, Robert N. 258
McLaughlin, K.A. 257
McMillan, Robert 110
Mean Group (MG) estimation model 187, 188, 192, 194
"measured uncertainty" 217
Mehra, R. 313
Mehta, Nirav 125
Mellor, J.W. 42
Melzer, Brian T. 255
Mendicino, C. 158
mental and psychological health 415–16
metropolitan statistical areas (MSAs) 167, 185, 186, 201
   coastal and inland 196
   by supply elasticity 197
Meyer, S. 417
Mian, Atif 224, 225, 241, 249, 250, 253–5, 260, 261
Michelsen, C. 151
middle-income households 92, 94, 126
   housing affordability for 93
Milbourn, Todd 246
Millimet, D. L. 428
"million-dollar plant" (MDP) 348
Mills, Edwin S. 107
minimum housing size for average household 95
model selection procedure 327–32
monetary policy 280–281
Monnin, P. 153
Monte Carlo Markov Chain Bayesian estimation method 213
Monte Carlo simulation method 169, 314, 316–17
Moore, J. 285, 286

Moretti, Enrico 282, 345, 349, 355
Morrow, Greg 281
mortgage-backed securities (MBSs) 21, 169, 247
mortgage-originating bank 242
Mu, Q. 420
Muellbauer, J. 5
Mueller, Holger M. 343
Mumtaz, H. 207, 211, 213, 216, 224
municipal revenue per capita 99
Murata, K. 5
Murray, Sheila E. 118, 127
Muth, Richard F. 107

Nadauld, Taylor D. 242
Nakamura, Emi 345
Nakamura, K. 153
Nakamura, S. 87
Naoi, M. 5
Nareit index 375, 393
Nathanson, C.G. 137, 138, 168–70, 179, 181
National Housing Bank (NHB) 90
National Sample Survey 88, 90, 91
NCREIF 377, 382, 403
    assets 380
    *versus* Nareit index 382
Nechayev, G. 179
Nechyba, Thomas J. 110, 112, 126, 127
Needham, B. 86
Neely, C.J. 213
Neidell, M. 417
Nelson, C.R. 213
Neri, S. 142, 285
net asset value (NAV) 372
net purchase amount by investor type 25
NFI-ODCE *versus* Nareit index 376, 392
Ng, C.Y.J. 40, 283–5, 287
Ng, S. 207
Nguyen Thanh, B. 209
Nichols, D.A. 39, 40, 44
Niizeki, T. 6
"NINJA" loans 169
Nogushi, Y. 158
nominal farmland price index
    as dependent variable 64–6
    in developed countries 75
non-durability and obsolescence of houses 90
non-end user rights motives land reform
        implementation on urbanization 60–62
non-marginal air quality improvements 420
nonparametric causality-in-quantiles test 209
non-rational bubbles 143
non-tradable service amenities 109
norm-based optimal housing 103
Norris, M. 83
Novy-Marx, R. 384, 404

Nunn, N. 45

Oates, Wallace E. 113
Office of Federal Housing Enterprise Oversight
    (OFHEO) 321
Ogawa, K. 5, 18
Ogura, Y. 18
Oliva, P. 416, 426
"open door" policy 170
open-end commingled real estate fund 375
optimal housing 103
ordinary least squares (OLS) regression 192, 276
Organisation for Economic Co-operation and
    Development (OECD) countries 208, 258,
    371
originate to distribute (OTD) model 242
Otrok, C. 211, 213
overcrowding in housing, indicators of 94
Owen, A.L. 217
Owens, Raymond 109
Oxley, L. 151

Pagano, M. 18
Pagel, M. 417
Pagliari, J. 384, 404
Pagliari, J. Jr. 372, 390
pairwise correlation analysis 215–16
Palayi, A. 90, 103
panel data evidence 14–17
panel data model specification 213–14
panel regression 181–6
Parker, Jonathan A. 260
Parkhomenko, Andrii 355
Pavan, M. 286
Pavlidis, E. 151
Payne, A. Abigail 119
pension fund-real estate marriage 401–2
pension funds 393
    concentration risks 397
    investment shares 399
    liabilities 384
pension funds and private equity real estate 371–2
    CRE allocations and PERE investment
        performance 386–95
    economic and financial stability 396–402
    ERISA and real estate alternative 373–7
    shifting capital sources 377–86
"Pension Obligation Bonds" 385
Pesaran, H. 214
Pesaran, M.H. 214
Peterson, Paul E. 127
Pew Charitable Trust 396
Phillips, P.C.B. 139, 149, 150, 158
Phillips–Perron test 7
physical health and mortality 415

Piazzesi, M. 40, 44
Pigorsch, C. 312, 314, 332, 333
Piskorski, Tomasz 244, 245, 261, 262
Place, F. 45
Platt, Glenn J. 110
Ploberger, Werner 276
Poi, B.P. 217
political economy approach 110
political economy in China 359
    allocation of industrial parks across cities 362–4
    economic cost of politically driven distribution of industrial parks 364–8
    industrial parks 360–362
Pollution information disclosures 418
Pooled Mean Group (PMG) estimations 192, 194
    Chinese housing price dynamics 193–5
    by city type 198
    results 187, 188
    United States housing price dynamics 186–92
pooled mean group model 179–81
Porter, R.D. 138
post-Lehman Brothers bankruptcy 254
Poterba, J.M. 169, 176
Pradhan Mantri Awas Yojana (PMAY) 84, 85, 88, 89, 91, 93, 98–103
Prescott, E. C. 313
Preve, D. 318
price-to-rent ratio, log of 151
pricing dynamics 178–9
private capital sources 377
private CRE fund performance 402
private equity real estate (PERE) 371, 386–90, 393, 401, 402
    investment performance 386–95
private-label mortgage securitization 249
private residential investment 272
privatization motive land reform implementation 56, 57, 72, 78
Priyaranjan, N. 90, 103
pro-poor land reform 48–9
pro-poor motive land reform implementation
    on manufacturing 80
    on urbanization 61, 74
pro-poor-type reforms 62
Prudential Property Investment Separate Account (PRISA) 403
"prudent man" investment approach 380
PSY-IVX procedure 149–50
public housing system 86
public market equivalent (PME) 390, 404
public pension fund allocations 386
Public Plans Database (PPD) 380, 385
public transit infrastructure 425–6

Puga, Diego 346, 349, 355
Purfield, C. 85
Purnanandam, Amiyatosh 242

Qian, N. 45
quantitative and qualitative monetary easing (QQE) 21, 23, 32, 35
quantitative easing (QE) 280

Rajan, Raghuram G. 262
Rajan, Uday 251
Ram, P. 86
Ramcharan, Rodney 254
random-coefficients estimator 217, 230–231
random-coefficients models 213
Rangazas, Peter 110
Rao, J. 86, 88, 91
Rapach, D.E. 213
rational bubbles 143
Rauh, J. 384, 404
Ravikumar, B. 110
real estate alternative 373–7
real estate assets 141
real estate bubbles 137–9, 142
    housing non-fundamental bubble detection for Japan 150–157
    real estate *versus* financial assets 140–142
    testing for bubbles in the price-to-rent ratio 148–9
    testing for bubbles on the filtered price 149–50
    theory of housing price boom-busts and bubble typology 142–7
real estate investment trusts (REITs) 21, 22, 28, 38, 141, 372, 397, 401, 403
    holdings 23
    market equity capitalization 379
    number and market capitalization of 24
    purchase behavior 30–34
    purchase operations 26
    share prices, effect on 34–5
real estate market and consumption 2, 6–13
    in Japan, relationship between 5–6
    panel data evidence 14–17
    time series evidence 6–13
real estate markets
    dual nature of 141
    in Japan 2
    transaction costs in 141
"real estate premium puzzle" 313
real estate sector (REU) 209
real estate *versus* financial assets 140–142
real house prices and residential investment in the United States 273
real housing prices 289, 301–3

Redding, Stephen J. 344
redistribution motive land reform implementation
 on manufacturing 81
 on urbanization 75
regentrification 109
regime shift model 186
regional convergence 346
regional disparity in economic growth 92
regional economy to macroeconomy 338
 agglomeration and aggregate growth 345–6
 aggregate effects of regional shocks 344–5
 extensions 343
 firms 341
 general equilibrium effects of agglomeration economies 354
 general equilibrium effects of changes in housing policy 354
 granular shocks and macroeconomics 343–4
 growth convergence (divergence) in the United States 346–7
 households 340
 inefficient spatial allocation of resources 347–50
 localization decisions by households and firms 355
 policy implications 353–4
 reorganization of economic activity *versus* economic growth 354
 simple conceptual framework 339–40
 spatial equilibrium 341–2
 transportation 350–353
regional shocks, aggregate effects of 344–5
regional taxes 350
regional variations
 in access to finance 95–7
 in implementation of PMAY 99–101
 in local governance 98–9
registered housing finance institutions 96
regression analysis 216–25
regression discontinuity design 424–5
regression models 113
remedies 259–61
rents *versus* dividends 142
rent-to-price ratio 194
Report of the Committee on Real Estate Investment Strategy 156
residential investment, interest rates on 281
residential land price 6, 7
residential location behavior of households 107
residential location choice and outcomes in United States
 analytical approaches 111–12
 community choice models 109–10
 evidence on outcomes of school choice 113–14

 hybrid residential choice models 110–111
 urban location models 107–9
residential mortgage-backed security 378
residual autoregression estimations 190, 199
residual autoregressive models 189
restitution 47
restitution motive land reform implementation
 on manufacturing 78
 on urbanization 57, 72
restitution-motive land reforms 63
Restuccia, D. 43
return decile dummies 32
return decile groups 33, 35
return targeting 385
Riddiough, T. 375, 390, 403, 404
Riegle–Neal Act of 1994 249
risk-seeking behavior 386
"risk-shifting problem" 404
Rivkin, Steven G. 120
road-watering policies 430
Roback, Jennifer 339, 344
Roback model 343
Rodríguez-Clare, Andrés 343
Rogers, William H. 255
Rogerson, Richard 110, 126
Romer, Thomas 110
root mean square error (RMSE) 318
Rosenthal, Stuart S. 109, 257
Ross, S. 109, 377
Ross, Stephen L. 111
Rossi-Hansberg, Esteban 344, 345, 348, 352
Rothstein, Jesse 114
Rouse, Cecilia Elena 127
Russell-NCREIF index 375
Ruttan, V.W. 39

Saita, Y. 153
Saiz, A. 191, 195
Salvanes, Kjell G. 113
*San Antonio School District* v. *Rodriguez* 117
Sanders, Anthony 251
Sanders, N. J. 426
Sandler, R. 423, 426
Schaal, Edouard 353
Schaller, H. 169
Schaz, Philipp 250
Scherbina, A. 137, 138
Schlusche, B. 138
Schneider, M. 40, 44
Schoenmaker, Dirk 258
school choice options 122
 charter schools 124–5
 evidence on outcomes of 113–14
 homeschooling 123
 interdistrict open enrollment 124

intradistrict open enrollment 123
school desegregation 119–20
school district consolidation 120–122
school finance court cases 114–19
school finance literature 110
school finance policies 110–112
school financing 116
school quality 113
    into housing prices, capitalization of 113–14
securitization 244
    of loans by banks 242–4
Sengupta, J. 87
Sengupta, U. 86
Serrano, R. 314, 315, 332, 333
*Serrano* v. *Priest* 117
Seru, Amit 262
Sherlund, Shane M. 242
Shi, S. 139, 149, 150, 158
Shiller, R. 145
Shiller, R.J. 138, 158, 166
Shilling, J. 313
Shimizu, C. 157
Shimizutani, S. 5
Shin, Y. 214
Shleifer, A. 45, 247
Shoag, Daniel 346, 347
shock propagation 285–6
short-selling and high transaction costs 140–141
Shulman, David 406
Sieg, Holger 110, 112
Siegel, L. 374, 403
Silva, Fabio 110
Silverman, B. W. 321, 334
Simeonova, E. 424
simple conceptual framework 339–40
simple granger tests 275–8
simulation-based model 112
Singh, C. 85
Singh, S. 86
Singleton, John D. 125
Smith, G. 145, 158
Smith, M.H. 145, 158
socio-demographic inequalities 83
Sonstelie, Jon 108–10
Sorensen, M. 391
spatial efficiency 354
spatial equilibrium 341–2
"spatial impossibility theorem" 339
spatial spillovers 347–8
special economic zones (SEZs) 361
square loss criterion (SLC) 319
state funding of schools 114–19
state funding program 116
state-level economic uncertainty 211
state net domestic product 100

state school revenue 116
state-specific uncertainty coefficient 220–223, 232–4, 237
state urban population 101
state-wise affordability analysis 101
state-wise distribution of assisted housing 85
Steiner, E. 403
Steinsson, Jón 345
Stevenson, B. 52
Stiglitz, J.E. 144
stochastic bubbles model 169
stochastic volatility factor, macroeconomic uncertainty on 218, 219, 236
Stock, J.H. 211
Strahan, Philip E. 250
Strange, W.C. 168
Strobel, J. 209, 210
structural change in the extensive margin (SCEM) 313
structural change in the intensive margin (SCIM) 313
Stucky, Thomas D. 256
Suárez Serrato, Juan Carlos 350
subprime borrowers, predatory lending to 241
Suburban communities 127
Sufi, Amir 225, 241, 249, 250, 253, 254, 260
Summers, L. 169
Supreme Court decisions 118
Suzuki, K. 18
Swamy, P.A.V. 214, 217
Swiss National Bank 36
Symbolic Transfer Entropy test 238

Taipalus, K. 179
Tan, J. 430
Tanaka, S. 426
Tang, Dragon Yongjun 246
Taylor series expansion 145
Tchistyi, Alexei 261
Technical Group of the Government for the Twelfth Five Year Plan 85
Technical Group on Urban Housing Shortage 84
Tekin, Erdal 257
tenure security arrangements 41
tenure security improvement 48, 53
    motive land reform implementation on manufacturing 79
tenure security motive land reform implementation on urbanization 73
Term Asset-Backed Securities Loan Facility 260
theory of housing price boom-busts 142–7
Tiebout, C. M. 109, 114, 121
time-dependent covariates, Cox hazard model with 29–30
time-series dynamics of excess return 315–16

time series evidence 6–13
time-varying factor-augmented vector autoregression (TVP-FAVAR) model 209
Tiwari, P. 84, 86–8, 91
Tokyo Stock Exchange (TSE) 21
TOPIX 25, 26, 28, 38
total suspended particulates (TSP) 414
"tournament competition" 428
Towe, Charles 256
trade-dependent economy 297
traditional debt and equity capital 377
traditional DiD estimator 51
traditional public schools 127
traditional reduced-form approach 344
transaction costs in real estate markets 141
transboundary air pollution 427
treasury inflation-protected (TIP) 272
Treasury Inflation-Protected Securities (TIPS) 181
Tremblay, Jean-François 110
Trichet, J. C. 312, 332
Tripathi, S. 95
Troncoso, R. 422
Troubled Asset Relief Program 321
Tse, Chung-Yi 248
Turner, Matthew A. 351
Twelfth Five Year Plan 84
Two Control Zone (TCZ) policy 426, 428
two-way differences-in-differences estimation 62–4
two-way differences-in-differences model 53
Tzavalis, E. 181

Udry, C. 42
Uesugi, I 18
unconventional monetary policy 22–4
unemployment, increase in 253–4
unemployment insurance (UI) 259
United Nations Committee on Economic, Social and Cultural Rights 85
United States 106
    housing markets 167
    interaction of policy and locational decisions 114–25
    residential location choice and outcomes 107–14
    school revenue 115
United States housing price dynamics 181–92
    data used 181
    long-/short-term mechanisms 186–92
    regime shift 181–6
unit root test results 214–15
urban land price index 2
urban local bodies (ULBs) 91, 98, 100–102
urban locational models 107–9, 111, 125

urban location theory 108
urbanization
    CICRT recognition motive land reform implementation 60
    CICRT recognition motive land reform implementation on 74
    combined end user rights motives land reform implementation on 73
    consolidation motive land reform implementation on 55, 71
    distributive motive land reform implementation on 55, 71
    land reform implementation on 58
    privatization motive land reform implementation on 56, 72
    pro-poor motive land reform implementation on 61, 74
    redistribution motive land reform implementation on 75
    restitution motive land reform implementation on 57, 72
    tenure security motive land reform implementation on 73
Urquiola, Miguel 114
US Clean Air Act 419, 426, 427
U.S. education system 115
US Environmental Protection Agency (EPA) 421
U.S. household borrowings 250
U.S. Interstate Highway System 353
US metropolitan statistical areas 172
US Nitrogen Oxides Budget Program 420

Vallascas, Francesco 258
value-add and opportunity funds 371
value of a statistical life (VSL) 415
van Benthem, A. A. 423
Van Hemert, Otto 241
van Horen, Neeltje 258
Van Nieuwerburgh, S. 372, 390, 392
Van Norden, S. 169
Van Order, Robert A. 166, 169, 178, 179, 181, 186, 191, 192, 201
variance decomposition
    of consumer borrowing 8, 11, 12
    of consumption 9–11
vector-autoregressive (VAR) models 4, 6, 7, 17, 18, 139, 207, 209
Viard, V. B. 422
Vickery, James 244
vintage-agnostic restrictions 422
vintage-based driving restrictions 423
vintage-specific registration fee 423
Vishny, Robert 247
Vissing-Jorgensen, Annette 158, 280
voluntary financial education program 262

Von Thünen, Johann 107

Walsh, Randall P. 126, 256, 413
Wan, J. 5
Wang, H.J. 19
Wang, J. 365
Wang, S. 197
Ward, B.A. 44
Warr, P. 42
Watson, M. 169
Watson, M.W. 211
wealth effect channel 4
Welch, Finis 120
Westerlund, J. 186
Whalley, A. 425
Wheaton, W. 179
Wheaton, William C. 108
White, Michelle J. 108
Whiteman, C.H. 169
Whyte, Ann Marie 249
Wilcox, D. 384
Wiley, J. 390, 404
Willen, Paul S. 262
Williams, A. 420
Williams, Sonya 256
willingness to pay (WTP) for air quality 419–20
Windsor, C. 19
Winter, William 255
Wolfers, J. 52
Wolff, H. 422

World Development Indicators (WDIs) 46
World Health Organization (WHO) 94, 413
Wright, Mark L.J. 345
Wu, J. 193

Xiao, J. 422
Xi Jinping 369
Xu, Y. 422

Yang, B. 139, 149
Yang, J. 422, 424
Yang, M. 427
Yao, Yuxi 344
Yilmaz, Kuzey 111, 119, 126, 127
Yilmazer, Tansel 257
youth unemployment 87
Yu, J. 139
Yukutake, N. 19

Zeng, Z. 286
Zhang, J. 420, 428
Zhang, S. 420
Zhang, Yunqi 259
Zheng, Angela 112
Zheng, S. 419
Zhi, T. 176
Zhong, N. 422
Zidar, Owen 350
Zisler, R. 377